CRIMINAL JUSTICE:
An Introduction to the Criminal Justice System in England and Wales

Second Edition

DAVIES, CROALL AND TYRER

CRIMINAL JUSTICE:

AN INTRODUCTION TO
THE CRIMINAL JUSTICE SYSTEM IN
ENGLAND AND WALES

Second Edition

Longman

An imprint of **Pearson Education**

Harlow, England · London · New York · Reading, Massachusetts · San Francisco
Toronto · Don Mills, Ontario · Sydney · Tokyo · Singapore · Hong Kong · Seoul
Taipei · Cape Town · Madrid · Mexico City · Amsterdam · Munich · Paris · Milan

Pearson Education Limited
Edinburgh Gate,
Harlow,
Essex CM20 2JE,
England

and Associated Companies throughout the world

Visit us on the World Wide Web at:
http://www.pearsoneduc.com

First published 1995
Second edition 1998

ISBN 0-582-35621-0 PPR

British Library Cataloguing-in-Publication Data

A catalogue record for this book is available from the British Library

Set by 35 in 10/12 pt Plantin
Printed in Malaysia, VVP

10 9 8 7 6
05 04 03 02 01

CONTENTS

LIST OF FIGURES

CHAPTER 11: RESPONDING TO CRIME

PREFACE TO THE
FIRST EDITION

In the last ten years criminal justice has emerged as a new field of study in Britain. New degree courses in criminal justice studies have been set up, and careers advisers point to an industry with over a quarter of a million employees; bigger than the British army and legal profession combined. As sure as night follows day, the arrival of new degree courses is followed by a demand for student textbooks. But what type of textbook is needed for criminal justice? It was our observation as lecturers on one of the first criminal justice degree courses in Britain that many texts were neither introductory nor comprehensive in coverage as they focused on particular aspects of the criminal justice process.

We felt that an introductory textbook, written for students, practitioners and volunteers, new to the subject, should provide basic information about the various agencies of the criminal justice system: police, Crown Prosecution Service, magistrates' courts, Crown Court, probation and prisons. We also felt that it was important to outline the basic elements of criminal law and procedure which define crime and the responses to it in England and Wales, along with an exploration of the philosophies, principles and models of criminal justice on which these are based. In addition we also wished to look at the many non-legal factors which affect the operation of these agencies and finally we wanted to identify some of the policy issues involved in the control of crime and the pursuit of justice which interest the public and practitioners.

The aims of this book are therefore to:

- introduce readers to the agencies of the criminal justice process in England and Wales and to outline their legal responsibilities and tasks;

- help readers to understand the contextual constraints which influence the operations of these agencies;

- explain the legal and sociological factors which have shaped the operations of the criminal justice agencies in England and Wales;

- illustrate the relationship between these agencies and their interdependency;

- by the inclusion of study exercises and review questions, to aid understanding.

xv

In this text we will therefore describe the legislation, history and organisational forms of the agencies operating within the criminal justice system. We did not wish our approach to be straitjacketed by any one academic discipline, be it law, sociology, criminology or administrative studies. We have therefore included insights into the principles of criminal law and its procedure provided by criminal lawyers, along with empirical studies of how these laws are implemented on a day-to-day level. Thus we have included findings of empirical research and statistical data in the hope of moving beyond an understanding of law as discussed in books to an appreciation of law in action. Moreover, we felt that readers should have an awareness of the system as a whole. The criminal justice system is more than the sum of its parts and an awareness of the interdependencies between the agencies in the system is as important as an understanding of the role of individual agencies.

Our approach is therefore intended to be both introductory and comprehensive. Thus we have included the role and functions of police, prosecutors and the trial and have looked beyond these into the working of the probation and prison services. These agencies and processes are all part of the criminal justice system, and their work is interdependent. They are all affected by the pervasive logic of the adversarial system, and by the goals and principles which shape the criminal justice process. The policies and procedures adopted at one stage of the system affect later stages.

This book is not, however, meant to be a detailed guide to either criminal law and procedure or criminology – many other texts perform this task adequately. It is intended to provide readers with a broad introduction to the present criminal justice system, to the principles which underlie it and to the many conflicting pressures on criminal justice policy to which current legislative changes and reviews are a response. Thus it should be regarded neither as a law nor criminology text, but rather as drawing on elements of law, sociology and criminology to introduce the many aspects of criminal justice and to place these in a broader socio-legal context.

The first three chapters aim to introduce students to the key elements of criminal justice and to the many ways of defining, explaining and measuring crime. Chapters 4–7 deal with the agencies and processes involved in investigating and prosecuting crime and determining the guilt or otherwise of those accused of having committed crimes. Chapters 8 and 9 explore sentencing and penal policy, introducing students to the main aims of punishment, and the many influences on sentencing decisions. The aims and purpose of imprisonment are considered in Chapter 10. The criminal justice process however has many limitations and recent pressures to reduce crime have led to the development of many initiatives involving the community in relation to crime prevention, punishment and policing. These will be discussed in Chapter 11. Finally, the implications of changing influences on policy for the future of criminal justice will be explored in Chapter 12.

Each chapter is followed by a number of review questions directed towards the student reader. In addition there are a series of exercises which student readers may attempt in order to further their understanding of some of the concepts and processes which we have explored. A list of key further reading also follows each chapter, to enable readers to increase their knowledge and understanding of the agencies or processes introduced.

We have included the many far-ranging changes to the criminal law and its procedures brought about by the Criminal Justice and Public Order Act 1994. The political controversy surrounding this hotch-potch Act was apparent in the debates in Parliament and in the street protests over the legislation. We do not think that the political implications of the criminal justice system can be ignored. However, we do not see our task as being to simplify issues as is apparent in the many partisan debates on topics of criminal justice, nor do we intend to present the text from any one theoretical or ideological perspective.

We are conscious that issues of criminal justice are now centre stage in the political drama and that the five Criminal Justice Acts passed in the 13 years since 1982 reveal not only a heightened audience interest on matters of crime and justice, but a desperate search to stage a happy ending – the retreat on unit fines was a prime example.

Given the continual review of aspects of criminal justice, it is possible that by the time this book is published, further changes will have taken place. No text can ever be fully up-to-date. It is hoped however that readers will be able to place such recent changes in the context of the many influences on policy that will be explored in this text.

Malcolm Davies,
Hazel Croall,
Jane Tyrer,
June 1995

PREFACE TO SECOND EDITION

Twelve criminal justice experts were blindfolded and asked to describe a creature, an elephant, they could touch but not see. The first holding the trunk thought it was a new hose that would be useful for controlling rioting crowds. One held the tail and thought it might be a rope, which could come in handy if hanging was ever restored. The penologist felt the hard pointed tip of the tusk and concluded that it was used for administering long, sharp shocks, obviously an additional sentencing option for use with adults. The expert holding the elephant's ear, noting that despite the thick skin it was extraordinarily manipulative, deduced that it must be something used by defence barristers. The criminologist measured its girth and concluded that it was big, although he could not explain what it was. The police chief decided that he didn't care what it was, anything that big ought to be locked up to protect the public. The liberal journalist warned the others not to be alarmist and that it was not as big as the others thought. The probation expert's PSR, Possible Solution Report, claimed that, following talks with the creature, the rumour of the beast's rogue nature was an unfair stigmatisation and was anyway explained by the harsh treatment it had received at the hands of its keepers. The expert who was a member of the Socialist Workers Party concluded, after the elephant refused to buy a paper from him, that it was a creature of capitalism. The offender profiler issued a statement saying that the creature was almost certainly male, aged between 18 and 30 years, and was unemployed and unmarried. The expert on juries said that he thought he knew how the beast moved but could say nothing because he was worried about being in contempt of court. The twelfth expert, a wise man who was also an expert on elephants, said nothing.

The criminal justice system in England and Wales is more complicated than an elephant and we are conscious of the risk of trying to describe it in one introductory textbook. However, we have forsaken the safe route taken by wiser heads than ourselves, and have attempted to say something about how the system works. In doing so we have aspired to describe three things in this book: firstly, to introduce the agencies that make up the criminal justice system in England and Wales; secondly, to look at some of the ideas, theories and principles about how the system operates; and, thirdly, to provide an overview to see how the different agencies and ideas blend together to form an operating whole, which, like the elephant, is bigger than the sum of its parts.

In this second edition we have added a glossary of terms, extra exercises, information about websites of interest and a new chapter on Responding to Crime in which we look at policy making and the administration of criminal justice, the influence of Europe, privatisation, co-ordination of the system, monitoring, accountability, complaints procedure, crime prevention and new ideas about restorative justice and zero tolerance of crime. We have updated the figures and added information about new bodies and agencies which include the Criminal Cases Review Commission, Youth Justice Board, National Crime Squad and the National Criminal Intelligence Service. Finally, we have included the changes enacted by the Criminal Procedure and Investigations Act 1996, Crime (Sentences) Act 1997 and the Crime and Disorder Act 1998.

Malcolm Davies,
Hazel Croall,
Jane Tyrer,
July 1998

We would like to dedicate this book to Michael Molyneux
for his inspiration as a teacher to generations of
students and colleagues in the Law School at
Thames Valley University

AUTHORS'
ACKNOWLEDGEMENTS

The authors are most grateful to the following scholars, researchers and practitioners who commented on the manuscripts: Bill Brown, penal policy lecturer at Thames Valley University; Jacqueline Burns and Jane Grant, research associates at the Criminal Justice Centre at TVU; Michael Molyneux, retired law teacher; Dr Alex Weich, from Westminster University; Clive Welsh of the Prison Service: and the three anonymous readers of the manuscript for their helpful comments and suggestions.

We are entirely beholden to Angela Legg, the administrator of the Criminal Justice Centre at Thames Valley University, for her tireless help with this book. To our students of criminal justice at Thames Valley we offer our thanks for their part in the development of this book.

In preparing the second edition of *Criminal Justice* we would like to thank Clive Coleman of Hull University, Professor Ken Plummer of Essex University, Les Johnston of Teesside University, Dr Sean Stitt and Professor Joe Sim of John Moores University, Liverpool, for their comments and suggestions for the new edition, also Christine Ivamy who diligently compiled the index. We are particularly indebted to Dr Tony Fowles of the Criminal Justice Centre, TVU, who provided a constant source of information and sound advice. Finally, we thank our Publishing Director at Addison Wesley Longman for his encouragement and patience, and our Editor, for the care and professionalism that went into the second edition of Criminal Justice.

PUBLISHER'S ACKNOWLEDGEMENTS

The publishers are grateful to the following for permission to reproduce copyright material:

Telegraph Group Limited for our Figures 1.2 and 4.2 © Telegraph Group Limited, London, 1994; HMSO for our Figures 1.6, 6.5, 9.2 and 10.6 Crown copyright is reproduced with the permission of the Controller of Her Majesty's Stationery Office; the author Michael King for Figure 1.7; Addison Wesley Longman Ltd. for Figure 3.3; News International for Figures 4.3 and 7.4 © Times Newspapers Limited, 21 February 1998 and 16 January 1992 also Photonews Service for the ear identification photograph in Figure 4.3; The Magistrates' Association for the three forms covered by Figure 8.2.

TABLE OF CASES

CHAPTER 1
CRIMINAL JUSTICE

- Defining Criminal Justice
- Criminal Justice in England and Wales
- Principles, Systems and Models of Criminal Justice
- Criminal Justice Legislation

INTRODUCTION

There are three criminal justice systems in Britain, with Scotland and Ulster having different criminal procedures from those in England and Wales, which is a single jurisdiction. European institutions also affect the operations and policy of criminal justice in this country.

Examining the criminal justice system involves many issues. Political issues are raised in asking what the aims of the system are and in whose interests it is run. Criminal justice also inevitably raises issues of fairness and freedom, as the system seeks to control and repress criminal behaviour. If it does this too vigorously, citizens may be arbitrarily arrested and unfairly accused of a crime they did not commit. We are all at risk however if crime is tolerated and the system cannot deal effectively with it. This in turn raises questions about how we understand and define crime, how we measure the extent of crime, the number of criminals and victims, and the effects of crime on victims and the community at large.

Before these questions are addressed we must first define what we mean by the phrase 'criminal justice system', understand how it works, what it is trying to achieve, and with what effect. This book sets out to examine these issues, and this chapter will define these questions more specifically. Criminal justice systems in all countries involve a vast and growing organisation, including many different agencies responsible for the detection and trial of suspected criminals and the punishment of those who are found to be guilty.

In this chapter the main agencies of the criminal justice system will be described and their expansion in recent years outlined. To comprehend criminal justice fully we also need to understand the principles underlying the system, and how these principles affect policy and practice. Like any other institution, criminal justice has to be organised and managed in the context of political and public pressures along with financial and resource constraints. Different models of criminal justice, which illustrate its conflicting aims, and the pressures these place on policy, will be explored. Finally, recent legislation will be briefly outlined to illustrate the conflicting pressures surrounding contemporary criminal justice. A short chronology of significant criminal justice legislation will complete this introductory chapter.

DEFINING CRIMINAL JUSTICE

How can a criminal justice system be defined and described? Criminal justice is about society's formal response to crime and is defined more specifically in terms of a series of decisions and actions taken by a number of agencies in response to a specific crime or criminal or crime in general. Following the recognition of a crime-like incident, or in seeking to prevent lawless behaviour, criminal justice agencies become involved. There are four key sub-systems of criminal justice:

- Law enforcement: involving the police and prosecuting agencies.

- Courts: making decisions about pre-trial detention, adjudication on the guilt of the defendant, deciding on the sentence for those convicted and ensuring that the rights of the defendant are respected.

- Penal system: involves probation and the prisons.

- Crime prevention: involves the above agencies who deal with individual offenders along with a wider group of agencies, some private, others governmental, who plan crime-free environments or seek to change the conditions that lead to criminal behaviour.

People are exposed in everyday life to images and realities of crime and criminal justice as victims, witnesses, professionals, offenders and as onlookers. We develop ideas about and images of the way the different agencies such as the police, prosecutors, courts, prisons, probation, local authorities and private security agencies respond to crime or its perceived threats. We are made aware through the media, official statements and political debates about the issues of crime and justice. In an effort to become more analytical in our approach to these issue, ideas and images, it is possible to conceptualise the criminal justice system in the following terms:

- Substantive law: The content of the criminal law provides the starting point of the criminal justice system by defining behaviour that is to be regulated through the use of the criminal law.

- Form: Who is given the task of responding to crime and what procedures must they follow?

- Functions: What are the intended consequences and aims of the system?

- Modes of punishment: What sentences are available to the courts?

- Criminal justice paradigms: What are the dominant ways of thinking about issues of crime, criminals and justice?

When we look at other countries we can see clear differences in the contents of criminal law, the procedures in the courts, the types of sentences, and the ways of thinking about crime and punishment. The purpose of the criminal justice system will be very different when a secular society is contrasted with a religious one. It becomes apparent that cultural factors are a major influence on the operation of a criminal justice system.

The O J Simpson and Louise Woodward trials generated immense interest about the system of criminal justice in the USA and led to discussion as to whether this type of case would be dealt with in the same way in this country. A trip around the world would show that many aspects of law, procedure and punishment vary considerably. In Scotland the age of criminal responsibility starts at 9 while in Finland it is 15. In France the law demands that a bystander must intervene to help a person being attacked. The legal system in California found O J Simpson responsible for killing his wife in the civil court while the criminal court found him not guilty, as in the case in England and Wales of Tony Dietrick who was found responsible in the civil court for the death of Joan Francisco (*The Times*, 25 March 1998: 1). Barbados, Jamaica and Trinidad & Tobago have threatened to leave the Commonwealth because the Privy Council in London have reprieved all death penalty cases. Nearly all the former colonies of the Caribbean retained the Privy Council as the final Court of Appeal. South Africa abolished the death penalty in 1995 at a time when many US states were about to implement it. In China during this decade the number of executions has been estimated at around 2,000 a year. In Saudi Arabia beheading is regarded as an appropriate mode of punishment, and two nurses found guilty of the murder of an Australian colleague were subject to bartering for their lives. People living in different jurisdictions are subject to different sets of laws. In Saudi Arabia there is no concept of rape within a marriage but alcohol is prohibited.

We use these illustrations from around the world, firstly, to demonstrate the many variations in the way issues of crime, guilt and punishment are approached in different jurisdictions. Secondly, so that students of criminal justice should be conscious of this diversity of approach. It follows that an awareness of different legal systems is required for those who wish to understand the complexities of other jurisdictions and the differences in the definitions of crimes and criminal procedures. Thirdly, we use these illustrations to show that beyond the legal details are issue of morality, politics and ethics that might require a strong stomach and a willingness to understand that issues of criminal justice raise many fundamental questions about the nature of humanity and society.

Content of the criminal law: what is penalised?

In most countries, particular kinds of behaviour are criminalised through the criminal law, formulated in some countries by a penal code. As we will see in Chapter 2, there is no simple way of defining what behaviour is criminal, and this may vary between different countries and over time. Nonetheless, in most Western societies similar kinds of behaviour are considered to be criminal including homicide, rape, arson, kidnapping, robbery, burglary, assault, theft, fraud and motoring offences. Thus according to Knut Sveri, 'if a person does something which is considered to be a crime in Sweden, it will practically always be considered to be a crime in New York' (Sveri 1990).

Form and process: criminal procedure and criminal justice agencies

Different countries have very different ways of investigating and prosecuting criminal cases, based on different principles and rules. Varying procedures and regulations govern such matters as the investigation of crime, the arrest and interrogation of suspects, prosecution decisions, bail procedure, trial procedures, rules of evidence and the role of the jury, if there is one. There are also differences in how courts decide on the guilt or otherwise of defendants.

This is in part because other countries have different agencies dealing with these matters. In France an investigating magistrate, the *juge d'instruction*, conducts investigations into serious crime, in contrast to the UK where the police have this responsibility. In Germany the public prosecutor, the *staatsanwalt*, has overall responsibility for pre-trial proceedings and advises the examining judge on bail and remand decisions. There is no equivalent in England and Wales to the Scottish Procurator Fiscal who also has an investigating and prosecuting role. Across the USA, each of the 50 states has its own penal code and each county within a state has its own criminal justice agencies such as district attorneys and sheriffs, in addition to the state and federal agencies.

It is important to appreciate how criminal justice agencies define and interpret their role and legal responsibilities. The criminal law does not enforce itself. To understand a system we need to consider how law enforcers, prosecutors, lawyers, magistrates, judges, probation officers and prison officers perceive their job and their function within the system. How they work will not only be affected by their official role but by political, financial, organisational and cultural influences. While Parliament and judges may create and interpret the criminal law, they do not implement it on a day-to-day basis. An appreciation of the everyday world of those who translate the law as described in books into the law in action is therefore essential to an understanding of how criminal justice agencies operate.

4

Fig 1.1 Agency-specific functions

Police
- Investigating crime
- Preventing crime
- Arresting and detaining suspects
- Maintaining public order
- Traffic control
- Responding to criminal and non-criminal emergencies

Some of these tasks are also carried out by private and other public law enforcement agencies such as Customs and Excise and environmental health and trading standards departments of local authorities.

Prosecution
- Filtering out weak cases
- Preparing cases for prosecution
- Prosecuting cases in the magistrates' courts
- Preparing cases for trial in the Crown Court by liaising with barristers for the prosecution before and throughout a trial

Courts
- Handling and processing cases efficiently
- Deciding on bail, remands, and mode of trial
- Protecting the rights of the defendant
- Deciding on guilt
- Passing sentence
- Hearing appeals against conviction and sentence
- Providing a public arena so that justice can be seen to be done

Prisons
- Holding persons remanded in custody by the courts
- Holding sentenced offenders
- Maintaining proper conditions for those held in custody
- Preparing inmates for release
- Attempting to rehabilitate offenders

Probation
- Preparing pre-sentence reports
- Providing bail facilities for and information to the courts on offenders' appropriateness for bail
- Working with offenders given a probation, community service, or combination order
- Running probation centres
- Supervising released prisoners and pre-release work with inmates in custody

Functions and aims of the criminal justice system

In exploring what a criminal justice aims to do, we need to distinguish between the goals of the system as a whole, and the functions of the different agencies who make up the system. Agency-specific functions are shown in Figure 1.1. Cross-system goals include:

- Protecting the public by preventing and deterring crime, by rehabilitating offenders and incapacitating others who constitute a persistent threat to the community.

- Upholding and promoting the rule of law and respect for the law, by ensuring due process and proper treatment of suspects, arrestees, defendants and those held in custody, successfully prosecuting criminals and acquitting innocent people accused of a crime.

- Maintaining law and order.

- Punishing criminals with regard to the principles of just deserts.

- Registering social disapproval of censured behaviour by punishing criminals.

- Aiding and advising the victims of crime.

Mode and distribution of punishment

Finally, variations between systems include differences in the modes and distribution of punishment, recognising that societies punish offenders in diverse ways. If one point of distinction in defining a criminal justice system is to establish what is punished, another is to describe the types or mode of punishment used.

The main penal sanctions or court sentencing options are imprisonment, fines, probation, community penalties, discharges, admonitions and cautions. The death penalty for murder was abolished in this country in 1965, and has also been abolished in most European countries although it is still in use in some states in the USA and in African and Asian countries.

The most noticeable difference between countries however is not merely in the mode of punishment but in the distribution of punishment, that is the range of sentences routinely given for particular offences. What is acceptable to a Swedish, British or USA court in terms of typical sentencing practice varies greatly.

In different cultures, ideas as to what constitutes an appropriate punishment will differ. A good illustration of this is provided in the extract from *The Daily Telegraph* (Figure 1.2) which looks at differences within Australia between the European and Aboriginal attitude towards punishment.

Criminal justice paradigms

In what ways are issues of crime and justice thought about in public debates and in everyday life? Are criminals regarded as an evil minority or just as ordinary people? Should the police be more concerned with strategies to

6

Fig 1.2 Tribal elders punish Aborigine car thieves

Six Aborigines have been beaten for stealing cars after Northern Territory police let their elders handle the matter in a traditional way.

The six, aged 15–25, were beaten with rubber hoses in front of the local council chambers in an Aboriginal community near Darwin.

Since the incident three months ago, only one minor offence of theft has been committed in the town.

It was not the first time Aborigines in the Territory have been handed over to elders by the Australian justice system for tribal punishment.

Earlier this year, Mr Brian Martin, the Chief Justice of the Territory, asked the Department of Correctional Services to monitor the tribal 'payback' spearing through both thighs of Wilson Jagamara Walker, an Aboriginal convicted of manslaughter. Mr Martin's decision was influenced by petitions from the man's tribal council and a group of senior women at Yuendumu, 150 miles southwest of Alice Springs, who warned him that innocent members of the man's family would be speared instead of him if he was jailed.

Taking this into account, the judge released Walker on a bond and asked that correctional services report on whether the spearing took place.

However, the judicial outcome remained unclear after officials said that the victim's family had decided not to proceed with the spearing even though Walker was prepared to submit to the punishment.

Mr Martin gave Walker a three-year suspended jail term and allowed six months, which expires in August, for the payback to occur. In the ritual, the convicted man will be speared through the thighs in front of the tribe by the younger brother of a man he stabbed to death in Alice Springs in a family feud last year.

Walker, who has accepted the tribal law and is said to be happy with the judge's decision, is now being cared for by relatives at an isolated settlement. He is said to be ready to return to Yuendumu for the spearing when preliminary tribal ceremonies have been completed.

My Kevin Kitchener, a barrister/ with the North Australian Aboriginal Legal Aid Service, said: 'Maybe we should go back to the old traditional ways. They seem to work.' Mr Kitchener, who related the beating incident to a conference on Aboriginal justice issues in Townsville, Queensland, said the youths had been surrounded in the street by Aboriginal male adults. They had not been seriously hurt because the adults knew how to beat them without causing permanent injuries.

'It sounds barbaric', he said, 'but the instant justice had an important further deterrent effect. They know that if they get into trouble again the same thing will happen. But next time women will be wielding the rubber hoses, which will give them an even greater sense of shame.'

Mr Kitchener said the day before the public beating another group of Aboriginal youths had been arrested in Darwin for similar offences.

'They told friends they were very glad to be facing white man's justice – not one of them wanted to face Aboriginal punishment,' he said.

by Geoffrey Lee Martin
in Sydney

Source: *The Daily Telegraph*, 18 June 1994: 13. © Telegraph Group Limited, London, 1994

prevent crime or to capture criminals? Should we spend more money on probation to help offenders or more on prison to punish them? Are the courts effective in ensuring fair trials and preventing miscarriages of justice? Should the phrase 'miscarriage of justice' apply only to those who are wrongly convicted of a crime they did not commit, or should it also apply to those who committed a crime but were convicted by improper use of evidence?

Should it even apply to those who avoid conviction although they have committed a criminal act? These questions and issues will depend on a number of assumptions and views about the nature and extent of the problems of crime and the justice and injustices associated with the way the agencies who operate on behalf of society go about their business. Therefore, in this book we have included chapters about images of, and the extent of, crime and in this opening chapter we introduce the reader to some of the key principles of criminal justice and the models and flow diagrams that provide ways of thinking about the criminal justice system in England and Wales, or elsewhere.

CRIMINAL JUSTICE IN ENGLAND AND WALES

The organisation and jurisdictional limits of criminal justice in England and Wales are determined by constitutional distinctions within the UK. In the UK, although Parliament passes legislation which may apply throughout, there are three distinctive criminal justice systems with separate procedures and agencies: England and Wales, Scotland, and Northern Ireland. Different government departments are responsible for criminal justice in these three regions – the Home Office for England and Wales, the Scottish Office and the Northern Ireland Office.

Other government departments such as the Lord Chancellor's Department and the Attorney General's Office are involved in the administration of criminal justice. Local councils have a statutory duty to establish a Social Services Department employing qualified social workers to deal with children in trouble with the criminal law. Criminal investigations are not made exclusively by the police but also by many other agencies such as investigators for the Department of Trade and Industry, the Serious Fraud Office, HM Customs and Excise and various local government bodies such as the Environmental Health and Trading Standards Departments.

In England and Wales criminal justice agencies such as the police, prisons and probation are funded primarily by central government. Policy is established in part by civil servants who advise ministers and by legislation enacted by Parliament. For administrative purposes agencies are divided into regional areas. The main agencies are briefly described below:

- *Police.* There are 43 regional police forces each under the direction of a chief constable and, except for the Metropolitan Police and the City of London police, local police authorities. Forces vary in size – the biggest being the Metropolitan Police with 28,000 uniformed officers. The Home Office is the government department responsible for the police.

- *Prosecutors.* The Crown Prosecution Service is divided into 42 areas and was set up in 1985. The Attorney General is answerable in Parliament for the Crown Prosecution Service which is headed by the Director of Public Prosecutions, a senior lawyer.

- *Courts.* Most criminal cases have to go to the magistrates' courts although more serious cases are ultimately dealt with in the Crown Courts. Officials in these courts include judges, magistrates, magistrates' clerks and ushers. The criminal courts come under the authority of the Lord Chancellor's Department which is responsible for the appointment of magistrates and judges.

- *Probation.* The Probation Service is responsible for preparing pre-sentence reports for courts, supervising probation orders and helping prisoners adapt to community life following release. There are 55 probation areas, and the service comes under the control of the Home Office.

- *Prisons.* The Prison Service is an executive agency, with policy direction from the Home Office and is organised into 15 regional areas, with responsibility for 133 prisons in 1998.

As well as the professions and officials in these agencies, many private citizens are involved in criminal justice. These include lay visitors to police stations, neighbourhood watch groups, victim support volunteers, members of juries, prison boards of visitors, and lay magistrates of which there were 30,374 in 1998.

There is also a growing army of employees in private security firms, of which Group 4, Pinkerton's, Securicor and Wells Fargo are the best known. There are also many smaller businesses, such as private detectives, locksmiths, bailiffs and credit investigation and information services. Although it is extremely difficult to estimate the total number of employees in this sector some have estimated the number to be as high as 250,000 although the most reliable estimate gives a figure of 162,303 (Jones and Newburn 1994a). The higher figure is about the same size as the numbers working for all government criminal justice agencies, thus the private sector plays a major and growing role in crime prevention. It is also becoming increasingly involved in other sectors of the system. In November 1991, Group 4 signed a contract to run the first private prison, the Wolds Remand Prison in Humberside. The second to be opened was Blakenhurst, a local prison, and Doncaster opened in 1994. Twelve prisons were initially planned to be put in private hands by the Prison Service.

Finally, the legal professions are a vital part of criminal justice. Barristers and solicitors are the two branches of this powerful professional group which is independent of government. Barristers are primarily court advocates whereas solicitors advise clients on a variety of matters and deal with clients prior to trial. The majority of advocacy in the Crown Court is done by barristers and the higher courts have only recently been open to solicitors as advocates. Both solicitors and barristers have the right to appear and represent clients, i.e. rights of audience, in the magistrates' court, where much of the work is undertaken by solicitors. A member of the public cannot directly seek advice from a barrister without first instructing a solicitor. A survey by the Law

Society (1989) showed that of the 26,670 solicitors in private practice, 62 per cent dealt with criminal matters. In 1992 there were 7,150 practising barristers, most of whom will have represented criminal clients in their career, and some of whom specialise entirely in criminal cases.

Expansion of the criminal justice system in the 1980s and 1990s

Whether we assess growth by expenditure, output or number of employees, the agencies making up the criminal justice system in England and Wales have all grown steadily over the last decade. Figure 1.3 illustrates the growth of employees in some of the main sectors, showing that in 1995/6 there were a quarter of a million employees. To this must be added the estimated 162,000 private sector employees.

In addition to the quantitative growth of this occupational sector, a qualitative change is also occurring as pressure mounts for greater professionalisation through degree level entry and an increasing emphasis on training. This is most evident in the police, prison and court services. This demand for greater professionalism reflects the greater complexity of the work of criminal justice employees in the 1990s. It is recognised for example that officials need to be responsive to the changing demands of society and the increasing complexities of the system. Social change and community demands have resulted in continual reviews and a re-examination of the function and practice of many agencies and professions. Further changes can be expected as the implications of greater European and international co-operation are examined. The introduction of new technology has increased demands for a more highly trained and flexible workforce.

The volume of recent legislation, government reports and commissions on aspects of criminal justice, which will be referred to throughout this book, reflects this state of change. Throughout the 1990s we have seen a steady flow

Fig 1.3 Employment in criminal justice

	1986/87	*1995/96**	*Growth*
Prisons	28,180	40,360	12,180
Police officers	121,542	126,878	5,336
Police civilians	45,185	52,933	7,748
Magistrates' court manpower	9,523	10,727	1,204
Probation officers	5,630	7,813	2,183
CPS	2,243	6,577	4,334
Total	**212,303**	**245,288**	**32,985**

* Relates to planned growth

Compiled from The Government's Public Expenditure Plans 1991–2 to 1993–4 for the Home Office and the Charity Commission, February 1991. Cm 1509. London: HMSO and Home Office Research and Statistics Directorate, 17 December 1996.

of legislation on matters to do with criminal justice (see the chronological section at the end of this chapter). The Royal Commission on Criminal Justice chaired by Lord Runciman examined options for reform of criminal procedure and reported in 1993. The Lord Chancellor's Department has established an agenda of reforms for the legal profession and the court services. Reviews of recruitment, functions and training are taking place in both the police and prison services. Virtually every aspect of the system is currently undergoing change.

This expansion has meant that the law and order budget has grown steadily. In the financial year 1993/4 the Home Office, Lord Chancellor's Department and the Attorney General's Office spent £9,424 million on criminal justice services. This compares with £35,675 million spent on health, £30,399 million on education and £22,757 million on defence. In recent years the Home Office has sought to improve the cost effectiveness of the system by contracting out some services and utilising performance measures and auditing techniques. The restructuring of the management of the magistrates' court services and the reform of legal aid have been influenced by fiscal pressures to reduce public expenditure.

It is clear, therefore, that criminal justice is currently undergoing considerable change, brought about by a number of different and often conflicting pressures. These also affect the perceived role and function of criminal justice and its many agencies. Before discussing this, we need to examine the principles on which the criminal justice system is based, and the different ways of looking at its role.

PRINCIPLES, SYSTEMS AND MODELS OF CRIMINAL JUSTICE

Principles of criminal justice

Unlike many other countries, England and Wales have no written penal code or definitive statement of the principles of criminal justice. Nonetheless some important principles guide criminal justice procedure. A crucial feature of criminal justice in England and Wales is the adversarial principle, which determines how guilt should be established. A central aspect of this is that the individual has rights; whether as a suspect, defendant or convicted person.

Adversarial justice

The main principle that underpins the system of criminal justice in England and Wales is adversarial justice. This requires the police to identify a suspect from the evidence available and, if there is sufficient evidence against him or

11

her, to prosecute that person and establish his or her guilt. An adversarial system does not seek to establish what happened or the truth about an incident, that is sometimes left to inquiries; the adversarial system only requires the police and prosecutor to identify a person, called a suspect. The logic of adversarial justice, however, requires that the police and the prosecutors will not continue with a case even if they are convinced that they know who committed a crime, until they have sufficient evidence to show beyond reasonable doubt that the person they accused of the crime did it. They will have to convince the magistrates in a summary trial, or a jury in the Crown Court.

Beyond reasonable doubt is a high standard of proof and this not only protects the innocent against wrongful conviction but also protects the guilty where the evidence is not available or exists but is not admissible. The adversarial system does not presume that all people arrested are innocent, otherwise no one would be arrested or remanded in custody. The presumption of innocence is a rule that governs the conduct of the trial stage only. It means in effect that the prosecutor must convince a jury or magistrates of the fact that the person accused of the crime did it by reference to evidence rather than assertion. The trial procedure is based on the assumption that the defendant is innocent and it is up to the prosecutor to demonstrate by evidence that the person is guilty beyond reasonable doubt. The trial and the system of appeals never establishes the innocence of the accused. Because a person is acquitted does not mean he or she was innocent in the commonsense meaning of the word.

The image of adversarial justice is of ranks of bewigged and articulate barristers using argument and evidence and cross-examination to establish the guilt or otherwise of the offender accused of a crime. This image is unrealistic as most defendants admit their guilt for an offence rather than have it established by trial. Thus in 1996 in magistrates' courts nearly three quarters of a million cases (732,300) resulted in convictions because the defendant pleaded guilty. Whereas in only 72,800 summary cases defendants contested their guilt by trial. In that same year in the Crown Court 65 per cent of 89,070 defendants pleaded guilty without a trial.

It is therefore arguable whether the adversarial nature of criminal justice is the dominant feature of a system in which only a small proportion of defendants exercise their right to trial. However, it is still accurate to describe the system as adversarial because the possibility of a trial, and the onus of having to prove beyond reasonable doubt the guilt of an offender, affects many parts of the system – particularly the way the police and prosecutors conduct their business. The police will need evidence that might be exposed to the full glare of a trial. A prosecutor's reputation will be adversely affected if he or she allows a case to proceed that does not meet the standards set in the Code for Crown Prosecutors for evidential sufficiency, which means the evidence must be admissible, credible and reliable such that it is likely to convince a jury that the person was guilty beyond reasonable doubt.

In adversarial systems therefore a trial does not establish whether the accused is innocent of the offence he or she has been charged with, but whether the evidence is sufficient, beyond reasonable doubt, to establish guilt. Criminal appeals examine the same issue, a point explained by Professor Michael Zander in the context of a Court of Appeal decision which overturned the conviction of Winston Silcott for the murder of PC Blakelock during the Broadwater Farm riot of October 1985.

In a letter to *The Times*, Zander explains the key logic of the adversarial system:

Guilt or Innocence?

Sir, In writing about compensation for Winston Silcott (August 3) Janet Daley says, 'He has now been declared innocent of one particular crime'. This commonly held view is incorrect.

Mr Silcott, whose conviction for another murder still stands, had his conviction for murder in the case of PC Blakelock quashed by the Court of Appeal. This no more represents a declaration of innocence than does acquittal by a jury.

A jury acquittal means that in the jury's view the prosecution have not proved beyond reasonable doubt, or that even if guilt has been established they are unwilling to convict. The quashing of a conviction by the Court of Appeal means that for one of a large number of possible reasons the conviction cannot stand. Very often the reason is that the judge directed the jury wrongly on law. In the Silcott case, the reason related to documents which the Court of Appeal considered had been tampered with.

Many people, including many commentators in the media, have confused these issues.

The question of whether someone is innocent is not one that is addressed in a criminal trial in our legal system (emphasis added).

(*The Times*, 12 August 1994: 15)

In the same way as the trial questions whether guilt has been established on the basis of evidence presented, an appeal after conviction considers whether the trial process was flawed. In neither case does the court ask 'Is the defendant innocent?'.

Principles, other than adversarial, can be found in policy statements by parliamentary bodies such as the Select Committee on Home Affairs and in the written aims of separate agencies in the system (see Chapter 11). General statements can also be found in policy documents such as white papers or as preambles to legislation. The Home Office and the Lord Chancellor's Department have overall responsibility for many aspects of the criminal justice system, but unlike other more centralised systems, a policy document from these departments is not regarded as a definitive statement of policy to be followed slavishly. This is partly because this would conflict with other principles such as the independence of the judiciary, professional autonomy and divisions of responsibility for the management and funding of criminal justice (see Chapter 11).

In contrast to our system, some countries have penal codes which contain clearly stated principles. An example of this is Finland where the basic principles of the criminal justice system have been set out in the Penal Code of 1889. Although these have been amended over the century, the Finnish Ministry of Justice identifies the fundamental principles in Finnish criminal law and procedure:

Today, the fundamental principles in criminal law include the principles of legality, equality, predictability and proportionality. Among the consequences of the strict interpretation given the principle of *legality* in Finland is that the court may not impose forms of punishment that are not specified for the offence in question. *Equality* demands that all cases falling within a specific category are dealt with in the same way. *Predictability* demands that it is possible to assess, in advance, the certainty and level of punishment for a given act. Predictability increases if the law is simple and legal practice is uniform. *Proportionality* requires that the sanction for an offence is in proportion to its blameworthiness. This principle, which also requires that consideration be taken of all official and unofficial penal and non-penal consequences of an offence, establishes the maximum punishment. It is not seen to prevent mitigation of punishment where this is deemed reasonable.

In Finland, as in all of the Nordic countries, it is generally felt that punishments primarily have, and should have, a general preventive effect. General prevention can be enhanced by two components, the *certainty* and *severity* of punishment. Finnish criminal policy emphasizes certainty, but not severity. General prevention also involves the maintenance of standards of morality through the public disapproval that punishment directs at criminal behaviour. Individual prevention, as a primary goal of punishment, has been rejected. The coercive rehabilitation of offenders was found to be based on flawed arguments and to raise problems with legal safeguards and the control of discretion.

(Joutsen 1990: 2)

Without a penal code or its equivalent the principles that govern criminal justice in England and Wales evolve from the system of parliamentary sovereignty and the principles of the rule of law. The system of parliamentary sovereignty means that Parliament is the supreme authority and the final arbiter of legality as defined by the enacted laws of the land. In recent years, since the Treaty of Rome, Parliament has not been the only source of rules and regulations and some aspects of the sovereignty of the British Parliament have been ceded to European institutions.

The basic principles of the rule of law were articulated by A V Dicey, who wrote:

No man is punishable or can be lawfully made to suffer in body or goods except for a distinct breach of law established in the ordinary legal manner before the ordinary courts of the land.

. . . no man is above the law, but . . . every man whatever be his rank or condition, is subject to the ordinary law of the realm and amenable to the jurisdiction of the ordinary tribunals.

. . . the general principles of the constitution (as for example the right to personal liberty, or the right to public meeting) are with us as the result of judicial decisions determining the rights of private persons in particular cases brought before the courts.

(Dicey 1959: 188–95)

14

The rights of the defendant, and the victim and the public at large, are derived from the provisions enacted by Parliament and interpretations of the ordinary courts. A primary principle of the rule of law is that everyone is subject to the law including those who enforce it. They can claim no special status unless given by the law and must always be answerable to the law.

In England and Wales official objectives are typically expressed in Home Office documents, such as *Criminal Justice: A Working Paper* (Home Office 1984). In the foreword the then Home Secretary, Leon Brittan, specified four objectives for criminal justice which would contribute towards sustaining the principle of the rule of law:

> A fair and effective criminal justice system marks the distinction between a civilised society and anarchy. If it works well, we as citizens can live our lives peacefully, and enjoy the rewards of our labours; if it works badly, many of us – particularly the elderly and the vulnerable – will have our lives marred by the fear, and sometimes the experience, of crime. . . .
> We needed a strategy. . .
> The central objectives of this strategy are to sustain the rule of law:
> a. by preventing crime wherever possible;
> b. when crimes are committed, by detecting the culprit;
> c. by convicting the guilty and acquitting the innocent;
> d. by dealing adequately and appropriately with those who are guilty and by giving proper effect to the sentences or orders which are imposed.

Principles of criminal justice, whether set out in penal codes, legislation or policy documents, attempt to capture a complex set of issues in grand statements which are supposed to guide the policies and actions of participants in the system. However, the world of human behaviour is not so easily captured into a few phrases and reality is necessarily more complex. The presumption of innocence, for example, sounds simple but raises complex questions. One of these is how many guilty criminals we are prepared to allow to escape apprehension and punishment in order to ensure that no innocent person is unjustly arrested and punished. We could punish those whom we are absolutely certain have committed an offence, but victims may feel aggrieved when cases fall on seeming technicalities and the release of too many apparently guilty persons could encourage vigilantism. Then the chances of justice being done would be even less likely.

Principles of criminal justice are abstractions which portray what ought to happen. Anecdotal insights, be they from police officers, solicitors, barristers, probation officers or recidivists, are frequently stories of the way the system failed to work as it is supposed. Empirical studies by criminologists and social scientists in recent years have given credence to some of these insights by revealing the gap between principles and reality.

It is very important for a student of criminal justice not to treat the principles as facts, but to regard them instead as criteria by which to judge the performance and practices of a criminal justice system.

15

Systems approaches to criminal justice

We have used the term 'criminal justice system' and must now look at what this implies. The term 'system' is often used to describe a designed unit such as a central heating or a recording system, or a natural phenomenon such as the solar system. It has also been used by social reformers who applied the term to the education or welfare systems and talked in terms of social engineering. The word 'system' conveys an impression of a complex object with interconnected parts and subdivisions with a flow from beginning to end.

Would it be accurate to describe criminal justice as a system? Certainly looking at the flow charts in Figures 1.4–1.6, it could well appear that there is a system at work which has a beginning and a number of predictable stages. The agencies in the criminal justice system are interdependent. One agency's output is another agency's input. Those who leave the courts with a custodial sentence become the intake into the prisons at the back-end of the system. The role of each agency depends on its particular function in the overall scheme of things. For instance, policing cannot be fully understood without an awareness of the role of the police in the overall context of the system. The system may therefore be seen as greater than the sum of its parts.

It is also useful to view criminal justice as a system when considering planning, organisation and policy. During the 1980s, for example, there were a number of attempts to encourage a systems approach towards criminal justice. The Home Secretary, Leon Brittan, in evidence to the Home Affairs Committee of the House of Commons declared:

> . . . on taking office I decided that we needed a strategy which would enable us to establish and pursue our priorities and objectives in a deliberate and coherent way. . . . Our principal preoccupation is, and I believe it ought to be, the criminal justice system which, incidentally, I wish to see treated in all that we do as a system.
>
> (Home Affairs Select Committee, 23 January 1984)

There are several implications of regarding criminal justice as a system. It recognises that agencies are interdependent. Hence, the work of the prison and probation services depends on the work of the courts who, in turn, depend on the filtering role of the Crown Prosecution Service, the generation of cases by the police and initially by the activities of lawbreakers. It is very important for financial and resource planning and is particularly crucial when considering reforms to recognise the interdependency of the system. Thus reforms proposed for one part of the system will often have an impact on other agencies not directly involved in the proposed changes.

This can be seen by considering how the prison population can be affected by changes in the law. In the last 50 years, the advent of the motor car has created the need for more regulation by the criminal law, as cars not only provide opportunities for theft, but also necessitate regulation of driving if others are not to be endangered or inconvenienced. This increases the number of people brought to court, which in turn affects the number in prison. Motoring offences have resulted in a rise in the number of receptions into prisons of those convicted of serious motoring offences such as causing death by dangerous driving, along with many fine defaulters initially convicted of a motoring offence.

A systems approach also encourages inter-agency consultation and co-operation. One recommendation from the Woolf Inquiry into the series of prison riots during 1990 was the need for greater co-operation and liaison between agencies in the criminal justice system. Thus prisons cannot be effectively managed without the fullest co-operation of all agencies respons-ible for dealing with offenders. The report recommended that a Criminal Justice Consultative Council (CJCC) be set up. This was done in 1991 and includes senior members of most of the agencies. Since then 24 local com-mittees have been formed. The aim of establishing Area Committees was to encourage better communications between agencies and to improve strategic planning by identifying common areas of concern, receive reports, collect and distribute information on agency and cross-agency activities, disseminate information regarding available resources and be a forum for addressing strategic developments that affect all agencies (see Chapter 11).

Greater co-operation between criminal justice agencies and external organ-isations was also encouraged during the 1980s in respect of crime prevention. Many partnerships were set up, encouraged by the Home Office, involving links between official criminal justice agencies, local government and the voluntary and business sectors. These will be explored in Chapter 11.

How systematic is criminal justice in England and Wales? It must be recog-nised that the multiple and competing aims of the system mean that different goals may be simultaneously pursued by different participants. These aims are not easy to reconcile, either in the system as a whole or within specific agencies. For example, should the judge give a sentence that deters the future lawbreaker or one that rehabilitates past lawbreakers?

These multiple aims also affect how those working in agencies see their role, and how, over time, they have developed their own ways of working within conflicting constraints. Thus agencies have developed what can be de-scribed as a distinctive working culture or professional ideology. One example of these kinds of conflicts can be found in the implementation of parts of the Criminal Justice Act 1991, which enacted curfew orders and electronic monitoring but did not provide details as to how or when they were to come into effect. These new sanctions were not popular with some sections of the probation service who regard themselves as a profession whose aim is to help or care for offenders, rather than to supervise or control them. So the central problem of describing criminal justice as a system is to recognise the prac-tical implications of these conflicting goals.

Another problem may arise where agencies are expected to co-operate with each other. There may, for example, be competition between agencies over the allocation of responsibilities or funding. Different working cultures which derive from different perceptions of the goals of the system may lead to mistrust between agencies. This may mean that they are reluctant to co-operate with each other and may inhibit the exchange of information, which affected the initial relationship between the police and the Crown Prosecution Service when it was established in 1985. Differing models, as described below, may be followed: the police, who have traditionally been seen as following a crime control model, may have difficulties in communicating with lawyers whose role derives from the due process model, or with social workers, who may be more committed to a rehabilitative model.

A certain level of conflict is designed into the system by the *adversarial* nature of criminal trials. It is the duty of the prosecution to prove the guilt of the accused 'beyond reasonable doubt', whereas it is the duty of the defence lawyer to plant that 'reasonable doubt' in the minds of the magistrates or the jury and so secure an acquittal. This adversarial nature of criminal trials has important consequences for other parts of the system. It affects the way the police, prosecutors and the probation service perceive and discharge their respective roles.

As we have seen, the trial seeks not to establish the truth, but provides a process for the conviction or acquittal of the accused which affects the kind of evidence the police must secure. The logic of the adversarial style of trial explains why the defence lawyer may cross-examine victims of crime, for example in rape cases, in a way that appears at times to be brutal and insensitive.

Flow charts of the criminal justice system

The interrelationships between agencies and stages in the system can be represented in flow charts which provide a helpful snapshot of the process to enhance understanding of the jigsaw of interrelationships in the system. Figures 1.4–1.6 illustrate the flow and stages of the criminal justice system from crime to prosecution, in the courts, and in the penal system.

Flow charts, however, provide a misleadingly simplistic picture of a system that involves encounters between human beings, all coming into the system with their own motives, be they criminals, victims or criminal justice officials. Each encounter involves an individual story, and has significance in the overall drama of society's response to crime. The drama, morality and social consequences of crime and punishment cannot be portrayed easily in such charts. In addition, while they show some of the ways in which agencies and the stages of the system interrelate, they cannot always reflect the complexities of how one decision, taken by one agency at a particular point in the system affects later decisions.

Some prefer to see criminal justice as a process – through which a case or a defendant passes. In this process all stages, each governed by a set of

Fig 1.4 Criminal Justice Flow Chart 1: from crime to prosecution (For routine cases involving adults)

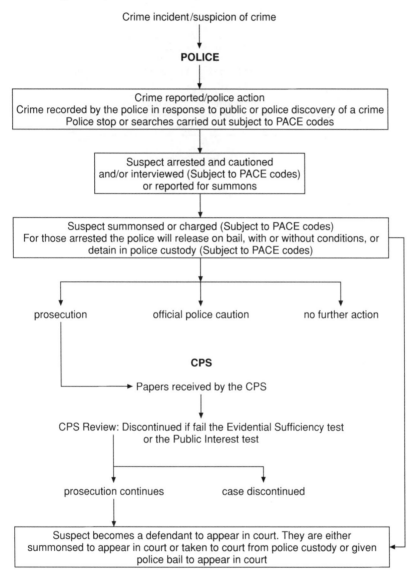

discrete rules, are interrelated and affect the eventual outcome. Whether a defendant pleads guilty or not guilty for example affects not only whether he or she is convicted, but whether and how evidence must be prepared, whether he or she is given bail, and it will almost certainly affect any sentence. At the same time, defendants' decisions about whether or not to plead guilty and, if so, when to plead guilty, will be affected by what might happen at later stages.

Fig 1.5 Criminal Justice Flow Chart 2: the criminal courts – from first court appearance to conviction (For routine cases involving adults)

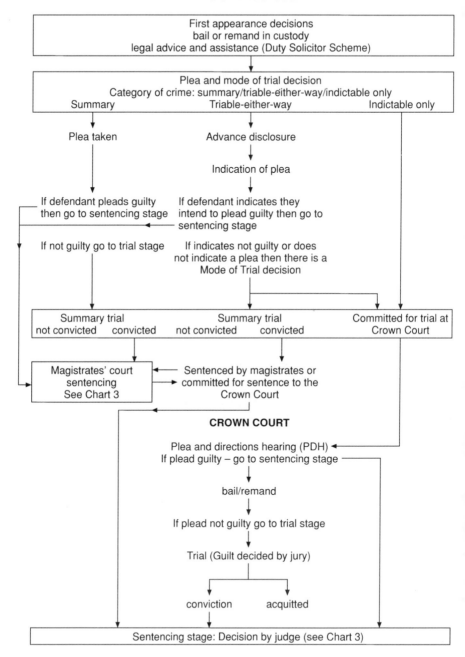

MAGISTRATES' COURT

First appearance decisions
bail or remand in custody
legal advice and assistance (Duty Solicitor Scheme)

Plea and mode of trial decision
Category of crime: summary/triable-either-way/indictable only

Summary   Triable-either-way   Indictable only

Plea taken   Advance disclosure

Indication of plea

If defendant pleads guilty   If defendant indicates they
then go to sentencing stage   intend to plead guilty then go to
                               sentencing stage

If not guilty go to trial stage   If indicates not guilty or does
                                   not indicate a plea then there is a
                                   Mode of Trial decision

Summary trial   Summary trial   Committed for trial at
not convicted   convicted not convicted   convicted Crown Court

Magistrates' court   ◄── Sentenced by magistrates or
sentencing   ──► committed for sentence to the
See Chart 3   Crown Court

CROWN COURT

Plea and directions hearing (PDH)
If plead guilty – go to sentencing stage

bail/remand

If plead not guilty go to trial stage

Trial (Guilt decided by jury)

conviction   acquitted

Sentencing stage: Decision by judge (see Chart 3)

Fig 1.6 Criminal Justice Flow Chart 3: inter-relationship of agencies in the penal system (For routine cases involving adults)

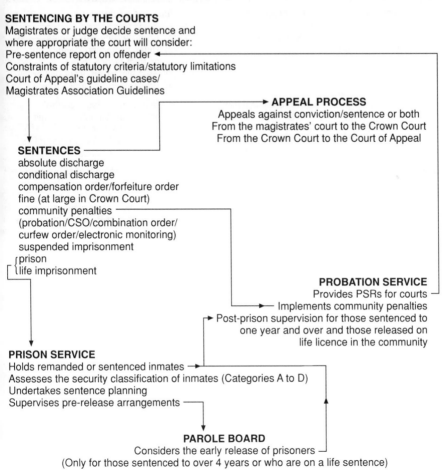

SENTENCING BY THE COURTS
Magistrates or judge decide sentence and
where appropriate the court will consider:
Pre-sentence report on offender
Constraints of statutory criteria/statutory limitations
Court of Appeal's guideline cases/
Magistrates Association Guidelines

APPEAL PROCESS
Appeals against conviction/sentence or both
From the magistrates' court to the Crown Court
From the Crown Court to the Court of Appeal

SENTENCES
absolute discharge
conditional discharge
compensation order/forfeiture order
fine (at large in Crown Court)
community penalties
(probation/CSO/combination order/
curfew order/electronic monitoring)
suspended imprisonment
prison
life imprisonment

PROBATION SERVICE
Provides PSRs for courts
Implements community penalties
Post-prison supervision for those sentenced to
one year and over and those released on
life licence in the community

PRISON SERVICE
Holds remanded or sentenced inmates
Assesses the security classification of inmates (Categories A to D)
Undertakes sentence planning
Supervises pre-release arrangements

PAROLE BOARD
Considers the early release of prisoners
(Only for those sentenced to over 4 years or who are on a life sentence)

Models of criminal justice

Models of criminal justice are essentially different perspectives on, or different ways of looking at, criminal justice, derived from the work of writers from a variety of legal, sociological, or administrative backgrounds. They provide a way of looking at criminal justice in terms of some general characteristics, principles or themes of a system. They help the person new to a system to come to terms with its complexities and to make some sense of it. But it should be remembered that, like all models, they are a scaled-down version of the real thing and will not capture all its complexities.

Herbert Packer first identified two alternative models – a crime control model which stressed the role of criminal justice in terms of the efficient

21

Fig 1.7 Models of criminal justice

Social function	Process model	Features of court
1. Justice	Due process model	(a) Equality between parties (b) Rules protecting defendants against error (c) Restraint or arbitrary power (d) Presumption of innocence
2. Punishment	Crime control model	(a) Disregard of legal controls (b) Implicit presumption of guilt (c) High conviction rate (d) Unpleasantness of experience (e) Support for police
3. Rehabilitation	Medical model (diagnosis, prediction, and treatment selection)	(a) Information collecting procedures (b) Individualisation (c) Treatment presumption (d) Discretion of decision-makers (e) Expertise of decision-makers or advisers (f) Relaxation of formal rules
4. Management of crime and criminals	Bureaucratic model	(a) Independence from political considerations (b) Speed and efficiency (c) Importance of and acceptance of records (d) Minimisation of conflict (e) Minimisation of expense (f) Economical division of labour
5. Denunciation and degradation	Status passage model	(a) Public shaming of defendant (b) Court values reflecting community values (c) Agents' control over process
6. Maintenance of class domination	Power model	(a) Reinforcement of class values (b) Alienation of defendant (c) Deflection of attention from issues of class conflict (d) Differences between judges and judged (e) Paradoxes and contradictions between rhetoric and performance

Source: King (1981: 13).

controlling of crime (the conveyor belt), and a due process model (the obstacle course), which stressed the importance of the rule of law and procedural safeguards (Packer 1968). These ideas were extremely influential, and later writers identified further models such as Michael King who outlined six such models (King 1981).

The first model, originally developed by Packer is the *due process* model, which represents an idealised version of how the system should work derived from the ideas inherent in the rule of law. It encompasses the principles of the defendant's rights found in textbooks and constitutional documents. It incorporates principles conveyed in well-known phrases such as the presumption of innocence, the defendant's right to a fair trial, equality before the law and that justice should be seen to be done. These phrases embody principles that underlie and allow us to interpret the many rules surrounding both the trial and the pre-trial processes. They protect defendants in order that the innocent may be acquitted and only the guilty convicted.

The second model is the *crime control* model identified by Packer and earlier explored by Jerome Skolnick in his book *Justice Without Trial* (Skolnick 1966). This stresses the role of the system in reducing, preventing and curbing crime by prosecuting and punishing those who are guilty of offences. It also stresses the importance of protecting citizens and serving the public by crime reduction. Thus the police and prosecution agencies may interpret their role primarily as crime fighters responsible for ensuring that the guilty are brought to justice. However, problems arise if this aim is pursued regardless of rules protecting the rights of the suspect. Fabricating evidence or neglecting to use search warrants could be seen as justifiable in order to ensure that an offender whom the police 'know' to be guilty is found guilty. This problem underlies many laws governing police procedure, seen most recently in legislative reforms of the 1980s. The Police and Criminal Evidence Act 1984 introduced the procedure under which the police tape recorded interviews with suspects in police stations, and the Prosecution of Offences Act 1985 led to the establishment of a prosecution agency independent of the police – the Crown Prosecution Service.

For many decades it has been accepted that offenders may not be wholly responsible for their own actions but that their criminality may spring from individual characteristics or social factors. These may be psychological disturbance or problems related to their family circumstances or the social environment. It may make little sense to punish such offenders without at the same time attempting to deal with these underlying issues. This is reflected in King's third model, that of *rehabilitation*, which has affected many parts of the criminal justice process. Under this model one of the major considerations at each stage is how best to deal with the individual offender, assuming that their criminality can be reduced by taking a rehabilitative approach. Thus it might be more desirable for the police to divert some offenders, especially young offenders, from the system, in circumstances where they feel that no benefit will be served by prosecution. The police have powers to caution offenders and refer them to social work agencies which may also help adult offenders. Social workers and probation officers become involved at the sentencing stage, by preparing pre-sentence reports on the offender's circumstances and outlining sentencing options which may involve counselling and treatment rather than punishment.

Rehabilitation therefore individualises decisions, requiring that the needs of the offender are taken into account. It gives all agencies far greater amounts of discretion. This may well conflict with other goals – for example with those of due process which seek to ensure that all offenders are treated equally, or with the crime control model which stresses the need to punish the guilty.

King's fourth model reflects the pressure on criminal justice officials to implement rules and procedures within the many constraints imposed by limited resources and public pressure to solve crimes. Agencies must therefore establish measures of *bureaucratic efficiency*. They must ensure that defendants are tried and sentenced as speedily and efficiently as possible. If defendants spend too long in prison before they come to trial, if trials take too long and are too costly, or if it is argued that too many defendants are acquitted or that there are miscarriages of justice, agencies and courts will come under considerable criticism. The cost effectiveness of law enforcement and court administration has become a major concern of the government in the 1990s.

Balancing the interests of due process with those of crime control and bureaucratic efficiency is not always easy. It is difficult for example to subject abstract principles such as justice to tests of cost effectiveness. How many defendants should be acquitted? How many should be tried rather than plead guilty? There are no straightforward answers to these questions – no yardstick against which to assess the efficiency of the system. Indeed in some instances the interests of justice may conflict with those of efficiency – as can be seen in the example of not guilty pleas. If the defendant pleads not guilty, the prosecution and the defence have to prepare a case which may involve collecting evidence, summoning witnesses and preparing the many documents involved in a trial. If the defendant pleads guilty, much of this work can be avoided. Guilty pleas are, therefore, cost-effective and save the time of victims, witnesses, police, courts and the Crown Prosecution Service. But any pressure on defendants to plead guilty could deprive them of their right to trial. However, if more defendants insisted on their right to trial the system could become overloaded and more costly.

On the other hand, the police might not have sufficient admissible evidence to proceed against a person they suspect is guilty. The due process model would result in no action being taken. However, there may be some concern about the resources expended on an investigation with no result. The tension between these models will result in a difficult decision on whether to charge the person and hope that he or she pleads guilty or to drop the case.

Some would argue that offenders should be publicly tried and sentenced in order to reflect the community's moral disapproval of offending behaviour. This is reflected in the fifth model identified by King – the *denunciation and degradation* model. In this model, public trial and punishment are necessary to underline the law-abiding values of the community. Some sociologists have argued that the criminal justice system serves an important social function in reinforcing social values. While this may conflict with the aims of rehabilitation, it can be argued that such public punishment and expression of society's disapproval can in itself be rehabilitative, as it may induce feelings of shame in offenders – a prerequisite for rehabilitation. John Braithwaite argues in favour of re-integrative shaming – offenders should feel ashamed of their offences but shaming should not be so extreme that it stigmatises offenders to a point where they cannot be re-integrated into the community (Braithwaite 1989).

Analysing criminal justice systems also raises questions about who makes the law and whose interests criminal justice serves. This is reflected in King's last model, the *power* model. Some, using a Marxist or conflict perspective, which will be outlined in Chapter 2, argue that criminal justice systems essentially reinforce the role of the powerful – those who make the laws and who are served by the many agencies of the system. Thus criminal law and its enforcement are influenced by the interests of dominant classes, elites, races or gender, depending on the particular version of domination used. The state is regarded in this model as acting in the interest of the dominant group who use the criminal law to further these interests. Advocates of this approach point to the over-representation of those from poorer sections of the community as defendants in the criminal justice system.

To King's six models of criminal justice we would add a seventh: the *just deserts* model. Combining elements of retribution for offenders with a notion of proper respect for the treatment of the accused or defendant, this model stresses the importance of punishing offenders in terms of their blameworthiness and the seriousness of their offence, not through crude revenge or incapacitation, but in response to the wrongfulness of their act. This brings together the principles of respect for the offender as a human being with certain rights, the need to establish the offender's culpability for the offence so as to punish only the guilty, and the right of society to exact retribution from those who have done wrong. This links punishment and crime to issues of morality and control.

How useful are these models of criminal justice? To an extent they focus on and magnify one feature of the system. They do, however, illustrate different ways of looking at the system and indicate very different influences on policy and practice. Most of these models have been developed by different academic disciplines such as criminology, sociology or law and more recently from systems analysis utilised by experts in management and auditing techniques. Not surprisingly these disparate disciplines provide different snapshots of bits of the system from their own perspective. Lawyers focus mainly on procedures before and during trial. Sociologists emphasise the informal influences that can lead to inequalities and injustice. Criminologists focus on crime statistics and explanations of crime. Systems analysts trace the aggregate flow of cases through the system, management consultants look at problems of accountability and effectiveness, while accountants examine the cost effectiveness of the entire system and agencies within it. This has led to the development of management by objectives and the use of auditing techniques in the criminal justice system.

These different models indicate the many different influences on policy which often conflict. It might be better to understand a criminal justice system by starting with its multiple goals and by understanding the influences on the agencies that seek to implement these goals, be they legal, political, administrative, professional or economic. The next section will briefly outline recent legislation and reports which have had an important impact on the system, and which illustrate these conflicting policy pressures.

CRIMINAL JUSTICE LEGISLATION

'The first five Criminal Justice Acts of the century were spaced out over nearly 50 years, from 1925 to 1972, whereas the last five have come in less than 20 years since 1972 and the current Act is the third in only five years.' Wasik and Taylor wrote this in 1991 since when there has been a major piece of criminal justice legislation in every year since 1993 (see the Chronology of Kay Dates).

This section aims to outline briefly recent developments in the 1990s, highlighting how these reflect the many conflicting goals and models of the system and their effect on policy. These are the Criminal Justice Act 1991, subsequently amended by the Criminal Justice Act 1993, the Criminal Justice and Public Order Act 1994, the Police and Magistrates' Court Act 1994, and the Crime and Disorder Act 1998. The final section of this chapter gives a chronology of key legislation and events which have had a significant impact on the system – many of which will be discussed in later chapters. But first let us look at the remarkable history of one recent example of criminal justice legislation, the Criminal Justice Act 1991.

Criminal Justice Act 1991

This Criminal Justice Act (CJA 1991) was preceded by an unprecedented amount of research, planning, consultation and training. An experiment on unit fines was carried out in magistrates' courts in Hampshire, and extensive training was given to those who were to enforce the Act. But despite the research and consultation that went into the Act, within seven months of its implementation the Home Secretary announced that amendments were to be made to it.

The CJA 1991 was hailed as a far-reaching systematic reform of sentencing, although it reflected many existing shifts in penal philosophy and sentencing policy. The underlying themes of this change were expressed in the 1990 White Paper, *Crime, Justice and Protecting the Public* (Home Office 1990a) and included the need for more consistency in sentencing policy and for sentences to be proportionate to the offence. In addition it introduced what has come to be known as a 'twin track' approach to sentencing, making a clearer distinction between property offences and violent crime. The former were to be dealt with by a greater use of punishment in the community, while

26

the latter, with a view to crime prevention, could result in longer prison sentences. The overall framework for sentencing otherwise was provided by a philosophy of 'just deserts': punishing in accordance with the current offence, rather than past crimes or possible future ones.

An example of this approach was the introduction of the unit fine system under which sentencers were to allocate points reflecting the severity of the offence. These points would then be related to the offender's income, producing a specific amount of fine. Unit fines almost immediately attracted criticism. The calculation for translating points into actual amounts meant that fines were not only higher overall, but that they were particularly severe for those on middle incomes, typically convicted for traffic offences. In a review of the impact of the CJA 1991, Martin Wasik comments that 'people on average incomes found themselves in the top band' (Wasik 1993: 15).

Vociferous criticism was made of another aspect of the sentencing reforms introduced by the CJA 1991. Section 29 had prevented judges and magistrates taking into account past convictions when sentencing except in limited circumstances. Furthermore, they could only take into account two offences when assessing seriousness for a person convicted of multiple incidents. Thus the burglar convicted of 20 burglaries would actually be sentenced on the basis of the worst two burglaries. Sentencers felt unable to reflect the frequency and history of offending in their disposals.

Criminal Justice Act 1993

Most of the provisions of the CJA 1991 came into effect on 1 October 1992. By Easter 1993, Kenneth Clarke, the then Home Secretary, announced that the unit fine system was to be abandoned. Legislation to this effect was added to the Criminal Justice Bill already before Parliament. Thus the CJA 1993, which dealt primarily with measures to combat anti-terrorist acts, drug trafficking and insider dealing, was used to amend the CJA 1991. Section 65 abolished the two main planks of the 1991 Act, unit fines and s. 29. The new Act provides that sentencers must take account of means when fining, and adjust fines up or down as appropriate, but without imposing a framework for doing so. In addition, the court can now consider all offences before the court and offenders' previous convictions or any failure to respond to earlier sanctions can be used by the courts when deciding on a sentence.

Criminal Justice and Public Order Act 1994

This Act deals with many aspects of the criminal justice system. Details of its provisions will be given in relevant chapters. Below are its main provisions:

- The introduction of a secure training order for 12–14-year-old persistent offenders. The first half of this order is to be spent in secure training units, and the second half to be spent under compulsory supervision in the community.

- The doubling of the maximum sentence for 15–17 year olds of detention in a young offender institution from 1 to 2 years (see Chapter 5).

- Curbing the right to silence by allowing a court to draw inferences from a defendant's silence during police questioning or in court.

- Section 25 of the Act provided that bail cannot be granted to defendants charged with or convicted of homicide or rape or who have a previous conviction for such an offence. Section 26 provided that persons accused or convicted of committing an offence while on bail need not be given bail (see Chapter 6).

- Pilot projects for curfew orders and electronic monitoring.

- With regard to sentencing, s. 48 of the Act, which dealt with discounts for guilty pleas, required the courts to take account of the timing and circumstances of a guilty plea in line with the recommendations of the Royal Commission.

- Tougher powers against trespassers and unauthorised camping were directed at new age travellers and rave parties of more than 100 people. A new offence of aggravated trespass was created in ss 68 and 69. In addition, the enhanced protection for property owners against squatters effectively amounted to the criminalisation of squatting.

- Changes to the laws in relation to obscenity to incorporate child pornography produced on computers and some restrictions on the classification of video recordings were directed against what are commonly known as 'video nasties'.

- Changes to sexual offences: s. 142 of the Act redefined the offence of rape which may now cover non-consensual intercourse with either a woman or a man – thus effectively recognising the offence commonly known as 'male rape'. Section 145 lowered the age of consent for homosexual acts from 21 to 18.

- The Act created other new offences including a new offence of intentionally causing harassment, alarm or distress by using threatening, abusive or insulting words, behaviour or displays, intended to apply to racial harassment. Other changes dealt with the use of embryos or foetuses, ticket touting at football matches and touting for car hire services.

The Police and Magistrates' Courts Act 1994

This made a number of changes in the organisation of the police and magistrates' courts, including proposals for reorganising police authorities and the introduction of devolved budgets and performance related criteria in the administration of them. See Chapter 4.

Crime and Disorder Act 1998

The main themes of this Act focus on strategies to combat criminal behaviour among younger offenders and to tackle crime at an earlier stage in the offender's history. An array of measures are introduced that permit intervention at an early stage and allow for a response to anti-social and criminal behaviour of children, including: a local child curfew scheme, parenting orders, action plan orders, and police reprimands and final warnings. Youth offending teams will be established on a multi-disciplinary basis to co-ordinate crime prevention and responses to youth crime.

New sentences for young offenders are introduced: the reparation order and the detention and training order replaces the secure training order. Secure training centres for those aged from 12 to 14 will be under the authority of a new Youth Justice Board. Tougher community protection laws with respect to sex offenders and anti-social behaviour and a new category of racially aggravated offence is created.

In the courts, procedural changes include speeding up the process of dealing with cases by imposing time limits, and the ending of committal proceedings for indictable-only offences. Reform of the CPS will allow lay employees to conduct pre-trial procedure such as bail hearings.

For sentencing policy a Sentencing Advisory Panel is to be established to advise the Court of Appeal on matters to do with sentencing guidelines.

CONCLUSION

In this chapter, we have suggested that to understand how a criminal justice system operates it is necessary to identify its many aims, to be able to describe its procedures, modes of punishments and the behaviour criminalised and to appreciate the interdependencies between agencies, which at a minimum allow us to call it a system. We have also indicated through the models of criminal justice many of the influences and principles that guide criminal justice agencies and placed this into the context of the political, economic and cultural factors that shape participants' views and actions, be they offenders, judges, police or probation officers. Finally we have illustrated how models of criminal justice help us to come to terms with the tensions between the formal goals and the real practices that go on in the world of those who enforce, interpret and implement the criminal law. That world is complex, given its many manifestations, aspirations and everyday encounters, and no one theory, model or principle will do justice to that reality. This book will attempt to reflect these many issues as we look at specific agencies and stages of the system.

CHRONOLOGY OF KEY DATES IN THE DEVELOPMENT OF CRIMINAL JUSTICE IN ENGLAND AND WALES

The following gives a list of significant dates referred to in this book. Added comments indicate key developments in the criminal justice system in England and Wales.

1717   Transportation Act
1779   Penitentiary Act
1784   Transportation Act
1816   Millbank penitentiary opened in London
1823   Gaol Act
1824   Vagrancy Act
1829   Metropolitan Police Improvement Act. The Metropolitan Police Force was established
1833   Factory Act
1842   Pentonville prison opened
1853   Penal Servitude Act. Ends short terms of transportation and Parkhurst Prison opens with a regime designed for young offenders
1854   Reformatory School Act
1856   County and Borough Police Act
1861   Offences Against the Person Act
1867   End of transportation
1877   Prison Act. The Prison Commission was established with responsibility for all prisons in the country: the first chairman was Sir Edmund Du Cane
1878   Criminal Investigation Department (CID) of the Metropolitan Police was established
1879   Prosecution of Offences Act
1895   Gladstone Committee Report
1898   Prison Act
1898   Criminal Evidence Act
1901   Borstal experiment introduced
1907   Probation of Offenders Act
1908   Prevention of Crime Act. Borstal system and preventive detention introduced
1908   Children Act. Restrictions on the imprisonment of children
1913   Mental Deficiency Act. Mentally deficient persons were diverted out of the prison system
1919   Police Act followed the Police Strike and the formation of the Police Federation
1925   Criminal Justice Act
1933   Children and Young Persons Act. Reformatories and industrial schools were replaced by approved schools

1936 Open prison was established near Wakefield
     Prison Officers' Association was founded
     End to arrows on uniforms and treadmills
1936 Public Order Act
1948 Criminal Justice Act. Abolished penal servitude, prison with hard labour and whipping. Introduced corrective training, preventive detention and detention centres
1949 Royal Commission on Capital Punishment
1957 Homicide Act
1961 Criminal Justice Act. Minimum age of imprisonment was raised from 15 to 17. Greater use was encouraged of borstal training instead of prison for offenders under 21
1962 Royal Commission on the Police
1963 Prison Commission abolished and replaced by the Prison Department
1964 Criminal Procedure (Insanity) Act
1964 Police Act
1965 Murder (Abolition of Death Penalty) Act
1966 Mountbatten Report. Following the escape of the Russian spy George Blake from Wormwood Scrubs prison, Earl Mountbatten conducted an inquiry into prison security
1967 Criminal Justice Act. Introduction of the suspended sentence and discretionary parole. Courts were empowered to suspend any sentence of imprisonment not exceeding two years. Parole allowed an inmate to apply for parole after serving one third of their sentence. Abolition of preventive detention and corrective training and corporal punishment in prisons. Introduction of majority jury verdicts
1968 Firearms Act
1968 Criminal Appeal Act
1969 Children and Young Persons Act. Introduced care and supervision orders and replaced approved schools and remand homes with community homes
1971 Misuse of Drugs Act
1971 Courts Act. Abolished Assizes and Quarter Sessions and established the Crown Court
1972 Road Traffic Act. Introduced the breathalyser
1972 Criminal Justice Act. Introduced community service orders
1974 Juries Act
1974 Rehabilitation of Offenders Act
1976 Bail Act
1977 Criminal Law Act. Allowed the court to suspend a sentence of imprisonment in part.
1979 Report of the May Committee on the Prison Services. A policy of positive custody was advocated
1980 Magistrates' Courts Act

1981   Scarman Report

1981   Contempt of Court Act

1981   Royal Commission on Criminal Procedure

1982   Criminal Justice Act. Reduction of the parole eligibility criteria from 12 to 6 months. Statutory criteria for sentencing young offenders to custodial sentences. Borstal training replaced by youth custody

1983   Mental Health Act

1984   Police and Criminal Evidence Act

1985   Prosecution of Offences Act. Established the Crown Prosecution Service

1986   Public Order Act

1988   Criminal Justice Act. Extension of statutory criteria for custodial sentences for young offenders

1988   Legal Aid Act

1988   Road Traffic Act

1990   White Paper, *Crime, Justice and Protecting the Public*

1991   Criminal Justice Act. Introduced the combination order and the unit fine

1991   Report on the Prison Disturbances of April 1990 (chairman, Lord Justice Woolf). It recommended wide-ranging changes to the nature of prison regimes and the need for greater co-ordination throughout the criminal justice system.

1991   Criminal Procedure (Insanity and Unfitness to Plead) Act

1993   Royal Commission on Criminal Justice (chairman, Lord Runciman)

1993   Bail (Amendment) Act

1993   Criminal Justice Act repealed the unit fine

1994   Sexual Offences Act

1994   Criminal Justice and Public Order Act. Secure training order, revised bail law, right to silence redefined, new offences relating to collective trespass, raves and squatters; new offence of male rape and reduction in the age of homosexual consent to 18.

1994   Police and Magistrates' Courts Act. New process of funding and monitoring police performance and changed the organisation and funding of magistrates' courts. Home Secretary was given the power to set the objectives for the Police Service which have to be included in the local policing plan.

1995   Criminal Appeal Act established the Criminal Cases Review Commission.

1995   Learmont report on prison security

1996   Criminal Procedure and Investigations Act introduced new rules on the disclosure of evidence and the timing of the plea. Restored committal proceedings to replace the unimplemented transfer proceedings and introduced plea before venue.

1997   Firearms (Amendment) Act outlawed ownership of handguns above .22 calibre.

1997 Protection from Harassment Act.

1997 Sex Offenders Act established the Sex Offender Register.

1997 Crime (Sentences) Act introduced mandatory life sentence for adults convicted of a second serious offence such as rape or robbery with the use of a firearm, and minimum custodial sentences of seven years for those reconvicted of trafficking in Class A drugs.

1998 Crime and Disorder Act.

Review questions

1. Identify and outline the characteristics of the seven models of criminal justice defined in Chapter 1.

2. Identify current issues and controversies affecting criminal justice (for example a current case, issue or debate in Parliament, statement by politicians or other public figures) and consider:

   (a) To what extent these reveal the conflicting goals of the criminal justice system?

   (b) How these would be approached by the different models of criminal justice outlined above?

Further reading

Ashworth A (1998) *The Criminal Process.* 2nd edn. Oxford: Clarendon Press

King M (1981) *The Framework of Criminal Justice.* London: Croom Helm

Sanders A and Young R (1994) *Criminal Justice.* London: Butterworth

CHAPTER 2

IMAGES OF CRIME

- Images and Definitions of Crime
- Criminal Liability and Criminal Defences
- Explaining Crime
- Crime and Victimisation

INTRODUCTION

What is crime? This is not such an easy question to answer as it might at first appear because a number of different meanings are associated with the words crime and criminal. In this chapter we will look at different aspects of crime, from the legal conception of crime used to establish a person's liability for criminal conduct, to some of the theories put forward by criminologists, psychologists and sociologists to explain crime. We will also look briefly at some contemporary concerns about crime such as how it is related to the family, unemployment and social exclusion and at why the victim is also an important element in understanding crime. These accounts of crime filter into everyday consciousness and affect the public's notions about the causes of crime and policies which aim to 'do something about crime'. They also influence the way that the professionals in the criminal justice process think about crime, be they probation officer or judge.

IMAGES AND DEFINITIONS OF CRIME

Legally, a crime is any act or omission proscribed by the criminal law and thus punishable by the state through the criminal justice process. The criminal law and its associated punishment are used against a very wide range of behaviour – from murder, rape and assault to driving with excess alcohol, parking on a yellow line and failing to comply with a plethora of health and safety regulations. While few would dispute that murder is and should be an offence, not all members of the public would think of someone who drives with excess alcohol in their blood as a criminal.

The public have a commonsense view of what they regard as crime. Behaviour which people disapprove of is often described as criminal to emphasise its seriousness and unacceptability. These commonsense images tend to be associated with the deliberate infliction of physical harm often involving a confrontation between an offender and a victim. Dishonesty, cheating or theft are also a key part of these commonsense notions of crime. Everyday conceptions of the criminal carry connotations of the wrongdoer who should be stigmatised. Stigma means that a person is not considered normal, or is deviant and should be censured as a person who behaves badly.

Yet not all activities proscribed by the criminal law are necessarily regarded as crimes, or their perpetrators as criminal. In the workplace, for example, employees may regularly fiddle the books or engage in petty pilfering. These activities are described euphemistically as perks or fiddles rather than as theft or fraud. Members of the public may inflate insurance claims or fail to disclose their full earnings to the Inland Revenue without regarding themselves as criminals, or being viewed as such by others. Drivers may regularly infringe road traffic laws without considering their behaviour as deviant. Different groups therefore may have different conceptions of where to draw the line between acceptable behaviour and crime.

Even where individuals are injured and killed as a result of illegal actions they may not always be regarded as victims of crime. Many injuries and deaths in the workplace are caused by neglect of health and safety regulations. Yet these are regularly dealt with as accidents rather than as crimes, and those responsible are rarely sanctioned as criminals (Wells 1988; Croall 1992). This may be because there is no immediate confrontation between offender and victim and because those responsible intended no harm. Many are also physically injured within the home, by the actions of their spouses, lovers, parents or children. Yet domestic violence was for many years not widely perceived as being as serious as other violent crime – partly because it takes place in the private sphere of the home.

Although there is considerable overlap between legal and everyday conceptions of crime there is therefore no necessary equation between the two. Public tolerance of different activities changes over time and legal categories are subject to change. The criminal law in our society is not based on a fundamentalist or absolutist conception of morality but shifts according to changes in public attitudes. This is reflected in political pressures to change legislation that defines crime. Thus over the last 50 years the way in which the law has dealt with drunk driving, homosexuality, prostitution and domestic violence has changed. Changes in the public's tolerance of activities leads to campaigns to criminalise some behaviours and to decriminalise others. As seen in Chapter 1, parts of the Criminal Justice and Public Order Act 1994 aimed to curb the activities of new age travellers and organisers of raves, while lowering from 21 to 18 years the age at which men may lawfully perform homosexual acts in private.

35

Hence the legal conception of crime is subject to change and depends, in a parliamentary democracy, on political as well as moral considerations. However, if the criminal law does not express and reflect public morality and concerns about harm to the community the public would have little regard for the law – it would lose its legitimacy. Furthermore, it would be seen as unduly oppressive – as an instrument of social control and political domination. Such laws are unlikely to inspire public trust, confidence or legitimacy. They would be difficult to enforce and would undermine confidence in the criminal justice process.

To avoid confusion between the more technical and legal conception of crime used by lawyers and its everyday usage, we suggest the following definition of a criminal.

> A person whose behaviour is in breach of legally prescribed rules which renders that person liable to criminal proceedings.

As a starting point this definition is useful because it focuses on the three elements that are indispensable if we are to understand and explain crime. They are: behaviour, rules and enforcement.

Behaviour

Criminal law is essentially concerned with the regulation of behaviour. This may involve prohibitions on some kinds of behaviour such as stealing another person's property or harming them deliberately. Some criminal laws may require a specific action, such as having insurance when driving a car, or complying with regulations. In some instances it is the combination of behaviour with a particular situation that defines a crime such as being drunk in a public place. In others it is the combination of status with behaviour such as the purchase of alcohol by someone under 16 years of age.

Illegality covers a multitude of actions, responsibilities, circumstances and statuses and hence the diversity of acts that may be characterised as criminal is considerable. Thus it is impossible to offer a simple explanation of why someone acts criminally. Furthermore, people do not act in an identical fashion. Some people are more prone to self-indulgence, others are more violent in character.

The causes of criminal behaviour are complex and multiple. They are multiple because crime does not relate to only one form of action. For instance, the causes of domestic violence by a woman may not be the same as when committed by a man. The causes that lead a teenager to commit arson may be very different from those that lead an old-age pensioner to fraud. Therefore, we should not expect to find a single cause for all types of criminality.

Furthermore, the complexity is apparent when we look at the range of factors used to explain delinquency. Contributing to the debate are criminologists, sociologists, psychologists, penologists, economists, biologists, geneticists, psychiatrists, town planners, architects, social workers, doctors, nutritionists, teachers and theologians. The potential list of causes is long: biological predisposition, lack of bonding between parent and child, inconsistent parenting, irresponsible parenting, failure at school, truancy, labelling, violent videos, hyperactivity, overstimulating foods, drugs, glue, alcohol, masculinity, testosterone, repressed sexuality, underdeveloped super ego, lack of discipline, peer influence, television, lack of moral training, racism, lack of legitimate opportunities and too many illegal opportunities.

Some accounts of criminal conduct seek to identify the cause, or causes, that lead to behaviour that is distinctively deviant and untypical, such as the murders committed by Frederick and Rosemary West in their home at 25 Cromwell Road, Gloucester. In contrast, other theories of criminal behaviour focus on the types of motives that might affect anyone such as greed, envy, lust and jealousy as causes of bad behaviour. We will discuss some of these explanations later in this chapter.

Rules

The rules which determine whether or not behaviour is criminal are found in legislation passed by Parliament or in decisions of the courts. These form the starting point for understanding crime as they provide the legal definition of criminal acts. As we have seen, these rules may change over time, and the number of potentially illegal acts may increase as new areas and types of behaviour are criminalised. For example, under the Firearms Amendment Act 1996, pistol owners were required to hand over to the police, before midnight on 30 September 1997, any hand guns over .22 calibre they possessed or face up to ten years' imprisonment. In 1977, what had become known as stalking was made an offence by the Protection from Harassment Act.

There are two sources of law in England and Wales: legislation and law based on decided cases. Legislation consists of Acts of Parliament (statutes) and statutory instruments (often called subordinate legislation). Case law is law that has been built up over the years by decisions of the courts in individual matters: these may include decisions on the meaning of statutes. The law of England and Wales is thus based on the accumulation of previous cases and is described as a common law system, which distinguishes it from European systems which are based on codes established by legislation.

Although many offences are now governed by, or were created by, statute, the general principles of criminal law are still matters of the common law, which also governs some of the most serious crimes, for example murder. The idea that the common law evolves from the piecemeal interpretation of the law by judges is an integral part of the legal tradition in England and Wales.

Enforcement and criminal proceedings

Behaviour is not self-defining nor are rules self-enforcing. Laws do not have an impact unless they are enforced, or unless there is the anticipation of enforcement. How then is behaviour interpreted as breaking the rules? By whom and how are rules interpreted and applied? The criminal law specifies who can enforce the law and what procedures are necessary to investigate and prosecute crime, adjudicate on guilt and decide on an appropriate sentence. Enforcement is the responsibility of specialist agencies or organisations specifically given the right to enforce the law, such as the police, Customs and Excise officers and crown prosecutors. Although the basic procedures and guidelines for law enforcement are set out in statutes and case law, it is inevitable that these cannot cover every situation. That is why it is important to understand that many factors in addition to legal rules influence the way the criminal law is put into action.

Resources are required to fund the agencies and organisations that enforce the law. To learn how these agencies operate it is necessary to establish how they deploy these resources and how they interpret their formal goals and objectives. Professional loyalties, training and commonsense notions of crime and the crime problem will influence the way officials decide on priorities and interpret their responsibilities. Also, as officials in criminal justice agencies do not normally come from outside the society in which they work, many of the taken-for-granted prejudices of the wider culture also influence how they see their role.

Edwin Schur wrote, 'Once we recognise that crime is defined by the criminal law and is therefore variable in content, we see quite clearly that no explanation of crime that limits itself to the motivation and behaviour of individual offenders can ever be a complete one' (Schur 1969: 10).

The three elements that constitute a criminal act – behaviour, rules and the enforcement of rules – are further refined by the concept of criminal liability. Not all actions by a person, that might appear to be in breach of the criminal law, are necessarily criminal because there may be an excuse or acceptable reason for their behaviour. In commonsense terms and in a legal sense they may not be blameworthy or culpable. Establishing the culpability of a defendant is therefore central to the criminal process and explains the central role of the trial as the mechanism of establishing criminal liability.

CRIMINAL LIABILITY AND CRIMINAL DEFENCES

One of the most fundamental principles of criminal law is that a person should not be punished unless he or she has both committed the act or omission in question and is blameworthy. This means that in order to be considered culpable, it must be established that an offender has not only committed an offence but is responsible for it. These two aspects are usually referred to as the *actus reus*, the guilty act, and the *mens rea*, the guilty mind. Both the act and the intention are generally required before someone is deemed to be guilty of a crime.

Some crimes, called crimes of strict or absolute liability, do not require a guilty mind. These include offences such as speeding, drinking and driving, and applying a false trade description to goods. These types of crimes tend not to attract the same level of blame or culpability as offences that involve intention.

To illustrate the concepts of *actus reus* and *mens rea*, it is useful to analyse the offence of theft, which is now defined by s. 1 of the Theft Act 1968 which states:

> A person is guilty of theft if he dishonestly appropriates property belonging to another with the intention of permanently depriving that other of it.

It can be seen that two different elements make up the offence. First, the act of appropriating property belonging to another person, and, secondly, the mental element of dishonesty and the intent to permanently deprive another person. If either of these elements is missing, the offence is not committed.

Someone is guilty of murder if that person kills another person either intending to do so, or intending to cause him or her serious harm. So, if a person shoots someone dead the pulling of the trigger and the consequent death constitutes the *actus reus*. The *actus reus* relates to the events and consequences. Despite the fact that someone died, the person with the gun might not be guilty of murder. In addition to the act, *mens rea* is necessary: the person who fired the gun must have intended to kill or cause really serious injury. If, for example, the gun was fired by mistake while it was being cleaned at home, or the victim was shot accidentally while straying onto a grouse moor, the person who fired the gun would not be guilty of murder: there was no intent to kill.

The significance of the concept of intent can be illustrated by the problem of dealing with those who take cars but abandon them after use. The takers never intended to keep the car, thus they cannot be guilty of theft, having no 'intention to permanently deprive'. Therefore a different offence had to be created if this conduct was to be punished as a crime. The offence, now in s. 12 of the Theft Act 1968, is, 'Taking a conveyance without the owner's consent'. This provision states:

> . . . a person shall be guilty of an offence if, without having the consent of the owner or other lawful authority, he takes any conveyance for his own or another's use or, knowing that any conveyance has been taken without authority, drives it or allows himself to be carried in or on it.

Different offences relating to similar behaviour, for example assault, may reflect different levels of intent and seriousness of injury. This can be illustrated by examining the different crimes relating to offences of violence, the seriousness of which is determined both by the injury inflicted and the level of intention, thereby combining an assessment of *actus reus* and *mens rea* in determining culpability.

Common assault is the least serious, and can only be tried in the magistrates' court and is punishable by up to 6 months' imprisonment. It is defined as the intentional or reckless causing of another to fear immediate unlawful violence. More serious is the offence of occasioning actual bodily harm under s. 47 of the Offences Against the Person Act 1861 (OAPA 1861). This can be tried either in the magistrates' court or the Crown Court and is punishable with a maximum sentence of 5 years' imprisonment. It is not necessary to establish that the accused intended the kind of injury that occurred. Actual bodily harm means any physical harm.

Another offence, higher up the ladder of seriousness, although attracting the same maximum penalty, is the offence under s. 20, OAPA 1861, of unlawfully and maliciously wounding or inflicting grievous bodily harm. Grievous bodily harm means really serious harm. More serious still, triable only on indictment, and attracting up to life imprisonment, is the offence under s. 18, OAPA 1861, of malicious wounding or causing grievous bodily harm with intent to do grievous bodily harm.

In 1998 the Government proposed reforms to the law governing violent offences against the person. These proposals seek to clarify the law on assault along the lines suggested by the Law Commission. With over 70 different types of assault in law, the intention is to abolish the 1861 Offences Against the Person Act and replace it with an Act that sets out to define violent, non-fatal crimes in clear terms using plain modern language and taking into account new types of crime. Thus there will be a new offence of intentionally transmitting a disease with intent to cause serious harm. Actions such as deliberately releasing anthrax spores into the atmosphere and injecting meat with salmonella would also be covered by the new law. It will also deal with attacks where people are stabbed or threatened with syringes containing HIV-infected blood. In November 1996 two prison officers were stabbed with a syringe by an inmate who was a heroin addict. The deliberate infection of another person with a disease was highlighted by the case of Janette Pink, a British woman who, on holiday in Cyprus, met Paul Georgiou from whom she contracted AIDS. The courts in Cyprus decided that he knew he was infected and did not tell her. He was sentenced to 15 months imprisonment in 1997.

A draft bill reformulates the violent offences, other than those resulting in death, based on a combination of motivation and outcome as follows:

- The most serious is **intentionally causing serious injury** and includes deliberately transmitting a serious disease (maximum sentence of life imprisonment).

- **Recklessly causing serious injury** is similar to the above without the degree of intent to cause harm (maximum sentence of 7 years).

- **Intentional or reckless injury** will apply to less serious injuries than the two offences above (maximum sentence of 5 years).

- **Assault** will replace the two existing offences of common assault and battery and will be triable as a summary offence (maximum sentence of 6 months).

It is not possible to analyse these provisions in detail here, but it can be seen that varying combinations are possible depending on the level of injury and the level of intent to do harm of the kind that resulted – the *mens rea*. Did the defendants mean to do any harm at all, or, were they reckless as to what harm was caused? Did they intend to cause harm of the level inflicted? What was the level of harm inflicted?

The most serious offence known to the criminal law is murder, which is punishable with a mandatory life sentence. This means that once a conviction is recorded, only a life sentence can be passed by the judge. However, the law has long recognised that deaths can be caused, even intentionally, in many different circumstances, not all equally blameworthy. This is reflected in three categories of homicide; murder, manslaughter and infanticide. Murder is described as unlawful killing involving intention to kill or cause grievous bodily harm. Murder can be reduced to manslaughter (for which the sentence is variable) because of 'provocation' by virtue of s. 3 of the Homicide Act 1957. This recognises that, under pressure, people may lose control and provocation is defined as a 'sudden temporary loss of self-control'. This provision has recently been the subject of much criticism. Particularly problematic has been the situation of women who have been systematically brutalised by partners and have planned to kill them. Decisions where such women have been prosecuted have underlined the requirement that the defence of provocation will be successful only if there is a sudden explosion of emotions so that the person is temporarily out of control as a result of a particular trigger such as a remark or incident. Sarah Thornton, who was prosecuted for murder, stabbed her husband while he was in a drunken stupor and did not succeed with the defence that she had been provoked. Kiranjit Ahluwalia was convicted of the murder of her husband and sentenced to life imprisonment in 1989 despite claiming she was 'provoked' by 10 years of abuse at his hands.

Murder is also reduced to manslaughter when killing takes place as a result of diminished responsibility, defined as an abnormality of mind which impairs the mental processes, or under a suicide pact. Both these circumstances are referred to as voluntary manslaughter, where the intent was to kill but in less blameworthy circumstances. Some abused women have succeeded in arguing that they should be convicted of manslaughter rather than murder as a result of diminished responsibility brought on by the abuse. Kiranjit Ahluwalia's conviction was thus reduced to manslaughter on appeal in 1992.

Manslaughter includes all other forms of unlawful killing when there was a lesser degree of intent than that required for murder. Manslaughter is therefore committed when death results in the course of an unlawful act, for example, burglary, and in other circumstances where death was not actually intended. Many different combinations of circumstances can be envisaged and have come before the courts: the defendants who threw a brick from a motorway bridge to deter a 'blackleg' (*R v Hancock and Shankland* (1986)) and the defendant who played 'Russian Roulette' with tragic consequences for his step-father (*R v Mahoney* (1985)).

The role of the law is to develop rules that reflect moral blameworthiness. But as the following case illustrates, it is not always easy to apply these principles in cases involving the deliberate commission of a dangerous act resulting in death. In one recent case the Court of Appeal, seeking to clarify the application of principles, listed the kinds of situation in which this type of offence, sometimes called involuntary manslaughter, arises (*R v Sulman and Others* (1993)). This particular case arose after a patient died following a negligently conducted operation. There had been negligence – did that create a criminal offence? Negligent inattention in the sense of mere inadvertence does not create criminal liability; the degree of fault has to be gross negligence, such as:

• indifference to a known risk

• foresight of a risk which is nevertheless undertaken

• appreciation of the risk, and an intention to avoid it, but coupled with a high degree of negligence in the attempted avoidance

• inattention to a serious and obvious risk.

Infanticide is also recognised as a special case by the law which provides that a different offence, less culpable than murder, is committed where a woman kills her child in the first year of its life, when the balance of her mind is affected by the birth.

Another situation recognised by the law is where death occurs as a result of a road accident. Legislation has taken a variety of approaches to these situations, the current position being that it is an offence to cause death by dangerous driving. Dangerous driving is defined as driving at a standard far below that of a competent and careful driver and where it would be obvious to such a driver that driving in that way would be dangerous.

The problem of basing criminal culpability on the offender's intention and not on the result of the offence can be seen in the increasing number of cases in which pedestrians or other car users are killed by a driver subsequently convicted of careless driving. While careless driving can kill, in many cases it has either no adverse consequence or only a trivial one. Outraged relatives have been appalled when drivers who have killed a member of their family have been given non-custodial sentences or even a fine. This outrage is further added to when the driver is proved to have been drinking and has a past record of driving with excess alcohol. Lee Taziker was 'over the limit' and driving at 56 mph when he swerved a 28-ton articulated lorry and hit and killed 17-year-old John Smith on a Somerset road in October 1993. Taziker was sentenced to 240 hours of community service and banned from driving for three years. Judge Willis, who gave the sentence, said, 'I do not think any useful purpose would be served by sending you to prison.' The victim's father, Steve Smith is quoted as saying, 'I simply cannot believe it . . . It just makes a mockery of the law. You get more than that for thumping somebody.' (*The Daily Telegraph*, 13 August 1994: 9).

Culpability under the criminal law stretches from those who deliberately set out to commit criminal acts such as a planned robbery, through those who behave recklessly and cause harm, to those who have no intention at all but nevertheless are guilty of a crime of strict liability. Failure to take steps to prevent harm can result in guilt: an offence of omission. The Court of Appeal upheld the decision of North Shield's magistrates' court who convicted Mark Greener under the Dangerous Dogs Act 1991, because he did not take sufficient steps to prevent his Staffordshire Bull Terrier from straying into a nearby garden and biting a young child's face. (Greener v DPP, *The Times*, 15 February 1996.)

Criminal defences

In criminal trials the defence may argue that although the defendant did commit the act they had an excuse for so doing. These excuses reflect an acceptance that in certain circumstances the defendant could not help acting in a particular way, was somehow forced into the action, or could not control his or her behaviour and is therefore not to blame. The *mens rea* element of the criminal trial focuses on blameworthiness or moral culpability and the defence counsel may use arguments known as criminal defences in an attempt to show that the defendant was not responsible or blameworthy for the act he or she did indeed commit.

Because they are not seen as responsible for their acts there are two categories of people who cannot be liable for criminal offences:

• children under the age of criminal responsibility

• those certified as mentally ill.

In the first category, children under 10 in England and Wales are, by law, deemed unable to commit offences: in other words they cannot be criminally liable. This is often referred to as being *doli incapax*. The mentally ill are not held responsible in law for their actions and if they do stand trial at all will be found not guilty by reason of insanity (see Chapter 5).

There are, however, other situations where, though the accused cannot escape liability because of age or mental incapacity, circumstances may provide a complete defence. If the defence is accepted the person is found not guilty. These circumstances are:

- *Duress:* where people are compelled by threats to do something criminal. The threat or danger must be severe – such as death or serious personal injury. This would excuse all offences other than murder and treason. In these circumstances, although the act is deliberate and intended, the offender is regarded as not responsible for the act committed.

- *Automatism:* where a person is not in control of his or her physical actions, such as during an epileptic fit.

- *Self-defence:* defendants are not seen as blameworthy when, in responding to another person's aggression, they cause injury in the process of defending themselves. The scriptures might require a person to turn the other cheek, the law does not.

In other situations, the defendant may be held less responsible or blameworthy, by relying on partial defences. A partial defence, as its name suggests, will partly exonerate the defendant. Whereas a successful complete defence means that the defendant is found not guilty of any offence at all, a partial defence means that, if successful, the defendant will be found not guilty of the major offence but guilty of a lesser offence. The situation arises only in the case of murder, where a successful defence of diminished responsibility or provocation will result in the accused being found guilty of manslaughter rather than murder.

A situation commonly found in criminal acts is that the defendant was affected by alcohol or drugs. The mere fact of being drunk is not a defence, even though it is recognised that drinking may reduce inhibitions. It may however be a defence where the alcohol or drugs had the effect that the offender was not able to form the intent required for the commission of the crime, such as murder or wounding 'with intent'.

Sentencing mitigation

Even where a legal defence – which removes all blame – is not available or has not been accepted by the jury or magistrates, other factors may reduce culpability. After a defendant has been found guilty or has pleaded guilty, the defence may offer a plea in mitigation to the court. This will introduce factors suggesting that the seriousness of the offence is not as great as it might be, or that the offender is less blameworthy.

Mitigation may relate to the offence: that the offender played a limited part, was led into the offence by others, or that it happened almost by accident. Defendants may claim they forgot to renew a licence or their motor vehicle insurance. Mitigation might also relate to the personal circumstances of the offender. It may be argued that offenders are in such difficult circumstances that he or she should not be blamed or punished any more than has already happened because he or she might have lost his or her job or have been deserted by his or her family. If you sit in court for any length of time you might be surprised to hear the same mitigation repeated, such as the number of recently convicted people who are starting a job next week or whose girlfriend has just discovered she is pregnant. This part of the criminal process allows the convicted person the opportunity to minimise their culpability for the offence and so increase their chance of a more lenient sentence.

The court must take all these factors into account in passing sentence, which may mean that individual sentencing decisions are unpopular. Some sentencing decisions cause outrage and public anxiety and have been widely criticised in the press, Parliament or on the radio and television. It is important to appreciate that members of the public may have very different perceptions of criminal responsibility from those of the court. Questions of crime and criminal responsibility generate many strong opinions and public conceptions may well conflict with legal concerns. Public views of crime are not necessarily informed by the somewhat narrow legal conceptions of culpability and blameworthiness outlined above, nor do the public always appreciate the technicalities of requirements to prove intent or to focus on the act rather than the result. Public discussion tends to be more general than legal discussion.

EXPLAINING CRIME

Public and political discussions of crime incorporate a variety of notions about how crime can be explained. Some see individual criminals as inherently bad or wicked. Others blame a general lack of discipline, particularly within families. Yet others argue that the culture of modern society with its emphasis on materialism and individual success may be related to crime, along with socio-economic factors such as unemployment or social exclusion. Academic research and analysis subjects these ideas to the tests of empirical validation through research. The wide range of activities which are encompassed by the criminal law, however, makes it impossible to attribute crime to any single set of explanations or causes and academic researchers have asked many different questions in the attempt to explain crime.

To early criminologists crime was seen as a pathology, as a problem which could be cured, in line with the rehabilitative model outlined in Chapter 1. The nature of this problem was, however, disputed. To some it lay in the individual characteristics of offenders who were assumed to be different from the so-called normal population. To others it was primarily a social problem emerging from the culture and organisation of society and was related to social deprivation and disadvantage. These theories asked why offenders turned to crime – a question which later approaches turned away from. To some, a more interesting question was why some actions and behaviour were labelled as criminal and what effects followed such labelling. To others the main question was how offenders, having chosen to commit crime, decided where, when and how to commit that crime – on the basis that, if this could be understood, crime could be prevented. These perspectives also help us to explore some of the questions raised in contemporary public discussions. How is crime related to the family, to unemployment, to social deprivation and social exclusion, and to drug use? What is the significance of white collar crime? And, while many of these approaches focus on offenders – is it important to also look at the victims of crime?

Crime as an individual problem

What are often called individual approaches assume that crime is 'caused' by characteristics which differentiate criminals from the non-criminal population. Many have asked, for example, whether crime is part of a person's biological inheritance; others, whether criminals are distinguished by some form of mental illness.

Born criminal – biological theories

An extremely pervasive notion is that a propensity to crime can be inherited, like height, weight or hair colour. In an early version of this approach the Italian criminologist Cesare Lombroso studied the characteristics of convicts in prisons, and claimed that criminal men were distinguished by what he called physical stigmata such as long arms, shifty glances, droopy eyelids, bushy eyebrows, large ears, twisted noses and abnormal mouths and skulls (Lombroso 1897). His theories were later discredited, particularly as many similar characteristics were found in the general population, but they stimulated further research relating criminality to physical and genetic characteristics. A variety of factors were related to crime such as body shapes, and later research looked at the possibility that chromosome abnormalities or biochemical factors such as vitamin deficiencies or food allergies were also associated with crime. In a celebrated case in the United States a defendant claimed in mitigation that he had a chemical imbalance in his brain caused by eating too much junk food – the so called 'twinkie defence', called after the offending sweet bar (Williams 1991: 119).

While these ideas have been influential the extent to which crime can be accounted for by biological factors is limited. The results of many studies were inconclusive and failed to distinguish offenders from those who had no criminal convictions. There are also problems with the assumption that a propensity to crime can be inherited. As we have seen, crime is a form of behaviour which contravenes rules made by society. Even if we could assume that people could inherit a propensity to behave aggressively, such aggression could have legitimate and illegitimate outlets – it could, for example, be legitimately channelled through sports or other activities. A further problem is determining whether behavioural traits are inherited or are learnt – often referred to as the nature – nurture debate. Was the Kray twins' life of crime influenced by their common genetic inheritance or socialisation, or both? Criminality involves issues of morality, a choice between right and wrong, learnt within the social environment. Thus it is virtually impossible to establish the extent to which characteristics are a result of genetic inheritance or socialisation.

Are criminals mad?

Another popular explanation of criminality is to imply that in some way criminals are mad, psychotic, or suffering from personality disorders and psychological research has explored a wide range of factors. Many have looked for evidence of a link between criminality and mental illness. Some mental illnesses such as schizophrenia can lead to delusions and hallucinations which may make the affected person feel that he or she has a 'mission' to rid the world of particular groups of people such as prostitutes. These conditions are, however, extremely rare and there is no general link between schizophrenia and criminality (Williams 1991). Similar problems occur when trying to link crime to other mental states such as depression which has been associated with murderers who murder their family and then commit suicide (West 1965). Again, this only affects a very small number of people. Problems also surround the popular description of criminals as 'psychopaths', which has proved difficult to define and measure. While some convicted offenders have been depicted as psychopathic – a condition associated with an inability to form loving relationships, a lack of responsibility for actions, a failure to feel or admit guilt for one's actions and aggressiveness – it has not been established that this condition is necessarily linked to crime. There may be many such people in the general population who have not been found to have committed crimes. One noted psychologist of crime has commented that psychopathy remains 'something of a puzzle' (Hollin 1989).

While many individual offenders may be suffering from some form of mental illness, many more are not, and in addition, the majority of people considered to be suffering from mental illness do not commit crime. Associating crime with mental illness may also involve a circular argument – as criminals are often seen as 'abnormal' or as 'nutters', their criminality is then explained by associating it with another abnormality – mental illness.

These individual approaches shared the assumption that crime is the product of some kind of 'pathology', implying that criminals are 'driven' to crime. While this may be the case with some offenders, it cannot account for all offending, particularly where crime is culturally tolerated. In addition, more recent approaches suggest that crime, rather than being the result of some predisposition, is the product of a rational choice on the part of offenders. Thus while individual approaches can be useful they cannot account for 'crime' in general.

47

Crime as a social problem

Crime is seen by some sociologists as a sign of wider cultural problems or as a symptom of the adverse effects of social and economic change. One sociologist to look at crime in this way was Emile Durkheim. To him, social and economic changes following the Industrial Revolution had led to the decline of communities and religion which provided people with guidance about morality and standards of behaviour. Rapid change could lead, he argued, to the development of anomie, or normlessness, in which individuals lacked such guidance. In addition, the growth of materialism led to people developing what he called 'boundless aspirations' which could often not be met (Durkheim 1970). These ideas were taken up by the American sociologist Robert Merton. In American society, he argued, goals of material success predominated. Socially approved norms exist to provide guidelines to achieve these goals by legitimate means such as hard work and educational achievement, but not all who work hard would achieve the goals. This strain could produce anomie, in which the norms of hard work are no longer relevant, especially to those at the bottom of the ladder (Merton 1938). People could adapt to this strain in different ways. While most continue to conform, some, whom he described as innovators, devise their own means to achieve the goals – stealing money instead of earning it, for example. Many theories developed out of this anomie paradigm, and while its original formulation had many limitations, the view that crime can be interpreted as a 'solution' to the problems of blocked aspirations influenced many subsequent writers, particularly those looking at criminal and delinquent subcultures.

Subcultural theory focuses on groups, often of young people, within which particular kinds of crime are seen as normal and where status may derive from delinquent or criminal activity. Many have a distinctive set of norms, values, language and dress and they may include a career structure through which younger members graduate from less serious activities to more serious involvement in crime. Examples of such subcultures include groups of joyriders, juvenile thieves and drug takers. To subcultural theorists, these emerge from a strain similar to anomie, whereby youth, faced with the difficulties of achieving culturally approved goals such as employment, material success or consumption, adopt different kinds of 'deviant solutions' such as becoming members of violent gangs, using illegal drugs or engaging in property crime. How any particular group adapts depends on what has been described as the structure of illegitimate opportunities of a particular neighbourhood (Cloward and Ohlin 1960). In areas with an existing criminal subculture, youth could learn how to engage in activities such as burglary or theft. Without this knowledge, and suitable outlets for stolen goods, such participation would be far less likely. Delinquent subcultures can therefore be interpreted as providing an achievable, if criminal, aspiration for youth who have failed to achieve different cultural goals transmitted through the media. This may be exacerbated where youth face unemployment, giving them little stake in society. Thus, for example, what is often described as joy riding may spring from the emphasis in advertising and the media on the desirability of cars and driving. Few unemployed youths can afford these status symbols and may be tempted to steal them to give themselves an illusion of participation.

These approaches raise important questions about the relationship between crime and social and economic change, and also point out that to some offenders crime performs a positive function. They also draw attention to the importance of the local structure of opportunities for participation in many criminal activities – insights which continue to affect analyses of crime. As will be seen below, recent social and economic changes may have contributed to rising levels of crime as many youth have few realistic hopes of stable employment. Crime may become an alternative means of participating in the lifestyles to which they aspire.

These approaches also have limitations. In some ways they provide almost too easy an explanation of many kinds of delinquency. If delinquent subcultures are so attractive, why do not all lower class youth, presumably facing the same problems, participate? One critic of early subcultural theories, for example, argued that they explained too much delinquency (Matza 1964). Like the individual approaches discussed above, they assume that crime results from some kind of predisposition generated by culture or the structure of society itself. It is difficult, however, as will be seen below, to establish how these factors are associated. They also took for granted that the majority of delinquents and criminals originated from the lower class which provided the link with deprivation and disadvantage. The lower class origins of many convicted offenders could, however, be a product of labelling, whereby the activities of lower class youth are seen as delinquent and more likely to be subject to police attention.

Crime as a label

Individuals and groups may become labelled as 'criminal' or deviant, which may affect how they are dealt with by law enforcement agencies. Many of the studies on which both individual and sociological approaches were based relied on comparing offenders with samples taken from the population at large who are assumed not to be criminal. As will be seen in Chapter 3, however, many offences are not detected and many offenders are not prosecuted – therefore some of the so-called non-offending population may in fact have committed crimes. The labelling perspective focuses on many of these questions. Actions or behaviour are not, as we have seen, intrinsically criminal – society defines which acts are against the criminal law. Those committing these acts are not defined as criminals until they have been caught and convicted. Thus to writers such as Becker, no behaviour is intrinsically criminal or deviant, these are labels applied by others (Becker 1963). An important distinction can also be made between primary and secondary deviance (Lemert 1967). Primary deviance refers to the initial act and secondary deviance follows initial labelling. Once a person is labelled as a thief or a delinquent, many consequences follow. He or she may feel stigmatised, cast out and may seek the company of other deviants. Stigma may make it difficult to return to a normal existence. The person may be mistrusted by friends, treated with suspicion by his or her family and find it difficult to obtain legitimate employment. Some, labelled as troublesome, may react with hostility to those who have labelled them – leading to a confirmation of that label – a self-fulfilling prophecy. It can also lead to a process of deviancy amplification, where the reaction to a deviant act produces more deviance. Therefore reaction to crime can produce more crime. This may also happen with subcultures and groups – young people, for example, are often seen as troublesome, and groups of youth apparently 'doing nothing' may attract attention from the police and public. This may provoke a further reaction and being formally processed as a 'delinquent' may harden offenders' commitment to a deviant 'identity' or subculture. Areas and neighbourhoods can also be labelled as 'high crime' or 'dangerous' areas, which affects how their inhabitants are perceived – youth coming from such areas may be denied jobs on the basis of such perceptions (see, for example, Anderson *et al* 1994).

The labelling approach has been enormously influential, and its practical implications extend to arguments to divert juveniles from custody and formal criminal procedures. It does not explain why people become deviant or turn to crime in the first place but draws attention to the way in which some groups or neighbourhoods may become the targets of police attention. Analyses of crime must therefore also include this labelling effect.

Crime and opportunity

The assumption that offenders were 'predisposed' to commit crime implied that crime could be reduced by identifying its causes and adopting strategies to eradicate the source of criminality. The rehabilitative approach, based on the medical model failed to substantially reduce crime and sociological approaches relating crime to poverty and social disadvantage were called into question when crime appeared to be rising during the relatively affluent 1950s and 1960s. New approaches were therefore sought and it was argued that rather than being 'predisposed' to crime, individuals make rational choices to commit an offence. When considering whether to commit crime, offenders may evaluate their chances of success, whether or not they are likely to be caught, and what their punishment might be. Whether or not a crime occurs may depend on the evaluation of risk and the opportunities provided by the situation (see, for example, Clarke 1980). Faced with an open till in an empty shop, a potential thief is more likely to steal than if the shop is crowded and has publicised video surveillance. Thus much crime is opportunistic, rather than being driven by individual pathologies or subcultural motivation.

This kind of approach has led, as will be seen in Chapter 11, to a wide range of policies aimed at crime prevention. In addition it prompted the widespread use of the victim survey to establish more precisely the kind of situations in which most crime occurs, and where risks of victimisation are highest. Like many other theories, these approaches also have limitations. If, for example, some crime is committed by individuals or groups who are determined or predisposed to commit an offence, they may be less deterred by crime prevention measures and may commit their crimes elsewhere. Moreover they do not ask why offenders are in the situation in the first place and therefore neglect the wider cultural and structural roots of crime pointed to in earlier theories (Downes and Rock 1995).

These different approaches to crime, along with others, provide many valuable insights into how crime can be better understood. They also provide a basis for exploring some of the questions which have been asked about contemporary crime, and which affect policies towards crime.

Crime and the family

Crime is sometimes popularly blamed on the family, with poor parenting, lack of discipline and family breakdown often being associated with youth crime. A recurrent theme in academic research has been to investigate the relationship between delinquency and a range of family related factors. Early studies explored child-rearing behaviour, parental discipline, the criminal histories of parents and family size and income. Popular theories in the 1950s and 1960s related juvenile delinquency to maternal deprivation, broken homes and to the growing number of 'latch key' children who were left unsupervised after school while their mothers went to work. All of these presaged current concerns with discipline and the role of single-parent families. What has emerged from this research is that some family factors are related to the likelihood of delinquency but that they must be considered in the context of the socio-economic circumstances of the family and other factors such as school and the peer group. The following factors have emerged as particularly important.

Parental discipline and supervision

Parental discipline has always been seen as a major factor underlying youth crime and it was found that inconsistent and erratic discipline are more likely to be associated with delinquency than lax or strict discipline (West and Farrington 1973, 1977). More recent studies have focused on the quality of parental supervision, often measured by whether parents know where their children are when they are not at home. A recent Home Office study, for example, found that supervision was strongly related to offending with higher numbers of those who were not closely supervised admitting offending. Around one-third of boys who were closely supervised had offended compared with over half of those who were not closely supervised (Graham and Bowling 1995).

Family structure

Large families and single-parent or reconstituted families have been associated with delinquency although a complex situation has emerged. While large families have been associated with delinquent children this effect is strongly related to household income and supervision – the stress of having a large family on a low income may lead to less supervision (Utting *et al* 1993; Graham and Bowling 1995). Some studies have found that fewer offenders come from families living with two natural parents, but there is no evidence to suggest that divorce, separation or single parenthood are criminogenic in themselves, as these are widespread throughout society and not always related to crime (Utting *et al* 1993; Graham and Bowling 1995). The Home Office study referred to above found that those living with two natural parents were least likely to offend and that those living with one natural and one step-parent were most likely to offend (Graham and Bowling 1995). These differences disappeared, however, when supervision and the quality of relationships within the family were considered.

The quality of family relationships

It has been argued that it is the quality of relationships within the family rather than its structure which may affect the likelihood of crime. Many studies have found that it is the conflict surrounding separation or divorce rather than family breakdown which may be significant (Utting *et al* 1993; Rutter 1985). Moreover, a single-parent home may provide the child with a caring and affectionate environment which may be far better than a home where two parents are constantly in dispute and have little time to pay attention to their children (Utting *et al* 1993). The Home Office study cited above confirms these points, finding that a bad relationship with a father had a strong relationship to offending for both boys and girls (Graham and Bowling 1995).

The socio-economic circumstances of the family

Supervision and the quality of relationships within the family may also be adversely affected by the socio-economic situation of the family. Thus many of the above factors are related to the additional stresses of unemployment and low income.

While this illustrates the importance of the family, it does not work in isolation. In the recent Home Office study, attachment to school and truancy also emerged as strongly associated with offending and, as children grow older, the influence of parents may decline in relation to that of friends.

Crime, unemployment and deprivation

As seen above, crime has also been related to social deprivation and, more recently, to the growth of unemployment. Exploring this association is far from easy, and statistical correlations between unemployment rates and crime rates are difficult to establish. Neither set of statistics is totally reliable and studies have failed to find strong or consistent relationships, although later work has found stronger relationships between youth crime and unemployment (Box 1987; Wells 1995). It is also difficult to separate the effects of unemployment from wider economic conditions such as growth and recession and different hypotheses can be advanced as to how these might be related to crime. On the one hand, it could be argued that during a recession, when unemployment rises and some incomes fall, some would have an increased motivation for crime (Pyle and Deadman 1994). On the other hand economic growth, when incomes rise, may produce increased opportunities for crime as there are more goods in circulation. The effects of these contrasting scenarios could cancel each other out and they may affect different kinds of crime in different ways.

A study carried out in the 1980s illustrates this. Field (1996) concluded that personal consumption, rather than unemployment, is the most important economic factor affecting crime, and that it affects personal and property crimes in different ways. He found that as personal consumption – the amount that each person has to spend during any one year – rose, property crime fell, whereas it rose again as personal consumption fell. This reflects the effect of both motivation and opportunity theories. Recession has an exaggerated effect on those most immediately affected – those who are most likely to become unemployed, and who, he argues, are most likely to turn to crime. As the economy recovers this group move back into legitimate work, and property crime falls. As the economy continues to recover, increased opportunities for crime produce higher rates of property crime. Crimes against the person, on the other hand, rises during periods of economic growth and decreases during periods of recession. This is less likely to be economically motivated and more likely to take place in and around pubs and leisure sites. It is therefore related to how often people go out – which is in turn related to personal consumption.

These kinds of studies may establish statistical correlations, but cannot explain them or establish that unemployment or other economic conditions 'cause' crime – not all unemployed people are likely to turn to crime and many people who are employed also commit crime. In order to fully understand the relationship it is necessary to explore the different ways in which economic factors may be experienced (Lea and Young 1992). Previous economic depressions, for example during the 1930s, were not associated with a growth in crime. This may have been because at that time people had lower expectations of economic achievement or consumption. If people expect to achieve a certain standard of living, they will feel more frustrated if they are denied the opportunity, particularly if they can see others succeeding. Crime may therefore be related to relative rather than absolute deprivation (Lea and Young 1992). The 1980s saw a polarisation in incomes – while incomes fell for those most affected by unemployment, other incomes increased. Where people have few legitimate channels for expressing their dissatisfaction such as through party politics or trade unionism, as might be the case for the unemployed and members of minority groups, crime may be more likely. This points to the significance of what is currently described as social exclusion.

Crime, the 'underclass' and social exclusion

Economic and industrial restructuring have, in recent decades, had an enormous impact not only creating long-term unemployment but also increasing the amounts of low paid, casual employment. Many of those who live in areas which have seen the decline of traditional industries can no longer expect stable full-time employment. This affects their ability to undertake financial and other commitments, such as buying a house or getting married. For young people it may mean a period of extended adolescence prolonging their entry into the world of work. Many of the communities most affected are also geographically isolated, some in peripheral estates outside towns and cities. This has led to what some see as a situation in which groups and whole communities are effectively excluded from participation in society. This has been further associated with family breakdown, the growth in single-parent families and the growth of an 'underclass' with high rates of participation in crime.

The notion of the underclass implies the existence of a distinct class below other social classes and both its existence and its relationship to crime are disputed. To those of the political right, such as the American commentator Charles Murray, the underclass emerges from an increasing dependence on welfare benefits which leads to the development of a dependency culture. In Britain, he argues, a growing number of people who are able to work but choose not to, live in a 'different world' from others. They do not obtain good work habits and discipline and their values contaminate 'the life of entire neighbourhoods' (Murray 1996: 123). Men in such communities cannot support families, leading to high rates of illegitimacy, and seek alternative, destructive means of proving that they are men. Whole communities are devastated by crime and young men look up to criminal role models.

While, to Murray, liberal welfare policies lie at the root of these problems, industrial restructuring, free market policies, housing policies, and the decline in real terms of welfare benefits, have also been associated with the existence of groups who are extremely disadvantaged. Murray's depiction of the 'underclass' has attracted considerable criticism, particularly in that, by arguing that people choose not to work and attacking the cultural values of whole communities, it blames the poor for their own predicament. On the contrary, many argue that people do not choose to be unemployed nor do lone parents choose to be dependent on benefits (Bagguley and Mann 1992). There is also, as seen above, little evidence that single parenthood in itself contributes to crime. Others argue that a reduction in real terms in benefit levels, rather than an excess of benefits, has contributed to social exclusion – drawing attention to the social and economic policies which have accompanied industrial restructuring (Taylor 1997).

Whether or not the underclass exists, most agree that industrial restructuring has led to the growth of communities within which the majority of inhabitants are excluded from work and its associated benefits, and that these are also characterised by high amounts of property crime, youth crime and illegal drug use. These effects, however, may not be inevitable but linked to the free market economic policies which accompanied these changes (Taylor 1997). Elliot Currie, for example, argues that unemployment, casual employment and low wages create a situation in which communities can no longer provide informal support and mutual provision – 'if you're having tough times, you can't lean on your neighbours' (Currie 1996: 346). Low wages, which emerged from free market policies, mean that, even in two-parent families, increasing numbers of parents have to work harder – reducing the time they have to spend with their children. Unemployment reduces the pool of 'marriageable men' leading to the growth of single-parent families. At the same time, other groups are becoming more affluent and high consumption levels are seen as desirable. This excludes the disadvantaged who may seek illegitimate channels to succeed. Thus many writers see crime as alternative means of pursing the 'high life', a lifestyle involving excitement, risk, danger, designer clothes and drug taking whose desirability is disseminated globally through the mass media, films and advertising (see, for example, Hobbs 1995; Collison 1996).

Crime and drugs

The neighbourhoods associated with the so-called 'underclass' are also those associated with high amounts of illegal drug use which, in itself, has had a major impact on crime, and concerns have also been expressed about the apparently growing extent of drug use among young people. In response to this in 1998 a 'drug Czar' was appointed by the Government to co-ordinate the multi-agency approach to curbing drug related crimes and a new style 'drugs offences' court was started in Wakefield. The consumption or possession of illegal drugs is in itself a crime. This creates a 'criminal industry' around the supply of illegal drugs and may also lead to increased property crime committed by those who need to resort to crime to support a drugs habit. Some of the questions raised by this are summarised below:

Do the physical effects of drugs lead to crime?

Different drugs have different pharmacological effects – some, like alcohol, are depressants, whereas others are stimulants. While drugs, particularly alcohol which depresses inhibitions, are often involved in offences, particularly violent incidents, the consumption of drugs does not in itself lead to crime – many who consume alcohol or other drugs do not commit crime (see, for example, Parker 1996).

How widespread is illegal drug use?

The possession or consumption of some drugs, such as heroin, cannabis or the new 'dance drugs', is in itself a crime which is seen to be rising. Some have argued that the increase from the 1980s to the 1990s is such that it has become 'normal' among young people irrespective of social class (Measham *et al* 1994). Care, however, must be taken when interpreting research – some studies refer to the numbers of people who have 'ever' tried an illegal drug – thus one recent survey found that 43 per cent of 15 and 16-year-old English boys and 39 per cent of girls had experimented with illicit drugs – the figures were lower for Wales (Miller and Plant 1996). Other surveys have produced even higher figures with the latest British Crime Survey (BCS) reporting that nearly one-half of those aged between 16 and 29 have at some time tried an illicit drug (Ramsay and Spiller 1997). These figures fall dramatically when respondents are asked about more recent consumption, with only 12 per cent reporting consumption in the last month. Many young people experiment with illegal drugs but do not go on to use them on a regular basis. The BCS also found that cannabis is the most commonly used illegal drug, with, for the 16–29 age range, ecstasy being the least popular. Just over a quarter had ever used any 'dance drugs' and consumption of heroin and cocaine was extremely rare with only 1 per cent having ever used each of these drugs (Ramsay and Spiller 1997).

Does using illegal drugs lead to property crime?

It is extremely difficult to estimate the extent of drugs-related crime which is often subject to exaggerated estimates. The majority of young people who do use illegal drugs use cannabis occasionally and do not resort to other forms of crime (Hough 1996). Others commit crime and use the proceeds to purchase drugs – thus crime can lead to drug taking. For some, crime and drug consumption may then increase in an escalating spiral and may be part of the thrill and buzz of a subcultural lifestyle (Collison 1996). The drug dependency of others leads to crime to fund an addiction. The size of this group is difficult to estimate although they may account for a large amount of property crime in relation to their numbers (Jarvis and Parker 1989). In a recent review, Hough (1996) argues that illegal drug use is responsible for a significant minority of crimes in England and Wales.

The illegal drugs industry

Substantial amounts of crime are also involved in the multi-national criminal drugs industry which involves traffickers, importers, distributors and sellers (Dorn *et al* 1992; Ruggiero and South 1995). The growth of this industry has very much altered the nature of organised crime in Britain, with many former bank robbers and criminal 'firms' having diversified into drug trafficking and distribution (Hobbs 1995; Ruggiero and South 1995). Traffickers also include those for whom drug importation is a sideline from legitimate, import/export businesses (Dorn *et al* 1992). The drugs industry includes highly organised entrepreneurs and their employees – often drawn from the ranks of the unemployed for whom work in the drugs market may provide an alternative to legitimate employment.

Legal drugs and crime

It is also important to recognise the contribution to crime made by legal drugs. It has already been pointed out that alcohol is involved in many offences and it is also an offence to drive and carry out other functions while under the influence of alcohol – drunk driving still causes many accidents and deaths. Alcohol and cigarettes are also subject to taxation which provides a market in contraband cigarettes and 'bootleg' beer – the latter amounting to a substantial trade with considerable profits.

White collar crime

Many of the above discussions have been related to the association between social exclusion, unemployment and crime, but it is also important to recognise the extent of crimes at work along with those committed in a professional and business context – called white collar crime. While this is often ignored in public discussions of crime, recent years have also seen a spate of high profile financial frauds such as the collapse of the Bank of Credit and Commerce International (BCCI), the Maxwell pensions scandal and the collapse of Barings Bank. Concern has also surrounded the unlawful activities of public appointees, government ministers, MPs and concerns about 'sleaze' affected the 1997 general election. Also included in this category is organisational or corporate crime in which the offender is a corporate body and where the offence involves the breach of criminally enforced regulations to protect consumers, workers or the public from fraud or physical harm caused by a neglect of trading or safety regulations. Breaches of safety regulations can have disastrous consequences as seen in cases such as the sinking of the *Herald of Free Enterprise* off Zeebrugge, or the drowning of four teenagers in Lyme Regis Bay while staying at an adventure centre – which led to two company directors being convicted of corporate manslaughter (Croall 1998a).

White collar crime may not be seen by some as a major crime problem, partly because the offences involved are seen as less serious and threatening than murder, rape or robbery. They are often less public than other crimes, taking place in offices rather than on the streets. The relationship between victims and offenders is indirect and, where breaches of safety regulations are involved, offenders have not intended to injure or kill their eventual victims. They often involve complex technological or financial issues, less easy to detect by either victims or enforcement agencies.

Many of the explanation of the causes of crime outlined above cannot readily be applied to white collar crime. It makes little sense to attribute major frauds such as those involved in BCCI to family problems or to biological or psychological abnormalities and few white collar offenders are suffering from poverty or social deprivation. The tolerance of many white collar offences such as tax evasion or insider dealing mean that offenders are less likely to be labelled as deviant and, indeed, many offences may be seen as perfectly acceptable within business subcultures. To some, 'greed' rather than 'need' motivates white collar crime, or the prioritisation, within organisations, of profits at the expense of the interests of consumers, workers or the general public. Thus many industrial accidents can be attributed to the strain between the need to comply with safety regulations and the need to cut costs. These attitudes, argue some, were particularly prevalent in the enterprise culture of the 1980s which may account for the apparent rise of financial frauds (Punch 1996). In addition, the privatisation of public services has been associated with the need for ever more stringent controls against fraud, bribery and corruption (see, for example, Doig 1996).

White collar crime also draws attention to the nature of the organisations. Managers may find themselves in a situation where loyalty to the organisation and organisational 'group think' blinds them to the nature of actions which they might otherwise see as 'wrong'. They might therefore continue to market a dangerous product by convincing themselves that it will not do any harm (Punch 1996).

Despite the adverse effects of white collar or corporate crime they are far less likely to be detected, prosecuted or severely sanctioned (Croall 1992). The reasons underlying this are extremely complex; however, they do lend some support to the arguments of critical criminologists that the offences of the powerful are less severely dealt with than those of the powerless. In addition, the treatment of white collar crime, and the tolerance of the many activities it involves, further reveals the complexities of attempting to define crime.

CRIME AND VICTIMISATION

All of the approaches to crime outlined above have focused on the offender rather than the victim. Yet the victim is most directly affected by crime, and in recent years criminologists and practitioners have shown an increasing interest in the victim. To early victimologists, victims could form part of the causes of crime, and some groups were seen as more 'prone' to becoming victims. The later focus on the situations in which crimes occurred also drew attention to the role of victims. If the situations which were more likely to lead to offending and victimisation could be identified, victims could play a major role in preventing crime. Surveys, such as the BCS, which look at the public's experiences of and attitudes to crime, have also revealed much about the impact of crime on individual victims and about the more generalised fear of crime on the part of the public, which some have seen as exceeding the 'real' risk of crime. This section will start by looking at images of victimisation and at some of the reasons why there has been a resurgence of interest in the victim. The growth of victim surveys and their findings about the impact and distribution of victimisation will be explored in Chapter 3 and the role of the victim in criminal justice in Chapter 11.

Like the concept of crime, the concept of the victim requires some exploration. Clearly, in order to be defined as a victim of crime, victims have to be aware that some harm has been done to them and that this harm can be defined as crime. In both commonsense and legal terms the notion of victim is linked to notions of crime. Where, for example, a victim is assumed to be 'innocent' the crime is seen as more serious than if the victim is seen to have provoked an offence – which can act as a form of mitigation. There is therefore a continuum ranging from the 'innocent victim' – examples of which might be children or the elderly who are set upon by an attacker – to victims who are seen to have invited trouble by, for example, appearing to provoke a fight or leaving their valuables fully visible in an open car. Some victims are therefore blamed for their own victimisation and seen as less deserving. These notions can affect perceptions of whole groups of offences and victims – women who have been raped can, for example, be seen to have 'asked for it' by dressing provocatively or appearing to have invited sexual activity. 'Date rape', in which defendants claim that women consented to sex or implied consent by, for example, accompanying men to their rooms, is seen as less serious than the less common 'stranger rape'. Victimisation, like crime, is therefore affected by circumstances and social perceptions.

'Blaming the victim', by assuming that he or she provoked the crime, has been a recurrent theme in victimology. Early victimologists hypothesised that some groups, such as children, the elderly, the weak or the depressed, were particularly prone to being victims and others argued that some victims precipitated offences, particularly in cases of murder and rape (see, for example, von Hentig 1948; Walklate 1989). Amir, for example, surveying police records, stated that 19 per cent of rapes were 'victim precipitated' in that women had initially agreed to sex but later changed their mind or had not resisted strongly enough (Amir 1971). Later victimologists focused more specifically on how people's lifestyles were related to victimisation, arguing, for example, that victimisation was related to the amount of time spent in public places where crimes were more likely to occur. Those who go out more often are more likely to be assaulted in the street than, for example, those who stay at home. If these situations can be identified then high risk lifestyles can be better avoided. Many of these approaches have been criticised as they are associated with 'victim blaming'. Feminists have argued, for example, that Amir's arguments blame women for inviting rape. Lifestyle theories, which have been linked to the opportunity theories outlined above, are useful for crime prevention but also have limitations. They identify situations in which people's lifestyles are 'risky' but they fail to ask why some are riskier than others. The poor, for example, may have little choice but to live in a high crime area and those whose work takes them through such areas also have little opportunity to avoid any risk. They also focus largely on the more public manifestations of crime, neglecting assaults and violence which take place in the home, or the many crimes in the workplace.

Nonetheless, looking at victimisation has become a very important part of studying crime and recent decades have seen what has been described as the 'rediscovery' of the victim. This emerged from diverse sources (see, for example, Zedner 1997). Women's groups were critical of the absence of support by the police and courts for women and children who were the victims of violence in the home. In addition, victims of violent crime, which could lead in severe cases to incapacitation, had no means of obtaining compensation from the state. A growing number of studies also revealed not only that victims in general felt that they needed help and support in the aftermath of an offence but that they were dissatisfied with their treatment in the criminal justice system. Often they were not informed about the progress of their case and, when needed in court to give evidence, were often ill prepared for this. These different arguments led to a number of policies, some of which will be outlined in Chapter 11 and include a new victim telephone helpline introduced in March 1998.

The increasing attention paid to the victim was also evident in the growing use of victim surveys in which random samples of the population are asked about their experiences of victimisation and their attitudes to a range of issues surrounding crime and criminal justice. This has produced a rich source of information about the extent of different forms of crime and their impact on victims – which will be outlined in Chapter 3 and subsequent chapters. They also provide invaluable information about which groups in what circumstances are more 'at risk' of becoming a victim. The result of these developments has been that studying the victim has become a major feature of criminology and that the needs of the victim have been more widely recognised in the criminal justice process.

CONCLUSION

This chapter has explored many dimensions of crime. We have identified the three interrelated elements that are vital to understand and explain crime; behaviour, rules and their enforcement. The legal conception of crime defined in terms of *actus rea* and *mens rea* focuses on the need of the criminal justice system to establish the blame or degree of blame with respect to behaviour either proscribed or required by the criminal law. Hence the importance of criminal defences such as self-defence or duress which might absolve a person of an act otherwise deemed criminal, and the mitigation statements put forward for those convicted in order to diminish their culpability for an offence.

Theories of crime, or a popular version of them, come to enter the public imagination and provide guides or cues to public debate about what is to be done about crime. The models of criminal justice discussed in Chapter 1 relate to these theories. The rehabilitative model is linked to the idea that offenders are in some way pathological. If, for example, crime is the result of some identifiable problem in the individual offender, then the problem may be addressed by developing suitable forms of 'treatment'. Sentencing policy could therefore be likened to a doctor's recommendations for treatment. The promise of these theories was however not fulfilled. Crime cannot be easily traced to an offender's individual characteristics – making it difficult to devise appropriate treatment programmes.

Furthermore, some research links criminality to factors outside the reach of sentencers. Not all football supporters are hooligans. Nevertheless it is obvious that football crowds in this country attract some young men looking for an opportunity for violent behaviour. To what extent male hormones or alcohol are contributory factors is not easily diagnosed. However, this does not mean nothing can be done. The sale and consumption of alcohol can be banned at a football ground, as can known offenders.

The labelling perspective has had a major impact on criminal justice polices. It suggested that intervention by criminal justice agencies can potentially increase the volume of crime and precipitate criminal careers. For many years, policies for young offenders have sought to divert children and young persons from the formal processes to avoid stigmatisation and labelling. These kinds of policies, however, may run counter to other models. The crime control model, for example, suggests that those who are guilty of a crime should be prosecuted and punished and the due process model requires that this should be done publicly and equally. Should some offenders therefore avoid such public trial and punishment? In addition the criminal justice process performs an important denunciatory role – which again requires that offenders be publicly held accountable for their offences. Labelling theory, however, suggests that such denunciation and punishment should not be such as to create outsiders or oppositional subcultures (Braithwaite 1989).

Some of the theories outlined in this chapter relate crime to the wider socio-economic context in which crime takes place. This raises a further set of questions. The criminal justice process deals primarily with individual offenders. It has no power over the economic system let alone the social structure. Yet the due process model requires that offenders are treated 'fairly'. This could pose problems, for example, in the sentencing of an offender claiming that offences had been brought about by the effects of unemployment. Should this be taken into account? If, on the other hand, it is the case that unemployment is related to crime it may also mean that the criminal justice process may be able to do little to reduce crime substantially. The causes of crime may quite simply lie outside its remit. Sentencers can scarcely provide jobs for offenders, remove them from a crime prone environment, or sentence them to marriage!

Review questions

1. How would you define a criminal?

2. List the ways in which the criminal law reflects a concern with blameworthiness.

3. In 1992 the Home Office published the results of a National Prison Survey of 4,000 randomly selected inmates. The prisoners were asked, 'whether any other member of their family had been convicted of a criminal offence; 43 per cent said this had occurred and 35 per cent replied that someone in their family had been imprisoned' (Home Office 1992: xii).

   How might you account for these figures in the light of the explanations of crime discussed in this chapter?

4. Which of the main perspectives on crime do you think help to give an insight into the reasons offenders commit burglary, business fraud, vandalism or murder?

Further reading

Croall H (1998) *Crime and Society in Britain*. London: Longman

Muncie J, McLaughlin E and Langan M (eds) *Criminological Perspectives*. London: Sage

Walklate S (1998) *Understanding Criminology*. Buckingham: Open University Press

Williams K (1994) *Textbook on Criminology*, 2nd edn. London: Blackstone Press

CHAPTER 3

HOW MUCH CRIME?

- Crime and its Impact
- Home Office Statistics on Crime
- British Crime Survey
- Public and Police Influence on Crime Statistics

INTRODUCTION

In Chapter 2 it was seen how difficult it is to define and explain crime, and many difficulties also surround its measurement. Thus before an offence is counted, behaviour must be defined as being against the criminal law and brought to the attention of a law enforcer. Chapter 2 also showed that as public tolerance of different activities changes, the criminal law itself can change. New crimes may be added to the statute book, increasing the total amount of crime. Technological and social change can also affect crime rates – if, for example, there are more cars on the road, there are more opportunities and temptations to steal them and more regulations concerning their use. The activities of law enforcement agencies can affect the volume and kind of crimes which are recorded. If the police associate certain areas with particular kinds of crime, they might pay more attention to these areas, thus producing more recorded crime.

Therefore criminal statistics must be interpreted with considerable caution. These statistics are often taken as a barometer of crime from which the media, politicians and the public shape their ideas about crime. This in turn affects criminal justice policy. It is important to realise, however, that these statistics are likely to be at considerable variance with the actual incidence of crime and that all attempts to calculate the crime figure are no more than estimates. Thus the Home Office *Digest 2: Information on the Criminal Justice System in England and Wales* comments that 'no-one knows the true extent of crime in this country' (Barclay 1995: 1).

This chapter will explore in more detail the available information about crime and convicted offenders, and will look at how this is constructed and interpreted. It will start by looking at some general indications about the

64

extent and impact of different kinds of crime and at statistics on offences, convicted offenders and victims. The main sources of crime statistics will then be outlined along with an indication of what they can and cannot tell us about the amount of different kinds of crime. We will then look at how the actions of the police, the public and victims influence these statistics. We will examine the insights into the extent of crime provided by the British Crime Survey and other assessments of the amount and impact of crime.

CRIME AND ITS IMPACT

There are a variety of ways of looking at the extent of crime and its impact including statistics based on police records, statistics derived from victim surveys such as the British Crime Survey, self-report studies and estimates of the cost of crime.

In recent years the official statistics, based on police records, have charted a steady growth in recorded crime between 1950 and 1992, illustrated in Figure 3.1. In the 12 months to June 1997, the police recorded 4.8 million offences in England and Wales. This compares with 2.5 million in 1980, 1.6 million in 1970, 0.5 million in 1950 and an annual recorded figure of 100,000 which was relatively stable between 1876 and 1920. But the population itself has grown and therefore it could be expected that crime would also rise. A less dramatic growth is indicated when population figures are taken into account. Methods of recording crime have also changed during the period that the table covers. Categories and definitions of crime have changed and new crimes have emerged. Furthermore, the Home Office has helped to promote more reliable and consistent data collection methods. Crime statistics may also be affected by the growth of the police – if there are more police to record and investigate crime, this will produce higher rates of recorded crime. Nonetheless, even when these factors are taken into account, the figures show a dramatic and sustained growth in recorded crime, tenfold since 1950, and they illustrate why crime has come to be seen as such a major social problem.

The total volume of crime known to the police is affected by many factors, not all of them directly related to actual increases in crime. Changes in the crime rate can be affected by wider changes in society as a whole. For example, mass car ownership in the twentieth century has resulted in the creation of new offences, such as reckless or dangerous driving, and has also led to the extension of offences such as driving without a licence or insurance. Motor cars parked in streets have created many opportunities for theft, both of the cars themselves and of accessories such as radios and spare parts. In 1997, vehicle crime accounted for around one-quarter of all notifiable crimes recorded by the police.

Another way of looking at crime is to explore its impact on the public, on victims and on community life in general. All members of the public are

Fig 3.1 Crime trends 1950–97 in England and Wales

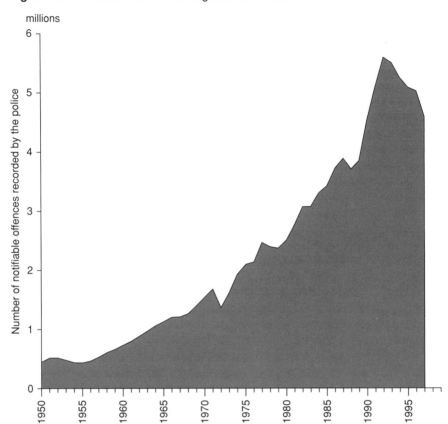

Compiled from *Criminal Statistics England and Wales*, 1950 to 1997.

affected by crime. They pay for crime through taxes which pay for the criminal justice system. They also pay higher insurance premiums to protect themselves from the financial losses incurred by property crimes. These taxes may be higher to compensate for the large amount of tax frauds and evasion. Prices in shops include an amount to take account of theft by customers and employees.

Our daily lives are affected by the impact of and the fear of crime. Houses must be locked and protected against potential burglars and many people are scared to go to certain areas through fear of being mugged, raped or assaulted. Valuable items are post-coded, car windows have numbers etched on them, car breakdown services are informed of lone female drivers and give them priority. Violent offences are most likely to have a psychological impact on victims and also have consequences for the community and the way people lead their lives. Many women avoid walking in the streets at night – potentially reducing their freedom to participate in a variety of leisure activities. The fear of crime may deter people from using public transport and going to public places and can thus dramatically alter the quality of people's lives.

Individual victims may be affected in many ways. As we have seen, many crimes involve property offences, such as those involving cars. While many may be insured and may not lose financially, others are not. Financial losses are exacerbated by the inconvenience and frustration involved in the immediate aftermath of an offence. To some, burglaries not only involve the loss of goods but the feeling that their homes and privacy have been violated. Victims of fraud may also experience these feelings (Levi and Pithouse 1992). In general, the extent of fraud and corruption in organisations can undermine the trust which people have in many public and private institutions (Croall 1992).

Another consequence of crime is its cost to the community and business interests. This is illustrated in a report, *Counting the Cost*, published by Crime Concern and the Thames Valley Crime Prevention Group in 1994. The report estimated that crime costs £24.5 billion a year. This estimate is based on government statistics, crime surveys and on the costs of lost and damaged property, policing, insurance and the cost of the criminal justice system. Thus in 1991/2 government expenditure was £9 billion and the cost of private security to companies, private individuals and public authorities was £1.6 billion. Burglary losses are set at £1 billion and theft losses at £1.9 billion including £775 million in stolen cars. Insurance companies estimate that arson accounts for £500 million annually and local authorities pay £500 million per year to deal with vandalism. The Confederation of British Industry and Crime Concern estimate that crime costs business £5–£10 billion per year – with losses of more than £3 billion in business fraud, £165 million per year on credit card frauds and £400 million a year through computer-based crime. While it is difficult to assess the accuracy of these or any such global figures they do illustrate the enormous financial costs of crime. Another way of assessing the impact of crime is by looking in more detail at the global figures and looking at some statistics on offences, offenders and victims. Statistics can be of considerable use and can often be contrasted with the images of crime presented in the media. This section will look at some aspects of statistics in relation to offences, offenders and victims.

Types of offence

Information about the extent of offences comes from police records which detail how many offences are reported to them, and from victim surveys which indicate the kinds of incident which victims have experienced. While the limitations of these figures will be explored later in this chapter, they provide a broad snapshot of the kinds of offence dealt with in the criminal justice process. They also correct some of the more misleading images of

Fig 3.2 Notifiable offences recorded by the police in 1997

Theft and handling stolen goods (excl. vehicle crime)	1,048,500
Vehicle crime	1,117,700
Burglary	1,015,800
Criminal damage	867,000
Violence against the person	253,100
Fraud and forgery	135,500
Robbery	64,100
Sexual offences	33,500
Other notifiable offences	60,000
Total	**4,595,200**

Compiled from *Home Office Statistical Bulletin*, 7/98: 2.

crime which can result from the tendency of the press, for example, to focus on more dramatic and newsworthy offences. Figure 3.2 shows, in descending order, the numbers of different kinds of crime reported to the police in 1997. This illustrates that violent and sexual crime, often seen as major problems, account for a relatively small proportion of the total volume of recorded crime with different kinds of theft, vehicle crime and burglary dominating the figures. Some of these categories will be explored below. The data on crime for 1997 continues a downward trend in crimes recorded by the police. This is the fifth year in succession that recorded crime has fallen.

Violent crime

Violent crime, which includes homicide and assaults, accounted for 7 per cent of recorded crime in the year to June 1997. Violent crime is sometimes described as 'contact' or 'personal' crime. There has been an increase in violent offences reported from the 1980s which is generally attributed to an increased willingness to report offences, particularly domestic violence, although this is generally recognised to be under-reported (Mirrlees-Black *et al* 1996). Of the violent offences reported to the most recent BCS, 1.7 million involved acquaintance violence compared with one million each for domestic and stranger violence – thus the majority of violent offences involve people who know each other. Some features of the main categories of violent offences are summarised below.

- *Homicide*: A general category that covers the offences of murder, manslaughter and infanticide and attracts a lot of public attention. Many of the most notorious criminal incidents that enter public consciousness relate to horrific cases, such as the Moors murderers Ian Brady and Myra Hindley, Peter Sutcliffe (the Yorkshire Ripper) and Frederick West, the Gloucester builder who committed suicide in prison in 1995 while awaiting trial for the murder of 12 people. Much public concern was aroused by the brutal killing of 2-year-old James Bulger, murdered in Bootle on 12 February 1993 by two 10-year-old boys, Robert Thompson and Jon Venables. However, stranger murders of children are relatively rare. Between 1977 and 1996 there were on average 7 deaths a year of victims under the age of 16 where the suspect had been identified and was not known to the victim. In 1987 one incident in Hungerford accounted for 16 deaths. Despite the impression given by high-profile cases, multiple murders account for 3 per cent of victims (Gresswell and Hollin 1994). Typically homicide is a crime in which relatives and acquaintances rather than strangers kill each other. In the 10 years between 1987 to 1996 there were on average 686 homicides a year and most victims were male.

- *Domestic violence*: In the 1995 BCS, 1.3 per cent of all women surveyed reported domestic violence compared with 0.7 per cent of men (Mirrlees-Black *et al* 1996). Women were more likely to have been attacked by their current or ex-partners (accounting for 80 per cent of reported incidents), whereas while 47 per cent of assaults on men were by current or ex-partners, half were by other household members and other relatives. Even more difficult to calculate is the number of children and the elderly who are also affected by violence in the home.

- *Assaults*: The picture which has emerged from victim and crime surveys is that many reported assaults take place in and around leisure sites such as pubs and clubs with the category of officially recorded assaults dominated by fights, largely between young men. Some assaults are summary offences and as such are not included in the criminal statistics based on police recording notifiable offences. Thus common assault, which was redesignated as a summary offence in 1988, is not included in official statistics on violent offences, nor is an assault on a police officer.

- *Violence in the workplace*: Violent offences may also take place at work – the 1988 BCS found that for those who worked, nearly a quarter of violent incidents were associated with work, with welfare workers, nurses, production and site managers, entertainment managers and security workers emerging as most at risk. Shop workers may also face violence as, of course, do the police and prison officers who deal with violent offenders.

While small in proportion to other forms of recorded crime, it is important to recognise that many violent incidents are not recorded, particularly where victims and offenders know each other – only one-third of domestic violent offences reported to the BCS were reported to the police compared with two-thirds of muggings (Mirrlees-Black *et al* 1996). To these figures must also be added the many common assaults, which include threats of violence, which are not counted as notifiable offences to be recorded by the police. A more accurate picture of the extent of violent crimes such as common assault is reported in the British Crime Survey.

Threats of violence, where no actual assault takes place, can for some people be more psychologically damaging than occasional incidents of actual violence. This might happen particularly within families, among neighbours or with persistent racial harassment which may involve verbal abuse, threats of violence, vandalism and daubing racist slogans on the homes or businesses of members of minority ethnic groups. To the catalogue of violence could also be added 'road rage' and reckless or aggressive driving.

Sexual offences

The offences recorded by the police in this category are rape, buggery, indecent assault on males and females, indecency between males, unlawful sexual intercourse with a girl under 16, incest, abduction, bigamy and gross indecency with a child, and offences to do with procuring people for sexual purposes such as prostitution. Offences in relation to prostitution, other than procurement, including kerb crawling, are summary offences and are not included in the statistics recorded by the police. Indecent assaults on women account for more than half of all recorded sexual offences, and indecent assaults on men is the next highest category. Many victims and offenders are known to each other – a recent survey carried out by the Home Office found that nearly two-thirds of rapes, three-quarters of indecent assaults on males and two-thirds on females involved family members. About a quarter of rapes involved strangers, with one-third involving spouses, lovers, parents and other family members and another third involving acquaintances (Watson 1996).

Property crime

As seen in Figure 3.2, property crime dominates officially recorded crime. Theft, which together with handling stolen goods accounts for around half of all recorded crimes, includes shoplifting, theft by an employee and theft from the person – many of these may involve relatively trivial amounts although their net cost is considerable. Property crimes also include:

- *Burglary*: The BCS estimated that, in 1995, 6.3 per cent of households experienced an actual or attempted burglary with some experiencing more than one. The majority of recorded burglaries (56 per cent) did not involve any loss – the offender either failed to gain entry or did not steal anything. The most common items stolen in burglaries are jewellery, video equipment and cash, and net losses vary enormously with over a fifth involving losses of less than £100, but a third involving losses of over £1,000 (Mirrlees-Black et al 1996).

- *Vehicle theft*: This category includes thefts of, and thefts from, cars. Thefts from cars, which include the theft of external items such as wheels and

badges and the theft of audio equipment, accounts for the largest proportion in this category. Thefts of cars include so-called joyriding and thefts of
cars for economic gain – with the latter having been estimated to have
risen in recent years (Webb and Laycock 1992).

- *Fraud and forgery*: This accounts for around 3 per cent of recorded crime,
  although it is generally assumed to be undercounted – many frauds are not
  detected by victims and the frequent use of one credit card may only be
  counted once (Coleman and Moynihan 1996; Maguire 1997). The largest
  category of recorded frauds involves stolen credit cards although much
  business and financial fraud is either not detected or dealt with by agencies
  other than the police.

Organised and white collar crime

Any snapshot of recorded crime must also acknowledge the extent of many
forms of crime which are less likely to appear in official statistics. These
include organised and white collar crime – sometimes referred to as 'economic' or 'business' crime. Taken together, these kinds of crime would add
enormously to the extent and impact of officially recorded offences as the
following examples indicate:

- *Professional and organised crime*: In contrast to one-off, occasional and
  opportunistic crimes the term 'professional and organised' refers to the
  structured and business-like approach of those involved, for example, in
  stolen cars whose parts are stripped and identities concealed before they
  are re-sold. Organised crime is generally involved in the sale of illegal
  commodities and services such as drugs, arms, pornography, gambling, sex
  or stolen goods, the transport of illegal immigrants and protection rackets.
  The growing profits of the drugs industry, which need to be 'laundered',
  have also led to the involvement of organised criminals in other activities
  such as financial frauds and the manufacture of counterfeit goods such as
  designer clothes, sports equipment, audio and video cassettes. While many
  organised criminals avoid violence as it increases their risk of detection,
  much organised crime relies on the threat of violence (Hobbs 1995).

- *White collar and corporate crime*: In contrast to the category above these
  crimes are committed by people already engaged in legitimate enterprises
  in business or the professions who use their position to commit offences
  such as financial or pensions frauds. These crimes can also affect the public
  service: the Healthcare Financial Management Association, for example,
  recently estimated that 'tens of millions of pounds are being lost by prescrip-
  tions frauds and false claims of payment by doctors, dentists, pharmacists
  and opticians (*The Guardian* 24 June 1997: 8). Frauds on the European
  Union are also said to be widespread, and to involve both legitimate and

illegitimate business enterprises. Chapter 2 drew attention to the vast area of white collar and corporate crime, whose real extent is impossible to estimate although many argue that it exceeds the costs of property crimes such as theft or burglary. The BCCI case, referred to in Chapter 2, was estimated to have cost as much as £15 billion pounds (Croall 1992).

Offenders

Statistics give details of the age and gender of offenders found guilty of or cautioned for offences. Information from the Home Office Offenders Index (which contains the criminal histories of people convicted of standard list offences since 1963) was used in a cohort study to trace the criminal histories of males born in 1953. It showed that by the age of 30, 36 per cent had been convicted of one serious offence, that most first convictions occurred at the age of 17, and that a few offenders (6 per cent) accounted for nearly two-thirds of all crimes resulting in a conviction.

In general, statistics show that recorded crime is very much a young person's activity, with just under 43 per cent of known offenders in 1994 being under 21. One-quarter of offenders were aged under 17. It should also be borne in mind that many young offenders caught for the first time may not be formally cautioned, but are given an informal warning and that 'young offender crime' such as vandalism and criminal damage is considerably under-reported, which is largely confirmed in self-report studies. The peak age for known offending is 18 for males and 15 for females.

A consistent feature of the statistics, not only in England and Wales but across Europe and America, is that far fewer women are convicted of crime than men – 81 per cent of offenders in 1994 were male, a proportion which has changed little over the years. Female offenders also show a different pattern of offending being less involved in violent offences and proportionately more involved in theft. In general most now accept that girls and women do commit fewer offences than boys and men.

Statistics do not give breakdowns of offenders by ethnic groups and information on this matter is somewhat inconclusive, having been gathered by a number of different research studies using only partial information. Broadly speaking, figures indicate that black people tend to be arrested, convicted and imprisoned in higher proportions than would be expected from their overall proportion of the population, with Asians being under-represented (Smith 1997). However, these figures are extremely difficult to interpret and could be affected by a variety of factors. For example, black people tend to be more concentrated in areas where more street crime occurs, and, compared to the white population, the black population has higher proportions of young people who, as we have seen, feature prominently as offenders. Thus it might be expected that higher proportions of black youth would appear as offenders although many argue that there is also discrimination against black people at different stages in the criminal justice process. Finally, black youth feature among those who might be considered to experience relative deprivation, as discrimination in relation to employment may mean that they are more disadvantaged than white youth (Lea and Young 1992).

These breakdowns may, of course, be affected by unreported crime. Fewer offences of domestic violence, white collar and organised crime are likely to be reported or detected so it could be argued that males over 21 are underrepresented in the statistics. Although the majority of convicted offenders are from lower socio-economic backgrounds, the relative absence of white collar offenders from reported crime means that we cannot necessarily conclude that the majority of offences are committed by lower class individuals. On the other hand, acts of vandalism are estimated to be one of the least reported offences. This might explain differences in interpretation of the current amount of youth crime. Some commentators claim that there is a decrease in crime among children and young persons. Others suspect the recorded crime figures on youth crime are far from reliable, with much youth crime being regarded as trivial, unreported and with many offenders being diverted from the formal system (see Chapter 5).

Victims

Victim surveys not only tell us more about the incidence of crime, but also help us to examine the relationship between offenders and victims, which also corrects some media stereotypes about crime. Moral panics about crime in the mass media have led, it has been argued, to a widespread fear of crime, which exceeds the risk of actually being a victim. The first British Crime Survey in 1982, for example, found that a statistically average person aged over 16 could expect a robbery once every five centuries, an assault once every century, and a burglary once every 40 years. But who is a statistically average person? Later locally based surveys such as the Islington Crime Survey, pointed out that the risks of victimisation are unevenly spread with those living in inner city areas being most at risk of being a victim of a burglary or car theft (Jones *et al* 1986; Walklate 1989).

Subsequent studies have revealed much more about the way in which victimisation is spread throughout the population, and about how, as indicated in Chapter 2, it is related to aspects of social class, gender, age, race and ethnicity and lifestyles. In general terms, victimisation is higher for those in certain types of areas which reflect a combination of geographical and social factors – thus:

- High-risk areas are found in metropolitan areas, high-status non-family areas and poorest council estates.

- Medium-risk areas are found in better-off council estates, older terraced housing and less well-off council houses.

- Low-risk areas are found in agricultural areas, better-off retirement areas, modern family housing for higher income groups, affluent suburban housing and older housing of intermediate status (Mayhew *et al* 1993).

This reflects a variety of factors. Some kinds of houses are more ready targets for burglars – burglary is higher, for example, in flats than in houses, in terrace-type houses than in detached houses, and in rented accommodation. While lower income groups have high rates of victimisation, the more affluent may also be more ready targets, especially of car thieves, as they presumably have more worth stealing. Victimisation also reflects, as suggested in Chapter 2, different lifestyles – thus those who go out more often are more likely to be the victims of public forms of violence. Young men are therefore more likely to be the victims of public assaults and robbery, although women are more likely to be the victims of 'snatch thefts' of handbags. Moreover, as indicated above, women are more likely than men to be victimised in the home.

Racial or minority ethnic status may also affect victimisation. More recent sweeps of the BCS have taken 'booster samples' of minority ethnic groups finding that both Afro-Caribbeans and Asians are more at risk than whites of household and personal offences with Pakistanis being particularly vulnerable to vandalism of houses and cars and to serious threats. Many of these differences can be explained by socio-economic factors, although for some, especially Asian groups, it remains significant and these groups also perceive more crime to be racially motivated. This is more prevalent for personal than for property crimes and around 4 per cent of Afro-Caribbeans and 8 per cent of Pakistanis reported having been victims of racially motivated offences in the 1992 BCS (FitzGerald and Hale 1996).

Victim surveys also attempt to assess the impact of crime on victims. As seen above, many violent offences do not involve serious injury, and many property crimes also involve trivial amounts. Many victims, therefore, may not be greatly affected by offences, with more severe effects being found among victims of robbery, wounding, burglary, threats and major vandalism (see, for example, Mayhew *et al* 1989). With burglary, the invasion of privacy emerged in the most recent BCS as a major upsetting feature; and, for men, mugging, and, for women, domestic violence, were the most upsetting kinds of offence (Mirrlees-Black *et al* 1996). A minority of victims report emotional effects such as sleeplessness and tearfulness with many reporting being angry about offences. In addition to financial losses and injury, many offences cause inconvenience – reports have to be made to the police, lost goods replaced or damaged items and houses repaired. This 'nuisance value' of crime is also reported by many victims.

Offences may also have indirect effects. Victims' families may be affected – most particularly in cases of murder and serious injury, but also in cases of burglary. Children in houses which have been burgled have been found to suffer from sleeplessness and bed wetting (Morgan and Zedner 1992). Witnesses to crime, particularly violent crime, may be emotionally affected and also have to suffer the inconvenience of giving statements to the police or attending court. In more general terms the quality of life of entire communities may be affected by high rates of crime, which may lead to the general 'decline' of an area, and high rates of prostitution or drug taking may further damage a neighbourhood's reputation and quality of life.

HOME OFFICE STATISTICS ON CRIME

The government publishes many different statistics on crime and the criminal justice process. The main source of information provided by the Home Office is the publication *Criminal Statistics England and Wales*. These statistics contain a wealth of information about the amount and kinds of offences dealt with by the police and the courts. They give details for example of the following:

- Numbers of offences recorded by the police, along with breakdowns of different categories of offences. This may differ from the numbers of offences reported to the police because the police, for reasons which will be explored below, may not record all offences reported to them.

- Proportions of offences 'cleared up' by the police. Not all offences reported to or recorded by the police will be attributed to a suspect. Thus the police may not clear up the crime.

- Numbers of offenders cautioned and convicted for offences, broken down by offence category, age and sex.

- Numbers of court proceedings and sentences – again broken down by offence category, age and sex.

- Increases and decreases in all of these categories.

More detailed information on specific offences such as different kinds of theft and fraud and less serious offences are given in the *Supplementary Criminal Statistics* which also show statistics by police area. A very useful summary of these statistics can be found in the *Criminal Justice Digest* which can be obtained from the Home Office, which also includes data from the British Crime Survey (see, for example, Barclay 1993). Selected statistics are also available on the internet (see Appendix on Criminal Justice Websites).

The Home Office's Offender Index holds data on individuals convicted of serious offences. Computerised in 1991, the index adds nearly half a million new pieces of data each year. Each record includes a name with initials, gender, date of birth, ethnicity and, if known, a CRO (Criminal Records Office) number. Six million individual criminal histories are available to the police with information about offences and sentences.

Official statistics refer to many different categories of offences. The main statistics refer to notifiable offences recorded by the police. This covers most serious crimes including indictable offences which must be tried in the Crown

Court, and others which can be tried in either the Crown Court or magistrates' courts. They also include some summary offences, which are less serious than indictable offences and are tried only in magistrates' courts. But few statistical details of summary offences are available. Statistical literature also refers to the category of grave offences. Broadly speaking, these are offences which attract a maximum sentence of life imprisonment and include homicide, serious wounding, rape, buggery, robbery, aggravated burglary and arson. Another way of classifying offences is 'Standard List' offences. These include all 'grave offences' along with violence against the person, sexual offences, burglary, theft and handling stolen goods, fraud and forgery, criminal damage (in excess of £20) and drug offences. They also include a variety of other offences including blackmail, kidnapping, offences against the state or public order, aiding and abetting an offender and firearms and public health offences.

The compilation and publication of criminal statistics involves considerable effort in bringing together data from many agencies including the 43 police forces and the resulting publication provides much detailed information about crime and the activities of the criminal justice agencies. The statistics could never be wholly accurate but, in any event, many offences are not included. They omit, for example, offences recorded by police forces outside the ambit of the Home Office such as the British Transport Police, the Ministry of Defence Police and the UK Atomic Energy Authority Police. Many other offences which are known to agencies other than the police are not prosecuted, and do not appear in the Home Office statistics. Thus the Inland Revenue, Customs and Excise and Department of Social Security may deal with many offences which they do not prosecute, as do the many regulatory agencies involved with public health, pollution or trading standards offences. Many of these are summary offences and statistics are only available for numbers of convictions.

Other factors may affect what is counted and how offences are classified. For example, changing views of the seriousness of offences may affect their classification and whether or not they appear in the main statistics. Mike Maguire cites the example of offences of criminal damage of £20 or less. These were not counted before 1977 but their re-classification as notifiable offences immediately raised the total volume of crime by around 7 per cent (Maguire 1997).

In addition, as seen previously, many potential offences may not be defined as criminal or reported to the police. Some kinds of offences are less likely to come to the attention of the police than others including:

- Offences which are not readily detectable by the police or public. These include offences which take place in private, for example domestic violence, sexual offences and drug offences.

- Offences with no discernible victim, often called victimless crimes – for example, prostitution, pornography, illegal gambling or drug abuse. These involve an exchange between consumers and suppliers of illegal commodities who are unlikely to report themselves to the police.

• Offences where victims are unaware that they have been a victim of a crime. Many frauds, for example, depend on victims not noticing that they have been defrauded. Other offences, such as the failure of businesses to comply with health, safety or environmental regulations, involve dangers which cannot be readily detected.

Many offences are therefore omitted from the statistics. Criminologists have long recognised that there is a large hidden or 'dark figure' of crime and that official crime rates reflect only those crimes reported to the police. Variations in crime rates therefore could be the result, not of differences between the real rates of offending, but of variations in reporting.

Even when crimes are reported to the police, they may not subsequently be recorded and counted as crimes 'known to the police'. In some cases the police may decide to take 'no further action' or decide that 'no crime' has been committed. This may happen, for example, where police are called to an incident such as a pub brawl and resolve it without arresting or charging someone, or where items are reported missing but it is unclear whether they are lost or stolen.

Statistics relating to offenders also have limitations. Clearly many offenders are never caught as their offences are invisible or not reported. In addition, the police only clear up a proportion of all crimes reported thus many offenders escape detection. Some crimes are easier to detect than others, which accounts for variations by offence in the clear-up rates given in the statistics. For example, many victims of assault know their assailant, leading to almost automatic clear up. If a fraud is discovered its perpetrator may be self evident.

The Home Office *Digest 3* (Barclay 1995: 26) reports that only 26 per cent of offences recorded by the police were cleared up. Reassuringly, 88 per cent of homicides were cleared up, as were 77 per cent of violent and sexual offences. Less than a quarter of thefts, burglaries and robberies were cleared up. The proportion of offenders detected becomes even smaller when the large volume of unreported crimes is taken into account. Thus only a very small proportion of offenders are ever caught.

Not even all known suspects and offenders are subsequently brought to court as the police or the Crown Prosecution Service may decide not to proceed with a case (see Chapter 5). The police have discretion when dealing with a case and may decide to take no further action, to caution offenders rather than bring a formal charge, not proceed with the case because they consider they have insufficient evidence, or proceed with the case and pass the papers on to the Crown Prosecution Service.

In effect, therefore, official statistics tell us which crimes the public choose to report and how those crimes are dealt with by the police. The data produced by the police will tell us as much about the method of policing and the

Fig 3.3 The process of attrition. Offences committed according to BCS, England and Wales

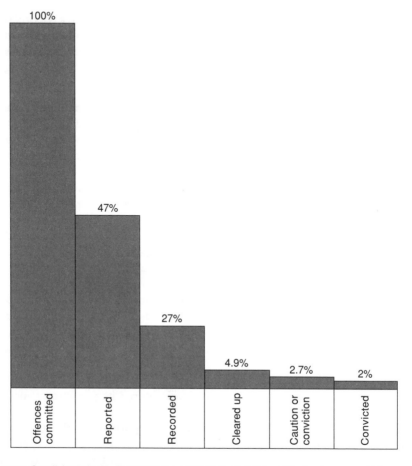

Source: Croall (1998b: 2). Reprinted by permission of Addison Wesley Longman Ltd.

level of public concern about crime as it does about the amount of crime. The report on the first British Crime Survey commented that:

> Variations over time or place in recorded crime rates can reflect the processes by which the statistics are complied as much as the condition they are intended to depict.

(Hough and Mayhew 1983)

This is illustrated in Figures 3.3 and 3.4 which show the sharp drop in numbers at each stage of the process. The British Crime Survey estimates that about 2 in 100 offences committed result in a criminal conviction. Variations occur between offences such as wounding where 14 in 100 offences result in a caution or a conviction while for burglary the figure is 3 in 100 and 1 in 100 for vandalism.

Fig 3.4 Attrition: specific offences

	Wounding (%)	Domestic burglary (%)	Vandalism (%)
Offences committed	100	100	100
Offences reported	54	69	27
Offences recorded	24	41	14
Offences cleared up	19	8	2
Offences resulting in a caution or conviction	14	2	3
Offences resulting in a conviction	11	2	2

(Compiled from Barclay 1995: 25)

Finally, the statistics may tell us about the numbers of different offences reported to the police, but little about how serious these offences are or the situations in which they occur. Many offence groups include vastly different kinds of offences. Thus categories of theft include very minor thefts along with serious ones, and frauds may involve very trifling sums or the millions of pounds involved in major frauds. In addition, as Maguire points out, a long-standing criticism of official statistics is that they cannot indicate changing patterns of crime – there may for example be changes in the kinds of typical thefts or robberies which are not reflected in broad classifications (Maguire 1997). More information about these kinds of issues can be found in victim and self report studies, which will be described below.

BRITISH CRIME SURVEY

One way of finding out more about crime is to ask the public what kinds of crime they have been the victims of and whether or not they have reported this to the police. This is done in what are called victim or crime surveys such as the British Crime Survey (BCS) which was first carried out in 1982. The BCS gives figures normally only for England and Wales – separate surveys have been carried out in Scotland. The 1996 survey estimated that a total of 19 million crimes were committed in 1995 against individuals and their property, of which only just over a quarter are estimated to be recorded by the police (Mirrlees-Black et al 1996).

This survey has become a regular feature of the criminological scene and further surveys were held in 1984, 1988, 1990, 1992, 1994 and 1996 and are likely to be conducted every two years in future. A random sample is used to select respondents. A core sample of 22,170 addresses in the 1996 sample led to 16,134 face-to-face interviews being completed. The survey asks members of the population how often they have been a victim of a specific offence in a specified time period. The scope of the questionnaire is extensive with 200 questions to elicit information on many aspects of crime, including:

79

- what kinds of crime people have been victims of
- what proportions of these offences are reported to the police
- why some offences are not reported
- what kinds of crime people are most worried about.

This information can be compared with police statistics to ascertain the difference between crimes known to the police and those experienced by victims. This data can be charted over time to give a more accurate picture of crime trends. Thus the British Crime Survey estimated that the crime rate in the 1980s rose at a slower rate than that suggested by recorded police statistics. Between 1981 and 1991, for the subset of crimes covered by the British Crime Survey, the police recorded a 96 per cent increase in crime, in contrast to a 49 per cent increase reported in the survey. However, between 1991 and 1993, the British Crime Survey indicated an 18 per cent rise in crime compared with a 7 per cent increase recorded by the police, and between 1993 and 1995 recorded crime fell by 8 per cent, whereas BCS figures for equivalent offences rose by 2 per cent (Home Office 1994; Mirrlees-Black et al 1996).

In addition to the comparisons with police figures referred to above, the survey can give useful information about unreported crime. The 1988 survey found that the following proportions of incidents were not reported to the police:

Vehicle vandalism	75%
Common assault	66%
Theft from the person	60%
Theft from vehicles	50%
Robbery	43%
Bicycle theft	37%

The 1996 survey estimated that the numbers of crimes committed exceeded the numbers recorded by the police in the following proportions:

- three times as many domestic burglaries
- four times as many thefts from vehicles
- four times as many woundings
- seven times as many offences of vandalism
- eight times as many robberies and thefts from the person.

Crime surveys can also compare the difference between the public's fear of crime and their actual risk from different offences, along with figures relating to the risks of victimisation for different groups such as the young and ethnic minorities and how these risks vary by neighbourhood. The survey can thus capture information on aspects of crime which escape official attention and indicates the types of crime that give the public most concern. Numerically, crimes associated with motor vehicles, such as vandalism to a vehicle and theft of, or from, motor vehicles, account for 24 per cent of all notifiable offences (Home Office Statistical Bulletin, 7/98: 1). This does not, however, cause as much anxiety as other types of personal crime such as robbery and burglary which are less numerous.

While producing much valuable information, the British Crime Survey has important limitations. It only includes private households and therefore does not include crimes committed in organisations and businesses (such as shop-lifting and pilfering from a workplace) and thus greatly underestimates the amount of theft committed. Many of the offences or incidents reported to the interviewers do not conform easily to legal classifications of crime and are therefore difficult to compare with police statistics. For example, if some-one reports an assault, how is it to be classified? Respondents' information may be inaccurate. They may forget some incidents or exaggerate others. In some circumstances they may be unwilling to reveal offences to interviewers that cause them embarrassment. Respondents may misunderstand a question or the meaning of a word. Victim surveys cannot cover crimes of which victims are unaware, such as consumer fraud or those which have no direct victims, for example drug offences. Some groups, many of which may be at risk from crime, are under-represented. Crimes against children are not in-cluded as only those aged 16 and above are included in the sample. Others, such as the homeless, are less likely to be on the personal address files which are the basis of the sample.

Self-report studies

Another way of attempting to find out more about crime is the self-report study. These ask groups of the population what kinds of crime they have committed in a given period. These may be used along with victim surveys, and crime surveys often include both victim and self-report questions. They have been used with schoolchildren to reveal large amounts of hidden delin-quency, with respect to crimes such as vandalism and shoplifting. These kinds of surveys, whose use has grown recently, can illuminate some of the many questions posed by the limitations of official statistics. They can be used, for example, to test the often made links between sex, class and delin-quency. Self-report studies have tended to confirm that girls are far less likely to commit delinquent acts than boys, although they do report many more offences than appear in the statistics (Heidensohn 1985). They have also been used to investigate the extent of drug taking among young people.

Self-report studies have many limitations, not least of which is the problem that however carefully anonymity is assured, respondents may not be honest in their answers: some may exaggerate the amount and seriousness of crimes they have committed. In addition, they tend, like victim surveys, to reveal vast amounts of fairly trivial crime which would probably not have been the subject of formal proceedings in any event. Like victim surveys they may also be difficult to compare with official figures as respondents' descriptions of activities may not be the same as legally classified offences. Self-report studies among adolescents are often carried out in schools, where researchers can find large numbers of young people in one place. This may not, however, be representative as school surveys will not include those who are truants or those in special establishments who may be the most likely to have committed offences (Williams 1991). In addition, because of their anonymity data cannot be independently checked against police records (Williams 1991).

Both victim and self-report studies are nonetheless invaluable sources of information about many dimensions of crime and they fill in some of the gaps left by official statistics.

PUBLIC AND POLICE INFLUENCE ON CRIME STATISTICS

As we have seen, official statistics are the result of actions and decisions of both the public and the police, which will be examined next.

Public attitudes to reporting crime

In Chapter 2 and in earlier sections of this chapter, it has been stressed that victims and the public play a key role in defining activities as crime and bringing these to the attention of formal agencies. In the British Crime Survey, respondents who have been victims of crime were asked, 'Did the police come to know about the matter? If "no", why not?' Respondents were allowed to give multiple answers to this question so they could give more than one reason. Data from the 1996 survey shows that the most frequent reason (40 per cent) for not reporting a crime to the police was that they thought the incident was not serious enough. Twenty-nine per cent thought the police would be unable to do anything and 20 per cent thought the police would not be interested. Nineteen per cent answered that it would be inappropriate to inform the police as they would deal with the matter themselves. Only 4 per cent cited fear of reprisal as a reason, and 4 per cent said it was inconvenient. Several factors might influence the decision to report a crime and the main ones are outlined below.

- *Awareness of victim status.* Quite simply, many victims are unaware of any offence having been committed against them. Citizens, for example, may be abstract or indirect victims of offences such as social security, tax or customs fraud. In more routine criminal cases the loss of property from an office or in a shop could be attributed to a misplaced or dropped wallet instead of a theft. In other cases, victims will not necessarily know that they have been a victim of a crime – for example, a young child in an incest case or the elderly relative who is forgetful and bedridden whose savings are used without prior consent by relatives.

82

- *Crimes without victims.* As seen above, some conduct defined as criminal does not have a victim in the traditional sense of the word in that there is no obvious person who is suffering and likely to complain about the offence, even when there is awareness that a crime has been committed. Drug abuse, some sexual offences, gambling and prostitution are therefore less likely to be reported.

- *Public tolerance.* For a crime to be reported, a victim or member of the public must feel sufficiently aggrieved to consider it worthwhile reporting – it must be something that exceeds their limit of tolerance. As seen in Chapter 2, public tolerance changes over time, and varies in different areas and within different subcultures. Thus, for example, people who live in the country may have a very different view of what activities are considered serious enough to report to the police than those living in towns, who may be more used to noisy parties or minor thefts from cars. Young people often experiment with different kinds of controlled drugs like cannabis and may not regard this as a real crime.

- *Seriousness or triviality of the offence.* One of the most common reasons given by victims for not reporting an offence is that it was too trivial to bother with. This will obviously be affected by levels of tolerance, but it is clear that a number of petty thefts or minor assaults are seen as insufficiently troublesome to bother the police with. On the other hand, serious offences are more likely to be reported, at least when victims are aware of them.

- *Lack of confidence in the police.* Some victims feel that even if they did report an offence the police would either not be able to solve it or would not pay much attention. Some crimes may be so trivial that the police will not bother to deal with them. Where sections of the population hold hostile attitudes towards the police they are less likely to report crime to them.

- *No motive.* A victim or a witness may conclude they have nothing to gain personally by reporting a crime and may consider the loss of time involved as not worth the effort. This might be counteracted by compensation or insurance incentives, or by public spiritedness.

- *Fear of reprisals.* Some victims may not wish to report offences because they are afraid that offenders may take some form of reprisal. This might be particularly the case with organised crime, school bullying and street vandalism where the offenders are known to the victim.

- *Embarrassment.* In some cases victims may be too embarrassed to report offences – victims of fraud or sexual assault may feel that they might be seen to have precipitated the offence and feel ashamed. In other cases victims may themselves have been indulging in behaviour they want to keep secret – clients who have their money stolen by prostitutes, for example, may well choose not to report an offence. Companies who find that senior executives have been embezzling funds may fear the public embarrassment following trial and conviction and decide to sack the executives concerned rather than call in the police.

- *Fear of self-incrimination.* Theft or violence against users of illegal drugs or illegal immigrants means that the victim has a difficult choice of revealing their own illegal behaviour if they choose to report an incident to the police.

- *Sympathy for the victim.* Where the offender is known to a victim as a friend or relative the victim may be reluctant to report a criminal incident as they do not wish to get the person into trouble. This can even be the case in crimes involving strangers, for example when the victim feels sympathy for the destitute state of the thief and decides not to report a loss.

Police influence on crime statistics

Crimes become 'known to the police' in two main ways. The vast majority of offences recorded by the police, about 90 per cent, are reported to the police by the public, the rest coming to their attention as they patrol the streets or carry out surveillance operations, as they might do to catch the suppliers of illegal drugs. It was pointed out above, however, that not all incidents reported to the police are recorded as crime. Furthermore, police priorities will be reflected in subsequent statistics as deployment of officers to cover one type of crime means that there are less to cover others. This will be discussed in more detail in Chapter 4, however it is important here to point out some of the ways in which variations in police practice affect the crime figures.

Different areas may have different rules regarding what should be recorded, which can affect local variations in crime rates. For example, the increase of 29 per cent in reported rape in 1985 by the Metropolitan Police did not necessarily represent an increase in the number of rapes or in the victim's readiness to report them, but reflected a change in police procedure in the recording of rapes. Policies of individual departments may produce apparent crime waves resulting from decisions to crack down, for example on street crime. Policy decisions by the chief constable will be reflected in the following year's criminal statistics, as arrest and summonses shift with the transfer of personnel from one type of work to another, for example, from the anti-burglary unit to the vice squad.

In other cases the police may decide that no crime has taken place. This might happen in case of domestic violence where after the police have been called in, they calm the situation down and the victim does not wish any further action to be taken. In many public order incidents it is the police who decide whether or not to take any further action. In other cases, as in the example of a missing purse or bicycle, the incident form may be completed by writing 'no crime' and no further action is taken. The attitude of the victim is also crucial here – if victims are unlikely to press for further action in a relatively trivial case, then it will usually be dropped.

No further action may result in a variety of other situations. The police may know who committed an offence but not be able to prove it. Gathering evidence may be costly and time consuming, as in the case of financial frauds, and allocation of budgets may mean that the case is not pursued. Alternatively the offence may be regarded as too trivial to pursue. In other cases, it may be decided that it is not in the public's interests to proceed – the offender may be seriously ill, very young or very old and therefore unlikely to repeat the offence.

Statistics also record the number of offenders cautioned or convicted. The basis for cautioning decisions will be discussed in Chapter 5 but it is important to recognise that here, as elsewhere in the criminal process, the numbers going forward to the next stage are dependent on the policy and decisions of a preceding agency.

In addition, there is no standard method of recording crimes used by all the separate police forces around the country. The story in Figure 3.5, 'Secret of a One-Man "Crime Wave"', provides an example of the difficulties of interpreting the data where there are a series of identical offences and the police decide to issue a summons for each breach of the criminal law.

Maguire also points out that there may be many different ways of counting an offence or series of offences (Maguire 1997). One offence may involve several offenders – is this to be counted as one offence or several? In other cases, a number of single offences may be counted as one or several. This could happen for example with a series of thefts of different items taking place in one location. Figures are also affected by how the police choose to classify an offence. While legal categories appear watertight, many offences may fall into several categories. When, for example, does an assault occasion actual or grievous bodily harm? The police may not have evidence to sustain one charge and therefore choose another.

An indication of how these many factors operate can be seen in a study to account for the differences in crime rates carried out in the 1980s. In 1981 Nottinghamshire had the highest recorded crime rate in the country, ahead of London, Liverpool, Manchester and Newcastle. In contrast, two of Nottingham's neighbouring counties, Leicester and Staffordshire, had a crime rate less than half that of Nottingham, as shown in Figure 3.6. A study by Farrington and Dowds in 1985 suggested an explanation for these differences. The British Crime Survey showed that there was indeed a higher crime rate in Nottinghamshire but there were other important factors, revealed by the greater number of recorded crimes originating from admissions to the police, usually after interviews with the police (Figure 3.7), and the

85

Fig 3.5 Secret of a one-man 'crime wave'

Buried in the annual report of the Northern Constabulary – a litany of highland crime, including malicious mischief, false fire alarms, and offences under the Deer (Scotland) Act – lies a staggering statistic: traffic offences in the Shetland Islands apparently rose by more than 400 per cent last year – **from 500 in 1976 to a grim 2,210**.

For a group of islands whose population is a mere 18,268, the figures seem to suggest some appalling sociological mutation.

The explanation is simpler, but no less bizarre. One man – an Irish lorry contractor called Darrall McKnight – has been summoned for what could be an international record of 1,380 alleged offences. Police in Shetland are still working on the formalities of this horrendous state of affairs.

McKnight, who also owns the Pig and Chicken restaurant near Belfast, had won a sub-contract to move rubble from a quarry on the island to a road construction site. At one point in the journey the lorries had to cross a public highway.

Lerwick police say that a constable making 'routine inquiries' discovered that McKnight's lorries did not have the appropriate operator's licence and that each time they crossed the highway they committed an offence.

Diligently he did his sums. He worked out how many times a day a single lorry crossed the road. He multiplied it by the number of lorries, and then multiplied it by the number of days they had been working on the contract. The grand total was 1,380.

Lerwick police listed each offence as a 'separate occurrence report' and sent the whole lot into the Procurator Fiscal for action. The procurator drafted an identical charge for each offence and then police carried the bundle of 1,380 summonses out to the construction site to confront McKnight.

There, however, they encountered Murphy's Law, whereby if anything can go wrong it will. McKnight had returned to Ireland. The police carried the unserved charges back to Lerwick.

Back in Belfast, McKnight was undaunted. 'They are just learning about traffic in the Shetlands', he said last week. 'They are just like a lot of childish policemen trying to make it sound like a murder case.'

But the Shetland police remain determined to get their man. A spokesman said that since they could not serve the summonses in person they intended to send all 1,380 of the charges to the Pig and Chicken.

by Michael Kerr

Source: *Sunday Times*, 23 April 1977.

Fig 3.6 Crimes recorded by the police per 1,000 population

Year	England and Wales	London	Liverpool	Notts.	Leics.	Staffs.
1981	60	88	87	90	45	42
1980	55	81	76	79	42	38
1979	52	77	71	75	36	38
1978	49	73	69	71	35	34
1977	50	73	76	76	35	32
1976	44	64	68	65	31	29
1975	43	60	68	65	29	27

Source: Farrington and Dowds (1985: 42).

Fig 3.7 How crimes were discovered: numbers and percentages

	Notts.	Leics.	Staffs.
Police, directly	19 (2.3)	17 (5.2)	26 (6.7)
Police, on admission	211 (25.4)	14 (4.3)	30 (7.7)
Public call at station	143 (17.2)	103 (31.3)	108 (27.7)
Public telephone call	340 (41.0)	178 (54.1)	203 (52.1)
Public call to patrol	111 (13.4)	9 (2.7)	20 (5.1)
Other	6 (0.7)	8 (2.4)	3 (0.8)
Total	**830 (100)**	**329 (100)**	**390 (100)**

Note: The 'other' category incudes burglar alarms, reports by letter, and the offender giving himself up. Percentage figures are rounded to one decimal place.

Source: Farrington and Dowds (1985: 58).

Fig 3.8 Value of stolen property: numbers and percentages

	Notts.	Leics.	Staffs.
£1 or less, nothing	167 (25.0)	38 (12.6)	43 (15.4)
£2–£10	154 (23.1)	50 (16.6)	57 (20.4)
£11–£25	79 (11.8)	33 (10.9)	48 (17.1)
£26–£50	67 (10.0)	51 (16.9)	35 (12.5)
£51–£100	66 (9.9)	43 (14.2)	34 (12.1)
£101–£250	67 (10.0)	37 (12.3)	26 (9.3)
£251–£500	41 (6.1)	30 (9.9)	21 (7.5)
Over £500	27 (4.0)	20 (6.6)	16 (5.7)
Total	**668 (100)**	**302 (100)**	**280 (100)**

Source: Farrington and Dowds (1985: 59).

greater number of property offences recorded involving property of little value (Figure 3.8).

They conclude that police interviewing and recording practice was a major factor explaining the differences between the three Midland counties. If the same recording practices had been used, the authors wrote:

> the crime rate per 1,000 population would have been about 57 in Nottingham, 48 in Leicestershire, and 36 in Staffordshire, in comparison with the observed figures of 87, 44, and 40. It was estimated from the study of police records that the greater number of crimes originating in admissions, and crimes involving stolen property of little value, amounted to a difference in crime rate between Nottinghamshire and the other two counties of about 31 per 1,000 population.
>
> (Farrington and Dowds 1985: 70)

CONCLUSION

We can see, therefore, that estimating the extent and impact of crime is extremely difficult and official statistics and crime surveys can only give a partial picture of the real extent of crime. In effect they may tell us more about what the public define as crime and what the police and other agencies choose to process. The above analysis of how these statistics are created has several implications for a consideration of criminal justice agencies and policy.

In the first place, it shows that the actions of the public and the police have an important impact on the crime figures. It is therefore important, in examining the role of criminal justice agencies, to also examine how they contribute to overall estimates of the extent of crime and how offenders are selected for subsequent stages. They reveal the considerable discretion which exists at all stages in the process. In addition, the public can also be affected by the images of crime portrayed in the media. If, for example, they learn that there has been an increase in a particular kind of crime, they may be more likely to report it. In addition, they may come to be more afraid of this kind of crime and take action to prevent it.

The analysis of crime figures also shows that public pressure and policy may be directed against a limited group of crimes, those which receive most attention in the media. Many crimes never reach the attention of the police and many more offenders remain undetected. Therefore those going through the criminal justice system may be a small and unrepresentative group of offenders. This raises important questions in relation to the role of criminal justice. How far can it seek to prevent crime, when it deals with only a proportion of those who commit it? A common response to a moral panic or a seeming spate of offences reported in the media is often to institute tougher penalties. However, if so many offenders remain undetected, how effective are these strategies likely to be? Should the system not focus on attempting to catch more offenders rather than punishing the ones that are caught? How much can sentencing policy really affect the volume of crime? These considerations underlie the current emphasis on crime prevention which will be discussed in Chapter 11.

However, other views (explored in Chapter 9) stress that the impact on the volume of crime is not the only purpose of sentencing. From the 'just deserts' and denunciatory perspectives it is important to punish wrongdoers regardless of their numbers. Whatever is considered the main objective of sentencing, it must first be understood that it occurs at a late stage in the criminal justice system, which starts with the police as the gatekeepers of the system. The following chapter will analyse their work in more detail.

Review questions

1. List the main factors which could account for an increase in crimes reported to the police in the last 40 years.

2. List offences which might be under-represented in the crime figures along with the reasons why they might be under-represented.

3. Discuss the factors which might explain why men are convicted of more offences than women and young offenders are convicted of more offences than adults.

4. List the main reasons why victims might not report crimes to the police.

5. See also Appendix 1, Practical Exercises, Exercise 1.

Further reading

Barclay G (ed). (1995) *Digest 3: Information on the Criminal Justice System in England and Wales*. London: HMSO
Coleman C and Moynihan J (1996) *Understanding Crime Data: Haunted by the Dark Figure*. Buckingham: Open University Press
Home Office (annually) *Criminal Statistics England and Wales*. London: HMSO
Maguire M (1997) 'Crime Statistics, Patterns and Trends: Changing Perceptions and their Implications', in Maguire M, Morgan R and Reiner R (eds) *The Oxford Handbook of Criminology* 2nd edn. Oxford: Clarendon Press
Walker M (ed) (1995) *Interpreting Crime Statistics*. Oxford: Clarendon Press

CHAPTER 4

THE POLICE

- The Role and Development of Policing
- Organisation and Accountability
- Police Powers and PACE
- Community Policing
- Discretion in Police Work
- Discrimination and Police Culture

INTRODUCTION

Policing attracts much public interest. Police dramas and documentaries nightly fill up television schedules and detective fiction and crime stories regularly feature in publishers' bestseller lists. But these popular images are often very far from the reality of policing. Police dramas feature murder, violent and organised crime, and investigations involve following up clues, dramatic car chases and confrontations. In reality murders are rare, most crimes are solved because the victim identifies the perpetrator, and in the life of an average police officer car chases and violent encounters with suspects are, perhaps fortunately, rare. The routine work of policing is less dramatic than television portrays, but is no less important for everyday life in the community as police patrol the streets, respond to a variety of incidents from lost keys to lost children, and endeavour to keep the traffic flowing safely.

There are other, less positive images of policing. In riots and demonstrations the police are seen in pitched battles with demonstrators and there have been allegations of planting evidence, 'fitting up' suspects and violence by the police. These different images illustrate some of the problems in defining the role of the police. Are they better described as a force or a service? Is it possible to talk about consensus policing or are the police essentially a paramilitary force waging a war against crime and disorder?

The conflicting demands of due process, crime control and bureaucratic efficiency strongly affect how the police are organised and evaluated. They are expected to find and bring to court those suspected of having committed an offence, but while doing so must stay within the law and the restraints imposed by the adversarial system of justice. The police must have powers to investigate crime but the public must be able to proceed without undue interference. Policing must be cost effective, but is difficult to subject to measurement – how, for example, can due process be measured? Having more police on the beat may make the public feel happier, but it might be costly and have little effect on crime.

Other models of criminal justice are also relevant to policing. While a key role of the police is to ensure that offenders are brought to court and punished, many offenders, especially young offenders, may have a better chance of being rehabilitated if they are diverted from formal proceedings. Thus the police play a role in both rehabilitation and denunciation. The police also play a role in preventing crime. This might conflict with their role of bringing offenders to justice. For instance, should an officer who observes suspicious behaviour intervene to prevent a potential crime happening or await the outcome of events and act only if a crime is committed? To critics following the class domination model, the police are essentially an organisation protecting the interests of the propertied and powerful and function as an arm of the state.

Two separate areas in which criticisms of police work have led to reforms are, firstly, in relation to the nature and extent of police powers and, secondly, the organisation and management of policing. A key piece of legislation on police powers was the Police and Criminal Evidence Act 1984. This brought together and rationalised many disparate rules relating to the investigation of crime to provide a clearer system of rules on matters of stopping, searching and questioning suspects. More recently major changes to police organisation and management have followed the Sheehy Report of 1993 and the subsequent reform enacted in the Police and Magistrates' Court Act 1994.

This chapter will examine many of these issues and explore the current organisation of policing in England and Wales. It will start by looking at the role and development of the police. It will then examine how the police are organised and how accountable they are. Legislation regulating how the police exercise their powers will be considered, followed by an outline of community policing. As we have seen, the police have considerable discretion and how they exercise this will be explored along with a discussion of the extent to which this involves discrimination against any particular group. Finally, at a day-to-day level, policing is strongly affected by how officers themselves interpret their role and the conflicting pressures on their work. This involves looking at what has been described as the occupational culture of the police.

Other chapters will explore further aspects of policing. The police role in cautioning will be looked at in Chapter 5, and some implications of current reforms will be taken up in Chapter 11. Many discussions of the police automatically refer to the police in the public sector, but it is important also to recognise, as seen in Chapter 1, that there is a vast and growing private security sector, who are carrying out an increasing number of police tasks. This chapter will look at the work of the public police service.

Fig 4.1 Public order snapshot

It was an ordinary winter's night, relatively mild for the time of year and uneventful as far as the general public and the media were concerned. In fact, as the public sat down to their breakfast that Saturday morning they would have had no idea what the police service had been doing on their behalf during the previous night.

During this eight-hour period, in fact, police officers responded to 20,932 separate incidents, that is 43 incidents every minute. 6,212 of these incidents (approximately 30%) were the result of 999 emergency calls which required an immediate response. There were four murders, seven rapes and 502 serious and indecent assaults, together with 112 cases of arson and 1,264 incidents of criminal damage to property. Robbery, burglary and car crime amounted to a further 3,045 separate incidents. 108 road traffic accidents involving personal injury included six fatalities. Minor assaults and drink-drive offences accounted for 1,548 incidents. 9,830 (47%) of the total incidents represented police attendance to matters not specifically identified but requiring advice and assistance.

In addition there were 4,458 incidents of public disorder ranging from 59 incidents of violent disorder and affray to almost 3,000 general disturbances in the streets. As a consequence of this 759 people were arrested, 30% of the total number arrested during the eight-hour period.

One of the most disturbing facts arising out of this survey is that, in this one short period, 54 police officers were assaulted whilst in the execution of their duty. In one area, three officers were injured whilst arresting a man for stabbing two other youths.

Source: (HM Chief Inspector of Constabulary, *Annual Report for the Year 1991/2*, p. 22)

THE ROLE AND DEVELOPMENT OF POLICING

Policing involves many different functions from patrolling and detection to traffic control, licensing and dealing with incidents which do not involve crime at all. This is illustrated in Figure 4.1, which is a snapshot survey of police work in 1991/2. This was conducted during an eight-hour period from 8 pm on Friday, 7 February to 4 am on Saturday, 8 February 1992 and while Fridays are not typical of other days in the week, it shows the range of incidents which the police are expected to deal with.

In his Annual Report for 1996 Her Majesty's Chief Inspector of Constabulary reported that in England and Wales the police responded to just under 19 million incidents of which 3 million required an urgent response. Over 7 million '999 calls' were answered, and over 1.75 million arrests were made; 1.3 million crimes were detected of which 15 per cent were considered to be serious.

The many tasks carried out by the police are often divided into three distinct roles. In the first place the police are responsible for law enforcement, for investigating crime, arresting suspects and deciding whether or not to pass the case on to the Crown Prosecution Service. This reflects their key role as enforcers of the criminal law. They are also the guardians of the Queen's Peace and preserving law and order in society. This involves tasks such as patrolling the streets and monitoring public gatherings, football matches or demonstrations. Less obvious is a third, social service role, in which the police deal with an enormous number of tasks which do not involve crime such as traffic management and dealing with accidents, deaths and emergencies. In practice, these roles are interrelated.

For example, not all incidents the police are called to can be clearly identified as crime, public order or social service – they are incidents requiring some form of action. Imagine, for example, a situation in which officers are called to investigate complaints about noise and disturbance in a street. In this situation they will principally be concerned to calm the situation which might be achieved by their very presence or might involve making arrests. If they behave too aggressively, however, they might exacerbate the situation. In other circumstances they may proffer advice and help or refer parties to another agency. Thus in many situations, all three roles are combined, and the police are dealing with 'potential crime' situations (Morgan and Newburn 1997). Studies of calls to the police have found that potential crime situations account for 53 per cent of all calls with 20 per cent involving social disorder, 18 per cent involving information or services and traffic matters accounting for 8 per cent of all calls (Morgan and Newburn 1997).

In other situations these roles conflict. For example, during the miners' strike of 1984, groups of police officers were accused of violence, harassment and intimidation. Afterwards, the local police in mining towns, who had by and large not been involved in these incidents, complained that their ability to enforce the law was impeded by the hostility which had developed towards the police in general. Indeed the police vitally need the support of the public to enforce the criminal law. As we have seen, the public play a crucial role in reporting crime, and the majority of crimes are cleared up on the basis of public information. If, however, the public mistrust the police they will be less prepared to volunteer information.

The adversarial system creates further dilemmas. As seen in Chapter 1 this system does not seek to establish the truth, but requires that a case is proved beyond reasonable doubt through the provision of legally admissible evidence. Thus the test of success for the police becomes whether an investigation leads to a prosecution and finding of guilt. In some of the cases which have been labelled as 'miscarriages of justice' it would appear that the police tampered with evidence or improperly gained confessions in order to provide evidence to support their view of the defendants' guilt. In other cases, victims and witnesses may privately offer details of an incident but refuse to give evidence in public. In such cases the police may stop the investigation because they have no evidence that can be used in court, or seek other ways of collecting evidence. If no other source of evidence is available they face the possibility that a guilty person will escape justice. In high-profile cases arousing public outrage, especially those involving terrorism, pressure to get a result may be sufficient to lead to the use of illegally obtained evidence. On other occasions the police can be said to provoke crime by acting as *agents provocateurs*, for example, by leaving goods where they might be stolen, or operating a business to encourage offers to sell stolen goods.

Fig 4.2 The death of Streetwise

Death in the Stables

It was at a tournament in Gainsville, Florida, in February, 1991, that the cops were waiting for 'Ray' (the name used on the charge sheet). Tipped off by Miller, they followed him from bar and motel to paddock and show jumping ring. The tournament passed: a horse called Streetwise performed badly, as usual, and afterwards the police followed Ray back through the rain back to the stables from a bar. Ray, who was travelling with an associate, Harlow Arlie,

loaded three horses, and then led Streetwise from his stall.

The rain gave Ray the perfect cover. Instead of leading the trusting animal into the horse box. Ray held it by its halter in the yard, while the burly Arlie took up a crowbar and smashed it against the horse's right rear leg. The horse fell, bellowing and then rose, broke free and stumbled into a paddock where it fell again.

The scene had shocked even Ray, but so far everything was going to plan. Ray called

the vet, with the story that Streetwise had fallen in the rain and broken a leg. The vet called the insurance company hotline, and was given authority to put the horse down.

Ray drove away with the three remaining horses, ready to collect his $5,000 fee, but ran straight into a roadblock which had been set up following the call of an Agricultural Department agent who had watched the whole performance from the top of a horsebox.

Source: *The Daily Telegraph*, 13 August 1994: 1 (Weekend Section). © Telegraph Group Limited, 1994

The interdependencies within the adversarial system is another reason why the police might appear non-active as they await evidence that can be used in a trial. In the following illustration from the USA (Figure 4.2) the priority was to establish evidence rather than prevent a crime from happening at a terrible cost to a horse named Streetwise. Timothy Ray was suspected of maiming and killing show jumping horses so that their owners could claim the insurance money. One wealthy show jumping figure, Barney Ward, was accused of having Ray kill four of his horses for an insurance payout of $570,000. The law enforcement agents from the Agricultural Department of the US government put the suspect, Timothy Ray, under surveillance so as to collect the evidence before they could arrest him.

Development of policing

Before the nineteenth century, no one public organisation was responsible for policing and different functions were carried out by what Brogden describes as a hotch potch of different arrangements (Brogden *et al* 1988). Local boroughs employed constables and watchmen who were not very efficient. Many other policing functions were carried out privately – individual businesses hired men to protect property and landowners employed gamekeepers. Towards the end of the eighteenth century, the famous Fielding brothers, magistrates at Bow Street, set up and financed the Bow Street runners to catch thieves. Industrialisation brought large numbers of migrants into urban areas and led to fears that public safety would be threatened by the 'dangerous' classes. Early calls for an organised police force were, however, resisted as a publicly financed police organisation was seen as a threat to the liberty of the individual citizen.

Campaigners such as Sir Robert Peel continued to press for a more organised system and, in 1829, the Metropolitan Police Improvement Act set up the Metropolitan Police Force. Initially this consisted of 1,000 officers controlled from No. 4 Whitehall Place – backing on to Scotland Yard. Similar forces were set up in municipal corporations and counties and, following the County and Borough Police Act 1856, there were 239 forces operating in England and Wales. These early police forces concentrated largely on patrolling the streets. In 1842, following two attempts on the life of Queen Victoria, a small detective branch was set up, consisting of two inspectors and six sergeants. By 1877 it had expanded to 250 men. A Fenian bombing campaign during the 1880s led to the formation of the Special Irish Branch, later to become the Special Branch, specialising in counteracting subversive political and industrial activity. As the police force grew and new technology became available, new specialist functions emerged. In 1901 the system of classifying fingerprints was introduced, and in 1910 the Metropolitan Police first caught a criminal using radio telegraphy. In 1920 the police acquired two motor vans – the birth of the flying squad. Women officers were introduced in 1919, although women, often police constables' wives, had been employed as 'matrons' to deal with female convicts and matters involving children. Until 1973, women were organised in a separate department and paid less than male officers. After 1973 the women's organisation was abolished and the force was integrated.

From their inception, the 'new police' were unpopular. The working classes saw them as a potentially oppressive force, popularly described as a 'plague of blue locusts', 'blue devils', or 'crushers'. The middle and upper classes saw a threat to their liberty from so-called government spies. Gradually, however, opposition from both groups was overcome and the police gained legitimacy. According to Robert Reiner:

> By the 1950s policing by consent was achieved in Britain to the maximal degree it is ever attainable – the wholehearted approval of the majority of the population who do not experience the coercive exercise of police powers to any significant extent and *de facto* acceptance of the legitimacy of the institution by those who do.
>
> (Reiner 1992a: 60)

This success was due, according to Reiner, to the policies adopted by early commissioners which created the distinctive style of English policing. Crucial to these policies, devised in an attempt to secure the support of the public at large, was the emphasis on the independence of the police from any particular class or political influence.

Reiner identifies several key elements of these early strategies. In the first place, a quasi-military command structure incorporated elements of rank, authority and discipline. This bureaucratic organisation, which included training and a career structure to attract high-quality recruits, distinguished the 'new' police from their disorganised and often corrupt forerunners. In addition the importance of upholding the rule of law was stressed, thus protecting citizens from any abuse of police powers. A policy of minimum force sought to allay fears of the working classes that the police would be unduly oppressive. This led to one of the most distinctive features of British policing – the absence of firearms in everyday duties and a reluctance to use paramilitary tactics more common in the US and many European countries. In addition, the police were to be non-partisan and impartial in their enforcement of the law, favouring the interests of neither one class nor the other. This impartiality was underlined by denying police officers the vote until 1887, and they are still not allowed to affiliate to political parties or have a trade union. The Police Federation represents police officers of the rank of constable (up to chief inspector) but they are not allowed to take industrial action.

The reluctance to expand the detective branch arose out of a deep-rooted suspicion of the plain clothes officer. Hostility was reduced as the new police gained a reputation for being relatively effective in preventing and detecting crime. Finally, argues Reiner, their legitimacy increased as a result of changes in society itself. By the 1950s there was less class conflict than before, the working classes had become more incorporated into society and were relatively homogeneous – thus the public as a whole tended to have a shared conception of what they expected from the police.

By the 1950s, generally depicted as a golden age of consensus policing, the legitimacy of the police was established. This was symbolised by the popular Dixon of Dock Green television series which portrayed a friendly local bobby whose knowledge of his patch helped him to prevent crime, catch local villains, and help many members of the local community. Dixon was followed by very different TV heroes in such programmes as The Sweeney and the Professionals in the 1970s and 1980s, and the popular series of the early 1990s Between the Lines dealing with police discipline and complaints.

From the 1950s the legitimacy which the police had established was challenged on several fronts. The urban disturbances of 1981, which led to the Scarman Report, were in part attributed to the frequent use in multi-racial areas of stop-and-search powers. Increasing evidence emerged of cases where the police were found to have tampered with evidence, secured false confessions and abused their powers. Other complaints concerned how suspects were dealt with in custody. This raised the issue of how accountable the police were – both in terms of individual complaints and police policy. What happened to change the image of the police, in Reiner's words, from 'plods to pigs'? (Reiner 1992a: 77).

The key factors which led to increased legitimacy, according to Reiner, can also account for its decline. Revelations about corruption on the part of police officers during the 1960s and allegations about improper behaviour severely dented the image of the police as a disciplined force, showing that they could readily break the law in order to enforce it. The 1970s and 1980s saw the increasing use of riot shields and other modern hardware in the control of industrial disputes and urban unrest replacing the 'pushing and shoving' strategy used in demonstrations during the 1950s and 1960s. The accidental killing of innocent citizens by armed police officers attracted much criticism, especially from their traditional supporters, the middle classes. The traditional political impartiality of the police was also questioned during the general election of 1979, when they campaigned vigorously for stronger law and order policies. Finally, society itself had changed. Whereas during the so-called golden age, the working class was a more homogeneous community, by the 1980s it was increasingly fragmented and divided with the growth of unemployment, the increasingly multi-racial nature of urban communities, and the growth of what some describe as an underclass. This made it more difficult for the police to satisfy the now conflicting expectations about how areas should be policed.

Police relationships with the public were also affected by the consequences of changes in the nature and organisation of policing. Like any organisation the police face pressures for efficiency and must respond to changes in crime which may lead to the use of more sophisticated technology. These pressures also produced specialisation. This necessitated organisational changes which vitally affected relationships between the police and local communities.

A simple example of this is the effect of expansion in cars, traffic and car ownership. The increasing volume of cars on the roads necessitated the development of techniques of traffic control and the enforcement of road traffic legislation. Specialist traffic control using increasingly sophisticated technology followed. As car ownership spread, many groups, particularly the middle classes, previously unlikely to encounter the police in their law enforcement role became the subject of police attention. This on occasion provoked the response 'why don't you go out and catch real criminals?'. Cars also became an essential tool in law enforcement and patrolling, and had a fundamental impact on the job of the police constable. The car chase has become a symbolic feature of policing in both popular imagery and police folklore. And, of course, as well as increasing the mobility of criminals, cars have provided multiple opportunities for crime – from vandalism to serious car theft, ramraiding and joyriding: for some joyriders part of the thrill is the chase with the police.

Similar points could be made about other technological developments – computers have radically changed the nature of policing as have developments in communications. The beat officer of 40 years ago could not instantly call on the police computer, let alone the local station, to provide instant back-up. Information had to be gathered directly from the public. While undoubtedly these developments have increased the ability of the police to respond quickly to emergencies, to call for help, and to sift through large amounts of information, they have had important consequences for relations between the police and public, and for the basic role of the police officer.

This can be seen in contrasting the work of officers during the period of the so-called golden age of policing, when officers were allocated a beat and were responsible for patrolling it, often on foot. This meant that officers got to know the local community – they would make purchases from shopkeepers, visit local cafés and come into contact with many residents. The intelligence they gathered from these natural social contacts may have helped when they came to investigate a crime. Armed only with a truncheon and a whistle to call for help, the constable had to rely on his or her own wits to handle troublesome situations. Communication with the station was made through the police box and incidents had to be handled on the spot.

This form of policing was, however, inefficient. One officer could only cover a limited area, whereas two officers, in a car, receiving their information from a radio link with the station, could cover a much larger area and arrive at incidents much quicker. The lone officer on patrol is also unlikely to catch many criminals – no self-respecting burglar is going to break in when they see a constable walking down the road. The growth of many specialised functions also fundamentally changed the job of the basic constable on the beat, who became less involved in detecting crime and proportionately more involved with the more mundane elements of police work such as dealing with drunks, vagrants or handling minor local incidents.

This affected relationships between the police and the public. Whereas the old style beat officer encountered many members of the public while pounding the beat, officers in cars had less immediate contact. The public were less likely to know or have encountered these officers, and information tended to come from the police station rather than from the public. The ability to call instantly for back-up meant that officers were less reliant on their own personal skills to handle situations and the cars and radios in themselves became symbols of authority.

Although there has been a loss of personal contact between the public and the police, the use of television programmes such as Crime Watch UK and Crime Stoppers has enabled a different style of relationship to emerge. In the task of fighting crime the police use video footage and the re-enactment of crimes on television to mobilise the public to act as informants as well as fostering public relations about the shared problems for police and public of fighting crime.

In addition, pressures for efficiency led to a stress on law enforcement as opposed to service or preventive roles – to the more readily measurable aspects of police work such as arrest rates, clear-up rates and response times – often described as fire brigade policing. This meant that other, less easily measurable tasks became seen as less significant. The 1970s and 1980s also saw the rise of what is often called paramilitary policing. A spate of urban disturbances and industrial disputes prompted the development of specialist squads trained to deal with riots and crowd control. These units, including the Special Patrol Group, were increasingly armed with the hardware used for disturbances in Ulster and abroad. Their tactics caused enormous controversy, especially during the miners' strike of 1984. Some were also used as a back-up for crime-fighting initiatives, which involved the intensive use of stop-and-search powers. These kind of tactics were found by the Scarman Report to have been partly responsible for local resentments which contributed to the breakdown in relations between the police and public preceding the Brixton disturbances of 1981.

All these factors illustrate the many tensions in the role of the police which has been questioned in recent years and there are different views about which roles the police should prioritise. The recent Audit Commission report, for example, recommended that the police should adopt a more proactive, 'intelligence led' approach involving targeting the most prolific offenders and using 'intelligence' gathered from informers and surveillance. This may conflict with public opinion which consistently indicates a preference for more 'bobbies on the beat' and foot patrols (Morgan and Newburn 1997). Research commissioned for the Audit Commission found that while the public were generally satisfied with police performance in relation to emergencies, motoring offences, traffic and riot control they were dissatisfied with their performance in relation to detecting burglaries and foot patrols. Other studies indicate a public preference for more community-based policing. This may, however, conflict with police officers' own preference for what to them is 'real police work' and is associated with action, arrests and catching serious offenders (Morgan and Newburn 1997).

ORGANISATION AND ACCOUNTABILITY

Policing in England and Wales is carried out by 43 forces. In 1996 these forces employed an average of 126,878 police officers – a rise of 4.4 per cent since 1986. Fourteen per cent of police officers are female and 1.6 per cent are from minority ethnic groups. The number of civilian staff has also grown by 17 per cent in 10 years and expenditure on the police rose by 30 per cent between 1984/5 and 1988/9. The largest force is the Metropolitan Police with 27,400 officers in 1998, and the smallest is the City of London with only 789 officers. The size of individual forces reflects the size of the population and the demands of the area. The ratio of police to population is one officer to 257 in the Metropolitan Police District, whereas in the non-metropolitan counties the figure is one officer to 497.

Police officers are distributed between various ranks, a feature introduced to maintain discipline. The rank structure was felt by the Sheehy Report to contain, 'too many chiefs and not enough indians' and the number of ranks was reduced by the Police and Magistrates' Courts Act 1994. From 1995, the rank structure is as follows:

OUTSIDE LONDON	LONDON (MPD)
Chief Constable	Commissioner (MPD)
	Deputy Commissioner (MPD)
Assistant Chief Constable	Assistant Commissioner
	Deputy Assistant Commissioner
	Commander

Superintendent
Chief Inspector
Inspector
Sergeant
Constable

Each force is divided into geographical areas or divisions with management and support services – including personnel, training and the inspectorate. Metropolitan Police District areas are headed by a Deputy Assistant Commissioner assisted by two Commanders. Each has its own headquarters and controls a number of support branches including dog sections, traffic patrols, area major incident teams, complaints sections, and child protection teams. There are also local crime squads, drug squads and robbery squads, depending on demand. Each area has patrol cars for rapid response, traffic cars and motorcycles.

The Metropolitan Police have a number of specialist squads and departments including the central drugs squad, the central cheque squad, the stolen motor vehicle investigation squad, the serious and organised crime squad (the gangbusters), the central robbery squad (flying squad or colloquially 'the Sweeney'), the regional crime squad, the fraud squad, football intelligence unit, special branch, the anti-terrorist branch and the international criminal police organisation (Interpol). These squads can all call on specialist departments such as the forensic science laboratories, the fingerprint branch, the photographic branch and the national identification bureau.

Because of its size, the Metropolitan Police also has a number of specialist departments including the traffic police, the Thames division which patrols the River Thames 24 hours a day; a mounted branch and an air support unit which assists with traffic and crowd control along with the royalty and diplomatic protection department, the special escort group and an art squad. Not all forces have such a large number of branches. Other responsibilities include public relations and the growing organisation around community policing which will be discussed later in this chapter.

While the police in England and Wales are organised primarily on a local level, the increasingly international and organised nature of serious crime has led to the development of nationally and internationally organised policing (Leishman et al 1998; Morgan and Newburn 1997) (see Chapter 11). This includes:

- *Regional Crime Squads.* These were set up in 1964 to deal with offences transcending the local boundaries of any one force. Their main functions are to identify and arrest those responsible for serious criminal offences; to co-operate with regional intelligence officers to generate intelligence; and to assist in the investigation of serious crime.

- *National Criminal Intelligence Service* (NCIS). This body, emerging out of the National Crime Intelligence Unit set up in 1990, will integrate the work of the existing Intelligence Units dealing with football hooligans, crimes involving art and antiques, drugs and professional and organised crime.

- *Interpol* is the oldest international police network which passes criminal intelligence between different countries. It has over 150 members.

- *Europe-wide police arrangements* include the Trevi Group, originally set up to deal with counter-terrorist measures, and the Schengen Group, which was set up following relaxed border controls in the European Union and provides for increased police co-operation, information systems and the ability of officers from one country to pursue offenders outside their own jurisdictions. *Europol* was set up following the Maastricht Treaty in 1993 to replace Trevi and it is intended to develop information exchanges to deal with terrorism, drug trafficking and other serious, organised crime.

Investigating crime

While it is important to understand the many functions of the police, such as emergency services and traffic control, they have a unique role in investigating crime. Apart from a few specialist agencies the police handle most crime investigation in this country. Thus most prosecutions depend on the routine information collected by uniformed officers and the detective work of their non-uniformed colleagues in the criminal investigation departments, the CID.

Criminal investigations over the years have stimulated the development of technical and expert services such as forensic services. Today's police have access to computer information systems such as those storing details of all car registrations, and more recently they have employed psychological profiling in murder cases, such as that of Rachel Nickell on Wimbledon Common. The Royal Commission on Criminal Justice 1993 recommended a national database and wider powers for the police to require suspects to give DNA samples, similar to the powers they have with fingerprints. In 1994 the Home Office announced that Britain was to have the first such database in the world. This will not only assist crime investigation, but might also be a deterrent in that a person listed might abstain from committing further sexual crimes as the chances of being identified are increased.

The most widely accepted form of forensic evidence is the fingerprint test. The idea was developed by Edward Henry, Inspector-General of the Nepal Police, who noticed its use in nineteenth-century India and the Metropolitan Police introduced it in 1901. Its use led to the conviction of two brothers – the Strattons – for murder in 1905. The assumption has been that no two sets of fingerprints are the same. Each fingerprint is based on the ridges made by the barely visible papillary lines on the skin's surface and each print can be classified in terms of the patterns of arches, whorls and loops that are displayed and the distinctive characteristics in a fingerprint – split, lake, island or end of ridge. By 2001, all police forces in England and Wales will have access to a National Automated Fingerprint Recognition Service. Fingerprints of arrested persons will be processed locally and searches will be made against a national fingerprint database. Fingerprinting until recently was widely regarded as foolproof and conclusive of guilt by police and juries. But doubt was raised about the ability of fingerprints to determine individual identity in the case of Neville Lee who was arrested, solely on the basis of a fingerprint left in blood in a lavatory cubicle after a brutal rape of an 11-year-old girl in Clumber Park near Worksop in August 1991. He was arrested by the Nottinghamshire police and detained in custody for six weeks before another sexual attack in the same park led to the arrest of a person who confessed to the rape of which Lee had been accused.

The use of DNA profiling was also regarded as reliable as fingerprinting to check the unique characteristics of an individual. Developed by Dr Alec Jeffries, the technique is now used in rape cases around the world. The DNA technique involves comparing a number of bands in the suspect's DNA with those of the DNA from body fluid or tissue involved in the crime. A calculation is then made on the probabilities of another person having a similar match. The Criminal Justice and Public Order Act 1994 allowed the police to take DNA samples, such as hair or mouth swabs, without consent of the accused, from offenders charged with, or convicted of, recordable offences – broadly those that are imprisonable. A national DNA database was started in April 1995 to provide information to police forces by matching DNA profiles taken from suspects to profiles left at the scene of a crime. By January 1997 there were 102,769 suspect samples on the database run by the Forensic Science Service at Birmingham.

While fingerprints and DNA profiling are familiar, at least in concept to most people, other identification evidence can be important, such as voice analysis or earprint identification as used in the conviction of Calvin Sewell for burglary in February 1998 (see Figure 4.3). A new aid to police investigation, a 'scent machine', is being tested which extracts skin cells left by humans at the scene of a crime. Items carrying human scents, in this case the victim's sweatshirt, are removed by the police and frozen. The process of storing the scent involves a vacuum machine which helps to preserve the skin cells. This method was used in evidence in a California court to convict Earl Rhoney for the murder of a 42-year-old Californian woman, who was beaten and then strangled in her bed. In October 1994, eight months after the murder, a suspect in the case, who admitted carrying out a series of burglaries in the district, was followed by the police into a crowded Orange County shopping mall. A bloodhound was given the scent and it identified Rhoney. Given the novelty of this new type of evidence, Rhoney was retried, convicted but subsequently released in 1998 after a judge ordered another retrial.

102

Fig 4.3 Earprint identification

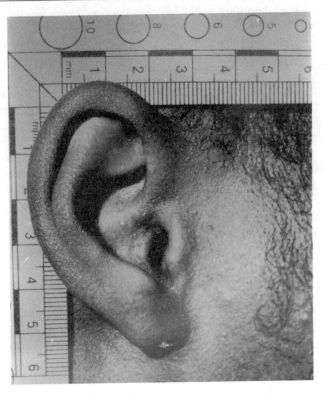

What's all this ear, then? The body part in
Calvin Sewell's downfall

Burglar let down by an ear for trouble

BY PETER FOSTER

Source: The Times, 21 February 1998. © Times Newspapers Limited, 1998. Photo ©
Photonews Service, 1998

Forensic evidence, based on scientific procedure, provides valuable evidence
for investigators and prosecutors in contrast to the unpredictability of human
witnesses. Scientific evidence can be used in all manner of circumstances, as
in the case of Tracie Andrews. She was convicted of the murder of her
boyfriend who, she claimed, was a victim of a road rage attack. Examination of a hat she said had nothing to do with her, showed hairs belonging to
her mother's cat. But the faith in scientific evidence has been shown to be
unjustified in dramatic cases such as the Birmingham Six convicted in 1975

for the murder of 21 people in 1974 after a bomb was left in a public house in the central shopping district. The conduct of the test to show that the suspects had been handling explosives was later to prove unreliable.

To whom are the police accountable?

A key issue in looking at police organisation is who they are answerable, or accountable, to. As we have seen, a major characteristic of the British police has been their independence from direct political control. This can, however, lead to a situation in which they could be seen to have too much autonomy from both central government or local communities. At the same time too much control from the centre is often criticised as leading to centralisation, thereby reducing the influence of local communities. Outside London, local police authorities (LPAs) are responsible for a variety of functions. Disciplinary and complaints procedures deal with individual matters, and the police are ultimately accountable to the law and the courts.

The Police Act 1964 set up what became known as a tripartite structure involving, outside London, chief constables, the Home Secretary and police authorities which were composed of two-thirds elected representatives from local councils and one-third justices of the peace. The Metropolitan Police area does not have a police authority and the Commissioner is directly answerable to the Home Secretary. By the 1990s these bodies were subject to criticism that they were large, some having as many as 46 members, and that their links with the local community and the extent of their powers were uncertain. While they were, for example, responsible, under s. 5(1) of the Police Act 1964, for 'the maintenance of an adequate and efficient police force for the area', exactly how they should do this was ambiguous. Two key roles were the appointment of a chief constable and approving the budget. The Home Secretary, however, approved the appointment of chief constables and in practice police authorities had little control over how budgets were spent or over police policy. While they could ask for a report from the chief constable, this could be refused if it would contain operational matters which it would not be in the public interest to disclose. A study by the Policy Studies Institute found that policy developments such as crime prevention, crimes against women and children and the diversion of administrative tasks from uniformed officers to civilian employees was increasingly determined by central government and that local police authorities had little influence over these developments (Jones and Newburn 1994a). This study also found that police authorities took too narrow a view of their role, lacked relevant information and expertise and were too large and cumbersome to carry out effective discussion.

The Police and Magistrates' Court Act of 1994 changed this structure. In controversial proposals the Government sought to make chief constables more responsible for budgets and to exert more control over their appointment. Many of the original proposals, which might have led to greater centralisation, were dropped, and the Act set up a new structure – aspects of which are summarised below (Leishman *et al* 1998; Jones and Newburn 1997).

- The primary duty of the police authority is 'to secure the maintenance of an efficient and effective police force for its area'.

- Each local police authority consists of a maximum of seventeen members consisting of three magistrates, five independent members and nine locally elected councillors.

- Independent members are selected through a complex procedure involving existing members of police authorities and the Home Office.

- Local police authorities are no longer committees of local authorities but free-standing authorities.

- Financial management is the responsibility of the chief constable, with authorities having a monitoring role.

- Each authority must develop a local policing plan, drafted by the chief constable, who must be consulted about any changes which the police authority, who retain 'ownership' of the plan, wish to make.

- The Home Office may affect the total spending of the police authority and the Home Secretary is empowered to amalgamate forces.

- The Home Office is also responsible for setting national objectives for policing which must be taken account of by local police authorities (see Chapter 11).

The effect of these changes is as yet unclear, although Jones and Newburn (1997), who carried out a study of the initial effects of the Act, comment that the changes have not been nearly as far reaching as was at first anticipated. Despite fears that the Home Office would seek to exert undue influence over the appointment of independent members, initial signs are that the views of the police authorities have prevailed. Local plans, drafted in the context of National Objectives, vary considerably, although chief constables have considerable influence with some police authorities acting as a 'rubber stamp' for initial proposals, while others play a more active role. Overall, they argue, police interests continue to be more influential than others.

Another way in which local communities may affect policing is via Police Community Consultative Groups (PCCGs) set up after the Scarman report. These consist of members of the public, usually invited from a number of relevant organisations and a number of local officers. They have no formal power, and tend to be drawn from a very small section of society, with few representatives from groups who are likely to suffer most from any abuse of police powers or from the adverse effects of policies (Morgan 1989). Morgan and Newburn (1997) argue that while they have had little effect on police priorities, they have played some role in improving police communications with surrounding communities, and could play an enhanced role in future arrangements.

Legal accountability

The police are not above the law. They must operate within the same laws as the public and to rules specific to the police. The Police and Criminal Evidence Act 1984 (PACE) and the codes made under its authority, outlined below, are there to protect the citizen from the abuse of police powers. In order to convict, a court must be sure that an offence has been committed and that the evidence to prove this is admissible in court. Thus the courts and the judiciary play a role in police accountability. Abuse of powers in the early stages could prevent a conviction being obtained.

Yet despite safeguards, courts do convict on illegally obtained evidence, if the judge and jury are convinced that it is reliable and relevant evidence. In court, in some cases the reality often is that it is a police officer's word against a defendant's. Given that the police are trained to present evidence in court they are likely to appear more credible witnesses, especially where they enjoy public confidence.

Aggrieved citizens can complain to the police force in question, and internal discipline within the police also protects the citizen. All complaints must be recorded and, if not dealt with informally, will be investigated under the auspices of the Police Complaints Authority (see Chapter 11). Complaints are investigated by an officer within the force, but if the complaint is serious or against a senior officer, an officer from another force will be appointed.

This structure has attracted criticism, particularly on the grounds that it is largely the police investigating themselves. This is justified on the basis that professionals such as the police, along with doctors and lawyers, are the only people with the necessary knowledge and expertise to investigate complaints. Nonetheless, the absence of an independent element in this procedure has attracted much criticism particularly since very few complaints are successful (Uglow 1988). Figures published by the Home Office show that a total of 22,500 complaints were received between April 1996 and March 1997 of which 834 were substantiated (Home Office *Statistical Bulletin*, Issue 21/97). Seventy per cent were withdrawn or informally resolved and one-third were investigated. Of those investigated 7.2 per cent were substantiated. The largest number of complaints (55 per cent) were for neglect of duty. In addition, in 1996, 377 officers were the subject of proven disciplinary charges; 77 were dismissed or were required to resign.

POLICE POWERS AND PACE

As we have seen, the exercise of police powers is subject to rules and guidelines, and the extent of police powers has occasioned considerable controversy since the inception of the 'new police'. On the one hand, the police clearly need powers to stop people on the street if they are suspected of a crime, to enter people's houses if they suspect that they are hiding stolen goods or firearms and to arrest people they suspect of a crime. They need to be able to interview suspects in the police station and may have to hold suspects in cells. On the other hand, individual citizens need to be able to carry on with their everyday lives without risking being stopped on the street, having their homes ransacked by the police and being arrested and taken to the police station. Suspects must be protected from torture, brutality and the extraction of false confessions. Special protection may be afforded to vulnerable groups such as the young and mentally ill. Legislation on police powers therefore must balance conflicting needs.

The Royal Commission on Criminal Procedure (RCCP) set up in 1978 found that the law on police powers was piecemeal and haphazard. Different provisions enabled the police to stop and search, and powers of arrest were included in 70 different statutes. In addition the Royal Commission felt that crime investigation should be separated from prosecution and accordingly recommended the setting up of a separate Crown Prosecution Service (discussed in Chapter 5). The subsequent Police and Criminal Evidence Act 1984 (PACE) sought to modernise and rationalise the law governing police powers and to reform aspects of the law relating to criminal evidence. One of its major innovations was to provide for the tape-recording of interviews in police stations. Other safeguards for suspects included provisions for the police to keep records on their dealings with suspects at all stages. PACE, as it has become universally known, fundamentally changed many aspects of policing.

The Act provides for the creation of Codes of Practice to deal with the minutiae of implementation. Codes are more easily amended than Acts of Parliament. These codes cover the following areas:

- Code A   Powers of stop and search
- Code B   Search of premises and seizure of property
- Code C   Detention treatment and questioning of suspects
- Code D   Identification procedures
- Code E   Tape recording of interviews

Breach of a provision of the code by the police does not of itself constitute an offence, but can be the basis of a complaint against the police which may lead to a disciplinary matter. Additionally, significant transgression of any code provision may mean that evidence obtained as a result might be excluded in any subsequent trial (see Chapter 6).

The Act sets out the powers of the police in various circumstances, and provides safeguards for suspects as to when the powers can be exercised. In some cases an officer can only act after authorisation from a senior officer (for example, in delaying access to legal advice). In certain situations reasons for a procedure must be given to a suspect – for example, the reason why an officer wishes to stop and search a suspect. On other occasions the police officer must formally explain the individual's rights – for example, when someone is arrested they must be informed of their right to remain silent and the consequences of so doing.

There is also a requirement for written records. Custody records must show all the details of a suspect's stay in police detention, and may be analysed by the defence. Any irregularities would support their argument for the exclusion of evidence.

The main provisions dealing with powers of search in PACE 1984 are as follows, although some items – for example, correspondence between the suspect and their solicitor, confidential personal records, such as those held by a doctor, and certain confidential trade documents – are not permitted to be taken in a search.

SEARCH POWERS: PACE 1984

Stop and search (ss 1–7)

Allows an officer to stop and search a person or a vehicle in a public place where there are reasonable grounds for suspecting that there are stolen goods, or weapons or articles for use in offences such as theft or burglary. Detention for a reasonable period is allowed, and the person searched must be told reasons for the search and of his or her right to a copy of the search record.

Search warrants (s. 8)

An officer can obtain a search warrant from a magistrate when it is reasonable to believe that there would be evidence relating to an offence (for example, drugs or stolen property) on the premises to be searched. With such a warrant, the officer may enter and search the specified premises, and remove any such evidence.

Entry for searching and arrest (s. 17)

Provides that an officer can enter property in order to carry out an arrest for the following reasons:

- with a warrant, for an arrestable offence
- for recapturing escaped prisoners
- for certain specified offences (arrestable offences, that is any offence for which the sentence is 5 years or more)
- to save someone from injury or prevent damage to property.

108

Entry and search after arrest (s. 18)

Allows a police officer to go into an arrested person's home or business premises to collect evidence about an offence, subject to getting the authority of an inspector.

Search on arrest (s. 32)

Allows an officer to search a person who has been arrested, or the premises where the suspect was found, for evidence, or for things that might help them escape, or with which they might harm themselves.

Searches of detained people (s. 54)

Sets out the responsibilities and powers of the custody officer and other officers in relation to search of people in police detention. The police must make a record of the arrested person's possessions. They are entitled to search for, and remove things, that might allow the person to harm themselves or someone else, or for things that might be used to escape. They must explain why such items are being removed.

Intimate searches (s. 55)

Limits the situations in which intimate searches can be carried out to searches for things that can harm the suspect, or injure other people, and drugs. The search can only be carried out by an officer of the same sex.

Further provisions in relation to stop and search are contained in the Criminal Justice and Public Order Act 1994, which allows certain exceptions to the 'reasonable suspicion' provision. Under these provisions the police will have powers to act when senior officers believe incidents involving serious violence may take place or to prevent terrorism. These powers will last for up to 24 hours, but may be extended if serious violence does break out. While introduced to allow the police to prevent serious violence, some fear that the abandonment of reasonable suspicion might lead to some groups being unduly harassed.

Sections 24–33 of PACE deal with powers of arrest. First, the Act lays down the circumstances in which any person, including a police officer, store detective or ordinary person carrying out a citizen's arrest, can arrest a person. They may arrest anyone who is, or whom they reasonably suspect to be committing an arrestable offence, and anyone who has committed or who can reasonably be suspected of having committed an arrestable office. Additionally, police officers have wider powers of arrest including the power to arrest someone they believe is about to commit an arrestable offence. An arrestable offence is defined as one for which the penalty is fixed by law (for example, murder), or, which carries a sentence of five years' or more imprisonment, or, as in the case of taking a vehicle without consent, is specifically made arrestable by statute.

Further, the police have specific powers of arrest where a break of bail occurs or is anticipated; for specific offences listed in PACE; and where the 'general arrest conditions' are satisfied. The 'general arrest conditions' allow the police to make an arrest, whatever the offence, to prevent injury, property damage, or where a person has given a suspicious name or address.

Although these provisions provide the police with wide powers, they are not limitless and any officer infringing them may be liable to civil or criminal proceedings or disciplinary action. Perhaps most importantly they risk losing an otherwise promising case as evidence obtained after a wrongful arrest may be excluded by the court. Where an arrest is improperly made the police may also be liable for damages to the wrongfully arrested person.

PACE also consolidated provisions about the suspect's rights on arrest and at the police station. On arrest, any person arrested on suspicion of committing a crime is entitled to be:

- told that he or she has been arrested and why
- arrested without excessive use of force
- cautioned
- taken to a designated police station for interview and not interviewed before arrival at the police station except in urgent cases.

At the police station PACE and the codes provide a comprehensive and detailed framework for the treatment of suspects and arrestees at the police station. Those in custody are the responsibility of the custody officer, a police officer not involved in the investigation. This officer is wholly responsible for all aspects of the period of custody, for any incidents which occur, and for the custody record. The Act provides a complex timetable for the review of detention before charge to ensure that arrested people are not kept in custody without charge for long periods.

On arrival at the police station the custody officer must ensure that persons arrested are informed about their rights. These include, first, a right to inform someone that they have been arrested. Secondly, any persons arrested have the right to contact and consult a solicitor in private. If they do not wish to or cannot contact a solicitor, or do not have one, free advice is available from a duty solicitor who can be contacted round the clock. Thirdly, arrested persons have the right to have access to PACE and the codes. This is to a certain extent window dressing, as few arrested persons are likely to pore over the minutiae of the codes, but it is an important reminder to suspects and the police of their provisions.

Prior to 1995, throughout the period of arrest and interview suspects had the 'right to remain silent' and were reminded of this in a caution given on arrest, before any interview, and on charge. Thus they should have been advised that:

> You do not have to say anything unless you wish to do so but what you say may be given in evidence.

The right to silence was redefined by the Criminal Justice and Public Order Act 1994. This, contrary to some assertions, does not remove the right, but affects the use that can be made of silence in the trial. Before 1995 juries were told that they should not assume a defendant was guilty because he or she failed to answer an accusation at the time of arrest or when interviewed at a police station. Under the 1994 Act, the jury will be told that they can, in certain circumstances, make 'adverse inferences' from silence.

The words of the caution needed to reflect the change. After much debate, in January 1995 the following new wording for the caution was prepared by the Home Office:

> You do not have to say anything. But it may harm your defence if you do not mention when questioned something which you later rely on in court. Anything you do say may be given in evidence.

Additionally, where a suspect is asked about his or her presence, at or near a scene of a crime, or, why he or she is in possession of an item, a warning must be given about the implications of failing to respond (see Chapter 7). Vulnerable groups are given extra protection by PACE in that young people should not be interviewed in the absence of an appropriate adult, usually a parent or social worker, and a similar provision protects the mentally ill. Those who do not speak English fluently, and the deaf, should have appropriate translators present at interview and foreign nationals must be told of their right to contact their embassy or High Commission.

Code C deals with the detention, treatment and questioning of suspects and seeks to provide that all people should be dealt with quickly and not detained any longer than necessary. It places the overall responsibility for the control, recording and supervision of the custody period with a custody officer: a police officer, usually with the rank of sergeant or above, who has overall responsibility for ensuring the correct treatment of those held at the police station. Many of the detailed provisions of this code set constraints on police conduct. They must keep a record of what happens to an offender during detention and provide information to suspects about their rights. Other provisions relate to the minimum level of comfort that should be provided to all suspects. Rules limit the time a suspect can be kept in police custody before being charged. The most important of these matters are described below.

- The custody record is made a fundamental part of the custody process, upon which must be written everything that affects the suspect while in the police station, including time of release, comments made by the suspect at various stages, and a list of the suspect's property. The suspect's lawyer has the right to examine this record at the police station or during any subsequent court proceedings. An examination of the record may reveal that procedures were not correctly followed, or indeed establish that they were, as the suspect will be asked to sign the custody record, for example, to indicate that legal advice has been offered. If the suspect refuses to sign when asked, that refusal must also be recorded. Any interview with the suspect must be recorded in full. This will usually be by means of tape-recorded interviews (governed by Code E) which replaced the old system of 'contemporaneous notes' as they were more susceptible to fabrication. Interviews should only be carried out at designated police stations, except when an interview is urgent, for example, to get information about an imminent attack on a person.

- When an interview forms part of the evidence against a defendant, he or she is entitled to a balanced summary of the recording, and can demand a copy of the tape. While the taping of interviews protects the accused, it may also prevent unfounded complaints against the police and allegations of false confessions.

- The code states that suspects should be held usually in single cells, which should be adequately heated, cleaned, lit and ventilated, with adequate clean bedding and access to toilet and washing facilities. They should be offered two light meals and one main meal in a 24-hour period, and a reasonable number of drinks. Medical assistance should be called if necessary.

Perhaps the most significant provisions relate to the continuing assessment of whether an arrested person can be charged or released. Detention in a police station without charge usually arises to allow the person to be questioned to obtain evidence. Once sufficient evidence has been obtained, and the suspect has said what he or she wishes to say, the questioning must stop and the suspect charged. After charge, suspects may:

- be released on bail to attend court for the start of proceedings against them
- be released and required to return later to the police station
- be kept in police custody and taken to the next sitting of the magistrates' court.

Whether it is necessary to keep the suspect any longer, or indeed whether the police have enough evidence to charge, must be considered at the following times:

- 6 hours after arrival at the police station
- then at not more than 9 hourly intervals from when the detention was first authorised, up to a total of 24 hours.

Further detention must be authorised after 24 hours. Any longer period must be authorised by an officer of the rank of superintendent or above. This further period can extend the period to 36 hours, and then only if necessary for the effective investigation of a serious arrestable offence.

- If the police want to interview the suspect further they must apply to a magistrates' court for permission to hold the person for any longer time. A court can authorise an extra 36 hours of detention, on two occasions. The overall maximum period of detention is 96 hours.

PACE was introduced amidst fears that it would vastly increase police powers at the expense of the civil liberties of defendants. The police feared that it would result in much extra paperwork and that its many safeguards would hamper their efficiency. Research since the Act indicates that neither of these sets of concerns has been borne out (Brown 1997: Morgan and Newburn 1997). There is little evidence, argue Morgan and Newburn, to suggest that police efficiency has been hampered and the police have come to accept practices such as the routine taping of interviews which initially attracted resistance. In a review of research, Brown found that the new powers have been used considerably and that, on the whole, custody officers do ensure that suspects are aware of their basic rights. There has been an increase in the demand for legal advice by suspects, although the quality of this advice is uneven. It has been estimated that suspects are protected by the tape recording of interviews in police stations and that the use of unacceptable tactics to secure confessions has declined (Brown 1997). While these procedures in the station have given suspects better protection, there are more problems outside the station where it remains difficult to determine the extent to which stop-and-search procedures are carried out with 'reasonable grounds'. This is more difficult to review objectively, as these decisions are difficult to monitor independently 'after the event', and, as will be seen later in the chapter, are heavily determined by the context in which they are made and the informal working rules of police officers 'on the street' (Brown 1997).

Fig 4.4 Aspects of the use of police powers under PACE in 1996

- The police stopped and searched a total of 814,500 persons and/or vehicles.
- Eleven per cent of searches led to an arrest.
- The most frequent reason (36 per cent) for stops and searches was to look for stolen property. Thirty-one per cent were to search for drugs, and a further 18 per cent were to search for articles which could be used in burglary or theft – 'going equipped'. Other searches were for firearms or offensive weapons.
- Some 550 persons were detained for more than 24 hours and subsequently released without charge.
- A total of 132 intimate searches were carried out – mainly for drugs.
- Over one-third of stops in England and Wales took place in the Metropolitan Police area.

Compiled from *Home Office Statistical Bulletin*, 27/97: 1.

COMMUNITY POLICING

Effective policing requires the co-operation and support of the community, and as has been seen, changes in policing and in the nature of communities have led to what was seen as a decline in police community relations in some areas. This led to the growth of a number of initiatives described, somewhat loosely, as community policing, which includes both the more familiar policing tasks of patrolling and investigating crime and strategies aimed at crime prevention and reducing the fear of crime. Schemes often involve the police working with local authorities, businesses and voluntary organisations.

It is difficult to define what, exactly, is meant by the phrase community policing, which emerged in the late 1970s. A pioneer of the concept was Chief Constable John Alderson of the Devon and Cornwall force, who argued:

> community policing would exist in its purest form where all elements in the community, official and unofficial, would conceive of the common good and combine to produce a social climate and an environment conducive to good order and the happiness of all those living within it.

(Alderson 1978)

In Alderson's version the community constable is seen as a 'social leader' working with the community and the emphasis is firmly placed on preventive rather than reactive policing. In theory, community policing is based on ideas that the police should consult and seek co-operation with the public and in 'general notions of creating a tranquil and safe environment' (Bennett 1994b: 6). On the basis of informal conversations with police officers Bennett found that these broadly conceived aims included stressing the benefits of public contact and reassurance along with deterrence, prevention, intelligence gathering and reducing the fear of crime (Bennett 1994a).

Many advantages are claimed for community policing. In addition to the obvious benefit of improving police relations with the community, it can also add to the effectiveness of the police in relation to law enforcement. Thus it is argued that if the community have more confidence in the police, they may be more likely to come forward with information and co-operation.

In practice, community policing encompasses a wide variety of different schemes and Bennett identifies five models or styles (Bennett 1994a). First, many schemes involve area-based policing, known variously as neighbourhood, zonal, team or sector policing. This involves a small team of managers, supervisors and officers being allocated to a local area. Sector policing was introduced in the Metropolitan Police and has been adopted by many other forces – Bennett cites a 1990 survey which found that over one-quarter of all forces operated some form of sector policing. These generally involve allocating community constables to small areas on a semi-permanent basis. In the Metropolitan Police Area, teams of officers, under an inspector are responsible for a small community area, or sector. This inspector, according to the Commissioner's Annual Report for 1991/2 will be responsible for:

ensuring that the policing arrangements are adequate and effective. The Senior Inspector, in consultation with the local community, will determine the style of policing for the sector, and set its priorities . . . Over a period of time the officers will come to identify more closely with that community and as a result will be more responsive to its needs. They will feel greater ownership of the community's problems, and will help to address underlying causes, rather than merely responding to the symptoms.

(Metropolitan Police Commissioner 1992)

Bennett's second model of community policing refers to the multi-agency approach, in which the police work in partnership with local authorities and voluntary agencies. These initiatives may be centred around law enforcement by, for example, targeting particular crimes, or may be more concerned with crime prevention or victim support. In an example of partnership policing in the King's Cross area of London the police and local authorities developed a co-ordinated range of environmental and policing initiatives to reduce prostitution and drug dealing. Local authority departments cleaned the streets, improved lighting and closed off places where drug dealers and prostitutes operated. High-profile policing, including videos of drug dealers carrying out their trade, led to an increase in convictions. It was claimed that drug dealing was reduced by two-thirds (*The Guardian*, 16 February 1994).

Another project in south London targeted a high rate of street robbery. In an area where there had been poor relationships between the police and the community a range of strategies were developed involving the police, the local authority, schools and community consultative groups. Safe routes were created and video cameras installed on selected streets; school campaigns against bullying and carrying knives were launched and the Department of the Environment funded a crime shop which offered help and advice on a local estate. Summer projects aimed to keep young people involved in sport. As a result it was claimed that robbery fell by 38 per cent (*The Guardian*, 4 April 1994).

A major focus of these schemes is crime prevention, the focus of Bennett's third theme. Community crime prevention partnerships include neighbourhood watch schemes, which will be discussed in Chapter 11. Bennett's fourth model identifies schemes which involve police contact with the public. This may be through foot patrols or setting up shops on estates and high streets away from the police station. It may also involve the police knocking on doors to contact the public directly. Fifthly, community policing refers to the consultation mechanisms outlined above and the introduction of lay visitors to police stations.

Despite the many potential benefits of community policing it has not proved easy to implement. Full implementation would, argue many, involve a total reorganisation of police forces in which prevention and service roles take precedence over law enforcement and public order roles. As has been seen, however, the law enforcement role is often prioritised and seen within police culture as real police work. Some have discerned a tendency for community police functions to be 'bolted on' to existing organisations and seen as an addition to, rather than the main purpose of, organisations (Bennett 1994a). Attempts to change styles of policing may encounter resistance from officers on the ground and it has been argued that they cannot be effective if they do not carry the support of these officers (Fielding 1988).

In addition, given the vast number of tasks which the police are expected to perform, there may simply not be enough officers to allocate to beats on a semi-permanent basis. In times of emergency they may be called off the beat to deal with football disturbances, public order incidents or other duties. This means that the community cannot rely on consistency of cover. In addition, community constables spend much time on administrative duties and in the police station, and relatively small amounts of time on 'community contacts' (Bennett and Lupton 1992). Moreover, in organisations where community policing has a low status officers may be keen to move on from such roles, meaning that few gather sufficient experience. Community policing has also been found to be more successful in smaller, suburban middle-class communities than in inner city areas where the greatest problems have occurred (Fielding et al 1989).

A study attempting to measure the impact of community policing found no change in public attitudes or rates of victimisation (Irving et al 1989). The reasons for this limited success of schemes may be that they did not fit well with other organisational priorities and faced resistance from officers. Some positive results have been associated with foot patrols – Bennett, for example, found that a scheme involving the police seeking direct contact with the public had little effect on crime or reporting rates but did lead to substantial improvement in public satisfaction with the police (Bennett 1991).

These results should not, however, be taken to indicate that all schemes are ineffective and there are examples of highly committed community officers. Some schemes may have little impact on crime or victimisation rates but reduce people's fear of crime. Some, on the other hand, may have an immediate success which is difficult to sustain over time as enthusiasm wanes. The limited evidence of success to date, however, raises important questions about the role of the police – to what extent should they be fostering community relations or focusing on law enforcement and public order? Community policing, while popular with the public, may conflict with pressures to give priority to other areas of police work which produce measurable results. Community-based schemes may not be seen as the most efficient use of police resources (Morgan and Newburn 1997).

DISCRETION IN POLICE WORK

The effectiveness of the rules on police work depends on how they are enforced and implemented on the street, in the police station and by the policies and priorities drawn up by chief constables. The police have considerable discretion at all stages of the criminal justice process – quite simply they cannot enforce all the laws all the time. To attempt anything approximating full law enforcement would result in extremely large numbers of police officers exercising surveillance over the population by means of video cameras and intensive patrolling. This would be extremely costly and would lead to what would be regarded as a police state. The police therefore have neither the numbers, resources nor technological expertise to enforce all laws fully. Thus law is selectively enforced even within the context of zero tolerance policing where a higher police presence on the streets aims to change the perception that minor crimes will be ignored by the police (see Chapter 11).

Chief constables must determine the style of policing and priorities for their area within their given budget and national and local policing plans. Some may favour an emphasis on community policing, others may target particular offences. These general policies are implemented by areas and divisions who may also interpret policy in the light of what they see as the most pressing problems of their area. In the police station yet more discretionary decisions are involved. How suspects are dealt with, interrogated, and charged are all decisions made at this level along with decisions about cautioning or proceeding with charges. Police officers on the streets have discretion in deciding where to patrol, what to investigate, whether and how to intervene in incidents, or whether to stop and search members of the public. Unlike many other organisations, where those at the top exercise the greatest amounts of discretion, police officers on the street have to make difficult decisions on the spur of the moment. This is illustrated in comments made by the Commissioner of the Metropolitan Police, Sir Paul Condon, who, in a speech in October 1993, said that many key decisions have to be taken by some of the most junior officers. He went on to say 'they are expected to be counsellors, negotiators, mediators, managers, advisers, experts, parental figures, law enforcers and humble servants, ready to make contentious decisions, some involving life or death'.

Of course priorities are not just about the deployment of police for street work. The whole range of police work has to be prioritised. Traffic flows in London are a top concern for most citizens yet only 600 officers in the Metropolitan Police are deployed full-time on traffic duties. Is this enough? In terms of crime work the Commissioner indicated the following top three priorities for 1994; terrorism, burglary and armed crimes. After a process of public consultation the Metropolitan Police identified the following three aspects of their work as the highest priorities for the public: provision of an emergency response service (999 calls); more visible street patrolling, even though this is unlikely to result in an increase in crime detection; and a decent crime investigation service with proper consideration being given to victims.

There have been many studies of aspects of police discretion exploring how decisions are made and how tasks are prioritised. Clearly the law constrains the use of discretion, but a variety of non-legal or extra-legal factors are also important, and there may well be a gap between the law in action and the law as described in books.

In general, while legal factors form a backcloth against which decisions must be made, the law is often ambiguous and requires interpretation – what situations, for example, amount to 'reasonably suspicious'? As seen in previous chapters, the police must judge when actions are to be defined as criminal. The immediate situation affects the way an incident will be dealt with. Outcomes may be affected by apparently trivial circumstances such as the weather, the officer's mood, or the time of day. For example, at the end of a long shift, an officer may not want to be delayed by the amount of paper work which could result from an arrest. Alternatively, on a wet cold night they might want to get back to the station and might even look out for people to arrest (Cain 1973). Many studies of police behaviour have found that a wide variety of factors affect how the police react to specific incidents such as drunken brawls, disturbances by youths or disputes between neighbours. Blitzes or purges may be made against particular offences as a result of public policy.

Whether a person is likely to be seen as 'suspicious' depends also on cultural cues. The police have a set of expectations about what kinds of people belong in a certain area, and when and in what circumstances one would expect to find them. Behavioural cues like walking slowly or quickly may also affect judgments of 'suspiciousness' – and these are also culturally determined. The local knowledge and experience of the officer is likely to be important here, as is the local police culture which defines certain areas and groups as representing trouble, and which also provides guidelines for appropriate responses.

Many studies of the exercise of police discretion have focused on street level discretion – perhaps because this aspect has been subject to so much criticism. It is also more visible and easier for researchers to investigate. Police policies and organisation, both national and local, also affect the use of discretion. They will determine the priorities and style of policing in any area and thus the areas and groups of the population that the police come into contact with. Policy is a crucial aspect of discretion, as it influences and informs other decisions. The sections which follow look at some of these decisions and illustrate the limitations of laws and guidelines.

The decision to stop and search

The significance of the words 'reasonable suspicion' in relation to stop-and-search powers has already been indicated. PACE codes state that this must not be based on someone's race or hairstyle, on the fact that they are members of a group or community that have a higher than average record of committing that type of offence, nor on the fact that they are known to have previous convictions for possession of an unlawful article. These guidelines however, like the law, are limited. Decisions to stop and search are made on the spot, and rely on the individual officer's judgment of the situation. In deciding who to stop, officers are looking for something incongruous, something which doesn't fit (Dixon *et al* 1989). They are encouraged to learn, as part of their training, to identify such situations. This in turn implies a conception of normal – what does fit, which may depend on factors such as age, sex, race, behaviour, dress, time and place. These are impossible to capture by guidelines. In addition, argues Dixon, laws such as PACE are limited because they view a stop as an isolated event with its own set of rules. Often, however, officers do not have any specific purpose in mind when they stop someone – they may be acting on a hunch, the reasons for which cannot be legally defined. Thus a decision to stop and subsequently to search is a process rather than an isolated event. Many studies have found that factors such as being 'known to the police' by virtue of previous convictions, or failing to show appropriate respect for the police officer's authority may constitute informal reasons for a stop or an arrest. A police sergeant in Dixon's study says:

> the bobby out on the street . . . doesn't appreciate what the rules are until he's back in here. He's got to make an instant decision; sometimes the rules and regulations go by the board and he uses his commonsense. Then he may find when he comes into the police station that he's done something he shouldn't have, or he's used a power that he didn't have. Then we have to sort of find a way round that . . . find him a power!
>
> (Dixon *et al* 1989)

In the police station

PACE also deals with the exercise of police discretion in the police station, where individual suspects are interviewed and decisions are made about how to proceed with a case. As we have seen it introduced requirements for the taping of interviews and custody records. Nonetheless, in any job, ways are often found to circumvent formal rules, and informal practices may become the norm. Simon Holdaway, for example, in a study written before PACE, found that the police attempt to prevent those with power to challenge their actions (such as doctors or lawyers) from entering the 'back regions' of the station – the interview or interrogation rooms (Holdaway 1983). In addition, just as the rules and guidelines surrounding stop and search cannot fully reflect the social processes underlying encounters, recorded interviews cannot capture the 'reality' of conversations with suspects. They cannot, for example, control the informal interviews which police have with suspects outside the police station, in the car or in the cells (Leng *et al* 1992). Such conversations are not officially defined as interviews. In this way, deals such as charge bargains can be made which must not form part of formal interviews. In addition, in recorded interviews, the fear of the suspect and the

119

attitude of the officer cannot be fully reproduced on tape. Thus even though confessions which are involuntary, or produced in oppressive circumstances, are inadmissible, these factors may still mean that tactics used by skilled and experienced officers may 'put words into' a suspect's mouth.

These considerations do not imply that the police act illegally – many practices are essentially a way around the constraints of law. To the police, obtaining confessions from someone they have good reasons to believe is guilty is part of their job. Nor does it mean that laws such as PACE are entirely without effect as they may curtail blatant abuses of police powers as was indicated above (Brown 1997).

DISCRIMINATION AND POLICE CULTURE

Discrimination

Residents of some areas may feel that they are being unfairly picked on if the police pay too much attention to them, whereas other groups may feel that the police neglect their problems. Thus women's groups may complain that the police pay insufficient attention to domestic disputes and complaints of rape, and some ethnic groups have complained that racial harassment has not been dealt with effectively. These allegations suggest that the police are discriminating – that is treating some complaints less seriously on the basis of either the gender or race of the complainants. In addition, throughout the 1970s and 1980s there were allegations that the police racially discriminated in stop and search and arrest decisions. It is difficult to find evidence supporting or rejecting such allegations. As the race of offenders is not collected in the criminal statistics, any research must be based on studies in individual areas. A number of studies have now been undertaken, however their findings require careful interpretation (see, for example, Smith 1997; Holdaway 1996, 1997).

Some studies have found that in many, though not all, areas black people were stopped in higher proportions than white. For example research by the Policy Studies Institute in the Metropolitan Police area found that proportionately nearly twice as many black males aged 15–24 were stopped as white youth (Smith and Gray 1985): 8 per cent of black males aged between 15 and 24 were stopped in the year preceding the study compared with 5 per cent whites and 2 per cent Asians. Other studies have found that black youth are proportionately more likely to be arrested than other ethnic groups. After examining the statistics for arrests in the Metropolitan Police area, Monica Walker concludes that 'black people must have four and a half times the chance of being arrested for a burglary . . . (compared to white) . . . to account for their over representation' (Walker 1987).

This does not necessarily mean that the police are dealing unfairly with black youth. Demographic factors may account for many of these differences. Higher proportions of the black population are younger, unemployed, come from lower class backgrounds and live in lower class areas – all characteristics associated with the likelihood of being stopped. Therefore we would expect a higher number of black youth to be stopped in proportion to white youth, especially where studies are carried out in large areas. Were the base of studies to be smaller, more homogeneous areas among groups of similar social class backgrounds, living in the same area, the results might be different (see, for example, Walker 1987).

In a more recent study in Leeds, it was found that while, overall, blacks were stopped twice as often as whites, a more complex picture emerged when the characteristics of individual areas were taken into account (Jefferson *et al* 1992). Thus black people were disproportionately stopped in areas where the majority of residents were white, but in areas where the majority of residents were black, white people were stopped more often. This could, argue the authors, reflect patterns of home ownership – where any group predominates they are more likely to be home owners, whereas the minority population are more likely to be in rented accommodation and to live in parts of the areas more likely to attract police attention.

Research conducted by Simon Holdaway and the Policy Studies Institute (PSI) found that police officers did use derogatory language when describing black people, and that the 'canteen culture' contained many racist elements (Holdaway 1983; Smith and Gray 1985). A report of the Chief Inspector of the Constabulary cites unacceptable levels of prejudice and sexist and racist behaviour on the part of the police as a disincentive for both women and ethnic minority individuals to join the police (*The Guardian*, 14 June 1994). But such attitudes do not necessarily lead to direct discrimination – which involves treating a group differently on the grounds of race. The PSI studies found little evidence of discriminatory decisions. What is more likely is that there may be indirect discrimination, which exists where the policies or practices of an institution are applied evenly, but have an unequal impact on different groups. Thus when the police prioritise lower class, high-crime areas containing a large proportion of ethnic minority residents, more lower class and black people became subject to stops, searches or arrests. Moreover, the race, ethnicity or socio-economic status of a suspect is only one among many other factors which may be relevant in an officer's decision to stop and search. It may or may not be the primary factor, which makes it difficult to establish statistically the influences on such decisions (Holdaway 1997). Wider social inequalities such as unemployment, poor housing conditions and family breakdown further compound the disadvantages of black youths as they enter the criminal justice system – as they may then be less likely to be cautioned or warned and more likely to be taken to court.

Nonetheless, the perception of inequality among black groups has had a number of effects. It may make black people more 'combative' in their attitude to the criminal justice process, which can affect relationships between the police and the black population. This may mean that the black population as a whole are less supportive of the police and less likely to co-operate.

Lea and Young suggest that this can start a vicious circle. If the black community are less supportive, then the police may have to use more aggressive styles in black areas, leading to more use of stop-and-search tactics (Lea and Young 1984). This may create 'flashpoints' where a seemingly trivial incident may provoke a more widespread disturbance. These kinds of considerations led, during the 1980s, to the development of more community based styles of policing.

Police culture

The informal rules which affect how the police behave in any particular incident or situation form part of what has been called the occupational culture of policing. Many occupations have associated cultures, within which members use a special language, and share a similar view of the world and their occupation. Anyone starting a job very quickly learns the distinction between how things should be done and how they really are done. These informal rules are learnt during what sociologists call occupational socialisation where a recruit learns the norms and values associated with the occupation. The expectations associated with the job and what constitutes success are part of such a culture as are attitudes about the role of the occupation. This is particularly the case where the occupation faces hostility or misunderstanding from the public – as may be the case with the police. In this case the culture may have a justifying role, justifying the job that members do.

In some occupations this culture is stronger than others – particularly where work spreads into other aspects of life and leisure. Policing is not a nine to five job from which officers can switch off when they leave the station. It makes heavy emotional demands on officers, involves high levels of stress and is a vocation as well as a job. A key aspect of policing is that it involves danger and on the beat the police face the ever present threat of physical harm. Violence against police officers has increased in recent years. The Annual Report in 1995 of the Chief Inspector of Constabulary gave figures that showed that 15,141 officers had been assaulted in 1994/5. Trefor Morris, the Chief Inspector, commented, 'The deaths of Sergeant Derek Robertson and Constable Philip Walters brings to 10 the number of police officers in England and Wales murdered since 1990 in the course of their duty' (HM Chief Inspector of Constabulary, *Annual Report 1995*: 51). Police officers therefore need to be able to rely on each other often in life threatening situations. This makes for closer relationships between officers and a stronger culture than in many jobs.

The police must display authority in order to handle some situations, especially where large numbers of people are involved. Police can only 'handle' situations if the public respect the authority of the police. This may affect decisions about suspects to the extent that those who appear to challenge authority may be more likely to be stopped, arrested or charged. Authority is re-enforced by the symbols of the job – cars, radios and uniforms all signify the authority vested in the role of police officer (Holdaway 1983).

Police officers are also geographically and socially isolated. Policing involves shift work, therefore they are often working when others are enjoying their leisure time, they may not be able to undertake many leisure pursuits involving the general public and may find it difficult to maintain friendships with non-police officers. In some areas, the police may live in police accommodation. Police officers tend to mix socially with other officers and they may prefer to let their hair down where they are not observed by the public.

All these factors give rise to a strong occupational culture within the police, described by writers such as Holdaway, Reiner and Brogden (Reiner 1992a; Brogden et al 1988; Holdway 1983). While it is impossible to make sweeping generalisations about this culture, certain themes appear to characterise police culture in Anglo-American societies.

Most studies emphasise that police officers feel that their job is important – they feel a sense of mission. They often see themselves as forming a 'thin blue line', protecting society from disorder. A key part of this mission is catching criminals, which attracts many to the job. Thus law enforcement tasks are described as 'real police work', making an implicit contrast with much hated desk or paper work, and reflecting an emphasis on action, seen most clearly in the imagery of the car chase. Car chases, according to Holdaway are often the subject of animated conversations in the dull moments in the canteen and they form an important part of the police folk lore. This may mean that the more mundane elements of policing are downgraded and seen as 'rubbish' rather than real police work. Nonetheless the emphasis on catching criminals is reflected in how the police are assessed – the clear up rates – and there is a great emphasis on the figures. Resolving a dispute without an arrest is less amenable to measurement and may be seen as less important.

There is an element of machismo within police culture with an emphasis on action and crime fighting. This, plus conservative views about gender relationships, affects their views towards women officers – who are treated protectively. Indeed attitudes about women officers demonstrate many elements of the police culture. Heidensohn found that a common objection to women officers is that they cannot handle a group of drunks. This implies, she argues, that a macho way of handling drunks is more appropriate than the persuasive 'soft cop' image associated with women police (Heidensohn 1992).

Reiner also sees police culture as containing strong elements of conservatism (Reiner 1992a). This does not imply that all police vote Conservative but that police tend to hold very traditional views about crime, the family, law and order and discipline. Indeed it would be surprising if they did not as they have chosen a job which involves upholding the law. These attitudes, however, may affect their judgments about the people they come into contact with most. It may also affect aspects of discrimination both in relation to the public, and within the force itself. The social isolation of the police further reinforces these beliefs.

An understanding of police culture is important when policy reforms are considered. For example, the view of police work which is associated with the love of action may mean that many officers resist community policing styles, and the elements of machismo, racism and conservatism may affect how well women and ethnic officers can be integrated. The occupational culture may also affect the emphasis placed on crime control and due process. This is not to say that attitudes cannot change and it is important not to paint too static or simple a picture.

There is more than one approach to police work as many of the studies on policing show. For example, detectives may have a perspective and a culture very different from uniformed officers and may need to adopt very different styles to perform their job adequately (Hobbs 1991). Different stations within a particular area may have very different cultures, affected by the policy of the division (Foster 1989). Some officers may value their role within the community, whereas others may see themselves more as crime fighters. Rural policing may be very different from urban policing with rural police being more involved in all the tasks of the police simply because of the time it may take to call in the specialists from the town (Cain 1973). Those involved in public order duties, especially those in special patrols may also come to look forward to a 'piece of action' (Jefferson 1990).

CONCLUSION

This chapter has shown how the police are organised and how different models may assess their role and function. It has also outlined the main laws governing police investigation along with how the police are made accountable. These rules and guidelines, however, provide only a backcloth against which the police operate on a day-to-day level, which is inevitably affected by their own perception of their job and how they interpret the many rules and guidelines. This is important for a number of reasons. Should the police, for example, perceive their main role as one of crime control, then they may be tempted to neglect due process in the interests of making sure that those guilty of crime are brought to court and found guilty. They may, as we have seen, downgrade the service or preventive aspects of their role. Discussions of police policy must therefore recognise the significance of discretion in police work and the role of the police culture and its influence on police work.

This chapter also raises questions about the role of the police vital to our understanding of the criminal justice process as a whole. What is the main role of the police? Should they be responsible mainly for law enforcement or should they also seek to prevent crime, protect the public, consider the welfare as well as the prosecution of suspects and perform many other services for the community? Should their time be spent chiefly on crime-related tasks while they pass other duties onto other agencies? And how might this affect their law enforcement role? One of the functions of the police not yet explored is their role in determining whether a suspect is prosecuted or diverted out of the criminal justice system. This will be taken up in Chapter 5.

Review questions

1. Outline the range of tasks carried out by the police service.

2. What are the main ways in which the police are rendered accountable? How and why have these arrangements recently been changed?

3. Look at the way in which the police are portrayed in the media through police dramas, documentaries or news stories. How does this reflect the different roles of the police?

4. Identify the possible infringements of PACE and Code C in the following:

> At 10 pm Alan is seen at the scene of a suspected burglary with a video camera thought to come from the burgled house. PC Bob asks him where he got the camera. Alan does not reply whereupon, without more ado, he is bundled into the police van and taken to the police station.
>
> At the police station, Alan is placed in a cell with three other people, and told he will be seen when the officer has time. The only light in the cell is broken. Four hours later Alan has not been interviewed. He wants to sleep but cannot as the only bed is occupied. Alan is very cold, and asks the custody officer for a cup of tea. He is told that there has been a problem in the canteen and he can have a glass of water. This arrives one hour later. At 6 am Alan is interviewed about his possession of the camera and suspected involvement in the burglary. He asks to see a solicitor, but is told the duty solicitor has just left and is not likely to want to come back before morning. Alan states that he stole the camera. Alan is 16.

To help you answer consider the following:

- Was Alan arrested properly?
- Should anything have been said when he was taken to the police station?
- Should anything have been said to him when he got to the police station?
- Where the conditions in his cell acceptable?
- Should he have been asked if he wanted to contact anyone?
- Should he have been given refreshments?
- Should he have been given anything else?
- Was the time during which he was kept at the police station acceptable under the code?
- Should he have been allowed to speak with a duty solicitor?
- Should anyone else have been present during the interview?

5. Read this letter, which was sent to *The Times* by the Chief Constable of Surrey. What policy objectives are referred to in this letter? What new Key Performance Indicator would you suggest to deal with the point he raises in his letter? (See Chapter 11.)

> Sir, Your account today (earlier edition) of the Audit Commission report on police performance makes a direct comparison between the crime detection rates of Kent Constabulary and those of Surrey Police, much to the detriment of the latter.
>
> If the debate was focused on levels of crime, rather than detection, the situation would be entirely different. While I congratulate Kent Constabulary on their detection rate and note that their rates of crime are falling, I must point out that Surrey remains the safest county in England in terms of crime rates, with a greater fall in crime over the last five years than any force in the South East. The likelihood of being a victim of crime in Surrey is almost half that in Kent.
>
> I am determined that Surrey Police will increase the likelihood of criminals being caught when they commit crime, but I am more interested in preventing that crime happening in the first place and I want to be measured on how successful I am in achieving that.
>
> I have the feeling that most people would rather not be burgled than be burgled and know that the burglar had been caught.
>
> Yours sincerely,
>
> Ian Blair
> Chief Constable of Surrey
>
> > (*The Times*, 7 February 1998: 23)

Further reading

Brogden M, Jefferson T and Walklate S (1988) *Introducing Police Work*. London: Unwin Hyman

Leishman F, Loveday B and Savage S (eds) (1998) *Core Issues in Policing*, 2nd edn. London: Longman

Reiner R (1992) *The Politics of the Police*. London: Harvester Wheatsheaf

Stephens M and Becker S (eds) (1994) *Police Force Police Service: Care and Control in Britain*. London: Macmillan

Uglow S (1988) *Policing Liberal Society*. Oxford: Oxford University Press

CHAPTER 5

PROSECUTION AND
DIVERSION

- Cautioning
- Prosecution
- Juvenile Justice
- Mentally Disordered Offenders

INTRODUCTION

Once the police are reasonably sure they have identified a suspect, they have several options. They may decide to take no further action at all, or give an informal warning, or decide to issue a formal police caution, or refer the case to some form of mediation. They may instead decide to pass the papers to the Crown Prosecution Service. Many criminal cases are therefore diverted from the criminal justice process without any public trial or hearing. The decision to prosecute is a vital one and we will look at the rules and guidelines surrounding this decision, at the agencies responsible for it, and at the issues raised for criminal justice.

Prosecution and diversion raise many issues which can again be highlighted by looking at the different perspectives on criminal justice. Under a crime control approach, for example, it is clearly important that guilty offenders are convicted and punished and the system would be seen to lack any deterrent potential if this does not happen. Principles of due process also require that the defendant should have the opportunity to be publicly tried and enabled to refute any allegations of guilt. In addition, the notion that all are equal before the law underlies the principle that justice should be seen to be done. Diversion of some at the expense of others might produce a situation where critics from a class domination perspective could argue that some groups of offenders enjoy advantages. In addition, it is important to proponents of a denunciatory approach that offenders ought to be publicly tried and punished for the system to perform its function of expressing society's disapproval of particular behaviour. Victims also may feel aggrieved if they do not see those that have harmed them publicly held to account. If suspected offenders are diverted from the system it implies that the police and prosecutors are making essentially judicial decisions which should be made formally in the public forum of the criminal courts to ensure just deserts.

There are strong arguments that all suspects should be prosecuted (Gross 1979). Such an approach, however, would pose considerable problems. The process of prosecution and trial is costly. Police officers, prosecutors and the legal profession must collect evidence and produce and contest it in court, which also occupies the time and resources of court personnel. Diverting offenders from the formal process can therefore produce considerable savings and reduce delays. In addition, there may be many circumstances in which diversion is desirable. The labelling perspective outlined in Chapter 2 suggests, for example, that the stigmatising effects of public trial and punishment could propel some offenders into more crime. For young offenders particularly it may be desirable in the interests of rehabilitation to avoid prosecution and eventual punishment. Some offenders, such as the very young or the mentally disordered may be considered to be not fully responsible for their own actions, making trial and punishment inappropriate.

In recent years a number of policies have encouraged diversion although not as we shall see without some criticism. This chapter will focus on four main aspects of prosecution and diversion. It will first look at the considerations surrounding the cautioning of offenders. It will then explore the decision to prosecute, and describe the agency responsible for the majority of prosecutions, the Crown Prosecution Service (CPS), along with a brief account of the work of other agencies involved in prosecution. Further sections will explore the treatment of two groups for whom diversion is often seen as appropriate, young offenders and the mentally ill. The arrangements for these offenders are clearly distinguishable from other offenders and we will outline the options available to the court and in the pre-trial stage to divert these offenders from being prosecuted.

CAUTIONING

Before looking at formal cautions given in lieu of trial and sentence, it is important to recognise that some cases are diverted from the system with no formal action being taken. Whereas an official caution is recorded and can be referred to on subsequent appearances, cases which result in no further action (NFA) or an informal warning are not recorded. While precise numbers are not officially recorded, on the basis of research it has been estimated that as many as 25 per cent of known offenders are so dealt with (Sanders 1997). This proportion varies both between and within police areas – one survey for example found variations of zero to 24 per cent, with an average of 10.6 per cent, reflecting different police policies (Evans and Wilkinson 1990).

No further action may be taken in a variety of situations. An individual officer may do nothing because the matter is too trivial and making an 'issue' of it could create further problems out of proportion to the incident. In other cases there may be a formal reason why the police cannot proceed with a prosecution, for example, where they cannot provide sufficient evidence for the court, or where the offender is too young. In other situations they may feel that no useful purpose will be served by taking matters any further, particularly where offenders are elderly or mentally ill.

The officer may, instead of doing nothing, give an immediate informal caution or warning. This might happen with trivial offences, such as where an officer observes young people riding bicycles on the pavement, and issues a few words of warning (Evans and Wilkinson 1990). This is only appropriate in less serious matters and is completely within the discretion of the officer. In some offences involving the maintenance of vehicles, an officer can issue a Notice to Rectify advising the motorist to correct the defect within a number of days, to avoid prosecution. Only if this is not done will prosecution result. A further option is the formal warning, a system which operates in some areas where a written warning is given in lieu of prosecution after the suspect has been reported for a possible offence. These alternatives are used for a variety of minor infringements – road traffic matters and very minor public order matters being the most common.

No further action may also reflect the use by the police of what Sanders describes as speculative arrests, which might occur where the police arrest people to encourage them to give information (Sanders 1997). Arrest may in effect be a strategy to assist further investigation and may not be intended to lead to prosecution.

The most significant alternative to prosecution is the formal caution, which is used in a wide range of offences of varying seriousness. The issue of a police caution is a regulated and recorded procedure whereby a potential defendant admits guilt without evidence being fully gathered and is formally warned by a senior police officer 'not to do it again'. Cautions are recorded at the local Criminal Record Office, retained for three years and may be quoted in court at the time of sentence. Although cautions are given most often to young defendants, including young adults, they are available for defendants of any age. The use of cautioning with young offenders was given statutory authority in the Children and Young Persons Act 1969 (see later section in this chapter for reforms to cautioning of young offenders introduced in the Crime and Disorder Act 1998). Use of cautioning with adults developed through Home Office policy in the 1980s.

Because cautions can be referred to in court, and because they constitute a significant diversion from prosecution, the system is regulated. A number of guidelines have been issued, including the Attorney General's guidelines entitled *Criteria for Prosecution* issued in 1984, and Home Office Circular 14 in February 1985 which encouraged the greater use of cautioning. In 1990, Home Office Circular 59 was issued to promote national standards for cautioning. Home Office Circular 18 in 1994 recommended limiting multiple cautions or cautions for serious offences. The Code for Crown Prosecutors also gives guidance on the use of cautioning. In some circumstances chief

Fig 5.1 Offenders cautioned or sentenced 1975–96

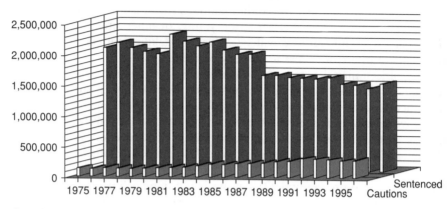

Compiled from *Criminal Statistics England and Wales*, 1975 to 1997.

constables issue internal guidelines indicating which offences are appropriate for a caution. The most important prerequisite for a caution is that the offender accepts guilt. In order for a caution to be administered the following conditions must be fulfilled:

- there must be sufficient evidence to warrant a prosecution
- the offender must admit guilt
- either the person being cautioned, or, in the case of a child or young person, the parent or appropriate adult, must consent to such a disposal after being warned that the caution may be cited in future court appearances.

A number of criteria guide the decision of whether to initiate a prosecution including the following:

- the nature and seriousness of the offence
- the likely penalty if the offender was convicted by the court
- the offender's age, personal circumstances and state of health
- the offender's character and previous criminal history
- the offender's attitude to the offence, including practical expressions of regret
- the view of the victim.

The 1990 circular indicates that 'courts should only be used as a last resort, particularly for juveniles and young adults', and that where the criteria for cautioning are met there should be a 'presumption in favour of not prosecuting'.

Cautioning grew in use throughout the 1980s to over 300,000 offenders cautioned annually, with an average increase of 6 per cent per year from 1985 to 1992. Since then the number has fallen and in 1996 there were 286,000 (see Figure 5.1). The usage still varied considerably with age and sex. In 1995 cautioning rates for males and females aged 14–17 in England and Wales were respectively 58 and 79 per cent of all those in that age group either convicted or cautioned for indictable offences; for 10–13 year olds the figures were 86 and 96 per cent (*Home Office Statistical Bulletin,* 16/97).

The 1990 standards were in part a response to the diversity in cautioning rates (see, for example, Evans and Wilkinson 1990; Ashworth 1994a). This variation can be seen in figures provided in *Digest 2: A Digest of Information on the Criminal Justice System,* which indicate that in 1991, 'The use of formal cautioning for indictable offences varies from 20 per cent of known offenders in South Wales to 45 per cent in Humberside' (Barclay 1993: 31). These variations, it comments, reflect the use of formal rather than informal cautioning.

They also reflect the high amount of discretion underlying these decisions. For example, guidelines do not specify precisely what account needs be taken of particular factors and the police may use the decision to caution or prosecute in a way that accords with their working rules. Thus officers may simply feel that some offenders deserve prosecution, and cautions may avoid unnecessary paperwork. Indeed, while cautions should only be given where there is sufficient evidence to prosecute, Sanders points to research indicating that some suspects were cautioned because there was insufficient evidence to prosecute – thus a caution can be used to clear up a case which might otherwise not have been prosecuted (Sanders 1997). Thus, argues Sanders, the low visibility of cautioning can enable the police to use cautions as a bargaining tool.

The exercise of discretion also raises issues of possible bias. As we have seen, girls are more likely to be cautioned than boys, although most research indicates that this reflects the tendency for girls to be first offenders and to have committed less serious offences (see Chapter 3 and Eaton 1986). Some differences have also been found in relation to race. One study found that white juveniles had a greater chance of being cautioned than black youth (Landau and Nathan 1983). A later study found that Asians were more likely to be cautioned than any other group while Afro-Caribbeans were less likely to receive a caution (Jefferson and Walker 1992).

As with the use of police powers, complex factors underlie these figures. Landau and Nathan, for example, conclude that while bias on the part of the police cannot be ruled out, much of the difference can be explained by the fact that more black youth had previous convictions, and came from what were seen as problem or one parent families. In addition we have already seen that offenders must plead guilty in order to receive a caution. Where there has been hostility between the black population and the police, the more combative attitude of black youth may mean that they are more likely to plead not guilty and go to trial (Jefferson and Walker 1992). Indeed some studies have found that more black people plead not guilty, and that more are acquitted (Walker 1987). The police in some areas may be more sensitive to such feelings, leading to changes in attitudes and policy.

There is also some concern that cautioning may have a built-in class bias. Many of the criteria relating to offenders' circumstances may unintentionally advantage better-off offenders or young people from middle-class homes.

Ashworth indicates how the criterion concerning attitude to the offence may work in this way. This criterion includes consideration of whether the offender has made some practical demonstration of regret, such as an apology to a victim or an offer to put matters right, for example by voluntary compensation. Thus, he comments, 'wealthy offenders might be able to buy themselves out of prosecution by offering payments to their victims, whereas impecunious offenders cannot' (Ashworth 1994a: 138–9).

In addition, the regulatory agencies, such as the Inland Revenue or local authority consumer protection departments, who are responsible for the prosecution of offences involving white collar or business offenders, often follow a policy of not prosecuting offenders and extensively use both informal and written cautions. Indeed these agencies regularly caution offenders on many occasions before a prosecution is considered and the extent to which offenders have sought to rectify matters is part of this decision (see, for example, Croall 1992; Ashworth 1994a and below).

The police are responsible for the decision to give a caution. The CPS may send the papers in the case back to the police with a recommendation that one is given. If a caution is given this normally means an end of the matter and the police and the Crown Prosecution Service will take no further action. However, it is possible for a private prosecution to be taken out against an offender who has been cautioned by the police. Thus, Mr Hayter instituted a private prosecution in Basildon against two youths who had assaulted his son. The police were of the view that a caution was the appropriate means of dealing with the matter, and both boys agreed after having legal advice. In the cautioning process, both were told that it did not prevent an aggrieved person bringing proceedings, and that is what Mr Hayter did. Although it was argued that the prosecution should not continue, the Queen's Bench Division of the High Court (QBD) decided that the case could continue (*Hayter v L and Another, The Times*, 3 February 1998).

Cautioning and young offenders

Cautioning was first put onto a statutory basis by the Children and Young Persons Act 1969 (CYPA) and its use increased as a means of diverting young offenders from the court system in the hope that they would behave better without the stigma of being labelled a criminal. Arguments critical of its use focused upon the problem of net widening, suggesting that the apparently more benign approach might be responsible for increasing the number of youngsters caught in the net of the criminal justice system. Other critics looked at the high proportion of crime committed by young offenders (see statistics in this chapter) to suggest that it was not an effective means to control delinquency.

The arguments about the use of cautioning with young offenders came under scrutiny in the Audit Commission's 1996 report *Misspent Youth*. The evidence focused on the limited effectiveness of repeat cautioning, the problems of inconsistent usage and to the fact that cautioning does not 'nip offending in the bud' (Home Office 1997b, para 5.10). In November 1997 a White Paper, *No More Excuses*, was published by the Home Office. The recently installed Home Secretary, Jack Straw, commented that the proposals represented 'the most radical reform of the youth justice system since the war'. In the preface he wrote, 'An excuse culture has developed within the youth justice system. It excuses itself for its inefficiency, and too often excuses the young offenders before it, implying that they cannot help their behaviour because of their social circumstances.' A reform of polices at all levels was promised from crime prevention strategies through diversion and court appearance to sentences.

The white paper referred to the proposals, later included in the Crime and Disorder Act 1998, to replace the current system of cautioning for young offenders with 'police reprimands' and 'final warnings'. Under the Act, when an offence is committed by a young person, the police can take no action at all, or give a police reprimand, or give a final warning, or start a prosecution. Normally for a first offence the police would decide upon one of the following:

- a police reprimand if the offence was not very serious
- a final warning if it was more serious
- a decision to prosecute.

For a second offence, if a reprimand had already been given, a further reprimand could not be given and the young person would be given a final warning, or prosecuted.

After any final warning the commission of a further offence would automatically result in criminal proceedings unless two years had elapsed from the warning and the new offence was minor. A final warning would usually involve offenders and their families in a community intervention programme aimed at trying to change offenders' behaviour to prevent further offences being committed. The community intervention schemes could build on those developed under the present Caution Plus programmes, such as in Aylesbury where young offenders are encouraged to apologise to victims and to discuss with them the effect of the crime.

The rights of both defendants and victims are affected by cautions. A caution can only be given following an admission of guilt. This raises the question of the extent to which defendants may be under pressure to admit guilt which they otherwise deny in order to avoid the stress of a court appearance. The low visibility of cautions raises concerns about how far defendants' rights are observed at this stage, especially since a caution may have a bearing on subsequent sentence.

There may also be a conflict between the benefits of diversion and the interest of victims. When offenders are cautioned, victims are deprived of the opportunity to obtain compensation (Ashworth 1994a). While some areas have provisions for offering mediation between offenders and victims as a form of diversion, this practice, which will be discussed more fully in Chapter 11, is by no means widespread.

A final concern about cautions, which involve the police making quasi-judicial decisions, is how accountable these powers are (Ashworth 1994a). Better record-keeping and some provision for legal advice before admitting guilt might answer some of these points, and the Royal Commission on Criminal Justice of 1993 recommended that police cautioning be governed by statute. Others have suggested a role for the CPS in cautioning decisions (see, for example, Ashworth 1994a). This however would involve far-reaching changes in the respective roles of the police and the CPS.

Once the police have decided that a prosecution rather than any other form of action is appropriate, the papers are referred to the CPS for consideration.

PROSECUTION

The vast majority of prosecutions are undertaken by the CPS, but a number of other agencies also have responsibility for undertaking criminal prosecutions. These include the agencies responsible for enforcing laws regulating many aspects of business, trade and commerce. Their work will be outlined following an examination of the CPS. Private bodies and individuals may also prosecute but this only accounts for a very small number of prosecutions.

Private prosecutions may be started by, for example, departmental stores to deal with shoplifting on their premises, or individuals who feel an issue should be dealt with by the courts, as when, in January 1998, 72-year-old Roy Edney of Harrow started proceedings against Bath rugby player Kevin Yates alleging that he had bitten a lump of skin from another player's ear during a match. Sometimes aggrieved victims and their families take up a prosecution, as with the Hayter case cited above and with the murder of Steven Lawrence, because they feel the police or the CPS have taken insufficient action. The right to start a private prosecution is subject to limitations:

- The magistrates may refuse to issue a summons.
- The Attorney General can stop what are called 'vexatious litigants' from bringing cases.
- The DPP has a power to take over prosecutions and end them.

The process of prosecutions is formally started either following the arrest and charge of a suspect by the police, or after a summons has been issued by a magistrates' court. The court issues a summons after receiving information from the police or other prosecuting bodies or from individuals about an alleged offence; this is referred to as 'laying an information'. There are many more summonses issued than people arrested and charged (see Figure 6.3). A large number of prosecutions for 'summary only' offences such as motoring offences are started this way.

The Crown Prosecution Service

Before the creation of the CPS in the 1980s, the police and the Director of Public Prosecutions (DPP) were responsible for prosecution. The office of the DPP was set up by the Prosecution of Offences Act 1879, and its task was to institute, undertake or carry on criminal proceedings, and to give advice and assistance to chief officers of police and other persons responsible for the prosecution of offences. The DPP was responsible for prosecuting cases of murder, along with those involving national security, public figures and police officers.

The police were responsible for the prosecution of routine offences in magistrates' courts, and there were 43 prosecution authorities in England and Wales. They were advised by solicitors, who were either employed or consulted by them, and who conducted more complex cases in the magistrates' courts. Cases in Crown Courts were conducted by barristers on behalf of the police.

The police were therefore both investigators and prosecutors, a dual role which caused considerable concern. It was argued for example that the crime control function of investigation could clash with the interests of due process in ensuring that prosecutions only be undertaken on the basis of sufficient evidence. The potential conflict was noted by Royal Commissions in 1929 and 1962 and the Royal Commission on Criminal Procedure, known as the Phillips Commission, which was set up in 1978 and reported in 1981. It pointed out that there was no uniform system of prosecution in England and Wales, and that there was a strong civil liberties case for an independent agency, other than the police, to review and conduct the prosecution of criminal cases. It argued that a new prosecuting agency would encourage greater consistency in approach to prosecution. It stressed that the roles of investigating crime, collecting evidence and arresting suspects were likely to interfere with the impartial review of a case and decisions about whether prosecution was necessary or likely to be successful. The dual responsibility for policing and prosecution could lead to the abuse of the rights of the arrested person by the police, born out of an anxiety to convict those whom the police believed were guilty. There were also concerns from an efficiency viewpoint about the number of weak cases where the evidence was insufficient to lead to a conviction, being taken to court and then thrown out as a result of a judge-directed acquittal, which was both costly and time consuming.

Following a debate in the House of Commons and the Bonan Working Party whose report was published in August 1983, a white paper proposed the setting up of a Crown Prosecution Service. The Prosecution of Offences Act 1985 established the CPS and specified its functions which included taking over the conduct of all criminal proceedings instituted by the police. As seen in Chapter 4, the introduction of the CPS was closely linked with the Police and Criminal Evidence Act 1984 (PACE).

There was much debate over whether the service should be a centralised national service or a local one or combine elements of both. In the end a national service was created: the CPS therefore represents a single independent and nationwide authority for England and Wales. It is independent of the police and has the power to discontinue prosecutions. Unlike prosecution agencies in other jurisdictions it has no powers to institute proceedings or to direct the police to carry out any further investigations. Its introduction had substantial constitutional significance for a number of reasons. For the first time there was a single state prosecuting authority charged with making decisions of a quasi judicial nature which could ultimately affect the rights and liberties of the individual. It also created a new legal interest group directly linked to government. These lawyers, although civil servants, were expected to be independent of government control, though little was put in place to guarantee this, save the *Code for Crown Prosecutors* and the existing *Codes of Professional Conduct for the Legal Professions*.

The introduction of the CPS as a body with a duty to review cases at every stage of a prosecution inevitably caused problems. Some of these sprung from initial rivalry between the police and CPS and misunderstandings about their respective roles. The necessary bureaucratic changes also produced problems – major delays followed changes in the system for transmitting files to court and prioritising cases. The Royal Commission on Criminal Justice in 1993 commented that the service was hastily conceived and inadequately resourced. A report in 1990 by the Public Accounts Committee on a Review of the Crown Prosecution Service (House of Commons 1990) found that estimates of how much the system would cost were initially too low and that many problems were caused by understaffing and inadequate resourcing.

The powers of the CPS to discontinue cases also caused friction with the police and frustration on the part of victims and courts. As we shall see below, the rate of cases discontinued continues to cause concern although one of the roles of the CPS was to reduce the number of trials aborted on evidential grounds. Other critics saw the CPS as a threat to civil liberties, as it intermingled judicial and executive functions.

The organisation and functions of the Crown Prosecution Service

In England and Wales the CPS has become the main agency responsible for the prosecution of offenders. It started in 1986 as a result of the Prosecution of Offences Act 1985 and its establishment was part of a complete reform of the laws governing police investigation (PACE 1984) (see Chapter 4) and the prosecution of offences. By 1996 it employed 6,000 people, of whom 2,000 were lawyers. They are responsible for carrying out the major tasks of the CPS which are:

136

- To review cases to decide whether to continue or discontinue them.
- To liaise with the police on matters of evidence and agreeing charging standards.
- To liaise with barristers who represent the prosecution in the Crown Court.
- To present cases in the magistrates' courts at all pre-trial and trial stages.

Their role as civil servants and crown employees is tempered by the *Code for Crown Prosecutors* and by their professional ethics as lawyers, with a primary duty to the court. The head of the CPS is the Director of Public Prosecutions (DPP). Barbara Mills was the DPP from 1992–8.

The work of the CPS is divided into different geographical areas. Between 1986 and 1998 there have been three reorganisations of the CPS. These have sought to create a balance between areas so that they have similar case loads while, where possible, having boundaries that are coterminous with other agencies, especially the police.

The Phillips Commission (1978–81) originally conceived of the CPS as a locally accountable organisation and recommended dividing the country into 43 areas reflecting the 43 police force areas. However, when introduced in 1986 the CPS was organised into 31 areas, in an attempt to equalise work-loads. In 1992, reorganisation to achieve a more cohesive national structure led to these being re-divided into 13 areas.

In April 1997 the Labour Party produced a policy document *The Case for the Prosecution*, suggesting another reorganisation into 42 areas, each with a Chief Crown Prosecutor with one to cover the entire area of the Metropolitan and City of London forces. Outside of London the boundaries are the same as for the police. The document underlined the need for an independent service but with opportunity for closer liaison with the police. After the Labour Party was elected, the new Attorney General announced that this policy statement would be put in force. However, in June 1997 the Glidewell review of the CPS was initiated with wide-ranging terms of reference covering the organisation and structure of the CPS with a view to enhancing the efficient prosecution of crime within existing resources. Specific questions were re-examined in connection with falling conviction rates, downgrading of charges and CPS relations with the police. The report, in 1998, recommended the boundary and administrative reforms outlined above.

Once an accused person has been charged or summoned the papers are forwarded to the appropriate branch of the CPS which deals with cases from the police station where the offence originates. On receipt of these papers the CPS is under a duty to review the case in accordance with two criteria involved in the decision to prosecute. These two criteria, which will be discussed in detail below, are (a) that there is sufficient evidence to continue the case and (b) that it is in the public interest to continue.

When the accused is brought to the magistrates' court in custody, the CPS normally receive the papers on the morning of the first hearing and are expected to represent the prosecution on adjournments and applications for bail. Once papers are received the CPS is entirely responsible for the conduct of the case. This includes deciding which charges should be proceeded with, what evidence is relevant and admissible and whether or not it is sufficient – in effect whether there is a reasonable prospect of success. It also includes assessing whether or not it is in the public interest to continue with the prosecution and, if so, ensuring that the case is prepared and ready for trial.

By 1998, as mentioned above, the CPS were waiting to implement the range of reform proposals emanating from the new Labour Government, incorporating the ideas from the Glidewell Review (1997–98) and the Narey report on the *Review of Delay in the Criminal Justice System* (Home Office 1997c). The Narey report made sweeping recommendations for all stages of the criminal justice system and may reflect a more systems-based approach to criminal justice involving greater co-operation and liaison between agencies (see Chapter 11). The recommendations affecting the CPS included:

- An enhanced role for CPS staff without legal qualifications to review files and to present non-contested cases in the magistrates' courts.

- An end to the discontinuance of cases on the public interest ground that they consider the case as not serious.

- Greater local autonomy.

- Closer co-operation with the police on the preparation of prosecution files to reduce delay. This includes a permanent CPS presence in police administrative support units with the aim of prosecuting, as soon as possible after the charge, those cases where a guilty plea is likely.

- Closer liaison with the courts and improved communications between the CPS and the magistrates' courts through daily telephone contacts on hearings listed for the next day.

The use of non-legal staff to take over some of the duties of legally qualified staff was enacted in the Crime and Disorder Act 1998. It allowed non-lawyers to review cases with regard to decisions whether to continue prosecution and also allowed a right of audience to present criminal proceedings in magistrates' courts, although they are not allowed to represent the prosecution at the trial stage. They will therefore have the right to conduct much more of the pre-trial stages in the magistrates' court such as hearings regarding bail. The Act defines the trial as starting at the stage when the plea is taken. However, it may be that structural changes are not the only ones in prospect: before their election the Labour party were proposing a District Attorney style prosecutor. This would involve greater local contact but without the direct democratic accountability that is achieved in the USA by the election of a District Attorney. The idea is to raise the local profile of the Chief Crown Prosecutor so that he or she becomes 'a named and known' individual.

The Code for Crown Prosecutors

The Code for Crown Prosecutors is a public statement of the guidelines to be applied to the decision on whether to prosecute an offender or not. In June 1994 the code was revised to simplify and clarify it. Two statements explain the CPS approach.

> One of the most important tasks of the CPS is its review function. This means that we consider the evidence supplied by the police, and any other relevant information, and make a decision . . . in accordance with . . . the Code. . . . At all times, we exercise an independent judgement about the case presented, on the basis of the tests set out in the Code . . .
>
> The decision to prosecute . . . is a serious step. Fair and effective prosecution is essential to the maintenance of law and order . . . a prosecution has serious implications for all involved – the victim, a witness and a defendant. The Crown Prosecution Service applies the Code . . . so that it can make fair and consistent decisions about prosecutions.
>
> (CPS *Annual Report 1993/4*; p. 6)

The code is the cornerstone of the CPS's review and decision-making role and embodies the values and principles of the CPS. It was issued under s. 10 of the Prosecution of Offences Act 1985 and reissued after a review in June 1994. It restates general principles concerning the fairness, objectivity and independence of the CPS, and gives guidance about their approach to cautions, charges, mode of trial and the acceptance of guilty pleas. The bulk of the code is concerned with the two tests involved in the decision to prosecute; the evidential sufficiency and the public interest test.

The evidential sufficiency test is applied first; if the case does not pass this test, no matter how serious, important, or publicly notorious, it will not go ahead. Only if the case passes the evidence test will the second test, public interest, be applied.

The purpose of the evidential test is twofold. First, on a financial and practical basis, there is no point in proceeding with a case which will inevitably be 'thrown out' by the court because there is not enough evidence. To proceed in such cases would be very wasteful of limited resources. Secondly, it follows the general principle underpinning the whole criminal justice system, that people should not be put at risk on insufficient evidence, and that the duty of providing sufficient evidence is always on the prosecution. Some might argue that in certain cases the high public interest in a prosecution – even if it is doomed to failure – overrides the lack of evidence: that it is important to air the matter, even the lack of evidence, in the public domain.

Evidential test

The CPS must be satisfied that there is a realistic prospect of conviction on the available evidence. The test must be applied in respect of each defendant and each charge. A realistic prospect of conviction means that – in the view of the CPS – the magistrates or jury, properly advised on the law, are more likely than not to convict. This involves considering the availability, admissibility and reliability of evidence. In reaching a view, the CPS must consider whether any of the available evidence:

- would be inadmissible as hearsay: if leave to admit evidence would be required, is it likely to be given?

- is likely to be excluded by the judge because it has been illegally obtained – for example, by breaches of PACE and its codes

- is confession evidence likely to be excluded because of a breach of s. 76 PACE, where the confession has been obtained by improper means

- emanates from witnesses who are legally incompetent (cannot give evidence); are unwilling and cannot be compelled to give evidence; or who are children to whom special rules and considerations apply.

In considering reliability the CPS will consider:

- the defendant's age, understanding and intelligence
- whether the witness has a motive to lie or 'adapt' his or her evidence
- whether the witness has a relevant previous conviction
- if identification evidence is involved, whether the evidence is strong enough, bearing in mind the special difficulties with identification evidence.

Public interest test

This refers to criteria by which the CPS may, even after satisfying the evidential sufficiency criteria, decide not to proceed with a case. The use of the phrase public interest is somewhat misleading as what is deemed to be in the public interest involves no consultation with the public, but relates to notional standards encompassing concepts of 'fair play', whether a prosecution is 'worth while' and so on. Why this was called a public interest criteria is difficult to discern. Until the revised Code for Crown Prosecutors (CCP) was published in June 1994, the criteria indicated a series of points which favoured dropping the case against a defendant. The public benefit being to save money. It assumed that only certain cases needed to go forward for the public interest to be served. This assumption generated concern from victims and the public. Lord Shawcross, a former Attorney General is quoted to justify this criteria:

> It has never been the rule in this Country – I hope it never will be – that suspected criminal offences must automatically be the subject of prosecution. Indeed the very first Regulations under which the Director of Public Prosecutions worked provided that he should . . . prosecute 'wherever it appears that the offence or the circumstances

Fig 5.2 Public interest criteria used by the CPS

Factors militating against prosecution
- The likelihood of a small or nominal penalty
- The offence was committed as a result of a genuine mistake
- The loss or harm was minor and the result of a single incident, particularly if caused by misjudgment
- There has been a long delay since the offence – except where the offence is serious; the delay was caused by the defendant; the offence has only just come to light or there has been a long investigation
- A prosecution will adversely affect the *victim's* physical or mental health (having regard to the seriousness of offence)
- The *defendant* is elderly, or at the time of the offence suffering from significant mental or physical illness, unless the offence is serious or there is a possibility of repetition
- The defendant has put right the loss (but defendants should not be seen as 'buying' their way out of prosecution)
- Details could be made public which in the public interest should not be revealed

Factors militating in favour of prosecutions
- The likelihood of a significant sentence
- Use of a weapon or violence threatened
- Offence against a person serving the public (for example, a police officer or nurse)
- Defendant committed the offence in a position of authority or trust
- Defendant was the prime mover in the offence
- Premeditation
- Group offence
- Victim particularly vulnerable, put in fear, or suffered personal attack, damage or disturbance
- Offence motivated by racial, sexual, religious or political discrimination
- Marked difference between ages (real or mental) of defendant and victim or element of corruption
- Defendant has relevant previous convictions
- Commission of offence whilst subject to court order
- Likelihood of repetition
- Widespread offence in area

Compiled from CPS *Annual Report 1993/4*: 46.

of its commission is or are of such a character that a prosecution in respect thereof is required in the public interest'. That is still the dominant consideration.

(Shawcross 1951)

In 1994, for the first time, the criteria in the CPS Codes indicated public interest criteria both in favour of and against prosecution. As a general rule more serious cases are less likely to be discontinued but the criteria must be applied in each case. The factors for and against prosecution must be weighed carefully. It is in this context that the greatest discretion lies, and where most concern or confusion is caused. Thus it is stated that the factors for and against prosecution are not exhaustive, must be considered where appropriate and that all factors do not apply in all cases. Prosecutors are specifically expected to consider the interests of the victim, of young offenders, the possibility of a police caution and guidelines for dealing with mentally disordered offenders. The criteria are summarised in Figure 5.2.

The criteria used by the CPS are broadly similar to those used in sentencing. In other words, the offences which will be perceived as less serious by a court, thus attracting the lowest sentence, are unikely to be prosecuted at all. This may have a number of implications for the criminal justice system. First, the 'bottom layer' of offences will be removed with the possible consequent down-grading of remaining incidents. Secondly, the CPS are applying a quasi-judicial function 'second-guessing' possible sentences. Thirdly, the public interest in the denunciatory effect of bringing a range of offences to court is weakened.

The code also sets out guidelines in relation to what charges should be made – for example which offences a defendant should be charged with. This can on occasion cause disquiet, where, for example, it appears that a defendant is being charged with a lesser offence than that merited by the facts of the incident. Charges should therefore be chosen, according to the code, to reflect the seriousness of the offence, and to enable the case to be presented in a straight-forward way.

In August 1994, the first charging standards were published, resulting from co-operation between the CPS and police to encourage consistency and understanding between the two agencies and those dealing with the courts. The first standards related to an area where most confusion and inconsistency is likely – that of assaults:

- Common assault will be the appropriate charge where the injuries include no more than grazes, scratches, abrasions, bruises, swellings, 'black eye', or superficial cuts.

- Assault occasioning actual bodily harm (ABH) will be appropriate where there is loss of, or a broken tooth, temporary loss of sensory functions, extensive bruising, displaced broken nose, minor fractures, minor cuts, or psychiatric injury more than fear.

- Examples of grievous bodily harm (GBH) are injury resulting in broken limbs, permanent disability, or more than minor, permanent visible disfigurement.

It should be emphasised that these charging standards are statements of prosecution practice, and the aim of publishing them is to foster a greater consistency of approach between agencies and areas. By 1998 further charging standards had been issued in relation to driving and public order offences.

The work of the Crown Prosecution Service

The following data shows the workload for the CPS in 1996/7 in the magistrates' courts and the Crown Court. The information from the CPS *Annual Report 1996/7* shows the number of cases continued and discontinued, the cases completed by a guilty plea or conviction or acquittal after trial in the magistrates' courts and the Crown Court.

Total CPS caseload and discontinuance 1996/7

- 1,330,317 magistrates' court cases were dealt with
- 154,391 (12.1 per cent) were discontinued
- 114,540 Crown Court cases were dealt with.

Cases completed in the magistrates' courts in 1996/7

902,536 CPS hearings were completed in the magistrates' courts in 1996/7 as follows (figures exclude committals, cases discontinued and other withdrawals):

- 734,229 (81.4 per cent) by guilty plea
- 97,145 (10.8 per cent) by proof in the absence of the defendant (which is done without a trial after the prosecution has presented the evidence)
- 53,393 (5.9 per cent) by conviction after a trial
- 17,769 (2 per cent) by dismissal (defendant found not guilty after a summary trial).

Cases completed in the Crown Court in 1996/7

94,371 cases were committed for trial and completed in the Crown Court in 1996/7 as follows:

- 76,936 (81.5 per cent) by guilty plea or trial
- 6,364 (6.7 per cent) by acquittal after a trial (found not guilty)
- 1,648 (1.7 per cent) by judge directed acquittal
- 1,130 (1.2 per cent) by bind over
- 6, 626 (7 per cent) were not proceeded with
- 1,167 (1.8 per cent) by disposal in some other way.

In assessing the effectiveness or otherwise of the CPS we need to consider their working relationships with the police. As we have seen, the police also consider the sufficiency of evidence and make decisions on whether to take any further action or to caution. In theory therefore the police should initially have sifted out cases which do not merit prosecution. Therefore, as Ashworth points out in relation to discontinuances on public interest grounds, these could either be interpreted as 'police failures' or 'CPS successes' (Ashworth 1994a: 182).

Thus to understand the developing relationship between the police, CPS and the courts we must recognise that:

prosecution decisions are taken not in a laboratory atmosphere but in a working context that brings the CPS into contact with the police, with victims, and with magistrates . . . any attempt to explain practical decision making must take account of the organisational and operational contexts in which the decisions tend to be made.

(Ashworth 1994a: 193)

It is apparent, that while the CPS is independent of the police, they are reliant on police information. And, given that the police have already sifted out cases, the CPS may have a tendency to assume that cases passed to them merit prosecution. In addition, developing working relationships and shared assumptions about which cases should be prosecuted may result in a reluctance on the part of the CPS to go against police advice, thus reducing discontinuance rates. Some research conducted in the early days of the CPS was critical of this tendency, and pointed out that the police tended to provide information which would support their decision to prosecute (Leng et al 1992).

In addition, the evidential sufficiency criteria essentially asks the CPS to predict the likely outcome of a case. This may change, however, as a case proceeds as vital witnesses may refuse to give evidence, or new evidence may come to light. The CPS does not know in advance what the defence is likely to be except in the Crown Court. Weak evidence may not, however, lead to a case being dropped, especially where defendants indicate at an early stage that they intend to plead guilty. Thus the CPS may feel that a weak case is worth proceeding with and one writer comments that 'it is the experience of prosecutors that weak cases commonly produce a guilty plea' (Leng et al 1992: 136). Other factors such as the attitude of local courts may also affect prosecution decisions in that prosecutors may second guess the likely attitude of the courts. This can produce local variations. The local CPS also build up working relationships with the local police, who in turn may come to anticipate the decision of the prosecutor. Figures on discontinuances therefore may reflect the operation of these informal factors. The statistics on the number of cases that are dropped or subsequently acquitted could be taken to indicate a failure of the review process. But the reasons why cases are dropped may not, as seen above, be evident at the start of a case, and may only emerge during the trial.

Rising numbers of cases discontinued in the early 1990s raised questions about the benefits of prosecution and diversion. In 1993, for example, a total of 193,000 cases were discontinued. If these figures are taken alongside the large numbers of cautions and the under-reporting of crime it means that fewer and fewer cases are being taken to court. This could be seen as reducing any deterrent, denunciatory or crime control potential of the criminal justice system. In addition, defendants who are repeatedly asked to attend court and then told that the case has been dropped may have a valid grievance: not least those who wished to clear their name positively in court. Such defendants do have the right to seek repayment of costs incurred by them

Fig 5.3 Results of CPS Discontinuance Survey (November 1993)

Insufficient evidence (43%)
- 11% of the cases discontinued related to insufficient evidence about the identity of the accused. For example, a witness identified a man she said she had seen committing a burglary, but she had seen him in poor lighting and had not had a good view of him. There was no other evidence to link the man with the offence.
- 13% of the cases dropped due to insufficient evidence were dropped because there was a legal element missing. For example, a defendant was charged with theft of a car radio cassette even though there was no evidence that it was stolen property.
- 19% of the cases there was an essential legal element missing

Prosecution unable to proceed (17%)
- 13% were because of a missing witness
- 2% related to offences already taken into consideration
- 2% case not ready and adjournments refused

Defendants produced driving documents in court for the first time (9%)

Public interest (31%)
- 9% were convicted or sentenced on other matters
- 6% a nominal penalty was anticipated
- 4% staleness
- 3% complainants' attitude
- 2% defendant's age
- 1% defendant mentally ill
- 6% other

Compiled from CPS *Annual Report 1993/4*: 15–16.

– for many this, combined with the relief of having the case dropped, is sufficient. For others there remains a lingering grievance against 'the system'.

On the other hand, many cases are dropped in accordance with the criteria, because of a 'missing legal element', which indicates that they should never have been commenced at all (see Figure 5.3). As we have seen, official policy has encouraged diversion, and it is clearly stated that it is not in the interests of efficiency or public interest to prosecute all cases. The CPS was indeed intended to reduce the number of weak cases coming to court. Other critics have argued that the CPS does not discontinue enough cases on public interest grounds and is therefore not sufficiently independent of the police (Leng *et al* 1992).

Studies show that the CPS do discontinue cases on public interest grounds as well as on the grounds of evidential insufficiency. This can be seen in a recent survey of discontinued cases carried out by the CPS (Crown Prosecution Service Survey, January 1994) of 11,000 cases in November 1993. Prosecutors across the country were asked to record the reasons for discontinuance under four main headings: insufficient evidence, public interest, prosecution unable to proceed, and defendant producing documents in court for the first time. Forty-three per cent of cases dropped or discontinued were through the application of the 'insufficient evidence' criteria and 31 per cent

145

through the application of the 'public interest' criteria. Forty-one per cent of all cases discontinued during the month of the survey were minor motoring offences. Figure 5.3 summarises the main reasons why cases were discontinued.

The most common single factor leading to discontinuance on public interest grounds was that the defendant had been convicted or sentenced for other offences, and in a further 6 per cent the court was expected to impose only a nominal penalty, such as an absolute discharge. An example of staleness was a case where a defendant was summoned for having no driving licence, test certificate or insurance. The CPS did not receive the papers until almost 33 months after the offences were committed. Examples of discontinuance using other criteria include that of a woman charged with being drunk and disorderly and subsequently admitted to a psychiatric hospital. Consistent with the spirit of the Home Office Circular on Provision for Mentally Disordered Offenders the CPS decided that the wider public interest did not demand a prosecution. In another case, an 82-year-old motorist collided with a parked car without causing injury. The motorist surrendered his licence to the Driver and Vehicle Licensing Agency so the CPS decided that it was no longer necessary to prosecute.

Other cases are not proceeded with or fail because of the non-attendance of witnesses. William and Valerie Wicks were jailed in November 1994 for four weeks for contempt of court after refusing to give evidence against a person charged with causing grievous bodily harm to Mr Wicks. The attack on Mr Wicks was witnessed by his wife. (*The Daily Telegraph*, 19 November 1994: 6). In another case an expert witness went on holiday instead of giving evidence at a rape trial. The defendant was acquitted, and Dr Kusum Agrawal (the police doctor involved) was fined £3,000 by an Old Bailey judge (*The Times*, 21 January 1995: 8).

A final issue to be raised is what role victims can or should play in the prosecution process. Recent attention to the victim in the criminal justice process lay behind the criteria that victims' interests should play a part. But to what extent does this conflict with other criterion? What, if any role, should victims play? If the victim does not wish to proceed with a case, and is unwilling to give evidence, then the prosecution may be unsuccessful. Thus the victim's role in the provision of evidence may be crucial, as in the Wicks case referred to above. In addition, as with cautions, a failure to prosecute may deprive the victim of compensation, although some diversionary schemes provide for mediation between victim and offender (see Chapter 11). Any further role for the victim is problematic as it could be argued that to take the victim's attitude into account might conflict with any public interest there may be in prosecuting the offender to ensure that they are duly punished.

Prosecution by regulatory agencies

While the CPS is responsible for the majority of prosecutions, many other agencies also undertake criminal prosecutions. These include local authority departments responsible for consumer protection and environmental health, the Health and Safety Executive, and agencies responsible for pollution. The RSPCA may prosecute those accused of neglecting or mistreating animals. Taxation matters are the responsibility of the Customs and Excise and Inland Revenue departments, and many more government departments are responsible for investigating frauds and other offences involving business, trade and financial services. These include the Serious Fraud Office and the Department of Trade and Industry. It was seen in Chapter 3 that many of these offences are not included in the criminal statistics, and statistics on how many offences are prosecuted in relation to known offences are not generally available. Research into these agencies, however, indicates that they prosecute only a very small proportion of known offenders. It has already been seen that they use the caution extensively and prosecution is often seen as a last resort (see, for example, Croall 1992).

It is interesting to examine briefly how these agencies proceed, as their attitude to prosecution is very different. In his study of the origins of the factory inspectorate, established by the Factory Act 1833, which regulated the labour of children and young persons in mills and factories, W G Carson made the following observation:

> We . . . need to understand the social origins of an enforcement agency which, from its very inception, has not seen itself as being busy about the business of catching criminals. In adopting this historically explicable stance, the Factory Inspectorate has played its own inadvertent part in perpetuating a collective representation which portrays crime as being concentrated in circumscribed and morally peripheral segments of the community.
>
> (Carson 1974: 138)

Different attitudes to prosecution are strongly related to the perceived role and function of these agencies. Many see themselves not as industrial police officers with a primary duty to prosecute the guilty, but as agencies responsible for improving standards of business, trade or commerce by ensuring that businesses comply with regulations. Securing compliance is therefore seen as their primary aim, and prosecution is only one of many tools to achieve this. Therefore they tend to pursue what are often described as compliance strategies, which can be compared with a prosecution strategy (see, for example, Hawkins 1984; Croall 1992). Under a compliance strategy, the prevention of offences is seen as paramount, with education, advice and persuasion being seen as preferable to prosecution. Prosecution is likely to be seen by many agencies as costly and counter-productive, as it may lead to poor relationships between agencies and businesses.

Cost-effectiveness underlies many of these strategies. In many areas prosecution involves high costs. Many offences in the world of business and finance are very complex, and investigation may involve gathering enormous amounts of evidence and interviewing many witnesses. Fraud trials for example can be lengthy and involve extremely complex evidence. The cost to

147

the taxpayer, for example, of the first series of trials in the celebrated *Guinness* case was estimated at around £3 million (Croall 1992). Fraud trials are also seen as risky – the chances of conviction may be lessened by the complexity of the case and the ability of defendants to contest it. If there is a chance for the matter to be resolved without trial an out-of-court settlement becomes an attractive prospect. For local authority departments, if a prosecution is unsuccessful, they may have to bear the costs of prosecution themselves, thus reducing the resources they have for investigation.

In addition, many agencies have options other than doing nothing, cautioning and prosecuting. Some, like environmental health departments, may be able to grant or withhold licences from offending businesses, thus effectively threatening their viability. Others, like the Inland Revenue, can impose sanctions or fines without taking offenders to court. Yet others can disqualify those who need licences to operate, such as financial service employees. Many would argue that these powers constitute a greater deterrent than prosecution which may be followed by only a small fine.

Prosecution may only result if compliance is not forthcoming after a series of other measures. A prosecution may therefore reflect enforcers' attitudes that defendants are more blameworthy and deserve prosecution. In addition, the threat of prosecution may be used as a bargaining counter in persuading offenders to comply (Hawkins 1984). In some cases however these considerations can be overridden where for example there has been considerable public interest in a case and where prosecution may be considered necessary given the seriousness of the case. This may happen following major incidents in which there has been large scale pollution or where members of the public have been killed or injured.

A number of issues are raised by this brief outline of regulatory enforcement. While there may be considerable concern over high rates of discontinuances by the CPS, little public outcry is aroused by the low rates of prosecutions of many business offenders. This may be because as seen in Chapter 2, these offences are not so readily regarded as crime. Nonetheless it could be argued that there is little equity in the treatment of different groups of offenders and that these differences amount to class bias, in that the CPS is likely to be dealing with primarily lower-class offenders, and regulatory agencies with primarily middle-class offenders (Sanders 1985). It also raises the question of the extent to which some offenders resolve matters, by negotiating an out of court settlement and indicating their intention to defend the case, and so effectively avoid prosecution.

Another issue of interest is the role of the prosecution agency. Regulatory agencies play a major diversionary role, and in addition some have powers to sanction offenders. Some argue that this means that justice is being done in private rather than in a public hearing. To others, these powers represent an important and cost-effective means of diverting offenders from the full process of trial and conviction and there have been suggestions that prosecution agencies such as the CPS should have similar powers. In Scotland, for example, there is a system known as the Prosecutor Fine, which the Royal Commission on Criminal Justice 1993 has recommended should be considered in England and Wales.

JUVENILE JUSTICE

The introduction to the Audit Commission's report *Misspent Youth* states:

> A disproportionate amount of crime is committed by young people, especially young males. In 1994, two out of every five known offenders were under the age of 21, and a quarter were under 18 . . . offenders under the age of 18 commit about seven million offences a year against individuals, retailers and manufacturers.
>
> (Audit Commission 1996: 5–6)

The report also estimates that for every 100 crimes committed by young offenders in 1994, 1.8 per cent result in a caution and 1.3 per cent in a summons or charge (Audit Commission 1996: 14). Within the criminal justice system the response to younger offenders is determined by special laws, procedure and philosophies. Young offenders are among those for whom cautioning and diversionary policies have been seen as most appropriate. The law also makes provision for different treatment for children and young persons, reflecting differences in the degree to which young offenders can be held responsible for their own actions. Cases against children and young persons are held in a special court, the youth court, and sentencing options are also different for children, young offenders and young adult offenders. This section will look, firstly, at the different legal arrangements regarding the culpability of younger offenders and the current system for dealing with them.

Age and criminal responsibility

The law distinguishes between different age groups in an effort to recognise differences in maturity and understanding. Section 107 of the Children and Young Persons Act 1933 (CYPA) defines:

- a child as a person under the age of 14
- a young person as someone who has attained the age of 14 and is under 18

and 'a young adult', not defined by statute, is a term used to describe those aged 18 to 20.

Children under 10 years of age are deemed by the law to be incapable of telling right from wrong and therefore incapable of doing wrong – in legal terms *doli incapax*. As they are not regarded as responsible they cannot be put on trial, punished or regarded in law as blameworthy. In a trial at the Old Bailey in January 1998, described later in this chapter, two 10-year-old boys were accused of rape in a West London school. A third boy was not prosecuted because he was 9 years old at the time of the offence. Until 1998, the prosecution could not start a case against a child aged between 10 and 14 until it had shown that the child knew the difference between right and wrong. This presumption of *doli incapax* for this age group was abolished in the Crime and Disorder Act 1998. The age at which children are regarded as responsible for their actions in law varies across Europe such that in Cyprus, Ireland and Switzerland it is 7, and in Scandinavian countries it is 15. Apart from legal liability for a crime, the age of an offender will also affect where and how the young person is dealt with in the criminal justice system.

Welfare or punishment

It has been accepted for many years that special procedures are needed to deal with young offenders, and a series of different arrangements have developed. These reflect conflicting views over how such offenders should be dealt with. In general, two broad approaches can be contrasted. On the one hand, what is often described as a welfare approach seeks to protect children and young persons from the potential stigma of a criminal prosecution and encourages courts to take the welfare of the child or young person into account at all stages. Under this approach, diversion is encouraged and prosecution should be a last resort, and when taken to court, special procedures should protect young people from the harshness of a criminal trial and ensuing punishment. The rehabilitative approach was of particular relevance for young offenders who were seen to be potentially more likely to respond to measures involving help, treatment, discipline and education. On the other hand, many of these measures have been criticised as ineffective, too soft, or as insufficiently deterrent or punitive, and have attracted recurrent calls for tougher measures.

The range of measures therefore has tended to reflect a mixture of approaches, and recent very serious incidents involving young offenders have renewed these conflicts. When the toddler James Bulger was abducted and murdered in Liverpool by two children in 1993, a shocked public was exposed to the views of the experts, whose opinions ranged from the call for more treatment to the demand for the punishment of the offenders. In January 1998 an Old Bailey rape trial involved two 10-year-old defendants who were eventually acquitted of raping a 9-year-old victim. The prosecution and trial of these boys highlighted concern and horror at the serious allegations, together with concerns over the way that such young defendants should be tried. Great efforts were made to make the courtroom less intimidating. A report in *The Times* described the scene:

Court 12 at the Old Bailey has been transformed like a stage set into a modern primary school classroom. The only thing missing is a sandpit, a lump of Play-doh or a large frieze showing the letters of the alphabet. . . . Four square tables have been arranged in the middle of the room . . . just as at school. The four barristers have dispensed with their wigs.

(*The Times*, 16 January 1998: 1)

In addition, as was seen in Chapter 1, the Criminal Justice and Public Order Act 1994 was introduced amidst concerns about increasing rates of offending by the young and introduced a number of tougher measures. Publicity given to cases where young offenders have been sent to holiday camps or abroad as part of their sentences attracted criticisms that offending youngsters should not be given advantages not enjoyed by their law-abiding counterparts.

Special provision for juveniles

Before the nineteenth century juvenile offenders were treated in the same way as adults and could be sent to adult prisons, hanged or transported. Throughout the nineteenth century, however, there was a gradual development of measures specifically directed at young offenders, influenced by arguments that juveniles could be 'saved' and rehabilitated. This led to the development of special institutions such as reformatories, whose very name indicated an emphasis on reform through education and training. Reformatories catered for those with criminal convictions and the industrial schools for children in need of care as manifested by truancy, vagrancy or were in the care of adults with criminal or drunken habits. They were established by the Reformatory Schools Act 1854. At this time a separate prison for boys was opened at Parkhurst on the Isle of Wight.

The Children Act 1908 set up the juvenile court and formally separated cases involving juveniles from adult courts. It also abolished the use of imprisonment for juveniles. A mixture of welfare and punitive philosophies can be seen in the comment of the minister responsible for introducing this Act, Herbert Samuel, who stated that the 'courts should be the agencies for the rescue as well as the punishment of juveniles' (cited in Gelsthorpe and Morris 1994: 951). Other institutions for juveniles also reflected a welfare and punishment approach – special institutions were set up as part of the prison system, the first being in Borstal in Kent. The Borstal system, as it came to be known, emphasised a mixture of discipline and training. Some Borstals stressed education, being strongly imbued with the values and traditions of English public school education, and later some adopted a therapeutic approach (see, for example, Hood 1965).

Further moves towards a more welfare-based approach included the Children and Young Persons Act 1933 which established a special panel of magistrates to deal with juvenile offenders and stipulated that the court should have regard to the welfare of the child. In addition the court could act in the place of parents, *in loco parentis*, and take such steps as necessary to ensure that the welfare of the child was being met (see, for example, Gelsthorpe and Morris 1994). Approved schools, established in 1933, were residential schools for primarily delinquent boys and girls. They included naval and agricultural colleges and were mainly run by charitable groups or local authorities. They had to be approved by the Home Office. They were later abolished by the Children and Young Persons Act 1969. In 1948 local authorities were enabled to take into care children considered to be 'in need of care and protection'. The same year, however, saw the introduction of detention centres and attendance centres which reflected a more punitive approach (Morris and Giller 1987). Detention centres were institutions in which young offenders could be sentenced to a short period of custody, in a regime intended to be tough and disciplinary. Much emphasis was laid on physical education although there were also elements of education and training. Attendance centre orders required juveniles to attend a centre, run mainly by the police, for a number of hours per week, often on a Saturday afternoon. They aimed to deprive delinquents of their leisure time and were often used in an attempt to take football hooligans off the terraces. Discipline was a key feature of early attendance centres which mixed elements of physical education with more practical pursuits.

Diversion

The argument that there is little point in punishing juveniles whose delinquency may be related to family or other problems continued to influence policy. Some went so far as to suggest that juveniles should be removed from the criminal justice system entirely, and dealt with by a family council or tribunal which would deal with all children with family or social problems. These proposals were resisted. However, such ideas strongly affected the next important piece of legislation dealing with young offenders, the Children and Young Persons Act 1969 (CYPA 1969). This Act, often seen as representing the peak of the welfare approach, was based on a mixture of welfare and diversionary policies and made several radical and controversial changes (Morris and Giller 1987).

The benefits of diversionary policies were stressed and it was proposed that all offenders under 14 should be dealt with by care and protection proceedings rather than by criminal proceedings. The police were encouraged to use cautions for juvenile offenders and only refer them to court following consultation with the social services. The expanding role of the social worker was also reflected in provisions for care orders, which, after being given by magistrates, were to be implemented by social workers. Social workers rather than magistrates, therefore, would make the key decision as to whether the young person would be sent to a residential institution or left at home. Community homes, which were to house all children in care whether or not they had committed an offence, replaced the approved schools which dealt only with delinquents. It was also intended to phase out Borstals and detention centres and to replace them with a sentence of intermediate treatment – again run by social services.

In the event, many sections of the CYPA 1969 were never implemented and it attracted considerable controversy and opposition among observers of and practitioners involved in the system. Magistrates, for example, felt that too much power had been lost to social workers and that they were powerless to determine what might happen to an offender. Rising rates of juvenile crime attracted criticisms that the system was too soft and was unable to cope with serious juvenile offenders.

Diversion increased in the years following the CYPA 1969 with an enormous rise in numbers cautioned by the Juvenile Liaison Bureaux set up by the police. In the 1980s there was a growing recognition of the limitations of custodial or institutional treatment. Not only was such treatment costly – with detention in some institutions costing more than boarding schools – but the vast majority of juveniles coming out of such institutions went on to reoffend. Recidivism rates for detention centres, for example, were as high as 80 per cent. Many also argued that institutions for juveniles acted like schools of crime where offenders perpetuated a delinquent or criminal subculture. Concern was also aroused by evidence of violence and bullying within institutions. Treatment in the community therefore was seen as being preferable and as no less effective in terms of reconviction rates.

The CJA 1982 introduced criteria to restrict the use of care and custodial orders and requirements for juveniles to be legally represented. Custodial orders were only to be made in cases where it could be established that the offender had failed to respond to non-custodial measures, where a custodial sentence was seen as necessary for the protection of the public or where the offence was serious. Borstals were abolished, removing any element of indeterminacy from the system. Until then offenders had been sentenced to a period of Borstal training, with the date of release of up to 3 years to be decided by those running the system. Borstal was replaced by a fixed-term youth custody order and the Act also abolished the use of imprisonment for offenders under the age of 21. New sentences were then introduced and abolished with bewildering speed. From 1983 a determinate sentence of youth custody was introduced for offenders aged 15 and under 21, with a maximum sentence for those aged under 17 of 12 months (raised to two years in 1994). A sentence of custody for life was introduced as the equivalent to life imprisonment when the offender was aged 17 and under 21. Detention sentence orders for males were changed so that the usual sentence ranged from 21 days to 4 months instead of 3 to 6 months. The CJA 1988 abolished the detention sentence order and youth custody. The new term for youth custody was to be detention in a young offender institution.

Diversionary policies continued throughout the 1980s with a series of Home Office circulars stressing that prosecution should be used as a last resort for young offenders. There was also encouragement for the greater use of informal warnings instead of cautioning to avoid net widening (Gelsthorpe and Morris 1994). The use of cautions for second and third offences was encouraged along with the development in some areas of caution plus schemes, which incorporate a caution with some form of supervised activity in the community.

Since the 1970s diversion policies have worked to keep children (10–13), young people (14–17) and young adults (18–20) out of the courts and out of custodial institutions during a period when crime was rising steadily. If we examine the period from 1975 to 1995 we can see this. Figure 5.4 shows the total number of male children in the criminal justice system between 1975 and 1995, and the total that were either cautioned or sentenced by the court and the type of sentence given. Figure 5.5 shows the same information for young people and young adults aged 14 to 20. For younger male offenders there has been a steady decline in the numbers being processed and sentenced and an increase in the use of cautioning. The use of fines and custody has fallen over the 20-year period. Figure 5.6 is taken from the Audit Commission report and shows the proportion of the age group 10–17 sentenced to a custodial sentence. The chance of receiving a custodial sentence fell in the 10-year period 1984–94 from a rate of over 2 per 1,000 of the age group to less than one. The demographic decline in the number of young people in the population during these years does not explain the considerable reduction in the use of custody in this age group.

Criticisms of diversion

By 1990 a new mood had set in and disillusionment with diversionary and welfare approaches to young offenders. This reflected a growing concern about a number of related issues about the control of delinquent behaviour. Criticism focused on the reluctance of the system to respond to younger offenders, the type of sentences given by the courts, the lack of control and the leniency of the treatment of delinquents. There was a view that the system had moved too far in the direction of concern for the welfare of the young offender. It was felt that the wish to avoid labelling young offenders had resulted in a diversionary approach where youngsters felt they could get away with most things and that the public was not being protected from dangerous or persistent young criminals.

Newspaper references to lack of action and derisory sentences illustrate the frustrations with the youth justice system. Referring to a case of a 17 year old sentenced by the Inner London Youth Court, the crime correspondent of *The Times*, Stewart Tender, wrote, 'A London court's decision to fine a teenager £1.60 for going equipped to break into a new BMW has left police furious

Fig 5.4 Children in the criminal justice system 1975–95. Males aged 10–13

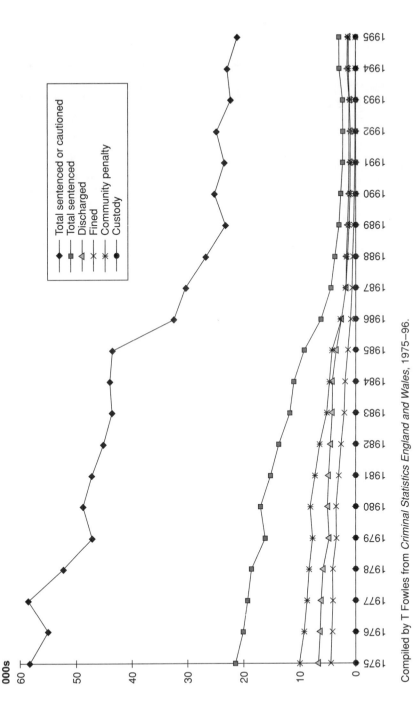

Compiled by T Fowles from *Criminal Statistics England and Wales*, 1975–96.

Fig 5.5 Young people and young adults in the criminal justice system 1975–95. Males aged 14–20

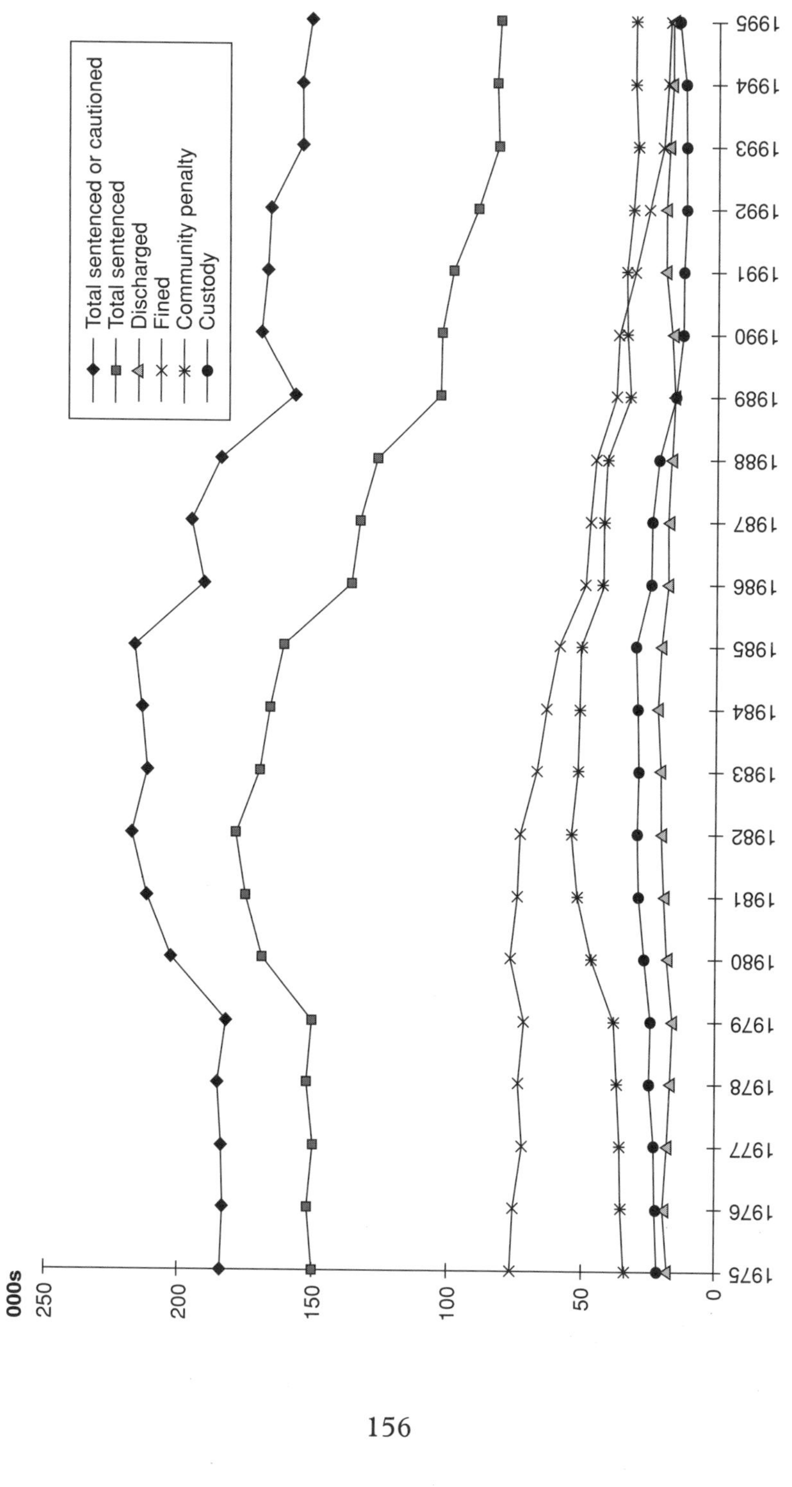
000s
250
200
150
100
50
0
1975
1976
1977
1978
1979
1980
1981
1982
1983
1984
1985
1986
1987
1988
1989
1990
1991
1992
1993
1994
1995
Total sentenced or cautioned
Total sentenced
Discharged
Fined
Community penalty
Custody

Compiled by T Fowles from *Criminal Statistics England and Wales*, 1975–96.

Fig 5.6 Males and females under 18 sentenced to immediate custody per 1,000 population of the age group

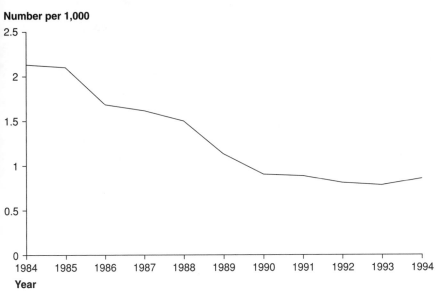

Number per 1,000

Source: Audit Commission (1996) *Misspent Youth*, p. 43.

after a case that involved six witnesses. . . . The teenager, with 22 previous convictions or findings of guilt, was on bail at the time of the offence' (*The Times*, 1 May 1993: 2). The frustration caused by persistent offending is evident in the statements released by the police in the West Midlands. Chief Superintendent John Jasper spoke to the press about his difficulties with a boy of 13 'who had committed more than 200 thefts and been arrested 50 times in five months. After various court appearances he was still in the care of social services who were powerless to control him . . . the boy remained above the law' (*The Times*, 9 September 1993: 2). From Havant in Hampshire another story of repeat offending was reported in the press: 'A gang of 5 youths has committed 228 offences between them. . . . The ringleader, whose list of crimes include 14 counts of theft, five of joint theft and two of burglary . . . has usually escaped with conditional discharges, supervision orders and attendance centre orders . . . he was sentenced to two months in a young offender institute. He served four weeks after being convicted of a public order offence, four counts of theft, affray and two counts of joint theft' (*The Daily Telegraph*, 28 May 1996: 10).

Another source of frustration concerns the lack of secure facilities to hold such offenders. In Cardiff, the police described their frustration at the situation where 'A boy of 14 who has been charged with more than 150 burglaries, drug offences and car thefts . . . was bailed by magistrates . . . for the 29th time this year . . . he cannot be sent to a detention centre until he is 15, while the only purpose-built "secure home" in Wales, run by social services and opened in Neath last month, is full' (*Sunday Telegraph*, 15 December 1996: 10).

The lack of facilities is not the only problem, as even where they exist they do not always ensure that the public are protected. A teenager accused of murder escaped while on a swimming trip with a social worker to Crystal Palace sports centre. In April 1996 Cleon Reid, aged 15, was remanded in custody in secure accommodation. He was accused of murdering 75-year-old Ted Howell who was stabbed, and died when he disturbed a burglar. An Old Bailey judge took the unusual step of lifting the restriction on naming him as he believed the 6-foot-tall schoolboy constituted a threat to the public and himself.

In 1997 a trial at the Old Bailey found a gang of seven youths aged between 14 and 17 guilty of the rape of a 33-year-old Austrian tourist. The attack took place by the Grand Union canal at King's Cross, London. After the assault and rape the victim was thrown into the canal even though she said she could not swim. These incidents highlight a number of problems about violent crimes committed by youth who seem to have no moral concern about their actions and who constitute a grave danger to the public. It also reveals a major weakness in the diversionary strategy of what to do with young criminals even after arrest. Six of the seven were on bail for robbery offences at the time of the attack, including the person identified as the gang leader, a 14 year old from Islington who was in the care of the social services at the time. His mother told a newspaper, 'He was out of control. He would go out at night and I wouldn't see him until the next day. In the end I couldn't cope and put him into care around 18 months ago. I blame the social services for this. They should have kept a closer eye on him. They let him run wild' (*Daily Mail*, 19 April 1997: 7).

Developments in the 1990s

During the 1990s both the Conservative Government and the Labour Government elected in 1997 introduced reforms to tackle the concerns raised above.

The Criminal Justice and Public Order Act 1994 introduced a secure training order for persistent offenders who will be held in secure training units. The new sentence is for persistent offenders aged from 12 to 14. If convicted of an imprisonable offence they will be eligible for the order if they have at least three previous convictions and have been convicted while subject to a supervision order. The minimum length of the order is 6 months; the maximum is 2 years. They spend the first half of their order in a secure training unit and the second half being supervised in the community. The Act envisaged that the regimes of the secure training units will provide a minimum of 25 hours a week training and education, tailored to individual needs, and aim to tackle offending behaviour in the context of secure accommodation with high standards of care and discipline.

The Crime (Sentences) Act 1997 extended the use of community sentences for younger offenders and allowed for electronic tagging of 10–15-year-old offenders. A pilot project was established in Norfolk and Manchester in 1998. In November 1997 the Home Office published a white paper, *No More Excuses*, based on the views of the Labour Government that had been elected in May that year and promised a radical overall of the youth justice system. The Crime and Disorder Act 1998 included the following provisions:

- Youth Justice Board for England and Wales, responsible for all secure facilities for young offenders.

- Youth Justice Service: local authorities, police and probation to combine to tackle crime by younger offenders.

- Youth offending teams: must include a probation officer, social worker, police officer, representative of the health authority and the local authority education department.

- Police reprimands and final warnings (see earlier in this chapter).

- Parenting orders: to help parents control their children. Parents will be required to attend counselling and guidance sessions once a week for a period up to 3 months.

- Reparation orders: will be available for younger offenders, which the courts will have to consider if compensation order is not imposed.

- Local child curfew: gives power to the local authority and the police to set up curfew schemes for children under 10. Such that in specified curfew area children under 10 should not be out without supervision late at night.

- Action plan orders: a new kind of community penalty for those aged 10 to 17 that will last 3 months and combine elements of punishment rehabilitation and reparation.

- Detention and training order (DTO): a new custodial disposal for those aged 10–17 years of age. This will replace the sentence of detention in a young offender institution and the secure training order.

The DTO sentence is likely to be ready for implementation in late 1999. It will be used for serious offences and in the case of 10 and 11 year olds for the purpose of protecting the public; for 12–14 year olds the DTO will only be used with respect to persistent offending; and, for 15–17 year olds it would be imposed for offences sufficiently serious to justify custody under CJA 1991. Half the term of a DTO will be spent in custody and the other half under community supervision. Offenders can be detained in a young offender institution, secure training centre, youth treatment centre or local authority secure unit supervised by the Youth Justice Board.

Youth courts

Youth courts were set up by the CJA 1991 and replaced and extended the jurisdiction of the old juvenile courts. They now deal with the majority of offenders aged 10 to 17, although some younger offenders may be dealt with in the Crown Court. The situations in which this occurs are as follows:

- where defendants are charged with homicide (murder or manslaughter) they must be sent to the Crown Court for trial (s. 53(1) CYPA 1933);

- defendants aged from 14 to 17 when charged with other grave crimes – defined as any offence which carries a maximum term of imprisonment of 14 or more years, plus indecent assault on women and dangerous driving – may be sent to the Crown Court for trial when the court of first appearance decides that if convicted, they should be given a longer sentence than the magistrates can give (s. 53(2) CYPA 1933);

- young defendants may be dealt with in an adult court if charged in association with another defendant, aged over 18, when both are to be dealt with in the adult court.

They may also be referred to the Crown Court for sentence. Guidelines from the Court of Appeal indicate that where, in the case of an adult, the sentence for the offence would be 2 or more years' imprisonment, it is appropriate for the youth court to refuse jurisdiction and commit the defendant to the Crown Court for trial.

The youth court has more informal procedures than adult courts, and special rules protect young people from publicity and contact with older defendants. Members of the public are not allowed to be present at a youth court hearing, and although members of the press are allowed to attend, they may not publish any information which can identify a young defendant. The CYPA 1933 empowers the court to restrict any reporting of cases revealing the name, address or school of a defendant or containing any particulars which could lead to the identification of any child or young person concerned in proceedings. This provision applies to witnesses as well as defendants, and may be applied in the adult court. A youth court may not be held in a courtroom that has been used in the preceding hour, or will be used within the next hour, for adult proceedings. This minimises the risk of young people coming into contact with adult offenders or members of the public. Most courts hold youth court hearings on a different day, or in a different part of the building, from the adult court. For defendants under 16 the court must require a parent or guardian to attend also. For those over 16 the court may require the parent or guardian to attend. Where a child or young person is in the care of the local authority, a local authority representative can be required to attend.

In Inner London, magistrates are appointed directly to the Youth Court Panel. In other areas a youth court panel is made up of magistrates especially chosen from the bench because of their special knowledge of, or interest in, young people. Because of this interest many magistrates sit in both the youth court and the Family Proceedings Court which deals with care proceedings. The bench dealing with a youth court hearing will be composed of two or more (usually three) members of the Youth Court Panel. A stipendiary usually sits with lay magistrates. The bench should contain at least one male and one female. A single-sex bench or trial by a stipendiary sitting alone is only permissible in the youth court in emergencies, where it is not possible to adjourn.

Magistrates have a wide discretion in the youth court but are guided by s. 44 CYPA 1933 which states that every court shall have regard for the welfare of the child or young person and, where proper, take steps to remove him or her from undesirable surroundings and ensure that adequate provision is made for training and education.

Sentencing in the youth court

Before sentence is passed, the offender, either individually, or through a lawyer, parent or guardian must be allowed to make representations and the court has to consider all available material concerning the offender, his or her background, education and medical history. It is usual to have reports from social or probation services, and often a school report.

The sentences applicable to a young offender vary according to the court in which they are being sentenced. Very often, where a conviction is recorded in an adult court, a young offender will be remitted to the youth court for sentence. Like adult offenders, young offenders can be given absolute or conditional discharges and compensation orders. Some special provisions relate to the sentencing of young offenders:

- *Fine.* The maximum fine payable by an offender under the age of 14 is £250, and for an offender aged 14 to 17 is £1,000. Where the offender is under 16 the court is under a duty to order that compensation is paid by the parent or guardian unless they cannot be found and it would unreasonable for them to be ordered to pay. For offenders over 16, magistrates have discretion to make such an order.

- *Parental recognisance.* The court may, with the consent of the parent or guardian, order them to enter into a recognisance to take and exercise proper control of an offender under 16. The parent then promises to pay a specified sum (up to £1,000) if they fail to do so.

- *Attendance centre order.* This sentence is only available for offences punishable with imprisonment in the case of an adult. The offender must not have received previous detention. The attendance centre must be reasonably accessible to the offender. The maximum attendance is 12 hours if

161

the offender is under 14. The maximum is 24 hours for offenders under 16 and 36 hours for offenders of 16 or 17.

- *Supervision order.* This is the equivalent of probation for young offenders and must not be longer than 3 years. An order may impose conditions of residence or intermediate treatment, either at the direction of the court or an appointed supervisor. A night restriction order can also be imposed ordering the supervisee to stay in a specified place for up to 10 hours per night. The restrictions cannot be imposed for more than a total of 30 days and cannot continue over a period longer than 3 months.

- *Community service.* This is available for offenders aged 16 and over, in the same terms as for an adult.

- *Secure training order.* Younger offenders with previous convictions may be sentenced to secure training orders, introduced under the Criminal Justice and Public Order Act 1994. These orders came into effect on 1 March 1998 and may be between 6 months and 2 years. They will be replaced by the DTO.

- *Detention and training order* (DTO). A sentence introduced as a generic custodial sentence for 10–17 year olds by the Crime and Disorder Act 1998. It is to be used for serious offences and in the case of 10 and 11 year olds for the purpose of protecting the public; for 12–14 year olds the DTO will only be used with respect to persistent offending; for 15–17 year olds it will be imposed for offences sufficiently serious to justify custody under the CJA 1991.

- *Action plan order.* A sentence introduced by the Crime and Disorder Act 1998 for 10–17 year olds providing for supervision for 3 months by a probation officer, social worker or member of the youth offending team. Before it is imposed by the courts a report from the local youth offending team will be produced. Following consultation with the young offender a detailed plan of action will be recommended and should be tailored to address the offending behaviour.

- *Detention in a young offender institution* (YOI). Young offenders are not sentenced to imprisonment, but to detention in a young offender institution, which deals with incarcerated offenders between 15 and 21. When the DTOs are implemented 15 to 17 year olds will be given the sentence of DTO rather than detention in a YOI.

As we have seen some young offenders are dealt with in adult courts. When a young person appears for sentence in the Crown Court, the court has similar sentencing options and additionally has powers to impose a sentence of 24 months' detention in a young offender institution – increased by the CJPOA 1994 – and there is a minimum period of incarceration of 21 days for those aged 18 to 21. The Crown Court may also impose longer sentences

162

for grave offences under s. 53 CYPA 1933 of up to the maximum adult sentence for that offence. Life detention during Her Majesty's Pleasure is imposed on offenders aged 10 to 17 convicted of murder. It is not possible to suspend a sentence of detention in a young offender institution.

It can be seen from the above that different notions of responsibility and the desire to divert and rehabilitate young offenders affects the treatment of children and young persons. The final part of this chapter will look at the treatment of another group requiring special consideration, the mentally disordered offender.

MENTALLY DISORDERED OFFENDERS

Like children and young persons, there are strong arguments for diverting mentally disordered offenders from the criminal justice system before trial and before punishment. At the same time, however, mentally disordered offenders may constitute a danger to themselves and others and may arouse fears on the part of the public. In order to protect the public, therefore, it may be seen as necessary to commit them to hospital, or, if this is not possible, to some form of containment, even where their offences are not so serious as to merit a prison sentence. Thus due process may conflict with a protectionist stance which raises issues concerning the rights of mentally disordered offenders.

Our approach to the mentally disordered offender, as it is with the younger offender, is affected by notions of responsibility and liability. The criminal law, as we have seen, depends by and large on the concept of a 'guilty mind' and harm to create criminal liability which provides the justification for intervention and punishment. It is important to recognise that the mental state of the defendant is considered at three stages in the criminal justice process. In the first place, there is the issue of whether someone is culpable for an act committed while they were suffering from some kind of mental disorder. A second question arises in establishing whether a person is mentally fit and able to undergo a trial. Finally, there is an issue as to whether someone who was mentally disordered at the time of the offence, or has subsequently become mentally disordered, can or should be punished.

Responsibility for the offence

The criminal courts do not regard a person as culpable or blameworthy for an offence who is deemed 'not guilty by reason of insanity', or where the court accepts the statutory defence of diminished responsibility, or the state known as automatism is established, as described below:

163

Insanity is governed by the M'Naghten Rules, formulated after the trial in 1843 of Daniel M'Naghten who, suffering from a delusion that he should kill the then prime minister, Sir Robert Peel, killed his secretary by mistake. The rules provide that a defendant is not guilty by reason of insanity if 'he was labouring under a defect of reason because of a disease of the mind so that he did not know the nature and quality of his act, or if he did know it, did not know it was wrong'. If found not guilty by reason of insanity, the court may make a hospital order, a guardianship order, a supervision and treatment order or an absolute discharge. There is a right of appeal against such a verdict.

This definition has caused many difficulties, principally surrounding what is to be counted as a disease of the mind. For example in the case of *Sullivan* in 1984 it was held that a minor epileptic seizure fell within the definition of insanity. In addition, courts have distinguished between defects of reason caused by internal factors such as medical conditions which can only give rise to an insanity defence or verdict and external factors such as a blow to the head or medication which can give rise to a non-insane automatism defence.

Automatism describes a condition where a person is not strictly in control of his or her actions. If a criminal act is not voluntary there is no *actus reus*. Where automatism is caused by something deemed to be a disease of the mind the verdict should be not guilty by reason of insanity. If the automatism is caused by any other reason, for example, an injury, the defendant should be acquitted. As described above, there has been much unease about the line between non-insane and insane automatism, first because of the possible stigma attached and, secondly, because of the consequent disposal.

Diminished responsibility is a special defence to murder and is defined in s. 2 of the Homicide Act 1957, under which a person who kills, or is a party to the killing of another, cannot be convicted of murder if found to be 'suffering from such an abnormality of mind as substantially impaired his mental responsibility for his acts or omissions'. The abnormality in question may arise from arrested or retarded development, an inherent cause or disease or injury. The onus of proving such an abnormality is expressly placed on the defence. Diminished responsibility is only a defence to murder, and if the *actus reus* is established the accused using such a defence will be found guilty of manslaughter instead. Diminished responsibility is therefore a partial defence, which reduces the level of culpability of the defendant and avoids the mandatory life sentence.

Before reaching a trial, defendants may be found unfit to plead. It is inherent in a criminal trial that a defendant is fit to plead – that a defendant knows and understands any charges and is able to instruct a lawyer. A defendant is held to be unfit to plead if he or she is either physically or mentally incapable of instructing legal advisers, following the proceedings or objecting to jurors.

The procedure of establishing fitness to plead is governed by the Criminal Procedure (Insanity) Act 1964 as amended by the Criminal Procedure (Insanity and Unfitness to Plead) Act 1991, which provide that the issue can be addressed by the court at any time up to the beginning of the defence case. Unfitness must be determined on the evidence of two or more doctors. If found unfit, the trial proceeds to establish whether or not the defendant has committed the *actus reus* – this is to avoid a mentally ill person being sentenced without proof of an offence. If the defendant is found fit to plead, the trial is carried on in the normal way, and any issues of mental disorder are raised in defence or mitigation. In cases where defendants are found to be both unfit to plead and have committed the *actus reus*, the court may make a hospital or guardianship order, a supervision order or impose an absolute discharge.

Police and the mentally disordered

In responding to a breach of public order or breach of the peace the police may find they have arrested a mentally disordered person. On other occasions a theft or violent crime may result in the police arresting and detaining someone who is mentally disturbed. In the main they will be taken to the police station. A Home Office Research Study commented, 'Up to two per cent of detainees are treated by the police as mentally disordered or mentally handicapped. In London, the figure may be nearer four per cent. Up to one-third are brought to the police station as a place of safety rather than on suspicion of committing an offence' (Brown 1997: 213).

If the police know or suspect that they have a person with a mental disorder or a mental handicap they must, under PACE, get an appropriate adult to attend the police station to be present at the interview. The arrested person may be regarded as unfit for interview. Often there is no interview. 'Custody officers often summon the police surgeon in the first instance and, acting on the doctor's advice, do not then call for an appropriate adult in many cases' (Brown 1977: 213). Mental health and social work specialists are also called in as an appropriate adult as they are able to respond quickly to calls from the police.

The police are unlikely to take further criminal proceeding with those they arrest that are certified as mentally ill. Usually no criminal charges are involved and the local health medical authorities are informed. In one Home Office study of 2,739 people arrested by the police, 18 were considered mentally ill and in need of care and control in a 'place of safety' (s. 136, Mental Health Act 1983). Of the remaining, 2,721, the researchers estimated that a further 37 showed signs of serious mental illness. Of these 52 per cent were arrested for breach of the peace or public order offences and they were much more likely to be released without further action (46 per cent) than detainees arrested for similar offences who were not considered mentally ill (11 per cent) (Robertson *et al* 1995).

Orders available to the courts for mentally disordered offenders

The courts have a number of options in dealing with mentally disordered offenders. These raise the issue of the rights of mentally disordered offenders, who may find themselves being deprived of their liberty for longer periods of time than if they were not mentally disordered, arising from the inevitable tension between the desire of the court to protect the public and the rights of offenders. In addition, diagnosing what form of mental disorder an offender is suffering from is not always straightforward, as is assessing how amenable the condition is to treatment. There are four types of mental incapacity defined in s. 1 of the Mental Health Act 1983.

Mental disorder is defined as 'mental illness, arrested or incomplete development of mind, psychopathic disorder and any other disorder or disability of mind'. More specifically, *mental impairment* is defined as 'a state of arrested or incomplete development of mind (not amounting to severe mental impairment) which includes significant impairment of intelligence and social functioning and is associated with abnormally aggressive or seriously irresponsible conduct on the part of the person concerned'. *Severe mental impairment* is defined as 'a state of arrested or incomplete development of the mind which includes severe impairment of intelligence and social functioning and is associated with abnormally aggressive or seriously irresponsible conduct on the part of the person concerned'. A *psychopathic disorder* is defined as 'a persistent disorder or disability of mind (whether or not including significant impairment of intelligence) which results in abnormally aggressive or seriously irresponsible conduct on the part of the person concerned'.

The main options for the court when dealing with a mentally disordered offender are outlined below.

- Supervision or probation with treatment if the court is satisfied on the evidence of an approved medical practitioner that the mental condition of the offender requires and may be susceptible to treatment but that the condition does not warrant a full hospital order.

- Mental health hospital or guardianship orders can be made if the court is satisfied, first, that the defendant is suffering from
  (1) a mental illness
  (2) a psychopathic disorder
  (3) mental impairment
  (4) severe mental impairment (see definitions above)
  and, secondly, that either the condition makes it appropriate for detention in a hospital for treatment (which, in the case of a psychopathic disorder

166

and mental impairment is likely to improve the condition) or the offender is 16 or over and the condition warrants a guardianship order and the court feels such an order is the most suitable disposal.

A hospital order lapses after 6 months but can be renewed and the detainee can be discharged at any time by the hospital managers or the medical officer responsible for the case. For a hospital order to be made the condition must be treatable – which is not required for a guardianship order. The order lasts initially for one year but is renewable. Hospital or guardianship orders cannot be made by an adult magistrates' court on a young person under 18. Both the Crown Court and the magistrates' courts can make interim hospital orders on the evidence of two registered medical practitioners initially for up to 12 weeks, but this may be renewed for periods of up to 28 days at a time for a maximum of 6 months.

- An order under s. 37(3) of the Mental Health Act 1983: where a person has been charged and the court would have power on conviction to make a hospital order, a magistrates' court may, if satisfied that the accused did the act, make a hospital order without a conviction. This section does away with the requirement for a finding that the *actus reus* was accompanied by the requisite *mens rea*.

- Restriction order under s. 41 of the Mental Health Act 1983: this power is not available to magistrates and can only be exercised by the Crown Court. The order provides for detention for a defined or indefinite period, so that the offender cannot be discharged from hospital without the permission of the Secretary of State or the Mental Health Review Tribunal. It may be imposed where it is felt necessary to impose such an order to protect the public from serious harm taking into account the nature of the offence, the history of the offender and the risk of future offending. Where magistrates, taking the same considerations into account, feel that a restriction order is necessary, they may commit the offender to the Crown Court.

- Hospital and limitation direction was created by s. 46 of the Crime (Sentences) Act 1997 for those suffering from a psychopathic disorder under which a court can impose a sentence of imprisonment and direct that the person be sent to a hospital.

In 1996, 1,057 restricted patients were admitted to hospital in relation to the following types of mental disorder: 935 for mental illness; 28 for mental illness with other disorders; 47 for psychopathic disorder; 18 with mental impairment; 6 had mental impairment with psychopathic disorder; and 3 for severe mental impairment (*Home Office Statistical Bulletin* 20/97: 17). Of the above patients 392 were admitted as a result of violent offences and, of these, 337 were categorised as suffering from a mental illness and 18 from a psychopathic disorder. The next highest offence category was burglary, with

103 patients admitted as a result of which almost all, 100, were diagnosed as mentally ill.

De-institutionalisation and care in the community

The Mental Health Act 1959 brought about a major revision in the treatment of the mentally ill. The policy of placing mental patients into mental hospitals had its origins in the county asylums of the late eighteenth century and early nineteenth century. The new approach was called 'community care' and was based on a new respect for the rights of the mental patient and a wish to avoid the use of the gloomy institutions that, in some places, held regimes that were brutal and uncaring. It was also believed that rehabilitation was more likely to take place in the more normal world of the community rather than the closed worlds of total institutions (Goffman 1961). Advancement in pharmaceutical drugs meant that new methods of treatment were available for the control of behaviour and the cure of patients. It was a policy that was also cheaper if measured in monetary terms. The number of beds available for psychiatric patients fell from 140,000 in 1959 to 37,000 in 1998.

While few would dispute that it is desirable to divert mentally disordered offenders from the criminal justice process or refer them for treatment rather than punishment, there are some concerns about the orders outlined above. Particularly problematic is the definition of different kinds of mental disorder. These definitions are somewhat narrow and may not accord with psychiatric diagnoses. The definition of psychopathy has raised special problems, as there is little agreement over what kind of underlying condition produces the behaviour which amounts to its definition. In essence, argues Peay, it is 'a legal category defined by persistently violent behaviour', rather than being a clearly defined mental disorder (Peay 1994: 1146).

A person's mental condition may change and indeed be affected by the process of being arrested or institutionalised, making predictions of whether and how the condition will respond to treatment extremely problematic. It is difficult therefore to state with any certainty how long a mentally disordered offender should be held in hospital. Given the fear that released offenders may re-offend this may lead to longer periods of hospitalisation than would be merited either by considerations of the offence or the needs of the offender for treatment.

However, recent tragedies have shown these fears are not imagined; fears which have been exacerbated by the current policy of treating mentally disordered offenders in the community. In December 1992 Jonathan Zito, a musician aged 27, was waiting for an underground train at Finsbury Park Station in London when he was stabbed in the face and killed by Christopher Clunis, a diagnosed schizophrenic. Clunis had a long history of violence which included stabbing a person in the neck. He had been released from prison to a mental hospital from which he had been discharged in 1992.

Community care and public safety

A report from the Royal College of Psychiatrists (17 August 1994) revealed in a survey of an 18-month period from July 1992 to December 1993, that 34 people were killed by newly released mental patients. William Boyd of the Royal Edinburgh Hospital investigated 22 of the 34 killings and discovered that all the perpetrators had been in the care of psychiatric services in the 12 months preceding the killings. Of the 22, 17 had histories of violence. Fifteen of the killings were committed by men, most of whom had been diagnosed as schizophrenic or paranoid psychotic. Nine of the 15 men had convictions for violent behaviour. The seven women in the study were mostly suffering from depression and six of them killed their own children.

Since the Clunis incident a number of changes of practice have been introduced to avoid the problem of dangerous mentally ill people being left unsupervised in the community. The Mental Health (Patients in the Community) Act 1995 introduced provisions that make it easier to return a mental patient to hospital. The Act gives the supervisor the power to take and convey the patient to any place where the patient is required to reside or to attend for the purpose of medical treatment. There is a new system in which each patient has a 'responsible medical officer' (a doctor), a 'key worker' (care/social worker), a 'key plan' and should be put onto a 'supervision register'.

While it is recognised that only a small proportion of offenders are considered to be mentally ill and that the vast majority of mentally disordered people do not commit crime, the assumption that mentally ill people were no less dangerous than other offenders has also been challenged by recent reports. In October 1997 the Zito Trust published the results of its survey on homicides by people released from institutions and who were being supervised in the community. Since January 1990 there have been 141 homicides, that is two a month on average, resulting in the death of 44 strangers, 23 acquaintances, 3 health professionals, 13 co-residents, 34 family members and 33 children under the age of 16 (Zito Trust 1997).

There is a problem of balance between patients' rights and the public's right to be protected from dangerous people. Doctors take as their priority the care and treatment of their patients. Community control by medically trained staff is a problem as they are likely to put patients' rights before the needs of the criminal justice system. When they wish to take action there is often a problem of lack of beds in the medium security wards available to the local health authority. There was also the problem of monitoring mentally ill patients released from secure accommodation. Lack of contact with their case workers and failure to take medication have been cited in inquiries into deaths caused by psychiatric patients.

Co-ordination of services and sharing of information were identified as problems in the inquiry led by Louis Blom-Cooper, a former chairman of the Mental Health Tribunal, into the case of Jason Mitchell. In December 1994 Mitchell was released into the community from St Clements Hospital in Ipswich on the advice of the consultant psychiatrist. He was staying in a halfway house when he broke into the home of a couple, both aged 65, and killed them before going to his father's home nearby in Bramford in Suffolk where he beheaded and dismembered him. The inquiry found that records from his time in a young offender institution, identifying him as a potential killer, had been lost and a later report on his attitudes revealing a violent disposition was ignored by doctors. In July 1995 he was given three life sentences and sent to Rampton hospital.

The balance between patients' rights and public safety is undergoing review. The Health Secretary, Frank Dobson, announced in 1998 that the policy of 'care in the community' had not been a success and a review was in process and added that 'Care in the community has become a discredited policy'. Future plans are for seriously disturbed psychiatric patients to be kept in secure units to protect the public. The plans include building new homes or converting old buildings into care centres for the mentally ill. Paul Boateng, a Health Minister, stated, 'There will be no return to grim Victorian asylums. But the old mantra, "community good, hospitals bad" is dead' (BBC, 17 January 1998).

CONCLUSION

In this chapter we have examined the pre-trial decisions by which some offenders are diverted out of the criminal justice system. Some are diverted because of their status either as young offenders or because they are mentally disordered; others are diverted because of decisions made by the police and the CPS. Many of the issues involved in these decisions and the policy that drives them have their roots in our concepts of criminal responsibility. Diversion also demonstrates the conflict in goals of the criminal justice system: to treat all equally before the law, to provide a cost-effective system, and to ensure judicial decisions are made openly, fairly and even-handedly.

It is, for example, clearly cheaper and less wasteful of resources to divert offenders who for various reasons might not be convicted, or if convicted would receive only a nominal penalty or some form of treatment rather than punishment. It may even be seen as desirable in the interests of equity and efficiency to allow prosecutors greater powers to impose sanctions for some offences without taking offenders to court. To prosecute all offenders uses up valuable resources which might be better used for the investigation and prevention of crime.

At the same time, however, this means that justice is being done in private rather than in public, which in turn means that it is less publicly accountable and that equal treatment cannot be guaranteed. Diverted defendants have less chance to dispute fully allegations, and treatment programmes which may seem more desirable than punishment may involve more control than punishment. In addition as we have seen it may be in the public interest to see offenders publicly tried and punished as well as giving victims the chance to obtain compensation and the satisfaction of seeing justice being done. Another consideration from a crime control perspective is the potential threat to the public of dangerous offenders, be they sometimes young or mentally ill, being released back into the community. Many of these considerations also affect pre-trial processes. The next chapter describes the procedures they will go through before they reach the trial stage.

Review questions

1. Identify the main considerations underlying the decision to caution or prosecute and relate these to the models of criminal justice.

2. What criteria do the Crown Prosecution Service use in deciding whether to continue with a prosecution? What reasons are given for discontinuing prosecutions?

3. (a) What are the main options available to the youth court in respect of different age groups of young offenders?
   (b) Look for some recent public statements about the treatment of young offenders. How do these reflect different views of dealing with young offenders?

4. (a) What are the four types of mental incapacity defined in s. 1 of the Mental Health Act 1983?
   (b) What are the main orders available to the courts in respect of the mentally ill?

5. At what stages are those suffering from mental incapacity dealt with differently from others?

Further reading

Ashworth A (1994) The Criminal Process. Oxford: Clarendon Press.
Newburn T (1998) Juvenile Justice. London: Longman.
Peay J (1997) 'Mentally Disordered Offenders', in Maguire M, Morgan R and Reiner R (eds) The Oxford Handbook of Criminology, 2nd edn. Oxford: Clarendon Press.

CHAPTER 6

CRIMINAL COURTS AND PRE-TRIAL PROCEDURE

- Magistrates' Courts and the Crown Court
- Rights of the Defendant in Court
- Bail, Custody or Summons
- Plea, Venue and Mode of Trial Decisions

INTRODUCTION

After a decision has been made to prosecute there are various stages that have to be gone through before an eventual conviction or acquittal. Criminal cases are dealt with in either magistrates' courts or the Crown Court. Nearly all start in the magistrates' court, and before a full trial or hearing the magistrates may have to decide whether or not the accused is to be held in custody while awaiting trial. In some cases the accused has to decide whether to have the case heard by magistrates or before a judge and jury. As with the decision to prosecute or caution, many issues are involved with conflicting pressures between the goals of due process, crime control and cost efficiency.

In a trial the defendant, according to the principles of due process, is presumed innocent until proven guilty. But before the trial stage, a defendant may be placed in custody, to ensure that they appear to answer the case against them, or to ensure that they do not interfere with evidence or with witnesses, or to protect the public. Crime control interests, therefore, may require that the defendant's liberty is restricted before they have been convicted. Other procedures seek to ensure that defendants' interests are protected, particularly in respect of their rights to legal representation, to a jury trial and to not being tried on insufficient evidence. In addition, the organisation of criminal proceedings seeks, by including lay persons in both the magistracy and the jury, to involve representatives of the community as well as professionals and experts. As we have seen in previous chapters, however, due process may be lengthy and expensive and pressures for efficiency have resulted in changes in these procedures. This has led to fears, particularly

172

from a class domination perspective, that too much power lies with the police and other professionals and that defendants' rights are being eroded.

This chapter will first describe the functions and organisation of different courts and how cases are classified. It will then look at how the system seeks to protect the rights of individual suspects and defendants and provides for their legal representation. It will then go on to consider crucial pre-trial decisions such as whether to remand on bail or in custody and the mode of trial decision before going on to examine the process of establishing guilt in Chapter 7.

MAGISTRATES' COURTS AND THE CROWN COURT

Different courts in the English legal system deal with different kinds of cases and proceedings. We are concerned with criminal cases which are generally contrasted with civil cases. In criminal cases, a prosecution is conducted on behalf of the state or the Crown, though occasionally privately, against a defendant in order to establish whether or not that defendant is guilty of a crime. Guilt may be proved by a verdict following a trial or accepted after a guilty plea, following which a conviction is recorded. This will normally be followed by a form of punishment referred to as a sentence.

Civil cases, in contrast, are mainly concerned with the settlement of disputes between two or more parties, often involving arguments over such matters as rent, boundaries, contracts, negligence, family disputes on the break up of marriage and inheritance. In civil cases a plaintiff sues another person – called the defendant – with a view to obtaining a judgment. A judgment may result in the court ordering the defendant to pay money as damages to compensate the plaintiff. Alternatively the court may issue an order or injunction requiring the defendant to do or to refrain from doing something. In other cases the court may make a declaration, or change the status of an individual – for example, by granting a divorce.

Different courts deal with different types of cases: the county court can only deal with civil cases – it has only civil jurisdiction. Other courts, for example the High Court and magistrates' courts, have jurisdiction in both civil and criminal matters. Magistrates' jurisdiction over civil law matters is limited to licensing matters and family proceedings.

A case may be transferred from one court to another. Nearly all criminal cases start in the magistrates' court and some, as will be seen below, are then passed to the Crown Court. Other cases may be heard by different courts because one or other party has appealed against the decision of the first court. Courts are therefore classified not only on the basis of the type of matter they deal with, but also in accordance with their jurisdiction to hear cases 'at first instance' or on appeal. Two criminal courts – the magistrates' courts and the Crown Court – deal with trials; they therefore have first

instance criminal jurisdiction. These courts will now be explored in mor
detail. We will start with the magistrates, those voluntary workhorses of th
system along with stipendiary magistrates, and then go on to examine procee
ings in the Crown Court, before the thoroughbreds of the process, the judge

Magistrates' courts

If you visit a magistrates' court, all of which are open to the public, excep
when dealing with family matters or young people, you will find that betwee
9.45 am and 10 am, when business normally starts, the lobby of a typica
urban court resembles a station ticket office during the rush hour. Defendant
are looking for their name on lists pinned to the wall and lawyers and proba
tion officers are seeking out their clients. Ushers and clerks are attempting t
impose order by checking lists to see which defendants have arrived. Victims
witnesses, reporters and the interested public are also attempting to find ou
what is happening, which is not always immediately evident. To the uniniti
ated the high turnover of defendants making short appearances may give a
impression of confusion with little being achieved.

Only very trivial and straightforward cases can be dealt with on the de
fendant's first appearance. Most defendants are making their second or thir
trip to the court after an adjournment. They are therefore appearing a
different stages of the pre-trial and trial process; some for remand or bai
hearings, others to enter a plea or decide whether a case is to be heard in th
magistrates' court or in the Crown Court. Other defendants will be returnin
for a summary trial to take place. Even that may not be the end of the matte
as proceedings may be adjourned again to await a pre-sentence report befor
a sentencing decision.

Magistrates

A magistrates' court is presided over either by lay magistrates, who are als
known as justices of the peace (hence JP), who usually sit as a bench of three
or by a stipendiary magistrate sitting alone. Lay magistrates are advised o
matters of law by a legally qualified clerk. A senior magistrate chairs th
bench and speaks on its behalf but all three magistrates have equal power. A
we have seen, a special panel of magistrates sit in the youth court.

In a summary trial, magistrates decide on guilt in cases where the defend
ant contests guilt, that is pleads not guilty. A contested case will involve
trial, which in a magistrates' court is known as a summary trial. Most de
fendants do not deny guilt, that is they plead guilty, and are sentenced by th
magistrates as are those who have been found guilty following a trial. Nearl
all criminal cases start in the magistrates' court and most, approximatel
93 per cent, end there.

DECISION MAKING BY MAGISTRATES

During the course of a case, the magistrates may make decisions about:

- whether to issue a search warrant
- whether to adjourn a case to another day, and how long the adjournment should be
- granting or refusing legal aid
- remanding the accused in custody
- remanding the accused on bail with or without conditions
- in TEW cases, where the case should be tried
- whether to hear a case in the absence of the defendant
- granting a warrant to arrest the defendant
- whether someone is guilty or not, in a trial
- asking for reports on a convicted defendant
- the sentence to impose if someone is found guilty, including imposing disqualifications, for example, from driving or from owning an animal
- sending cases to other courts, for example, to another magistrates' court so that a number of matters can be dealt with together, or to the youth court if a young person has been charged with an adult
- sending cases to the Crown Court for sentence or for trial
- whether to impose a different or further sentence if someone breaks an order of the court
- enforcement of fines.

The justices' clerk is responsible for the administration of the court, and for the legal advice given to justices. The clerk should advise magistrates on legal matters only, which includes guidance on their powers of sentence, but should never seek to influence them on questions of fact, such as whether they believe a witness, nor on the actual sentence to impose.

Stipendiary magistrates sit in larger urban courts and have exactly the same powers as lay magistrates. They sit alone and can exercise all their powers alone. They are paid, and are professional lawyers with at least seven years' experience as a barrister or solicitor. In 1997 there were 90 stipendiary and 83 acting stipendiary magistrates.

Lay magistrates are unpaid, sit part time, and are not required to be legally qualified, though they undergo introductory and continuing training. On 1 January 1997 there were 30,374 lay magistrates in the 550 petty sessional divisions in England and Wales: just under half of these were women. Magistrates are appointed by local panels which include experienced magistrates, under the jurisdiction and direction of the Lord Chancellor. Individuals may put their own name forward for appointment, others are nominated by existing magistrates, charitable bodies, political parties, trade unions or other organisations. Suitable candidates are then interviewed by the appointments panel who are concerned to appoint magistrates who, as far as possible, represent a cross-section of the community. They therefore attempt to balance the bench in terms of sex, age, political affiliation, ethnic origin, and background.

The overriding consideration for appointment is that the candidate is suitable in terms of integrity and local standing. Thus anyone who is an undischarged bankrupt or has a conviction for a serious offence or a number of minor offences is unlikely to be appointed. Certain categories of people employed in enforcing the law are ineligible to apply, even when retired. This includes police officers, members of the special constabulary, traffic wardens, civilians working for the police and members of the armed forces.

An applicant will not be appointed to a petty sessional division if he or she has a mother, father, son, daughter, brother or sister who is a police officer, special constable, traffic warden or JP in that district. No one may be appointed with a close relative who works for the Crown Prosecution Service or the magistrates' courts in that district, or is a retired police officer, traffic warden or a special constable. You cannot apply to be a JP in a petty sessional division if you are a Member of Parliament, are adopted as a political candidate, or are a full-time political agent in that petty sessional division.

All of these restrictions are based on the need to keep those who adjudicate on the law separate from those who make or investigate it. A key feature of criminal justice in England and Wales is that magistrates are generally lay, as opposed to professional or expert. They are therefore clearly distinct from other participants in the adversarial system such as the police, prosecution or defence and from other professionals such as probation officers. The magistracy is therefore independent of any other interest, and its members are there to represent the wider community.

The constitution of the magistracy has occasioned some criticism. It has been argued, for example, that it makes little sense for such vital roles as the adjudication of guilt and the sentencing of the offender to be carried out by amateurs, who cannot be expected to appreciate the finer points of criminal liability, let alone the complexities involved in making sentencing decisions. It could therefore be argued that criminal justice should be in the hands of full-time professionals.

On the other hand, leaving these decisions in the hands of professionals and experts could be seen as leaving too much power in the hands of experts, power which the involvement of lay persons in the system can check. Magistrates themselves clearly value their independence and argue that their experience and common sense are valuable assets in making the system work (see, for example, Parker *et al* 1989). Sentencing, they feel, is not a task for experts, but is more akin to an art. Magistrates also tend to resent any

attempts to curtail their powers, by, for example, standardising court procedures and sentencing practice. Some magistrates resigned at the time of the
introduction of the unit fine in the Criminal Justice Act 1991 because they
felt that this reduced their discretion.

Others are critical of the composition of the magistracy on the grounds
that they are not elected and are not representative of the general population.
The magistracy is often perceived to be dominated by middle class, middle
aged white professional groups. Women are well represented, although ethnic
minority numbers are lower than their proportion in the population. Critics
have also focused on the social class profile of magistrates. Recent figures on
the class composition of magistrates are hard to come by (see Dignan and
Wynne 1997), but it is likely that the middle classes are over-represented for
the following reasons.

Being a magistrate takes up a considerable amount of time. Many people
are not able to leave young children, the office, the schoolroom or the factory
floor for extended periods. This inevitably means that some groups, such as
middle-class housewives or the relatively affluent self-employed, are over-
represented and others, such as manual workers, are under-represented.
Also the latter are less likely to be proposed, or to be seen as having 'local
standing' – a point which also militates against the appointment of the
unemployed, the young and recently settled members of ethnic minorities.

The issue of representativeness is not, however, easy to resolve. What
would a more representative magistracy achieve and just what, or who, should
it represent? A representative magistracy on the grounds of demographic
characteristics alone may not make different decisions in relation to either
guilt or sentencing from the current magistracy. Women magistrates appear
no more sympathetic, for example, to female offenders, who often come from
very different socio-economic backgrounds (see, for example, Eaton 1986),
and there is also little evidence of any direct bias on the grounds of social
status in respect of business offenders (see, for example, Croall 1991).

Should magistrates in some way represent the views of the community?
Should they be elected? In California judges have to go through an election
or re-confirmation process. This means that they must campaign for office
as if a politician. This could itself be seen as undesirable as the magistracy
should be free from political commitments – they are supposed to make
decisions on behalf of the whole community, not just those who vote for
them. Should the magistracy be selected on the basis that they represent the
views of the population on punishment? Representativeness in terms of community values could, for example, see a magistracy in which a large proportion would welcome the restoration of capital punishment. A 1993 survey of
social attitudes confirms previous findings from opinion polls in that 74 per
cent of respondents thought that, for some crimes, the death penalty was
appropriate (Jowell et al 1994: 78).

The magistracy represents a lay element in the system which means that the
public, albeit a somewhat selected group, play a part in the administration of

justice and sentencing. A professional magistracy, which as we have seen would place more power in the hands of professionals, would also be less representative in terms of social class.

The Crown Court

The Crown Court is presided over by a judge. Usually this will be a circuit judge, a full-time judge appointed by the Lord Chancellor from the ranks of barristers and solicitors to the circuit bench. In 1997 in 91 Crown Court centres there were:

- 529 judges
- 884 recorders and
- 360 assistant recorders.

Recorders and assistant recorders are part-time judges drawn from the ranks of barristers and solicitors of a number of years' standing. A High Court judge presides over the most serious criminal cases. The role of the Crown Court judge is explained in Chapter 7.

The Crown Court system was introduced by legislation in 1971 and replaced the older system of assizes and petty sessions. Technically there is one Crown Court in England and Wales sitting at a number of locations or Crown Court Centres. Although the Crown Court has a limited civil jurisdiction on appeals, the vast majority of its work is on criminal matters. It is a first instance court which deals with more serious matters than the magistrates' court and also hears appeals against conviction or sentence from the magistrates' court.

Criminal cases come to the Crown Court in three main ways. Some have been previously sent to the Crown Court for trial from a magistrates' court. These may not always lead to trials, as defendants may change their mind at the last minute and plead guilty. Other cases have been sent on from a magistrates' court for sentence and yet others involve appeals against decisions of guilt or sentence at a magistrates' court.

The Crown Court, High Court and Court of Appeal all have appellate jurisdiction which means the right to hear an appeal. Most appeals against conviction and sentence from the Crown Court go to the Court of Appeal, Criminal Division. A few appeals on points of law will go to the High Court which is divided into Divisions and it is the Queen's Bench Division which deals with appeals on criminal matters. The Court of Appeal has a wider appellate jurisdiction hearing both criminal and civil matters, and the Criminal Division of the Court of Appeal is the usual venue for appeals from the Crown Court. An appeal from the Court of Appeal goes to the House of Lords, which is the highest domestic appeal court. In certain cases there is an appeal to the European Court of Justice (see Chapter 8).

Fig 6.1 Magistrates' courts: number of completed cases

	1992	%	1994	%	1996	%
Heard in court	1,025,800	70	939,300	69	900,200	71
Discontinued	193,100	12	159,800	12	153,300	12
Committals for trial	119,600	8	104,600	8	96,700	8
Written Off	88,000	6	132,000	10	102,200	8
Bound Over	28,800	2	23,600	2	20,000	2
Total	**1,455,300**	**100**	**1,359,300**	**100**	**1,272,400**	**100**

NB. The figures above refer to the number of cases and is different from the number of defendants. In 1996 the magistrates dealt with 1.92 million defendants. If an accused person is bound over to keep the peace there is no trial and it is not a sentence. Cases are written off usually because a defendant cannot be traced or has died. Percentage figures are rounded to one decimal place.

Compiled from *Criminal Statistics England and Wales*, 1996.

Fig 6.2 Crown Court caseloads 1991/2, 1993/4 and 1996/7

Category	1991/2	%	1993/4	%	1996/7	%
Committed for trial	119,170	82.6	91,748	80.1	94,370	82.4
Appeals	14,729	10.2	18,124	15.9	14,606	12.8
Committed for sentence	10,427	7.2	4,603	4.0	5,563	4.9
Total	**144,326**	**100.0**	**114,475**	**100.0**	**114,539**	**100**

Compiled from CPS *Annual Report 1993/4* and CPS *Annual Report 1996/7*. Percentage figures are rounded to one decimal place.

The number of cases dealt with in the magistrates' courts and the Crown Court is given in Figures 6.1 and 6.2. Figure 6.1 shows the total number of hearings, that is decisions on guilt or not; the cases not continued by the CPS; and the number of committals to the Crown Court. Figure 6.2 shows the Crown Court caseload in recent years and indicates the number of cases committed for trial from the magistrates' courts. It also gives the number of appeals that were sent to the Crown Court, either against conviction or sentence, and the number of cases sent to the Crown Court from the magistrates' court for sentencing.

The jurisdiction of magistrates' courts and the Crown Court

Jurisdiction for criminal cases – that is, where cases can be tried – is determined by a number of factors. The first is the type of offence. Criminal offences are divided into three categories as follows:

- summary offences
- offences triable on indictment only
- offences triable either way, i.e. summarily or on indictment.

The latter two categories are referred to as indictable offences. Cases triable only on indictment must be tried at the Crown Court. An indictment is the formal document used in a Crown Court trial setting out the charges against the defendant. The magistrates' court has power to hear summary offences and offences that are triable either way where a decision has been made to try them summarily, that is in the magistrates' court. In 1996, 1.92 million defendants were proceeded against, of which:

- 465,000 were indictable
- 608,000 were summary non-motoring
- 847,000 were summary motoring.

The time and place at which the alleged offence was committed can also affect where it is heard. Magistrates' courts can only try offences committed in their area and normally proceedings for summary offences must be started within 6 months of the commission of the offence. Indictable offences may be tried in any Crown Court and there is generally no time limit for the commencement of proceedings except in a few cases such as some Customs and Excise offences where there is a 20-year time limit.

Classification of offences: summary and indictable

Summary offences are comparatively less serious crimes. Most motoring offences are summary, including driving with excess alcohol, but there is a wide variety of other summary offences, including common assault, assaulting a police officer, and taking a motor vehicle without the owner's consent. All summary offences are made so by statute.

Generally speaking, the maximum penalty for a summary offence is six months' imprisonment or a £5,000 fine or both, but many summary offences carry much lower maximum penalties, and many are not imprisonable at all. The maximum financial penalties are determined in accordance with a range of levels established by Parliament. Level 1 offences currently carry a maximum fine of £200 and level 5 offences carry a maximum fine of £5,000. The offence of being drunk and disorderly for example is a level 3 offence with a maximum five of £1,000. These five levels were introduced by the Criminal Justice Act 1982 and they mean that as inflation erodes the value of money, fine maxima can be simply adjusted by legislation altering the value of the levels: the CJA 1991 raised the maximum to £5,000.

Offences triable only on indictment are very serious matters, including murder, rape, blackmail, robbery, and wounding with intent. For those convicted of murder the only sentence available to the court is life imprisonment. Maximum penalties for other offences are laid down by statute and may include a discretionary life sentence or a simple term of years. For example, 14 years is the maximum custodial penalty for blackmail and

180

burglary of a dwelling, while 10 years is the maximum for burglary of a non-dwelling. Financial penalties for offences tried on indictment have no limit but fines are rarely imposed for such serious offences.

Triable-either-way (TEW) offences include theft, burglary, assault occasioning actual bodily harm, and unlawful wounding. This category covers many offences where the offence's relative seriousness can vary tremendously depending on the facts. Theft, for example, includes stealing a bottle of milk from a doorstep, shoplifting and stealing from an employer. The seriousness of these matters is affected by the value of the theft and all the circumstances surrounding it, including the relationship between thief and victim.

Criminal damage is another offence where the circumstances can vary tremendously. The offence is committed when someone knowingly or recklessly inflicts damage on the property of another person and it is generally a TEW offence. However, in criminal damage cases not involving threat to life or arson and where the value of the damage inflicted is £5,000 or less, the charge is regarded as summary with a maximum penalty of 3 months custody or a £2,500 fine. When the value of the damage is over £5,000 the offence remains triable either way.

Successive Acts have attempted to reduce the numbers of TEW offences, in part to reduce costs and to spread the work more efficiently between the courts. During the discussion of the Criminal Law Bill 1977 proposals were made to change the classification of some offences including criminal damage and theft. These changes were criticised on the grounds that they reduced the defendant's right to a trial by jury. In respect of theft, it was felt that anyone threatened with a conviction for dishonesty must retain this right, however trivial the offence. Proposals for changing the classification of offences were also made by the 1993 Royal Commission.

An offence which was reclassified in response to changing legislative and public perceptions of seriousness was taking a vehicle without the owner's consent, an offence under s. 12 of the Theft Act 1968. This, in its original form, was a TEW offence. In the Criminal Justice Act 1988 it, along with common assault and driving while disqualified, became triable in summary proceedings only. The early 1990s saw an increase in public concern about offences involving a number of widely reported incidents where such cars were used to commit robberies, or resulted in the deaths of the drivers or bystanders. Vivid newspaper reports about ramraiders fuelled political disquiet. In response Parliament created a new indictable offence, 'Aggravated Vehicle-Taking', to cover the situation in which a car, taken without the owner's consent, was involved in an accident or crime.

As we will see below with TEW offences a decision has to be made as to where the case will be tried. Before looking at these pre-trial decisions however, we will first examine what rights the defendant has in court along with the arrangements for legal aid for criminal cases. Figure 6.3 shows whether offenders were summonsed, or were on bail or in custody. Figure 6.1 gives the breakdown of the number of cases completed in the magistrates' courts.

Fig 6.3 Arrest or summons: offenders in the magistrates' court 1980, 1988 and 1996

	Number of persons proceeded against (in thousands)		
	1980	*1988*	*1996*
Indictable offences			
Summoned	136 [24%]	109 [19%]	50 [10%]
Arrested and bailed	364 [63%]	391 [67%]	386 [76%]
Arrested and held in custody	74 [13%]	81 [14%]	72 [14%]
Total	574 [100%]	582 [100%]	508 [100%]
Summary non-motoring offences			
Summoned	271 [58%]	364 [72%]	406 [70%]
Arrested and bailed	165 [35%]	124 [25%]	160 [27%]
Arrested and held in custody	31 [7%]	15 [3%]	16 [3%]
Total	467 [100%]	503 [100%]	582 [100%]
Summary motoring offences			
Summoned	1,334 [99%]	733 [89%]	703 [84%]
Arrested and bailed	15 [1%]	85 [10%]	125 [15%]
Arrested and held in custody	2 [–]	6 [1%]	10 [1%]
Total	1,351 [100%]	823 [100%]	838 [100%]
All offences			
Summoned	1,741 [73%]	1,205 [63%]	1,159 [60%]
Arrested and bailed	544 [23%]	600 [31%]	671 [35%]
Arrested and held in custody	106 [4%]	102 [5%]	98 [5%]
Total	**2,391 [100%]**	**1,908 [100%]**	**928 [100%]**

Compiled from Home Office *Criminal Statistics England and Wales*, 1989 and 1996.

RIGHTS OF THE DEFENDANT IN COURT

A person suspected, arrested, prosecuted or convicted of an offence has rights under the law at each stage of the criminal justice system. These are there to protect the suspect or defendant against the greater power of the state as embodied by the police, the courts and the prison system, and are a key feature of the due process model. As seen in Chapter 1, the most important protection for the citizen is that no official is above the law and that all officials are accountable for their actions regardless of their rank. It was also seen in Chapter 4 how laws relating to police powers seek to balance the interests of the citizen with those of efficient law enforcement. Along with this general principle established by the rule of law, the citizen has specifically defined rights at each stage of the system. Many of these arise from the key principle that the prosecution must prove beyond reasonable doubt that the accused person is guilty of a crime and that it is not the duty of the suspect to help them to prove guilt.

First appearance at court

Prosecutions can be started by the accused being arrested and charged or by the laying of an information and the issue (by the court) of a summons or arrest warrant. Many minor offences, particularly road traffic offences, are started by the summons procedure. After the police or other prosecuting authority form a provisional view that an offence has been committed they will usually (and in the case of some driving offences, must) warn the person that they may be prosecuted. A decision will then be made whether to commence proceedings or to caution the suspect informally. If the decision is made to proceed to prosecution, a document is prepared called an 'information'. This informs the magistrates' court for the appropriate area of the details of the alleged offence, the name and address of the accused and the informing officer. This is sent to the court (laid) within 6 months of the date of commission of the offence. Provided it appears in order, the court will then issue a summons based on the allegation, and it will be served on the defendant by post. The summons, as its name suggests, summons the defendant to court at a specified date and time to answer the charge.

Having been charged by the police, an arrested or summonsed person now becomes a defendant and is entitled to certain rights even before the case is heard. These include the following:

- To know the nature and brief details of any charges.

- The opportunity to be legally represented by a solicitor or barrister.

- An entitlement to unconditional bail except where there are reasons for not granting bail, described below.

- If remanded in custody defendants are entitled to apply again for bail on their next appearance if their circumstances have changed.

- To jury trial in TEW cases.

- To advance disclosure of the evidence in any TEW offence.

- To see unused prosecution evidence before Crown Court trial and be notified of witnesses interviewed by the prosecution but not called. The prosecution has a general duty to give the defence information of use to them, now governed by the Criminal Procedure and Investigations Act 1996.

During the trial

Defendants have the right to a fair trial in which they are entitled to challenge any evidence or witness used in the case against them. They are also entitled to call witnesses and evidence on their own behalf to counter the accusations of the prosecution. The defendant should expect to be found not guilty unless the case has been proved beyond reasonable doubt. The defendant should be assured that the usual established procedure for trial applies to him or her. In particular they have the following rights:

- To seek legal representation, and to have it free if the criteria on merit and means are fulfilled (see below).

- To have the assistance of a Mackenzie friend (someone to assist them if they are unrepresented).

- To challenge any number of jurors, if they have a good reason (i.e. cause).

- Not to give evidence, though this may prompt an 'adverse inference' (see Chapter 7).

- Not to have previous convictions mentioned during the trial stage except in limited and well-defined circumstances.

- To insist that, if acquitted, their fingerprints and photographs be destroyed.

- To argue that the prosecution has not made out a case to answer.

Legal aid and the duty solicitor scheme

For many defendants the key to their protection is the assistance of someone who understands the issues and the legal system. This section will briefly outline a defendant's rights to legal representation. Where defendants have insufficient resources to pay for their own lawyer, they are entitled, in certain circumstances, to assistance by means of legal aid. The legal aid system is under the overall control of the Lord Chancellor and it provides financial assistance for suspects and defendants to pay for legal advice in a number of different ways. The most significant are under the *duty solicitor scheme* and *criminal legal aid*, but two other provisions, the *green form scheme* and *advice by way of representation*, provide help in criminal matters. Much legal aid is means tested, which means that its availability is dependent on the financial circumstances of the defendant. An assessment is made of the disposable income and capital of the defendant and a calculation made as to whether legal aid can be granted and whether any contribution to legal costs will be required from the defendant.

Duty solicitor scheme. The duty solicitor scheme has two aspects: the police station advice scheme for suspects being interviewed, and the court scheme to assist defendants, which covers most magistrates' courts. The scheme provides financial assistance, in that legal representation or advice is provided free of charge (without any means testing). The system depends on a rota of lawyers.

At the police station, PACE 1984 provided for a 24-hours duty solicitor advice scheme for those being questioned by the police whether arrested or attending the police station voluntarily. The solicitors involved will attend calls on a rota basis and will be members of a locally appointed panel.

At court, a defendant can seek advice from the member of the duty solicitor panel in attendance that day. The solicitor can give advice on straightforward matters to enable defendants to deal with cases themselves or can represent clients in court on simple matters such as bail applications and pleas in mitigation after a guilty plea. They can also apply for an adjournment to allow the client to apply for full legal aid for more complicated matters. The court scheme does not apply to very minor incidents such as most motoring matters.

Criminal legal aid. Full legal aid subject to the means of the defendant satisfying the criteria is always available for defendants in the following circumstances:

- where the defendant is committed for trial for murder
- where the prosecution is appealing to the House of Lords
- in the magistrates' court where the defendant is in custody or is likely to be remanded in custody.

This is referred to as mandatory legal aid. Discretionary legal aid is available if it is desirable in the interests of justice and the defendant has insufficient means. The means criteria in 1998 for this type of legal aid allows for legal assistance to be provided free of charge for those whose income was below £50 per week and with less than £3,000 of capital. Above those limits some contribution to the cost would be necessary. If legal aid is refused there are rights of review. In determining whether legal aid should be granted the clerk of the court will consider whether the case involves any of the following:

- a possible loss of liberty, livelihood or reputation
- a substantial question of law
- a defendant whose command of English is poor or who is hampered by physical or mental infirmity
- the tracing and interviewing of witnesses
- interests of persons other than the defendant are at stake.

Assistance by way of representation (ABWOR). This allows a solicitor to provide assistance in court – for example, where a defendant has not been granted legal aid yet and is applying for bail, or is at risk of imprisonment for fine default. Under 1998 limits it is free to those with a disposable weekly income of under £72 and capital of under £3,000.

Green form. This allows defendants to obtain up to 2 hours of preliminary legal advice, and to find out whether they will be entitled to full legal aid. It is available free to those who, after deductions, are left with a weekly disposable income and disposable capital below a specified amount. In 1998 the amounts were £80 and £1,000 respectively.

185

Many aspects of the current provisions have been criticised and are under review. There has been a tendency to restrict the availability of full legal aid, much driven by the high costs of the system. In 1995/6 the total cost of the legal aid service for criminal cases was £748 million, and 446,000 people received legal aid to contest a criminal case. As a result of spiralling costs the government has consistently sought to reduce eligibility for legal aid and to reduce the amount it pays to the legal profession to administer the system. Thus in 1992, Lord Mackay, the Lord Chancellor, announced that a ceiling was to be put on available funds and that only those whose need was greatest should receive legal aid. In addition the fees paid to defence lawyers would also be reduced (Burton 1994).

In 1994, changes to the income limits were introduced and defendants with over £45 per week disposable income had to contribute towards the costs of a case. In addition anyone with capital assets of over £3,000 had to contribute the excess towards legal fees. When they were announced the then Lord Chief Justice, Lord Taylor, commented that 'a large band in our community will become ineligible for legal aid and will have no access to the courts unless they are willing to appear without a lawyer' (quoted in Burton 1994: 1491).

In addition, the government has altered the way legal aid fees are calculated for solicitors for legal aid work which in itself may be a disincentive for some solicitors to accept legal aid work. The provision of legal aid is a further example of how pressures for cost clearly conflict with the interests of due process. This will also be seen when we consider the issues underlying many of the pre-trial processes explored below, starting with decisions regarding remanding a defendant on bail or in custody.

BAIL, CUSTODY OR SUMMONS

The court process starts with the attendance of the defendant. Most will have been summonsed, normally by post, as is the case, for example, with minor motoring offences. Some will have been arrested and may have been held overnight in police custody, or released on police bail to attend court. Yet others may have been remanded in custody and arrive from a prison. Cases are not normally heard on their first appearance and most are adjourned. This is necessary to allow both the prosecution and the defendant time to prepare their case, to seek legal or other expert advice or to contact witnesses.

Both the police and the courts can make decisions about holding an accused person in custody prior to conviction. The police must decide whether to release arrested persons or to detain them in police custody. In 1996 the police arrested and detained in custody 5 per cent of those who were prosecuted. They released on bail a further 35 per cent. Most (60 per cent) of those prosecuted were summonsed (see Figure 6.3). Following their first appearance in the magistrates' court, defendants may be released to await trial or may be remanded on bail or in custody by the magistrates. Similar decisions have to be made by the judge if the case goes to trial in the Crown Court. In 1996, 27 per cent of offenders prosecuted were granted bail by the magistrates, 3 per cent were remanded in custody and 70 per cent were released with no conditions (*Criminal Statistics England and Wales*, 1996: 194).

Less serious cases will simply be adjourned and defendants notified of the date of the next hearing. In more serious cases, however, defendants will be remanded either on bail or in custody. Remands can only be for a fixed period of time, and remand length varies in relation to whether or not the accused is held in custody. There are fixed limits to the length of time that a person can be detained by the police at a police station and by the magistrates when remanding an offender in custody.

As seen in Chapter 4, PACE governs police powers in relation to detention without charge. Under a strict timetable, a suspect may only be held for questioning for a limited time before being charged. If the time limit is reached the suspect must be charged or released. PACE also provides that once a suspect has been charged they may be released by the police on bail to attend the magistrates' court at a specified time. Under the Criminal Justice and Public Order Act 1994 the police can to impose conditions of bail which will prevent the necessity of referring the matter to court when a simple condition would meet their concerns.

Defendants may be detained without charge initially for 24 hours. If, in the opinion of the police, the offence is a 'serious arrestable offence', then the period of detention by the police may be extended for a further 12 hours on the authorisation of a senior officer of superintendent rank or above. After 36 hours accused persons must be presented at a magistrates' court, who may return them to police custody for a further 36 hours. After this time they must again be returned to the court, when the magistrates may decide on a further period of remand. The maximum total period of remand without charge in police custody is 96 hours. Thereafter the suspect must be charged or released. After charge, further decisions on remand in custody or bail are made and if remanded in custody, the accused will be held in a remand wing or centre in a prison service establishment.

Unconvicted defendants may not be initially remanded in custody by magistrates for more than 8 days at a time. They may be remanded for up to 28 days, however, if they have been previously remanded in custody for the same offence and are present in court. A convicted defendant can be remanded in custody for up to 3 weeks for reports. In order to prevent repeated custodial remands, custody time limits were introduced following the creation of the Crown Prosecution Service. These provide a maximum time limit for proceedings where the defendant is in custody. When the limit is reached, leave to extend the period must be applied for or the defendant must be given bail. Under the Prosecution of Offences (Custody Time Limits) Regulations 1987 the limits are 70 days between first appearance and summary trial or committal proceedings, unless the decision to have summary trial is reached earlier than 56 days in which case the limit is 56 days. The maximum period for holding a defendant in custody between committal to the Crown Court and trial is 112 days.

Bail

The operation of the bail system in England and Wales is governed by the Bail Act 1976. If a person accused, convicted or under arrest for an offence is granted bail, he or she is released under a duty to attend court or the police station at a given time.

Bail may be granted subject to certain conditions, which aim to ensure that the defendant appears for the next hearing. The court may ask for a *surety*, someone who will pledge to pay an amount of money set by the court should the defendant not turn up, or may require a *security* – the deposit of a sum of money. In other circumstances, the court may require that the accused lodge their passports with the police to ensure that they do not flee the country, or the court may decide to restrict defendants' movements by imposing a curfew order, or insisting they report daily to a police station, or ban them from making contact with witnesses or victims.

Those who are granted bail must appear at the time and place specified, which they will be given written details of. If they do not surrender to custody, they are guilty of an offence, except when they are prevented from so doing because of, for example, an accident. A warrant may be issued for their arrest and if found guilty of the offence of failing to attend they risk a fine of up to £5,000 from the magistrates' court or up to 3 months' imprisonment. The police may also arrest someone on bail if they have reasonable grounds for believing that any conditions are not being met or that the accused is unlikely to surrender.

Criteria for bail

The criteria for granting and refusing bail are also dealt with by the Bail Act 1976. In general there is a presumption in favour of bail for unconvicted defendants but there are some important exceptions. Bail need not be granted to defendants charged with imprisonable offences, if:

- the court or the police (for police bail) think there are substantial grounds for believing that, if released, the defendant
  - will fail to return to court
  - will commit an offence
  - will interfere with witnesses, for example by contacting them about the court proceedings, or otherwise obstruct the course of justice

- the defendant is already on bail at the time and is charged with a new indictable offence
- it is necessary for the defendant's own protection or, if a young person, for his or her welfare
- the defendant is already in custody on other matters
- the defendant has already absconded in the present proceedings
- it has been impracticable to obtain information in order to make a bail decision.

In deciding whether grounds exist for refusing bail and in deciding whether to impose any conditions on the bail, the court or police will consider:

- the nature and seriousness of the matter and the probable sentence
- the character and previous convictions of the defendant
- neighbourhood ties such as family, job, property
- any previous bail record (has the accused always attended court when asked?)
- strength of the evidence against him or her
- any other relevant information.

In cases involving charges of murder, rape or manslaughter, courts must give reasons for granting (rather than refusing) bail. No bail will be granted for those who already have a previous conviction for one of those offences. For convicted offenders bail can be withheld if it is necessary to hold the person in custody to allow a report to be compiled.

Concerns about bail

As a result of increasing concern about the possibility of dangerous offenders being released on bail, the Bail Amendment Act 1993 gave the Crown Prosecution Service limited rights to appeal against a bail decision made in a magistrates' court. In addition, the Criminal Justice and Public Order Act 1994 aims to ensure automatic remand in custody with no opportunity for bail for those charged with murder, manslaughter or rape who have been convicted previously of those offences. The case of Andrew Hagans in 1992 highlighted the public disquiet caused by releasing convicted violent offenders charged with another serious violent offence.

Andrew Hagans was released from prison in July 1991. He was 25 years old and had 28 convictions, mainly for violent and sexual offences. At the age of 15 he was placed under supervision after holding three women at knifepoint and indecently assaulting them. A year later he was again placed under supervision for 3 years for burglary with intent to rape. On 4 August 1991, 3 weeks after release from prison, he was arrested and charged with raping a woman in Cheltenham. After a week on remand in jail he was given bail by the magistrates' court, despite strong opposition from the police. The condition of his bail was that he lived in a bail hostel and did not go to Cheltenham. Sixteen days later Hagans was in Gloucester where he raped and murdered 23-year-old Anna McGurk. In June 1992 he was jailed for life at Bristol Crown Court.

When bail is refused the court must consider whether it ought to be granted on subsequent occasions. This does not mean that the accused can make repeated applications on the same grounds. After bail has been refused for any of the stated reasons, other than insufficient information, only one further bail application is usually allowed and the court does not have to hear further applications unless there has been a change in circumstances. A remand in custody on the basis that there is insufficient information is not a refusal of bail as such and does not count as a bail application so that the accused may still make two applications.

Some concern has been expressed about the length of adjournments, especially where defendants are remanded in custody. This clearly causes immense stress to defendants, let alone the cost to the taxpayer. In addition, those remanded in custody and subsequently acquitted are not entitled to any compensation. For defendants remanded in custody throughout their proceedings, the average time spent in custody was 6.5 weeks in 1992 (*Home Office Statistical Bulletin*, 32/93, December 1993) rising to 9.5 weeks in 1996 (*Judicial Statistics*, 1996: 69).

The issues underlying the granting of bail again illustrate the conflicting models of, and pressures on, the criminal justice system. As we have seen, there is an assumption that a defendant, who has not yet been proven guilty or sentenced by the court, should have a right to bail. Placing defendants, who may yet be found not guilty, in custody involves depriving possibly innocent persons of their liberty, disrupting their lives and possibly endangering their employment opportunities. The high cost of custodial remands also causes concern. In Autumn 1991, remand and unsentenced prisoners constituted 21 per cent of the average daily prison population. The weekly cost per inmate in local prisons and remand centres, where most of those remanded in custody are held, was £437 per inmate in 1991/2 (Prison Service 1993: 80). In 1996 the average daily remand population was 11,600 (*Home Office Statistical Bulletin*, 18/97).

On the other hand, it is important from the point of view of due process, just deserts, crime control and denunciation that those who are suspected of a crime appear in court to be tried and sentenced. In 1996, 13 per cent of those granted bail in the magistrates' court and 6 per cent of those granted bail by judges in the Crown Court failed to appear. Remands in custody are also necessary from a crime control perspective as the public require protection from offenders who may commit further offences while awaiting trial.

This can be seen in the concerns voiced in 1994 about the numbers of so-called bail bandits: offenders, mainly young offenders, who continue to commit crimes while on bail. The full extent of this problem is difficult to assess. A Home Office study suggested that around 10 per cent of those on bail commit offences, and that as many as 16 per cent of burglaries are committed while offenders are on bail (Morgan 1992).

Evidence from local police forces suggests not only higher figures, but that the pattern of offending while on bail varies as is indicated in this summary by Nick Cohen, the Home Affairs correspondent of *The Independent*.

> The Northumbria Survey, which was monitored by the University of Newcastle, was based on an examination of 3,960 people arrested in North Tyneside in 1989. It found that 23 per cent of all arrests were of people who were on bail for other offences. Bailed defendants committed 40.1 per cent of detected crimes in the area, and about half the detected burglary and motor offences . . .
>
> A study by the Metropolitan Police earlier this year estimated that only 16 per cent of crimes were committed by defendants on bail.
>
> (*The Independent*, 17 September 1991: 6)

In July 1991 the Avon and Somerset Police issued the results of a survey which found that between 24 and 39 per cent of crimes committed in the county were committed by offenders on bail (*The Independent*, 4 September 1991: 6). These figures must also be treated with caution, it may be, for example, that the offences of those granted bail are easier to detect as the individuals concerned are watched more closely. In addition, police figures include offences taken into consideration (TIC), whereby offenders admit to many offences at the one time to avoid separate proceedings for each (Morgan 1992). Whether or not fears of excessive numbers of offences committed by those on bail are justified, they led to the provisions in the Criminal Justice and Public Order Act 1994 to remove the right to bail for a person charged with a further indictable offence while on bail.

Remands in custody

Remanding defendants in custody raises important issues concerning civil liberties. Around 14–15 per cent of untried prisoners are subsequently acquitted or not proceeded against, and a further third will not receive custodial sentences (Morgan and Jones 1992). In a letter to *The Times*, Stephen Shaw, Director of the Prison Reform Trust, wrote:

> Some 40 per cent of those who are remanded in custody are eventually found not guilty or are given a non-custodial sentence. Clearly there are individuals who could, and should, have been granted bail.
>
> (*The Times*, 17 September 1991)

This argument reflects a view that some defendants are being unfairly dealt with – especially those who are eventually acquitted. It could be argued that depriving a person of their liberty before trial amounts to the police or the courts pre-judging guilt. On the other hand however, as we have seen, conflicting arguments surround the granting of bail. If a person has been accused of a very serious offence, the interests of public protection require that they should be prevented from committing a 'further' offence. If they should re-offend, the public might well query why they were released back into the community. Also, as argued above, due process is not well served if defendants abscond and do not appear to answer any charges.

The other part of the argument concerns those who, having been remanded in custody, are subsequently given non-custodial sentences. Yet the principles underlying bail or custody decisions are different from factors shaping sentencing decisions. Remand in custody is not a punishment for an offence not yet proved, it is a preventative measure; to prevent further offending, interfering with witnesses or evidence or absconding. In the case of remand, as we have seen, public protection may be a paramount interest, and full information about the risk posed to the public by a defendant may not be available. Defendants may, before sentencing, provide sufficient mitigation to limit their culpability by giving information which may not be available at the time of the decision on remand.

Time spent in prison on remand will be deducted from any eventual sentence. Furthermore, the fact that a defendant has had a 'taste of prison' may be a factor militating against an eventual custodial sentence. This is certainly an argument much used by defence counsel. On the other hand, it would not justify the use of such a 'taste of prison' as a tactic by magistrates to deter the offender before guilt has been proven. This again illustrates how difficult it is to examine any one stage of the criminal justice process in isolation from other stages. While theoretically separate, decisions on remands in custody and sentencing are necessarily interrelated.

While remand prisoners enjoy certain privileges compared to sentenced prisoners, there is considerable evidence that conditions in remand prisons can be severe – thus adding to the stress and frustration of those awaiting trial and sentence (Morgan and Jones 1992). However, although remand prisons and centres are among the most overcrowded, they do allow more freedom and they are usually nearer the defendants' home as they are often in urban areas. This may explain the finding of a survey asking defendants why they opted for trial at a Crown Court, in which 24 per cent responded that they wished to serve part of an expected sentence on remand (see Figure 6.5). So despite the poorer conditions found in many remand wings, the extra privileges of being on remand and the proximity to where they lived were an inducement for those who expected to be found guilty. Yet again we see how decisions which are theoretically separate are interdependent and how informal considerations influence these decisions.

Whether or not it is felt that too many, or too few, defendants are granted bail, it is clear that the decision whether to remand on bail or in custody is a crucial one both for individual defendants and for the system as a whole. Accordingly, a number of initiatives have been suggested to assist magistrates in their assessment of which offenders are most suitable for bail. These include the use of information schemes which aim to provide more information about defendants on their first appearance. Bail can be denied if, at an early stage of the proceedings, there is insufficient information to make a decision. This may happen when the individual refuses to give a name and address, or where the court doubts the reliability of the information given. In these cases bail information schemes have proved successful in enabling the courts to make decisions based on reliable and accurate information. Bail support schemes, involving a mixture of advice, counselling and surveillance, have also been suggested to cut down the numbers remanded in custody awaiting trial.

Bail hostels, run by the probation service, are available in some areas, providing accommodation for defendants awaiting trial. This provides a fixed address suitable for those of no fixed abode or where 'home' accommodation is considered to be related to the offending. Hostels provide a measure of freedom mixed with some supervision and enable those remanded to attend work. Many have argued for the provision of more of these hostels. In 1991, for example, there were only 559 places available in such hostels in England and Wales with an additional 1,782 in joint probation and bail hostels (cited in Ashworth 1994a).

We can see from this discussion of remand that not only do the conflicting pressures on criminal justice operate on pre-trial proceedings, but also that one stage cannot be treated in isolation from others. Whether or not the accused is remanded in custody or on bail is only one of many decisions taken before trial and magistrates also deal with cases that have moved further on in the process. One crucial decision with triable-either-way offences is the mode of trial decision.

PLEA, VENUE AND MODE OF TRIAL DECISIONS

In summary cases and those that can only be tried on indictment, there is no choice as to where the case will be dealt with. For triable-either-way cases (TEW) a decision has to be made about which court will hear the case. This is called the mode of trial decision.

Prior to the implementation of the Criminal Procedure and Investigations Act 1996 (CPIA) the mode of trial decision was made before any plea was entered and without regard to any subsequent plea, but since s. 49 of the Act came into force in October 1997, the situation is reversed and the defendant is asked about any plea in advance of a decision on venue.

Before any decision on plea can be made, the defendant needs to have some knowledge of the case against him. The Magistrates' Court (Advance Information) Rules 1985 provides that for any TEW offence, if asked, the prosecution must give the defendant a copy of, or summary of, the statements or other evidence on which they intend to rely. This rule does not apply to summary offences, though often the CPS will voluntarily provide information in those cases. When the advance disclosure is provided, accused persons and their solicitors may well wish to have time to consider it, in order to make decisions about whether they wish to plead guilty or not. In those circumstances, the defendant may ask for an adjournment for that to take place. In other cases, defendants will be clear about which course they wish to take, and may not even wish to see the papers before pleading guilty immediately.

Once the court is satisfied that the defendant has had an opportunity to consider the evidence, or does not wish to take advantage of this process, the defendant will be asked to indicate a plea of guilty or not guilty. The defendant will be told, in the event of a guilty plea, that the magistrates will deal with the case, but that they nevertheless may come to the conclusion that their sentencing powers are insufficient and may send the case for sentence to the Crown Court. If a defendant indicates a guilty plea, then the magistrates move immediately to the sentencing stage. If the defendant pleads not guilty or is unwilling to indicate a plea, then a mode of trial decision is required. This takes the following form:

- The prosecution outlines the basic allegations, highlighting points relevant to its seriousness.

- The prosecutor gives a view as to where the case should be tried (see criteria below).

- The defendant, or their representative, may make their view clear as to the choice of venue, though probably that will not be necessary if the intention is to elect trial by jury in any event.

- The magistrates make their decision on whether they will accept jurisdiction, on the basis that if the defendant were to be convicted, the case is within their powers of sentencing.

- If it is decided that the case can be heard in the magistrates' court, the clerk will tell the defendant that the magistrates are willing to deal with the case, but that the defendant has a choice whether to *consent to summary trial* or to *elect trial by jury*. At this stage defendants are warned that if they were tried in the magistrates' court and found guilty, the magistrates might send them to the Crown Court if they felt their powers of punishment were insufficient.

- If the defendant consents to a summary trial they will then be formally asked to plead not guilty.

- If the magistrates decide that their powers of punishment are insufficient or that the Crown Court is a more appropriate venue for other reasons, they will refuse to hear the case and will *direct* that it is sent to the Crown Court. The case will then be adjourned for committal proceedings to take place. No plea will be taken, and the defendant will not be given a choice.

For the purpose of the mode of trial decision, the court assumes that the prosecution allegations are correct, and assumes that the defendant has no previous convictions. The decision is based, in part, on whether the sentencing powers of the magistrates would be adequate. The normal maximum powers of the magistrates' court in sentencing is 6 months in custody or a fine of £5,000 for one offence, with an overall maximum of 12 months custody for two or more TEW offences tried together. (A higher maximum is possible for specific sentences.)

When magistrates make their decision on mode of trial they must consider, by virtue of s. 19 of the Magistrates' Courts Act 1980:

- the nature of the case

- the seriousness of the offence

- the magistrates' powers of punishment (including compensation)

- other circumstances making one venue more suitable than the other

- the representations of prosecution and defendant.

National Mode of Trial Guidelines were issued in October 1990 by the Lord Chief Justice and amended in January 1995 by the Criminal Justice Consultative Committee (see Chapter 11) to give guidance to magistrates on the mode of trial decision and to encourage them to commit fewer cases to the Crown Court for trial. These list the factors that should be considered in mode of trial decisions in general and give particular guidance in respect of the most common offences. General guidance includes the following:

- the decision should never be on grounds of convenience or expediency

- a difficult question of law or fact should be dealt with on indictment

- subject to the defendant's consent, the presumption is in favour of summary trial.

They also list specific factors that may make a case not suitable for summary trial, the overriding factor being the magistrates' powers of punishment. For example, for offences of violence that are TEW (s. 20 and s. 47 Offences Against the Person Act 1861), the guidance states that summary trial should take place unless one or more of the following features are present:

- use of a weapon of a kind likely to cause serious injury

- a weapon is used and serious injury is caused

- more than minor injury is caused by headbutting, kicking, or similar forms of assault

- serious violence is caused to someone working with the public, for example a taxi driver, publican, or police officer

- a particularly vulnerable victim, for example very young or elderly

- the offence has a clear racial motivation.

Fig 6.4 Mode of trial decisions

Crown Court: source of committals for trial 1991/2, 1993/4 and 1996/7

	1991/2	%	1993/4	%	1996/7	%
Magistrates' direction	61,867	51.9	46,954	51.2	49,028	52.0
Defendants' elections	35,584	29.9	25,249	27.5	21,472	22.8
Indictable only	21,719	18.2	19,545	21.3	23,872	25.3
Total	**119,170**	**100**	**91,748**	**100**	**94,372**	**100**

Compiled from CPS *Annual Reports 1993/4* and *1996/7*.

Appropriate guidelines are given for other offences. As jury trial is seen as a cornerstone of the criminal justice system, it is important that defendants are aware of their rights and can make an informed choice. The mode of trial procedure is therefore mandatory for a TEW offence unless the defendant indicates a guilty plea. Figure 6.4 shows the number of cases between 1991 and 1996 committed to the Crown Court either as result of the magistrates' direction or because the defendant chose or elected to have the case dealt with there.

Defendants' choice may be influenced by a number of factors, and research published in 1992 indicated that 70 per cent of defendants who opted for jury trial did so on the advice of their lawyer (Hedderman and Moxon 1992). Almost a third of defendants thought opting for Crown Court would delay the trial, whilst just over a third thought it would be quicker. Rather unusually, 59 per cent of respondents in the survey thought that they would receive a lower sentence in the Crown Court, a perception which does not reflect the sentencing powers of the two courts. It may reflect a tendency for the Crown Court to give sentences at the lower end of their spectrum for TEW offences. And as seen above, almost a quarter of defendants were influenced by the consideration that they would, by delaying the trial, spend longer in remand prisons.

The most common reason given was the increased chance of acquittal (see Figure 6.5). It is generally believed that juries are more likely to acquit than magistrates, and there is some justification for this view as the acquittal rates in the Crown Court have been found to be higher than in magistrates' courts (Vennard 1985). It is also generally believed that magistrates' courts tend to accept police evidence more readily (Ashworth 1994a). It may be, therefore, that defendants are encouraged to elect jury trial whenever the case against them is not very strong. However, the study also found that 70 per cent of those defendants who elected trial at the Crown Court pleaded guilty to all charges on the day of the trial.

Since this research was carried out, important changes in the law have been introduced that are likely to affect the numbers of defendants committed to the Crown Court for trial. These are, firstly, the change described above so that defendants who plead guilty are dealt with in the magistrates'

Fig 6.5 Reasons defendants and solicitors gave for preferring Crown Court trial

Reason	Defendants (%)	Solicitors (%)
Better chance of acquittal	69	81
Magistrates on the side of the police	62	70
Lighter sentence	59	38
To get more information about the prosecution case	48	45
Would be sent to Crown Court for sentence	42	40
More likely to get bail	36	11
Crown Court quicker	34	6
Delay start of trial	28	19
Co-defendant wanted Crown Court	26	19
To serve part of sentence on remand	24	Not asked
Easier to get legal aid	19	4

Source: Hedderman and Moxon (1992: 20).

court, and, secondly, the so-called discount for a guilty plea set out in s. 48 of the Criminal Justice and Public Order Act 1994. This provides that courts in sentencing must take account of the fact that the defendant pleaded guilty, and consider reducing the sentence, but in particular will take account of the stage of proceedings at which the guilty plea was entered. This means that defendants' sentences will often be significantly reduced if they plead guilty at an early stage. The figures for committals will therefore reduce dramatically in the future, as will the figures for guilty pleas in the Crown Court.

One of the reasons behind the series of reforms that now encourage defendants to indicate their intention to plead guilty at an earlier stage of proceedings than was the case before October 1997, was the aim to reduce the number of 'cracked cases'. These are cases in which preparations for a contested trial at the Crown Court have been made with witnesses, and evidence assembled and barristers briefed; and if, at the start or during the trial, the defendant changes his plea to guilty, then an enormous amount of effort, time and money is wasted. In 1996, of the 16,212 cracked trials, 10,722 (66.1 per cent) were as a result of a late guilty plea (*Judicial Statistics 1996*).

The cost of a Crown Court trial far exceeds that of a summary trial. It is perhaps unsurprising therefore, that on the grounds of cost-effectiveness there have been successive attempts to reduce the number of TEW cases.

Committal and pre-trial review

The procedures for sending a case from the magistrates' court to the Crown Court are known as committal proceedings. These are held for cases that must be tried in the Crown Court (indictable only) and those that are TEW where a decision has been made to send them to the Crown Court. Committal proceedings were originally intended to allow the lower court to examine cases and sift out those that had insufficient evidence. Committals eventually took two forms: one without considering the evidence, and the other which provided for the calling of witnesses and their cross-examination. The procedure was criticised in the Royal Commission which stated:

> We accordingly recommend that, where the defendant makes a submission of no case to answer, it be considered on the papers, although the defence should be able to advance oral argument in support of the submission and the prosecution should be able to reply. Witnesses should not be called: the right place to test their evidence is the trial itself. We do not accept that they should be required in effect to give their evidence twice over. Quite apart from the time and trouble wasted by unnecessary duplication, we agree that there is a significant risk that some of them will feel so intimidated on the first occasion that they will be unable to give their evidence at the trial satisfactorily or perhaps at all. We believe that a hearing on the papers would be sufficient to enable the court to prevent from proceeding to trial cases too weak to deserve it.
>
> (Lord Runciman 1993: 90)

From October 1997 committal evidence is tested by an examination of the documents only. The requirement for witnesses to be called to give oral evidence was removed. To that extent the recommendations of the Royal Commission of 1993 were accepted. Committal proceedings for indictable only offences were abolished by the Crime and Disorder Act 1998.

Once committed to the Crown Court the case would formerly be listed 'for plea' so that an indication of the progress of the case could take place, but, as has been already seen, many cases were prepared for trial and a guilty plea was entered at the last moment. While it is unlikely that the problem of 'cracked trials' can be completely eradicated, some of the efficiency measures have been specifically aimed at reducing their number.

In the Crown Court a procedure called the 'plea and directions hearing' (PDH) has been introduced and is compulsory in all cases other than serious fraud (Practice Direction: Crown Court (Plea and Directions Hearings) [1995] 1 WLR 1318). This is administered by a judge, often at the time when the defendant is arraigned (i.e. the plea to the indictment is formally taken) so that it can be seen whether a guilty plea is expected at this stage, and administrative and legal matters are canvassed which will affect the time the trial will take and the state of readiness of the parties. The purpose of many of the questions on the Plea and Direction questionnaire is to save matters suddenly arising at trial and causing delay.

In long or complex cases the CPIA makes provision for preparatory hearings, as has been done in serious fraud cases, which allows the trial judge to make decisions on the case without the jury needing to attend, thus limiting sometime lengthy debate in the absence of the jury in such cases, with consequent waste of court and juror time. There are rights of appeal from rulings made in these hearings and limits on what can be reported in the press, so the eventual jury in the cases will not be affected by media reports.

CONCLUSION

It can be seen from the above discussions that many important processes precede a full trial or hearing, and that complex issues are involved in pretrial procedures. We have also seen the interdependency between different stages of the process. Although very different considerations and rules surround decisions to grant bail and the sentencing decision – in practice what happens at one stage affects the later stage. A remand in custody may affect the eventual sentence and become part of defendants' calculations on mode of trial or plea decisions (see Chapter 7).

The pre-trial processes show the conflict between the different goals and models of criminal justice, and further illustrate how difficult it is in practice to balance these competing pressures. The due process model stresses the rights of the defendant throughout the process. Yet the crime control model requires that those who are guilty of crime be brought to court, convicted and punished. Due process requires procedures to assure that defendants are able to take advantage of their rights. Any erosion of defendants' rights places more power in the hands of the police and professional experts and may have serious implications for underprivileged defendants. Similarly, erosions of the right to legal aid deprive some defendants of the opportunity to resist such power.

As seen above, the issues raised by bail or custodial remands are particularly difficult to resolve. It is clearly in the interests of due process that citizens are not deprived of their liberty until proven guilty. On the other hand, there is understandable concern that dangerous offenders may be allowed to return to the community and that many property offences may be committed while offenders are on bail. Crime control and prevention aims nonetheless conflict with due process.

The cost of keeping offenders in custody is high, and bureaucratic and financial pressures also indicate that remands in custody should be kept to a minimum and that court adjournment periods should be kept as short as possible. Many of these issues are also seen in Chapter 7, which deals with the processes by which guilt or not is established.

The bureaucratic efficiency model of criminal justice underlines the need for speed, efficiency and cost effectiveness. The cost and speed of justice has become an increasingly important issue.

Currently a visitor to any magistrates' court would see many cases adjourned, almost without consideration because they are 'first time in', where a culture has grown up that no progress is expected. Others will not be able to progress as expected because 'the defendant needs legal advice', or the prosecution papers are not ready, or available, or have not been shown to the defence in sufficient time for them to be considered. Suggestions to remedy some of the delays in the system have included proposals to reform the bureaucracy by improving liaison between the CPS and the magistrates' court administrators. Other more radical proposals involve starting 'indictable only' cases in the Crown Court, and a fundamental constitutional change of removing the defendant's right of election of jury trials in TEW cases.

In October 1996 the Home Office set up a review of delay in the criminal justice system, which reported in February 1997, *Review of Delay in the Criminal Justice System* (Home Office 1997c). Its terms of reference were wide-ranging over all aspects of the system and not limited by existing legislation. Its recommendations included matters concerning reorganisation of the CPS and the method of Legal Aid decision making. Fundamental suggestions about case management in the magistrates' court were made, including: giving justices' clerks wider powers, introduction of early administrative hearings to encourage and hasten the obtaining of legal advice and, perhaps the most optimistic suggestion of all, that likely guilty pleas could be listed for hearing the next sitting day after charge.

It remains to be seen where exactly the balance between efficiency and justice will fall.

Review questions

1. What are the advantages and disadvantages of having lay people make the decision on the guilt of the defendant?

2. List the three categories of criminal offences dealt with by the courts and describe the circumstances in which a mode of trial decision is made.

3. A person has been charged with assault occasioning actual bodily harm and intends to plead guilty. Identify in the correct sequence the following stages and decisions between arrest and trial:

   plea/police bail or remand/access to legal advice/mode of trial decision/ magistrates' court bail or remand/committal proceedings/plea and direction hearings

4. Gary Fowles appears at the magistrates' court after being arrested the previous night and held in police custody for burglary. He is 25 years old and lives with his girlfriend and their six-month-old child. They have lived together in their council flat since the birth of their child. He works on a market stall selling CDs. He takes home approximately £150 per week. His girlfriend does not work.

   He has previous convictions (see below) and is currently undertaking a 150-hour community service order (CSO) for a previous conviction of burglary. He has an absconding conviction.

   Gary was arrested coming out of a house last night carrying computer equipment worth £500. He had entered through an unlocked door. He made a full confession to the police and is anxious to be released on bail to return to his girlfriend. He is willing to comply with any conditions the magistrates may impose, but cannot offer any surety.

He has the following previous convictions:

Date:	Conviction for:	Sentence:
2 years ago	Common assault	Fine of £150
1 year ago	Taking vehicle without consent	Fine of £200
6 months ago	Burglary	CSO for 150 hours
6 months ago	Absconding (missed court appearance)	Fine of £20

Questions:

(a) Might the police or CPS object to bail?
(b) On what grounds might they object?
(c) If bail were granted, what conditions might be appropriate?
(d) What do you think the magistrates should do?

Further reading

Ashworth A (1998) *The Criminal Process*. 2nd edn. Oxford: Clarendon Press

Sanders A and Young R (1994) *Criminal Justice*. London: Butterworth

Sprack J (1997) *Emmins on Criminal Procedure*, 7th edn. London: Blackstone Press

CHAPTER 7

ESTABLISHING GUILT

- Role of the Trial
- Participants in the Trial
- Trial Procedure and Evidence
- Lay Perceptions of Court Proceedings
- Plea and Sentence Negotiations
- Appeals

INTRODUCTION

Court proceedings are the most public manifestation of the criminal justice process, the arena in which justice is very literally 'seen to be done'. This is especially true of the trial, generally assumed to be the stage in the process where the defendant has his or her day in court and the opportunity to assert innocence. The trial is a vital part of the adversarial system, and as we have seen the right to trial by one's peers, represented by the jury system, is seen as a fundamental protection for the defendant against the power of the state. In the trial the defendant is presumed innocent until proven guilty beyond reasonable doubt. Rules of evidence, which seem technical and abstract, embody the principles of due process, and are there to protect the defendant from unfair or unsuitable allegations. In addition the trial plays a key role in denunciation and just deserts – it is the arena in which society expresses its moral disapproval of wrongdoing and it is important in the interests of justice that all accused persons are publicly tried.

As we have seen, however, only a minority of defendants exercise their right to a full trial, with many being diverted before prosecution and yet more pleading guilty. Indeed only a very small minority of defendants contest their guilt. Nevertheless the court system is still subject to delays and is very costly. The system operates with only a small number of defendants pleading not guilty and going to a full trial. Is there a pressure on defendants and officials in the system to speed up the process? Are defendants pressurised into pleading guilty? Are defendants aware of their rights and of the protection offered to them by rules of evidence? One commentator from the USA was argued that the pressures of crime control and cost-effectiveness may lead to what is in essence a presumption of guilt, whereby defendants are processed through the system like cars on an assembly line (Blumberg 1967).

Although so few defendants exercise their right to a trial, whether in the magistrates' court or the Crown Court, it is nonetheless regarded as the epitome of the adversarial process. This chapter will begin by looking in more depth at the role and function of the trial and at its participants. In criminal courts in England and Wales the guilt of the defendant is in most cases determined by representatives of the public: lay magistrates or the jury. In Chapter 5 we looked at the role and function of magistrates in summary trials. In this chapter we will look at barristers, judges and juries – the major participants in the trial in the Crown Court, and we will outline the various arguments for and against the retention of the jury. We will then examine the rules of evidence and procedure which aim to ensure that defendants are dealt with fairly. As we have seen in previous chapters however, the practical impact of all rules and procedures is subject to how they are applied by court personnel and how they are affected by informal processes and working cultures. These will be explored before finally inquiring into the implications for concepts of justice of the idea of plea and sentence negotiation; another topic which clearly illustrates the problems of balancing the due process and just deserts models of criminal justice with those of bureaucratic efficiency and crime control.

ROLE OF THE TRIAL

A Crown Court trial has some of the appearance of a theatrical performance with costumes, ceremony, dramatic setting and seating for an audience. These dramatic qualities are also evident in the cross-examination of witnesses to see who will play their part well, and the speeches of counsel to win the sympathy of the jury. They play out their roles in line with the adversarial principles of the trial. The prosecution and defence counsel present their arguments before a judge whose role is to ensure a fair trial, and the jury, who must decide on the guilt, or not, of the defendant. The real life drama of the trial lies in its public examination of and formal adjudication upon matters of human weakness and wickedness.

At a more prosaic level the trial seeks to establish the guilt, or otherwise, of the accused. Whether a trial takes place in the magistrates' court or the Crown Court, the key issues are the same and relate to the principle of the presumption of innocence and the application of the adversarial approach to justice. The rules are largely the same though differences do arise to take account of the different participants. In a summary trial the magistrates determine the facts, including guilt or innocence, apply the law and, if appropriate, determine sentence. In a Crown Court the jury determine the facts while the judge alone is concerned with sentence.

203

At the trial stage a presumption is made that the defendant is innocent, and it is the duty of the prosecution to try to establish guilt: the trial is based on the principle that the burden of proof is on the prosecution. The prosecution must provide evidence to establish the defendant's guilt 'beyond reasonable doubt'. If the jury or magistrates suspect a person has committed a crime, they should not convict unless convinced that the evidence clearly demonstrates guilt beyond reasonable doubt. It was seen in Chapter 1 that in an adversarial system a trial does not set out to establish the truth but whether there is sufficient evidence to establish that the accused is guilty of the offence. Hence, the trial is the quality control mechanism to try to ensure that only the demonstrably guilty are convicted and punished. Of course in the end this is a matter of human judgment and it does not guarantee that the jury or JPs will not make mistakes, but the legal principle influencing the procedure of the trial is that a person is innocent unless and until proved guilty by a verdict of the court. If acquitted, does that mean the defendant is – in reality – innocent?

As pointed out by Lord Donaldson, Master of the Rolls from 1982 to 1992, this does not follow. In a letter to *The Times* he wrote:

> A 'guilty' verdict means that in the view of the jury the accused undoubtedly committed the offence. It is not only the innocent who are entitled to a 'not guilty' verdict. They are joined and, in my experience, are heavily outnumbered by the almost certainly guilty. This is as it should be because, as every law student is taught, it is far better that ten guilty men go free than that one innocent man be convicted.
>
> (*The Times*, 19 August 1994: 17)

Thus a jury might well suspect from what they have heard that the person has committed a crime but they cannot be certain beyond reasonable doubt. They must therefore find the accused not guilty. Everyone is innocent until proven guilty in legal doctrine but this does not always reflect commonsense notions of responsibility for a crime. In Scotland, besides guilty and not guilty there is a third possible verdict of 'not proven'. A 'not proven' decision by a jury does not result in any punishment and means the prosecution may not reopen the case, but it might more accurately reflect the opinion of the jury on the evidence.

Rules of procedure and evidence have developed to try to ensure that only the guilty are convicted, and they take account of and reflect our adversarial system. Some rules seek to prevent the jury being misled or unfairly prejudiced by information which is not strictly relevant to the question of whether the defendant committed the offence in question. Thus rumour, gossip about the defendant or facts about the defendant's previous criminal behaviour is not normally allowed as evidence. Anyone who has been involved in the case or who knows witnesses or the defendant can therefore not sit on a jury. Other rules reflect our increasing understanding about human memory and observation and therefore limit or prevent the admission of certain types of

Fig 7.1 Crown Court results 1996/7

Completed case results	Numbers	%
Guilty pleas	66,938	69
Conviction after trial	11,982	12
Acquittals after trial	6,364	7
Judge directed acquittals	1,648	2
Cases not proceeded with	6,626	7
Bind overs	1,130	1
Other disposals	1,667	2
Total	**96,355**	**100**

Compiled from CPS *Annual Report 1996/7*: 38–9.

evidence. In criminal cases it has for long been recognised that there is a need to limit the extent to which defendants' confessions can be used in evidence against them. Out-of-court confessions are in principle admissible – why would a defendant say something against his or her own interests unless it was true? Rules are necessary, however, to protect those who might have been induced by the police into making confessions. Section 76 of PACE provides criteria which must be met before a confession can be adduced in evidence. Confessions obtained as a result of pressure by the police will be ruled as inadmissible.

Strict rules of procedure also determine the order the proceedings should follow and determine how and when evidence can be presented and challenged. This means that trials are formal proceedings which use legal rather than everyday language, which can often be confusing for the lay participant or observer (see the section later in this chapter). This, however, ensures that the proceedings are regulated and that only the right kind of evidence is brought to the court. It also ensures that the defence have the opportunity to challenge evidence and witnesses in a systematic way.

Figure 7.1 shows the number of cases resolved by the Crown Court. As seen in Chapter 6, most defendants, having reached Crown Court, enter a plea of guilty (69 per cent). Cases not proceeded with account for some 7 per cent of the total. Cases are not proceeded with for a variety of reasons – it was seen in Chapter 5 for example that the CPS have a continuing duty to review the case. Cases are not proceeded with for the following reasons. A defendant may already have been dealt with by the Crown Court for other offences, or it may be found that the defendant has a serious medical condition. In other cases, witnesses may fail to attend to give evidence, or the CPS may feel that the evidence is not sufficient to proceed. In these latter cases, no evidence is offered by the CPS and the judge will order a formal verdict of not guilty. In Figure 7.1 the numbers of 'other disposals' refer to situations where defendants fail to appear for trial, have died, or have been found unfit to plead as a result of mental illness. Bind overs refer to cases where, without trial, the defendant is bound over to keep the peace.

PARTICIPANTS IN THE TRIAL

Role of the prosecutor

The duty of prosecutors is to present the evidence fairly, and to seek a conviction on the most serious offence warranted by the evidence. Their role is not to seek a conviction at all costs: they should prosecute not persecute. As seen in Chapter 5, the Code for Crown Prosecutors also indicates that the prosecution must have an eye to the public interest which includes, 'consideration of *inter alia*, financial matters – the cost to the public purse in prosecuting'. The legal staff of the CPS have, until recently, only been able to appear and personally act as prosecutor in the magistrates' court. In the Crown Court independent barristers are instructed by the CPS. An announcement that legally qualified CPS staff would be able to present cases in the Crown Court was made by the Lord Chancellor in January 1998.

Lawyers are bound by codes of conduct, which provide that they must never knowingly mislead the courts. Barristers and solicitors are deemed to be officers of the court, and must assist the court in the administration of justice. Although these general rules apply equally to the defence, the prosecution is charged, in furtherance of the concept of fairness, to disclose information that might be of assistance to the defence. This includes details of previous convictions of prosecution witnesses, and unused witness statements. Judith Ward's conviction for terrorist offences was overturned by the Court of Appeal in June 1992. In this case witness statements obtained by the prosecution which undermined their case had not been made available to the defence. The Court of Appeal strongly underlined the principle that the defence is entitled not only to information that the prosecution intend to use in the trial but also to any information collected by the police in the process of investigating a case which may assist the defence.

Since the introduction of the Criminal Procedure and Investigations Act 1996 a policy of increasing disclosure of pre-trial information affecting both the prosecution and, in the Crown Court, the defence, was introduced. It was hoped that this would provide a balance between (a) continuing prosecution disclosure so that defendants are properly able to meet the case against them, and (b) introducing defence disclosure so that, in turn, the prosecution is not taken by surprise by an 'ambush' defence in the midst of a trial.

Role of the defence lawyer

The lawyers dealing with the defence case will include a solicitor, who is instructed directly by the defendant, will take his initial instructions, and may represent the defendant in the magistrates' court. If the trial takes place in the Crown Court, the lawyer appearing there will usually be a barrister, although increasingly solicitors have 'higher rights of audience'. The role of he defence lawyer is influenced by the fact that the prosecution must prove he case, and that – strictly – the defence need do nothing. However, in recent years, as a result of changes to the law introduced by the Criminal Justice and Public Order Act 1994 and the Criminal Procedure and Investigations Act 1996, there are disincentives to the defence in failing to state their account or give an explanation. This is because the court may be able to draw an 'adverse inference' from the fact that a defendant does not give evidence – that is, make assumptions about the reasons why the defendant has not given an explanation.

Defence counsel must represent the defendant fearlessly, without regard to his or her own view of the case or his or her own interests. This latter point is reflected in the so-called cab-rank principle, which demands that a barrister must always represent a client when asked, provided the barrister is not otherwise engaged, they practice in the relevant court and are offered a suitable fee. This means that defendants with unpopular beliefs and those accused of even the most unpleasant crimes will be represented.

Role of the judge

The role of magistrates as triers of facts and sentencers is discussed in Chapter 6. In Crown Court procedure, the content and style of a trial are different to take account of the split in functions between those who decide on the guilt of the offender – the jury, and the person who decides on the sentence – the judge. In the Crown Court, the presence of, and separation of functions between judge and jury creates the need for special procedures and rules. Before these are considered in relation to the trial, we should put the trial process into the context of the judge's overall work, described below by the then Lord Chief Justice:

What do judges do?

Many people believe that when judges sit in the morning from 10.30 to 1 pm and in the afternoon from 2 to 4.30 pm, they have a very cushy life. First of all, as any juror would confirm, sitting in court for 5 hours in the day is very exhausting in itself. It cannot be compared to attending an office or other workplace for 5 hours. Time in court requires concentrated attention on the evidence and the submissions. There is no scope for day-dreaming, telephone calls, cups of coffee, badinage with a fellow employee or even visits to the lavatory. But on top of that, what the public see of a judge's work between 10.30 and 4.30 is only the tip of the iceberg. He has to read all the papers and consult any legal authorities before coming into court. He also has to deal with paper applications, and find time to write reserved judgments. Most judges have in addition a number of extra-mural commitments, for example, Presiding Judges on the Circuits have much administrative work to do, others as members of the Parole Board, the Judicial Studies Board, Area Committees of Court Users and there are many other commitments.

(Lord Taylor 1993)

Court proceedings are the most visible part of judges' duties. In a trial the role of the judge is to direct the jury on the law, determine questions of the admissibility of evidence, determine sentence if the defendant is found guilty and generally to be 'in charge' of the proceedings. For trials to be regarded as fair it is important that judges are regarded as independent and not subservient to political or other interests. Lord Taylor also explains the importance of the independence of the judiciary.

> To maintain not only the fact of judicial independence but its appearance, judges have to be cautious in their social activities and must avoid politics. The result of all this care to guard judicial independence is that litigants can be confident the judge will try their case on its merit and as the judicial oath requires: Without fear or favour, affection or ill-will.
>
> (Lord Taylor 1993)

During the trial the judge's function is to direct the jury on the law. The jury must accept these directions, but any views the judge has or expresses on the facts can be disregarded by the jury. The judge is entitled to comment on the facts, and a very important part of the judge's role is to help the jury assess the relevance of evidence, and to marshal what is often a large body of material into some order. It is often very difficult, therefore, to gauge when the judge oversteps the line and begins to usurp the jury's function by determining or appearing to determine issues of fact. If, however, the judge does exceed his or her function, convicted defendants may use this as a ground for appeal.

The judge's influence is paramount where it is argued that evidence (usually but not always prosecution evidence) should not be admitted in the trial. This could be an argument that the evidence fell within a category which is not admitted, or an argument asking the judge to exercise his discretion to make a judgment to exclude certain evidence. For example, the judge in a criminal trial has the power to exclude – that is, prevent evidence being put before the jury where its prejudicial effect outweighs its value as evidence. In addition to this general discretion the judge has discretion under s. 78 of the Police and Criminal Evidence Act 1984 to exclude evidence whose admission would be unfair in all the circumstances, including the manner in which the evidence was obtained. This section is often relied upon in cases involving breaches of the codes of practice under PACE (see Chapter 4).

Judges have often been criticised as being out of touch, an impression fostered by media reports of judges who are unaware of current popular music or sporting icons. In recent years attempts have been made to address this impression, partly by the appointment of some younger judges. Criticism of the racial composition of the judiciary has been addressed by the Lord Chancellor, Lord Irvine, in a speech to a Minority Lawyers Conference in London in November 1997. He said he wished to encourage ethnic minority applicants for appointment, and also made the point that he would like to remove some of the perceived secrecy about judicial appointments.

Juries

In the Crown Court, the body charged with determining guilt or not is the jury. Defended by some as the bastion of democracy, castigated by others as an unwieldy anachronism that allows miscarriages of justice to take place, the jury has been part of the criminal justice system in one form or another since the twelfth century. Juries are currently composed of 12 men and women drawn from the register of electors for the area in which the trial is to take place. The qualification for jury service is now laid down in the Juries Act 1974. To be eligible for jury service a person must be:

- between 18 and 70
- ordinarily resident in the UK for at least five years since the age of 13
- not ineligible
- not disqualified.

Members of the judiciary and legal profession, the clergy and the mentally disordered are ineligible. Disqualified categories of persons include anyone who has received a custodial sentence of more than 5 years or a life sentence, those who have been sentenced to probation within the last 5 years, or to community service or imprisonment within the last 10 years. Added to this list of those debarred from jury service under the CJPOA 1994 are those on police or court bail. Other categories have a right to be excused jury service if they so wish, including the medical profession, armed forces, MPs and those over 65. Although all other persons called for jury service are expected to attend, and can be prosecuted for failing to do so, it is also possible to apply to be excused on grounds either that the potential juror is connected with the facts of the case or the people involved, or because jury service will cause personal hardship. Many categories, such as sole traders, or those responsible for the care of young children, find even a two-week stint, the usual period, of jury service impossible. On application to the court, they are normally allowed to be excused or to defer jury service.

Each Crown Court Centre summons more jurors than they need for the start of each trial. This group of people form the jury panel, from which 12 are selected. Selection is done in the court of trial by the random selection of names. The 12 selected will then try the case unless any of them are challenged by prosecution or defence or asked to 'stand by' for the prosecution. This may be done if a juror is known to someone involved in the case or appears unable to understand the proceedings, by virtue of mental disability or language difficulties. Jurors who may be biased can be challenged also, but as there is no normal power of jury vetting, by either side, it is unlikely that prejudices would be known. There is no power to create specifically a racial or gender balance, or indeed imbalance, on a jury, other than by the random selection process itself. There is a limited power of jury checking in cases involving national security, terrorism, or where there is reason to believe that disqualified persons are present on the panel.

Once jurors have been called and not challenged, they take the jury oath and a place in the jury box. The complete jury is then charged with returning a verdict on the charge or charges in the indictment. A jury is of course only required when the defendant pleads not guilty, so a plea is taken before the empanelling of the jury. Once the jury is sworn in the trial can begin. The randomness of the jury selection process is often fiercely defended as its greatest strength. In principle, this ensures that no one grouping of opinion can dominate the outcome, and thus limits the ability of outside individuals or bodies to affect decisions. However, by definition this means that a randomly selected jury could all belong to one sex, one political party, one religion or one race.

In a criminal trial the function of the jury is to determine the facts of the case, including the most significant fact – whether the defendant is guilty of the charge on the basis of evidence. The jury will be told by the judge that it is their duty to seek to arrive at a unanimous verdict. Majority verdicts have been possible since 1967, but are only acceptable when the jury have been deliberating for a long period (at least two hours in straightforward cases, longer if the issues are complex) and have been directed by the judge that a majority verdict (a verdict of at least 10) is acceptable. The judge will stress however, that though prepared to accept a majority view, the jurors should still strive to achieve unanimity. When a majority verdict of guilty is accepted, the foreman is asked to announce the number comprising the majority and minority (10–2 or 11–1). When the verdict is not guilty, no information is sought about the distribution of views among the jury. In Scotland the jury consists of 15 people and a simple majority verdict is acceptable.

In England and Wales if at least 10 of the jury are unable to agree and there seems no prospect of agreement the judge will discharge the jury from giving a verdict. If the defendant has been convicted on other matters, the charge may be allowed to lie on the file or the prosecution may decide not to proceed. Normally, however, the defendant will be retried at a later date by a different jury. The judge may or may not be the same.

Proceedings within the jury room are entirely privileged. Jurors are forbidden to discuss the case or their deliberations with anyone else, for fear of distorting the trial process. If they do they may be charged as being in contempt of court. The Royal Commission on Criminal Justice 1993 has, however, recommended that the Contempt of Court Act 1981 be amended so that properly authorised research can be carried out into the way juries reach their verdicts. The secrecy of jury deliberations also has the result that alleged irregularities in the jury's discussions cannot be a ground for appeal. Misconduct by the jury or a jury member outside the confines of the jury room can, however, be a ground for appeal. If the problem is discovered during the trial, it can be a reason for the judge to discharge the juror, or the whole jury. An example of where this might happen is when information inadvertently falls into the jury's hands about previous convictions of the defendant, where such matters were not admissible in the trial.

Figure 7.1 above shows the outcome of cases heard in the Crown Court, in terms of the number of guilty pleas, convictions after trial, acquittals, and cases not proceeded with, or dealt with by the defendant being bound over to keep the peace. Eighty-one per cent of all cases resulted in a conviction. Figure 7.1 also shows the number of defendants acquitted by the jury after full trial, and the number acquitted at the direction of the judge. These judge-directed acquittals accounted for 2 per cent of all cases in the Crown Court in 1996/7.

Research carried out for the Royal Commission on Criminal Justice 1993 considered the reasons for ordered acquittals (before the trial begins) and directed acquittals (after the commencement of trial). Of the sample of 100 acquittals examined, 45 were found to be unavoidable – arising due to unforeseen problems. Fifty-five were probably foreseeable and at least 15 should have been foreseen before the committal stage. This means that the CPS review procedure, intended to reveal weak cases, was failing to 'weed out' a sufficient number of cases (Block *et al* 1993).

The CPS conduct, for example, in prosecuting Colin Stagg for the murder of 23-year-old Rachel Nickell on Wimbledon Common in July 1992, drew adverse criticism from the trial judge (Mr Justice Ognall) in September 1994 for proceeding without sufficient 'proper' evidence. The police investigators knew that a person fitting Stagg's description, and identified as him by an eyewitness in an identity parade, was on the Common at the time of the murder. Psychological profiling had further persuaded the police that they had the 'right person' so they used a female undercover officer to feign a relationship with Stagg. It was to her that Stagg claimed in a letter to have committed a murder, in response to her boast that she was a psycho-sexual murderess who could not love anyone who was not the same. The judge stopped the trial before the jury were asked to decide on Stagg's guilt on the basis that there was insufficient evidence.

The use of juries has been the subject of conflicting views among lawyers, politicians and the public at large. Some of the arguments advanced in favour of and against juries are set out in Figure 7.2.

The arguments in favour of the jury involve fundamental principles developed over the centuries. The right to a trial by jury involves the concept of being tried by one's peers. It is therefore essential to this principle that jury members be chosen from a random selection of the population. In this way lay members of the public are involved in justice. Fears of oppressive laws and governments also underlie the argument that juries can affect the law itself. In so-called 'equity' verdicts juries have acquitted on the grounds that they do not think that the law is right even where the accused has quite clearly committed the act. This was apparently the situation in 1986 when Clive Ponting was prosecuted under the Official Secrets Act and acquitted by the jury despite a clear directive by the judge that he had no defence. Jurors may not wish to see the defendant receive a harsher punishment than they feel is deserved – juries during the 1950s, for example, often acquitted drivers

211

Fig 7.2 Debate on the jury

Arguments for retaining the jury
- Juries represent a cross-section of the population so the accused is tried by his or her peers.
- Juries enable the public's view of the criminal justice system to be reflected.
- Juries ensure that unpopular or 'unjust' laws cannot be enforced.
- There is no acceptable alternative.
- Jury members are not 'case-hardened'.
- The jury system is the cornerstone of our criminal trial process.
- Fact assessment is a common sense matter best left to lay people.

Arguments against retaining the jury
- Juries are not representative of society as a whole.
- Juries are not able to handle complex issues, particularly in fraud trials.
- Juries are subject to prejudice and irrationality.
- Jurors are not treated with consideration, and are expected to perform a difficult important function in uncomfortable surroundings and without preparation.
- Juries prolong the length and therefore the cost of trials.
- Juries acquit the guilty.
- Juries convict the innocent.
- Juries are too ready to believe the prosecution evidence.
- Juries are reluctant to believe the police.

accused of manslaughter. Because of this, a new offence of causing death by reckless or dangerous driving was introduced in 1956. On the other hand, juries are costly largely because they slow down the process of justice.

In a complex society, ensuring trial by a random sample of one's peers can also raise difficult issues. Should minority groups, for example, be able to ensure that a sample of their group is on the jury? Seeking, as some have argued, a racially balanced jury, necessarily militates against randomness. It is often suggested that juries, especially in cases involving a racial incident, should be racially balanced, or that trials of rape or other sexual offences should be equally composed of men and women, or even have a predominance of women. It is difficult to reconcile these views with the principles of due process – that all defendants should be tried in the same way – or with the existence of the jury at all. To seek a specially composed jury for certain cases suggests that the ordinary random jury is not able to perform its task in the required way. If that is the case, then surely the whole jury system should be reformed, and not merely in certain cases. Another problem is that some crimes have become more complex – especially frauds, where trials are lengthy and the ability of the jury to follow often complex financial evidence has been questioned. Yet frauds inevitably involve complex issues and judges themselves are not necessarily financially qualified. There is a danger that the jury has become a scapegoat for other failings in the prosecution of serious frauds (see, for example, Levi 1987).

Other arguments are extremely difficult to assess, particularly in relation to whether or not juries are likely to be swayed by eloquent arguments and produce 'perverse' verdicts. As no research on real life juries has been permitted it is difficult to produce firm evidence. The only research possible has been with either mock or shadow juries. The former consisted of a jury randomly chosen from the public who watched films of trials. Shadow juries watch the trial as a real jury and proceed to act as a jury. In general these studies found that juries did proceed in a rational manner, rarely disagreed over verdicts and that shadow juries tended to agree with the real jury (McCabe 1988). It can readily be objected that these juries were not dealing with real life cases and were knowingly participating in a research activity – both of which might affect their discussions.

Another method is to question participants in the trial about how they viewed the verdict. Here, a slightly different picture emerges. Baldwin and McConville (1979) found that out of 114 acquittals, judges expressed satisfaction in 70 and dissatisfaction in 41 cases. In many of the latter there appeared to be some reasonable explanation of the result, such as a weakness in the prosecution case. It is normally the trial judge who criticises the jury for being perverse and yet one of the main arguments for the jury is that they are there to counterbalance the judge. Thus can there ever be a perverse acquittal? Lord Devlin argued, 'perversity is just a lawyer's word for a jury which applies its own standards instead of those recommended by lawyers' (Blackstone Lecture 1978 cited in Harman and Griffith 1979).

The approach to jury composition in England and Wales is in stark contrast with that in the US, where jury selection and challenging potential jurors is a recognised and extensive part of the pre-trial process, especially in cases with emotive issues, as was seen at the jury selection in the trials of O J Simpson and Louise Woodward. In these cases, shadow or test juries and jury consultants were used extensively to assess not only which jurors would be more likely to be amenable to one side or the other, but also what arguments would be likely to find favour with them.

The trial of nanny Louise Woodward in 1997 in Massachusetts for the murder of Matthew Eappen, a baby in her care, occasioned much debate about the value of juries. The US system has significant differences in such matters as jury selection, access to jurors, the roles of participants and culture of the courts, which is illustrated by the amount of access to the courtroom of the media during a trial. Nevertheless, much of the press discussion focused on factors that, though possibly extraneous to the court decision, might have affected the jurors' minds, and are equally applicable in British courts.

Some have advocated the abolition of the jury; replacing the jury with lay assessors, or allowing the judge to decide not only on the law, but also on guilt and innocence. Others fear the power which would be placed in the hands of legal 'experts' were the jury to be substantially altered. The Report of the Royal Commission on Criminal Justice (Lord Runciman 1993) did not recommend the abolition of juries but recommended that the law be amended to enable research to be conducted in order that the matter could be fully assessed.

Having identified some of the participants, we will now examine the principles and procedures to be followed in the trial, which as we have seen are guided by the due process model, and affected by – or created for – the adversarial system in England and Wales.

TRIAL PROCEDURE AND EVIDENCE

Visitors to courts are often surprised by the significance attached to, and the time taken by, matters of procedure. This may be particularly noticeable at the pre-trial stage, but may loom large also at the trial stage. Procedure can have immense significance for the outcome of a trial and, even where it does not directly affect the outcome, a knowledge of the structure and format of legal procedure is necessary to understand the context and significance of criminal proceedings. Rules of evidence, which are in part procedural and in part substantive legal rules, very often play a decisive role. The significance of procedural rules is partly practical – cases should finish within a reasonable time and impose a recognisable pattern on the trial process. Procedural rules are also affected by jurisprudential considerations, such as the need to seek justice by the even-handed application of rules. The system has its critics and currently there is much legal and public debate over whether changes in the procedure of criminal trials could remedy perceived shortcomings. The adversarial system, in which two opposing sides contest the evidence, also affects the procedure of the trial.

The main stages in procedure will be outlined below, but it is important to note that, as indicated above, there are some differences between the magistrates' court and the Crown Court. The differences in procedure between magistrates' courts and the Crown Court reflect a functional difference: while juries are not trained in any way for their role, even lay magistrates have considerable training and, of course, regular experience on the bench.

The structure of a trial in the magistrates' court highlights the adversarial nature of the trial process, with magistrates acting as independent arbiters, not investigators involved at first hand in the proceedings. Whether the offence is only triable summarily, or a decision has been made to try a triable-either-way offence summarily, the first stage is that the charges are read to the accused, and the defendant then pleads guilty or not guilty to each charge.

Where the defendant pleads not guilty, the prosecution outline the case and call evidence in support of it. After the prosecution evidence has been called and challenged if desired by the defence, the defence will call the evidence in support of its case. This can be challenged by cross-examination on behalf of the prosecution. Cross-examination of either side is seen as the essential way of testing the truthfulness of a witness. At the end the defence will make a closing speech, putting any argument on the facts and the law to the magistrates. The prosecution may reply only on matters of law. When all the evidence has been heard, and all arguments made, the magistrates will reach a verdict.

Where a lay bench is sitting, they will usually retire to discuss their views. Where there is a disagreement, the majority view prevails, but normally magistrates will try to come to a unanimous decision. Whether the decision is unanimous or by a majority the verdict is announced without explanation. If the verdict is guilty the accused is said to have been convicted and will then be sentenced to some form of punishment, even if it is only a token form such as an absolute or conditional discharge. If the verdict is not guilty the accused is acquitted.

When a defendant decides to enter a plea of guilty, the prosecution outlines the facts and information is provided on the background of the offender including any previous convictions. The defence can make a plea in mitigation and then the court proceeds to sentence, often after an adjournment in more serious cases to receive a pre-sentence report (PSR) from the probation service.

Trials in the Crown Court have a similar format to trial in the magistrates' court, but some differences reflect the presence of the jury as the fact-finding body, and of the judge as the arbiter of legal issues and procedure such as the admissibility of evidence. The most significant differences are that both prosecution and defence make closing speeches after all the evidence, and that the judge will thereafter sum up to the jury. In the summing-up the judge will direct the jury on the law and remind them of the evidence. The jury will then retire to consider their verdict and return to court to deliver it when they have agreed.

The format and structure of the trial process is affected by the rules of procedure. The content is affected by the rules of evidence, discussed below.

Evidence

As we have seen, defendants can only be convicted on the basis of evidence. A criminal trial is founded on the presentation of admissible evidence with a view to persuading the tribunal of fact, that is the magistrates or the jury, of the soundness or otherwise of the prosecution's case. A trial determines whether or not the defendant is guilty as charged on the basis of evidence. Rules of evidence determine what must be proved, what can and cannot be used as evidence, along with who must prove the issues and to what standard. These rules will be referred to later, but it is important first to consider what is meant by the word evidence.

> Evidence is any material which tends to persuade the court of the truth or probability of some fact asserted before it.
>
> (Murphy 1992: 1)

Evidence thus can take many forms, and can be described in different ways, either in terms of how it is presented to the court, in terms of the legal rules applicable, or in terms of the function it fulfils. In relation to how the evidence is given in court, it can include the following:

- Oral testimony of witnesses.

- Documentary evidence in, for example, business records and witness statements, and computer print-outs.

- *Real* evidence such as exhibits of items to be displayed in court – for example, a murder weapon, fingerprints and other forensic items.

- Evidence of video and audio tapes and photographs.

As far as identifying its nature and persuasiveness, evidence is often described in the following ways:

- Eye witness evidence from an observer of the facts.

- Evidence of alibi, indicating that the defendant could not have been at the place claimed.

- A confession from the accused, usually obtained when they are interviewed by the police.

- Character evidence about a witness's history and background.

- Opinion evidence from an expert to interpret specialist matters to the court.

- Circumstantial evidence from which inferences can be drawn about matters relevant to the case.

Circumstantial evidence can be very weighty. It refers to deductions which can be reasonably made from the circumstances. For example, if there is evidence that a person accused of murder was in the habit of wearing a distinctive item of clothing, and that such an item was found at the scene of the crime, then that is some evidence of involvement. Evidence legally categorised as hearsay (reference to a statement made out of court) is less reliable because its truth cannot be checked in court by cross-examination and will not usually be admissible. Rules relating to the admissibility of evidence means that much material is not permitted to be put before the court.

The law of evidence is concerned with the rules governing these issues. It is a body of procedural or adjectival law, in contrast with what is termed substantive law – for example, the law of crime or contract. It should not be thought that rules of evidence constitute a dry body of regulations unrelated to the social context of law – the development of evidential rules over the years has reflected social and moral concerns with the protection of the defendant, the delimitation of police powers and notions of justice as well as purely theoretical legal concepts. Fears that evidence may be unreliable or concocted have strongly influenced the development of the law of evidence – the hearsay rule in particular has developed to minimise the danger of unreliable evidence. This rule has been continuously refined especially in relation to confessions because of concerns over methods of police interrogation. In addition, as mentioned above, many rules develop out of fears that the jury might be unfairly prejudiced against the defendant.

Evidence should not be confused with proof. Evidence is the means by which some fact is proved or disproved or rendered more or less likely. Neither should be confused with truth: as we have already seen the court aims to establish guilt beyond reasonable doubt in the light of the evidence presented at the trial.

When considering evidence, three basic principles need to be considered: relevancy, admissibility, and weight. The relevancy of a piece of evidence is determined largely as a matter of common sense but tempered by legal rules for the protection of defendants. Nothing can be admitted in evidence unless it is relevant to a matter before the court. But some relevant evidence may be inadmissible because of a procedural rule. Such evidence is often excluded to protect the defendant or to prevent the jury being misled. For example, previous conduct of the accused is usually deemed irrelevant to the current charge. This means that a jury or magistrates will not normally be told about any previous convictions of the defendant – at least not unless and until the defendant is found guilty.

The weight or cogency of evidence is not normally related to its admissibility, but to its reliability or credibility – how persuasive it is likely to be. A jury or magistrates, when assessing the weight to be attached to evidence of a witness in court, may, for instance, consider whether they believed the witness, whether the witness's memory was likely to be reliable, whether the witness had a reason to fabricate the evidence, or to misinterpret an incident. They are thus assessing the weight to be attached to that evidence. Similarly where two witnesses give conflicting evidence, the jury will need to assess the weight to be attached to each witness in order to determine whether they prefer one witness to the other. Oral witnesses may often give a version which contradicts documentary evidence – the jury will need to consider whether the documentary evidence is preferable to the oral evidence, which might be affected by how well the witness can remember an event which might have involved traumatic circumstances.

As we have seen, the criminal law determines that in order to prove theft, it must be established that the defendant:

> dishonestly appropriated property belonging to another with the intention of permanently depriving that other of it.
>
> (s. 1 Theft Act 1968)

If Mrs Smith is charged with stealing a frozen chicken from a supermarket, the prosecution must prove that Mrs Smith (and not someone else) is guilty as described above. The prosecution may be able to bring evidence from a store detective that Mrs Smith was seen taking the chicken from the display and hiding it inside her coat, and leaving the supermarket without paying for it.

In the absence of a credible explanation, the prosecution, if the above evidence is believed, will be able to show an appropriation of property (the chicken) belonging to the supermarket. What of dishonesty? That can be assumed or inferred from the action: who hides a frozen chicken in their coat if they are not dishonest? What of intention to permanently deprive? Intention is one of the most difficult elements to establish – as it is known only to the defendant. But intention too can be inferred from conduct.

The criminal law defines what must be proved; the law of evidence determines how that can be done, with rules concerning the admissibility of evidence and the burden and standard of proof. Although in some cases failure to explain may lead to an 'adverse inference' being drawn against the defendant, the defendant need do nothing, and is not compelled to give evidence or indeed to offer any self-defence. The defence may simply say, in effect, to the prosecution, 'Prove it'. This reflects the principle outlined above that the burden of proof lies with the prosecution with the standard of proof being that it is proved beyond reasonable doubt. This means that the triers of fact – magistrates in the magistrates' court, the jury in the Crown Court – must be satisfied of guilt to that standard. Although the precise formulation of the standard may be varied, by for instance the use of the phrase 'satisfied so you are sure', the famous time-honoured formulation 'beyond reasonable doubt' is still that most favoured in the courts. The rules concerning the burden and standard of proof are the most significant of all rules of evidence.

These two concepts must be examined closely as they underpin any criminal trial and set the parameters for determination of guilt. The phrase 'burden of proof' indicates where the onus of proving a case lies. In a criminal case as we have seen this burden lies with the prosecution. The only exceptions are where the defendant is seeking to rely on insanity as a defence, or where statute expressly or impliedly puts the burden on the defendant. The fact that the prosecution has to prove its case – and every element of it – is reflected throughout the trial process. That the defendant is 'innocent until proven guilty' is the popular statement of the rule and the right for the defendant to remain silent during and before the trial is a natural concomitant of it.

However, certain statutes explicitly place the burden of proof on the defendant. Perhaps the clearest example of this is where someone is charged with not having a licence, for example a driving or shotgun licence. The relevant statutes place the burden of proof to disprove the allegation on the defendant, who must show the court that he or she did have a licence. The rationale for this is that it is a matter specifically within the defendant's own knowledge, and also because it is much easier to prove a positive than a negative.

As previously mentioned, the defendant is not compelled to give evidence on their own behalf. However, there are circumstances where their failure to do so, or their failure to give explanations at an early stage, can be construed against them at trial. This means that when defendants are on trial, evidence can be given to the court that when they were arrested for an offence they failed to answer questions in any of the following matters:

- why they were at the place where and when the offence was committed

- why they had in their possession items (such as tools that could be used in burglary, or scales usable for drug dealing) relevant to the offence in question

- why they had in their possession substances (such as acid that might inflict property or personal damage) that could relate to the offence

- why at the place of arrest there were items (such as drugs) relevant to the offence

- why there were bodily marks (for example traces of dirt gained in a burglary, or cuts gained in a fight) that could relate to the offence.

In any of the above cases, or at trial, where a defendant

- uses an excuse that could have been mentioned when first interviewed or charged, but was not, or

- does not give evidence at all, or

- fails to conform to the disclosure provisions of the Criminal Procedure and Investigations Act,

then the court (that is, the jury or magistrates) can take that into account with other evidence in deciding whether or not they find the defendant guilty. In doing so they must consider whether the defendant could or should have explained. Was there a good reason not to explain at the time? Was the defendant hiding some other, non-criminal, behaviour? Were they too ill or too frightened or too drunk to explain?

Presentation of evidence

These are rules governing the order in which witnesses are called and evidence produced. The prosecution starts the proceedings and the defence responds, or decides not to respond to the prosecution case. After outlining the case, the prosecution calls the prosecution witnesses in the order that enables the case to be presented most coherently. The defence are then entitled to call witnesses but need not do so. If the defendant is to give evidence, he or she will appear before any other defence witnesses. Each witness will be asked questions initially by the counsel who has called them. They may then be cross-examined by the opposing side, to elicit inconsistencies or weaknesses, and may also be re-examined by the original questioner. Although, as has been stated above, evidence can be in documentary or real form, the most common type of evidence is oral evidence given in the witness box and referred to as testimony. Most of the discussion below refers to testimony. In order to appreciate the process by which evidence is advanced, we will first examine the course of evidence and consider how the trial process takes place.

In the course of producing evidence, each side must be aware of what evidence is inadmissible. The scope of this book does not allow for a comprehensive discussion of all the principles involved, but a brief explanation of two of the most significant areas of inadmissible evidence will be provided. These are hearsay evidence and evidence relating to the bad character of the defendant. These are common kinds of contested evidence and they also arouse public confusion and criticism.

The hearsay rules come into effect when a witness states in court what someone told them. The rules are applied when a witness refers to a statement, comment or opinion made by another person. The reason for the hearsay rule is because unlike the person in the witness box, the originator of the statement is not available to be cross-examined on the accuracy of the statement.

In criminal cases, hearsay evidence is usually inadmissible. An important exception relates to confession or admissions of guilt made out of court. It has long been recognised that as confessions constitute very powerful evidence against any defendant, the desire on the part of the police to obtain this evidence may result in defendants being pressured into making confessions. There is also a growing awareness that some people do confess when they are in fact innocent. A series of measures are in place to avoid this. PACE provides that confessions will only be admissible if the prosecution can show that they were not obtained by oppression, or in consequence of anything said or done that would render a confession unreliable (s. 76). If the way in which the confession was obtained is called into question, the prosecution must establish beyond reasonable doubt that it was not obtained in contravention of the Act. Breaches of the codes of practice under PACE are often relied on in arguments based on the potential unreliability of a confession.

In the case of *R v Paris and Abdullah* in 1992, the defendants were being interviewed by the police about the murder of a prostitute in Cardiff. One defendant denied being involved over 300 times before eventually confessing. The Court of Appeal ruled that the confession should have been excluded because it was obtained by using oppressive methods. It also castigated the police officers for their manner of interview and the accused's legal representative who had been present at the interviews and allowed it to continue.

Understandably, a confession can be a powerful piece of prosecution evidence, as is the information about the defendant's previous convictions. The general approach in a criminal trial is that the jury or magistrates do not know about such information during the trial. The jury would not know, for example, in a rape case, if the defendant has been convicted of previous rapes. This is because it is thought that knowledge of previous criminal history would unfairly prejudice the jury against the defendant. Having

220

committed a previous offence does not necessarily mean the defendant is guilty of the present one – the law deems the previous matter irrelevant to proof of the current one.

There are exceptions, however, with regard to the admissibility of previous convictions. The first concerns what is known rather inaccurately as the 'similar fact' rule where it would fly in the face of common sense to disregard previous matters. This could happen in cases where, for example, previous convictions are cited because they show that the same individual was responsible for a series of offences, perhaps because they have a distinctive pattern.

The difficulties inherent in this rule are demonstrated by the case of *R v Kevin Johnson* in 1994. The case turned on the identity of a masked intruder who had burgled, robbed and attempted to rape a woman. The victim and her boyfriend identified the voice of the defendant on tape as that of their attacker. The trial judge allowed evidence to be given of the defendant's two previous convictions for rape. In all the three cases reference was made to the rapist's 'gentleness' – thus the judge took the view that the previous convictions for rape could be put before the jury. The Court of Appeal held that the judge had erred in allowing the information of previous convictions to be used in evidence.

The second exception is where the defendant makes his or her own character an issue by falsely stating that he or she is of 'good character'. Thirdly, if a defendant attacks the character of a prosecution witness or a deceased victim, or gives evidence against a co-accused, he or she can be cross-examined about his or her own character, including previous convictions. But this third exception only arises if the defendant actually gives evidence. This exception, embodied in the Criminal Evidence Act 1898, was enacted as part of a fundamental change in the law. Until that time, defendants were not able to give evidence in their own defence as it was felt that such evidence was so obviously biased that it was of no value. When the law was changed allowing defendants to be witnesses, they were also protected by the prohibition on questions about previous convictions, as it was felt that this would be too prejudicial. In order, however, that the defendant should not shelter too easily behind this protection, a 'tit-for-tat' rule was included whereby defendants are safe unless they try to mislead the court about themselves or to malign prosecution witnesses.

The effect of hearing about the previous convictions of the defendant is well-illustrated by the case of *R v Bills* (set out in Figure 7.3) where it appears that the jury's minds were changed after hearing the defendant's previous convictions. This led to the unusual situation – and subsequent appeal – described.

Although the rules of evidence may be complex, the crucial task for those charged with determining the facts, who are usually lay people, is to assess the evidence submitted. This means they must decide whether they believe the evidence, and, if so, what it tells them about the facts in issue. This may

Fig 7.3 Jury's change of mind

Jury changed verdict after hearing antecedents
Regina v Bills

Before Lord Justice Russell, Mr Justice Hooper
[Judgement February 17]

Although there was no fixed rule of principal or of law that once the jury had been allowed to reconsider their verdicts, it could not be considered safe for them to reconsider when they had heard evidence of the defendant's previous convictions.

The Court of Appeal, Criminal Division, so held in allowing the appeal of Adrian Mark Bills against his conviction in April 1994 at Wolverhampton Crown Court (Judge Malcolm Ward and a jury) of wounding with intent to do grievous harm, contrary to section 18 of the Offences Against the Person Act 1861, for which he was sentenced to three and a half years imprisonment.

Mr Patrick Darby, assigned by the registrar of Criminal Appeals, for the appellant; Mr Michael H J Grey for the Crown.

LORD JUSTICE RUS-SELL, giving the judgement of the court, said that the defendant had been charged with an offence of wounding with intent to cause grievous harm, contrary to section 18 of the 1861 Act, but the jury had acquitted him of that offence and had convicted him of the lesser offence of unlawful wounding, contrary to section 20 of the 1861 Act.

After the trial judge had accepted that verdict, and while the jury remained in the jury box, prosecuting counsel dealt with the defendant's previous convictions which included other offences of violence such as assault occasioning actual bodily harm and robbery. The jury were then discharged. What happened thereafter was unique in the experience of the court.

It appeared that immediately upon leaving court a juror spoke to the court usher and told him that the jury foreman had given the wrong verdict. The judge was informed. He decided to reconvene the jury and invited them to explain themselves. They indicated that the wrong verdict had been returned. The judge clarified the three possible verdicts and the unanimous altered verdict of guilty of the more serious offence was given and recorded.

It seemed to their Lordships that the original verdict was plain and unequivocal and they were abundantly satisfied that no adequate explanation had been put forward as to the jury's change of mind. It could not be gainsaid that the jury had heard material which they had no right to hear, namely the previous convictions of the defendant.

Wherever the truth lay, that course of action had led to a verdict which was unsafe and unsatisfactory and the appropriate course would be to reinstate the jury's original verdict of guilty of the section 20 offence and to alter the sentence to one of 30 months.

Solicitors: CPS, Midlands.

---

involve weighing up the reliability of witnesses: whether they could observe, interpret and remember key incidents, whether they could identify participants, whether they had a reason to lie. Where witnesses give evidence they may support each other or conflict: could one or both be mistaken? Often, direct evidence of what a witness perceived gives only half the story, it is circumstantial evidence. What inferences or deductions can be made from those circumstances? Sometimes expert witnesses will be called to assist the court on matters outside the court's knowledge. Doctors, engineers, forensic scientists or psychiatrists might be called to explain the significance of evidence to the jury or to magistrates: this might result in the fact-finders being 'blinded by science' rather than being helped to determine the facts.

LAY PERCEPTIONS OF COURT PROCEEDINGS

It is clear from the above that the rules surrounding court proceedings, based on adversarial principles, aim to protect the innocent from unfair conviction. The due process model underpins the formulation of these rules. But what is their effect in reality? While in theory the onus of proof is on the prosecution, and defendants should be treated equally and fairly, many observers of courtroom proceedings have found that these aims are difficult to achieve. In the day-to-day operation of a court, it may be all too easy to assume that the police rarely make mistakes and that those who find themselves in the position of being accused are more than likely to be guilty. This is especially so where such large numbers actually plead guilty. Indeed to plead not guilty can be a high-risk strategy as it may involve challenging the statements and credibility of victims and witnesses, in effect saying that they are either mistaken or are lying. In these circumstances, if found guilty, it makes it more difficult to provide strong mitigation at the time of sentence – after all it is difficult to say on the one hand that 'I didn't do it', and subsequently to argue that, 'I'm terribly sorry and won't ever do it again'.

The complexities of procedural rules may indeed mean that the courtroom is an alien environment to lay observers, jury members, witnesses and defendants. Court proceedings are highly structured and those most aware of the rules, the police, court personnel and lawyers are all familiar with the rules and the language in which proceedings are conducted. The defendant, on the other hand, may not understand these rules and needs to be guided through them by legal representatives or court personnel. Some argue that court proceedings can be likened to a game of bridge – with the experts as regular players and the defendant as the dummy player (Carlen 1976).

Defendants, for example, may simply want to tell the court their story in commonsense language. This may not conform to the rules and order of the court proceedings. The events may be complex, and commonsense perceptions of guilt or innocence are often different from the precise legal concepts of *mens rea* or *actus reus*. In telling their story defendants may try to use inadmissible or irrelevant evidence – some may even give indications of their own bad character, by referring to previous encounters with the police or courts. In addition, only some kinds of questions are allowed and proceedings must follow the order laid down by the court. For example, at the start of the proceedings defendants are asked how they will plead. Some defendants assume that this is their chance to begin their story and they may reply to the question by saying, 'Well ... I did it ... but ...' as a preamble to

223

arguing that they didn't mean any harm, or that 'it just happened'. The defendant may then go on to challenge the word of the police or prosecution witnesses often in commonsense language and unrelated to the evidence. For example they may argue that they were 'picked on' unfairly, or that the police had 'no right' to be where they were. Very often they will be stopped from dealing with legal irrelevancies, thus disrupting the flow of their story. This is more likely to happen to defendants who attempt to conduct their own case (see, for example, Carlen 1976; Croall 1989).

Even where defendants are represented, as most are except in the most trivial cases, they may still feel left out of the proceedings. They may only see their lawyer for a few minutes before the case and fail to appreciate what the lawyer is trying to do. Many plead guilty on the advice of their lawyer – yet in commonsense terms legal representatives are expected to be on the same side as the defendant. Questions may be asked about the defendant's personal circumstances to provide mitigation, yet the defendant may fail to see their relevance. In addition, the defendant is often discussed as if he or she weren't there, and may fail to understand the meaning of the proceedings. In some cases it is apparent that the defence solicitor or counsel has not spent much time with the defendant and has to keep interrupting the flow of the proceedings to check the defendant's current address or earnings.

In September 1994 the General Council of the Bar made suggestions to change the Bar Code of Conduct to include a rule that counsel should always see their client before the day of trial in any contested matter. This suggestion no doubt surprised many who would have expected such consultation to take place in every case.

Some defendants may feel that they have not had a chance to give their side of the story. The following comments from two defendants in a study of magistrates' courts by Bottoms and McLean illustrate this:

> I felt awful; I was in a daze most of the time . . .

> The police statement of the facts . . . gave completely the wrong impression. But I wasn't given a proper chance to explain – I was so amazed at what the police said that I couldn't say anything.

(Bottoms and McClean 1978: 135)

Thus while the rules of evidence are quite clearly there to protect the defendant, they can, in some circumstances, do this at the expense of distancing the defendant from the proceedings. Some argue that this underlines the power relationships inherent in the trial – symbolically demonstrated by the spatial positions of the participants. Judges and magistrates are separated from the rest of court – often on a raised platform or bench – indicating their authority. The defendant, on the other hand, is 'in the dock' serving to underline their position as supplicant. Indeed one sociologist has described the trial as a degradation ceremony (Garfinkel 1956).

The remorse expected by the court from those convicted, and the recital of the defendant's personal circumstances in court, can be viewed in commonsense terms as humiliating. To avoid this some defendants would prefer to admit guilt or lie about their guilt to minimise the shame of a court appearance. However, not all defendants respond to the court in the same way, and it is possible to identify a number of different typical demeanours among defendants: the remorseful, the inadequate, the bemused and overwhelmed, the unemotive professional criminal, the arrogant, the angry, the innocent, and the manipulative who knows 'how to play the game'.

'Playing the game' includes demonstrating expected levels of respect for the court, judged by such factors as dress, demeanour or respectful speech. This may well advantage the better-off defendant who is more likely to present him or herself as a respectful, well-dressed and responsible citizen. Wearing scruffy clothes, slouching, swaggering or chewing gum or using insolent language are all attitudes which may attract negative responses from magistrates and juries. One study, for example, found that magistrates paid considerable attention to demeanour and felt that they could judge the character of defendants (Parker *et al* 1989). While this may appear trivial, it underlines the fact that demeanour, speech and body language are an important part of the way in which defendants may be assessed. Demeanour can be indicative of a defendant's respect for the proceedings in particular and hence the rule of law in general. But this has implications for the impartiality of justice. Different groups in society may have different cultural standards of dress and respectful behaviour. Some defendants may be disadvantaged by different interpretations of body language and their responses to questions. What might appear to be 'shifty' to some might in fact be a symptom of shyness or fear to others.

The subjective experiences of the trial process by defendants, victims and witnesses may be compounded by the somewhat confusing hustle and bustle in an average lower court, where those administering the system may be anxious to bring proceedings to a speedy conclusion, thus exacerbating the confusion. Victims in particular confirm the view that the experience of giving evidence and being cross-examined can be particularly confusing and upsetting (see Chapter 11). In recognition of this the victims of sexual attacks and of blackmail are protected by being granted anonymity when they give evidence. In 1984 the Criminal Law Revision Committee recommended that in rape cases the defendants should also be granted anonymity unless and until found guilty. This was not accepted. Calls have again been made for the introduction of such a provision after Surrey police officer Michael Seear was acquitted in February 1995 of raping a fellow officer at a New Year's Eve party, and again after Professor John Cottingham was cleared of indecently assaulting two of his students. The students' identity was protected, but the professor's was not.

In this chapter we have outlined the participants in the trial and the principles and procedures to be followed in the trial, consistent with the due process model of criminal justice. In the final section we will examine another issue affecting the actual outcome of this procedure in terms of the defendant's readiness to plead guilty and not exercise his or her right to trial. The realisation that the overwhelming majority of defendants plead guilty without a trial, in the context of the adversarial system where the onus is on the prosecution to prove guilt, suggests that other factors are at work influencing the guilty plea decision. The bureaucratic model of justice focuses on the need to understand the way the courts deal with such a large number of cases (see Figures 6.1 and 6.2). One answer is the inducement to defendants to plead guilty in return for a more certain or more lenient outcome.

PLEA AND SENTENCE NEGOTIATIONS

One of the most important decisions facing a defendant is whether to plead guilty or not. As we have seen, few defendants exercise their right to a trial. While it might be assumed that the vast majority of defendants are guilty, the decision to plead guilty may be affected by many considerations. In some situations, for example, defendants may feel that while they have committed the act in question, and are therefore 'technically' guilty, they did not intend the outcome – therefore there is no *mens rea*. Or they may know they didn't do it but feel that it is only their word against the police. They may be further persuaded that to persist in a plea of not guilty would protract the case and that if they plead guilty they will be able to have the matter dealt with immediately, thus avoiding the cost to the public purse of a trial and avoiding embarrassment to themselves, victims and witnesses. They may also be aware that they are likely to get a lighter sentence if they plead guilty. The Court of Appeal has indicated that a discount of between a quarter and a third is appropriate for those who plead guilty and statutory force was given to the concept of reducing sentences for a guilty plea in the CJPOA 1994. A plea of guilty may follow a process of negotiations about admitting guilt to a lesser charge, involving the defendant, their legal representative, the prosecution, and in some cases the judge.

The term 'plea bargaining' is used to describe negotiations that may take place between prosecution and defence before, or in the early stages of a trial. The phrase derives from the American process where it is a regular feature of trials. Albert Alschuler (1992) comments that:

> Plea bargaining appears in all common law jurisdictions. Nevertheless, the practice seems most intense in those nations whose trial procedures are most elaborate. For example, plea bargaining seems more firmly entrenched in the United States than in Canada – and more frequent and more intense in Canada than in the United Kingdom, New Zealand and Australia. (On the European Continent, simpler trial procedures apparently have made plea bargaining unnecessary in most serious cases, although Italy has exuberantly embraced the practice and, especially in cases of white-collar crime, Germany has begun bargaining sub rosa.)

A defendant may agree to plead guilty to an offence because of a promise that more serious charges will be dropped, or because the sentence will be less severe. This is unlikely to occur when either the defendant is convinced of his or her innocence or the prosecutor is confident in the strength of evidence. Giving a reduction in sentence for a 'timely' guilty plea is formalised by s. 48 CJPOA 1994 and this, together with the plea before venue procedure (see CPIA 1996) for TEW offences, may discourage the late entering of guilty pleas in many cases. However, there is still an advantage for some offenders, especially those remanded in custody, to delay entering a guilty plea to enable a longer period of time being spent on remand rather than as a convicted inmate. Also there is always the hope that the longer the delay, witnesses might die, become ill, move abroad or that evidence might get lost.

The importance of appreciating the interdependence of different stages in the criminal justice system is highlighted in this extract from an editorial in *The Times*.

Pressure put on a defendant to plead guilty, especially if the pressure is from a judge, will almost always lead to a successful appeal. The Court of Appeal has made this clear often enough for it to be standard doctrine in every English criminal trial. This is the reason plea bargaining is not accepted practice in the English courts. In America, practice is wholly different. Such bargaining usually includes a formal offer from the judge of a reduced sentence, and sometimes a reduction in the seriousness of the charge, if the defendant pleads guilty.

English law is too fastidious about such oiling of the gears of justice. A form of plea bargaining already happens, though surreptitiously. In many a barristers' robing room before the trial, defence counsel has hinted to prosecuting counsel that an adjustment in the charge downwards, say from grievous bodily harm to actual bodily harm, might result in a change of plea, to the benefit of swift justice. This cannot be admitted; and as a result the justice is rougher and not as transparent as it ought to be.

Plea bargaining should be legitimised. With suitable safeguards it would increase rather than reduce the accuracy of the criminal justice system and make it cheaper and more efficient. The strongest argument for plea bargaining comes from regular practitioners in the criminal courts. They say that what professional criminals most want to know, before a trial, is what punishment is likely. Dreading the uncertainty of sentencing and the risk of exceptional severity, the defendant often pleads not guilty on the off-chance of an acquittal. It is not a strictly rational choice, but nor is a life of crime.

(*The Times*, 2 July 1992)

There is often a link between the defendant's decision on plea and mode of trial. This was confirmed in the research by Hedderman and Moxon (1992) on mode of trial decisions. The Hedderman and Moxon study found that in their survey of convicted offenders, 40 per cent originally pleaded not guilty to all charges at the magistrates' court but that figure fell to 12 per cent by the time the final plea was taken. The reason given by 51 per cent of respondents for the change of plea was that they expected some charges to be dropped or reduced, resulting in a lighter sentence. A further 22 per cent claimed there was no chance of their not guilty plea succeeding.

In England and Wales there is currently no systematic plea bargaining but two separate situations may arise where negotiation takes place. The first is better described as charge bargaining, where the defence may offer a plea of guilty to one offence in exchange for a more serious charge being dropped. For example, dangerous driving gets reduced to careless driving, murder is reduced to manslaughter, rape becomes indecent assault.

It is a matter for the prosecution to decide whether to accept a plea of guilty to a lesser charge, or to some counts on the indictment and to take no action on the others. In coming to a decision, the public interest in the prosecution of offences must be weighed against the public interest in minimising expense. Account will be taken of the overall seriousness of the matters charged, the strength of the evidence and the likelihood of conviction.

The second situation is where a judge gives an indication of the likely sentence. This is better referred to as the sentence canvass. While it is obviously an advantage to all parties that all are aware of the range of sentence that the judge has in mind if the defendant is convicted so that appropriate advice can be given, this may be seen as putting pressure on the defendant whether by counsel or by the judge. Although sentences can be explicitly reduced to take account of an early guilty plea, and some reduction may follow from a guilty plea even at the door of the court, the choice of plea is the defendant's own and should be entered freely. Defence lawyers, however, have a duty to explain to their clients the advantages in terms of sentence from pleading guilty. Guidelines have therefore been laid down by the Court of Appeal (see the case of *Turner*, referred to below) stressing the role of both judge and counsel in sentence canvass and advice. These state that a judge should never indicate that a different form of sentence would be imposed if the defendant pleaded guilty, but the counsel might be informed of the likely range of sentence the judge had in mind, irrespective of plea.

What is not approved of is an indication that a contested trial, if lost, will result in a custodial sentence but a guilty plea will mean a non-custodial one. What the judge may say is that the sentence will be of a particular order, whatever the plea. This may therefore encourage a guilty defendant to accept guilt, knowing the likely sentence, rather than gamble on being acquitted after a contested hearing, through fear of an unknown sentence. The guidelines emphasise that although counsel must be able robustly to advise a client to plead guilty if all the evidence points to guilt, they should not persuade a client to plead guilty when the defendant wishes to plead not guilty.

Court of Appeal decisions on plea negotiation

Two-thirds of appeals to the Court of Appeal (Criminal Division) are against sentence rather than against conviction. In some of these appeals the argument is based on the claim that insufficient discount was given by the sentencing judge for a plea of guilty by the defendant. Although normally a third or a quarter discount is given, the Court of Appeal in 1992 established that this was not an absolute or automatic right (*R v R* (a Juvenile) (1992)). The reasons for this are explained in the extract in Figure 7.4. In *R v McGill* (1965) the Court of Appeal said that it was wrong to add on an additional length of sentence if a defendant had contested a case, but it was correct to give credit and so reduce the sentence length when a defendant had pleaded guilty and had shown remorse.

In *R v Behman* (1967) the trial judge made a statement that the defendant's plea of not guilty had led to an increase in sentence. This was wrong. In *R v de Haan* (1968) the Court of Appeal took the view that: 'It is undoubtedly right that a confession of guilt should tell in favour of an accused person and that it is clearly in the public interest.' The appeal against sentence by de Haan led to a sentence of 4.5 years being reduced to 3 years. The Court of Appeal held that the judge had given insufficient allowance for the plea of guilty.

The case of *R v Turner* (1970) highlighted – not for the first time – some of the dangers of advising on plea. The defendant, Turner, had reluctantly pleaded guilty to a charge of theft after strong advice from his counsel. The Court of Appeal set out four rules:

- Counsel must be completely free to give the accused the best advice, albeit in strong terms. This will often include advice that a plea of guilty, showing an element of remorse, is a mitigating factor which may well enable the court to give a lesser sentence than would otherwise be the case.

- The accused, having considered counsel's advice, must have complete freedom of choice whether to plead guilty or not guilty.

- There must be freedom of access between both counsel for the prosecution and the defence and the judge. Any discussion must be between judge and counsel for both sides. It is desirable that such discussions should be in open court, but it is sometimes necessary that they should be in the judge's room: for example, counsel may by way of mitigation wish to tell the judge that the accused had not long to live, is suffering, maybe from cancer, of which they should remain ignorant. Again counsel on both sides may wish to discuss with the judge whether it would be proper, in a particular case, for the prosecution to accept a plea to a lesser offence.

- Subject to one single exception the judge should never indicate the sentence likely to be imposed. Under the exception it is permissible for a judge, if he or she feels able to do so, to indicate that, whatever the accused's plea may be, the sentence will or will not take a particular form. A statement by a judge that, on a plea of guilty, they would impose one sentence, but that, on a conviction following a plea of not guilty, they would impose a severer sentence is one which should never be made.

In *R v Pitman* (1991) the Court of Appeal again drew attention to the difficulties of visits to the judge to discuss sentence. Such visits should only

Fig 7.4 Sentence discount for guilty plea is not a right

No discount for guilty plea Regina v R (a Juvenile)

Before Lord Lane, Lord Chief Justice, Mr Justice Kennedy and
Mr Justice Jowitt
[Judgment January 14]

The granting of credit for a plea of guilty was not to be taken as an inflexible rule. Some offences were so serious that the public interest required imposition of a maximum sentence despite guilty pleas.

The Court of Appeal so stated when giving judgment dismissing an appeal by R, a juvenile aged 15, against sentences imposed at Durham Crown Court by Mr Recorder S Spencer, QC, where he had been committed for sentence to be dealt with under sections 37 and 56 of the Criminal Justice Act 1967, on pleas of guilty to two charges of taking a conveyance without authority, allowing himself to be carried in a motor vehicle knowing it had been taken without the owner's consent, reckless driving and driving uninsured.

For reckless driving he was sentenced to nine months detention in a young offender institution, ordered to run consecutive to three months detention on each of the other offences, except uninsured driving for which no separate penalty was imposed. He was disqualified for holding a driving licence for two years.

Mr Jamie R Adam, assigned by the Registrar of Criminal Appeals, for the appellant.

MR JUSTICE JOWITT, giving the judgment of the court, said that the appellant unlocked and took a car parked at Teesside Airport and two days later took a high performance car from its garage in South Tyneside.

He was seen driving that car soon after 4 am on July 5, 1991 on a Sunderland housing estate and was pursued by a police patrol car. Then, on the appellant's part, there was driving of the most appalling recklessness.

He drove through red traffic lights at speeds in excess of 80 mph, reached speeds of 100 mph and drove the wrong way round a roundabout. When the car finally came to a halt, he ran off, pursued by police.

He was on bail when he committed his final offence of being carried in the vehicle which he knew had been taken without consent. He had a history of failing to respond to non-custodial sentences and was unable or unwilling to respond to them.

The reckless driving offence was too serious to allow of any but a custodial sentence. Had he been 21 or over, an immediate custodial sentence would have been inevitable.

Their Lordships took the view also that, having regard to the offence of reckless driving even without his history of offences, a custodial sentence was necessary to safeguard the public from serious harm by the appellant.

The only live point in the appeal was that, although the appellant pleaded guilty, he received the maximum custodial sentence: 12 months for a juvenile. It was submitted that meant he was given no credit for his pleas of guilty.

The first and foremost answer to that submission was that, although in most cases, the court would give credit for a plea of guilty, the public interest dictated that was not to be seen as an 'inflexible rule'.

There were cases in which, despite the plea of guilty, the offences were of such seriousness, the more so when it was so prevalent in a locality as the instant offence was and potentially highly dangerous to life and limb, the public interest required the imposition of the maximum sentence.

If ever there was such a case the present was it. That point alone was sufficient to dispose of the appeal which was dismissed.

take place if there is no alternative and should be recorded by the shorthand writer.

Advantages and disadvantages of plea bargaining

The issue of plea bargaining yet again reveals the tension between due process, just deserts and bureaucratic considerations. While undoubtedly most participants, including defendants, benefit from plea bargaining or negotiation as it saves time and money, and may reduce the eventual sentence, the system goes against the principle that people should be charged and sentenced for what they did, rather than for what they are able to negotiate. Because of the link between sentence discount and remorse the defendant has to make a difficult decision. Maintaining innocence may involve the defence in trying to discredit the veracity or character of the witnesses and the victim. Afterwards it is difficult to appear remorseful and contrite if found guilty.

With plea bargaining the state is spared the expense of a contested trial and the defendant, by accepting responsibility for a lesser charge, escapes being at risk of conviction of the greater. Plea bargaining saves police time as detectives do not have to attend the trial as witnesses. Staging a trial involves solicitors, barristers and the CPS in preparing their case in readiness for a trial. Plea bargaining also reduces the uncertainty of outcome associated with the trial process for both the defendant and prosecutor. It assures the defendant that the likely penalty is not going to be too draconian, and it ensures a conviction for the prosecutor and police.

It can mean that the victim or witnesses in a trial are spared from an embarrassing public performance and the subsequent publicity. In 1986 the Court of Appeal in *R v Billam*, commented with regard to sentencing in rape cases:

> The extra distress which giving evidence can cause to a victim means that a plea of guilty, perhaps more so than in other cases, should normally result in some reduction from what would otherwise be the appropriate sentence. The amount of such reduction will of course depend on all the circumstances, including the likelihood of a finding of not guilty had the matter been contested.

The sentencing discount, while it may be perfectly fair for sentencers to reward those who show signs of remorse by accepting their guilt, unintentionally disadvantages those who exercise their right to a trial. In addition it may run counter to the principles of just deserts – as defendants may be sentenced not for the offence they have committed, but for the offence that they have pleaded guilty to. Justice may not be done as in some cases the innocent agree to plea guilty. Also worrying to the public and victims is the number of criminals who may be convicted and sentenced for lesser crimes than they committed. This can cause outrage to the public, the victim and the

Fig 7.5 Judge comments on dropped charges

Rape Decision 'Means Justice Not Done'
By Craig Seton

A judge said yesterday he had no confidence that justice had been done after charges of rape or attempted rape were dropped against four men who subjected two teenage girls to a sexual attack.

Mr Justice McCullough, sitting at Birmingham Crown Court, imposed a fine of £250 on Iftikhar Ahmed, aged 17, who pleaded guilty to indecent assault after a charge of rape was withdrawn. But the judge told Ahmed, of Sparkhill, Birmingham: 'Had you stood trial, as I think you should, of being an accessory to the rape of one of the girls and you had been convicted by a jury, you would have lost your liberty for a number of years'.

The court was told that two of the other three men were alleged to have confessed to rape in Cannon Hill Park, Birmingham, last year in interviews with police. The judge said the prosecution had decided to accept lesser pleas because some evidence was unsatisfactory.

'I am not saying that these men were guilty of the offences for which they were not tried, but I have no confidence that justice has been done', he said.

Mahboo Khan, aged 18, from Balsall Heath, Birmingham, was sentenced to 27 months' youth custody after admitting attempted rape: a charge of rape and indecent assault were withdrawn. Nahim Ashad, aged 18, of Moseley, Birmingham, received 12 months' youth custody after admitting indecent assault; two charges of attempted rape were withdrawn. Razak Malik, 21, of Sparkhill, Birmingham pleaded guilty to indecent assault after an attempted rape charge was dropped. He was given a three-month jail sentence, suspended for a year.

Source: *The Times*, 2 February 1989; © Times Supplements Limited, 1989.

investigating police who collected the evidence. This concern prompted the comments in Figure 7.5 of a trial judge on dropped charges in a rape case.

APPEALS

There are provisions for appealing against most of the decisions made in the court process, and against decisions such as those relating to bail and legal aid, but the most significant areas for appeal are the two decisions that most directly affect the offender: the decision to convict and the decision on sentence. The prosecution only has limited rights of appeal in these matters: against conviction only on a point of law, which does not affect the acquittal; and on sentence against unduly lenient sentences in a limited number of more serious cases.

A defendant convicted after a trial in the magistrates' court can always appeal to the Crown Court against conviction and/or sentence. After a guilty plea the appeal is only against sentence. The appeal must be lodged within 21 days or any extended period granted by the Crown Court. The appeal takes the form of a fresh trial in the Crown Court, but the format is that of a summary trial, so there is no jury: the verdict is reached by the judge sitting with two lay magistrates. Their powers are to make any order that the original magistrates had power to impose. This means that a defendant can be more severely punished by the Crown Court on appeal and is a factor that may deter some appellants. Alternatively, an appeal arguing that a procedural error took place goes to the Queen's Bench Division of the High Court.

Appeals from Crown Court trials are generally made to the Court of Appeal, Criminal Division, against either sentence or conviction or both. Before a person can appeal they must obtain permission to do so. This permission can be given by the trial or sentencing judge granting a certificate that the case is fit for appeal, or by the Court of Appeal granting leave to appeal. The former is rare, except where a novel point of law is involved and both sides accept that the matter would inevitably need resolution by a higher court, and the vast majority of cases are dealt with by the Court of Appeal first as applications for leave. The court will allow an appeal against conviction only if it is felt that the conviction is unsafe (Criminal Appeal Act 1995). If they do allow it they may quash, that is overturn, the conviction, convict the defendant on another lesser offence or order a retrial in the Crown Court. Where the appeal is against sentence (except where the prosecution has used the special procedure to appeal against an unduly lenient sentence) the court may not impose a more serious sentence than the original sentence appealed against. Appeals from the Court of Appeal are made to the House of Lords by either side if leave is granted, or a certificate that a point of general public importance is involved.

CONCLUSION

This chapter has reviewed many aspects of the trial, looking at its participants and at the rules surrounding evidence and procedure. It is clear that while the trial is central to the due process model, many factors affect its outcome. The problems of reconciling the many goals of the criminal justice system are clearly seen in respect of plea negotiation. Few dispute that this greatly reduces the costs of the system and that in many cases it is advantageous for all concerned; indeed the consequent reduction in trials may ensure the system can function. Yet its popularity undermines many other goals of the system. It is, for example, in the interests of justice that offenders are punished for what they have done rather than what they are prepared to plead guilty to. A denunciation model would require that punishment should reflect society's disapproval of criminal acts – not reward them.

These matters are not easy to resolve, as seen in the continuing controversy over matters such as the right to silence, the admissibility of evidence and plea negotiation. In general, pressures for cost effectiveness may well conflict with those for crime control, just deserts and due process. When we add to this considerations which are more relevant to sentencing decisions, such as denunciation, rehabilitation and deterrence, the situation becomes even more complex. These sentencing decisions and policies will be the subject of Chapter 8.

Review questions

Write short notes on the following:

1. Does the trial in England and Wales establish the innocence of the defendant?

2. Why do rules of procedure and evidence exist?

3. What is meant by the terms 'burden' and 'standard of proof'?

4. Is there an acceptable alternative to the jury system?

5. How would the different models of criminal justice respond to the issue of plea bargaining?

6. Below are six examples of types of evidence presented during a criminal trial.

   (a) Classify them using the following categories of evidence:

   Character evidence
   Eye-witness identification evidence
   Expert evidence
   Alibi evidence
   Computer evidence
   Real evidence

   (b) Classify the following examples of evidence in terms of whether they are: oral, documentary or an exhibit:

   (1) Mrs Green states in the witness box that she recognised the defendant coming out of the shop where the robbery took place.

   (2) A report from a professor of mechanical engineering is presented to the court, setting out the damage to a car and explaining the likely speed of impact.

   (3) A till roll from an electronic checkout machine is presented showing there was no entry in respect of items found in Mr Brown's shopping basket.

   (4) A quantity of white powder, found in the defendant's car, is produced.

   (5) Mr White says that the defendant has worked for him for 10 years and has always been a model of probity.

(6) Miss Scarlet states in her evidence that Rhett, the defendant accused of arson, was with her the whole of the night during which the offence is alleged to have taken place.

7. What are the arguments for and against broadcasting of trials on television?

Further reading

Ashworth A (1998) *The Criminal Process*. 2nd Edn. Oxford: Clarendon Press
Darbyshire P (1991) 'The lamp that shows that freedom lives: is it worth the candle?', *Criminal Law Review*: 740. London: Sweet & Maxwell
Murphy P (1997) *A Practical Approach to Evidence*, 6th edn. London: Blackstone Press
Sanders A and Young R (1994) *Criminal Justice*. London: Butterworth

CHAPTER 8

SENTENCING PROCESS AND PROCEDURE

- Aims of Sentencing
- Types of Sentence
- Sentencing Procedure
- Factors Influencing Sentencing Decisions
- Structuring Sentencing Decisions

INTRODUCTION

Sentencing is a key function of the criminal justice process and involves many different and often conflicting considerations. The models of criminal justice explored in previous chapters indicate some of the issues to be addressed by an exploration of sentencing decisions and policy. Should sentences aim to punish or rehabilitate the individual offender or protect society from the risk posed by particular offenders? Should sentencing perform a broader role of expressing the community's condemnation of particular kinds of behaviour as the denunciation model suggests? Can or should the criminal justice process attempt to reduce crime, either by devising sentences aimed at individual offenders or at potential offenders in the general population? Can any criminal justice system reasonably aim to do all of these things or should the role of sentences be a more restricted one? Should sentences be individually tailored to the needs and risks of an offender, or is consistency more important? As with other aspects of the process, a balance must be sought between the often conflicting pressures of different goals.

In this chapter we will focus on sentencing decisions and the mechanisms and procedures which affect the sentencing process. We start by examining the multiple aims of sentencing which affect the choice of sentence: a choice increasingly curtailed by statutory and other considerations. The Criminal Justice Act 1991 (CJA 1991) set out to impose a coherent theoretical approach to sentencing. The implications of this Act, along with other legislation are considered when we examine the types of sentence available to the courts and the criteria and procedure for their imposition. The philosophical underpinnings of the CJA 1991 will be examined in Chapter 9.

236

We will look at the range and pattern of sentences given by the courts and the influence of statutory criteria, magistrates' guidelines and Court of Appeal decisions. The next section will examine overt and other less obvious influences on sentencing decisions, some of which have caused concern on the grounds of bias or inconsistency. Many suggestions have been made to limit inconsistencies and increasingly emphasis has been placed, especially in the magistrates' court, on a rational – perhaps rigid – approach to sentencing in order to ensure that relevant issues are considered appropriately.

AIMS OF SENTENCING

In 1996 1.44 million offenders were sentenced by the criminal courts in England and Wales (see Figure 8.1). To discover more about why all these people were sentenced in the way that they were, we need firstly to distinguish between the aims of sentencing, the justification for sentences and the distribution of sentences.

The *aim* of sentencing is the purpose or objective that the sentencer or policy maker is seeking to achieve. Does the sentence aim to rehabilitate, punish, or deter an individual offender or mark the seriousness of offence in some way? The *justification* for sentencing involves considering why the aims are desirable, especially where sentences aim at some beneficial consequences. The justification for sentencing policy may be that it can reduce crime, prevent private vengeance, or mark unacceptable behaviour. The *distribution* of punishment allows us to examine who is punished, and how they are – or should be – punished. Should the convicted criminal in a particular case be executed, locked away or made to pay a penalty? How long should they be locked away for? How much should they be required to pay if fined?

A sentence might involve some form of *punishment*, and a key feature distinguishing criminal from other branches of law is that it involves the possibility of the state imposing a punishment on an offender. Such punishment however must follow a finding of guilt in accordance with due process. This distinguishes state punishment from private vengeance. One definition of punishment in this context is provided by H L A Hart (1968).

- Punishment must involve pain or other consequences normally considered unpleasant.

- It must be for an offence against legal rules.

- It must be of an actual or supposed offender for an offence.

- It must be intentionally administered by human beings other than the offender.

- It must be imposed and administered by an authority constituted by a legal system against which the offence is committed.

237

Fig 8.1 Offenders sentenced in 1996

	Total no. of offenders	Indictable offences	Magistrates' courts Summary offences		% of those sentenced		
			non-motoring	motoring	indictable	summary non-motoring	summary motoring
Absolute discharge	19,900	2,400	5,700	11,800	1	1	2
Conditional discharge	102,000	50,100	43,200	8,700	22	9	1
Fine	1,069,700	81,900	402,300	585,400	36	83	90
Probation	43,800	26,300	7,900	9,500	11	2	1
Supervision order	10,300	8,000	1,900	400	3	0	0
CSO	36,800	19,700	8,100	9,000	9	2	1
Attendance centre	7,400	5,300	1,900	100	2	0	0
Combination order	14,300	7,400	2,100	4,900	3	0	1
Curfew order	200	100	0.0	0.0	0	0	0
YOI	11,200	7,400	1,900	1,900	3	0	0
Prison	30,000	14,600	4,400	11,000	6	1	2
Other	18,600	6,100	6,800	5,500	2	1	1
Total	**1,364,200**	**229,300**	**486,200**	**648,200**	**100**	**100**	**100**

Crown Court

	Total no. of offenders	Indictable offences	Summary offences		% of those sentenced		
			non-motoring	motoring	indictable	summary non-motoring	summary motoring
Absolute discharge	100	100	0.0	0.0	0	0	0
Conditional discharge	2,700	2,200	400	0	3	21	2
Fine	3,400	2,700	400	300	4	18	38
Probation	7,200	6,900	200	100	10	11	12
Supervision order	600	600	0.0	nil	1	0	nil
CSO	9,000	8,600	400	0.0	12	19	6
Attendance centre	100	100	0.0	nil	0	0	nil
Combination order	3,000	2,800	100	0.0	4	3	7
Curfew order	0.0	0.0	nil	nil	0	nil	nil
YOI	9,500	9,300	100	0.0	13	7	3
Prison	33,900	33,500	300	200	47	16	24
S53 CYPA 1933	600	600	n/a	n/a	1	n/a	n/a
Other	3,600	3,500	100	0.0	5	4	7
Total	**73,700**	**70,900**	**2,000**	**600**	**100**	**100**	**100**

Compiled from *Criminal Statistics England and Wales 1996*: 163.

(The statistics are rounded up and a 0.0 means less than 50: and, 0 means less than 500)

Through punishment it is often hoped to achieve one or more sentencing aims, often described as theories of sentencing. Six main theories are found in most jurisdictions, although the balance between different theories varies according to the prevailing sentencing policy of any individual system, which may place a greater emphasis on one aim or on a particular combination. The six theories are retribution, incapacitation, rehabilitation, deterrence, denunciation and restitution.

These theories affect what the sentencer hopes to achieve by a sentence and what considerations should be taken into account. Thus if the aim is to rehabilitate, the needs of the offender must be considered; if to protect the community through incapacitating dangerous offenders, the risk of future danger must be calculated. If the aim is to deter, an evaluation of what will make an impact on those considering criminal acts in the future must be made; if to denounce, the moral expectation of the community must be signalled; if to seek retribution, the right balance must be found between the seriousness of offence and severity of sanction.

The theories can be distinguished in terms of what they wish to achieve. Three of the objectives are sometimes described as offender-instrumental in that they aim to affect the future behaviour of individual offenders. Rehabilitation aims to change future behaviour through counselling, treatment and training. Deterrence aims to make the potential offender think again through the anticipation of future sanctions. Incapacitation seeks to restrain offenders physically to make it impossible for them to re-offend. However, the impact on the offender is just one aspect of sentencing, for there is another audience: the public and its desire to see criminals punished and to be protected from physical injury and loss of personal property. This is reflected in the aims of retribution, denunciation and incapacitation. Restitution also seeks directly or indirectly to recompense the victim for the harm suffered.

Thus sentences may be individualised, that is based on a consideration of their impact on individual offenders. This means that the circumstances of the offender and the risk they pose must be taken into account. On the other hand, sentences may be based primarily on the seriousness of the offence in that they aim to reflect public disapproval or attempt to punish in proportion to the seriousness of the offence. In addition, it is often seen as desirable that sentences should be concerned with justice for, and fairness to, individual offenders, as implied by the due process model. Thus if different sentences are given for similar offences to offenders with similar circumstances and background, they could be seen as unjust or unfair. This is known as sentencing disparity, and is more likely to happen, according to Andrew Ashworth, when the sentencer can draw on any one or any combination of the six theories to justify a decision. Different sentencers may have different aims and different conceptions of distribution, producing little consistency of approach. Therefore, unless a priority is established and agreed, individualised sentences will lead to disparities. Ashworth argues that 'unless decisions of principle are taken on priorities among two or more sentencing aims, the esultant uncertainty would be a recipe for disparity' (von Hirsch and Ashworth 1993: 258).

Turning penal aims into sentencing policy is not however easy, especially as most jurisdictions attempt to combine elements of the six theories so that sentencing policy simultaneously seeks to:

> denounce the wrongful, deter the calculating, incapacitate the incorrigible, rehabilitate the wayward, recompense the victim and punish only the culpable.
>
> (Davies 1989: 6)

In addition, different theories may be more influential at different times and the shifting balance between them is apparent not only in England and Wales but in other jurisdictions. These shifting penal paradigms will be examined in detail in Chapter 9. It is helpful however, when exploring the influences on sentencing aims and practice, to look at policy pronouncements on these issues. In the 1990 white paper, *Crime, Justice and Protecting the Public*, which led to the CJA 1991, the following balance between objectives was articulated:

> The first objective for all sentences is the denunciation of and retribution for the crime. Depending on the offence and the offender, the sentence may also aim to achieve public protection, reparation and reform of the offender, preferably in the community. This approach points to sentencing policies which are more firmly based on the seriousness of the offence, and just deserts for the offender.
>
> (Home Office 1990a: 6)

Although regarding the two goals of denunciation and retribution as primary, the statement makes it clear that they are not the exclusive aims of sentencing and it also refers to public protection, reparation and reform of the offender (Home Office 1990a: 6). Note the absence of a reference to deterrence.

There is rarely agreement among policy makers about the ideal form of sentencing. Translating sentencing objectives into a range of penalties and disposals for the courts, and providing a framework of principles to apply, is no easy task because of the multiple aims we simultaneously seek to achieve through sentencing. While philosophical, criminological and legal principles are important they are not the only considerations. The introduction of unit fines in the CJA 1991 and their subsequent repeal shows the importance of public confidence in such matters. Even if we devise a tariff of penalties and disposals within a just deserts framework, and ignore other claims, we would still have problems as the tariff cannot be derived from the scientific calibration of seriousness of a crime or the severity of a sanction as the tariff is not a fixed currency but moves with the public mood.

The CJA 1991 was passed following a period of unparalleled consultation and planning yet it was subject to fundamental amendments after only 6 months of operation by the CJA 1993. Since then, further, albeit less significant, alterations to the CJA 1991 have followed in the Criminal Justice and Public Order Act 1994, the Crime (Sentences) Act 1997 and the Crime and

Disorder Act 1998. Sentencing policy, perhaps more than any other aspect of the criminal justice system, is constantly being re-examined and reflected upon in terms of 'Does it work?' and, 'Is it credible?'.

The history of sentencing policy is a history of changing emphases on the six sentencing goals which we will now examine in turn.

Retribution

As we have seen, many theories see the purpose of sentencing as to reduce crime or change offenders' behaviour or attitudes. Retributionists do not use this rationale. The purpose of retribution is to seek vengeance upon a blameworthy person because they have committed a wrongful act. While some versions of retributive theory sought to justify punishment by talk of redressing the moral balance or atonement for wrongs committed, the more straightforward versions merely state that some acts are wrong and deserve to be punished, thus punishment is an end in itself.

This theory is sometimes referred to as an 'eye-for-an-eye', but if taken literally this would require the duplication of the offence as the punishment. Thus proponents of capital punishment use the phrase 'a life for a life'. However, punishment based on the literal duplication of the crime could be seen as unethical, especially where the crime was a particularly cruel murder. It is also impractical for most other crimes. For instance, what would be the eye-for-an-eye for offences such as burglary or handling stolen goods? Even more problematic would be deciding what punishment should be given to a serial killer, a rapist or a child molester. The eye-for-an-eye is more helpful as a metaphor to suggest that there should be some balance between the wrong done by the offender and the pain inflicted on that offender in the form of a punishment, popularly expressed as 'let the punishment fit the crime'.

In a retributive approach the calculation of punishment depends on two factors. First, culpability or blameworthiness. Retributionists insist that only blameworthy offenders should be punished. Therefore as seen in Chapter 5 children and the mentally ill are absolved of blame for their criminal conduct and need not be punished. We have also seen that a crucial issue in criminal liability is not only the *actus reus* but the *mens rea*. Thus before conviction for murder, the court must establish whether the defendant is blameworthy or as in a case of self-defence, acted in an acceptable way and is therefore not culpable of murder. Also, as we saw in Chapter 2, different defences and mitigating factors are used to absolve the defendant, or reduce the level of culpability.

Once culpability is established the retributionist will look at the seriousness of the offence to determine the deserved penalty. In this respect retributive theory refers to commensurate punishment, a concept not used so much today because it implies a notion of equivalence. The term 'proportionate sentence' is preferred because this suggests that offences and penalties can be anged from more to less severe without any suggestion that there can be an exact measurement of equivalence. Thus what is generally referred to as a tariff of penalties is notionally arranged in order of severity. There is no assumption, however, that they are somehow equivalent to the harm done by the offender.

ncapacitation or public protection

We have already seen how considerations of public protection influence all stages of the criminal justice process. These underlie the aim of incapacitation, the purpose of which is to impose a physical restriction on offenders which makes it impossible or reduces the opportunities for them to re-offend. The most common way of incapacitating offenders is through long periods of imprisonment justified on the grounds that they prevent persistent or serious offenders from re-offending. Thus the Prevention of Crime Act 1908 introduced a new measure of preventive detention to deal with 'habitual criminals' who made a career from crime. Section 10 of the 1908 Act allowed an addition of 5 to 10 years' detention on top of the original sentence for the current offence. The term applied to those who were persistently leading a life of crime and had three convictions since the age of 16. The extended sentence which replaced preventive detention in the CJA 1967, the discretionary life sentence and the retention in the CJA 1991 of discretionary parole for offenders sentenced for over 4 years in custody were similarly justified in terms of public protection. The Crime (Sentences) Act 1997 provides minimum sentences for repeat offenders in drug trafficking and a mandatory life sentence for some serious offences.

There are other ways of incapacitating offenders. Disqualification of drivers convicted of serious motoring offences aims to stop them driving and company directors convicted of serious fraud and other business offenders may also be incapacitated by disqualifications or by withdrawing licences which make it impossible for them to carry on in business. Offenders convicted of mistreating animals can be banned from owning them. Normally incapacitation is linked to the type of crime committed but a generally incapacitative sentence is introduced by the Crime (Sentences) Act 1997 under which a driving disqualification can be imposed for any offence. More recent 'high tech' forms of incapacitation, including electronic surveillance by the use of electronic tags and curfew orders, have an incapacitative element. Most controversial has been the use of medical means of incapacitation including the sterilisation of persistent sexual offenders. The common justification for these approaches is that they prevent a future offence from being committed and thereby protect the public.

In the USA, public protection was the justification given for the 'three strikes and you are out' policy of incapacitation of those criminals convicted of three felonies. In 1994 in some US jurisdictions legislation was introduced to make a mandatory prison term applicable after the third similar offence – whatever the mitigation. This same incapacitative logic is to be found in the justification of the reforms found in the Crime (Sentences) Act 1997.

Incapacitation and retribution are often contrasted in terms of sentencing aims and effects. Retribution relates to punishment for the wrong done, whereas incapacitation relates to the prevention of future wrong where exceeding any notion of proportionate sentencing is justified on the grounds that the offender is a continuing risk. The contrast is often articulated as 'deservedness versus dangerousness' (von Hirsch 1986), and both ideas are given as criteria for imprisonment in the CJA 1991. One of the major problems with incapacitation lies in how offenders are selected for extended periods of imprisonment or other forms of incapacitation. As this involves longer and more severe sentences than would be considered appropriate by other theories, it raises issues not only of fairness, but of how accurate predictions of the risk of further offending are likely to be.

Incapacitation seems to have been uppermost in Mr Justice Butterfield's mind when he sentenced Victor Farrant for murder and attempted murder in January 1998. On passing the mandatory life sentence for murder and 18 years for the attempt, committed within weeks of being released after serving 7 years of a 12-year rape sentence, the judge said

> This murder was so terrible and you are so dangerous that in your case the sentence of life should mean just that – you should never be released. You have devastated the lives of many people. The opportunity to do so again should not be allowed to you.
>
> (*The Independent*, 30 January 1998: 13)

Rehabilitation

We have seen in previous chapters how the rehabilitative model affects not only the sentencing process but permeates the entire criminal justice process. As a sentencing goal, rehabilitation is concerned with the future behaviour of an offender and aims to reduce the likelihood of future re-offending. Thus the use of welfare and treatment strategies targeted at individual offenders. The justification for this is that if successful, fewer people will be future victims of offences committed by these offenders.

As seen in Chapter 2, in the 1960s the emergent social sciences appeared to hold out the hope that crime could be reduced humanely. It was believed that through the application of science the causes of crime, which was seen as a kind of illness, could be diagnosed and treated. Criminals therefore were in need of treatment rather than punishment. Rehabilitative sentences, therefore, must consider the needs of the offender rather than issues of morality, the seriousness of the offence or criminal responsibility. Thus sentences with a rehabilitative aim may be very different from those indicated by other approaches. Rehabilitation could justify a longer sentence than the seriousness of the offence might suggest to allow for a programme of treatment to be carried out, or alternatively might suggest treatment outside institutions although this would mean less protection for the public. Rehabilitative ideals have strongly influenced penal policy in many jurisdictions and led to the development of social work and psychiatry in the penal system and of special institutions to cater for offenders considered to be in need of psychiatric help. The claims for rehabilitation are now much more modest for reasons which will be explored in Chapter 9.

Rehabilitation thus necessitates a sentencing policy that allows for the sentence to fit the individual rather than the offence. To this end, rehabilitative sentencing policies require the following:

- *Monitoring and classification.* Pre-sentence reports are required by the courts to assess needs prior to sentencing and constant monitoring is required during a sentence to establish progress.

- *Individualisation.* A flexible range of sanctions and resources should be available so as to be able to respond to the individual needs of each offender in the hope of changing their future behaviour. Some offenders will need counselling with regard to drug dependency; others will need social skills training.

- *Indeterminacy.* If the offender has committed a sufficiently serious offence, or is deemed a danger to the public, institutional containment in prisons or hospitals might be necessary. However, rehabilitative and treatment needs mean that the length of such incarceration should be flexible, to allow for the response of the offender, now classified as an inmate, client or patient, to a treatment programme. Thus sentences may be indeterminate, where the amount of time is not fixed at the time of sentence but is dependent on the progress of treatment.

Deterrence

The object of deterrence is to reduce the likelihood of crimes being committed in the future by the threat of punishment. It is based on the assumption that offenders, fearing punishment, will refrain from criminal behaviour. Deterrent policies may be aimed at individual offenders, thus we talk of individual deterrence, or it may aim to affect the behaviour of others who may be contemplating committing a crime, known as general deterrence. Deterrence is used in everyday life – it is, for example, the theory underpinning a threat issued to encourage people to comply with rules or refrain from infringing them, and is a principle well known to most parents: 'if you do that again I will . . . (threat), or you won't . . . (reward)'.

Deterrence, like rehabilitation and incapacitation, aims to reduce the likelihood of an offence being committed in the future. Thus they are described as 'consequentialist' theories as the focus is on the consequences of sentencing. Deterrent theory is not concerned with issues of fairness and justice but with the question of effectiveness. Does it work? This question can be looked at theoretically and empirically.

At a theoretical level the theory makes certain assumptions. It assumes that before engaging in criminal acts criminals calculate how unpleasant a sentence might be. This involves three other assumptions. First, that crimes occur as a result of individuals exercising free will and acting out of choice. Secondly, that these individuals consider the consequences of their acts and the likelihood of being caught. Thirdly, that the potential criminal regards the potential sentence as undesirable.

Objections might be made that many criminal acts do not match these assumptions. In particular, the most serious crimes such as homicide are not usually carried out after calculation, but result from anger, fear or a momentary loss of control. Other, and possibly most, offenders do not expect to be caught – so the likely sentence is far from their thoughts. Some serious crimes may be affected – offenders may for example think about the repercussions when deciding whether to use a weapon in a robbery. At the other end of the offending scale, in road traffic matters, deterrence has apparently had some effect. Sir Paul Condon, the Metropolitan Police Commissioner, is reported as commenting that 'fatalities on stretches of roads in West London are down by one-third since the introduction of law-enforcement cameras' (Condon 1994).

Although as we have seen deterrence was not given much credence in the 1990 White Paper, Court of Appeal judges continued to use it to justify sentencing decisions. In May 1993 the Court of Appeal reduced a 12 months' custodial sentence for Nicholas Decino to 10 months. Mr Decino had a 10 months' suspended sentence for burglary and possession of drugs activated after he was convicted of theft from a telephone kiosk. The Court of Appeal thought this was so serious as to justify a prison term but made it run concurrently so that the total term would be 10, not 12 months. Lord Justice Beldam explained the sentence of the court:

> . . . this was the kind of offence which was capable of depriving members of the public of the use of the public telephone which, to many people, was a lifeline. Of necessity telephone boxes were left unprotected. It was a matter of public policy to deter thefts from such boxes.
>
> (Law Report, *The Times*, 10 May 1993)

Denunciation

The denunciation model stresses the role of the criminal justice system in publicly expressing society's condemnation. Thus sentences can be used to underline the community's outrage at the particular offence and crime in general. Denunciation is concerned with the impact of the sentence on the community and how this in turn affects the demarcation of the moral boundaries of society. Thus by identifying what behaviour is unacceptable, societies define themselves.

Under denunciation theory, sentencing is an act of official disapproval and social censure. It shares with retribution a focus on the morality of the act, but unlike retribution it looks beyond what should happen to the offender and examines the impact of a sentence on the community. It thus brings to centre stage issues of morality and how community perceptions of crime and punishment may conflict with those of the state and the law.

> The impact of punishment is not a private matter between offender and victim, for it also involves the community's expectations about appropriate standards of behaviour . . . The criminal provides us with a living example of our moral boundaries: by our outrage we come to recognise our shared fears, rules of communal living and mutual interdependency. We collectively define what sort of people we are by denouncing the type of people we are not.
>
> (Davies 1993: 15)

Thus one of the key functions of sentencing is to portray, however impressionistically, the public's mood about unacceptable behaviour, and to represent a collective expression of right and wrong in response to offensive behaviour. Judges, in passing sentence, sketch the official portrait of public morality but the community's response to sentencing decisions provides the fine detail. Sentencing decisions are on some occasions unpopular and judicial pronouncements are criticised as too avant garde or too dated.

This can be seen in cases where sentencing decisions have become the focus of public debate about the society we live in as they draw attention to the offence committed and the response. Of course, not all sentencing decisions evoke a moral debate; many, if not most, go unnoticed. However, occasionally sentences receive considerable publicity and criticisms of their appropriateness. In more routine cases the audience for the moral drama may only be the jury, victim and witnesses or their neighbours, friends and relatives. The message they receive may be distorted by their limited understanding of criminal procedure and law. But they will form an impression of the state of public morality, which, while affecting them only directly, will influence their perception of the type of community they live in.

Everyday morality is constructed, in part, in this way. In a more individualistic and pluralistic society, the attempt to express the community's view becomes more difficult but even more important as an effort to identify commonly-held expectations about how we should behave towards each other. If unacceptable behaviour is not acknowledged and assumed morality is not reinforced by the courts, it might be concluded that there is no shared definition of unacceptable behaviour. This could enhance individualistic responses to crime and break down collective expectations, thus creating unpredictability and uncertainty and undermining the basis of citizenship. It is also likely to encourage people to take action themselves against crime by, for example, acts of vigilantism. This latter point has led to recent suggestions that there is possibly a further aim of sentencing – to maintain law and order and prevent such private responses to crime. We will look at vigilante response to crime in Chapter 11.

Restitution or reparation

Increasing concern with the interests of victims has led to a growth of interest in reparation and restitution which aim to compensate the victim of crime, either specifically or symbolically, usually through a financial payment or services provided. Thus an offender can be ordered to make financial compensation to individual victims, or to symbolically pay back society or the state for the harm done. Experimental reparation schemes have involved bringing offenders and victims together to attempt not only reparation, but also conciliation (see Chapter 11 on restorative justice). Outside the sentencing sphere, the Criminal Injuries Compensation Scheme provides a government fund whereby the state rather than the offender compensates the victim for harm done by violent crime. This however may be more akin to a state based insurance scheme: it is not a sentence, though it seeks to make reparation. These measures will be further explored in Chapter 11.

The potential effect of reparation is greatest perhaps with property crime and in circumstances where victims are willing to participate and offenders can make some kind of meaningful reparation. Their application is less appropriate in cases of serious violent crime, where it is unlikely that the offender can make any meaningful reparation. A symbolic form of reparation underlies some other sentencing options, as it can be argued that there is a notion of reparation in community service orders, in that the offender is in some way giving something back to the community.

Having looked at the theories underlying sentencing, we will now outline the main sentences available to the courts and, in general terms, ask which of the sentencing aims may be fulfilled by them.

TYPES OF SENTENCE

Four main categories of sentence – discharges, financial penalties, community sentences and custodial sentences – are available to the courts. All are available to both magistrates' courts and the Crown Court but the magistrates' court has an upper limit for financial and custodial sentences. In addition, the court may bind over a defendant, defer sentence or impose a range of ancillary orders.

Discharges

There are two main forms of discharge. An absolute discharge in effect means that although the conviction is recorded, nothing will happen to the offender. A conditional discharge means that if, for the duration of the order, a specified period of up to 3 years, offenders are not found guilty of any other offence, they will receive no punishment. If, however, during the period of the discharge, they are sentenced by a court for another offence, they may be sentenced not only for the new matter, but also for the offence for which they were originally discharged. Under the Powers of the Criminal Courts Act 1973 a court may impose a conditional or absolute discharge where it is of the opinion it is 'inexpedient to inflict punishment'.

A discharge is thus a sentence that does not seek to punish. The main sentencing aim that would appear relevant therefore is denunciation – merely acknowledging that an offence has been committed – but in the circumstances it is accepted that is unnecessary to punish. The conditional discharge also has a deterrent purpose: 'Do this again and you will be punished.' It is used in a wide variety of circumstances, but most commonly for first offenders who commit a less serious offence.

Financial penalties

A fine is the most common penalty, and is the most likely result for summary offences and many triable-either-way (TEW) offences heard in the magistrates' court. Where a case is sentenced in the magistrates' court the maximum fine is governed by the statutory maximum for that offence. Summary offences range from level one (maximum £200) to five (maximum £5,000). Most TEW offences are governed by the overall magistrates' court maximum, currently £5,000 for adult offenders. However, a few trading and environmental offences carry a penalty of up to £20,000 or £50,000. In the Crown Court fines are 'at large', which means there are no limits. Fines must be assessed in relation to the seriousness of the offence, and it has long been a principle of sentencing that the level of fine imposed on an individual should take into account the offender's means and income and vary the fine accordingly. The fine, therefore, can be accurately adjusted in terms of proportionality, and is usually thought of as a deterrent or retributive sentence. Some would urge that a fine can also have an incapacitative effect in limiting an offender's opportunities perhaps by preventing the offender from buying alcohol when the offence is drink related.

Compensation must be considered by a court when dealing with a case that has resulted in personal injury, or property damage. It can be ordered instead of, or in addition to, another order (Powers of the Criminal Courts Act 1973 as amended). If the court fails to order compensation in such circumstances, it must state its reasons. If a compensation order is made, it means that the offender should pay a stated amount to the person harmed by the offence. A compensation order is the prime reparative disposal.

Costs are also frequently ordered against offenders and may represent a substantial part of the financial effect of a court order. Costs may be awarded against any convicted offender, but rank after compensation and fines in order of payment: if the offender's means are insufficient to meet all three compensation to the victim takes priority.

Community penalties

The following are community sentences: probation order, community service order, combination order, curfew order, supervision order, or attendance centre order. The combination and curfew orders were introduced by the CJA 1991.

The criteria for the imposition of a community sentence were laid down by the CJA 1991, later, as we have seen, amended by the CJA 1993. Consequently a community sentence can only be imposed if the offence or offences are serious enough to warrant its imposition, if the combination of orders is suitable for the offender, and the restriction on liberty of the offender is commensurate with the seriousness of offending. A presentence report must be obtained before assessing whether or not the offender is suitable for an order when any of the following are being considered: combination order, community service order or a probation or supervision order with additional requirements. The 1991 Act also contains a requirement that the reasons for giving such an order, and the precise effect of it should be explained in ordinary language.

In addition to the general criteria laid down by the CJA 1991, individual sentences are considered appropriate in different situations. A probation order is available for an offender of 16 or over where the court feels such an order is desirable to rehabilitate the offender, to protect the public or prevent offences. Thus the specific aims that the court is seeking are clearly stated. Orders must be for a specified period, from 6 months to 3 years, and can be combined with a financial or other community order except a community service order. Under the Act, a probation order with additional requirements may be made such as an order of residence, an order to engage in certain activities such as attendance at anger management or impaired driver groups or desist from others, or to attend a probation centre. Extra requirements may be imposed for sex offenders or those in need of treatment for alcohol or drug abuse or mental illness and these need the consent of the offender before they can be imposed. Probation orders are still seen as primarily rehabilitative, although the 1991 Act sought to redefine all community sentences as punitive.

A community service order (CSO) requires the offender to do unpaid work for the community for a specified number of hours, ranging from a minimum of 40 hours to a maximum of 240, over a period of a year. It is available for offenders aged 16 and over convicted of any imprisonable offence. The court may hear from a probation officer as to the offender's suitability and must be satisfied that work is available. A CSO satisfies simultaneously many penal objectives. It includes a symbolic element of reparation, if not to the individual victim, then at least to the community. It also involves denunciation particularly if the imposition of the sentence is followed by a visible performance of the work, and the restriction on liberty is intended to have a punitive impact so as to deter and punish offenders. Others point to the rehabilitative effect of doing valuable work for the community.

The combination order was introduced by the CJA 1991, and is available for offenders who are 16 or over, where the offence is imprisonable and the court feels that such an order is in the interests of rehabilitation or of protecting the public or preventing offences. A combination order combines probation of 12 months to 3 years with community service of 40–100 hours, and was intended by the policy makers to be the most severe of all the community sentences.

A curfew order is a sentence of the court which can be imposed in association with another sentence, or alone. The Crime (Sentences) Act 1997 allows for the imposition of curfew orders with electronic monitoring (for up to 180 days) or 20–100 hours of CSO to be imposed on fine defaulters. Persistent petty offenders can also be punished by a curfew order or 40–240 hours of community service.

The courts' approach to a breach of the terms of any community order or of the commission of further offences during the period of an order was rationalised by the CJA 1993. For failure to comply with the terms of an order the offender can be ordered to pay up to £1,000 fine or to perform up to 60 hours of a CSO. If the offender already has a CSO, the total hours must not exceed the maximum applicable. The court may revoke the community sentence and impose a different penalty for the original offence. For offenders under 21, an attendance centre order may be made. If the offender wilfully and persistently refuses to comply with the order, this may be taken as refusing consent to it and the court can impose a custodial sentence. For the commission of a further offence the order can be revoked and the offender dealt with in some other way. The order can also be revoked and dealt with in some other way for good progress.

Sentencers also have various ancillary orders available, including orders allowing the confiscation of the proceeds of crime, the forfeit of money or property associated with offences and the destruction of items such as weapons or drugs. Other penalties relating specifically to motoring offences are worthy of note: the imposition of penalty points and disqualification from driving. Advertising campaigns, particularly over the Christmas period focus on the potential harm caused by driving with excess alcohol, to enhance the denunciatory effect and stress the impact of the penalty, i.e. disqualification from driving, highlighting the deterrent element of the sentence.

Custodial sentences

As a result of successive legislative efforts to reduce the numbers of offenders receiving prison sentences, a prison sentence (which includes the suspended sentence) may only be passed where one of the following criteria is satisfied:

- The offence is so serious that only a custodial sentence is justified.

- The offence is one of sex or violence and only a custodial sentence is sufficient to protect the public.

- The offender has failed to consent to a requirement in a probation or supervision order.

A custodial sentence of up to 2 years may be suspended for between one and two years, but only if there are exceptional grounds to do so. Commonplace grounds such as the youth of the offender will not justify suspension of the sentence. Suspended sentences are in any event not available for offenders who will serve their sentences in a young offender institution. The length of the sentence is also determined by the assessment of seriousness, or the need for public protection.

A life sentence is the most severe penalty available. It is a mandatory sentence for those found guilty of murder, and thus the judge has no choice. It is also a discretionary maximum sentence for those convicted of serious indictable crimes such as manslaughter, arson, rape, robbery, aggravated burglary, causing grievous bodily harm, wounding with intent, supplying class A drugs and kidnapping. Under the Firearms Act 1968 crimes of assault, theft, arson and resisting arrest carry a maximum sentence of a life sentence if the offender is carrying a gun.

Custodial sentences can be justified by most of the major theories of sentencing. A prison sentence can be seen as a deterrent and it is still commonplace to argue that prisons should be austere places which should not provide comforts not generally available outside. The forbidding nature of prisons also underlines society's disapproval of inmates. The essential punishment involved in imprisonment is the deprivation of a person's liberty, and thus a prison sentence can be retributive, with the length of a sentence being determined by the seriousness of the offence. Prisons also take offenders out of society and thus protect the public and as we have seen, they are the main form of incapacitative sentence. And as will be seen in Chapters 9 and 10, a major influence on penal policy and on the development of prison regimes throughout the twentieth century has been the belief that offenders can be rehabilitated while in prison.

Enforcement of sentences

Each type of sentence brings with it particular problems in relation to dealing with the offender who fails to comply. For some sentences the approach is simple: it is an offence to escape from prison and an escaped prisoner will be given an additional sentence. Committing an offence during the currency of a conditional discharge means that the offender can be sentenced for the original offence as well as the new offence.

Community sentences and fines pose particular problems. During the period of a community sentence two problems may arise:

- failure to comply, for example, by behaving badly or working poorly on a community service placement or not attending probation meetings

- committing further offences during the period covered.

With the first problem, *National Standards for the Supervision of Offenders in the Community* have sought to establish a consistency of approach; for example, only two warnings were to be given before breach proceedings are instituted. Ultimately the court can fine up to £1,000, impose a CSO of up to 60 hours, impose an attendance order or, in cases of serious breach, revoke the order and deal with the original offence in another way.

With the second type of problem (of re-offending) this can be dealt with by revocation of the order and re-sentencing in some other way.

Enforcement of fines perhaps causes the most difficulty, not least because it is the most used sentence. Much time and cost are spent chasing recalcitrant payers: some, who are well able to pay but are simply avoiding payment; others, who are financially inept; others, who are genuinely in difficulty or who find their finances worsen after the imposition of the fine.

In 1996 over a million offenders (1,069,700) were fined in the magistrates' courts. When imposing a fine magistrates must take into account the offender's means as measured in terms of income and expenses. However, circumstances may change and the offence and the sentence may lead to a worsening of the offender's financial situation: a drink driver might not be able to get to work after disqualification, or might lose their job; a man who assaults his wife might have to find alternative accommodation; an employee who steals from an employer will usually lose their job.

If the offender cannot pay immediately, time to pay can be, and usually is, allowed. If the offender still falls behind, a number of measures to obtain payment can be used:

- attachment of earnings, where a specified sum is deducted monthly or weekly from the earnings by the employer and sent to the court

- distress warrants, allowing a bailiff to seize goods to the value of the outstanding fine, other than clothing, bedding or tools of the person's trade

- (since 1992) deduction from benefit up to a maximum of £2.40 per week.

Since the Crime (Sentences) Act 1997 other measures for responding to fine default have been introduced:

- curfew with electronic monitoring

- CSO of 20–100 hours

- driving disqualification of up to 12 months.

Other measures available to deal with outstanding fines include:

- overnight detention in a police station in lieu of a fine

- remission of fines, by reducing the original fine because of subsequent hardship

- writing off of fines as an administrative act of the court

- imprisonment where the offence for which the fine was imposed is itself punishable by imprisonment and the offender is able to pay and refuses to do so.

In 1996 the average time served in prison for fine defaulters was 7 days for males and 5 days for females (*Prison Statistics England and Wales 1996*: 104). For a fine defaulter imprisoned for a separate offence the fine can be disposed of by serving days in lieu of payment. This is normally served concurrently so, in effect, no extra days are served in prison.

Despite difficulties of enforcement, the fine is by and large a simply administered sentence and gains revenue. Because the fine is a flexible punishment it can be used in a wide variety of cases and is popular with policy makers.

Distribution of sentences

In 1996 the magistrates' courts sentenced over a million offenders (1,364,100) and the Crown Court 73,800. Figure 8.1 shows the numbers and the percentage distribution of sentences given to offenders for indictable, summary motoring and summary non-motoring offences. In total 1,437,800 were sentenced. The figure shows the range of sentences available and the frequency of their use by judges and magistrates. Magistrates gave 102,000 offenders a conditional discharge, sent 30,000 adults to prison and 11,200 younger offenders to custody in young offender institutions. The Crown Court gave 2,700 a conditional discharge and sent a total of 34,000 adults to prison and 9,500 to young offender institutions. Three-quarters of all offenders leave the court with a fine, which is the most popular sentence (1,069,700 in the magistrates' courts and 3,400 in the Crown Court). Sentencing trends showing the change in use of different types of sentences over the period from 1950 to 1997 will be illustrated in Chapter 9.

SENTENCING PROCEDURE

Between the determination of guilt and decision on sentence there are various stages to go through, including a hearing of the mitigation the defendant may wish to offer in an attempt to reduce the severity of the sentence. Only in the most serious and the most trivial of cases will sentencing be carried out immediately after the decision on guilt. There is as we have seen a mandatory life sentence in cases of murder, and for many petty offences a discharge or small fine is likely and can be imposed immediately.

If the sentence follows a trial, the facts will have been presented. If there has been a guilty plea, the facts must be presented to the court by the prosecution. Occasionally there may be a dispute over the facts which affect the plea; for example the defendant may admit to an assault with fists, but deny kicking the victim. If the dispute is likely to affect the sentence, the sentencer must either sentence on the basis of the facts most favourable to the defence, or there must be what is called a 'Newton' hearing. This is like a mini-trial, where evidence is taken, but only on the specific issue involved

The defendant may ask for offences to be taken into consideration (TIC). This means that the court takes them into consideration when sentencing, though there has been no formal conviction. This procedure is often used where a number of related offences have been committed, but the police may have been unable to prosecute them successfully, for example, where the defendant has confessed to a number of thefts from cars, or several cheque frauds. They may also form part of the plea negotiations discussed in Chapter 7.

There is no statutory basis for the TIC procedure, but it is recognised by the courts. Lord Goddard described the process as:

> simply a convention under which, if a court is informed that there are outstanding charges against a prisoner, the court can, if the prisoner admits the offences and asks that they should be taken into account, ... give a longer sentence than it would if it were dealing with him only on the charge mentioned in the indictment.
>
> (*R v Batchelor*, 36 Cr App R 64)

The effect of having offences taken into consideration does not mean that the defendant is convicted of them. Strictly, a defendant can be charged with the offence taken into consideration, but no additional penalty can be imposed. In practice, once an offence has been taken into consideration by a court, it is not the subject of later charges.

Whether or not there are offences to be taken into consideration, the court will then need to know whether the offender has any previous convictions and whether they are in breach of any existing orders.

The defendant, personally or through an advocate, may then put forward any mitigation in respect of the offence or their own circumstances. This is known as making a plea in mitigation, and is the opportunity for the defence to put the offending behaviour into the best possible light in order to gain the lightest sentence. This is the point at which financial information may be also given to the court. Financial details are relevant not only to show why a defendant may have committed an offence, but also because the court must take the means of the offender into account when imposing a financial penalty. Apart from the details of the case, such as that the defendant only took a small part, sentence mitigation will include factors such as that the defendant pleaded guilty, especially if the guilty plea was entered early (CJPOA 1994, s. 48), and that they were of previous good character, that is have no previous convictions. Defence counsel may argue, for example, that in some way the offender was pressured into committing the offence by financial or family problems. They may argue that while they have admitted the offence and can offer no defence that nonetheless they did not intend the harm done and that the offence occurred almost by accident, with no planning or forethought. This is especially the case where the offence is one of strict liability which does not require intent, or where the offence has involved an omission to do something. Thus defendants may claim that they simply forgot to renew a licence, but had always intended to do it or that they forgot to tell the Inland Revenue about their earnings from a part-time job. Others may claim that they didn't anticipate driving home after going to the pub. As seen in Chapter 2, these mitigating factors attempt to reduce the culpability of the offender and thus seek to influence the eventual sentence.

Before proceeding to sentence the court may require further information about the offender's circumstances, including their physical or mental health. In many cases before the Crown Court and in the more serious cases in magistrates' courts a pre-sentence report is required. For adults, this is provided by the probation service and its preparation typically involves an adjournment of three weeks. The report contains information considered relevant by the probation officer and may cover such matters as home life, medical, psychiatric details, criminal background and schooling or employment. In the report the probation officer or social worker is asked to make an assessment of the seriousness of the offence and to consider the impact on the victim, although information on victims is often not available. In addition it should consider the possible sentences and the likely impact of such sentences on the offender. Before sentencing the judge or magistrates will hear from the convicted person's defence counsel to remind the court of any mitigating circumstance and will also consider the pre-sentence report. This double exposure of mitigation before sentence has led to the criticism that it focuses too heavily on the circumstances, background and personality of the convicted person and insufficiently on the offence. The introduction at this stage of a victim impact statement has been suggested to provide a more balanced hearing for the purpose of sentence.

FACTORS INFLUENCING SENTENCING DECISIONS

Many factors influence sentencers' decisions. In respect of a particular case, the judge or magistrate must consider how serious the particular offence is in relation to other similar offences and assess whether or not the offence had any particular mitigating or aggravating factors. For example, if the offence has involved harm to a particularly vulnerable group such as the elderly this would be an aggravating factor, whereas absence of direct physical harm to a victim is more likely to be seen as a mitigating factor. And as seen above, the defendant may provide information about mitigating factors. Sentencers are also likely to take into account the previous convictions and record of an offender, and the recommendations in the pre-sentence report.

Sentencing is not done in a legislative or policy vacuum. First, there are the statutory requirements. We have a mandatory life sentence in the case of murder. All offences have statutory maximum sentences such as 14 years for burglary of a domestic dwelling, even though this maximum is rarely, if ever, used. It provides an indication however of Parliament's view of the seriousness of the offence and so helps to set the sentencing tariff. There are a few minimum sentences for first offences, such as the two-year disqualification for those convicted of causing death by dangerous driving under the Road Traffic Act 1988. Offenders convicted of driving with excess alcohol will receive a minimum period of 12 months' disqualification. The Crime (Sentences) Act 1997 introduced a mandatory minimum 7-year sentence for a third conviction for drug trafficking in Class A drugs. For serious violent and serious sexual offences such as murder, manslaughter, rape or robbery with a firearm, an offender aged over 18, convicted for a second time of one of these offences, will be given a compulsory life sentence unless there are exceptional circumstances.

Statutes can provide limitations on sentencing in other ways; for example, children under 15 years cannot be sent to a YOI. They can also limit sentencing powers by providing statutory criteria for the use of certain powers such as custody. The statutory criteria for the use of imprisonment were set out in the CJA 1991 with respect to adults, as had previously applied since 1982 for young persons, (described earlier is this chapter). Magistrates are further curtailed by legislation which limits their powers to send a person to prison and imposes maxima on the fines they can give.

Other jurisdictions use legislation to indicate more precisely the power of sentences. In California the 1976 Uniform Determinate Sentencing Act specified the prison terms that a judge could give with respect to each criminal offence. Thus at that time, although subsequently amended upwards, the sentence for rape would be 3, 4 or 5 years. The judge would choose which of these three terms to give depending on the aggravating and mitigating factors of the case. The middle term would be used in typical cases. Thus a system of presumptive, or expected, sentences was established and these sentences were determinate, that is fixed in length by statute.

In the magistrates' courts, sentencing decisions have increasingly been influenced by guidelines issued by the Magistrates' Association, an example of which are illustrated in Figure 8.2. These were originally issued in the 1970s in respect of motoring offences in an effort to curb complaints of inconsistency

Fig 8.2 Magistrates' Association Sentencing Guidelines

Theft Act 1968 s.9 Triable either way - see Mode of Trial Guidelines Penalty: Level 5 and/or 6 months	Burglary (Dwelling)

CONSIDER THE SERIOUSNESS OF THE OFFENCE
(INCLUDING THE IMPACT ON THE VICTIM)

GUIDELINE: ➤

IS COMPENSATION, DISCHARGE OR FINE APPROPRIATE?
IS IT SERIOUS ENOUGH FOR A COMMUNITY PENALTY?
IS IT SO SERIOUS THAT ONLY CUSTODY IS APPROPRIATE?
ARE MAGISTRATES' COURTS' POWERS APPROPRIATE?

 ## CONSIDER AGGRAVATING AND MITIGATING FACTORS

for example
- Racial motivation
- Deliberately frightening occupants
- Group offence
- People in house
- Professional operation
- Forcible entry
- Soiling, ransacking, damage

- Offence committed on bail
- Previous convictions and failures to respond to previous sentences, if relevant
This list is not exhaustive

for example
- Low value
- Nobody frightened
- No damage or disturbance
- No forcible entry
- Opportunist
This list is not exhaustive

CONSIDER OFFENDER MITIGATION

for example
- Age, health (physical or mental)
- Co-operation with the police
- Voluntary compensation
- Remorse

CONSIDER YOUR SENTENCE

Compare it with the suggested guideline level of sentence and reconsider your reasons carefully if you have chosen a sentence at a different level.
Consider a discount for a timely guilty plea.

DECIDE YOUR SENTENCE

NB. COMPENSATION - Give reasons if not awarding compensation

Remember: These are GUIDELINES not a tariff

Issue April 1997

Fig 8.2 (*cont'd*)

Offences Against the Person Act 1961 s.47 Triable either way - see Mode of Trial Guidelines Penalty: Level 5 and/or 6 months	**Assault — Actual Bodily Harm**

CONSIDER THE SERIOUSNESS OF THE OFFENCE
(INCLUDING THE IMPACT ON THE VICTIM)

GUIDELINE: ➤

IS COMPENSATION, DISCHARGE OR FINE APPROPRIATE?

IS IT SERIOUS ENOUGH FOR A COMMUNITY PENALTY?

IS IT SO SERIOUS THAT ONLY CUSTODY IS APPROPRIATE?

ARE MAGISTRATES' COURTS' POWERS APPROPRIATE?

 CONSIDER AGGRAVATING AND MITIGATING FACTORS

for example

Racial motivation

Deliberate kicking or biting

Extensive injuries (may be psychiatric)

Group action

Offender in position of authority

Premeditated

Victim particularly vulnerable

Victim serving public

Weapon

Offence committed on bail

Previous convictions and failures to respond

to previous sentences, if relevant

This list is not exhaustive

for example

Impulsive

Minor injury

Provocation

Single blow

This list is not exhaustive

CONSIDER OFFENDER MITIGATION

for example

Age, health (physical or mental)

Co-operation with the police

Voluntary compensation

Remorse

CONSIDER YOUR SENTENCE

Compare it with the suggested guideline level of sentence and reconsider
your reasons carefully if you have chosen a sentence at a different level.
Consider a discount for a timely guilty plea.

DECIDE YOUR SENTENCE

NB. COMPENSATION - Give reasons if not awarding compensation

Remember: These are GUIDELINES not a tariff

Issue April 1997

Fig 8.2 (*cont'd*)

Public Order Act 1986 s.3 Triable either way - see Mode of Trial Guidelines Penalty: Level 5 and/or 6 months	**Affray**

CONSIDER THE SERIOUSNESS OF THE OFFENCE
(INCLUDING THE IMPACT ON THE VICTIM)

GUIDELINE: ➤

IS COMPENSATION, DISCHARGE OR FINE APPROPRIATE?
IS IT SERIOUS ENOUGH FOR A COMMUNITY PENALTY?
IS IT SO SERIOUS THAT ONLY CUSTODY IS APPROPRIATE?
ARE MAGISTRATES' COURTS' POWERS APPROPRIATE?

 ## CONSIDER AGGRAVATING AND MITIGATING FACTORS

for example
Racial motivation
Busy public place
Group action
People actually put in fear
Vulnerable victim(s)

Offence committed on bail
Previous convictions and failures to respond
to previous sentences, if relevant
This list is not exhaustive

for example
Offender acting alone
Provocation
Did not start the trouble
Stopped as soon as the police arrived
This list is not exhaustive

CONSIDER OFFENDER MITIGATION

for example
Age, health (physical or mental)
Co-operation with the police
Voluntary compensation
Remorse

CONSIDER YOUR SENTENCE

Compare it with the suggested guideline level of sentence and reconsider
your reasons carefully if you have chosen a sentence at a different level.
Consider a discount for a timely guilty plea.

DECIDE YOUR SENTENCE

NB. COMPENSATION - Give reasons if not awarding compensation

Remember: These are GUIDELINES not a tariff

Issue April 1997

between benches. These had some success, especially for offences which could be easily compared – thus a speeding offence on the M1 is very similar to a speeding offence on the M25. Their use, after consultation with the Justices' Clerks' Association and the Lord Chancellor's Department, was extended in 1989 to most offences dealt with in the magistrates' courts. More guidelines were issued to clarify the implementation of the CJA 1991 and reflected not only the framework of that Act but also the move towards more structured decision making discussed in the next section of this chapter. The guidelines were re-issued in 1993 to reflect the changes in the CJA 1993 and in particular the abolition of unit fines and again in April 1997.

As can be seen, the guidelines indicate, by means of an arrow, the likely sentence for a typical or average case of its type. They also contain a list of factors that make a 'typical offence' more or less serious. Although the guidelines inevitably lead to greater consistency, their influence can be a source of concern when sentencers feel unable to give a sentence they think to be appropriate in an individual case. The concern is that the guidelines, which are merely advisory, become the basis of rigid tariff. Changes to the guidelines have been made so that in the 1993 guidelines, for example, a community sentence was advised as the likely sentence or entry point for the offence of actual bodily harm. In 1997 custody was indicated.

A major influence on sentences in the Crown Courts in England and Wales is the appeal system. In 1907 the Court of Criminal Appeal was established to promote some degree of judicial self-regulation. Renamed the Court of Appeal, this deals with appeals from the Crown Court against conviction and sentence. Most appeals are, however, against sentence. In 1996, 8,898 offenders appealed to the Court of Appeal (Criminal Division): 6,495 appealed against their sentence, 757 against their conviction and sentence and 1,646 against conviction only (*Home Office Statistical Bulletin* 5/98).

In the 1980s and 1990s the Court of Appeal gave guidance to sentencers with a series of guideline cases. These include *Bibi* in 1980 on the use of custody, *Brewster* in 1997 on burglary offences; *Roberts* in 1982 and *Billam* in 1986 on rape; *Barrick* in 1985 and *Price* in 1993 on theft. For drug dealing a number of guideline sentencing cases include *Aramah* in 1983, *Aranguren* in 1994 and *Warren and Beeley* in 1996.

The Court of Appeal sentencing guidelines play a decisive part in fixing the appropriate tariff for an offence. Guideline cases are those where the appeal court has taken the opportunity to lay down detailed guidance to assist courts in sentencing. For example, in 1986 in *Billam*, the Lord Chief Justice made both a general statement of principle: that rape should be followed by a custodial sentence, and laid down a list of aggravating features which would call for a longer sentence than the norm, which he set at 5 years. Similarly in the case of *Barrick*, which involved theft in breach of trust, for example from an employer, guidelines as to the length of a custodial sentence were given in terms both of the amount stolen, and the degree of

261

trust broken. In the case of *Aramah*, and subsequent cases, guidelines were set out in terms of street value and class of drugs imported or supplied.

While these cases are an important and influential guide for lower courts in sentencing – and indeed for defendants and those advising them as to the likely sentence in a given case – they have limitations. First, the Court of Appeal can only respond to cases brought before it: therefore no systematic approach to offences or a certain range of offence can be made. Secondly, the cases that come before the Court of Appeal have, until recently, been a result of appeals against sentence on behalf of the defence.

The prosecution has only limited rights to appeal against unduly lenient sentences by virtue of the changes made in s. 36 of the Criminal Justice Act 1988. This allowed the Attorney General the right to refer to the Court of Appeal sentences that seem unduly lenient. This system of reference was not an automatic right for the prosecution to appeal routinely on sentences. It applies to sentences for those convicted of offences that are triable only on indictment, so that it does not apply to TEW offences. Despite this system of reference on unduly lenient sentences, the Court of Appeal tends to be concerned with lengthy custodial terms, as defendants receiving community sentences are not likely to appeal. It is comparatively rare, therefore, for short custodial or non-custodial sentences to be considered. The Sentencing Advisory Panel, created by the Crime and Disorder Act 1998, provides a means to develop a more systematic approach to sentencing guidelines.

All these are relatively open and identifiable influences on sentencing. As with any other discretionary process however, informal factors also play a role. As we have seen, sentences may be directed towards different aims and many different considerations affect the decision. How, therefore, do sentencers approach individual decisions?

In a detailed review of sentencing decisions in the Court of Appeal, David Thomas identifies a twofold sentencing process. In the first, or primary sentencing decision, judges decide on the basis of the individual case whether a 'tariff' sentence, primarily a retributive deterrent sentence, is appropriate or whether the sentence should be individualised – that is, based primarily on rehabilitative grounds (Thomas 1979). Individualised sentences may also be based on incapacitative and deterrent considerations with respect to the individual offender before the court, and will depend on an assessment of the likelihood of their re-offending and the danger they may be to the public. The secondary decision is which sentence will be imposed. Factors affecting the primary decision include both the personal characteristics of the defendant such as age, sex and previous history along with relevant personal circumstances and the seriousness of the offence. Where sentences are individualised it is extremely difficult to discern whether or not they are consistent as so many factors may affect the individual case (Thomas 1979).

Sentencers themselves may have their own individual approach, or philosophy, based on a mixture of the theories of sentencing outlined above. They may also be affected by the attitudes and opinions prevailing on their own ench. In a study of disparities in sentencing motoring offenders, Hood ound that many could be accounted for by local bench cultures. Thus within ndividual benches, sentencing norms evolved which could be affected by ocal considerations producing local variations (Hood 1972). These local bench cultures' may affect the perception both of offences and offenders and underlie sentencing disparities. Thus some studies have found that some ourts consistently impose more severe sentences, while others sentence more eniently (see, for example, Parker et al 1989). This combination of sentencers' ndividual philosophies and bench cultures may also become a filter through which information about offences and offenders is received. Thus some magistrates and judges are known by participants in the system to be tougher on ome kinds of offence than others, which may lead to attempts to put ases in front of selected benches or judges. Parker and his colleagues also ound that some benches paid more attention to school reports than probation officers' reports, believing that probation officers could be too soft on offenders, whereas school reports told them more about work habits and discipline (Parker et al 1989). They also found that magistrates who regarded entencing as an 'art form' felt that they could judge many aspects of defendants' character from their general demeanour and bearing in the court. These ttitudes were also reflected in a belief in the necessity to judge each case on ts own merits, an approach which underlay magistrates' resistance to any ttempts to reduce their discretion. This investigation was carried out before he CJA 1991 and it is not clear how far the changes introduced in the Act, nd the magistrates' guidelines, have affected this approach.

All these influences undoubtedly contribute to the variations found throughout the country which have caused so much concern. They may also, arguibly, produce disparities not only when individual offenders are compared but when groups of offenders are compared. There has been criticism, for example, about the fairness of sentencing policy in relation to women and ethnic minorities. Concerns about the treatment of both unemployed and white collar offenders raise issues of how far socio-economic status affects entencing decisions. The next section will look briefly at these issues.

Race and sentencing

According to Home Office figures, in June 1997 there were 11,500 people rom ethnic minority groups in prisons or young offender institutions.

> Ethnic minorities accounted for 18 per cent of the male prison population and 24 per cent of the female population compared with 6 per cent of the male and female general population of England and Wales.
>
> (*Home Office Statistical Bulletin*, 5/98: 9)

The higher proportion of ethnic minorities in female prisons, in contrast to nales from ethnic minorities, is explained by the higher proportion of foreign nationals – often imprisoned for illegally importing drugs. If we look at adult

British nationals in the prisons of England and Wales in 1997 we find the black and Chinese population over-represented in prisons and South Asians under-represented (*Home Office Statistical Bulletin*, 5/98: 10). This over-representation or under-representation in the prison population does not in itself necessarily indicate any prejudice or discrimination on the part of sentencers although it has caused much concern particularly throughout the 1980s. As we have seen in respect of earlier stages in the process, many other factors may account for this over-representation, indeed earlier stages of the process may affect sentencing outcomes. The legal and procedural factors which affect sentencing may account for many of the differences. Thus sentences are affected by the nature of the offence, the characteristics of individual offenders and whether or not defendants have pleaded guilty. We have already seen, for example, that more black offenders elect Crown Court trial and plead not guilty. This means that if convicted they would receive sentences that would not include a discount given for a guilty plea.

There has been considerable concern about whether ethnicity influences way people are dealt with in the criminal justice system. In one study to estimate the size of any race effect in sentencing, Hood (1992) found that a limited part of the difference in custodial rates between white and non-white offenders might be attributable to racial factors. Flood-Page and Mackie refer to research showing that: 'ethnic minorities are treated and act in different ways at the key stages in criminal process. For example, there is a lot of evidence that Afro-Caribbean's are less likely to admit an offence and therefore make themselves ineligible for a caution . . . This also means that they are less likely to benefit from the discount for a guilty plea.'

A Home Office research study of sentencing (Flood-Page and Mackie 1998: 116) highlights one of the difficulties of research into difference of sentencing patterns for racial groups:

> . . . it needs to be borne in mind that the fairly crude ethnic breakdowns used in most studies (including this one) simplify a complex picture. Among the 'Asian' group are a number of ethnic minorities who differ in their socioeconomic position (e.g. Pakistanis and Bangladeshis suffer higher rates of unemployment than Indians and East African Asians) and there is some evidence that, while the proportions of Indians and Bangladeshis in prison is the same as in the general population, there are a disproportionately high number of Pakistanis in prison . . . There are also important differences between black people of Caribbean origin (most of whom are British citizens) and Africans (some of whom are temporarily in the UK).

In their sentencing study based on 3,000 cases in 25 magistrates' courts and 1,800 in 18 Crown Court centres Flood-Page and Mackie conclude:

> Asian men were significantly more likely to be sentenced to custody than would have been expected on the basis of their offence and other factors. However, variables such as the type and number of offences, their plea, whether they were subject to a court order when they committed the offence, being mentally ill or whether the offence was premeditated explained more of the variations in custody rates than ethnic origin . . .

That ethnic minority males were not significantly more likely to receive custodial sentence than white males when other factors were taken into account was confirmed by further analysis. The differences in custody rates were explained by variables such as the type and number of offences, their plea, whether they were subject to a court order when they committed the offence, being mentally ill or whether the offence was spontaneous.'

(Flood-Page and Mackie 1998: 118–120)

Sentencing women

Women are generally assumed to be sentenced more leniently than men, often attributed to a 'chivalrous' attitude on the part of sentencers who may assume that a woman's crime is more likely to be related to mental illness or medical problems, and be reluctant to send women to prison, especially when they have children. On the other hand, some argue that women may be more harshly dealt with by the courts, as women who have offended may be seen as 'doubly deviant' – deviant as offenders and deviant as women.

Recent Home Office studies have looked at these issues. (Hedderman and Hough 1994) and reported that:

- Women are far less likely than men to receive a custodial sentence for virtually all indictable offences except drugs.

- When women do receive prison sentences these tend to be shorter than men's.

- One of the reasons for this is that women are less likely to be dealt with at the Crown Court.

- Women are less likely to receive prison sentences irrespective of the number of previous offences.

These findings, they argue, 'call into question claims that the criminal justice system is systematically more severe towards women than men. If anything, the evidence points to more lenient treatment of women.' However Mary Eaton found that courts tended to look carefully at female offenders' family and domestic situations, which might lead to the effect of more indirect forms of differentiation, reflecting notions of the 'ideal' woman, related to family and domestic considerations. Where a woman was seen to be capable of looking after her children and her husband was available to support her, the courts may be more lenient (Eaton 1986).

Hedderman and Gelsthorpe's study in 1997 found that women were more leniently treated than men. However, the situation was complicated because the courts fined women less frequently than men, and more were likely to impose a discharge. As a consequence repeat female offenders were more likely to be given a community penalty for subsequent offences. In 1995 statistics show that twice as many men (9.5%) as women (4.6%) sentenced for indictable offences received a custodial sentence. Men were also more likely to be fined than women, with a higher proportion of women receiving a conditional discharge. Just under 30 per cent of both men and women received a community penalty though more women were given probation and more men CSOs (*Criminal Statistics England and Wales 1995*).

Home Office researchers who conducted a study of 3,000 sentencing cases in the magistrates' courts and 1,800 in the Crown Court commented:

> Even allowing for their much lower rate of offending, females are much less likely to be prosecuted: in 1995, 59 per cent of women convicted or cautioned for indictable offences were cautioned, compared to 37 per cent of men . . .
>
> In this study a higher proportion of male first offenders received a custodial sentence than female first offenders in the Crown Court. So few first offenders received custodial sentences in the magistrates courts sample that the difference was not significant. Men with previous convictions were four times as likely to receive a custodial sentence than women who were repeat offenders in magistrates courts. In the Crown Court male repeat offenders were one-and-a-half times as likely to receive a custodial sentence as women.
>
> Further analysis confirmed that men had a significantly higher probability of receiving a custodial sentence than women even when other factors were taken into account.
>
> (Flood-Page and Mackie 1998: 121–2)

In respect of the sentencing of women one question is to ask whether they are sentenced more leniently or harshly. Another issue is to consider the differential impact of sentences on men and women. Answers reveal that issues of justice are hard to resolve and come down to whether it should be the offender or the offence that provides the primary focus when determining sentence. It may well be reasonable for sentencers to refrain from sending women to prison to avoid adverse effects on their children, but this is scarcely fair on fathers and their families.

Socio-economic status

The effects of both gender and ethnicity may also be related to the socio-economic circumstances of offenders. Thus it is more likely to be women in adverse socio-economic circumstances who end up in prison and, as seen above, many black offenders are unemployed. Thus the potential effect of socio-economic status on sentencing must be explored.

This can be seen in the situation of the unemployed, which provides a clear example of indirect and 'unintentional' discrimination. It is routinely stated in mitigation for offenders that they are in employment and that imprisonment would lead to the loss of such employment. Such employment is generally regarded as being a sign of good character (Cavadino and Dignan 1997) and a factor that might help promote good habits and so reduce the likelihood of future offending and thus appeal to sentencers seeking a rehabilitative approach. On the other hand the unemployed, having less to lose, may be more likely to end up in prison. It is also more difficult to find unemployed offenders.

The situation of the unemployed offender contrasts starkly with that of the middle-class and particularly the white collar offender. Many such offenders, for example, may plead in mitigation that they have much to lose – that a prison sentence would harm their innocent families and they might lose their house and their 'standing' in the community. Again, while it may be fair to take such factors into account, it may discriminate, albeit unintentionally, against offenders who have little to lose, let alone any 'standing' in the community (see, for example, Croall 1992; Levi 1989). Few studies have, however, found that social status or class alone affects sentencing outcomes. Indeed, judges, concerned to be fair and seen to be fair, may be conscious of any likely partiality on the grounds of class. Thus Mr Justice Henry, on refusing leave to appeal against a £5 million fine levied on one of the Guinness defendants, commented that:

> punishments are after all intended to be punitive and the court must ensure that a man's wealth and power does not put him beyond punishment.
> (*The Guardian*, 3 October 1990; quoted in Croall 1992: 119)

At the same time however, few offenders could pay a massive fine and the ability of wealthier offenders to pay both large fines and substantial compensation may make a financial penalty more likely. In addition, they are better able to employ legal representation which may affect how they present their case. Other factors may operate to reduce the severity of sentences for white collar offenders. The absence of direct victimisation in many white collar offences and in some the apparent lack of intent may also lead to less severe sentences (Croall 1992).

On a more general level, lower-class offenders may appear in court to be less likely cases for sympathy. As indicated above, sentencers may make judgments based on the demeanour and bearing of offenders and look for evidence of character, remorse and an acceptance of the courts' authority. Decisions earlier in the criminal justice process may also demonstrate a differential approach where the police may be more likely to caution middle-class youths – a decision which may reflect home circumstances and the employment of parents (Cavadino and Dignan 1997).

Taken together, consideration of the effects of ethnicity, gender and socio-economic status on sentencing decisions reveals how difficult it is to determine whether any discrimination exists on the part of sentencers. Nonetheless at the end of the criminal justice process there are differences in the proportions of some groups of offenders who receive different sentences. These raise important questions about the calculation of 'just deserts', which will be discussed in Chapter 9.

STRUCTURING SENTENCING DECISIONS

We can see from the above that a variety of factors directly and indirectly influence sentencing decisions, many of which have been associated with disparities. Concerns over these issues reflect two different goals in respect of sentencing policy:

- the need for consistency so that justice is even handed
- the need for flexibility so that sentences can be matched to the individual circumstances of the case.

These concerns have generated a desire to achieve a more consistent approach to sentencing without creating too much of a straitjacket. There have accordingly been various attempts to encourage a structured approach to sentencing decisions.

The 1990 white paper which preceded the CJA 1991 pointed out that 'there is still too much uncertainty and little guidance about the principles which should govern sentencing. . . . The Government is therefore proposing a new and more coherent statutory framework for sentencing' (Home Office 1990a: 1). The white paper goes on to argue that 'to achieve a more coherent and comprehensive consistency of approach in sentencing, a new framework is needed for the use of custodial, community and financial penalties' (Home Office 1990a: 5). The CJA 1991 sought to provide a firm basis for such consistency. Magistrates' training has increasingly focused on a structured approach following a systematic path to the sentence, ensuring that factors are considered in the appropriate order. Examples of the Magistrates' Association Guidelines are shown in Figure 8.2. Magistrates start by considering the seriousness of the offence, taking account of any aggravating or mitigating factors of the offence and of any previous convictions of the defendant. The second stage is to consider whether there is any mitigation in favour of the defendant, such as remorse or a guilty plea. The third stage requires a decision about the sentence, bearing in mind the entry point at the top of the guideline.

A number of initiatives have been introduced with the aim of achieving a more consistent or structured approach. The Judicial Studies Board is now responsible for collecting and disseminating statistics and for arranging Judges' Conferences and training sessions on sentencing. As already mentioned initiatives from the Magistrates' Association led to the development of guidelines to foster a more consistent approach to sentencing.

One suggestion aimed at achieving greater consistency is that a sentencing council or commission be established. This would be a body comprising a variety of criminal justice personnel and experts, who would produce ceilings or bandings for different offences along with articulating the principles to be used in calculating the precise sentence to be given. It would also consider how to deal with persistent or multiple offenders (Ashworth 1989). This has been popular in some states in the USA and Figure 8.3 shows the Minnesota sentencing grid to show how sentences are arrived at in that state. The two axes of the grid represent the main factors of seriousness of offence and the offender's previous criminal history. The bold line represents the in/out, or custody or not, presumption set out by the sentencing commission. Below

268

Fig 8.3 Minnesota sentencing grid

Severity levels of conviction offense		Criminal history score						
		0	1	2	3	4	5	6 or more
Unauthorized use of motor vehicle Possession of marijuana	I	12*	12*	12*	15	18	21	24 23–25
Theft-related crimes ($150–$2,500) Sale of marijuana	II	12*	12*	14	17	20	23	27 25–29
Theft crimes ($150–$2,500)	III	12*	13	16	19	22 21–23	27 25–29	32 30–34
Burglary – felony intent Receiving stolen goods ($150–$2,500)	IV	12*	15	18	21	25 24–26	32 30–34	41 37–45
Simple robbery	V	18	23	27	30 29–31	38 36–40	46 43–49	54 50–58
Assault, second-degree	VI	21	26	30	34 33–35	44 42–46	54 50–58	65 60–70
Aggravated robbery	VII	24 23–25	32 30–34	41 38–44	49 45–53	65 60–70	81 75–87	97 90–104
Assault, first-degree Criminal sexual conduct, first-degree	VIII	43 41–45	54 50–58	65 60–70	76 71–81	95 89–101	113 106–120	132 124–140
Murder, third-degree	IX	97 94–100	119 116–122	127 124–130	149 143–155	176 168–184	205 195–215	230 218–242
Murder, second-degree	X	116 111–121	140 133–147	162 153–171	203 192–214	243 231–255	284 270–298	324 309–339

Structuring Criminal Sentences Presumptive sentence lengths in months

* One year and one day

Note: Italicised numbers within the grid denote the range within which a judge may sentence without the sentence being deemed a departure. First-degree murder is excluded from the guidelines by law and continues to have a mandatory life sentence.

the line incarceration is presumed, above it the judge may substitute a community penalty. But if they decide to give custodial sentence above or below the line, the range of sentences is set out for all categories of crime except for first-degree murder.

Sentencing commissions are another initiative introduced in recent years in several states in the USA as well as for sentencing in the federal courts. Michael Tonry, writing for the National Institute of Justice, commented:

The Minnesota and Washington experiences suggest that the combination of sentencing commissions and presumptive guidelines is a viable approach for achieving consistent and coherent jurisdiction-wide sentencing policies. However, the experiences in Maine, New York, Pennsylvania, and South Carolina counsel that the sentencing commission approach won't necessarily succeed. Six jurisdictions are too few to support any but the most tentative generalizations about success and failure. Still, it is clear that most local legal and political cultures shape the environments in which the commissions work. Minnesota and Washington, for example are both relatively homogeneous states with reform traditions. In neither state were criminal justice issues highly politicized. New York and Pennsylvania, by contrast are heterogeneous states in which criminal justice issues are highly politicized and law-and-order sentiment is powerful. In some states, especially where trial judges are elected, judges may vigorously resist efforts to limit their discretion. Perhaps the only generalization that can be offered concerning political and legal culture is that the potential and the effectiveness of a sentencing commission will depend on how it addresses and accommodates constraints imposed by the local culture.

(Tonry 1987: 59

It seems, therefore, that the legal and political culture of the jurisdiction contributes to the success or failure of such an approach. This point was reflected in the UK in the consultation leading up to the CJA 1991 when the idea of a sentencing council was rejected. John Patten, a junior minister at the Home Office in 1991, identified the traditions of the criminal justice system as a reason why he thought the idea of a sentencing council would not work in England and Wales. In a letter to *The Times* he wrote:

Sentencing councils are the most fashionable nostrum these days for how much that advice (on sentencing) might be formalised. There seems to be almost as many recipes as there are cooks, producing councils, commissions or whatever; they vary in how much guidance or instruction should be given to the courts on sentencing and by whom it should be given.

At the end of this road stands Minnesota in the United States. There, I am told the local sentencing commission has produced tight numerical guidelines for prison sentences, which have taken the form of a 'sentencing grid'. Two axes determine the presumptive sentence. Along one side are the offence categories and along the other categories of 'criminal history'. So the ultimate sentence really depends on where the points along each axis occupied by the offender meet in the middle . . .

Those who ponder sentencing councils must not ignore that which is already in place, potentially providing so much of what they want to see, but in a way that works with the *grain of the criminal justice traditions* in this country. For there is a fast developing framework for judges and magistrates.

In no particular order, first, there is the coherent statutory framework for sentencing in the new criminal justice bill, as we do not think that Parliament has said enough about the principles that govern sentencing decisions. Second, there is the power for the Attorney-General to refer cases to the Court of Appeal, where sentences are allegedly over-lenient. Third, the powerful effect of guideline judgments with the Court of Appeal is self-evident. Last, the work of the Judicial Studies Board seems to be of ever-increasing importance in training and guiding the sentencers in their work.

(*The Times*, 5 February 1991; emphasis added

In England and Wales the provision for a Sentencing Advisory Panel has been included in the Crime and Disorder Act 1998. This is not a US-style sentencing

commission. It will collate information and views from a range of interested
parties such as the police, probation and victims. The panel will be appointed
by the Lord Chancellor after consultation with the Home Secretary and the
Lord Chief Justice. The Act allows the panel to suggest to the Court of
Appeal that guidelines for particular offences be formulated or existing ones
revised. In formulating guidelines the court must consider:

- the need to promote consistency
- the current sentencing practice in the courts
- the cost of sentences
- the effectiveness in preventing re-offending
- the need to promote public confidence
- the views of the Sentencing Advisory Panel.

Essentially the perennial difficulty remains – a multitude of objectives and the
conflict between the desire to individualise cases, taking account of personal
circumstances, character and history, always unique to the offender, and the
desire to have a consistent approach so that similar cases are dealt with in the
same way, in the interests of fairness, just deserts and due process.

CONCLUSION

This chapter has indicated the many issues involved in sentencing decisions.
In the first place, the different theories of punishment embody the different
aims which sentencers may take into account. The present range of sentences
available to the court reflect these different aims, and many sentences may be
directed to achieve a combination of these aims. Before the CJA 1991 and
other reforms attempted to impose greater consistency in sentencing policy,
sentencers could in effect choose between a range of different sentences in
what has been described as a 'cafeteria' approach (Ashworth 1989). The
tradition of judicial independence and the tendency of both magistrates and
judges to judge each case on its merits may produce the disparities which have
caused so much concern. As Ashworth (1994b: 852) comments: 'unstructured
discretion leaves leeway to the personal preferences of the judge, and if the
concept of the "rule of law" has any stable meaning, it must exclude such
preferences.'

As we have seen, therefore, there have been a variety of attempts to
encourage a more consistent approach to sentencing, including the use of
statutory criteria, voluntary guidelines and Court of Appeal guideline cases.
The CJA 1991 also attempted to introduce a more coherent approach and
went further than much previous legislation to spell out the priority to be
given to the various sentencing aims. It indicates the primacy of retribution,
denunciation, incapacitation and to a lesser extent restitution, and a declining
faith in rehabilitation or deterrence as having any substantial effect on individual offender's propensity to re-offend. This clearly reflects a changing

emphasis on the different aims of sentences. The reasons for this shift in emphasis will be explored in more depth in Chapter 9.

Review questions

1. Contrast the six major theories of punishment in terms of:
   (a) What do they seek to achieve?
   (b) Which are concerned primarily with the impact of the sentence on the offender before the court? Which are concerned with the impact on the public at large?
   (c) Which aim to reduce crime in the future?
   (d) If the judge or magistrates wish to achieve two objectives with the same sentence, which of the theories are compatible and which are not?

2. What are the main sentences available to the court? How can they be related to each of the major aims?

3. List the major factors which will influence sentencers in reaching a sentencing decision. Which factors are likely to produce disparity?

4. What are the main arguments underlying attempts to achieve a more structured approach to sentencing? How is this achieved in England and Wales?

5. See Exercises 4 and 5 on sentencing in Appendix 1.

Further reading

Ashworth A (1992) *Sentencing and Penal Policy*, 2nd edn. London: Weidenfeld & Nicolson

Ashworth A (1997) 'Sentencing', in Maguire M, Morgan R and Reiner R (eds) *The Oxford Handbook of Criminology*, 2nd edn. Oxford: Clarendon Press

Cavadino P and Dignan J (1997) *The Penal System: An Introduction*, 2nd edn. London: Sage

Flood-Page C and Mackie A (1998) *Sentencing practice: an examination of decisions in magistrates' courts and the Crown Court in the mid-1990's.* Home Office Research Study No. 180. London: Home Office.

Walker N and Padfield N (1996) (1985) *Sentencing: Theory, Law and Practice,* 2nd edn. London: Butterworth

Wasik M (1998) *Emmins on Sentencing*, 3rd edn. London: Blackstone Press

CHAPTER 9

PUNISHMENT PHILOSOPHIES AND SHIFTING PENAL PARADIGMS

INTRODUCTION

We saw in Chapter 8 that policy makers, judges and magistrates have sought to find a balance between the six major theories of sentencing, and the twentieth century has seen a change in the emphasis given to these goals. This chapter will focus on these shifting penal paradigms, that is ways of thinking about the causes and consequences of crime and how we should respond to them. The beginning of the century witnessed a growth in what was seen as a modern or progressive approach which believed that punishment could be replaced with treatment and welfare stratagems to cure criminals through a rehabilitative approach. This was to give way to the back-to-justice approach of the late 1960s as disenchantment with the rehabilitative model set in.

This chapter will start by looking at the history of penal reforms in the twentieth century in terms of innovations in the form of new sentences and institutions and the abolition of certain other types of sanctions. Then we will consider the ways of thinking about punishment, the penal paradigms, that influenced sentencing reforms and penal practice in this century. First we will trace the influence of rehabilitative approaches and then look at the Probation Service and its role in the sentencing process and the role of community

273

sentences. Next we will examine the justice approach based on just desert ideas of punishment and fairness. The impact of imprisonment on offender will be considered and we will discuss whether imprisonment works an whether it can deter. Finally, we will examine the question that arises at th sentencing stage, namely: who is sentencing for?

SENTENCING REFORMS AND TRENDS IN THE TWENTIETH CENTURY

By the beginning of the twentieth century the prison was the dominant pena sanction. Transportation had been formally abolished in 1867 and the numbe of offences that warranted the death penalty had been reduced to four (arso in Her Majesty's Dockyards, treason, piracy and murder) and was primaril used for murder. The Royal Commission on Capital Punishment (1949–53 recorded that for the decade 1900 to 1909, 257 men and 27 women wer sentenced to hang; 103 of the men and 22 of the women were reprieved. I contrast, in one year alone in 1900, there were 149,397 offenders of bot sexes and of all ages given a custodial sentence by the courts. By 1910 the num ber had risen to 179,397, whereas the number of adult and younger offenders both male and female, given a custodial sentence in 1990 was 57,600.

The term 'custody' covers a variety of sentences given different names ove the century, which includes for adults:

> imprisonment, life sentence, corrective training (1949–67), preventive detentio (1908–67), extended sentences (1967–91) and the partially suspended sentenc (1982–92);

and for younger offenders:

> borstal training (1908–83), those children sentenced under s. 53(1) and s. 53(2) o the Children and Young Offender Act 1933 for murder and grave offences (193 onwards), approved school order (1933–70), detention centre order (1953–88) youth custody order (1983–8), detention in a young offender institution (198 onwards), secure training order (1998 onwards), and detention and training orde when the Crime and Disorder Act 1998 is implemented.

Over the twentieth century the absolute and relative use of custody by the courts for sentencing has declined.

> In 1894, the total number of convicted criminals sent to prison in that year wa 156,466, which represented 526 persons per 100,000 of population. . . . In 1994 the number given an immediate custodial sentence was 60,800 . . . representing 118 persons per 100,000 of population.

> (Davies *et al* 1996: 75)

The decline in the use of custody began during the 1914–18 war. By 1920 the number sent to custody had fallen to 35,439. After the 1939–45 war the numbers sentenced to custody began to rise again and they rose from a total

274

umber sentenced to custody of 33,875 in 1950 to a high of 83,300 in 1985,
The trend from 1986 to 1993 was downwards, with 58,400 sentenced to
ustody in 1993. Since then numbers in prison have been going steadily up-
wards again with an average daily population of 61,100 in 1997 (*Home Office
Statistical Bulletin*, 5/98: 1) and with 65,227 in custody on 31 May 1998
Occupation of Prisons, Home Office, 24 February 1998).

The use of physical or corporal punishments was reformed and then stopped
during the twentieth century. In 1908 a person under the age of 16 could no
onger be executed. This was raised to 18 by the Criminal Justice Act 1948
and this reform led to one of the prolonged controversies about the death
penalty when Derek Bentley was hanged in 1953 and his more culpable 16-
ear-old accomplice escaped the death penalty (see Chapter 11). The CJA
1948 also abolished hard labour, and abolished corporal punishment as a
sentence of the court, although it was still allowed as a punishment within
penal establishments until the CJA 1967. The Murder (Abolition of the
Death Penalty) Act 1965 abolished capital punishment for murder and the
ast execution for murder took place in 1964. The Criminal Damage Act
1971 abolished the death penalty for arson in Her Majesty's Dockyards. The
death penalty existed for the offence of high treason and piracy with violence
until the Crime and Disorder Act 1998, though the last person executed for
reason was William Joyce in 1946, who made pro-German wireless broadcasts during the Second World War.

The sentence most often given by the courts is the fine. Its use grew
throughout the first half of the twentieth century so that by the 1970s it
was used for half of all indictable offenders sentenced by the courts. Although
its use has declined (see Figure 9.1) with indictable offenders since 1978,
t is still the most frequently used sentence and was given in 83 per cent
of summary non-motoring offences in 1996 in the magistrates' courts (see
Figure 8.1), and despite its fall in use was, in 1996, along with community
sentences, the most frequently used sentence given for indictable offences
(see Figure 9.1).

The use of community sentences has grown over the century as new types
of sanctions have become available. These, with the date of introduction,
include:

- probation (1887 and 1907)
- attendance centre orders (1948)
- community service order (1972)
- curfew orders for younger offenders (1982)
- combination orders (1991)
- curfew orders for adults (1991).

In 1996, of those sentenced for indictable offences, 28 per cent received
community penalties and the same proportion received a fine. Community
sentences were used more frequently than custody, which was used for 22
per cent of those sentenced for indictable offences (see Figure 9.1).

275

Fig 9.1 Sentencing patterns 1975–96

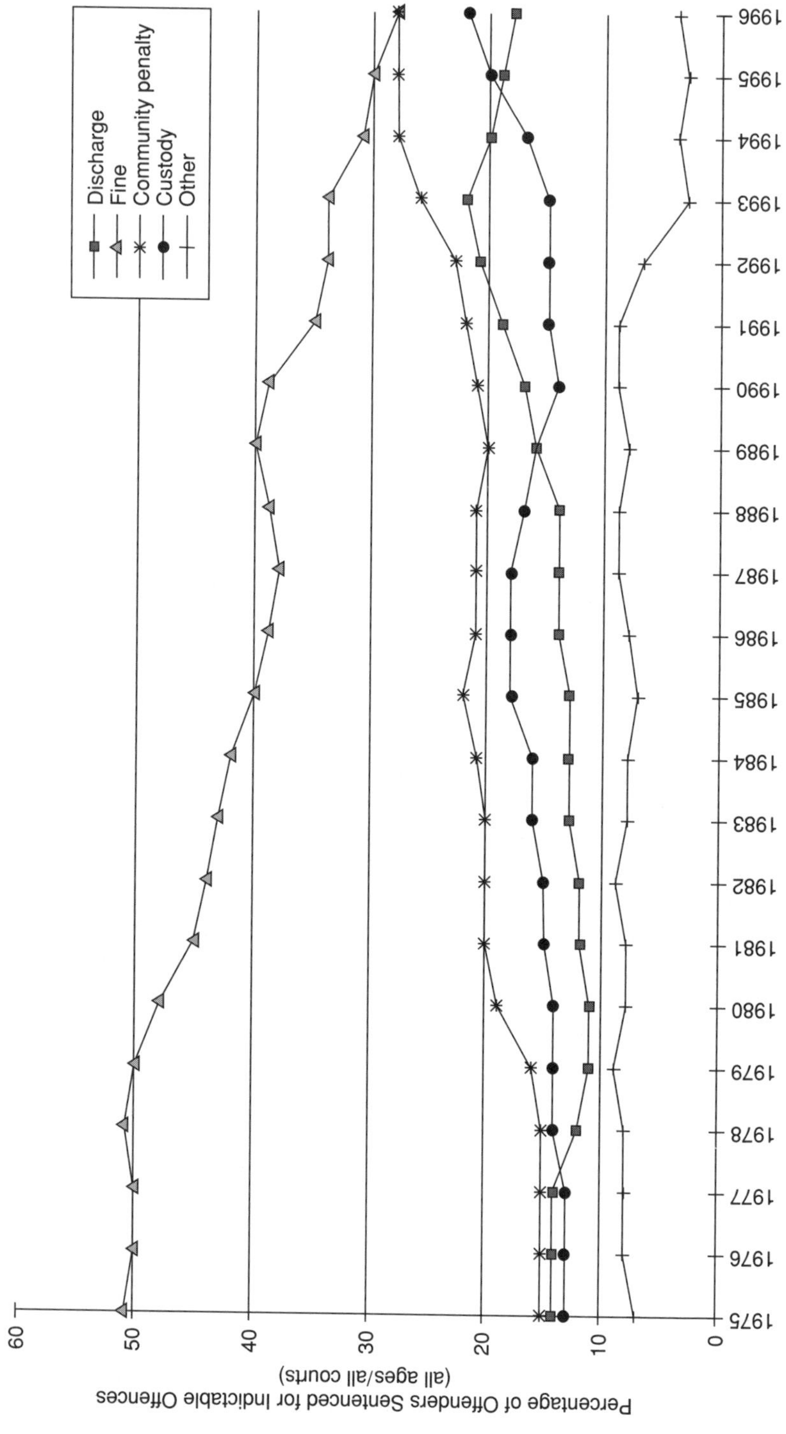

Compiled from *Criminal Statistics England and Wales 1975 to 1996*

276

In the last quarter of the century there were more efforts through sentencing to include measures that benefited victims, such as compensation orders and schemes involving reparation to victims and the community. The shift away from offender-instrumental theories was also evident as new orders were introduced to prevent offenders benefiting from their crime, as with forfeiture orders (from 1983) and confiscation orders, introduced under the Drug Trafficking Act 1986.

Trends in sentencing those convicted of indictable offences from 1975 to 1996 are shown in Figure 9.1.

THE ERA OF REHABILITATION

During the twentieth century, penal policy throughout Europe and the USA has been strongly influenced by the theory of rehabilitation. This moved away from earlier emphases on retribution and deterrence which were less concerned with the causes of crime and its treatment than with the justification for and distribution of punishment. Crime was seen as an immoral act which was in need of punishment which was justified primarily on deterrent or retributive grounds. To rehabilitationists, however, crime, like any other social problem, could be studied scientifically to establish its causes. In what came to be described as a medical model, crime was likened to an illness which could be diagnosed and treated, and through work with individual criminals and social reform, eventually cured. Thus from the start of the twentieth century experts from the world of medicine, the growing professions of psychiatry and social work, educational specialists and social reformers became increasingly involved in the courts and penal system. Rehabilitation offered the promise that crime could be almost eradicated by these scientific and professional approaches – an orthodoxy which dominated penal policy until the 1960s.

There were many different views on how rehabilitation could be achieved which led to a variety of different strategies. First, the medical model stressed the need to diagnose, treat and cure criminals. This led to a growing involvement of doctors and psychiatrists in the criminal justice process, providing medical and psychiatric reports to the courts and working in prisons and other institutions. Secondly, others believed in the value of discipline and work, and advocated methods such as industrial and vocational training to encourage offenders to develop self-discipline and good work habits. Unlike medical and psychiatric treatment these measures aimed not to reform offenders from within but to equip them with better skills which would, it was hoped, keep them from committing crimes. Thirdly, the growing profession of social work advocated the use of case work and counselling for offenders both inside prisons and through the work of the Probation Service. This led to the widespread use of pre-sentence reports outlining the circumstances of offenders, and also influenced the growth of after care provision for

277

ex-prisoners. Fourthly, many believed in the power of moral awakening either through religion, or more recently by confronting the offender with the harm they had done. Early prison regimes encouraged offenders to contemplate on their wrongdoing and religion has always played a role in prisons. Fifthly, others welcomed rehabilitationist strategies as a more humane way to treat prisoners which ameliorated the degrading and brutalising aspects of prison life. Thus penal reformers, who had for long sought to improve the conditions of prisoners and who felt that prison could make people worse supported rehabilitative measures enthusiastically. Lastly, rehabilitation was linked to the ideas of social engineers who identified social deprivation as the root of all social problems and put their faith in growing affluence and the welfare state.

In England and Wales, the rehabilitative paradigm was officially recognised in 1895 in the report of the Home Office Departmental Committee on Prisons chaired by Herbert Gladstone (Home Office 1895). The committee found that 'the moral condition in which a large number of prisoners leave the prison, and the serious number of re-committals have led us to think that there is ample cause for a searching inquiry into the main features of prison life'. It went on to state, 'we start from the principle that prison treatment should have as its primary and concurrent objects deterrence and reformation', and in what became one of the most influential statements about the aims of prison continued that:

> . . . prison discipline and treatment should be more effectually designed to maintain, stimulate or awaken the higher susceptibilities of prisoners, to develop their moral instincts, to train them in orderly and industrial habits, and whenever possible to turn them out of prison better men and women, both physically and morally, than when they came in.
>
> (Home Office 1895: 8)

The first decade of the twentieth century saw the development of many rehabilitative policies such as the introduction of probation in 1907, of Borstal in 1908, special provision for child offenders in 1913 and new arrangements for the mentally deficient offender in 1914. Welfare officers, psychiatrists and psychologists were recruited into the prison service and in 1919 the prison warder was replaced by the prison officer, a title which marked a changing role. The annual reports of prison commissioners revealed a new mood in which prisons were increasingly seen not negatively, as institutions for incarcerating the bad, but positively, as institutions which could act as agencies of human change.

Although our focus here is on penal philosophy, the growth of rehabilitative policies, especially in prisons, was strongly influenced by individuals. One particularly influential individual was Alexander Paterson, who was involved in social work with the Oxford Medical Mission in Bermondsey where he also worked as an elementary school teacher. Although never chairman of the Prison Commission he was its most dominant figure and his liberal reform values were evident in penal documents from 1921 until his death in 1947. This was a period in which the approach embodied in the Gladstone Report began to crystallise into the dominant penological paradigm. Thus Lionel Fox commented that 'it was in 1921 that gusts of fresh air began to blow through the pages of the reports of the prison commissioners' (Fox 1952). The 1930s were characterised as an age of optimism in penal reform (Hood 1974).

This spirit of optimism is illustrated in extracts from Paterson's evidence to the 1931 Persistent Offenders Committee. This committee also provides a good example of how changing views about the role of prisons legitimated the participation of medical experts. Of the 68 people who gave evidence to the committee, 13 were drawn from the medical world, working within the system as medical superintendents in prisons or in psychiatric hospitals. The growing influence of the medical model and the treatment approach is confirmed in Paterson's evidence. Thus:

> The English Courts today, facing a young offender under 21 in the dock, are not concerned like their predecessors to weigh out a dose of punishment appropriate to the proved offence, but exercised rather to diagnose his condition and to prescribe the right form of training or treatment for the condition. This more thoughtful, sensible and expensive way of dealing with the young offender has inevitably resulted in a marked fall in the number of professional recidivists.
> (Evidence to Persistent Offenders Committee 1931: vol 3: 669)

The significance to rehabilitation of other measures was also noted. Thus Paterson comments:

> There has ensued in the last 25 years a whole series of changes in law and practice. The Children's Courts have been established to discover and check the potential tendency of the child offender; the probation system has emerged as a common-sense alternative to the imprisonment of the first offender of any age; the reformatories and industrial schools are no longer convict prisons for turbulent children, but take their place among other educational agencies, as special schools for the backward and the forward; the adolescent offender is sent in increasing proportion for training in a Borstal Institution rather than confinement in a prison.
> (Evidence to Persistent Offenders Committee 1931: vol 3: 669)

Paterson was well aware of some of the problems and what have come to be called the 'pains' of imprisonment and the full impact on the individual offender and their families of a period of imprisonment.

> Imprisonment is to be avoided whenever possible. It is often but a clumsy piece of social surgery, tearing a man away from the social fabric of home and work and club and union that has woven round himself, causing distress to others and rendering his replacement in social and industrial life a matter of grave difficulty.
> (Evidence to Persistent Offenders Committee 1931: vol 3: 675)

He wished to abolish prisons, and replace them with other institutions which were primarily concerned with reform – thus he also wrote:

279

I propose to abolish all prisons.

I propose to replace the prison commission with a Board of Welfare, whose members shall under a director administer:

(a) Probation and Aftercare
(b) Reformatory and Industrial Schools
(c) Borstal Institutions
(d) Examination Clinics
(e) Training Centres
(f) Places of detention

There shall be no more places called prisons.

(Evidence to Persistent Offenders Committee 1931: vol 3: 675)

While Paterson's ambition of the abolition of prisons was not achieved, his thinking, and the goal of rehabilitation, was paramount in the penal approach. However, the result of rehabilitative policies may have had a surprising outcome: an increase in prison sentence lengths. As we saw in Chapter 8, one implication of rehabilitative theory is that sentence lengths should be flexible and responsive to the needs of the offender. From this came the argument that sentences should be indeterminate along with the idea that offenders needed to be sent to prison for a sufficient time for treatment and training to take effect. Thus Paterson said, 'if we are concerned to train him, a few weeks in prison will be an idle pretence . . .' (Paterson 1927). This was a view clearly held by those running the prison system in the inter-war years. Thus the Report of the Commissioners of Prisons for 1925/26 stated:

> . . . the short sentence remains an outstanding defect in our penal system and difficulty in prison administration. Repetition on this point is not amiss.
>
> The highest administrative and judicial authorities have taken the same view, and have drawn attention to the uselessness of the short sentence. The International Penitentiary Congress in August 1925 passed a resolution to the same effect. There is not doubt but that the prospect of prison has a strong deterrent effect on those who have never yet passed its gates; nor that, once the disgrace of imprisonment has been incurred, much of that effect has been lost. It can also be readily understood that an impediment to the development of a sound system of prison training is the presence of a number of men who only come in for a few days, and cannot therefore be taught any work other than the simplest. The difficulty, of course, is to find proper alternatives. The most hopeful prospect lies in the development of the probation system. A point may be reached where many offenders can be so well supervised in the open that, if they fail, a period of custodial training of substantial length will be justified.

(Paterson 1927: xiii)

This extract makes it clear that the prison commissioners did not seek longer sentences for all prisoners. Indeed they advocated non-custodial alternatives for less serious offenders. However, if offenders were to go to prison, the logic was clearly that short sentences would not allow sufficient time to treat and train them to lead a good and useful life. The Prison Rules, first introduced in 1949, took the view that the task of the prison service was to 'encourage

Fig 9.2 (a) Length of prison sentence imposed 1913–1975

	1913	*1938*	*1948*	*1958*	*1968*	*1975*
Up to 2 weeks	80,961	8,820	3,366	3,030	2,932	3,161
Over 2 weeks up to 5 weeks	30,359	7,475	5,595	4,922	3,765	5,069
Over 5 weeks up to 3 months	16,862	7,043	8,925	8,398	6,930	10,126
Over 3 months up to 6 months	5,070	3,947	6,447	6,710	7,801	7,483
Over 6 months up to 12 months	2,873	1,881	4,775	4,843	5,858	7,418
Over 12 months up to 18 months	1,033	694	2,361	2,085	3,179	4,546
Over 18 months up to 3 years	774	581	2,478	2,906	4,059	6,197
Over 3 years up to 5 years	231	158	617	733	1,086	1,749
Over 5 years	120	47	123	348	364	532
Life	13	14	30	40	95	153

(b) Length of prison sentence expressed as percentages

	1913	*1938*	*1948*	*1958*	*1968*	*1975*
Up to 2 weeks	58.6	28.7	10.0	8.9	8.1	6.0
Over 2 weeks up to 5 weeks	21.9	24.4	16.7	14.5	10.5	10.9
Over 5 weeks up to 3 months	12.2	23.0	24.7	24.7	19.2	21.8
Over 3 months up to 6 months	3.7	12.9	18.3	19.7	21.6	16.1
Over 6 months up to 12 months	2.1	6.1	14.3	14.2	16.2	16.0
Over 12 months up to 18 months	0.7	2.3	7.1	6.3	8.8	9.8
Over 18 months up to 3 years	0.5	1.9	7.4	8.5	11.3	13.3
Over 3 years up to 5 years	0.2	0.5	1.0	2.1	3.0	3.8
Over 5 years	0.1	0.2	0.4	1.0	1.0	1.2
Life	–	–	0.1	0.1	0.3	0.3

The data includes periods imposed in cases of fine default but excluding sentences of corrective training or preventive detention. The data also includes male and female offenders.

Source: **Prison and the Prisoner** 1977: 157–8.

and assist the inmate to lead a good and useful life'. In their Annual Report for 1949, the commissioners repeated the need for longer sentences in the context of discussing the new Criminal Justice Act 1948. Thus they argue, 'the purpose of the Act was not to provide some new form of training but to give the courts power to pass sentences long enough to enable the methods of training already developed in training prisons to be effectively applied'. This can be contrasted vividly, as we shall later see, with theories based on punishment and deterrence where the 'short sharp shock' or the 'clang of the prison gates' is urged as the most effective part of imprisonment. The effect of this policy is shown in Figure 9.2, which shows prison terms from 1913 to 1975 in absolute and percentage figures.

Figure 9.2 shows that sentence lengths increased between 1913 and 1975. This is partly explained by the increasing use of non-custodial sentences from 1913 which meant that fewer petty criminals were sent to prison for short periods of time – thus increasing the average sentence length. The figures also include offenders of all ages, and are therefore affected by the growing use of Borstal and detention centres for those under 21, and by statutory restrictions on sending younger offenders to prison. A major factor in the increase however is the influence of the rehabilitative arguments outlined above. By 1975, over 28 per cent of offenders sentenced to custody received terms of imprisonment of over 12 months, compared with less than 1.5 per cent in 1913. Thus policies based on rehabilitation appear to have led to longer prison sentences.

The 1979 May Report on the prison service also noted the link between sentences and rehabilitation and commented:

> However, confidence in the treatment model as it is usually called has now been waning throughout the Western world for some years. The drive behind the original borstal ideas has fallen away and there is now no belief that longer sentences may be justified because they make actual reformative treatment more possible.
>
> (Home Office 1979: 63)

This last quote indicates that, certainly by 1979, the influence of rehabilitation had waned: the reasons for this will be discussed below.

Rehabilitation reassessed

Rehabilitation fell out of favour largely because its promise was not achieved – it became a faith dashed on the rocks of the unprecedented rise in recorded crime in the post war years. As this coincided with the growing post-war affluence of the 1950s, it also challenged reformers' claims that crime would be reduced with the growth of social welfare. Thus a 1959 white paper, *Penal Practice in a Changing Society* (Home Office 1959), lamented,

> It is a disquieting feature of our society that in the years since the end of the war, rising standards in material prosperity, education and social welfare have brought no decrease in the high rate of crime reached during the war: on the contrary, crime has increased and is still increasing.

There were several main sources of the declining influence of rehabilitation. The medical model, whose influence has been illustrated above, began to come under considerable criticism. By the 1960s it was apparent that it could justify a range of treatments which seemed far from humane. Many feared the development, for example, of the use of surgery and drug treatment which could readily be used to produce docile inmates. When medical intervention took these more dramatic forms many of the liberal reformers, who supported rehabilitation as a more humane approach, came to realise that punishment might be a better alternative. In addition, the increase in sentence lengths mentioned above, along with the use of indeterminate sentences, made rehabilitative treatments appear harsher than those which would be justified by retributive approaches. Hence, the support from liberal and civil rights groups in the 1970s for the back-to-justice movement, to be discussed below.

A further problem with rehabilitation was its link, seen most clearly in the medical model, with a view that criminality resulted from the pathologies of individual offenders. Yet despite a large volume of research attempting to discover how the characteristics of individual offenders could be related to their criminality, the pathological causes of crime proved hard to identify and apply in individual cases. As seen in Chapter 2 there were also many other approaches to explaining crime, and many offenders possess no clearly identifiable pathology. In addition, from a labelling perspective, excessive intervention risked increasing crime, and adherents advocated the use of minimal intervention (Schur 1973). Thus the promise to diagnose and therefore to devise suitable treatments for offenders was never fulfilled.

One of the greatest problems with the rehabilitative strategies was that they failed to live up to the claim that they would reduce recidivism. The lesson that prisons were not likely to reform offenders was slow to be learned. The results of research seeking to establish the impact of rehabilitative measures led to the gloomy conclusion that 'nothing works' (Lipton *et al* 1975). During the 1960s the coalition of interests that made up the rehabilitative lobby in Europe and North America began to fall apart.

By the 1980s prison service policy documents had abandoned the ambitious mission statements of previous penal epochs, and referred to the much more basic functions of prison. Thus in 1988, a statement by the prison service contained the message that 'Her Majesty's Prison Service serves the public by keeping in custody those committed by the courts'. They had not abandoned, but diluted, the rehabilitative aspirations of the prison and strengthened the concern with humane conditions. 'Our duty is to look after them (inmates) with humanity and to help them lead law-abiding and useful lives in custody and after release' (Prison Service 1988).

By the 1980s the view was established that if rehabilitation was to be achieved then imprisonment was not a suitable location: 'it made bad people worse', to summarise the prevailing orthodoxy. While not claiming that prisons should give up their attempts to rehabilitate inmates, the argument prevailed that if rehabilitation was the primary aspiration of the court at the time of sentence then it would be better to leave the offender in the community. Thus community sentences and the probation service became the main focus of rehabilitative ambitions.

PROBATION SERVICE AND COMMUNITY PENALTIES

The probation service play their role in sentencing in three ways.

- They write pre-sentence reports to provide information about the offender, the offence and may recommend sentences to help the court in reaching their decision as to an appropriate sentence.

283

- They organise and carry out the sentences of the court that involve a supervisory role as with probation orders, community service orders, or combination orders to ensure compliance with the sentence of the court.

- They supervise prisoners in the community after release from prison or a young offender institution. There is a statutory requirement (CJA 1991) that all offenders sentenced to one year and over in prison should be supervised in the community for a period equal to one-quarter of the length of their sentence.

The historical development of probation was linked to reforms brought about by the Summary Jurisdiction Act 1879, which introduced conditional discharge for younger and first-time offenders. The court could add the requirement of supervision. Volunteers and friends offered to supervise, and from this developed the role whereby people, sometimes police officers, supervised and acted as mentors to offenders. The Probation of First Time Offenders Act 1887 specified the term 'probation' and defined the role of probation. The Probation Offenders Act 1907 established probation officers and defined their duties.

The idea that offenders can be dealt with in the community has a long history. In the late nineteenth century many juvenile offenders were 'saved' from prison by police court missionaries who agreed to be responsible for them – the forerunners of the probation service. The Probation of Offenders Act 1907 provided that the courts could appoint and pay probation officers who were to advise, assist and befriend offenders. The Criminal Justice Act 1925 formalised the role and required each petty sessional division to employ at least one probation officer.

Since then the work of the probation service has expanded. Probation officers became responsible not only for work in the criminal courts but also for civil work involving divorce. They provided social inquiry reports to the court giving information about offenders' circumstances and attitude to offences and gave the court advice about what sentence would be appropriate. They also began to work with ex-prisoners, reflected in the use of the term probation and after-care service. Their role was linked to the rise of rehabilitation and the service became professionalised and was linked to the development of social case work in the penal system. Most probation officers are trained as social workers.

In 1996 there were 54 probation areas in England and Wales employing 7,313 probation officers who wrote 219,000 pre-sentence reports. They supervised 114,700 offenders who were starting community sentences and 47,700 following a prison sentence, including those sentenced to life imprisonment released on licence and sex offenders (*Home Office Statistical Bulletin*, 13/97).

The scope of work carried out by the probation service is illustrated in a National Probation Survey (May 1992). This found that, typically, probation officers spent 23 per cent of their time on probation and other criminal supervision, 8 per cent on community service orders and 14 per cent on after care which includes work with offenders before and after release. Court duties took up 15 per cent of their time and the preparation of social inquiry reports (now called pre-sentence reports) a further 11 per cent. Office duties occupied 3 per cent of time and civil and other work 26 per cent. The precise activities of individual probation officers will depend, however, on whether they are part of a team attached to a court, a prison, a bail project or are one of several area teams working with offenders in the community.

Once on probation, community service or combination orders, offenders face a variety of experiences. These may include a programme of meetings with their supervising officer or attendance at counselling or therapy sessions for alcohol and drug abuse or anger management. Some will require help finding accommodation and work, others with welfare and social security applications. Others may participate in a variety of projects such as motor projects which provide offenders who have been involved in car crime with an opportunity to drive and work with cars legitimately. Other offenders are sent on programmes involving physical exercise to improve their ability to use leisure time constructively and co-operate within teams and groups.

An example of the latter kind of project is Essex Challenge run by the probation service (*The Daily Telegraph*, 23 October 1994). In this scheme persistent criminals are introduced to windsurfing, potholing and sailing. Offenders spend one week at a 'spartan' hostel and the next four weeks on outdoor sports. Intended as a last chance for offenders aged between 17 and 21, it is not, argued a council spokesperson, a soft option and aims to break the cycle of offending behaviour.

In a community service scheme in Manchester, offenders undertake a variety of decorating jobs which involve learning a trade. One such was in a nursery school. According to a senior probation officer this scheme puts offenders in contact with disadvantaged groups in the community such as the elderly or the disabled. This, he argues, means that offenders are put in contact with people coping with worse conditions than their own. Indeed, he adds, some carry on working as volunteers and others have obtained permanent jobs. At the same time however it is a punishment – if their work is unsatisfactory or they fail to comply they can lose hours and be sent back to court (*The Guardian*, 23 October 1994).

These kind of schemes have attracted criticism on the grounds that they are insufficiently punitive, comments which reflect an underlying tension in the role of community sentences. This role has always been problematic. When, for example, community service was introduced during the 1960s discussions referred to 'treatment in the community'. In the 1990s, however, the predominant phraseology was 'punishment in the community', for example the green paper issued by the Home Office in 1995 was entitled, *Strengthening Punishment in the Community*. This changing emphasis indicates some potential conflicts.

What is the role of the probation officer? Is it primarily to help offenders, who in the past were described as clients, or to serve the court and the public by ensuring that offenders do not re-offend? This care or control dilemma refers to the tension between the rehabilitative, and the control and penal aspects of probation. The tradition of the probation service has been mainly rehabilitative, providing 'treatment' for offenders who were referred to as 'clients'. The CJA 1991, in contrast, stressed the deprivation of liberty and the element of punishment. However community sentences are often seen as soft. This was particularly evident during 1994, when much publicity was given to a small number of offenders who were sent abroad or to holiday camps as part of their community sentences. The strong reaction this provoked led to measures to toughen up community sentences, illustrating the shift towards a more punitive role.

Many have seen the primary role of community sentences as being to reduce the prison population. These arguments influenced the introduction of new measures during the 1960s and 1970s. Parole and the suspended sentence were introduced in 1967 and the Criminal Justice Act 1972 introduced community service orders (CSOs), made available nationally in 1975. CSOs proved popular because they combined so many sentencing aims, and by 1988 they accounted for 8 per cent of all sentences for indictable offenders. While the legislation itself made no specific reference to their use for those who would otherwise have been sent to prison, they were expected to be used primarily as an alternative to prison (Cavadino and Dignan 1997). Later policies were also influenced by the disillusionment with rehabilitation which in some ways left the probation service without a clear function.

During the 1970s and 1980s new elements were added to community sentences. In 1973 provisions were made that offenders on probation could be required to attend day training centres. The Criminal Justice Act 1982 provided that courts could require full-time attendance at day centres for a maximum of 60 days. Day centres were viewed with concern by many probation officers who saw their use as increasing their control function (May 1994). Other policies during the 1970s involved targeting selected offenders for intensive probation supervision and during the 1980s some schemes involved tracking offenders.

Throughout the 1980s the Home Office policy sought to reduce local variations in community sentences and to increase their punitive elements. They thus attempted to exert greater control over community sentences seeing the strong welfare orientation within the probation service as an impediment (May 1994). In 1984 a Statement of National Objectives for Probation (SNOP) was issued which stated that the priorities of the probation service were to provide alternatives to custody and prepare social inquiry reports for the court. A major theme was that offenders with a high risk of imprisonment were to be targeted, signalling a shift away from the traditional role of the service as dealing with less serious offenders who would benefit from treatment, help or support (May 1994). In 1988 an Action Plan called on every local probation area to develop its own strategy for targeting more intensive supervision on young adult offenders.

Changes were also made to community service orders. In 1989 a set of national standards for community service was introduced which encouraged the adoption of more exacting procedures for dealing with lateness, non-compliance and unsatisfactory behaviour (*National Standards for the Supervision of Offenders in the Community*). A strong preference for manual labour was indicated, laying emphasis on tasks such as cleaning up graffiti.

In the 1990s controversy followed the news of offenders being sent to holiday camps, and the sentencing of a wife batterer to an 'anger management' course run by the probation service. The Home Secretary expressed these concerns in an address to the annual conference of the Central Probation Council in May of 1994, where he commented that 'probation services are working with offenders but for the community and not the other way round'. The courts and the public, he went on to say, must have confidence in community sentences as punishment, and, while he was in favour of programmes making demands on offenders, they should not be given 'privileged access to opportunities which law-abiding members of the community cannot afford'.

In August 1994 the Government announced new national standards including a ban on safari and domestic holidays and requirements that work on community sentences should be demanding and physical. Other proposals aimed to introduce stricter supervision and provisions that offenders would be sent to prison if the terms of a sentence were not met. Offenders would receive two formal warnings if they failed to comply with the terms of an order. After which, further breaches would result in a return to court. A different approach to the preparation of the all-important pre-sentence reports was introduced, underlining the role of probation officers as officers of the court, responsible for helping the court assess the risk of re-offending. Criticisms that probation officers had often made unrealistic suggestions as to the appropriate sentence were answered by making probation officers assess offending seriousness in the same way that a court might.

The many criticisms of community sentences imply that they may not be very effective. Given the different aims of community sentences however it is not entirely clear how they should be evaluated. Is their effectiveness to be judged in terms of how well they provide an alternative to prison? Or in terms of how many offenders are diverted from further crime? Alternatively, given the high costs of imprisonment and pressures for cost effectiveness should we subject community sentences to a cost benefit analysis? Finally, irrespective of any of these measures, should we look at the extent to which offenders are helped by these schemes, whether or not they re-offend?

In relation to the first question – their effectiveness as alternatives to prison – evidence is mixed. The prison population continued to rise despite the introduction of measures which aimed to reduce it, and it appeared that the so-called alternatives to prison acted instead as alternatives to existing non-custodial sentences. This may even have resulted in more people being sent to prison – if, for example, they failed to comply with an order or committed further offences, they could be sent to prison – thus moving more rapidly up the tariff than they might otherwise have done. What appeared to be happening was that the courts, viewing community sentences as too soft, were not prepared to use them for offenders that they would otherwise have sent to prison.

One argument in favour of community sentences is that they are cheaper. The National Probation Survey, for example, found that probation orders cost £1,060 per annum in 1990/1, and community service orders £1,020 (May 1992). Comparing this with the high costs of imprisonment it is evident that community sentences offer a cheaper alternative – but how effective are they in reducing recidivism?

Statistics on community sentences are difficult to compare with those on prison as the measure of success is often the number of offenders who successfully complete orders, rather than being returned to court for breaching orders. In 1996, 28 per cent of offenders on community service orders and 12 per cent on probation orders were the subject of breach proceedings (*Criminal Statistics England and Wales* 1996: 191). While these might be regarded as a success by those familiar with the problems of dealing with offenders, from another perspective they represent a failure of offenders to complete the sentence given by the court; a sentence usually proposed in the pre-sentence report by the probation service.

Statistics on reconviction indicate that 60 per cent of offenders given probation orders in 1993 were reconvicted within two years. The equivalent figure for community service orders was 52 per cent and for combination orders it was 61 per cent. Reconviction rates were highest for those who had previous custodial sentences or a large number of previous convictions (see Figure 10.5). In general these figures indicate that community sentences are no more successful than prison in terms of rehabilitation. These figures, however, are very limited as only two in every 100 crimes result in a conviction, their use as a measure of re-offending must be seriously questioned. The data only relates to a follow-up period of two years after release from prison or commencement of a community sentence. These figures tell us little about any positive help the offender may have received.

It is also important to consider the conflicting objectives of community sentences. The increasing emphasis on cost effectiveness and the deprivation of liberty may have an impact on how offenders respond to some schemes. For example, pressures of cost effectiveness may lead to more offenders being placed on any one scheme reducing opportunities for individual work. The recent stress on tough and demanding work may also have an effect. A report on community service projects in Scotland found that offenders responded better to schemes which provided contact with those who benefited from their work, where provision was made for the acquisition of new skills and where the work was seen to be useful (McIvor 1991). The author questions

he stress in the National Standards on hard manual labour which is less
ikely to be seen by offenders as useful and which provides few opportunities
or direct contact with the community and learning new skills. It has also
been argued that if community service becomes more punitive offenders
will become more hostile and resistant which might make them less willing to
comply (May 1994; Vass 1990).

While some in the probation service remain committed to the ideal of
rehabilitation through community penalties, their lack of success in rehabilitative terms undermines these claims. The rationale of community penalties
has moved on from an alternative to custody approach towards an intermediate sanction rationale in which success will be measured in terms of just
deserts and denunciatory goals. In this respect the shift reflects a greater
sensitivity to the concerns of the community rather than the needs of the
offenders.

Alternatives to custody or intermediate sanctions?

Many of the new types of sentences introduced from the 1960s onwards,
such as the community service order, were presented as alternatives to custody. That is they were to be regarded as equivalent to custody, and only
imposed in circumstances where a prison sentence would have been considered. This implies that the sentences can be substituted for prison and
are equivalent. And indeed the Court of Appeal established that 190 hours
of community service were equivalent to 9–12 months of imprisonment
(R v Lawrence 1982). When the community service order was originally
introduced, courts were enjoined to indicate whether the order was a direct
alternative to custody or not, and to record that fact in the court register
(Home Office 1986: 43).

The problem with this kind of approach is that many sentencers and the
public simply do not see community penalties as in any way equivalent to
prison. Thus there was a tendency for the new, so called alternatives to
prison to be used instead as alternatives to probation. In addition, the mixed
rationales underlying the community service order made it difficult to approach in terms of the tariff – how, for example, did such sentences match
the seriousness of the offence? If, however, the use of imprisonment was to
be reduced while at the same time maintaining a notion of tough sentences,
new approaches to community sentences were necessary.

Such new approaches were influenced by the justice model. The logic of
just deserts and proportionality implied that penalties should be differenti-
ated according to the severity of the crime and the culpability of the offender.
In practice, prison terms are measured in terms of the degree of restriction
on the offender's liberty. Community sentences could also, it was argued,
be justified in this way. It was suggested that community penalties could

be made tougher. This could be done by increasing sentencing options and introducing tougher penalties between probation and prison, thus producing a continuum or gradation of penalties which would reflect sentencers' need for sanctions proportionate to the seriousness of the offence.

The 1991 Criminal Justice Act made community sentences part of a frame work of sentences based on a just deserts approach. These sentences, a revised by the Act, provided for a range of community penalties with some being more demanding than others. They were no longer merely alternative to prison but intermediate sentences, a sentence in punitive terms some where between prison and probation, and became sentences in their own right with specific aims.

Despite the new role for community penalties as intermediate sanctions research suggests that some magistrates perceive community penalties a insufficiently demanding to provide the structured steps in a hierarchy o punitiveness between probation and prison. This is illustrated by the follow ing comments from magistrates about the implementation of communit service orders:

To me it's not structured enough. They come and go as they please.

I wouldn't say it was terribly demanding necessarily, only the discipline of having to be there and doing it . . . I wouldn't think they'd break out in a sweat.

I think they tend to lose credibility with me when we have breach hearings and you hear how often the administrator has really bent over backwards to accept their excuse.

The underlying view I think of probation officers would not be to divert peopl from crime but to divert people from prison.

(Davies *et al* 1996: 94–5

The Government, however, continues to place reliance on community sen tences. The 1997 white paper *No More Excuses* (Home Office 1997a) state that the Government will extend the range of community sentences for young offenders to allow a pilot scheme to evaluate the use of electronic tagging with curfew orders. The white paper indicated the Government's faith in the same scheme as used for adults (s. 5.17). The report also indicates the intention of introducing a new community penalty for younger offenders: the action plan order. This will involve a short, intensive community programme combining elements of punishment, rehabilitation and reparation (s. 5.18).

THE JUSTICE APPROACH

The declining faith in rehabilitation along with the continuing rise in re corded crime led to a reappraisal of sentencing aims in the late 1960s and 1970s. Extremely influential in this process was what came to be known as a back-to-justice policy which affected legislation throughout the 1980s and most particularly the CJA 1991. There was no one single and comprehensive formulation of the justice model, but it developed out of a number of publications by American academics such as K C Davies (1969), D Fogel (1975), M Frankel (1973) and Andrew von Hirsch (1976). In the USA, where the justice model developed and influenced policy more directly, it was influential in shaping reforms of the juvenile courts and the introduction of determinate sentencing laws in California in 1976. These reforms were strongly influenced by the problems of rehabilitative sentencing policies. The long and seemingly harsh sentences associated with rehabilitation, the uncertainty produced by indeterminate sentences and the individualisation of sentences were seen to conflict with the rights of offenders to receive predictable and proportionate sentences. Thus the justice model argues that sentencing should be fair and not aim to achieve anything other than punishing offenders in proportion to the harm they have done. It developed directly out of a critique of rehabilitation and as Messinger and Johnson (1978) comment 'it represented . . . an outright rejection of previous sentencing policy and seems to be based on the opposite assumptions in every respect'.

The justice model is often linked to and is not logically incompatible with retributive theories; however it emphasises fairness while retribution is often popularly distorted to support demands for vengeance or harsher sentences. Thus while the justice model stresses punishment as an end in itself it was not called 'back-to-punishment', and von Hirsch (1976) described it as 'vengeance with fairness'. This approach is incompatible with rehabilitation as a primary goal of punishment. It can, however, be included as a secondary aspect of sentencing provided it does not distort the length or type of sentence in terms of the principles of just deserts. There is no clearly articulated theory of just deserts, however there are four main sets of assumptions and principles that can be identified. These include assumptions about human behaviour, the objective of punishment, the distribution of punishment, and the extension of due process into the prisons.

Assumptions about human behaviour

To advocates of the justice model, individuals are responsible for their own behaviour. Criminal behaviour therefore, like any other, is thus a result of conscious decisions made by responsible, autonomous, self-determined individuals. Thus the rehabilitationist notion that criminality results from some individual pathology or is attributable to the offender's social, economic or personal circumstances was rejected. While it was accepted that these factors could affect behaviour they should not neglect what is seen as the moral imperative of regarding human action as primarily attributable to individual choice. Thus offenders have made a free choice to commit crime, and should therefore be punished. Where they have not been able because, for example,

of age or mental disability, to make a free choice, they are not fully responsible for their actions and need not be punished.

The objective of punishment

Punishment is seen as an end in itself and a just and condign reward for
morally wrong behaviour. It does not have to be justified by social protection
or on the grounds that it is likely to reduce the future likelihood of crime. It
should therefore be based simply on the notion of just deserts: culpable criminals should be punished in amounts proportional to or commensurate with
the seriousness of the harm done.

This raises important questions. By whom, and how is culpability to be
assessed? What constitutes the proportionate level of punishment for each
offence and who should determine this? Thus there can be moral and political objections to this approach. In unequal or unjust societies, just deserts
may be determined by those in power and may be far from just to those at
the receiving end. In addition, in pluralist societies, cultural differentiation
makes shared agreement as to what is right or wrong difficult to assess.
Decisions as to how serious a crime is and what its 'just' punishment should
be may open up a wider debate on moral, social and political issues. It might
not be easy, for example, to distinguish between different offences in terms of
seriousness. How can the respective seriousness of rape, burglary or tax fraud
be assessed? As we have seen, the public may have very different views over
what should be criminalised, and how to rank crime in terms of seriousness.
Disagreements are inevitable when citizens are asked to consider the harmful
consequences of crime; and the merits of different modes of punishment.
However, even if agreement cannot be reached as to what is 'just', it does
keep the debate about punishment associated with issues of morality and
justice. This point is made by C S Lewis:

> The humanitarian theory removes from punishment the concept of Desert. But the
> concept of Desert is the only connecting link between punishment and justice. It is
> only as deserved or undeserved that a sentence can be just or unjust . . . we may
> very properly ask whether it is likely to deter others and to reform the criminal. But
> neither of these two last questions is a question of justice.

(Lewis 1953)

Von Hirsch, discussing the twin objectives of deterrence and deserts makes
it clear that the deserts principle is more important for decisions about the
distribution of punishment. Thus he argues:

> . . . we think that the commensurate deserts principle should have priority over
> other objectives in decisions about how to punish. The disposition of convicted
> offenders should be commensurate with the seriousness of their offences, even if
> greater or less severity would promote other goals.

(von Hirsch 1976)

292

The distribution of punishment

Once culpability is established the main determinant of the type or amount of punishment will be the seriousness of the offence. A secondary consideration once this has been established is the degree of responsibility. Thus both mitigating and aggravating circumstances in relation to both the offence and the offender form part of the consideration of the sentence to be given.

Proponents of the justice model aimed to reduce individualised sentencing strategies, which as we have seen underlie sentencing disparities, and to eradicate indeterminacy. Thus they wished to see fixed and determinate sentencing with an established tariff for each offence, and uniformity of sentences for offenders committing the same offence in similar circumstances. Hence the move towards more constraints on judicial discretion at the sentencing stage throughout much of the USA and the UK.

Legalism: the extension of due process

Indeterminate prison sentences created a situation whereby the length of a prison sentence depended on discretionary decisions made within the prison. This led to many problems, which, especially in the USA, were associated not only with increasing sentence lengths and thus an increase in the prison population, but also with unrest within prisons. Prisoners could not predict how long their sentences were to last nor could they always predict what they had to do to ensure an early release. This could also lead to a situation where release dates and parole decisions could be used as a means of control within the prison system. It also led to apparent injustices as offenders sent to prison for similar offences could in effect serve very different lengths of sentence. This not surprisingly led to much discontent and feelings of inequity. Thus a major argument of the justice model was to extend the principles of due process into the prison system. The clearest impact on prison regimes was achieved by David Fogel, who, as Commissioner for Prisons in Minnesota from 1971 to 1973, attempted to apply the principles of the justice model to prisons. He advocated reforms which would involve more due process; greater openness in decision making and accountability according to the demands of natural justice. His reforms emphasised prisoners' rights and a belief that in the world of the prison community there should be an atmosphere of justice and fairness. This view was later echoed in the Woolf Report 1991 (Home Office 1991a) into prison disturbances in 1990, which will be discussed in Chapter 10.

In the UK the justice approach made its mark in a more diffuse way than in the USA. By the end of the 1970s aspects of prison policy were being scrutinised by the courts and greater attention was paid to prisoners' rights. The indeterminate sentence of Borstal training was replaced by the determinate sentence of youth custody in 1982. Also, as we have seen in Chapter 8, increasing guidance was given to courts to reduce sentence disparity. The 1990 white paper and the subsequent legislative reforms in the CJA 1991 gave the clearest message that just deserts should be the primary principle for sentencing decisions in England and Wales.

LIMITING THE USE OF PRISON

The declining influence of rehabilitationist arguments and the growing attention to a justice model were accompanied by arguments that the use of prison should be drastically reduced. It was gradually accepted by most commentators, policy makers and administrators that despite the good intentions of penal reformers prisons had not achieved the goals claimed by their protagonists and were not likely to rehabilitate offenders. Today prisons are primarily justified by notions of retribution and denunciation, the uncertain impact of deterrence and a claim to incapacitate. The existence of violence, gangs and drug use within the prisons means that even the claim to incapacitate is only partially true.

In addition prisons are costly institutions and there have been recurrent concerns over the overcrowding of existing prisons and conditions within them. Many prisons in the UK were built in Victorian times and have few modern facilities. Concerns about overcrowding on the part of the Prison Officers' Association were evident in Britain as early as the 1940s and the Prison Commissioners' Annual Reports repeated the warning from 1955 until their demise in 1964. The degrading conditions within prisons also caused considerable concern and were described as an 'affront to civilised society' by the Director General of Prisons in the Annual Report of the Prison Department in 1980.

Out of these concerns grew what came to be known as the 'prison reductionist' movement. Some focused on degrading conditions and overcrowding, while others focused on the adverse effects of prisons and claimed that sentencers were sending too many people to prison. By the 1970s liberal and welfare oriented groups who had supported rehabilitation came to argue for a reduction in the use of prison. Their message was underlined by media stories of overcrowded cells, antiquated conditions and incidents of unrest in prisons. Thus there has been a regular theme in the British press over the last 20 years of prisons in crisis.

Of course, one solution to problems of overcrowding and degrading conditions would be to build more prisons. Moreover, the argument that sentencers send 'too many people' to prison is a difficult one to evaluate given the different aims underlying a prison sentence. Nonetheless, the argument of the reductionists, who shared a common view that the size of the prison population should be reduced, became an influential one. A key part of this argument was that as prison could no longer be seen to rehabilitate and indeed could have an adverse effect on prisoners, their use should be curtailed.

This influence was evident in the parliamentary debate on the 1967 Criminal Justice Bill. Thus Roy Jenkins, then Home Secretary, echoed the reductionist position in his speech on the Bill in which he stated that 'the main range of the penal provision of the bill revolves round the single theme, that of keeping out of prison those who need not be there . . . the overstrain upon prison resources, both of buildings and men, is at present appalling'.

From the 1960s official documents started to move away from the grander claims made during the heyday of rehabilitation and towards an acceptance that prisons were not appropriate places to reform individual inmates. It began to be argued that prisons had an adverse effect on inmates, making them reliant on institutional life, and could further deepen their commitment to crime as they mixed freely with other criminals: the prison as the university of crime. In addition, ex-prisoners might face considerable stigma, making it more difficult for them to gain housing or employment. Thus a more limited rehabilitative rationale emerged in arguments that if rehabilitation was sought by sentencers it was not likely be achieved in prison. This was made most apparent in the arguments in the green paper, *Punishment, Custody and the Community* (Home Office 1988a) and the subsequent white paper of 1990 (Home Office 1990a).

During the late 1980s and early 1990s the reductionist message was paramount. The arguments of those who wished to see prisons reduced on the grounds that they were ineffective and inhumane were echoed by more pragmatic reductionists concerned with the costs, efficacy and the strains caused by the numbers in the system. Thus from the 1980s onwards, as we have seen, successive legislation and policy initiatives began to encourage more consistency in sentencing and imposed limitations on the use of imprisonment such as the introduction of statutory criteria on the use of prison in the Criminal Justice Acts 1982, 1988 and 1991.

In 1990, explicit recognition was given in a white paper to the idea that imprisonment has a limited role to play in penal policy. The report is discussed in Chapter 10. Changing prison regimes alone however could not alleviate the problems of the prison system and the white paper argued that prison overcrowding could not be solved in isolation from sentencing policy. Hence the search for sanctions which could be used instead of prison, not necessarily to act as an alternative sentence, but to be placed on the tariff below prison. These sentences should it was argued be less severe than imprisonment, but be demanding enough to encourage sentencers to use them for the less serious offences that had previously attracted a prison term.

SHIFTING PENAL PARADIGMS

By the 1980s therefore many factors suggested that there was a need for a review of penal policy. It had been largely recognised that the individualised sentencing associated with rehabilitation had produced disparities and what were seen by proponents of a justice model as injustices. It had become associated with longer and indeterminate sentences, far out of proportion to the crime committed. The belief in the positive rehabilitative effects of custody may have produced a rise in the prison population. However there were strong arguments in favour of substantially reducing the use of imprisonment, on the grounds of the relative ineffectiveness of prison in terms of rehabilitation and also on the grounds of its cost-effectiveness. At the same time, however public concern over rising crime rates, particularly in offences of violence suggested that reducing the use of imprisonment could be seen as paying insufficient regard to the protection of the public. Community sentence lacked credibility. These issues were reflected in a series of discussion documents and government papers (notably the 1988 green paper, *Punishment Custody and the Community*, and the 1990 white paper, *Crime, Justice and Protecting the Public*) preceding the CJA 1991, which promised to be one of the most thorough overhauls of sentencing policy. We have already outlined many of the changes brought about by this legislation, some to be quickly overturned in the CJA 1993. This section will place these changes in the context of the shifting penal paradigms outlined in this chapter.

The difficulties of the deterrent approach to sentencing was developed in the white paper:

> Deterrence is a principle with much immediate appeal. Most law abiding citizens understand the reasons why some behaviour is made a criminal offence, and would be deterred by the shame of a criminal conviction or the possibility of a severe penalty. There are doubtless some criminals who carefully calculate the possible gains and risks. But much crime is committed on impulse, given the opportunity presented by an open window or unlocked door, and it is committed by offenders who live from moment to moment; their crimes are as impulsive as the rest of their feckless, sad or pathetic lives. It is unrealistic to construct sentencing arrangements on the assumption that most offenders will weigh up the possibilities in advance and base their conduct on rational calculation. Often they do not.
>
> (Home Office 1990a: 6)

According to Ashworth, 'The origins of the new law were in the government's white paper of 1990, which stated that desert should be the primary aim of sentencing, that rehabilitation should not be an aim of sentencing but should be striven for within proportionate sentences, and that deterrence is rarely a proper or profitable aim for a sentencer' (von Hirsch and Ashworth 1993: 285–6). The white paper rejected deterrent sentencing and, while it saw a role for rehabilitation, rejected any notion that rehabilitation should be a primary goal. Denunciation was also seen as significant: thus the 1990 white paper stated that 'the first objective for all sentences is denunciation of and retribution for the crime' (Home Office 1990a: 6). The emphasis on just deserts meant that the seriousness of the offence was to be the primary criteria for determining the sentence, and it was also envisaged that it should limit the severity of a sentence. This can be seen in the following extract:

... the severity of the sentence in an individual case should reflect primarily the seriousness of the offence which has been committed. Whilst factors such as preventing crime or the rehabilitation of the offender remain important functions of the criminal justice process as a whole, they should not lead to a heavier penalty in an individual case than that which is justified by the seriousness of the offence or the need to protect the public from the offender.

(Home Office 1991b: 1)

This extract also shows that while just deserts is a major principle, the protection of the public is also important, thus the Act contained an important incapacitative element. What is often known as bifurcation or a twin-track approach was introduced on the principle that for most offenders the sentence was to be based on the seriousness of the offence, except in circumstances where, as, for example, with sexual and violent offenders, incapacitation was seen to be necessary. This was described largely in terms of distinguishing property offences from those involving violence. While the courts were to be encouraged to use non-custodial sentences for property offenders where possible, prison terms, and terms longer than the offence itself merited, could be used for violent offenders.

One controversial provision of the Act provided that previous convictions should not be looked at when assessing seriousness (s. 29), the only exception being where earlier offences were taken as aggravating features of the current offence. The offender was to be sentenced on the basis of the current offence and not previous convictions. Another controversial section, referred to as the 'two offence rule' meant that regardless of the number of offences only one offence (the most serious) and only one other would be considered to determine the sentence in typical cases. This was, as had been intended, given a very narrow interpretation by the courts. Both provisions were heavily criticised as limiting the powers available to courts when sentencing the persistent offender whose offences taken individually were not counted as 'so serious'. The CJA 1993 altered this position by repealing these two sections, allowing judges to consider previous offences and the number of offences when sentencing.

A second implication of the approach was that any restriction on liberty should be commensurate with the seriousness of the offence. This applied to both custodial and community sentences. As we have seen, the 1990 white paper made it clear that imprisonment should not be used for rehabilitative or deterrent motives but might be justified in particular cases on retributive, denunciatory and incapacitative grounds. This is the significance of the statutory criteria to restrict the use of imprisonment, particularly aimed at property offenders. Just deserts was also used to determine lengths of custodial sentences.

In addition, the element of indeterminacy implied by parole was also changed with the introduction of provisions to clarify release dates from prisons with the reform of the system of parole and remission, discussed in Chapter 10.

The Act also changed the role, function and organisation of communit
sentences. Indeed the 1990 white paper devoted four out of nine chapter
to exploring the role of community penalties. To make changes that wer
acceptable to the public meant that they had to be tied into the just desert
approach, and had to be credible punishments in their own right. Thus th
1990 white paper referred to a continuum of penalties involving an increas
ing degree of restriction on the offender's liberty with custody at one en
and probation at the other with a range of intermediate punishments in th
community. This new approach was based on the assumption that the pun
ishment was to be the degree of restriction on the offender's liberty.

Thus it was argued that imprisonment should be retained as the means c
punishment for the most serious offences, and fines and discharges for th
least serious offences. The green paper clarified this point, 'Liberty under th
law is highly valued by all of us. The deprivation of liberty is the most sever
penalty available to the courts' (Home Office 1988a: 8). Apart from financia
penalties, most court disposals place restrictions on offenders' freedom c
action. The degree of restriction on the offender's freedom of action thus pro
vides the link between community based forms of punishments and imprison
ment. Custody is at one end of the continuum of restrictions on offender
freedom of action:

> The effect of custodial sentences is to restrict offenders' freedom of action b
> removing them from their homes, by determining where they will live during th
> sentence, by limiting their social relationships and by deciding how and where the
> will spend the 24 hours in each day.
>
> (Home Office 1988a: 3.

Thus the CJA 1991 was a logical development in the context of the shif
ing penal paradigms explored above. In addition, it stated, more clearly tha
before, the main principles to be used by sentencers, and thus hoped t
encourage consistency. Consequently an editorial in the *Criminal Law Revie*
on the introduction of the Act commented that 'it can be claimed that th
1991 Act differs from its predecessors in one significant respect: its sentenc
ing provisions have some fairly coherent themes' (Ashworth 1992b: 229
Ashworth comments, 'it introduced a primary rationale for English sentenc
ing (desert) and clarified the extent to which other "aims" such as publi
protection, rehabilitation and deterrence should play a part' (Ashworth 1994
853).

The aims and principles of the Act were welcomed by many though th
details of its implementation, for instance, the system of unit fines, led t
opposition in some quarters. Of course, not everyone accepted a sentencin
policy based primarily on a just deserts approach which fitted sentences t
the seriousness of the offence. One of the problems was that the Act gav
little guidance on how this seriousness is to be assessed. There is an assump
tion, for example, that violent and sexual offenders are more serious tha
property ones, but in practice the delineation of seriousness is far mo

omplex, and perhaps leaves space for both individualisation in terms of idging offence seriousness and discretion. In addition, some argue that just eserts policies can lead to an increase in the tariff. This can come about by ery different calculations about what kind of sentence is appropriate for ifferent levels of offence. This is not inevitable however – just deserts models ave led to more severe sentencing approaches in California (Davies 1989), but ot in Scandinavian countries (Ashworth 1997b; Davies *et al* 1996; Hudson 993). Much depends on exactly how maximum sentences are conceived nd how actual sentencing lengths are determined in practice.

DOES PRISON WORK?

enal reform groups, prison reductionists and policy makers in the 1990 'hite paper claim that a deterrence approach to sentencing is an unrealistic olicy because it assumes that criminals make calculations about the likeli-ood of being detected, arrested and punished and mostly they do not, as 10st crime is opportunistic or carried out by people who do not make stimates of the likely consequences of their actions. Further, as only 2 per ent of offences result in any sentence (see Attrition Statistics in Figure 3.3) is assumed that not many people are affected by sentences. In addition, :conviction rates show that majority of imprisoned offenders will be recon-icted of a new offence in the 2-year period following their release from rison (see the recidivism rates in Figure 10.5). Thus prisons, it would seem, either deter nor rehabilitate the majority of offenders who are sent there. 'hese points add up to a view that prisons do not work and that the deter-ent theory of imprisonment is invalid. The 1990 white paper claimed that, t was unrealistic to construct sentencing arrangements on the assumption 1at most offenders will weigh up the possibilities in advance and base their onduct on rational calculation' (Home Office 1990a: 6).

For other critics of imprisonment the question is not whether prison works ut whether there are more effective ways of using resources. If the reconviction ites of those sent to prison and those given community sentences are sim-ar, they would argue that it is better to use the cheaper option. Other critics f the use of imprisonment recognise its value for locking up only potentially angerous offenders.

However, the problem with these different criticisms of prison – that it oes not work, or it works but is too costly, or that it should be reserved or dangerous offenders only – is that they focus exclusively on offender-istrumental considerations as if sentencing is only about the consequences n the future behaviour of those already convicted of crimes. These critics :nore the impact on other participants in, or audiences for, the sentence; the ublic and the victims. The public will include potential offenders who may 'ell be influenced by the general deterrent effect of the sentence and do make stimates as to whether the potential risks of offending are outweighed by the

possible gains; and also includes the law abiding who wish to be reassure
that offending does not pay and that the rules of the community are bein
respected, and when they are not, a person pays for this in the hard coinag
of punishment. Thus a concern with general deterrence, retribution an
denunciation means that prisons may well play an effective part in maintair
ing a stable and law-abiding society.

It can be argued that prisons do not need to be justified in terms (
whether they rehabilitate or deter the offenders sent to them, but in term
of the impact on those who do not go to prison. Prisons, it is argued, ca
work for the following sentencing reasons. Firstly, on retributivist ground
because they are regarded by the bulk of the public as suitable institution
for punishing people who have done wrong and have been convicted of
sufficiently serious crime such that the offence cannot be ignored and
considered worthy of a serious punishment such as incarceration. Secondl
on denunciatory grounds, because they underline society's commitment t
defining rules about the appropriateness of certain type of behaviour an
censuring others as unacceptable. Thirdly, on grounds of incapacitation, i
that certain dangerous and sometimes persistent offenders need to be locke
up to protect the public. There is a fourth justification based on a gener
deterrence view that prisons deter crimes from happening because of th
fear of punishment. As we have already seen, there is a strongly held vie
among policy makers that crime is often opportunistic and not based on pr
meditated calculations of potential gains and losses. However, not all crime
are spontaneous and it is likely that the calculations about the chances (
being discovered and punished may well deter some people who contempla
crime. Testing this idea is difficult because it requires a measure of why peop
do or do not act in a criminal manner.

One theorist who has taken up the issue of the deterrence role of imprisor
ment is Charles Murray, who challenges the liberal orthodoxy of the priso
reductionists in *Does Prison Work?* Murray states the case for the theory (
general deterrence and the impact of imprisonment, concluding that polic
directions have been taken since the 1950s that have helped to promo
rather than inhibit the growth of crime. Murray argues that, 'incarceratin
people will not, by itself, solve the crime problem . . . But if the question
"How can we deter people from committing crimes?" then . . . prison is b
far the most effective answer short of the death penalty' (Murray 1997: 20

He shows that the chances of a convicted criminal going to prison ha
fallen dramatically in the period from 1954 to 1994. The prison reductioni
claim about the overuse of custody is unconvincing when one contrasts, a
Murray does, the steady but slow rise in prison population figures (double
in 40 years) with the far more dramatic growth in crime over the perio
Murray concludes over the period, 'The risk of going to jail if you commit
crime was cut by 80 per cent' (1997: 1). By contrasting the number (
recorded crimes for a particular offence against the numbers given custod
in the form of prison or borstal, he concludes:

The reduction varied from crime to crime. In 1954, the number of people sentenced to prison or borstal for felonious wounding represented one out of five such felonious woundings; in 1994, one out of eight – a drop of 45 per cent. For rape, the number of people sentenced to custody went down from one out of three to fewer than one out of twelve – down 77 per cent. For burglary, from one out of ten to one out of a hundred – down 87 per cent. For robbery, from one out of three to one out of twenty – down 86 per cent.

(Murray 1997: 1)

he evidential basis of his views relates to statistics on offenders sentenced
or indictable offences and total crimes recorded taken from *Criminal Statistics England and Wales*. We saw in Chapter 3 that these official statistics can
e misleading, but Murray argues that the upward trends in recorded crime
om the 1950s represents a real growth in crime. This interpretation is
onfirmed by data from the British Crime Survey from 1982 onwards. Other
vidence for the thesis is given in Figure 9.3, which shows the number of
ecorded crimes from 1950 to 1996 and the numbers of offenders given a

ig 9.3 Crime and custodial trends 1950–96 in England and Wales.

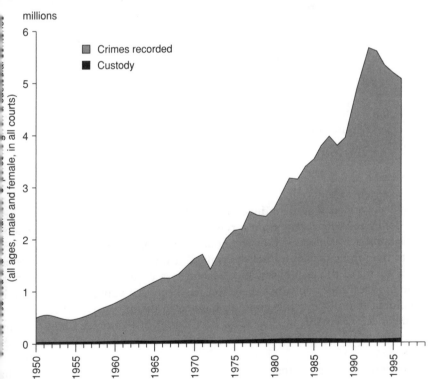

ompiled from *Criminal Statistics England and Wales*, 1950 to 1996.

Fig 9.4 Sentencing trends and use of custody 1950–96 in England and Wales

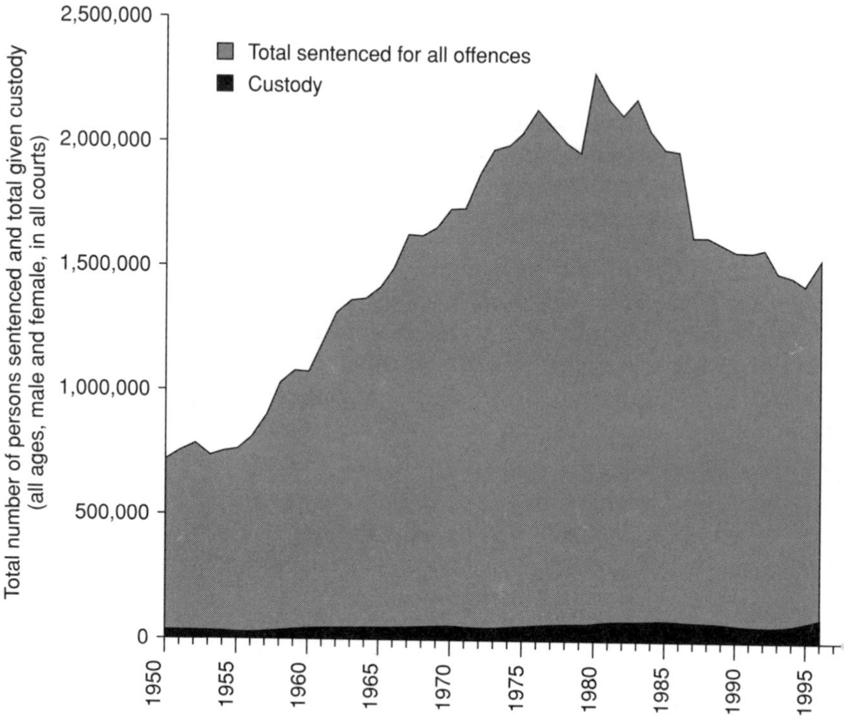

Compiled from *Criminal Statistics England and Wales*, 1950 to 1996.

custodial sentence of any form (see the list at the beginning of this chapt
for a description of types of custodial sentence) in all courts for men ar
women of all ages. Figure 9.3 shows a huge growth in recorded crime ov
the 46-year period but a far less dramatic rise in the use of custody, whic
provides a small proportion of all those sentenced over the same period, a
can be seen in Figure 9.4.

Murray argues that the reduced risk of imprisonment was part of a delibe
ate policy to switch away from a reliance on custody and towards diversio
This approach is illustrated by the policies as regards younger offenders. 'F
more than three decades, English criminal justice policy has taken successi
steps to make the criminal justice system less punitive towards youngster
The motives were noble, but the effect has been that young offenders can b
confident that not much is going to happen to them for any offence short
a major felony' (Murray 1997: 25). In Chapter 5, Figures 5.4 and 5.5 co
firm the trend away from the use of custody for younger offenders in th
1980s.

Murray also argues that something can be done about crime and tha
'the public is not upset about the crime problem only because the crime ra

as gone up. Much of the public's anger and anxiety arises from two other aspects of the crime problem: a breakdown in lawfulness and a breakdown in public civility' (Murray 1997: 23).

Prison is one part of a strategy to reduce crime and restore public confidence, built on a deterrence and just deserts approach. He believes that public confidence is likely to be undermined in a system of criminal justice if lawlessness is tolerated such that crime is ignored or criminals go unpunished. 'To help restore public confidence Murray argues that we need to discard most of the system's sympathy for the offender' (Murray 1997: 26). The criminal justice system is not primarily designed to engage in social work solutions. It is first and foremost designed around the principles of retribution to establish the culpability of the accused for the offence. In an adversarial system this puts the offender into the limelight. But after conviction there is no logical reason why offender-instrumental considerations should have priority over the interests of either the victim or the community.

In addition to the deterrence and retributive functions of imprisonment, Murray identifies the denunciatory functions of sentencing. He says:

> The court . . . is a stage in the never-ending morality play. It is a public forum in which the peaceful members of the community assert their superiority over the outlaws. It dispenses just deserts.
>
> (Murray 1997: 24)

The combination of denunciation and deterrence is also found in the Government's white paper about tackling youth crime, *No More Excuses* (Home Office 1997a). 'Punishment is necessary to signal society's disapproval when any person – including a young person – breaks the law and as a deterrent' (Home Office 1997a: 18). In the final section of this chapter we will be looking in more detail at a penal paradigm which, by the end of the twentieth century, has moved away from an almost exclusive focus on offender-instrumental theories of sentencing to an approach that incorporates a concern about public confidence and the impact on law-abiding citizens as well as the potential law breakers.

SENTENCING FOR WHOM?

We have seen above how penal policy has changed, and how new policies and the philosophies underpinning them are based on criticisms of the policies they replace. Shifts in the penal paradigm usually represent a change in the balance between the claims of many different theories and considerations. One of the questions that underlines the different theories of punishment is whether it is possible for sentencing decisions to reconcile the different needs of the offender, victim and community. We could also question who sentencing is for – the offender? the victim? or the wider community?

The dilemmas of sentencing policy are often popularly encapsulated seeking a balance between the offender and the offence. Thus should t punishment fit the crime or should punishment fit the offender? Many di cussions of sentencing policy focus on the individual offender or on t individual offence as is evident in the just deserts approach. But denounce and those who stress public protection would argue that this focus neglec the wider role of sentencing policy in expressing the public's disapproval crime and recognising their need for protection. Others see the victim as forgotten player in the drama of crime and punishment (see Chapter 11).

It is not surprising that a criminal justice system based on adversari principles should produce a sentencing policy that is geared towards t individual offence, offender and the circumstances of the case. The crimin justice system is after all primarily concerned with implementing the rul which determine criminal liability and it deals with individual cases ar individual offenders. Thus as Judge Rhys Davies comments, 'Judges . . . mu look at the person before them, and all the circumstances, and do what th know to be right conscientiously. That's their duty' (*The Times*, 28 June 199 11). To sentencers therefore what is fair in the individual case is likely take priority over abstract principles of justice. This is compounded by t case law tradition of English law in which, as we have seen, there are r penal codes stating general principles but a tendency to judge each case c its merits.

The individualisation of sentencing has also of course been justified by t offender instrumental approach which argues that sentences should aim prevent further criminality. Also in the adversarial system, defendants ha the opportunity as required by due process to present factors in mitigatio All of this encourages a focus on the circumstances of the convicted crimina

This individualisation, however, neglects a key person in many offences the victim. While there is a focus on the harm done, the victim would appe to be little involved in sentencing other than as the potential recipient a compensation order. As we have seen some argue that there should be victim impact statement and others have gone so far as to argue that victim opinions be sought. This might seem fair in some respects but is ofte rejected also on the grounds of fairness and justice. It is, for example, r garded as a key part of criminal law that punishment is undertaken by t state on behalf of the general public (see, for example, Ashworth 1997b An offence, unlike a civil dispute, is not a private matter, it is a public on Therefore, the victim should have no role in sentencing, other than whe compensation or reparation is considered. In addition, such victim involv ment might further compound disparities when different sentences are give to similar offenders on the basis of victim participation. This would add y further individualised circumstances, this time based on the opinion of t victim, and could produce highly unpredictable sentencing decisions, furth undermining any notion of fairness.

In terms of considering fairness, therefore, current discussions focus on fairness to individual offenders and fairness in terms of the sentence being proportionate to the crime. In recent years the balance has shifted with more weight being given to the seriousness of the offence and less to the needs and risks of individual offenders. However, the justice approach does restrict the severity of sentencing and encourage consistency, thus increasing justice to offenders. A major advantage of including in the aims of sentencing the retributivist concern with just desert is that it sets, in principle, limits on that system as to who, how and when it can act against an individual and thus provides the justification for civil rights within the criminal justice system.

But, as we have seen, fairness to individual offenders is not easy to achieve. How much, for example, should their individual circumstances be a factor in sentencing? And how might this lead to other kinds of inequities in sentencing? This can be seen when, as in Chapter 8, we look at the sentences given to those from different socio-economic backgrounds. Thus offenders' domestic, financial, and social circumstances may mean that they are judged favourably or adversely by the court. They may affect how they can present themselves, whether or not they can pay a fine, and the kind of mitigating factors they may put forward. In addition, sentences may have an unequal impact on these different groups.

Some of the above points indicate that sentencing policy cannot hope to include what some would see as the root causes of crime if these lie in social inequalities and the individual circumstances. This brings us back to the limitations of current offender-instrumental approaches to make much of an impact on the volume of crime. To what extent therefore, can the public be protected or reassured through sentencing policy?

In answer to this it could be argued that tougher policing and tougher sentencing policies are only likely to have a marginal effect on crime prevention. This is because as we have seen only a minority of cases reach the courts in comparison with the totality of crime. Less than 100,000 cases reached the Crown Court annually in recent years, and the number is falling, whereas the British Crime Survey suggests that 19 million crimes are committed each year. Even if the police force caught twice as many criminals, the courts could only be dealing with less than 1 per cent of those responsible for criminal acts. Currently, the Home Office figures on attrition suggest that only 2 per cent of known crimes result in a conviction (see Figure 3.3) and of these the overwhelming majority are offences that do not result in a prison sentence. Thus the offender instrumental approach can at best have only a marginal impact on the amount of crime that the community is subject to. Furthermore, as we have seen, the promise of rehabilitation that crime could be cured and the arguments of deterrent theorists that it could be prevented have not been fulfilled.

Thus the criminal justice process appears to have an intrinsically limited role to play in reducing or preventing crime. What implication does this have for sentencing policy particularly in respect of its credibility with the public The furore caused by unpopular sentencing decisions and the unit fine introduced by the CJA 1991 illustrates however that the public do perceive sentencing policy as important. To the denunciation model, as we have seen punishment is not only a matter for offenders and victims but also involve the community's expectations about standards of behaviour and appropriate punishment. The criminal endangers their civil liberties by threatening their property, physical well-being and shared values.

The CJA 1991 also recognised the denunciatory role of punishment Thus the 1990 white paper stated that, 'Punishment can effectively denounce criminal behaviour and exact retribution for it. The sentence of the court expresses public repugnance of criminal behaviour and determines the punish-ment for it' (Home Office 1990a: 5). The CJA 1991 therefore could be seen as advocating what has been described as a denunciatory-retributivist per-spective which by focusing on the morality of the act looks at the consequence of punishment for society as a whole rather than on the convicted criminal (Davies 1993).

Sentencing, after all, is a judgment about an appropriate sentence for wrong done and is in effect morality in action. The judge condemns the offender in the name of the community and so re-enforces standards of morality. Thus a denunciatory-retributivist approach to sentencing recognises the moral censuring role of sentencing; and that in a democracy the tariff of sentencing should reflect and articulate the moral concerns of the commun-ity as well as ensuring fairness to the individual offender before the courts.

Denunciation could add a more positive dimension to a sentencing policy which in many ways has accepted the rather gloomy prognostication that 'nothing works'. One strength of rehabilitative and deterrent arguments was that they appeared to do something positive, they focused on the future rather than on the past. Just deserts focuses on the harm done in the past and therefore could be seen as negative – punishment, however fair, for its own sake. Denunciation on the other hand stresses the key role of punishment in focusing public attention onto issues of morality and right and wrong. This in turn draws attention to the social function of punishment. Thus David Garland (1990) comments:

> In designing penal policy we are not simply deciding how to deal with a group of people on the margins of society – whether to deter, reform, or incapacitate them and if so how. Nor are we simply deploying power or economic resources for penological ends. We are also and at the same time defining ourselves and our society in ways which may be quite central to our cultural and political identity. An important part of a society's penal rhetoric is taken up with the suggestion of a social vision.

Thus the importance of punishment for community and society should be recognised. The values embodied in the criminal law demonstrate a society's moral views of right and wrong and those who breach the laws are doing more than just the physical and financial damage they do to the individual victim, they are challenging the values of society, and threaten the individual's definition of normality. Therefore, the purpose of punishment for the denouncer is not directed at the criminal act or the criminal actor, but at the values which define the rules embodied in the criminal law. The audience neither the criminal nor victim but the public at large.

Thus the link between punishment and the public involves more than protecting individual citizens from individual criminals, though it is one essential role of the criminal justice system. Thus crime does more than threaten the individual, it is a threat to the community itself. 'The real significance of crime', wrote Joseph Conrad, 'is in its being a breach of faith with the community of mankind.'

CONCLUSION

This chapter has looked at how sentencing policy must be placed within the context of changing views about the causes of crime and the role of the penal system, especially prison. Thus the rehabilitative model was based on the idea that the problems which caused crime could be established and therefore alleviated. A sentence of imprisonment could be likened to a period of hospital treatment, an approach which had great appeal to reformers who also saw it as more humane. After decades of influence however the key ideas of rehabilitation were discredited. Rehabilitative policies were criticised as inhumane and inefficient. To some indeed they represented another way in which the powerful in society could enforce their values on others. Where, for example, did rehabilitation stop and enforced conformity, 'thought reform' or brainwashing begin? Did offenders who were effectively sentenced to be helped not have rights? Were these sentences fair?

The justice model aimed to provide an answer to the many problems of rehabilitation and other offender-instrumental policies. Punishment should not aim to do good, but to do as little harm as possible. Harsher sentences on the grounds of rehabilitation or deterrence could be limited by an approach which stressed linking the sentence to the harm done by culpable offenders. Yet, as we have seen, the application of the justice model raises questions about what is meant by justice and fairness in relation to sentencing.

A key feature of sentencing policy has also been an acceptance of the prison reductionist's aim, whether for idealistic or practical reasons, to reduce the use of imprisonment. This involved stressing the punitive nature of community sentences so as to make them credible to the police and sentencers. Whether or not this will be successful either in terms of reducing the use of imprisonment or making community penalties acceptable as a punishment, remains to be seen.

Changes in penal policy reflect the efforts of policy makers to find a balance between the various aims of sentencing as well as the aims of the

criminal justice process as a whole. There is a constant tension between th
need for due process, which extends beyond conviction to the sentencin;
process and the penal system, and the often conflicting claims of publi
protection. While the CJA 1991 defined the primary aim of sentencing as jus
deserts it also, with the twin track approach, allows for incapacitation throug
larger sentences for some violent and sexual offences. Incapacitation may con
flict with the interests of due process, particularly where an assessment need
to be made of the circumstances in which a particular offender is assesse
as dangerous enough that a sentence out of proportion to just deserts i
justified.

The declining role of rehabilitation and offender-instrumental strategie
may require a re-evaluation of existing sentencing practices and penal sanc
tions. How, for example, might this affect prisons? How will the new em
phasis on punishment in the community affect the operation of communit
sentences previously seen as rehabilitative and offender focused? And how
far is the community served by the criminal justice process and sentencin;
policy? Some of these issues will be taken up in the next two chapters
Chapter 10 will look at prisons and Chapter 11 will explore developments in
crime prevention.

Review questions

1. Explain why the principles of individualisation and indeterminacy fol
   lowed from a rehabilitative approach to sentencing.

2. What is meant by the term 'disparity'? Explain how it is affected by
   individualistic strategies of sentencing.

3. What are the main elements of a justice approach to sentencing?

4. Explain the difference between a rationale for community penalties tha
   aims to achieve an 'alternative to custody' and a rationale that seeks an
   intermediate sanction.

5. What information would you need to be able to assess the question o.
   whether prison works from a sentencing point of view? Consider the question, firstly, from the point of view of the likely impact of imprisonmen
   on those offenders given a custodial sentence and, secondly, from the
   perspective of the general public.

Further reading

Cavadino P and Dignan J (1997) *The Penal System: An Introduction*, 2nd edn.
London: Sage

Davies M (1993) *Punishing Criminals: Developing Community-based Intermediate Sanctions*. Connecticut: Greenwood

Duff A and Garland D (1994) *A Reader on Punishment*. Oxford: Oxford University Press

on Hirsch A and Ashworth A (eds) (1993) *Principled Sentencing*. Edinburgh: Edinburgh University Press

CHAPTER 10
PRISONS

- Origins of the Penitentiary
- Prisons in England and Wales in the 1990s
- Prison Population
- Impact of Imprisonment on Inmates
- Aims and Performance of the Prison Service
- Prison Disturbances and Escapes in the 1990s

INTRODUCTION

In October 1993 in a speech to the Conservative Party Conference, the Home Secretary, Michael Howard, stated that:

> Let us be clear. Prison works. It ensures that we are protected from murderers, muggers and rapists – and it makes many who are tempted to commit crime think twice.

The considerable public debate which followed demonstrated conflicting views about the role, aims and functions of prison along with continuing concerns about aspects of prison regimes, conditions and security. In general terms prisons have credibility with the public as an institution for punishment – the punishment being loss of liberty. This serves a retributive and denunciatory purpose. Prisons are also seen as a potential deterrent for the general public and they incapacitate dangerous and persistent offenders for the period of time they are incarcerated. Whether prisons can rehabilitate inmates or deter them from committing further offences is far less obvious in the light of statistics on recidivism. Indeed some argue that it may increase the likelihood that offenders will continue their life of crime – not only have prisons been characterised as schools of crime but they remove offenders from the stabilising effect of their families and the likelihood of obtaining gainful employment. Yet others feel that the prison experience is insufficiently punitive.

On the other hand, it has often been argued that prison *is* the punishment, and is not *for* punishment. Poor conditions within prisons have been blamed for riots, violence within prisons and for inhibiting prospects for ehabilitation. To those who run prisons, the day-to-day problems of security ensuring that prisoners do not abscond) and control (attempting to prevent iots and violence) may well take precedence over more abstract goals of ehabilitation or deterrence.

This chapter will explore many of these issues. It starts by examining the origin of the penitentiary, and how the use and aims of prison have developed over the last century. We will outline the current organisation of the prison system in England and Wales, and we will look at the numbers and characteristics of the prison population. We will examine the experience of imprisonment, the aims of prisons, and explore the issues involved in assessing whether or not prison can be said to work (see Chapter 9). Finally, we will consider reports written during the 1990s about major incidents that led to official inquiries into the way the Prison Service operated.

ORIGINS OF THE PENITENTIARY

The prison as we know it today is a relatively recent social experiment which began 200 years ago. Before that time people were not usually given a sentence of imprisonment. The prisons, dungeons and gaols were owned by a variety of municipal and private bodies, and were used to hold debtors or people who had been arrested and were awaiting trial at the quarter sessions (quarterly sittings of the court). They also held those awaiting the implementation of a sentence. For serious offenders, transportation or execution was the main punishment. For lesser offenders, prison was used to encourage a person to pay a fine and short periods of confinement were prescribed for offenders too poor to pay a fine.

John Howard, in his survey of prisons in the 1770s, estimated a prison population of 4,084. His census of 1776 calculated that the prison population was made up of debtors (59.7 per cent), felons awaiting trial, execution and transportation, along with a few serving a prison sentence (24.3 per cent), and petty offenders (15.9 per cent). Howard was appointed to the post of High Sheriff for Bedfordshire in 1773. One of his duties, usually neglected by other sheriffs, was to report on the prisons in his county. The conditions he encountered so shocked him that he undertook a more widespread review of prison conditions that was printed in 1777, entitled *The State of the Prisons*.

Punishment in the eighteenth century for those convicted of misdemeanours consisted of the stocks, corporal punishment or fines. For serious offenders the sanction was the death penalty, or a substitute. During the eighteenth century, the number of capital offences rose from 50 to 225, and the death penalty became the prescribed punishment for most offences classified as felonies. Juries, however, were often reluctant to convict a person knowing that the person would be executed. 'Pious perjury' according to William Blackstone, became more popular after 1750. By re-evaluating the value of goods stolen to less than a shilling, juries convicted offenders for

Fig 10.1 Distribution of punishments, Old Bailey 1760–94

Year	Per cent death sentence	Per cent transported/hulks	Per cent whip/brand/fine	Per cent imprisoned
1760–64	12.7	74.1	12.3	1.2
1765–69	15.8	70.2	13.4	0.8
1770–74	17.0	66.5	14.2	2.3
1775–79	20.7	33.4	17.6	28.6
1780–84	25.8	24.1	15.5	34.6
1785–89	18.5	50.1	13.2	13.3
1790–94	15.9	43.9	11.7	28.3

Source: Ignatieff M (1975: 81).

petty larceny rather than the capital offence of grand larceny. Despite the growth in the number of capital offences, the number of executions declined over the century and transportation became the typical sentence by the end of the eighteenth century. As Figure 10.1 shows, in the five years from 1765 to 1769, 70 per cent of criminals sentenced at the Old Bailey were transported.

The Transportation Act 1717, providing for transportation to the American colonies as a punishment, was introduced with the purpose of deterring criminals and supplying the colonies with much needed labour. It became common practice to commute a death penalty to transportation. Although transportation did not stop immediately with the American Revolution of 1776, prisoners began to be housed in hulks which were permanently moored ships. A House of Commons Committee review of transportation in 1779 recommended the continued use of hulks and that two new penitentiaries be built. The idea of the penitentiary was therefore seen at this time as a way forward, even though alternative locations were also being examined to permit the continuation of transportation.

Transportation came under scrutiny because some felt it was not a sufficient deterrent. Indeed, despite the health hazards of the journey it was said that some committed crime in order to be transported. A Transportation Act was passed in 1784 at a time when there was nowhere to send convicts although the Beauchamp Committee of 1785 reported favourably on the practice and cited its potential for reform, its cheapness and the advantages to the colonies of a convict workforce. Alternatives considered included Algiers, Tristan de Cunha and sending convicts down the coal mines, but Australia was preferred.

Transportation to Australia reached its peak in the 1830s and 1840s with between 4,000 and 5,000 convicts being sent each year. There were also periods in the early nineteenth century when 70 per cent of convicted felons were imprisoned in hulks. The use of hulks and transportation declined after the prison building programme of the 1840s. By 1853 the idea of penal servitude as a substitute for transportation was introduced for those sentenced o under 14 years. In 1857 the last prison hulk went out of service and transportation formally ended in 1867.

Ideological and practical considerations changed the conditions within, and the function of, prison. Among the new penal ideas that emerged at the end of the eighteenth century the penitentiary style of prison was advocated as a place that could change criminals' behaviour by making them penitent. Places of detention were to be transformed from gaols for holding criminals into penitentiaries for transforming them into law-abiding citizens. This new ideo-ogy was influenced by a combination of ideas about religious salvation, humanitarian concern with the conditions of prisons and control concerns about the growing urban population. The penal ideology of the era was also shaped by the theories of rehabilitation which we discussed in Chapter 9. These involved isolating the offender from the bad influences of the com-munity in 'total institutions' (Goffman 1961) which cut off the inmate from the environmental sources that were considered by some to be the cause of crime (Rothman 1980). This penal ideology also focused on the importance of surveillance and styles of discipline which could transform prisoners into self-disciplined workers (Bentham 1791; Foucault 1977).

These new ideas were prevalent across the emerging industrial societies of Europe and the USA. They were embodied in reforms influenced by Quaker thinkers in Pennsylvania and prison reformers such as John Howard and Elizabeth Fry in England (Rothman 1980). They also represented a shift in views about how to control problem groups in the community (Scull 1977). By the end of the eighteenth century not only prisoners, but orphans, men-tally ill, sick and unemployed were being assigned to new style institutions such as prisons, orphanages, asylums, hospitals and workhouses. The grand Georgian and late Victorian style of institutions were invented at this time as the solution to deal with 'problem' categories of the population.

The Penitentiary Act 1779 provided the first indication of the new role for prisons as institutions to reform and deter criminals. The influence of John Howard, Sir William Blackstone and William Eden was apparent in the new direction to penal policy. This positive role for prisons was re-echoed in the report of the May Committee on prisons as late as 1979, and in the state-ments of the Chief Inspector of Prisons in the 1990s, Judge Stephen Tumin. Many ideas on prisons and their roles were utopian – such as Jeremy Bentham's panopticon, a model discussed below (see Figure 10.2). However, these ideas offered a way forward for a penal system which faced three main practical problems.

First, the concern about growing numbers of migrants coming to the cities in search of work. The old style welfare system, based on parish relief, was no longer viable as the new factory system needed a more mobile labour force. It was no use having large pools of unemployed workers in isolated rural areas away from the new sources of work. Hence, the problem of how to care and control those who were moving to rapidly expanding urban areas. This encouraged the search for innovative solutions and the invention of new

Fig 10.2 The Panopticon

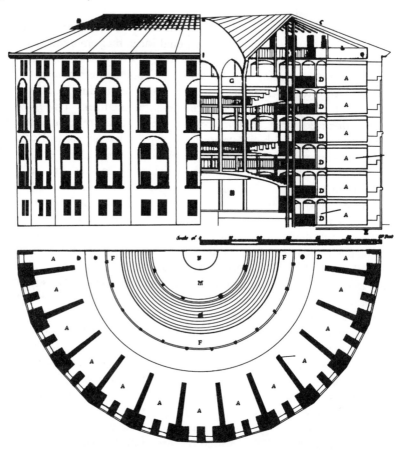

Source: Bowering (1843) *The Works of Jeremy Bentham*, Volume IV, 172–3 cf: 201.
Reproduced by permission of The British Library.

institutions to cope with those deemed to be either a threat or inadequate – thus the workhouse, asylum and orphanage as well as the penitentiary.

Secondly, there was the practical problem after 1776 that transportation to the colony of Virginia was no longer available as a result of the American Revolution. Thirdly, there was growing disquiet among reformers and thinkers such as Blackstone, Romilly and Beccaria about the large numbers of capital offences. The ideas of Cesare Beccaria about the use of the death penalty influenced debates in the House of Commons. He attacked the widespread use of capital punishment arguing that the death penalty brutalised rather than deterred the population. His views were espoused by William Eden in the reform debates in Britain. Eden's book, *Principles of Penal Law*, was published in 1771. Sir Samuel Romilly took the lead in the parliamentary campaign to reduce the number of capital offences. He realised that to relinquish one mode of punishment the public and Parliament would need to be reassured that a satisfactory alternative was available. Thus some promoters of the penitentiary argued that it was a more humane alternative to the death penalty, not that it was more efficient, as Bentham and Howard were to argue.

It took 50 years for prisons to become the main mode of punishment used by the criminal courts in Britain. The views of Howard and Bentham influenced prison policy for the next two centuries. Prison became not merely a substitute for the death penalty and transportation but a positive institution in which regimes, if sufficiently constructive, could rehabilitate those sent to them. Regimes were also to be sufficiently austere to deter future lawbreakers. The principle of 'less eligibility' implied that prison conditions were not to be more favourable than those found in the homes of the honest poor lest it encouraged crime.

The most celebrated of the novel ideas for bringing about constructive rehabilitation of convicts was the panopticon design proposed by Jeremy Bentham. The panopticon style prison involved a central viewing tower with rings of cells on each floor facing inwards to be visible to the observation tower. Observation and inspection were the keys to Bentham's approach to a more humane and effective mode of punishment. The panopticon would permit surveillance to allow prison officials to make assessments of prisoner's rehabilitation by constantly monitoring their behaviour.

The coliseum style and circular design of the panopticon was to prove difficult to build and was also inefficient. Pentonville was opened in 1842, and became the model for most Victorian prisons. It had stacked galleries on landings along a central straight corridor. Each corridor met at a central location in a fan-shaped floor plan with a central control and observation point permitting uninterrupted observation of each wing.

This systematic approach to prison design and administration reflected a growing interest in penal reform, which was wider than that of mere philanthropy. As the nineteenth century progressed a growing number of professional experts such as architects and doctors began to take an interest in penal affairs. The intervention of central government into penal policy meant that resources were made available to those who appeared to offer a solution to the problems of crime. Government involvement had been spurred by the problems of where to ship those sentenced to transportation. Having resorted to housing increasing numbers of prisoners in the hulks, it was then necessary for the government to find them work such as river dredging.

For the next 200 years, the Government became increasingly concerned in the administration of prisons. The second half of the nineteenth century saw the gradual transfer of responsibility for monitoring conditions and the administration of prisons to central government. This process began with the Gaol Act 1823, in which Peel's administration set out the first comprehensive statement of principles about the running of local prisons. The Act imposed health requirements; required inspection by visiting justices; banned the consumption of alcohol and demanded the classification of inmates and the segregation of different categories. There were to be five classes of inmates with male separated from female prisoners and an annual report on the prison had to be submitted to the Home Secretary.

In 1877 all prisons were nationalised in a Prison Act which brought all prisons under central government control. The Government established the Prison Commission to run prisons and the first of a number of influential chairmen of the commissioners was appointed, Sir Edmund Du Cane. Some commissioners led the debate on penal reform and were strong advocates of a modern penology based on better prison conditions and strategies to achieve the rehabilitation of inmates. They represented the age of optimism, documented in Chapter 9, about the positive aspects of penal institutions as places of reform. This commitment to the belief that through positive regimes inmates could be encouraged to lead good and useful lives was given official recognition in the Gladstone Committee of 1895 and became one of the leading principles of the prison service when incorporated into the Prison Rules in 1949. This states that the purpose of imprisonment was 'to encourage and assist the inmate to lead a good and useful life'.

During the 1930s the treadmill and arrows on convict uniforms were abolished. During this period also experiments with open prisons for adults were started at Wakefield Prison in 1936, when selected inmates from the prison slept in non-secure accommodation at New Hall Camp. In 1963 the Prison Commission was abolished and prisons were run by the prison service, a branch of the Home Office. The aim was to allow penal policy to be more fully integrated into a more general approach to crime control. This changed in 1993 as we will see in the following section.

PRISONS IN ENGLAND AND WALES IN THE 1990s

The prison service has the responsibility of operating the prison system in England and Wales, including the prisons operated by private companies. The Prison Act 1877 had created a state monopoly and brought under the control of the Prison Commissioners all those prisons that had previously been in local and private control. On 1 April 1993 the prison service became an executive agency of the Home Office. Agency status gives some degree of independence from Home Office control of daily operations and responsibility for budget and expenditure. The first director of the prison service under these new arrangements was Derek Lewis, who was dismissed in October 1995 and succeeded by Richard Tilt.

In 1998 there were 133 prison service establishments in England and Wales, including the privately run, contracted out prisons of Blakenhurst, Buckley Hall, Doncaster and the Wolds. The range of prisons reflects the variety of tasks they are used for. Some need to be near criminal courts in urban areas to house those remanded in custody while awaiting trial or sentence. Others deal with specialist populations such as young offenders or females. Others hold inmates for relatively short periods while others need to offer a regime for those prisoners who might spend the rest of their life inside a prison. Some can pay less attention to security because they house prisoners who have shown they can be trusted, while others must contain inmates convicted of serious violent offences who would be a danger to the public if they were to escape, and remain a danger to those inside prison while they are there. The Prison Service classifies prisons as local, training and dispersal prisons, young offender institutions, remand centres and women's prisons. Closed prisons have most security and surveillance to prevent escapes, whereas open prisons have more relaxed security. Open prisons include Ford near Worthing and Leyhill near Bristol. They have little, if any, perimeter security and house Category D prisoners posing a minimal risk to the public. Ford is renowned for the celebrities and white collar criminals who have spent time there and include George Best who served 3 months for a drink-driving offence, Lord Brockett the insurance fraudster and the Guinness trio of Gerald Ronson, Ernest Saunders and Anthony Parnes.

Local prisons are used to hold those remanded in custody awaiting trial or sentence. After conviction and sentence to a period of incarceration the observation, classification and allocation unit in the local prison carries out an initial assessment and classification. This determines which prison the prisoner will be sent to, depending on security categorisation, the length of sentence and the training, medical and other needs of the inmate.

Those sentenced to a short period in prison will probably stay in the local prison. This is usually near to where they live and so helps facilitate family visits. The local prisons tend to be the older prisons built in the Victorian era and found in urban built-up areas. A new local prison, Belmarsh in East London, was opened in 1991, but this is unusual as most expenditure on prison building went on new training prisons. These are convenient for proximity to the courts and to the prisoners' families but are often the most overcrowded with the oldest facilities. All 37 local prisons are closed establishments.

Remand wings and centres are used in addition to local prisons for holding remand prisoners. In 1998 there were 31 remand centres or local prisons with adult remand wings for males. Remand centres were created specifically for young offenders in response to growing concerns about mixing young remand prisoners with adults and, in particular, about the level of suicides and self-inflicted harm amongst remand prisoners under 21.

Dispersal prisons have regimes designed to ensure no escapes as they hold prisoners with the maximum security classification. All sentenced prisoners on arrival in a prison are given a security rating. This ranges from Category A for those whose escape would constitute a serious risk to the public, to Category D for those who can be sent to open prisons.

The escape of the Soviet spy, George Blake, from Wormwood Scrubs prison in 1965 led to an inquiry by the Mountbatten Committee (Home Office 1966). Their report in December 1965 recommended that all high-risk inmates

317

be held in one maximum security prison. This recommendation was not approved and, after a further proposal from a committee chaired by Leon Radzinowicz which reported in 1968 (Home Office 1968) it was decided that high security prisoners should be dispersed among a number of prisons with maximum security facilities; hence the term 'dispersal prisons' of which there were six in 1998 holding 3,250 prisoners. Three of these have special security units for those Category A inmates most likely to try to escape.

The need for security classifications was another of the recommendations of the Mountbatten Report. Initial classification is based on the crime committed and the reports made by the assessment unit in the local prison. These categories are reassessed at regular intervals and most inmates are reclassified downwards during their prison term. Category A is for prisoners whose escape from custody would be highly dangerous to the public or to the security of the state. In 1995 there were 750 Category A prisoners (Learmont 1995: 129). Category B is used to classify inmates who do not constitute such a serious risk. Category C is applied to prisoners who cannot be trusted in open prisons but are deemed unlikely to make an effort to escape, and category D is for prisoners who can be trusted to serve their time in open prisons where the security aspect of the regime is minimal.

Training prisons hold long-term inmates. There are 71 training prisons and they can be open or closed. They provide training facilities, vocational courses and the opportunity to work in the prison industries. At Coldingley Prison, a closed prison, inmates can work making motorway signs or in the large industrial laundry that has a contract with hospitals in the region. Grendon Underwood, opened in 1963, offers a specialist regime based on the therapeutic community concept pioneered by Maxwell Henderson in psychiatric hospitals.

Young offender institutions hold offenders aged between 15 and 21 years of age. There are 29 young offender institutions. Places for incarcerating younger offenders have changed over the years since the Victorian era when the first efforts to separate younger inmates from adults were made with the introduction of reformatories and industrial schools. Borstals were introduced in 1901 and made fully available after the Prevention of Crime Act 1908. Detention centres were introduced in the Criminal Justice Act 1948. In Chapter 5 we described the changes since 1982 to the name of institutions holding younger offenders. The names may have changed more rapidly than the nature of the regimes that the changes were supposed to signify.

In April 1998 Medway Secure Training Centre was opened near Rochester, Kent. It is the first of a new type of custodial institution for 12 to 14 year olds who have committed serious offences. The offenders, called trainees, spend between 3 months to a year in a regime designed to rehabilitate and punish. Trainees are required to attend educational course and programmes to address offending behaviour. It is run by a private firm, Rebound ECD, which is owned by Group 4. This type of secure accomodation for younger offenders is not a prison service insitution and will come under the Youth Justice Board established by the Crime and Disorder Act 1998.

Female establishments in 1996/7 held an average total population of 2,365. There are 15 female institutions; most of which are small, holding less than 100 inmates, except for the local prison at Eastwood Park, the open prisons of Askham Grange and Drake Hall, the closed training prisons at Brockhill and Cookham Wood and the largest, Holloway in London, with an average of 576 inmates (*Prison Service Annual Report and Accounts 1996/7*: 63).

Special hospitals are used for offenders who need treatment for mental disorders under conditions of special security because of their violent or criminal behaviour. These offenders can be sent to one of three special hospitals: Broadmoor, Rampton or Ashworth. These have maximum security facilities similar to a dispersal prison. Special hospitals are run by the Department of Health. All the other types of prisons mentioned above are the responsibility of the prison service.

The prison service is not now the only agency allowed to run prisons. The Criminal Justice Act 1988 allowed for private companies to take over the operation of remand prisons, a sector of the prison establishment where the worst conditions were usually found. Since then companies such as Group 4 have been involved in operating prisons. The prison service has overall responsibility for the 'contracted out' prisons run by the private sector. All contracted out prisons have a prison service controller of governor grade to monitor the delivery of the contract with the prison service, and to undertake adjudications for prisoners charged with offences against disciplinary rules.

First to open was The Wolds private remand centre near Hull. Others include Blakenhurst near Redditch, and Doncaster which opened in June 1994. The Government's aim to break down the prison service monopoly in this area was not only influenced by their ideological belief in the virtues of competition. Two other factors played their part. First, a desire to inject new ideas into the running of remand prison regimes and, secondly, after a series of industrial disputes, a determination to undermine the powerful trade union, the Prison Officers' Association, that represents prison officers.

The influence of the Prison Officers' Association has been apparent in a number of industrial disputes over the years. The Labour Government of James Callaghan established an inquiry to look into questions associated with the administration of prisons and in particular resources and staff relations with management. The resulting Home Office report was published in 1979 (*The Report of the Committee of Inquiry into the UK Prison Service*, Cmnd 7673). It was chaired by Mr Justice May and its report was known as the May Report (Home Office 1979). More than one Home Secretary would have agreed with Merlyn Rees, Home Secretary between 1976 and 1979, when he said, 'As Home Secretary I did not control the prison service' (University of London Conference, 26 April 1980).

The May Committee was set up after a long period of deteriorating industrial relations in prisons in England and Wales. It examined the prison population, objectives and regimes, the organisation of the system, resources, the roles of prison officers and governors, pay and allowances, industrial relations and working conditions. It concluded that, 'Central administration ought to have shown itself more responsive to growing feelings of dissatisfaction with the organization and management and service as a whole, especially in the field of personnel management.' With reference to the importance of having clear and agreed aims for prisons – discussed later in this chapter – it commented:

> A great deal of the evidence we received maintained that at the present time these objectives (of imprisonment) were unclear or confused or both, and that this had brought about or contributed not only to a lack of incisive and purposeful leadership but also to indecision, frustration and the consequent lowering of morale throughout the prison service . . .

> (Home Office 1979: 1961)

The May Report found that over a quarter of junior prison officers were working more than 60 hours overtime a week, boosting a modest basic salary into reasonably high average earnings. In response to these staffing costs, a new higher basic wage for a 39-hour working week was introduced for prison officers in exchange for abandoning some of the expensive shift work practices.

Fresh Start, as the initiative was called, was introduced in 1987 in an attempt to overcome these staffing costs. The Prison Officers' Association agreed to the scheme because of the rise in basic pay, pension benefits, and officers were allowed to, and given financial inducements to, buy their own living quarters. This created a longer-term problem for the prison service as it reduced geographical mobility due to the lack of affordable accommodation in some regions.

Industrial disputes were not overcome by the Fresh Start programme and the Government sought other ways of curtailing the influence of the Prison Officers' Association. The introduction of 'contracting out' of prison service work to private companies should be seen in this context. The CJPOA 1994 curtailed the right of prison officers and governor grade staff to go on strike.

In 1993/4 the average cost of imprisonment was calculated at £22,006 per inmate per year. However, this does not mean that sending one less person to prison would save this amount as most of these costs are relatively fixed. Three-quarters of prison service expenditure is attributable to staffing costs. In 1995 the prison service employed 38,800 people, of which 24,000 were uniformed officers. This represents a ratio of just over two inmates per officer and compares with a ratio of three to one in 1980. This is a very generous ratio of officers to prisoners compared with prison services around the world. In 1994, there were 1,020 governor grade posts.

The prison service is open to inspection by the *Inspectorate of Prisons*, established by statute in 1982 after a recommendation in the 1979 May Report. The Chief Inspector in 1998 was Sir David Rambotham. Members of the inspectorate can make unannounced visits as well as having a number of scheduled visits to certain prisons each year. After a visit a report is made highlighting the strengths and weaknesses of the establishments visited. Some reports have been very damning about conditions in prison establishments and the treatment of prisoners.

Each prison has a *Board of Visitors*, who oversee the administration of the prison, made up of lay members of the local community, usually JPs, doctors and other local people. Until 1992 the Board of Visitors adjudicated on matters of discipline where an inmate might be liable to lose remission for disciplinary offences. As a result of the CJA 1991 prison governors have the right to order up to 14 'added days' for disciplinary offences. The Board of Visitors at Wandsworth prison in the 1980s were among the first to publish a public report, describing the insanitary conditions associated with slopping out and the health hazards of a cockroach infestation near the kitchen area.

In April 1994, the Board of Visitors at Whitemoor prison in March, Cambridgeshire, published a report about the conditions and regime in the prison, which held 514 inmates, 20 per cent of whom were classified as Category A. These included Dennis Nilsen and IRA terrorists. Another 20 per cent were life sentence prisoners. It was in this prison that Leslie Bailey, a paedophile convicted of serious sexual offences against children, was found strangled in his cell in October 1993. The report describes the prison as dirty and the Board of Visitors condemned the illegal brewing of 'hooch' by inmates. The main concern expressed by the Board in their report was that management had lost control of the situation and they quote a governor who was of the opinion that the prisoners and not the staff were virtually in control of the prison – an allegation that was to be prescient in the light of the subsequent escape attempt in September 1994 by five convicted IRA prisoners who were able to obtain guns in which one prison officer was shot and wounded. All the prisoners were recaptured within hours of the escape. In the same month, quantities of the explosive Semtex were found at Whitemoor. These incidents raised many questions about why no action had been taken and led to demands for the resignation of the Home Secretary, as did the escape in January 1995 of three Category A offenders from another dispersal prison, Parkhurst, on the Isle of Wight. Two reports on these security matters, the Woodcock and Learmont reports, are discussed later in this chapter.

Information about accountability, monitoring and performance measurement in prison is to be found in Chapter 11, with further details about the Board of Visitors, the Prison Ombudsman, Prison Inspectorate and Key Performance Indicators (KPIs).

PRISON POPULATION

We saw in Chapter 9 that concerns over prison overcrowding, conditions and the size of the prison population led to policies to reduce the numbers sent to prison. At the same time a prison building programme started in 1982 designed to improve facilities and reduce cell sharing. The routine of 'slopping out' caused by the lack of toilet facilities in the cells of the Victorian prisons led to the daily morning practice in the cell blocks of prisoners forming a queue to the washrooms to dispose of the contents of their chamber pots.

Fig 10.3 Population in custody: annual averages 1988–97

Year	Under Sentence	Remand	Total
1988	38,300	11,400	**50,000**
1989	37,900	10,500	**48,600**
1990	35,500	9,900	**45,600**
1991	35,400	10,100	**45,900**
1992	35,400	10,100	**45,800**
1993	33,300	10,700	**44,600**
1994	35,800	12,400	**48,800**
1995	39,100	11,400	**51,000**
1996	43,000	11,600	**55,300**
1997	48,400	12,100	**61,100**

Compiled from White and Woodbridge (1998) 'The Prison Population in 1997', *Home Office Statistical Bulletin*, 5/98, Table 3; and *Prison Statistics England and Wales 1992*: 21.

NB. The numbers do not add up to the total as the totals include non-criminal inmates. Sentenced inmates includes those in custody because of default of a fine, compensation order or costs. The remand population includes those awaiting trial and those convicted but awaiting sentence and those held in police cells.

The prison service accepted the February 1996 deadline set by Lord Woolf for an end to slopping out. In fact most prisons completed their programme of modernisation to end this practice by 1994.

The daily population in prison varies depending on the time of year. It usually drops in December and rises to a high point in March. The average daily prison population in England and Wales in 1993 was 44,600. This was over 1,000 lower than the year before and the lowest population since 1984. The prison population peaked in 1988 at 50,000 and then fell to the 1993 level (see Figure 10.3). Since 1993, the prison population has steadily risen, almost reaching the 50,000 figure in October 1994. On 30 April 1998 the prison population had reached a high of 65,507 (*Occupation of Prisons, Remand Centres, Young Offender Institutions and Police Cells on 30 April 1998*, Directorate of Research and Statistics, Prison Service). To measure the degree of overcrowding, the prison population is compared with the Certified Normal Accommodation (CNA). In March 1998 the prison population was 108 per cent of its official capacity. Local prisons were most overcrowded with 122 inmates for every 100 places. Some institutions were undercapacity with open young offender institutions only three-quarters full.

The annual averages of the population in custody over the 10-year period 1988–97 is given in Figure 10.3.

European comparisons

It is often claimed in the press and in broadcasts that the courts in England and Wales make more use of custody than other European countries.

Fig 10.4 European prison populations

	1993*		1994*		1995*		1996†
	(a)	(b)	(a)	(b)	(a)	(b)	(a)
Austria	7,099	91	6,806	85	6,108	85	6,778
Belarus	–	–	45,814	445	52,033	505	–
Belgium	7,203	72	7,138	65	7,561	75	7,763
Bulgaria	8,364	99	8,495	95	9,289	105	–
Croatia	–	–	2,388	50	2,572	55	–
Czech Republic	16,567	165	18,753	180	19,832	190	20,949
Denmark	3,702	71	3,508	72	3,438	65	3,194
England and Wales	**45,633**	**89**	**49,393**	**96**	**51,265**	**100**	**55,537**
Estonia	–	–	4,220	270	4,034	270	–
Finland	3,132	62	3,322	59	3,018	60	3,248
France	51,134	86	53,758	90	53,178	90	54,014
Germany	65,838	81	67,626	83	66,146	80	71,047
Greece	6,524	68	5,852	71	5,897	55	5,427
Hungary	13,196	132	12,754	125	12,455	120	12,763
Ireland	2,108	60	2,053	60	2,054	60	2,139
Italy	50,794	89	52,041	90	49,642	90	48,747
Latvia	–	–	9,457	365	9,608	375	–
Lithuania	10,324	275	12,782	340	13,228	355	–
Macedonia	–	–	–	–	1,132	55	–
Moldovia	–	–	9,781	260	10,363	275	–
Netherland	7,843	51	8,737	55	10,200	65	11,931
Northern Ireland	1,902	118	1,911	117	1,740	105	1,640
Norway	2,607	60	2,677	60	2,398	55	2,558
Poland	61,895	160	62,719	165	61,136	170	57,320
Portugal	10,904	111	10,023	101	12,150	125	13,743
Romania	46,189	200	43,990	195	46,456	205	–
Russia	–	–	885,000	590	1,018,123	695	1,051,515
Scotland	5,900	115	5,594	109	5,626		5,861
Slovakia	7,221	136	7,412	140	7,899	145	–
Slovenia	–	–	1,019	50	630	25	–
Spain	45,711	115	41,169	106	40,157	105	42,105
Sweden	5,794	66	5,768	66	5,767	65	5,757
Switzerland	4,128		4,188		4,104		4,026
Turkey	31,304	52	43,432	72	49,895	90	
Ukraine	–	–	180,000	345	203,988	390	

* (a) Prison population; (b) Prisoners per 100,000 population.

† The number of prisoners per 100,000 population for 1996 is not available.

This figure was compiled from various sources: some of the data has been revised in the light of more recent estimates. The reliability of data will vary from country to country. For most countries the data is based on the numbers in prison on 1 September in the relevant year. Countries with prison populations of under 1,000 have been excluded from the figure: Cyprus, Iceland, Luxembourg and Malta. Compiled from *Prison Statistics England and Wales 1994*: 37; *Prison Statistics England and Wales 1995*: 29; *Prison Statistics England and Wales 1996*: 30; *Criminal Statistics England and Wales 1996*: 32. The original source of this information was the Council of Europe.

Sometimes it is stated that England and Wales is at, or near, the top of the European league table for the use of custody. But Figure 10.4 shows that in 1993, for instance, France, Germany, Poland, Romania and Spain held more

323

prisoners than England and Wales. Thus we were in sixth place in the European league in 1993. However, use of total numbers in prison does not take into account the relative size of the populations, such that no one would expect smaller countries such as Denmark to have the same custodial population as Germany. Therefore some comparisons look at the rates of imprisonment per 100,000 of population. With this measure we find that England and Wales at 100 per 100,000 of population in 1995, was in 17th place across Europe. Demographic comparisons might, of course, be misleading as some commentators (Pease 1994a/b) have suggested that it might be more useful to compare the numbers in prison with the amount of crime to assess comparisons between countries. The problem with comparisons based on the population is that it takes no account of the amount of crime committed, which is, after all, the main reason why people go to prison. The demographic comparative data does not take into account the differences in usage of imprisonment or the risk of imprisonment because of the age of criminal responsibility. Information comparing use of custody per 100,000 crimes recorded is used in Figure 10.7 in the review questions at the end of this chapter.

Categories of prisoner

Not all inmates held in Her Majesty's Prisons are of the same status. As we have seen in Chapter 5, some defendants are remanded in custody and held in prison. These unconvicted prisoners have rights distinguishing them from other inmates such as daily access to visitors. There are also those who have been convicted but have not yet been sentenced. In Figure 10.3 these two groups are identified as remand prisoners and constitute approximately one-fifth of the average prison population.

Fine defaulters in prison

Although there are many ways in which a fine can be enforced by the courts, as outlined in Chapter 8, the ultimate sanction for non-payment of fines or compensation orders is imprisonment, as indeed it is for non-compliance with community sentences. Fine defaulters are not, however, automatically sent to prison as Mark Romer, a Metropolitan Stipendiary Magistrate explained in a letter to the *Independent*:

> Fine defaulters are not imprisoned because they cannot pay their fines but because, often after many attempts to get them to pay, they will not. Magistrates are forbidden by law to imprison fine defaulters unless either they refuse to pay or, having had the means to pay and other methods of enforcing payment (e.g. by a bailiff's warrant) having failed, they do not pay.

(*Independent*, 5 March 1995: 24)

The average population of fine defaulters in prison in 1997 was 141 *Home Office Statistical Bulletin,* 5/98: 6). The drop in recent years is in part because of a Queen's Bench Judgment on 28 November 1995 (*R v Oldham Justices and Another, ex parte Cawley*) that the courts must consider all other methods of enforcing the fine before committing a fine defaulter to prison. The Magistrates' Association and the Justices' Clerks' Society produced guidelines that required the magistrates to take each enforcement measure in turn to consider whether each measure is appropriate or not. Good practice guidance notes were issued to the courts in July 1996 regarding the enforcement of financial penalties. Under the Criminal Procedure and Investigations Act 1996 the method of initiating an attachment of earnings order, in the case of fine default, was changed to allow Justices' Clerks to take proceedings without reference to the magistrates.

The average time served by fine defaulters in 1996 was 7 days for men and 5 for women, although in that year 44 offenders served between 3 and 6 months because of fine default: of these, 2 were originally fined for violence against the person, 2 for burglary or robbery, 6 for theft and handling stolen goods, 2 for fraud, 1 for drunkenness and 22 for motoring offences (*Prison Statistics England and Wales 1996*: 108).

Life sentence inmates

In contrast to those who enter prison for a week or two the offender given a life sentence has a very different situation to face. Life sentence prisoners spend some time after sentence at a life sentence unit to undergo counselling and preparation for their future life in prison or on licence. They have no entitlement to automatic release but are eligible to apply for *release on licence.* This is discretionary and if released the person is on licence for the rest of his or her life and may be recalled to prison at any time.

In 1996 there were 3,489 inmates in prison with a life sentence, of whom 124 were women, and most (2,815) had convictions for murder, 191 for rape, 142 for manslaughter and 76 for arson (*Prison Statistics 1996*: 119). Between 1972 and 1994 an average of 70 'lifers' each year were released for the first time on licence. The average time served prior to first release was 13.9 years in 1996.

Release on licence for those sentenced to a mandatory life sentence requires the authority of the Home Secretary following a recommendation of the Parole Board. The Murder (Abolition of the Death Penalty) Act 1965 allowed the trial judge to specify a minimum period that must be served. The Criminal Justice Act 1967 made it a statutory requirement that the Home Secretary must consult with the trial judge and the Lord Chief Justice whenever a life sentence prisoner is due for release.

The statutory framework concerning the recall of lifers is set out in s. 39 CJA 1991. When a licence is revoked the person must be told the reason and of his or her right to make representations to the Parole Board. The Parole Board must consider the likely risk to other people when considering to release a person on licence and the extent to which he or she has complied in the past or is likely in the future to comply with the conditions of a licence. Of those released on life licence between 1972 and 1990, 20 per cent were reconvicted of a standard list offence within 5 years and 21 were reconvicted for homicide (*Home Office Statistical Bulletin*, 2/97). Life licencees can be recalled to prison at any time if they commit an offence or otherwise fail to comply with their conditions of licence.

The time served before release on licence varies depending on the nature of the crime and the perceived risk to the community of releasing a life sentence inmate. Some inmates may never be released. Such is likely to be the situation of Ian Brady, the Moors murderer, convicted with Myra Hindley in 1966 at Chester Assizes for the murder of Lesley Anne Downey, aged 10, and Edward Evans, aged 17. Hindley later confessed to her role in the murder of three other children. Both have now been in prison for over 30 years.

Time served

The time served in prison is not usually the amount of time imposed by the judge or magistrate for three reasons. First, time is deducted for pre-sentence periods in custody awaiting trial or sentence while on remand. Secondly, because prisoners (except for those serving 4 years and over) are entitled to remission or what is now called automatic release, and, thirdly, because of parole.

The Prison Act 1898 allowed the use of remission of part of the sentence for the good conduct of inmates. The maximum remission, for those given penal sentences, was a quarter for men and a third for women. In the 1940s, this was changed to a third for all inmates. Parole was introduced in 1967 and allowed inmates to apply for early release in addition to remission. This was a discretionary element and, unlike remission, was not automatic. Prior to the changes brought about by the CJA 1991, parole release time was in addition to the one-third deduction from sentence length for remission. Thus with remission (one-third) and parole eligibility starting at the one-third stage of the sentence, before the changes brought about by the CJA 1991, an inmate might be released soon after the one-third stage of their sentence.

Time actually served prior to the Criminal Justice Act 1991

Let us take an example of a prisoner who had been given a custodial sentence of 6 years before the implementation of the CJA 1991. The deductions

om that 6-year period would be a one-third deduction for remission as the
arliest date of release: 4 years is the most the prisoner would have served
nless days of remission were lost for breaches of the prison rules. With a
eduction for time on remand in custody prior to sentence, of 4 months, for
xample, the actual maximum time served would have been 3 years and 8
nonths. However, the prisoner would have been eligible to apply for parole
t the one-third stage of sentence, i.e. after 2 years. In this example the pri-
oner was held on remand in custody for 4 months and therefore would be
ligible to apply for parole in 20 months' time.

Thus although the court had sentenced the offender to 6 years in prison,
he longest time in prison from time of sentence would be 3 years 8 months,
nd if immediately successful with an application for parole, the prisoner
ould have been released in 20 months. The situation for prisoners serving
inder 12 months was different and they were released at the 50 per cent
tage of sentence time.

Sentence calculations after the Criminal Justice Act 1991

Sentence calculations changed with the abolition of the terms 'remission' and
parole' by the CJA 1991. All inmates were now to serve half of their sen-
ence with full allowance for time held on remand in custody. For breaches of
prison rules an inmate may serve up to 14 'added days'. Three sets of rules
govern release as a consequence of the CJA 1991.

● *Those serving a sentence of under 12 months* would be automatically released
  at the 50 per cent stage as before. This is referred to as automatic unconditional release (AUR).

● *Those sentenced from 1 to 4 years* will serve 50 per cent of the time but on
  release will be supervised in the community until the three-quarters period
  of time. So a person sentenced to 2 years will be released after 1 year,
  allowing for time spent on remand in custody, and supervised for a further
  6 months. This is known as automatic conditional release (ACR).

● *Those sentenced to 4 years and over* must serve half their sentence, with an
  allowance for time spent in custody while on remand. But they must still
  apply after the 50 per cent stage of sentence for release. This is a discretionary decision. They might not be successful in which case they will serve
  up to the two-thirds stage of sentence time. Whether they are released at
  the earliest opportunity (50 per cent stage) or serve all their time to the
  two-thirds stage, the released prisoner will be supervised in the community
  after release until the three-quarters stage.

Thus a prisoner sentenced to 10 years who had spent 6 months awaiting trial
and sentence would, from the time of sentence, be able to apply for release

after a further 4 years 6 months. If successful the prisoner would be super
vised on release in the community for a further 2 years and 6 months, i.e. to
the three-quarters stage. If unsuccessful in a bid for early release the prisone
would be released finally at the two-thirds stage. That is, at 6 years 8 month
minus the 6 months served on remand. The prisoner would then be super
vised in the community for a further 1 year and 4 months, i.e. a total perio
either in prison or under supervision in the community of 7 years 6 month
for a sentence of 10 years.

Parole

Parole was introduced in the Criminal Justice Act 1967. It allowed a prisone
to be released early, for in addition to the one-third off for remission, afte
1967 they could apply for parole at the one-third point of their sentence
Those released on parole were supervised by the probation service. Befor
1967 they would have been released at the two-thirds stage. Introduced a
part of a prison reductionist strategy, the parole system provided for an
indeterminate element in a sentence between the one-third and two-third
stage. The decision about suitability for release was made by a Local Review
Committee who dealt with short-term prisoners and made recommendation
for other prisoners, including life sentence prisoners eligible for release on
licence, which went to the Parole Board for consideration and finally to the
Home Secretary who could veto a recommendation. The Parole Board was
composed of criminologists, judges, probation officers, psychiatrists and
independent members. All were part time.

The system was changed by the CJA 1991 which allowed for automatic
release at the 50 per cent stage of sentence for all prisoners serving under 4
years. The Local Review Committee was abolished. The Parole Board was
left to consider all cases of prisoners sentenced to 4 years and over. It make
the decision in the case of prisoners serving 4 to 7 years and sends recommendations in the case of those sentenced to over 7 years to the Home
Secretary. There are now full-time officials in addition to the part-time members. Following recommendations in a review of parole by the Carlisle Committee in 1988, the CJA 1991 introduced a more complex criteria system to
be used by the Parole Boards when reviewing cases. The Home Secretary was
given the task of constructing the criteria which is based primarily on an
assessment of the risk of re-offending. Offenders released under the conditions of parole are supervised in the community by a probation officer up to
the three-quarter point of those with a determinate sentence. In 1996/7 the
Parole Board received 4,899 cases of which 36 per cent were considered
eligible for parole by the board (*Report of the Parole Board for 1996/7*).

The length of time served is one calculation that the sentenced inmate will
be keen to work out soon after reception. However, other considerations will

328

ffect the nature of the prison experience that the inmate will face during his
r her prison term. Having explained the quantity of time that an inmate will
ave to serve, what factors influence the quality of time served?

IMPACT OF IMPRISONMENT ON INMATES

For 200 years since the introduction of the penitentiary the impact of prison
ife on the inmate has been debated. As we saw in Chapter 9, some believed
hat prison life could provide a positive and constructive experience that
would rehabilitate, while others argued that the consequence of imprisonment is to lock an offender further into a life of crime. Recent opinion, as
xpressed in the 1990 white paper, *Crime, Justice and Protecting the Public*
Home Office 1990a), makes it clear that the effect of imprisonment is
unlikely to be beneficial in rehabilitative terms. It is important to bear in
mind, however, that individual inmates vary in character and that general-
sations about the impact of prison regimes will not hold for every inmate.
Empirical studies of how inmates experience and adapt to prison help to
hed light on the consequences of being incarcerated, and explain why they
have not matched the good intentions of those who saw prison as a means of
esocialising inmates.

Toleration of life in prison varies from inmate to inmate. Some will feel
heir conviction or sentence was unjust, others will accept it, and others will
be grateful that the sentence length was no longer. Each prisoner will bring a
ange of pre-existing impressions and knowledge of prisons. The National
Prison Survey 1991 showed most (57 per cent) sentenced inmates had been
n prison before (Walmsley *et al* 1993). The survey of 4,000 inmates was
conducted in January and February 1991 and covered the background characteristics of inmates and asked questions about the regimes and the condi-
ions of imprisonment from the inmates' perspective.

Cell sharing was most evident among the remand population where only
18 per cent had a cell to themselves, compared with 52 per cent of the total
sample. Overcrowding was most apparent in local prisons, with 13 per cent
of prisoners in cells accommodating three people. The average time locked
up in a cell was 14 hours. Most, 66 per cent, said they had unlimited access
o baths and showers and a further 12 per cent reported that they had three
or more baths or showers in the preceding week. Questions about the quality
of food revealed that 51 per cent thought the quality was bad and 13 per cent
thought it was good.

Asked about how they got on with staff, 9 per cent said they had been
treated badly but most (41 per cent) said the prison staff treated them well.
Personal safety questions showed that while most (71 per cent) agreed with
he statement that 'most prison officers treat prisoners fairly here' a quarter

also expressed agreement with the statement that 'some prison officers assault prisoners here'. They expressed concern about their personal safety 18 per cent replied that they did not feel safe from being injured or bullied by other prisoners and 9 per cent reported that they had been assaulted by another inmate in the last 6 months.

These physical aspects of the regime such as food, overcrowding, the time locked up in a cell, access to bath and toilet facilities and staff attitudes are vital to the trouble-free running of a prison as will be shown in the final section of this chapter which looks at the findings of the Woolf Report on the riots in 1990.

Regimes, sentence planning and privileges

A framework of privileges and incentives was introduced into prisons in 1995. Intended by the Home Secretary, Michael Howard, to ensure greater discipline, the scheme allows for a greater number of visits, more disposable cash and community visits for those who comply with the regimes. There are three levels based on the facilities provided:

- Basic: the minimum level of facilities to which the prisoner is entitled by law regardless of performance and behaviour of the prisoner.

- Standard: set above the legal minimum requirements.

- Enhanced: at this level prisoners become eligible for additional privileges

The aims of the scheme were to ensure that privileges for prisoners are earned through good behaviour and are removable if prisoners fail to maintain acceptable standards of responsible behaviour. The scheme encourages hard work and rewards participation in constructive activity by prisoners The scheme also enhances the role of sentence planning. Finally, the scheme has a control function in that it seeks to create a more disciplined, better controlled and safer environment for prisoners and staff.

The earnable privileges include:

- access to private cash above a set minimum
- extra visits
- eligibility to take part in enhanced earning schemes
- community visits for Category D inmates
- permission to wear one's own clothing
- time out of cell in association.

Sentence planning was introduced in 1992 following the recommendations of the Woolf report, to encourage inmates to identify a way of progressing throughout their time in prison so that they might acquire skills and attempt to address their offending behaviour. Following discussion between staff and

he inmate, targets are set which aim to reduce future re-offending by agreement to undertake training programmes and activities such as drug coun-
elling or sex offender treatment programme. At the start of the sentence,
nformation is put together about the inmate's community and family ties,
prior training and educational attainments. Information is collected about
ubstance abuse, criminal history and self-harm history. During the period of
ncarceration comments are kept on file about how the prisoner co-operated
vith the wing or unit's routines, and how he or she related to other inmates
ind staff. This information is open to inmates to read and challenge if they
egard it as inaccurate.

nmate adaptation to prison life

Iow do people cope with being deprived of their liberty? Prisoners do not
have the same degree of freedom to decide their daily routines, eating habits,
ocial contacts and sleeping arrangements. Studies of how inmates adapt to
prison life illustrate its impact on the inmate and how this is likely to affect
heir potential for successful rehabilitation. These sociological and psychological studies of prison life give clues about the causes of prison disturbances
ind riots that we will look at in the final section of this chapter (Cohen and
Taylor 1972; Fitzgerald 1977; King and Elliott 1977).

How people cope with prison depends on a number of factors. First, if
hey have had prior experience of prison, they will have some understand-
ng of the routines of prison life. For the novice, initial acquaintance with
prison life might be overwhelming and intimidating. Erving Goffman uses
he term 'mortification', to describe the induction process in which supports
or the person's individuality such as personal name, clothing and hair style
ire replaced by a prison number, uniform and hygiene requirements (Goffman
1968). This can be lessened and some prison administrators have introduced
egimes to normalise some aspects of prison life by, for example, less insist-
ince on uniforms and less restrictions on what might be allowed in a cell,
although this might conflict with the needs of containment and security
is was suggested in the case of the IRA prisoner escape from Whitemoor
Prison.

Prisoner adaptation, whether the inmate is an 'old hand' or a novice, will
depend on individual circumstances. Most important is the length of sentence. The nature of the crime committed also influences the prison experi-
ince. Thieves, fraudsters and robbers are often regarded with relative degrees
of respect and contempt by other inmates, but they will not suffer the fear
elt by those convicted of sexual crimes, especially those where the victim was
a child. To avoid attacks from other inmates, the 'nonces', as they are called
n prison argot, often request to be housed in vulnerable prisoner units and
egregated for their own protection under Prison Rule 43, which states:

Where it appears desirable for the maintenance of good order or discipline or in his own interest, that a prisoner should not associate with other prisoners, either generally, or for particular purposes, the governor may arrange for the prisoner removal from association.

Another factor influencing prisoners' adaptation is relationships in the outside world. One of the realities of prison life is that inmates are cut off from ordinary routine interactions with the outside world. Goffman calls prisons, along with other institutions such as monasteries, mental hospitals and boarding schools, 'total institutions'. They are 'total' in that all aspects of life such as sleeping, eating, working and leisure are conducted within the one organisation (Goffman 1968). This means that the array of contacts and opportunities are severely confined and the impact of the outside world is limited. However, this does not mean that there is no outside contact and weekly visits, access to telephones for prisoners and outside visits in pre release schemes have all been extended in recent years. Of course, the main leisure activities such as watching television, listening to the radio and reading newspapers and magazines mean that inmates in prison can keep up with events that interest them. Regimes will vary between prisons and some, such as open prisons, allow inmates two days a month out of the prison for 'town visits'.

The loss of daily contact with the home or workplace is no hardship for some inmates. Others suffer mental anguish when they think about their outside lives, homes and families. The shame of imprisonment on the family and themselves will have an impact on some of those sentenced to imprisonment. Some argue that these factors are of particular significance to women prisoners, especially where they have children (Eaton 1993).

A further factor shaping the way in which inmates adapt to prison life is their attitude towards their offence and sentence. While some accept their guilt and feel ashamed, others feel no remorse. This might be because they are professional thieves who have made a career out of criminal activity and regard imprisonment as an occupational hazard. Individual inmates will vary in their response to conviction. Those incorrectly convicted are entitled to feel outrage and anger. Others are outraged because of the type of person they are. Some are resigned to their fate and 'do their time'. Others will be influenced by the type of company they come into contact with in the prison. Although there is no one factor that determines how a prisoner responds, a number of research studies have indicated patterns of adaptation (Cohen and Taylor 1972).

Some theories accounting for offender adaptation have stressed the importance of institutional traditions and opportunities, particularly focusing on the impact of inmate subcultures and the deprivations associated with a 'closed' institution. Theorists in this tradition include Donald Clemmer, Gresham Sykes and Erving Goffman. Other theorists have focused on the 'importation' model, where the prisoners' adaptations will depend on their pre-institutional careers and lifestyles (Schrag 1944). Schrag's work showed ow the social role adopted in prison depended on the inmate's previous festyle before imprisonment.

John Irwin's study, *The Felon* (1970), found three types of response among umates in California prisons: 'jailing', 'doing time' and 'gleaning'. These esponses tended to reflect the prisoner's personal history, although Irwin nakes the caveat that inmates did not always fit into only one response nodel and that the three main response patterns did not cover every inmate. Thus 'jailing' was characteristic of 'state raised youth' who had prior institu-ional contacts from an early age and knew how to exploit the opportunities n a total institution to achieve maximum benefits and status through the ackets and gangs. Prison was not too burdensome for them as they usually had little status outside the institution other than in gang life, which con-inued in prison. The professional and more mature thieves who were career riminals adopted a different response. Their predominant aim was to get hrough their sentence as quietly and as quickly as possible. Therefore they vere not interested in the rehabilitative programmes of the institution except vhere it meant an easier life inside or the chance to get out of prison more quickly. Nor were these inmates interested in campaigning or confrontation vith the authorities, as were the 'jailing' inmates. The third pattern of adapta-ion described by Irwin was 'gleaning'. These inmates engaged in the oppor-unities offered by education, counselling, therapy and work programmes to ncrease their opportunities of being granted parole and of changing their ifestyles.

In a later study, *Prisons in Turmoil* (1980), Irwin points out that the models of inmate subcultures were easier to identify in the traditional style of penit-entiary with more rigid and authoritarian regimes. Clemmer's study in 1940 ound a very distinctive and conformist prisoner culture, with an inmate ode, defined and enforced primarily through the inmates (Clemmer 1958). Since that time the nature of the prison experience has become more diver-ified, as new types of inmate and values have been brought into prison. The ommitment to rehabilitative strategies in the 1950s brought about more iberal regimes with less emphasis on the convict culture found in many orisons before 1950. The new mix of inmates also undermined the single nmate culture. In the USA in the 1960s, as with the British prisons during he period of World War I, political prisoners objecting to the war generated a more articulate and politically sophisticated inmate. In the USA the black oower movement created another form of politically orientated inmate. Younger nmates convicted of drug and gang-related crimes were not so easily im-oressed by either the formal or informal cultures of prison life and had their own support and reference groups as gang and drug activities meant that orison contacts became an extension of street life.

More recent theorists and studies have stressed the greater diversity of nmate culture as less strict regimes and more diverse pre-institutional life-tyles become more apparent in prison in the 1990s.

If prisons were no longer to be regarded as institutions seeking to rehabilitate

offenders, then what was their purpose? The next section will set out th
aims of the prison service in 1990 and asks 'Do prisons work?'.

AIMS AND PERFORMANCE OF THE
PRISON SERVICE

Does prison work, as Michael Howard asserted in the quote at the beginnin
of this chapter? To answer this it is necessary to ask what the goals of im
prisonment are. In clarifying these goals we must distinguish between th
function of imprisonment within the criminal justice system – that is, to carr
out the sentence of the court – and the specific goals of prisons as institution.

Thus prisons work in one sense if they deprive offenders of their liberty fc
the period of time specified by the court. Hence the main purpose of impri
onment is in terms of sentencing goals. When assessed in terms of whethe
prisons fulfil this function they are successful if general deterrence, denuncia
tion and just deserts goals are achieved; and at the minimum they fulfil a
incapacitative function of keeping away from the community offenders wh
would, and will, when released, continue criminal activities.

However, the prison service has its own institutionally specific goals re
flecting the penal paradigms explored in Chapter 9. In 1979 the report of th
May Committee referred to the loss of faith in the treatment objective i
prison and recommended the rewriting of Prison Rule 1 and adopting th
idea of custody which is both 'secure and yet positive'. 'Positive custody' wa
defined in four ways. It should (Home Office 1979: 67):

- create an environment which can assist them (the inmates) to respond an
  contribute to society as positively as possible;

- preserve and promote their self-respect;

- minimise, to the degree of security necessary in each particular case, th
  harmful effects of their removal from normal life;

- prepare them for and assist them on discharge.

In the 1990s the prison service set out the following goals of imprisonmer
in its mission statement:

> Her Majesty's Prison Service serves the public by keeping in custody those com
> mitted by the courts. Our duty is to look after them with humanity and help ther
> lead law-abiding and useful lives in custody and after release.

Therefore, in terms of the institutional goals the prison service has set itsel
prisons can be assessed as to their effectiveness by monitoring their succes
at achieving the objectives set. Key Performance Indicators (KPIs) wer
introduced for this purpose. The Home Secretary's list of objectives for th
prison service and the KPIs are set out in the Review Questions at the en
of Chapter 11. The first test is that those sent by the courts are retaine
until the proper release date. The escape and absconder rates from priso

tablishments in England and Wales could be looked at to test whether they
e serving the courts effectively by holding those sent there by the courts.
Between 1 April 1996 and 31 March 1997, 33 inmates escaped from
osed establishments. A further 98 escaped from their escort outside of the
ison, often on their way to court. Most escapes are from open prisons but
e referred to by the prison service as absconders. In addition, in 1996/7
ere were 1,116 absconders from open prisons or from outside working
rties or while on an outside visit. Most escapees and absconders are caught
thin the year.

Secondly, the prison service aims to look after inmates with humanity. This
quires providing decent conditions for inmates and meeting their physical
eds. The aspiration to look after inmates with humanity also implies a style
regime that allows inmates the opportunity to lead a full and responsible
e within the constraints imposed by costs and security. Apart from basic
aterial and medical needs a measure of the success of prisons, in terms of
eir declared aims, could include the number of inmates engaged on and
e average time devoted to educational, work and leisure activities.

The goal of humanity can be audited in general terms by such contra-
dicators as overcrowded cells, poor food, insulting behaviour by staff, time
lowed out of the cells and slopping out. Slopping out is condemned as
nacceptable by the criteria set in the European Prison Standards (Casale
984; Stern 1987; Morgan 1997).

Thirdly, do inmates lead law-abiding lives while in prison? One measure
ould be to look at inmate-on-inmate assault rates. In October 1993, Leslie
ailey, an inmate at Whitemoor Prison in March, Cambridgeshire, was
rangled in his cell. He was a convicted paedophile, a category of offender
equently the target of attacks in prison by other inmates. A murder in
rison is unlikely to support a view that inmates are secure from physical
ssault; surely a first condition for humane containment is the personal safety
f those sent to prison. Therefore the number of assaults on inmates and staff
one aspect of any measure of the success of the goal of helping inmates to
ad law-abiding lives while in custody. Between April 1996 and the end of
1arch 1997 there were 2,531 assaults on staff and 2,748 assaults on inmates
Prison Service Annual Report and Accounts 1996 to 1997: 59–65).

Fourthly, do prisons work to achieve the aim of helping inmates to lead
w abiding and useful lives after release? The prison service seeks to offer a
ositive environment so that offenders have an opportunity to address their
ffending behaviour. The 1990 white paper made it clear that judges should
o longer use imprisonment as a sentence if they seek to bring about the
ehabilitation of the offender. Prisons, the report concludes, are counter-
roductive in this regard. The report states:

It was once believed that prison, properly used, could encourage a high proportion
of offenders to start an honest life on their release. Nobody now regards imprisonment, in itself, as an effective means of reform for most prisoners . . . however

much prison staff try to inject a positive purpose into the regime, as they do, prisc
is a society which requires virtually no sense of personal responsibility fro
prisoners. Normal social or working habits do not fit. The opportunity to lear
from other prisoners is pervasive. For most offenders, imprisonment has to t
justified in terms of public protection, denunciation and retribution. Otherwise
can be an expensive way of making bad people worse.

(Home Office 1990a: (

The green paper *Punishment, Custody and the Community* can be seen as
formal recognition of the limitations of prisons as places for rehabilitatin
offenders (Home Office 1988a). They have not achieved the ambitious goa
claimed by the protagonists for the penitentiary 200 years ago. If custody
to be used it should be for purposes other than a belief that it will help th
offender to lead a 'good and useful life' or even a 'law-abiding and usef
life'. The green paper cites the many unintended consequences of imprisor
ment which made them counter-productive in rehabilitative terms.
Paragraph 1.1:

... they are not required to face up to what they have done and to the effects o
their victim.

Paragraph 1.1:

... if they are removed in prison from the responsibilities, problems and tempta
tions of everyday life, they are less likely to acquire the self-discipline and sel
reliance which will prevent re-offending in the future.

Paragraph 1.6:

Imprisonment is likely to add to the difficulties which offenders find in living
normal and law-abiding life. Overcrowded local prisons are emphatically not schoo
of citizenship.

Paragraph 2.15:

[With regard to young offenders] Even a short period of custody is quite likely t
confirm them as criminals, particularly if they acquire new criminal skills fror
more sophisticated offenders. They see themselves labelled as criminals and behav
accordingly.

(Home Office 1988a

However, it might be correct to recognise that while prisons do not work t
resocialise offenders, it is important to prevent further desocialisation whil
in prison. Therefore projects within prison that encourage self-responsibilit
and help inmates to maintain their links with the family and the outsid
world might help to achieve this. Treating inmates with respect can also b
an aspect of a positive regime. With this in mind it might be worth foster
ing constructive and positive goals in rehabilitative terms because it migh
encourage staff to treat inmates with some degree of decency.

The test of the proposition that prisons reduce the future criminality of those released from prison – whether through rehabilitative strategies or via the impact of individual deterrence – can be tested by an examination of recidivism rates. They measure what proportion of offenders have been reconvicted for a further offence in a 2-year period from release. These figures are not entirely accurate as measures of re-offending as, first, they include some 'pseudo-reconvictions' being convictions recorded after the original sentence, or offences committed before (Lloyd et al 1994).

Secondly, they will not include offences committed by those in the sample which remain unknown, unsolved, or unsuccessfully prosecuted. Figure 10.5 shows the reconviction rate for those discharged from custody or commencing probation, combination orders and community service orders.

These figures show that going to prison is likely to be related to future re-offending. However, they also show that non-custodial sanctions are not much better at reducing the likelihood of re-offending. Perhaps sentencing an offender, whether to prison or in the community, has little to do with the influences on offending behaviour. Certainly it is difficult to accept the proposition that prisons work to reduce criminality in the sense of their impact on individual offenders. The usefulness of imprisonment should be assessed in terms of its functions other than those to do with its effect on individual offenders (see Chapter 9).

So the answer to the question of whether prisons work is that it depends on what we expect of them. The failure to meet the original high expectations of those who pioneered the idea that the penitentiary would be an institution to change offenders into law-abiding citizens is apparent. But prisons meet other demands, particularly as the most credible way to achieve retribution, denunciation, general deterrence and incapacitation.

Finally, no doubt the 'success rate' of imprisonment, in terms of any of its aims could be improved if more money is spent on the prison system. What would be the cost of ensuring no escapes? Would the taxpayer wish to pay this cost? For those who think prisons have failed in all or most respects, the onus is on them to say what they would put in its place as the major institution symbolising punishment.

Fig 10.5 Reconviction rates England and Wales 1993. Percentage reconvicted after 2 years (all ages)

Sentence	Number of previous convictions					
	None	*1 or 2*	*3 to 6*	*7 to 10*	*11 or more*	*All*
Probation	31	50	63	71	77	60
Combination orders	35	54	65	73	75	52
Community service	26	45	62	67	71	52
Immediate custody	14	37	58	65	73	53

Compiled from, Kershaw C and Renshaw G (1997) Home Office Statistical Bulletin, 5/97: 20.

PRISON DISTURBANCES AND ESCAPES IN THE 1990s

On April Fool's Day 1990, prisoners rioted at Strangeways, a local prison Manchester. Strangeways was built in 1868 and at the time of the riot ha 1,647 inmates. The riot started during the Sunday morning chapel servi and resulted in violent attacks on prison officers and Rule 43 prisoners. It too 25 days for the prison authorities to gain control of the prison. The damag to the prison was valued at £30 million. Rioting was not to be confined t Strangeways as prisoners at other institutions followed their example. Th worst were at two other local prisons at Bristol and Cardiff; at the Categoi B training prison, Dartmoor; and at the young offender remand centres Glen Parva and Pucklechurch.

An independent public inquiry was established under the chairmanship Lord Justice Woolf to look at the causes of these riots and to make recom mendations. The report *Prison Disturbances, April 1990* was published in 199 (see Home Office 1991a). The first half of the report, written by Lord Justic Woolf, examined the causes of the riots. The second half of this extensive 60 page report was written by Lord Justice Woolf and Judge Stephen Tumin Her Majesty's Inspector of Prisons, and provided an overview of priso conditions and made 12 key recommendations and 204 specific proposals.

The inquiry gathered data from a number of sources, including inmate perceptions as to the causes of the riots. A content analysis of the lette submitted by prisoners indicated six possible causes of the riots: physic conditions, particularly poor sanitation; overcrowding; prisoners being locke in their cells for long periods of time and limited association, referred t as being 'banged up'; complaints about food; the attitude of staff toward inmates; and, finally, the letters indicated the 'copycat' influences on the rio as bored or hostile inmates emulated actions in other prisons. Figure 10. shows the perceptions of inmates in the six different prisons at the time c the riots and their views about the causes of the disturbances.

Woolf's conclusions about the causes of the riots pointed to individu reasons at each prison. For example, at Bristol the combination of prisoner being locked in their cells for long periods and limited facilities had fuelle inmate grievances, added to which was the influx of prisoners from Dart moor prison to a wing which already housed many disruptive prisoners.

The riot spread quickly because keys were taken from two officers attacke at the beginning of the riot. Their keys opened all the doors on the wing. I addition to the individual factors that played their part in each of the dis turbances, the report made a general comment on the way to achieve a mor stable prison system:

> The achievement of this role, however, depends on there being a proper balanc within prisons between security and control on the one hand and humanity an justice on the other.

> (Home Office 1991a: 245

g 10.6 Prisoners' letters on the causes of the 1990 riots

omplaints	Strangeways %	Glen Parva %	Dartmoor %	Bristol %	Cardiff %
anitation	55	7	22	24	20
vercrowding	50	–	–	16	18
ang up'	43	4	15	26	24
oor food	40	20	37	16	10
oor staff attitudes	27	13	39	22	22
opycat	N/A	32	21	26	16

esults from letters submitted to the public inquiry from prisoners involved in the sturbances. The results indicate the main sources of complaints within prisons.

ote: Results from Pucklechurch have not been included because the total set of sponses from this establishment was too small.

ource: Home Office (1991a).

The Woolf Report made 12 major recommendations aimed to reduce ature conflicts between inmates and the prison authorities. These recommendations not only apply to the internal running of prisons but make the oint that prisons should work more closely with other agencies in the criminal justice system. They recognised that prisons are at the back-end of he system and that prison managers have very little control over the numbers who are received into prisons, making it difficult to plan ahead to provide adequate and appropriate facilities. The 12 major recommendations are:

- Closer co-operation between the different parts of the criminal justice system. For this purpose a national forum and local committees should be established.

- More visible leadership of the prison service by a Director General who is and is seen to be the operational head and in day-to-day charge of the Service. To achieve this, there should be a published 'compact' or 'contract' given by ministers to the Director General of the prison service, who should be responsible for the performance of that 'contract' and publicly answerable for the day-to-day operations of the prison service.

- Increased delegation of responsibility to governors of establishments.

- An enhanced role for prison officers.

- A 'compact' or 'contract' for each prisoner setting out the prisoner's expectations and responsibilities in the prison in which he or she is held.

- A national system of accredited standards, with which, in time, each prison establishment would be required to comply.

- A new prison rule that no establishment should hold more prisoners than is provided for in its certified normal level of accommodation, with provisions for Parliament to be informed if exceptionally there is to be a material departure from that rule.

339

- A public commitment from ministers setting a timetable to provide access to sanitation for all inmates at the earliest practical date, not later than February 1996.

- Better prospects for prisoners to maintain their links with families and the community through more visits and home leaves and through being located in community prisons as near to their homes as possible.

- A division of prison establishments into small and more manageable and secure units.

- A separate statement of purpose, separate conditions and generally a lower security categorisation for remand prisoners.

- Improved standards of justice within prisons involving the giving of reasons to a prisoner for any decision which materially and adversely affects him; a grievance procedure and disciplinary proceedings which ensure that the governor deals with most matters under his present powers; relieving Boards of Visitors of their adjudicatory role; and providing for final access to an independent Complaints Adjudicator.

(Home Office 1991a: para 15.5)

In response, Kenneth Baker, the Home Secretary at the time of the publication of the Woolf Report, had already begun to introduce some of the proposals recommended by Woolf to improve conditions within prisons. An increase in visits, letters and access to telephones was implemented together with the start of a programme of works to meet the Woolf deadline of February 1996 for ending the practice of slopping out. The planning and building of new prisons also continued in order to reduce the overcrowding described in the Woolf Report. By early 1994 the prison service could claim that there were no cases of three inmates having to share a prison cell designed for one. Sentencing planning for inmates was introduced on 1 October 1992 for inmates serving 4 years and over and for Category A inmates. For inmates serving between 12 months and less than 4 years the scheme started on 1 November 1993. The CJA 1993 removed the disciplinary powers of the Board of Visitors in line with the recommendations of the Woolf Report; and National and Area Criminal Justice Consultative Councils were established. However, there has been less development with regard to community prisons and a national system of accredited standards.

On 9 September 1994, six prisoners escaped from the high-security prison at Whitemoor. An inquiry was conducted by Sir John Woodcock into that escape and, following the publication of his findings in December 1994, the Home Secretary announced a review of 'physical security and security procedure in the prison service in England and Wales'. This was to be conducted by Sir John Learmont. In the month in which the inquiry team started, Frederick West committed suicide in Winston Green Prison on 1 January 1995 and on 3 January three prisoners escaped from Parkhurst Prison on the Isle of

Vight. Whitemoor and Parkhurst were dispersal prisons with regimes designed to prevent the escapes of inmates regarded as a danger to the public. The inquiry found that one of the Parkhurst prisoners was a sheet-metal worker who was given access to workshops where he made the key used in the escape. The inquiry focused primarily on security in dispersal prisons.

The Learmont report (see Learmont 1995), *Review of Prison Service Security in England and Wales and the Escape from Parkhurst Prison on Tuesday 3rd January 1995*, made 127 recommendations regarding security in dispersal prisons, including the following:

- a daily audit of tools and materials used in workshops

- review of the training facilities available to inmates in dispersal prisons

- visitors to be subject to rub down searches and x-ray checks and efforts made to prevent smuggling

- 360 degree CCTV surveillance in visiting rooms

- end family visits in dispersal prisons

- cell searches conducted in accordance to the *Manual on Security*

- the volume of inmates' possessions should be limited to that which would fit into two transit boxes

- introduction of electronic or magnetic locks

- Parkhurst should be downgraded in security terms and another dispersal prison introduced

- wings and units should each have a single manager

- the statement of purpose of the prison service should be revised to make custody the primary purpose

- KPIs should be reviewed to show progress towards preventing escapes rather than just measuring the number of escapes, and should include assessment of staff training, staff morale and recidivism rates for inmates and the degree of success at dealing with the drug problem in prison

- the concept of drugs-free wings and of drug testing should be implemented where appropriate

- early release should be a privilege earned through good behaviour

- all prisoners should be offered meaningful work and wages

- the £40 limit per week for phonecards at Parkhurst must be reviewed and set at a lower level and telephone privileges should feature in an incentive scheme

- television in the cells should be an aspect of the privileges schemes an earned through good behaviour

- the problems for the staff, of intimidation, manipulation and boredom must be addressed

- the role of the Prison Inspectorate should be extended to include securit issues

- a new security classification system should be introduced.

A possible new security classification system was outlined in the report with six categories as below:

New category	Existing category	Type of prison
1	A (Exceptional Risk)	Dispersal
2	A (High Risk)	Dispersal
3	A and B (Standard Risk)	Dispersal
4	B	Closed cellular
	C	Training
5	C	Closed non-cellular estate
6	D	Open

Thus the report made recommendations with regard to details of practice in workshops and visiting rooms, proposals to restate the prison service object-ives to emphasise the primacy of security, suggestions to improve the culture of prisons to improve staff morale and training, and inmate behaviour by linking good behaviour to earned privileges and incentives.

CONCLUSION

We can see from this chapter that prisons have been expected to perform many functions. The rehabilitative paradigm discussed in Chapter 9 influ-enced the design, organisation and regimes of prisons from their inception to around the 1960s. Thus prisons were seen not as degrading and punit-ive institutions but as institutions where inmates should be encouraged and assisted to lead a good and useful life through a regime of treatment and training. These ideals, however, were not achieved, and some of the reasons why prisons may not be able to achieve rehabilitation have been noted. They are after all institutions in which inmates are deprived of their liberty, which may have an adverse effect on their sense of individuality and purpose. Some prisoners are wedded to a life of crime, others, particularly those on long sentences, may simply wish to forget the outside world and see no hope for the future. Prisons indeed may have a damaging rather than a positive effect.

The demise of rehabilitative goals, however, had a profound effect on the institutions making up the prison system. At the same time conditions within risons worsened due to the increasing numbers which the system had to deal with. One attraction of rehabilitative goals to penal reformers was that it held out the promise of treating prisoners with humanity. With its demise, these conditions also declined, many training programmes ceased and prisoners were locked up for longer periods in their cells. These conditions arguably contributed to the disturbances in the early 1990s.

As we have seen it is important to distinguish between the aims of sentencers in sending offenders to prison and the aims of the prison system itself. Thus while sentencers and policy makers talk of incapacitation and the deprivation of liberty, these do not provide constructive goals for the institutions who must carry out these aims. Reducing the goal of prison to that of simply keeping offenders from escaping until they are due to be released ('warehousing') might further distance staff from inmates and undermine programmes aimed at reforming them.

Prisons must deal with those whom the courts send to them and attempt to prevent them escaping and creating disturbances. Yet the interests of security and control may run counter to positive regimes and humane conditions in a cost-conscious climate. The debate over the balance between security, control, costs and changing offender behaviour in prison is likely to continue into the next millennium.

Review questions

1. What are the different categories of prisons run by the prison service in England and Wales?

2. Calculate the actual amount of time served by an inmate if he or she is sentenced to (a) 8 months, (b) 2 years. What rules apply to the prisoner sentenced to over 4 years?

3. What are the different aims of imprisonment? What kind of evidence should be examined to explore whether or not these aims are being achieved?

4. What arguments are involved in considering whether more prisons should be built or greater efforts should be made to reduce the prison population?

5. Look at the information in Figures 10.4 and 10.7 about the comparative use of imprisonment in European countries.
    From an examination of Figures 10.4 and 10.7, answer the following questions:

    (a) Using Figure 10.4, calculate where England and Wales is ranked among the countries and jurisdictions listed, in terms of the numbers of prisoners in the years indicated:

343

1993: . . . . .e.g. . . . . . . Answer – 6th . . . .
1994: . . . .
1995: . . . .
1996: . . . .

(b) Using Figure 10.4, where is England and Wales ranked among th
    countries listed in terms of the numbers of prisoners per 100,000 o
    the population in:

1993: . . . . .e.g. . . . . . . Answer – 13th . . . .
1994: . . . .
1995: . . . .

(c) In Figure 10.7 the data shows the use of imprisonment as a propor
    tion of the number of crimes recorded. Where is England and Wale
    ranked among the countries listed in 1995?

(d) The comparative information in these two figures shows the tota
    numbers in prison, the numbers compared with the population as
    whole, and the numbers compared with the amount of recorded crime
    Which of these do you regard as the more useful for assessing claim
    about the overuse of custody in England and Wales?

(e) Examine the percentage change in the numbers in custody betweer
    1987 and 1995 (see Figure 10.7). Does it show that the prison popu-
    lation in England and Wales has increased more than other Europear
    countries over that period?

Fig 10.7 Some European prison populations in 1995, and percentage increase
since 1987

Country	1995	% increase 1987–95	Per 100,000 recorded crimes in 1995
England and Wales	51,265	9	1,005
N. Ireland	1,740	–6	2,528
Scotland	5,657	4	1,125
Republic of Ireland	2,032	5	1,983
France	53,178	5	1,451
Belgium	7,561	12	1,053
Germany	68,408	–	1,026
Austria	6,180	–17	1,280
Netherlands	10,329	106	839
Norway	2,621	36	1,189
Sweden	5,767	34	591
Denmark	3,421	7	635
Finland	3,092	–27	811
Portugal	11,829	40	3,622
Italy	49,102	41	2,165
Greece	5,878	47	1,786
Spain	40,157	70	–
Switzerland	4,104	19	1,183

Compiled from *Criminal Statistics England and Wales 1995*: 25.

Further reading

Cavadino M and Dignan J (1997) *The Penal System: An Introduction*, 2nd edn. London: Sage

Harding C, Hines B, Ireland R and Rawlings P (1985) *Imprisonment in England and Wales*. London: Croom Helm

Morgan R (1997) 'Imprisonment' in Maguire M, Morgan R and Reiner R (eds) *The Oxford Handbook of Criminology*, 2nd edn. Oxford: Clarendon Press

CHAPTER 11

RESPONDING TO CRIME

- Administrative, Political and Policy Context
- Implementing Criminal Justice Policy
- Monitoring, Accountability and Complaints
- Community, Victims and Vigilantes
- Strategies for Tackling Crime

INTRODUCTION

Protecting the public is a major theme in political rhetoric that legitimate or justifies, the very existence of government. While the provision of school hospitals and roads is important, they become secondary when citizens fea for their safety in the communities where they live. As Thomas Hobbe pointed out in the seventeenth century in *Leviathan* (1650), there are limi to the extent to which individuals can protect themselves and therefore one the major responsibilities and purposes of government is to provide securi against threats to personal safety from others. Thus criminal justice system are expected to protect both the citizen and their property.

In a democratic society there may be differences of opinion as to ho public protection, and the process of reassurance that goes with this, can be best achieved. Since the late eighteenth century we have seen a steady growt of interest in all aspects of criminal justice. With this has come innovativ modes of intervention with:

- the development of professionals such as the police, psychiatrists an social workers;

- new institutions such as borstal and youth courts;

- a succession of ideas about how best to curb crime, deal with criminal maintain law and order, and provide due process to ensure justice fc those accused of a crime.

It is evident that ideas about these issues are subject to change and th plethora of criminal justice legislation at the end of the twentieth centur

346

illustrates that we live in a society where the response to crime is a major feature of government and politics.

In this chapter we will identify the main features of the administrative, political and policy-making context of the criminal justice system in England and Wales. Key players are to be found in Whitehall and Westminster but we will be looking beyond the UK to the increasing internationalisation of crime policy, particularly the growth in European co-operation. We will examine issues to do with the implementation of criminal justice policy such as the problems of co-ordination between the agencies, the increasing role played by private industry and the continuing and considerable role played by the lay and voluntary sector. Pragmatic and political issues are raised by the system for evaluating and monitoring the effectiveness of agencies through such innovations as performance indicators. Despite greater efforts to clarify objectives and assess performance, the issue of accountability is still relevant as it affects public confidence in the system and whether they feel it works to protect people's safety and property. The political and public reaction to crime policy will involve issues of how crime is represented in the media and the attitudes of the public to issues of crime and punishment. This leads on to the role that the public may play in responding to crime, either through initiatives such as Neighbourhood Watch or through vigilante activities. The public might also become involved as victims of crime and we will discuss some of the recent reforms that focus on victims.

Ideas change and policy experiments and initiatives do not wait for legislation but enter the fray of public discourse. Fashions change about the proper way to respond to crime, and new theories, policies and slogans may become encapsulated in crime strategies and new policy directions. We will look at current ideas about community crime prevention, zero tolerance and restorative justice.

ADMINISTRATIVE, POLITICAL AND POLICY CONTEXT

Who makes crime policy?

The most fundamental statement of criminal justice policy is to be found in legislation. Acts of Parliament provide both the starting point for defining many crimes and also the criminal justice agencies' powers and responsibilities in their response to crime.

In the UK, central government plays the dominant role in legislative reforms. Laws may start out as ideas in ministerial speeches, parliamentary statements and election manifestos. After a period of 18 years in opposition the newly formed Labour Government set out its approach to crime in the Crime and Disorder Act 1998. At other times the Government may be responding to a new or newly perceived problem as a result of a single incident which reflects wider public anxiety. Following the stabbing of head-master Philip Lawrence outside his school in Maida Vale the law was changed to prohibit children under 16 from buying knives.

Where legislation is approaching the planning stage, the Government may issue a green paper, a general discussion document inviting comment on particular ideas or proposals. Subsequently a white paper may be published which gives firm detailed proposals taking account of the feedback from the green paper. The white paper is the most definitive statement of the Government's policy and usually forms the basis of subsequent bills although many bills are introduced without this preliminary process of deliberation. All bills must go through a number of stages in both the House of Commons and the House of Lords before being transformed into an Act of Parliament. This process is not a formality and parliamentary debate may lead to amendments to the original details set out in the bill.

Policy can emerge in forms other than legislation and can be influenced not only by ministers or other politicians. Permanent officials in government departments will also have a departmental view on such issues as prison reduction and police powers. Policy statements are not always embodied in statute and innovations such as the Prison Ombudsman and cautioning in lieu of prosecution by the police has no statutory basis but emerged from decisions within the Home Office. Documents published by the Home Office are most influential on a range of matters concerning the police, probation and prisons. The Lord Chancellor's Department is important on matters relating to the judiciary and the courts.

Whitehall – a term that refers to both ministers and civil servants – is not the only source of policy statements. The work of the Home Affairs Committee at Westminster is important as are the views of the non-elected members of the House of Lords who include senior members of the judiciary, the Lords of Appeal who sit in the Upper House. During Michael Howard's term as Home Secretary senior members of the judiciary in the House of Lords spoke strongly against proposals in the Crime (Sentencing) Bill that proposed mandatory prison sentences for those re-convicted of serious violent or sexual offences, drug trafficking and for those convicted for a third time for burglary of a domestic dwelling. They were very critical of Michael Howard when Home Secretary and claimed he was pandering to public opinion in introducing tougher penalties that would increase the prison population. The Police and Magistrates' Courts Act 1994, described in Chapter 4, was also contested in the House of Lords with critics including former Home Secretaries.

It would be simplistic to think that policy making is restricted to Whitehall and Westminster. Policy is also found in the many documents defining the role and approach of the various agencies and professional and voluntary bodies that make up the criminal justice system. The process of policy making is very complex and reflects the fact that government is only one of a number of key players in the system. Other influential players in the process of consultation are professional groups, pressure groups and lay participants who have a unique role in criminal justice in this country when compared with others. The Magistrates' Association, for instance, has played an important role in developing sentencing guidelines.

Professional bodies are of considerable influence in England and Wales and include:

- Association of Chief Police Officers (ACPO)
- Police Federation (represents the ordinary police officer)
- National Association of Probation Officers (NAPO)
- Prison Officers' Association (POA)
- Prison Governors' Association
- Bar Council and the Criminal Bar Association (represent barristers)
- Law Society (represents solicitors)
- Justices' Clerks Society

The most powerful of professions on matters of criminal law, procedure and prosecution are the lawyers represented by the Bar Council, Criminal Bar Association, Law Society and the judiciary (judges) both individually and through bodies such as the Council of Circuit Judges and the Judicial Studies Board. The judiciary, although small in number, is powerful in defence of the principle of the independence of the judiciary, and is regularly consulted about new legislation. Lawyers' views are sought and listened to by the major government departments such as the Office of the Attorney General, responsible for the Crown Prosecution Service, and the Lord Chancellor's Department which is responsible for the appointment and training of judges, legal aid and the administration of the Crown Court and Court of Appeal through the Court Service and Public Trust Office, (an executive agency).

Several government departments play a role in the development of policy but the lead department for developing policy in criminal justice is the Home Office.

Home Office

The Home Office is the single most important government department with respect to criminal justice policy. As a source of ideas and funding, its role is pivotal in determining reforms of the criminal law and the direction of criminal justice policy. The Home Office has responsibilities for the police, the courts, prisons, probation, reviewing the criminal law, crime prevention and victim support. It has other non-criminal duties regarding the fire service, immigration control, dangerous dogs, national security, licensing of gambling and sales of alcohol, passports and applications for British citizenship.

While it is wrong to suggest that there is only one source of influence on criminal justice policy in England and Wales, the Home Office is the government agency with an overall view of the system. Issues of public confidence in the system of justice in terms of effectiveness, efficiency and fairness would normally be regarded as the responsibility of the Home Office, although the Lord Chancellor's Department and the Attorney General have an interest in such matters.

The Home Office has responsibilities regarding the criminal justice system in the following areas:

- legislative reform of the criminal law and criminal procedures

- public safety and responding to public disasters

- sentencing policy

- policy, funding, training and the efficiency of the police service, including setting performance indicators and vetting senior appointments

- the probation service

- policy and the funding of the prison service (an executive agency)

- forensic services

- appointments to the Parole Board and responding to its recommendations about the release of those sentenced to over 4 years and those serving life sentences for release on licence

- appointment of the Prison Ombudsman

- exercising the prerogative of mercy

- dealing with foreign jurisdictions on matters of common policy, for example Europol, and individual decisions regarding the extradition of suspects and the transfer of convicted prisoners

- mentally disordered persons subject to restriction orders

- producing annual statistics on the work of the criminal justice agencies and commissioning and conducting research into policy developments

- providing information to Parliament in response to parliamentary questions about activities under its control and providing information for government inquiries and Royal Commissions on criminal justice topics

- promoting crime prevention policy

- co-ordinating and funding Victim Support schemes

- conducting the British Crime Survey

The responsibilities and duties of the Home Office have changed over time. For example, the administration and control of prisons between 1877 and 1963 was the responsibility of the Prison Commission. In 1964 prisons came under the direct control of the Prison Department in the Home Office. The Permanent Secretary at the Home Office at that time, Charles Cunningham believed the advantage of amalgamating the prison service into the Home

Office was that it would bring the key law enforcement and crime control agencies under one roof to allow for a more integrated approach to crime prevention and permit better planning of the forces available to the state to combat crime. The idea of co-ordinating the work of criminal justice agencies and involving the voluntary and business communities in multi-agency approaches will be discussed later in this chapter, and it is clear that in the 1980s the Home Office gave a lead on this issue in the field of crime prevention.

However, by the 1990s it was also clear that Government was attempting to devolve and diversify responsibilities for the day-to-day running of criminal justice agencies and the courts. In 1993 the prison service became an executive agency. This signalled the beginning of a fundamental change in the administration of powers and budgets and management responsibilities. However, the extent of the separation of this new agency from Home Office control was not entirely clear and a major political and constitutional row took place when the Home Secretary, Michael Howard, sacked the first Director General, Derek Lewis, in 1995, after the publications of the Woodcock and Learmont reports on the security lapses following escapes from the maximum security prisons at Whitemoor in September 1994 and Parkhurst in January 1995.

Home Secretary

The Home Secretary, one of the major political figures in government, is responsible for promoting criminal law reform and has a general responsibility for the criminal justice system. During the 18-year period of Conservative governments, from 1979 to 1997, influential figures were appointed to the post: William Whitelaw, Leon Brittan, Douglas Hurd, David Waddington, Kenneth Baker, Kenneth Clarke and Michael Howard. In 1997, Jack Straw became the first Labour Party Home Secretary since Merlyn Rees in 1979. It is a demanding office to hold, and regarded as potentially disastrous for those who have further political ambitions, despite being one of the three great Offices of State, with the Chancellor of the Exchequer and the Foreign Secretary. Only two twentieth-century Home Secretaries, Winston Churchill (1910–11) and Jim Callaghan (1967–70) were to become Prime Minister.

Some of the momentum for reforms that laid the foundations for new agencies in the system of criminal justice came from influential nineteenth-century Home Secretaries. Robert Peel (1822–7 and 1928–30) played a vital role in the foundation of the Metropolitan Police Force. Lord Palmerston (1852–5) introduced a number of penal reforms during his period at the Home Office. The Penal Servitude Act 1853 abolished transportation and substituted the sentence of penal servitude. The Reformatory Schools Act 1854 meant that boys sentenced to a term in prison could be transferred after a period of time to a new style rehabilitative school.

351

Palmerston's responsibilities on matters of policing meant that a political row blew up when the political refugee Louis Kossuth was exiled to London. He was a radical who led the independence movement to free the Magyars from the Austrian Empire. His activities were investigated by plain-clothed policemen and he was implicated in a plot to manufacture arms and send them to Hungary for use in an uprising. Parliamentary questions, threats of prosecution and press coverage, particularly in *The Times*, led to the type of high-profile public controversy that most Home Secretaries can expect to cope with.

Home Secretaries are vulnerable to the type of political rows that get front page press coverage. They are expected to respond to public disquiet following major crime stories such as those about Jack the Ripper in 1880 or Peter Sutcliffe in Yorkshire a century later. Very emotive issues have to be considered, such as hanging and deaths in custody, and appropriate responses put in place following miscarriages of justice, corruption within the police force, disasters such as at Hillsborough and Dunblane and prison escapes such as those by the Great Train Robber Ronnie Biggs, the KGB spy George Blake and IRA terrorists.

In addition to the potential political rows following major crime and related incidents, the Home Secretary has a minefield to tread in the area of civil liberties. Unlike other government departments where the Minister is responsible for the broad issues of policy, the Home Secretary has discretionary powers to make decisions affecting individuals in a number of ways, such as in deportation cases. In the case of mandatory life sentence prisoners the Home Secretary makes the final decision whether to release a person on licence (for example, Myra Hindley). For those sentenced to a non-life prison sentence the Home Secretary has the final decision whether to accept recommendations from the Parole Board to release a prisoner on parole if he or she is serving a sentence of 4 years or more. In March, 1998 Jack Straw was under criticism for his decision to refuse a request from the German prosecutors to allow the extradition of Roisin McAliskey. She was a suspect in a terrorist trial in Germany involving the bombing of a British Army base at Osnabruck. She was arrested in Northern Ireland and subsequently gave birth while on remand in Holloway prison in London. She became emotionally ill and was moved to the Maudsley psychiatric hospital in south London. The Home Secretary claimed it was because she had been declared unfit to attend court by psychiatrists at the Maudsley hospital that he had made his decision and that he was uninfluenced by political considerations.

The Home Secretary exercises the prerogative of mercy on matters of reprieves and pardons. In the period before the death penalty was abolished in 1965, the Home Secretary made decisions as to whether to reprieve condemned persons or let them hang. Chuter Ede, the Home Secretary in 1950 decided that the case against Timothy Evans was strong enough to allow him to hang for the murder of his wife and daughter. A later Home Secretary in 1966, Roy Jenkins, decided that a posthumous pardon was the the right course of action, given the possibility of the involvement of John Reginald

Christie who lived at the same address as Evans and was subsequently hanged for the murder of at least six women whose bodies were found in the house at 10 Rillington Place in 1953. There were many other high-profile cases involving the death penalty and much subsequent public discussion and disquiet, particularly in the cases of Derek Bentley, James Hanratty and Ruth Ellis. Ellis was the last woman to be hanged in this country on 13 July 1955, provoking the headline in *The Mirror*, 'Should Hanging be Stopped?'.

Despite its abolition, death penalty cases continue to involve the Home Secretary and in 1992 Kenneth Clarke announced that he had rejected the application for a posthumous pardon for Derek Bentley who was hanged aged 19 in 1953 for the murder of PC Sydney Miles. Bentley and an accomplice, Christopher Craig, had broken into a warehouse in Tamworth Road, Croydon. They had been seen climbing over the gate and the police were alerted. As the murder was a joint enterprise, the execution was legal although by today's standards considered harsh as Craig, who was by law too young at 16 to be executed, had pulled the trigger that had killed the police officer. Craig was released from prison in 1963 but the campaign to get Bentley pardoned continues and the case was submitted to the newly formed Criminal Cases Review Commission in 1997 and was heard by the Court of Appeal in 1998.

Parliament and the Select Committee on Home Affairs

A system of select committees was introduced in 1979 allowing for committees of the House of Commons to monitor the work of government departments. The Select Committee on Home Affairs has over the years held public hearings and issued reports on a number of criminal justice topics such as improving the machinery for investigating complaints against the police (1981), administration of the prison service (1981), the state and use of prisons (1987). Similar topics have been revisited in recent years: police disciplinary codes and complaints procedure (1997–8), and the use of custody in 1998.

The committee can ask interested witnesses to give evidence before it and senior civil servants and agency heads may also be required to give evidence. The 1997 inquiry into police disciplinary codes and complaints procedure heard evidence from Paul Condon, the Metropolitan Police Commissioner, Barbara Mills, head of the Crown Prosecution Service, as well as from the Police Federation, Police Superintendents' Association, Police Complaints Authority, and the pressure group Liberty. In 1997 Frederick Crawford, chairman of the new Criminal Cases Review Commission, gave evidence about the work of the commission, and the Lord Chancellor, Lord Irvine, gave evidence about the work of the Lord Chancellor's Department. The Committee can set its own agenda and may develop its own particular perspective on issues. Its prison reductionist agenda has been apparent for some time regardless of the party in government. In 1998 the Committee inquired into the use of custody and alternatives to prison sentences with the aim of seeking 'to reduce the prison population' (Home Affairs Committee, Press Notice, 31 July 1997).

In January 1998 the committee published a report which was very critical of the existing procedure for dealing with complaints against the police, outlined in Chapter 4. Its 43 recommendations included proposals to improve the system of dealing with corruption by police officers and reforming the complaints and disciplinary system. The report sought a change to the rules in disciplinary hearings involving police officers moving away from the existing standard of proof, beyond reasonable doubt, as used in criminal court cases, to the civil court standard based on the balance of probabilities. Furthermore, at present an officer acquitted in a criminal case will not face subsequent disciplinary charges. While open to the argument of double jeopardy the report recommends allowing the possibility of further action when an officer is found not guilty in court. Other recommendations related to holding disciplinary meetings in public and making it easier to sack police officers who are guilty of serious misconduct. These views were accepted by the Home Secretary who announced reforms, to take effect in 1999, to the way the police complaints and disciplinary system works (see later in this chapter).

Established parliamentary lobby groups also work within Westminster. The Parliamentary All-Party Penal Affairs Group (PAPPAG) started in 1979 and is aided by a clerk, Paul Cavadino, who worked as the senior information officer for NACRO. This lobby group has led the prison reductionist argument in Parliament with considerable success. For example, the introduction of statutory criteria for the use of custody for those under 21 in the Criminal Justice Act 1982 led to a substantial drop in the use of custody with offenders under 21. Other campaigns have not been so successful as with the attempts to reform the mandatory life sentence for murder.

Reformers have persuaded Parliament to take a lead on some criminal justice issues such as the abolition of the death penalty against the wishes of the majority of the voting public. Since the Murder (Abolition of the Death Penalty) Act 1965, the House of Commons has held 14 debates and votes between 1969 and 1994 and each time there was a clear majority against the restoration of capital punishment. Public opinion has consistently shown about a 70 to 30 per cent divide in favour of the death penalty but, despite this, MPs have consistently voted against its restoration. This is possibly because the government of the day has not regarded this issue as a matter of government or party political policy but left it to a 'free vote' in which MPs are asked to follow their conscience.

Europeanisation of criminal justice policy

The increasing interdependency of the European states has meant that many policy developments are no longer the sole responsibility of Parliament in the UK and today policy is shaped by a need to take account of other jurisdictions.

most notably those in the European Union. Apart from the gradual process of European harmonisation, the exploitation of relaxed border controls and new forms of crime have prompted the governments of Europe to take initiatives to combat cross-jurisdictional crimes such as drug trafficking and international fraud. Cross-jurisdictional co-operation, such as that outlined in Chapter 4, has become essential given the limitations of crime policy based on the nation state and its restricted geographical boundaries.

In January 1998 the British Government took over the presidency of the European Union. Countries take it in turn for a 6-month period and crime issues feature large in the rhetoric of each country's agenda for the period. Jack Straw, as Home Secretary, declared that, 'Organised crime is no respecter of borders and it is crucial that we recognise that reality' (*The Daily Telegraph*, 29 December 1997: 2). The areas of primary concern were identified as paedophiles, drug trafficking, money laundering, electronic fraud and industrial and political espionage. Priority was given to improving arrangements for the extradition of suspects, introducing video links to interview suspects and witnesses and greater powers to intercept messages sent via the internet, referring to the cyber-criminals such as terrorists groups and paedophiles who use modern technology, especially coded e-mail messages, to organise their criminal activity.

In 1995 all members of the European Union agreed to the establishment of Europol (see Chapter 4). The UK became the first country in the European Union to ratify the Europol Convention in December 1996 which provided for a pan-European law enforcement organisation for the exchange and analysis of crime intelligence responsible for drug trafficking, unregulated dealing in nuclear and radioactive substances, illegal immigrant smuggling, motor vehicle crime and terrorism.

In Moscow in January 1997 Michael Howard, the Home Secretary, met the Russian Interior Minister to discuss greater co-operation to deal with organised crime. He commented:

Serious, dangerous criminals do not respect national borders. . . . Organised criminals run their operations across the whole of Europe, including Russia. We need to find their ring-leaders and bring them to justice. The UK has helped set up Europol – for the exchange and analysis of criminal intelligence which will help catch and convict international villains.

(Home Office press release, 25 January 1997)

International co-operation

Bilateral agreements between two countries to combat crime indicate the greater cross-jurisdictional awareness among governments of the need to co-operate to deal with a problem that is not retricted within national boundaries. Successful criminals have exploited the differences in the law and legal procedures to avoid detection or, if discovered, prosecution.

Bilateral international co-operation has been given a lead by the USA. The UK/USA Drugs Agreement of 1988 provides for co-operation in the investigation of drug-trafficking offences, the freezing and confiscation of the proceeds of drug-related crimes, providing for the exchange of document and banking evidence, allows for the transfer of prisoners with their consent to give evidence, and carrying out requests to search and seize property. On 2ᵗ February 1997 Poland and the UK signed a mutual co-operation agreement to work together to deal with the illegal distribution of weapons, drugs and organised crime. This allows for swifter extradition orders, intelligence gathering on illegal arms and drug sales and powers to confiscate the proceeds of crime that have been moved between the jurisdictions. Poland signed a similar agreement with the USA in 1996.

International co-operation involved the Forensic Science Service (FSS conducting DNA tests in 1992 in response to the Russian Government's approach to check the remains of a group of people, thought to be the remains of the Romanov family, the Russian royal family that disappeared, presumed murdered on the night of 16 July 1918, or soon after. Using bone material the FSS concluded that the DNA test supports the view that the family found in the mass grave was the Romanovs.

International co-operation is increasingly evident between the 176 member countries of Interpol. Within the National Criminal Intelligence Service (NCIS), Customs and Excise manage a network of Drugs Liaison officers (DLOs) who work with their counterparts in Europe and around the world. The success of the policing of Euro 96, when between a quarter and half a million foreign football supporters came to England, was due in part to the role played by the NCIS who helped to plan the policing of this event by putting together a team of experts on football hooliganism from different forces across the country, and liaison officers from each of the competing countries, as well as relying on information from Interpol.

Politicians and political parties

Policy cannot be divorced from politics and crime is a salient issue on the political agenda in the UK. As seen in the earlier section of this chapter, the Home Secretary plays a high-profile role in the politics of law and order and in influencing policy developments. Politicians quite properly talk about issues which worry the public and there can be little doubt that crime is a major election topic.

But who do the politicians listen to? We can see from the previous section of this chapter that, on the issue of the restoration of the death penalty politicians chose to disregard public opinion. However, they cannot completely ignore the public mood among voters and the fact that they can afford to do this at all illustrates the nature of the system of parliamentary government. Political office, and hence influence on decision making, depends on

ie fortunes of political parties in which voters primarily focus upon decid-
ig which political party they wish to see in office. The democratic process
ieans that politicians are at the centre of a number of influences and ideas
bout how best to respond to crime.

Politicians can provide leadership on issues such as hanging but will follow
ie public mood on other matters. They also have to negotiate their position
'ithin the party and the annual party conference. Politicians are answerable
ɔ their party activists and even Ministers may feel embarrassed by the need
ɔ explain themselves and their policies to the annual party conference. William
Vhitelaw, a Conservative Party Home Secretary (1979–83), regarded as a
beral on sentencing matters, wrote that he 'dreaded and disliked the pros-
ect of the law and order debate, for the atmosphere was so strangely hostile
nd so different from that accorded to one's colleagues' (Whitelaw 1989).

There was a time when crime policy was not at the centre of party political
isagreement with a cross-party consensus about many aspects of criminal
istice policy, but in the 1950s and 1960s crime issues started becoming
iore politicised. There are those who blame right-wing politicians for ex-
loiting the fear of crime issues by presenting their opponents as soft on
rime. Another factor was the level of public interest in the death penalty.
he moves towards abolition in 1957 and 1965 involved parliamentary deb-
ites that generated considerable media coverage and public interest. What it
ighlighted, of course, was the strong division between parliamentary opin-
ɔn as represented by MPs who voted for abolition and the public who then,
s now, wish to retain the death penalty. It seems likely that public interest in
iatters of law and order may well have been stimulated initially by the high
rofile given to the death penalty debate, as well as by the steady rise in the
ecorded crime from 1950 to 1990.

In the 1979 General Election, the Conservative Party was able to represent
he Labour Party as soft on crime and the criminal. (See the poster repro-
uced in Figure 11.1.) In recent elections the Labour Party have sought to
hange their image as being the softer party on matters of crime. In 1994
he Labour Party spokesman for Home Affairs, Tony Blair, popularised the
logan that a Labour Government would be 'tough on crime and tough on
he causes of crime'. These causes may well include wider social factors. Thus
e argued:

> nobody excuses crime because of social conditions but it is plain common sense
> that if young people are brought up in a culture of no job prospects, poor educa-
> tion, violence, drug abuse and family instability then they are less likely to grow up
> as individually responsible citizens.
>
> (*The Guardian*, 21 March 1994)

Political controversy is likely to continue even though the ideological gap
etween the parties has narrowed dramatically on the issue of crime. There
as been, for example, considerable political disagreement over the extent
ɔ which rising crime can be attributed to greed or badness on the part of

Fig 11.1 Conservative Party publicity on crime in the 1979 General Election

MUGGING UP 204%*
CRIMINAL DAMAGE UP 135%†
ROBBERY UP 88%†

Labour's record on crime is criminal. Crime is one of the few things in Britain that is booming under Labour.

In England and Wales last year, over 800,000 more crimes were recorded than in 1973. That's a rise of almost 50%. And yet since Labour came to power, police strength has risen by a mere 7%.

Perhaps if Labour had been more concerned with creating wealth rather than re-distributing it, they might have found it easier to be able to afford to increase policemen's pay. But it's not just more pay our policemen need.

The Government have a duty to be seen to support law and order, to protect people and property.

It certainly doesn't make the police's job any easier when some Labour Ministers are seen associating themselves with potentially violent situations, as they did at Grunwick last year.

The police are doing a difficult job, in difficult times-and they need the support of all the people-and that includes Government Ministers.

Many policemen feel there's only one way they can make the Government understand their plight. And that's by leaving the force.

IS IT SAFE TO VOTE FOR ANOTHER LABOUR GOVERNMENT?

VOTE CONSERVATIVE X

* Figure for London between 1973–1977. † Home Office Annual Criminal Statistics for England and Wales between 1973–1977

individuals, to family problems or problem families, or whether it is related to wider social factors such as unemployment. The Conservative Party expressed the following view during the 1987 General Election:

> The origins of crime lie deep in society in families where parents do not support or control their children; in schools where discipline is poor and in the wider world where violence is glamourised and traditional values are under attack.

Suggestions of a link between crime and unemployment, poverty or deprivation were dismissed as, in effect, excusing crime. In 1988 Margaret Thatcher commented that:

> If anyone else is to blame it is the professional progressives among broadcasters, social workers and politicians who have created a fog of excuses in which the mugger and burglar operate.

> (Loveday 1992: 302)

The link between poverty and crime was rejected in a Conservative Political Centre pamphlet in 1994. David Hunt, the Employment Secretary at the time, wrote:

> some of the so-called cultures springing up in our country reject all decency and civilised values . . . the bulk of thieving today, of course, has nothing to do with poverty. It is the result of wickedness and greed.

> (*The Guardian*, 21 March 1994)

ressure and interest groups

olitical parties are not the only representative groups to engage in debates out crime. A number of other bodies representing professional interests so contribute to discussions of crime policy. They may participate officially Royal Commissions, appear on current affairs programmes or contribute ewspaper articles. These bodies include, as we stated earlier in the chapter, the Police Federation, ACPO, NAPO, POA, the Bar Council, the Law Society, nd the Justices' Clerks Society. Voluntary groups such as the Magistrates' ssociation and the National Association of Victim Support also contribute this way.

Pressure groups also have an important role in shaping attitudes about enal policy. The Howard League for Penal Reform, the Prison Reform Trust nd the National Association for the Care and Resettlement of Offenders NACRO) have played a key role in changing opinions. NACRO, for ex-mple, carries out research, sponsors projects, runs conferences and provides uch useful information to its members, along with schools, colleges, journal-ts, policy makers, politicians and academics. NACRO aims to ensure that ne case for improved prison conditions and less frequent use of custodial entences is put effectively both in Parliament and in the mass media.

In a study of the impact of pressure groups on penal policy, Ryan (1978) escribes the history of the Howard League and the considerable influence xercised by its representatives Margery Fry and George Benson MP, during ne 1950s and 1960s, in Whitehall and Westminister. It was an acceptable ressure group: reliable, practical and trusted. In contrast, Ryan outlines the te of RAP (Radical Alternatives to Prison), which did not have status as an cceptable pressure group in its campaign to abolish all prisons. The differ-nces in resources, contacts, access and the degree of ideological congruence etween lobbyist and officials are important if a group is to have an influence n public policy.

The mass media has considerable influence on the way policies are pre-ented. The opportunity for making political gains are evident if a good ound bite or slogan can be found. In the 1979 General Election campaign ne Conservative Party, on advice from Saatchi and Saatchi, ran a poster ampaign on the theme of crime and whether it was safe to vote for Jim Callaghan's Labour Government. The poster, shown in Figure 11.1, made se of official statistics to highlight the growth of mugging, robbery and riminal damage.

Media

ome people find out about crime and form views on the basis of their own xperiences or those of their family, friends or neighbours. In large part, owever, their views are also influenced by information in newspapers or on

359

television. This may include coverage of individual cases, and some ma
follow discussions on crime by politicians and commentators.

Most people are influenced to some extent by the mass media – news
papers, television, books or films. This is because the majority of the publi
have limited first-hand knowledge about crime or the criminal justice syste
unless they are victims or perpetrators. Newspapers and television coverag
of crime stories will influence people's knowledge about crime and ma
enhance their fear of becoming a victim. Media coverage in itself may affe
people's behaviour – women and the elderly, for example, are often scared t
walk the streets at night for fear of being raped or mugged, and parents ma
be frightened to let their children out of the house alone through fear o
kidnapping, sexual assault or murder.

Crime is, of course, a popular subject in the mass media and, as man
point out, crime, especially sexual crime, sells newspapers (see, for exampl
Schlesinger and Tumber 1994; Soothill and Walby 1991). Crime dramas ar
also extremely popular, as seen in the high ratings given to TV detective
such as Inspectors Morse, Taggart or Wexford. Few, of course, believe tha
drama gives a real picture of crime or policing – otherwise the murder rate i
Oxford, Glasgow or Kingsmarkham would be the subject of national concer
and police clear-up rates would be vastly improved!

A new type of television documentary such as Crime Watch UK ha
become popular in recent years in which the police provide information an
CCTV photographs to encourage the public to telephone in with informa
tion about crimes and suspects. Police videos are broadcast on television tha
show drivers at their worst, as in Police, Camera, Action! Thus informatio
blends with entertainment.

High-profile cases provide a fascination that might be untypical and coul
lead people to draw general conclusions based on limited knowledge gleane
from such cases as the Louise Woodward trial in Massachusetts. Dere
Bentley and Myra Hindley have become household names because of th
interest taken by the mass media. But the focus on these selective and unusu
cases may not provide for a reliable impression of the crime problem. Thi
selectivity means that a very unrepresentative picture of crime may be give
by the media. From all the possible news stories about crime, the media ca
only select a small number. This selection will depend on decisions as t
whether or not such stories are newsworthy. What makes a story newsworth
is likely to be its novelty or dramatic elements. Thus cases reported in news
papers are likely to be unusual or have elements capable of providing dram
or titillation (Chibnall 1977; Soothill and Walby 1991). Most researche
would appear to agree, for example, that sexual and violent crimes, whic
play on the public's fear, are more likely to be reported than more commo
kinds of crime such as theft or vandalism (Ditton and Duffy 1983). I
addition, these kinds of crime are also selectively reported with an ove
emphasis on, for example, serial killers or rapists (Soothill 1993). Many hav

rgued that the reporting of rape tends to focus on the 'sex fiend' who attacks women in public places, whereas in reality women are more likely to be aped in private places, by people they know (Soothill 1993).

Newspaper reports also tend to simplify crime stories, providing little by way of extended analysis (Schlesinger and Tumber 1994). News reports about crimes are necessarily abbreviated accounts of events, focusing on those aspects considered likely to attract the public's attention. This is also the case when the criminal statistics are reported. Although these are complex documents requiring careful interpretation, reports in the media tend to focus on simple questions about whether some kinds of crime have risen or fallen.

The media may also set in train what is called a moral panic about a particular kind of crime (Cohen 1980). This happens where a spectacular incident or series of incidents – for example, a riot, a series of child abuse cases, or someone being killed by joyriders – alerts the public to a particular problem. The media may effectively create a new form of crime as the example of road rage and horse slashers demonstrates. Road rage was a term coined to describe violent incidents between motorists triggered by a dispute over such things as parking, driving styles or accidents. In 1992 a series of injuries to horses in certain areas of the country caused great public outrage and anxiety, with newspaper articles about attacks on horses. Many routine equine injuries were attributed to 'horse-slashers'. Yet of course, horse slashing, however unpleasant for its victims, is scarcely a typical crime.

The press are blamed by some criminologists for generating public anxiety in order to sell newspapers. However, many of these stories are newsworthy not just because they are printed in the papers but because they capture a fascination about a bizarre or horrific event that would be in itself of public interest. Deviancy, as the sociologist Emile Durkheim pointed out, provides a community with a concrete example of unacceptable and censored behaviour and thus gives a collective focus to re-evaluate and rethink its values. The press might also justify their coverage as campaigning newspapers when the criminal justice system appears to let victims down or wrongly convicts an innocent person. Campaigning programmes on the television and reports in the press have helped to clear innocent people and convict guilty ones. Frustration with the lack of action in the murder inquiry following the death of the black teenager Stephen Lawrence led the *Daily Mail* to take the unprecedented step of printing the names of five men they believed responsible for his death under the headline, 'Murderers'. The *Daily Mail* commented:

> We are naming them because, despite a criminal case, a private prosecution and an inquest, there has still been no justice for Stephen. . . . One or more of the five may have a valid defence to the charge which has been repeatedly levelled against them. So far they have steadfastly refused every opportunity to offer such a defence.
>
> (*Daily Mail*, 14 February 1997: 1)

IMPLEMENTING CRIMINAL JUSTICE POLICY

Co-ordinating criminal justice

Developments within the international community to improve co-operation on matters of crime have helped bring attention to the need to do more to promote better co-ordination within the criminal justice system in England and Wales. This has many parts and, like the twelve blind men describing different parts of the elephant (see Preface to this edition), has many different agencies with distinctive functions and styles of operating. This fragmentation leads to discorrespondence in two senses of the word; in that agencies do not always communicate effectively with each other, and, that the work of different agencies does not always fit together to provide for an efficient system. The origins of the fragmentation are complex and are to do with the distinctive constitutional, political and cultural histories of the agencies and professions, each having a unique agenda of interests and concerns. The judiciary in England and Wales come from a strong profession with deep traditional roots that are well embedded in the system of power and influence in this country. Thus when issues of policy such as a proposal for a sentencing commission is perceived as threatening the independence of the judiciary we can be sure that much pressure will be brought to reformulate the proposal. Traffic wardens, in contrast, do not have this degree of influence.

Co-ordination between agencies has also been a problem because of the principles inherent in our adversarial system, which puts the offender in centre stage with defence counsel and probation officers taking a pro defendant line and the police and prosecutors doing their best to convict the accused. The combative nature of the contest encourages strategies among the participants, such as appealing to prejudice, lack of frankness regarding the facts, and undermining the confidence of a witness, which may have more to do with winning the case rather than discovering the truth, with public interest and justice sometimes taking second place. The different working cultures adds to the difficulties of getting better co-operation between the agencies.

Until the 1950s governments took an interest in but did not seek to directly intervene on routine matters best left to judges and other professional groups. A more interventionist role for government on matters of crime control was revealed in the white paper, *Penal Practice in a Changing Society* published in 1959:

> The Government's responsibility does not end with ensuring that the efficiency of the police is maintained and that the courts are equipped with adequate machinery Behind these front lines of defence the counter-attack on crime must be mounted It is to the development of the means of dealing with the individual offender who has been sentenced by the courts to some form of detention that this Paper is principally directed.
>
> (Home Office, 1959: s. 16

It has fallen to the Home Office to take on the task of organising and planning an approach to crime control that is more comprehensive than maintaining law-enforcement agencies and punishment options. This task involves the need to develop strategies at a number of levels, provide adequate funding and most difficult to achieve co-ordination between the differing agencies involved on both the 'front line' and in the 'counter-attack on crime'.

Since Leon Brittan's period at the Home Office there has been a more concerted effort to generate greater attention to inter-agency consultation and regard for the general objectives of the criminal justice system as a whole. This has involved two developments in which the Government has come to take a more central and corporatist role to crime and widened its approach by moving from a reactive to a preventative approach to crime; and, secondly, by taking the initiative to co-ordinate the activities of the different criminal justice agencies, which because of their own institutional histories have tended to regard themselves as not part of a system.

The problems of co-ordination are threefold: firstly, getting agencies performing the same tasks to work together (for example, will the Metropolitan Police Force co-operate with an investigation originating from the Merseyside Police?); secondly, getting the different agencies in a region to work more co-operatively together (for example, the probation and prison services having an integrated post-release supervision programme for prisoners before and after release); and, thirdly, ensuring that the regional work of the agencies operates within a framework of priorities that reflect national and, nowadays, internationally established objectives.

One solution to improve the collaboration between the police and the CPS, was proposed in a Labour Party document, *The Case for the Prosecution*, in April 1997. It proposed the creation of 42 CPS areas to relace the current 13 to coincide with the police forces in England and Wales (the London area CPS to cover the work of the Metropolitan and the City of London police).

Awareness of the way that administrative boundaries provide potential hindrance to crime prevention and investigation is revealed in a survey of 39 police forces in England and Wales. *Tackling Cross Border Crime* (Porter 1997). Its main recommendations were to encourage neighbouring forces to establish collaborative arrangements, such as regional crime groups to share intelligence on crime and criminals, and appointing inter-force liaison officers and joint operation teams.

Another report, *Getting to Grips with Crime – A New Framework for Local Action* (Home Office 1997b), proposed a new statutory duty on the local authority to take into account the impact of crime when making decisions on planning, housing, social service and locating schools. The intention is to make the police and local authorities jointly responsible for crime prevention and in meeting targets for crime reduction set by the Home Secretary. Recognising that the police cannot combat crime on their own, and building on the Safer Cities and Crime Concern experiments in multi-agency co-operation the report makes it clear that business, health authorities, schools, colleges and local people have their part to play in crime reduction strategies. Targets will be set and the police and local authorities will be expected to provide leadership for a co-operative community-wide approach to crime. Local crime audits will be required, with published targets for reducing crime and monitoring of the results.

At the national level the *National Criminal Intelligence Service* (NCIS), referred to in Chapter 4, was established in 1992 to co-ordinate the approaches of law enforcement agencies. It provides nationwide and international intelligence to law enforcement agencies by collecting and analysing information about serious and organised crime. The NCIS gathers information on offenders engaged in money laundering, gun running, counterfeiting, drug trafficking, paedophile groups and on potential violence at football matches. It provides the British link with Interpol. The NCIS represents the police and 12 other law enforcement agencies and has staff from the police, Customs and Excise and the Home Office. John Abbott was appointed as its first Director General in 1998.

The Police Act 1997 provided for another new agency, *National Crime Squad*, to deal with crime across police areas in England and Wales and the NCIS to cover the whole of the UK and to provide co-operation with European police forces. John Wheeler was appointed in July 1997 as chairman of the two service authorities who oversee the work of the NCIS and the National Crime Squad. The National Crime Squad is the first operational national police force in this country although it is not envisaged as the British equivalent of the FBI and will work though existing police forces and regional crime squads. The National Crime Squad started operating on 1 April 1998, with 1,450 detectives seconded from local forces and regional crime squads. It operates from 44 centres across the country. The first Director General, Roy Penrose, sees a major role for the squad being to combat organised criminal drug groups and, in addition, to pursue 'about 180 major British criminals, and their teams, and this could take them to Europe' (*The Guardian*, 13 March 1998: 7).

The *Criminal Justice Consultative Council* (CJCC) was established in 1991 to promote greater awareness between agencies of their common purpose. The first recommendation of the Woolf Report on prison unrest in 1990 was the need for closer cooperation between the different parts of the criminal justice system and proposed a national forum and local committees. The CJCC was given the task of improving communications, co-operation and co-ordination by improving consultation and information sharing. To help do this it publishes an annual report. It was set up with 23 area committees and membership is drawn from the judiciary, police, social services, criminal justice agencies and government departments. In 1997 the chairman, Lord Justice Rose, said that the CJCC provided a unique opportunity to promote 'a greater awareness between agencies of their common purpose'. It has looked at video evidence fast tracking cases involving child witnesses, racial issues, and standardising definitions in child abuse cases.

Lay participation

An unprecedented role in criminal justice in England and Wales is played by unpaid volunteers who contribute in many different ways. There are over 30,000 lay magistrates whose vital role in pre-trial procedure and in making decisions about guilt and sentencing is described in Chapter 6. Victim Support is a charity that provides practical and emotional support to victims of crime. The Home Office in 1998 funded 500 paid co-ordinators who supervised 11,250 volunteers. There are special constables and lay visitors to police stations and Boards of Visitors for each prison.

The significance of lay participants has to be understood in terms of a political culture in which society has not wanted to become over-reliant on state functionaries and professional elites. This aspect of civil liberties is often misunderstood by those who question the representativeness of magistrates. They represent decision makers who do not have to take orders from government or follow the strictures of professional interest. They represent the laity and are expected to bring a common sense to the process of decision making. This may not make better decisions but it might at important times represent another point of view independent of the latest orthodoxy as laid down by government or professions.

There are 130 Boards of Visitors in England and Wales, one for each prison and young offender institution. These were established under the Prison Act 1952, and each has on average 15 lay members who receive no payment. They are independent of the prison service and must provide an annual report to the Home Secretary on the running of the prison. They must visit the prison regularly and hear complaints from prisoners and have a general concern for the treatment of inmates. The report from the Board of Visitors at Whitemoor Prison correctly predicted future security problems before the escape from their maximum security unit in 1994. The 1997 annual report of the Board of Visitors at Wormwood Scrubs Prison referred to allegations of abuse and assaults of inmates by prison officers. In March 1998 several officers were suspended awaiting investigations of these allegations by the police.

In 1983 pilot schemes introduced lay visitors to police stations after recommendations in the Scarman Report on the Brixton riots in 1981. 'I recommend provision for random checks by persons other than police officers on the interrogation and detention of suspects in the police station' (Scarman 1982: para. 7.7–7.10). In 1986 a Home Office circular recommended that they be established in all areas. Lay visitors to police stations are volunteers aged between 18 and 70, but Justices of the Peace, retired police officers and people convicted of a serious crime cannot be appointed. Lay visitors have the right to visit police stations to check on the treatment of people held in custody. They may arrive unannounced, and usually in pairs, and the police must allow them immediate access to custody areas of the police station. They will typically ask the custody officer how many detainees are being held and are then shown around the cells, escorted by an officer. Cells that a occupied will be opened and the officer will tell the detainees the reason f the visit and asked whether they would talk with the visitors. If they agree th will be asked questions about how long they have been held by the police, hav they contacted a solicitor, do their relatives know they are here, and wheth they have received food and drink. If any of the detainees are drunk, viole or hostile the visitors may talk to them through the grill in the cell door. La visitors are expected to talk with all those detained in police custody and th prepare a report. The report is sent to the secretary of the lay visitor pan and a copy to the officer in charge of the police station. If they find anythir wrong in their visits they should talk directly with the officer in charge of t station and expect an immediate response.

Under new management: privatisation and agency status

The political economy of crime control has changed in a very obvious sens in the 1990s, during which a shift from the public to commercial sector ha taken place. Some Prisons are now run by Group 4, Securicor, Wackenhu Corporation and UK Detention Service Ltd and a private security industr at least the size of the police service provides security for paying client Business interests are evident in other ways such as sponsorship of Safer Cit and Crime Concern projects. Finance and auditing methods have change for those agencies remaining within the public sector. The prison service now an executive agency with control over the budget allocated to it. Th police service must now charge the economic costs for activities such a maintaining order at football matches.

In addition to the greater privatisation and commercialisation of the secto and the devolution of budgets there has been an associated change in th culture of management in which a more aggressive accounting approach i adopted by management with performance indicators used to assess eff ciency. The Conservative Governments of the 1980s were determined t tackle what was regarded as a corporatist and overly intrusive system of gov ernment that generated a bureaucratic and costly approach to public secto funding and management. By 1990 reform ideas were emerging by which th public sector agencies had to cope with objectives that could be measured b performance indicators relating objectives to funding.

The police and prison service were to undergo radical organisational an managerial reforms. The prison service had been involved in a long runnin battle with the Prison Officers' Association over the way prisons were man aged. In 1978 the *Committee of Inquiry into the United Kingdom Prison Servic* (Home Office 1979) was set up following 'a long period of deterioratin industrial relations, especially in England and Wales' (para. 1). A new pa structure was established under the Fresh Start programme in 1987 bu industrial conflict was to continue. In this historical context the late 1980 nd 1990s saw the introduction of initiatives to save money and undermine aditional styles of doing business that included: private prisons, new funding initiatives such as the Private Finance Initiative (PFI) to raise capital om the private sector, financial targets, Key Performance Targets, and structural reforms that redesignating the prison service as an executive agency, nd the contracting out of prison escort work. They bore the hallmarks of the ew management culture.

MONITORING, ACCOUNTABILITY AND COMPLAINTS

By the 1990s the new management culture went hand in hand with new ideas about monitoring performance and the accountability of the services. The political agenda on accountability had moved on from the political issues raised about who controls police work and how is it to be accountable o the local community to monitoring in a very different sense in terms of auditing performance targets set centrally but delivered locally. The agencies had to meet specific criteria established by Key Performance Indicators (KPIs) and respond to a new breed of HM inspectors who monitored regimes in prisons and the performance of the probation and the police services. KPIs provide targets by which agency performance can be measured. For the probation service, KPI 1 aims 'to lower the actual reconviction rates for all types of order and achieve rates lower than those predicted'. This is monitored by the Home Office. The CPS in 1994/5 met the target of maintaining an average processing period of less than 3 months in the magistrates' courts. The objectives and the KPIs for the police and the prison service are given in detail in the next section.

Key performance indicators: police

Police forces must monitor their performance against five performance targets set by the Home Secretary. The Home Secretary's key objectives for policing were issued in 1995 and the KPIs used to assess these are as follows:

Policing objectives and KPIs (in brackets)

1. To maintain and if possible increase the number of detections for violent crimes (KPI: number of violent crimes detected per 100 officers).

2. To increase the number of detections for burglaries of people's homes (KPI: number of burglaries of dwellings detected per 100 officers).

3. To target and prevent crimes which are a particular problem in partner ship with the public and other local agencies (no KPI).

4. To provide high visibility policing as to reassure the public (KPIs: Publi satisfaction with the levels of foot and mobile patrols/number of polic officers available for ordinary duty per 1,000 population/proportion o uniformed constables' time spent in public).

5. To respond promptly to emergency calls from the public. (KPIs: the per centage of 999 calls answered within the local target time/the percentag of responses within the local target time to incidents requiring immediat response).

The local forces will establish their own targets. For instance, in the case o objective 5 they will have to decide their local target time for answering 99 calls, and the time to reach the incident in the case of an emergency cal requiring an immediate response. They will then, at the end of the year calculate what proportion of calls are answered within that target time. Mos forces aim to answer a 999 call within 10 to 15 seconds. In Cambridgeshir in 1995/6 they sought to answer 999 calls within 12 seconds and did thi in 80 per cent of all such calls. In responding to emergencies that require immediate response, they set themselves a target of 10 minutes in urba areas and 18 minutes in rural areas, targets which were met in 72 per cent o call outs.

Key performance indicators: prisons

While the police force have targets against established KPIs set locally, prison service targets are set centrally. The *Prison Service Annual Report and Account* shows the performance of the prison service with respect to KPIs (detailed below). Thus one objective, keeping prisoners in custody, is measured by the number of escapes from prisons and escorts. In 1996/7 the prison service se itself the target that no Category A prisoner would escape. It met this target. To assess how well the prison service met the objectives of helping to prepare prisoners for their return to the community they used a KPI which looked at the number of prisoners completing accredited programmes in reducing re-offending. The target for 1996/7 was aimed at getting 1,300 prisoners to complete accredited programmes. In that year 1,373 courses were completed (*Prison Service Annual Report and Accounts:* 6).

Prison Service objectives and KPIs (in brackets)

1. Keep prisoners in custody (KPI 1: The number of escapes from prison and escorts).

. Maintain order, control discipline and a safe environment (KPI 2: The number of assaults on staff, prisoners and others which results in a disciplinary adjudication. KPI 3: The rate of positive random drug testing).

. Provide decent conditions for prisoners and meet their needs, including health care (KPI 4: The number of prisoners held in units of accommodation intended for fewer prisoners).

. Provide positive regimes which help prisoners address their offending behaviour and allow them as full and responsible a life as possible (KPI 5: The number of hours which, on average, prisoners spend in purposeful activities. KPI 6: The proportion of prisoners held in prisons where all prisoners on standard or enhanced regimes are unlocked for at least 10 hours on a weekday).

. Help prisoners to prepare for their return to the community (KPI 7: The number of prisoners completing programmes accredited as effective in reducing re-offending).

. Deliver prison services using the resources provided by Parliament with maximum efficiency (KPI 8: The average cost of a prison place. KPI 9: The amount of staff training).

Her Majesty's Inspectors

There is a system of inspection for magistrates' courts, prisons, police and probation. Her Majesty's Inspectors provide independent expert advice to the Secretary of State. They may publish detailed reports on specific inquiries conducted and are required to produce an annual report for Parliament on the efficiency and effectiveness of the organisations for which they have responsibility.

• Her Majesty's Inspector of Constabulary was established in 1865. It is not primarily a policy-making body and its main function is monitoring, although it offers a source of consultation and advice on objectives, performance indicators, and on senior police appointments. It helps to disseminate good practice throughout the 43 forces in England and Wales. The annual report provides a source of information on the overall picture of police work in England and Wales such that in 1996/7 we learn that the police responded to just under 19 million incidents, 7 million 999 calls and made 1.75 million arrests. The report provides basic information about the size of the 43 forces and their performance against the Home Secretary's objectives. Home Office policies on policing and local targets are set out in the police authority's policing plans.

- The probation service inspectorate was established in 1936. The current system of inspection was established in 1985 and given a statutory role in the Criminal Justice Act 1991. The first annual report from Her Majesty's Inspectorate of Probation was published in 1994. It covers all of the 54 probation areas in England and Wales. The Chief Inspector is Graham Smith. The inspectorate looks at all aspects of the work of probation officers, including their role in the magistrates' and Crown Courts.

- Her Majesty's Inspector of Prisons reports on specific aspects of operations within a prison following a visit as well as on general issues affecting prisons. The focus is on management practice, spreading good practice and identifying bad practice. In December 1995, David Ramsbotham was appointed Chief Inspector of Prisons.

- Her Majesty's Magistrates' Courts Service Inspectorate (MCSI) started in 1995 and was given statutory authority by the Police and Magistrates Courts Act 1994. It reports to the Lord Chancellor's Department. Its task is to inspect and report on the organisation and administration of magistrates' courts for each magistrates' courts committee area. It is not involved in considering the judicial process or decision making. The Chief Inspector in 1996 was Rosemary Melling.

Complaints: Prison Ombudsman

The Prison Ombudsman was set up in 1994 following the recommendations of the Woolf Report 1991. The report referred to the importance 'of a proper balance between security and control on the one hand and humanity and justice on the other' (Home Office 1991a: para. 10.44). It went on specifically to recommend an independent complaints adjudicator to investigate individual grievances and act as the final avenue of appeal against findings of disciplinary hearings (paragraph 14.347). The Government accepted the need for an independent element in the complaints procedure and the 1991 white paper *Custody, Care and Justice* (Home Office 1991c) stated, 'there should be an independent avenue of appeal against disciplinary findings once avenues within the prison service have been exhausted' and 'appeals against decisions made in response to complaints should also be considered by the same independent body' (para. 8.8).

Appointed by the Home Secretary, the Prison Ombudsman only considers grievances from prisoners, including those about disciplinary offences, once all internal procedures have been exhausted. (These start with grievance complaints to the wing governor, the governor of the prison, to the Prison Service and then beyond that to the Prison Ombudsman.) The Ombudsman is able to investigate nearly all matters for which the prison service is currently responsible with respect to individual prisoners, including contracted-out prisons and contracted-out services within a prison.

The Prison Ombudsman only takes complaints from prisoners or their legal representative acting on their behalf; he does not act on complaints from relatives, neighbours or friends. The range of complaints typically cover food, assault, loss of property and complaints against adjudication decisions. He does not deny the right of the prisoners to go to court – they can still sue in the civil courts and can still seek judicial review. Most complaints are from long-term prisoners.

Of the 2,050 complaints referred to it in 1995, 500 were investigated. Most were not eligible under the terms of reference for the Prison Ombudsman. Those that are investigated and upheld will lead to a recommendation or action that is sent to the prisoner and the prison service. They are not made public. The Prison Ombudsman's remit is not to investigate prisons as a whole, as that is the responsibility of the prison inspectorate; he deals solely with grievances from individual prisoners who have written to him.

The Prison Ombudsman may make the following types of recommendation. For instance, if there is negligence regarding a prisoner's property that gets lost, he may recommend compensation. If there is a complaint about a transfer from one prison to another, he may suggest returning the prisoner to the original situation or, if it is too late, may recommend a written apology from the prison service. He may recommend changes in the security classification or review of a prisoner's security classification. These are only recommendations to the prison service but the Ombudsman estimates that originally 4 per cent recommendations were accepted, increasing in 1996 to 95 per cent. This followed 445 full investigations with the prisoner's complaint upheld in 86 cases resulting in 221 recommendations to the prison service.

Police Complaints Authority

The Police Complaints Authority (PCA) deal with complaints from the public (see Chapter 4 for details of the number of complaints and disciplinary charges). If their investigation shows that a criminal offence has been committed by a police officer they will pass the papers on to the CPS to make a decision about prosecution. Where there is no criminal offence their report goes to the chief officer of the force involved who must decide whether to take disciplinary action that can result in dismissal or, for less serious matters, an apology. The PCA will write to the complainant to explain what has happened. If the complainant agrees, minor matters can be dealt with informally.

Some high-profile cases become the subject of inquiries conducted by the Police Complaints Authority as happened in the case of the murder of Stephen Lawrence. An inquiry conducted for the PCA by the Deputy Chief Constable of Kent, Robert Aylingon, into the police handling of the investigation of the murder of the black teenager, Stephen Lawrence, aged 18, in Eltham in April 1993, found that the Metropolitan Police Force was insufficiently thorough in their investigation. Relatives of the murder victim claimed that

the police wasted time checking the possible links between Stephen an
black gangs and should have made house to house enquiries earlier. Th
police denied the accusation of bias or lack of professionalism and claimed t
have conducted interviews with 2,500 people without finding any reliabl
witnesses. An inquiry under Sir William Macpherson, a former High Cour
judge, started in March 1998 and a CID officer faced a disciplinary charg
for neglect of duty with respect to the case.

Complaints to the PCA do not prevent individuals who have been subjec
to unlawful acts at the hands of the police from using the civil court proced
ure to seek compensation. In serious miscarriages of justice the police wil
sometimes offer compensation. In 1997 George Lewis received £200,000 i
compensation after serving 5 years of a 10-year sentence for burglary an
robbery after the police, he claimed, had concocted the evidence. The polic
officer involved, Detective Constable John Perkins, was a member of the Wes
Midlands Crime Squad and had been cited in 23 cases where fabricate
evidence had led to convictions, including the arrests and imprisonment o
those convicted of killing Carl Bridgewater. The West Midlands Crime Squa
was disbanded in 1989 following a number of allegations about faked confes
sions and malpractice by the detectives in the squad. Subsequently 20 long
term prisoners had their convictions overturned as their cases relied heavil
on the evidence provided by the squad.

In March 1998 the Home Secretary, Jack Straw, announced reforms to th
system of handling police complaints and dealing with disciplinary matter
(see Chapter 4). Under his plan, disciplinary hearing against police officer
will come to decisions based on the civil law standard of the balance of prob
abilities rather than, as previously, on the criminal law standard of beyon
reasonable doubt. To avoid disciplinary hearings in the past some officer
have taken early retirement on health grounds to avoid punishment. This wil
no longer be permitted. Also some officers have avoided disciplinary hear
ing by going on sick leave. The plan is to change the regulations to allow
hearing in the absence of the officer complained about if he or she is on sicl
leave. An officer acquitted of a criminal offence may also face a disciplinar
hearing; the right to silence by an officer is to be abolished in disciplinar
hearings, and permit officers convicted of crimes to be sacked within a fe
days. The complaints against the police are to be registered, and the Hom
Secretary announced that the PCA is to have the power to fund independen
investigations into complaints.

Criminal Cases Review Commission

The Criminal Cases Review Commission (CRCC) was set up in 1997 fol
lowing the Criminal Appeal Act 1995. Its task is to investigate suspecte
miscarriages of justice and, where appropriate, refer cases to the Court o

Appeal. One aim of this reform is to make the process of dealing with allegations of miscarriages of justice less political by putting such matters, previously dealt with by the Home Office, into the hands of an independent commission. The Home Office transferred 180 cases to the new authority. High-profile miscarriage of justice cases, such as those dubbed by the media as the Bridgewater Three, Birmingham Six and the Guildford Four, had encouraged the view that it was important to establish an independent system of review of such cases.

Based in Birmingham, its first chairman is Sir Frederick Crawford, and had 14 members in 1998. It has the power to direct and supervise investigations into possible miscarriages of justice in England and Wales and Northern Ireland. It can investigate possible miscarriages of justice in both the Crown Court and magistrates' courts and can refer cases to the courts on matters regarding conviction or sentence.

In referring a case back to the Court of Appeal it must provide a statement for its reasons within the framework of the Criminal Appeal Act 1995 and explain why it considers the conviction unsafe. The first case referred back to the Court of Appeal by the Commission in July 1997 was that of Mahmood Mattan, who was hanged in South Wales in 1954. Further reviews were being made with respect of two of the three men convicted of the M25 murders and the case of Derek Bentley (see the section in this chapter on the Home Secretary).

COMMUNITY, VICTIMS AND VIGILANTES

Communities and crime

Crime has an enormous impact on the community in terms of the quality of life of citizens, the neighbourhoods they live in and the business life of a locality. Everyday decisions about how to get the children to school, when to go shopping and whether to go out at night are affected by views on crime. As we have seen, however, the agencies and formal processes of the criminal justice system have a limited direct effect on the volume of crime.

In this section we will consider victims' experiences in the criminal justice process along with policies to provide victims with support and compensation. Those most frustrated by the limited impact of the criminal justice system on crime may be tempted to engage in crime prevention and even retribution – to become vigilantes. Vigilantism, often seen as the ultimate threat to justice in the community because of its lack of due process, could also be seen as leading to a genuine involvement of the community in all aspects of criminal justice. But great dangers also accompany its growth which may involve untrained and inexperienced members of the community taking the law into their own hands.

Victims

Before the introduction of professional police forces in the nineteenth century and the effective nationalisation by the state of criminal justice by the
twentieth century, the victim had a crucial role in that it was the victim who
initiated criminal prosecutions. While the victim still has a legal right to bring
a prosecution, the system is geared to the official agencies dealing with crime
and few victims either know about the right or could afford it if they did. By
the late twentieth century it was often said that victims were the forgotten
element in the criminal justice process.

What came to be called the victim movement drew attention to the problems faced by victims at all stages of the criminal justice process. A number
of studies during the 1970s and 1980s, including the British Crime Surveys,
revealed that victims were often dissatisfied with many aspects of their treatment by criminal justice agencies (see, for example, Maguire and Pointing
1988). Once they had reported their case to the police, little else seemed to
happen. Yet victims might require both practical help, such as re-installing
locks and repairing damage, and emotional support to get over the trauma
involved in the offence. In addition, victims complained that they were often
unaware of the progress of their case, were not informed when cases were to
be tried unless they were called as witnesses, and if called as witnesses were
often given little information about what was expected of them.

In court, they could find themselves confronted by offenders' friends and
relatives in the waiting room. Giving evidence might involve reliving the
offence, and cross-examination could be particularly traumatic as one feature
of the adversarial system is that the defence may attempt to discredit the
victim's story. This can be particularly acute for female victims of rape or
sexual assault, whose own history and character can be called into question
(see, for example, Walklate 1989).

The victims might speculate about why they were picked on and fear that
it might be repeated or further contact might be regarded as likely and
unwelcome. Mike Maguire found that, with regard to burglary, the victim
feared that the offender was possibly, 'somebody local' and this realisation
was 'likely to prolong the worry caused by the incident' (Maguire 1982: 127).
Some victims suffer intimidation, threats and retaliation from the offender
Shapland *et al* (1985), in their study of 278 adult victims of violent crimes,
showed that 14 per cent suffered retaliation.

The emotional aspects of being a victim are illustrated in the case of Alison
Kennedy, victim of a violent attack. She wept outside the Old Bailey after
the conviction of Robert Buckland for attempted murder in January 1998.
She told reporters that she felt 'a great sense of relief at the result and the
satisfaction to have been here to see the verdict for myself' (*The Daily Telegraph*, 8 January 1998: 1). Buckland had attacked her on a deserted train in
March 1997 as she travelled from Waterloo to Guildford. The 18-year-old
stabbed her in an unprovoked attack with a five-inch serrated blade that was

embedded in the top of her head, and a surgeon claimed that it was a miracle that she lived.

Victim frustration is considerable when they believe they know who the criminals are yet the police or courts will do nothing because of the lack of admissible evidence. The frustration over the lack of a prosecution for the death of teenager Stephen Lawrence led the *Daily Mail* to declare on its front page 'Murderers: The Mail accuses these men of killing. If we are wrong, let them sue us' (*Daily Mail*, 14 February 1997). Underneath they printed the names and photographs of the five young men they alleged killed Stephen Lawrence. It would appear that there is insufficient evidence under our adversarial system of justice to have any likelihood of convicting them in a criminal court.

In the light of the Lawrence case one radical response to help victims is the proposal that a fundamental review of the adversarial process be undertaken to make it easier to prosecute criminals. Less radically, reforms in the USA have seen a much greater role given to the victim in terms of participation in the criminal justice process, most evident in the right of allocution, that is, the right to address the court about the offence and the offender at the time of sentence. In the UK the response to meeting the needs of victims has more narrowly focused on the provision of support and services for the victim and financial compensation. Helen Reeves, Director of Victim Support, wrote in a letter to *The Times* in 1995:

> Offenders have clear rights in our system of justice but victims have no enforceable rights under the law. Victims should have the right to be protected and respected and know what is happening in their case and why.
>
> (*The Times*, 22 February 1995: 7)

Meeting victims' needs in the UK

A number of disparate movements led to a recognition of the needs of victims and measures to improve their situation. The victim's movement has demanded the right to information and explanation, the right to compensation and the right to protection. Women's groups who drew attention to the plight of women victimised by rape, sexual assault and domestic violence formed part of this movement. They not only campaigned for better treatment but set up a number of initiatives themselves. In 1972 Erin Pizzey established the first refuge for victims of domestic violence in Chiswick. Rape crisis centres were also developed during the 1970s, and by 1988 there were 40 such centres (Zedner 1997). These, staffed mainly by volunteers, offer a helpline and a 24-hour counselling service. Many police forces also developed specialist units to provide a better service for women and child victims, and some set up special interview suites in police stations staffed by trained teams of female officers.

A Home Office Circular (69/1986) to chief police officers offered advice on better treatment for victims of rape and domestic violence. This included the provision of suitable private facilities for the examination of victims, reference to advice and counselling services, and police training. It also expressed an overriding concern with the safety of victims of domestic violence and the need to reduce any risk of further violence. In addition the CJA 1988 contains tougher provisions to ensure the anonymity of rape victims. The woman's identity is safeguarded, subject to the oversight of the courts, from the moment of allegation, whether or not any proceedings follow, and for the rest of her life. The protection of the identity of rape victims illustrates the point that the injury to the victim is emotional as well as physical and is not over with the crime.

Victim Support and the Victim's Charter

Victims' needs were supported by other developments, particularly by the growth of victim support schemes, first set up in Bristol in 1974. Nationally, these are regulated by the National Association of Victim Support Schemes (NAVSS) which receives financial support from the Government. By 1991, 370 schemes were affiliated and, in 1990, a total of 7,000 volunteers contacted almost 600,000 victims (Zedner 1997). Victim Support, as it is now known, is a charity which, in addition to providing individual support for victims, aims to influence the provision of services for victims and campaigns on matters relating to compensation and provision for the victim in court. It has also launched a special initiative on children affected by crime.

The major role of victim support is to provide services, on a voluntary basis, to individual victims at the local level. Each victim support scheme is run by a management committee and a co-ordinator collects details of victims from the police. Under local agreements the police give the local victim support scheme information about victims, including their name and address unless the victim asks them not to. These details are then distributed to a pool of volunteers who contact victims either by letter, telephone or doorstep visits.

Schemes provide help over practical matters or the provision of information. The emphasis of victim support has mainly been on short-term help and support on a 'good neighbour' principle by providing a shoulder to cry on (see, for example, Gill and Mawby 1990). Until recently, the emphasis was mainly on victims of burglary, robbery or theft although victim support has now expanded its work to include more long-term work with the victims of sexual and violent crime, the families of murder victims and some schemes include a service for those involved in serious motor accidents.

Victim support has also been involved with the provision of schemes to help victims in court, arising out of victims' complaints about their experiences. Initially a number of pilot schemes were set up. One such scheme is described by Rock (1991), who found that the main role of volunteers was to offer 'companionship and solace' during the long periods of waiting and confusion. These have been followed by a growing number of court schemes and the appointment of court staff with specific responsibility for liaison with victims.

A Victim's Charter was introduced in 1990 and a second edition in June 1996. Provisions of the charter state that the victims should be given details of the officer dealing with the crime. The police should have details of the loss to the victim, which they should pass on to the CPS if someone is charged so that they might obtain compensation. The police should give information about the progress of a case, trial dates and bail and sentencing decisions and should tell the victims if a decision to caution the offender is taken and remind them that they might obtain reparation in the civil courts and the availability of compensation from the CICB. Whenever an offender is convicted, the courts must consider ordering compensation for the victim. In addition, the charter gave a commitment to improve facilities for victim witnesses called to court, to reduce waiting times and to take the special needs of victims into account in new court buildings, by providing, for example, separate waiting rooms.

Despite the recognition of the needs of victims in the Victim's Charter, progress towards better provision has been slow. In October 1993, the Home Secretary announced that the government had accepted recommendations made by the Royal Commission on Criminal Justice including the provision of better information on the progress of cases, better consultation with victims and better court facilities. In addition, he announced extra funding for victim support to enable witness support schemes to be set up in all 78 Crown Court centres.

Two groups of victims have had their particular difficulties in the court recognised. Child witnesses may have their evidence pre-recorded on video tape, be cross-examined by TV link from outside the court and may not be cross-examined by the accused personally. Rape victims are prevented from being asked about their sexual experience with people other than the defendant. New measures were to be introduced in 1998 to prevent the defendant in a rape case from personally cross-examining the victim when they conduct their own defence. This followed trials where defendents carried out prolonged and intimidatory cross-examination of victims.

Victims and sentencing

When considering the role of victims in court a major issue is whether they should have any role in sentencing. At present in England and Wales there are, as we saw in Chapter 8, provisions for compensation orders which involve the victim being directly compensated by the offender. Other proposals for bringing the victim into the sentencing stage have been made. In the USA, for example, there are provisions in some states for victim impact statements to precede the court's consideration of compensation and sentencing. In some cases victims may state an opinion about the sentence. In California the courts and the parole boards must listen to representation by victims, their relatives or legal representatives at the time of sentencing or in hearings regarding early prison release.

These ideas have some strengths. Lucia Zedner, for example, argues that they recognise the victim's role in the dispute and could psychologically benefit the victim. In addition, victims might be encouraged to co-operate with the police and the court would have better information about the harm suffered by the victim thus assisting their assessment of how the sentence can be made proportionate to the harm done. On the other hand, continues Zedner, further victim involvement may limit the prosecutor's discretion and there is a danger that the victim's subjectivity would undermine the objectivity of the court. Disparities in sentencing could result whereby those guilty of similar offences received very different sentences. Finally, she argues, victims may not wish to be involved as it might prove yet a further burden (Zedner 1997).

Others, such as Ashworth (1993), have pointed out that a victim's participation in sentencing undermines one of the most fundamental principles of criminal law – that of culpability and intent. It is what the offender intends, not what the victim suffers, that should be the basis of the sentence. Furthermore, it undermines idea of consistency of sentencing as victims will have different motives towards offenders and ideas about punishment.

In the UK the National Standards for Probation state that the Presentence report should include:

> an assessment of the consequences of the offence, *including the impact on the victim* as set out in victim impact statements or other papers available from the Crown Prosecution Service (CPS) or the damage otherwise done by the offence.
>
> (Home Office 1995: 9)

Principles of restitution and reparation have become more popular in recent years. The restorative justice approach to sentencing seeks to bring offender and victim together in a conference. There has also been a growth in mediation schemes, which involve meetings between offenders and victims by which some form of compensation might be agreed. This may be an alternative to the formal trial process, it may be part of a community sentence, or it may be carried out while the offender is in custody. In one example, a victim whose car had been stolen and damaged, and who had himself been run down when he tried to intervene, met twice with the offender. These meetings were arranged at the local social services department, after the offender had given himself up to the police and had agreed to attempt mediation. In the first meeting, offender and victim confronted each ther, with the victim expressing strong feelings about his experience. In the second meeting the offender agreed to compensate the victim for the damage to his car (*The Guardian*, 24 August 1994).

Restorative justice

Many of the previous attempts to introduce mediation schemes were set up by agencies who were primarily interested in diverting offenders from the formal process of criminal justice. The criticism of these was that they were too offender focused. The restorative justice schemes aim to accommodate the needs of the victim and the offender. Some proponents of restorative theories of justice challenge the state involvement in responding to crime and argue that 'compensating individual victims . . . should be the primary aim of the criminal justice system' (Zedner 1997). Seeking to replace punishment models that are preoccupied with censuring law breakers they wish to focus on restoring individual damage and repairing 'ruptured social bonds' (Zedner 1997).

Restorative justice involves mediation and possibly reparation, bringing offender and victim together in a conference with a mediator to benefit both the victim and the offender. Victims might wish to take part because they want to find out more about the person who burgled their house or attacked them and why they were picked on by the criminal. It provides the victim with the opportunity to confront the offender and state the victim's feelings and experience of the crime. It is claimed that this last aspect might help to educate offenders about the impact of their behaviour and so contribute to their rehabilitation. It is concerned with the moral awakening of offenders by helping them to understand the seriousness of their crime and become aware of the harm they have done. Should they offer compensation and apology, then the offender might benefit.

Pioneered in New Zealand, the family group conference has been introduced by Charles Pollard, Chief Constable of Thames Valley Police, using a scheme based on the principle of restorative justice for some offenders who are to be cautioned. Called a 'community conference', the victim, offender and their families and friends are asked to meet with a police officer who has been trained as a conference facilitator. Pollard claims that, 'The highly successful Milton Keynes retail theft initiative has already seen a 50 per cent reduction in police time'.

While these schemes clearly help some individual offenders and victims, their potential may be somewhat limited. They may be more appropriate for less serious offences than for those involving serious loss and especially physical injury. Not all victims might wish to confront offenders. It can also be asked who benefits most from such schemes. Walklate comments that they may benefit offenders who receive a reduced sentence or have their case diverted. They may benefit the state by being cheap. But while they may benefit some individual victims, they are of dubious benefit to others (Walklate 1989). Where the loss has been great either in monetary or in physical terms such schemes are unlikely to provide anything like adequate compensation which may be either impossible or well beyond the offender's means.

Financial compensation

The idea of financial compensation to victims by either the state or the criminal was proposed in the 1959 White Paper *Penal Practice in a Changing Society*:

> The basis of the early law was personal reparation by the offender to the victim a concept of which modern criminal law has almost completely lost sight. The assumption that the claims of the victim are sufficiently satisfied if the offender is punished by society becomes less persuasive as society in its dealings with offender increasingly emphasises the reformative aspects of punishment. Indeed in the public mind the interest of the offender may not infrequently seem to be placed before those of his victims.
>
> (Margery Fry, Home Office 1959)

Margery Fry, Director of the Howard League, quoted in the 1959 white paper, argues that the redemptive virtue is likely to be increased if sentencing contained an element of personal reparation to the victim as this would help to bring home the realisation of the harm done to the victim.

However, the 1961 Home Office publication *Compensation for Victims of Crimes of Violence* did not include provisions for direct reparation but favoured state compensation. The Criminal Injuries Compensation Board (CICB) was started in 1964. Claims were evaluated on the basis of criteria which include an assessment of the victim's co-operation with the police, whether or not the victim precipitated an incident and a consideration of the character and conduct of the applicant. Victims with previous convictions might not receive an award. The system therefore embodied the notion of a 'deserving victim' (Walklate 1989). Thus Michael Hecker, shot while fleeing from a burglary for which he was later convicted, was turned down by the CICB (see section below on vigilantes).

Following the Criminal Injuries Compensation Act 1995, in April 1996 a new system came into force based on a tariff set according to the nature of the injury with additional allowances for special conditions and loss of earnings. This moved away from the previous system in which applications were considered on a case by case basis with loss of earnings and medical costs used to calculate the compensation. The 1995 Act renamed the Board the Criminal Injuries Compensation Authority (CICA). In 1996/7 the CICA resolved 13,566 claims, making awards to 8,432 victims and paying out £19.2 million.

The levels of compensation from the CICA are based on a tariff that ranges from 1 to 25 and represent £1,000 to £250,000. An indication of amounts under the CICA tariff is indicated below:

	Level	Amount
Blurred vision lasting 6–13 weeks	1	£1,000
Minor head bruises	3	£1,500
Dislocated jaw	5	£2,000
Loss of thumb	15	£15,000
Loss of both eyes	23	£100,000
Paralysis of all four limbs	25	£250,000

In addition to the above awards from central government funds, compensation orders were introduced in the Criminal Justice Act 1972 which provided that courts could make an ancillary order for compensation in addition to the main penalty in cases where injury, loss or damage had resulted. The Criminal Justice Act 1982 provided that a compensation order could be the sole penalty, and, where it was used with a fine, would take priority over the fine. The CJA 1988 required the courts to consider a compensation order in every case of death, injury, loss or damage. To increase the use of compensation it also requires courts to give reasons why they had not made orders when they could have done. The police have been asked to ensure that the information on the victim's injury or loss is obtained and the CPS will present it to the court. The CJA 1991 increased the maximum sum which can be awarded by magistrates' courts from £2,000 to £5,000. In 1996, 19 per cent of offenders convicted of indictable offences in magistrates' courts, and 8 per cent in Crown Courts, were ordered to pay compensation. The figure for Crown Courts is lower as compensation is not normally combined with a custodial sentence. The average amount of compensation in magistrates' courts in 1996 was £194 for indictable offences, and in Crown Courts, £1,072. In the magistrates' courts 53 per cent of all offenders sentenced of violence against the person were ordered to pay out on average £200 (Criminal Statistics England and Wales 1996: 187).

While compensation orders are clearly seen as important elements in sentencing, their effect can be somewhat limited. Like fines, they may not be paid. A Mail on Sunday investigation claimed that as many as two in three orders result in no payment, following which the Home Office undertook to investigate this problem (Mail on Sunday, 26 June 1994). Like mediation schemes, compensation orders may also be limited by the offender's means and the nature of the offence. Where, for example, non-monetary harm is involved, they may be inappropriate or inadequate. Both mediation schemes and compensation orders may therefore be more applicable to minor property crimes and are difficult to apply to more serious crimes where the trauma suffered by the victim cannot readily be translated into a monetary value.

Fig 11.2 Man electrifies car

Man who electrified car to deter thieves wins jury's sympathy

An engineer who electrified his high-performance car to protect it against persistent thieves was cleared of assault and weapon offences by an Old Bailey jury yesterday.

As Roderick Minshull, 48, left court he said he would swap the Ford Sierra Cosworth for a diesel van. A lawyer described the case as another example of the public showing sympathy for people who risked the law to fight crime or defend themselves.

He said his only intention was to protect his property and, as a qualified electrical engineer, he made sure the car was safe and would not cause serious injury.

Mr Minshull took action after thieves tried at least ten times to steal the car.

Mr Minshull used a £200 device known as an ESB200. The equipment, which could deliver a peak power of 10,000 volts, was placed in the boot and linked to the car battery.

Guy Holloway, a guard at the Hilton, saw a wire and heard ticking. . . . When he investigated further he touched the wire and received a shock through his hand into his chest.

After the case Steven Kay, secretary of the Criminal Bar Association, said: 'I don't know whether it will encourage others but the interesting thing is the public and juries are probably understanding more why people take steps to protect their property. They are becoming more sympathetic. I think this is disturbing as a trend, particularly as innocent people could get themselves injured.'

Kevin Delaney, the RAC's traffic policy manager, said: 'In this case the victim was someone who was quite robust. What if a small child had touched the car or an old person fallen against it? What we are seeing in this case is the frustration of the ordinary man in the street with car crime.'

The frustration felt by Mr Minshull to protect his car was obviously the same frustration felt by the jury that acquitted him at the inability of society to deal with car crimes.

Source: *The Times*, 30 June 1994, © Times Supplements Limited, 1994.

Vigilantes

Many of the issues and policies reviewed above have developed out of the recognition that the formal agencies of the criminal justice system have in reality a limited effect on the incidence of crime. One result of this perceived inadequacy may be that the public may quite literally decide to take the law into their own hands – by patrolling streets, apprehending offenders and punishing them. Extreme versions of such vigilantism can involve groups conducting their own trials and sentencing processes. In Northern Ireland, for example, informal justice has been carried out by paramilitary organisations on both sides against burglars, thieves and robbers. While their punishments – which have included injuring and 'knee capping' so-called offenders – have been severe they have enjoyed a degree of popular support (Johnston 1992). Other individuals who have sought to take the law into their own hands have received some sympathy, as seen in Figure 11.2.

Lord Chief Justice Taylor warned about the dangers of individuals taking the law into their own hands and reminded victims that the law only allows reasonable force to citizens to defend themselves. He was discussing the case, on appeal, of Duncan Bond and Mark Chapman who were sentenced in 1993 for kidnapping a teenager they suspected of theft and driving him round to frighten him. They were given a 5 year prison sentence, reduced to 6 months on appeal.

However, individual judges and juries are likely to look sympathetically on crime victims who use force. Barrie Richards legally possessed a shotgun which he fired at two people who, at night, broke into garages at the flats where he lived. Mr Richards said he fired over their heads but one of the thieves, Michael Hecker, was hit by pellets in his neck, wrist and face. The jury and judge believed that Richards had not intended to harm the intruders and the judge took the opportunity to comment on the fact that the case had been brought to court. Judge Fox, referring to the CPS's decision to prosecute, said, 'I would invite the attention of those who, in their discretion, decided that this prosecution should be brought, to the fact that it took the jury only a few minutes to determine that the right verdict was not guilty.' Hecker's claim to the Criminal Injuries Compensation Board was turned down and he was given an 8-month sentence (*The Times*, 29 November 1995: 3).

The response of the authorities in England and Wales shows they are keen to discourage citizens taking the law into their own hands. Encouraging 'active citizens' to deal with crime involves a different attitude in France where citizens are encouraged to intervene in criminal incidents rather than, as in the UK, leave it to the professionals. The French Penal Code makes it an offence not to go to the assistance of a person in danger. Penalties may follow if a witness of a violent crime does not try to help a person being attacked. The public are also allowed to carry mace gas for self-defence, although not knives or guns.

There is, of course, a very narrow borderline between the involvement of citizens in crime prevention or Neighbourhood Watch schemes – which, as we have seen, has been encouraged in recent years – and what is often seen as an alarming spread of vigilantism. The difference is that Neighbourhood Watch and other schemes involve members of the public working with, and under the supervision of, the police. It is a scheme that involves giving information and not taking action. Vigilantism, on the other hand, may not involve the police and raises the possibility that small groups of untrained citizens lacking the expertise of the police may be involved in patrolling and preventive duties. A major objection to vigilantism is that the power of such groups is uncontrollable as they are not accountable to law. Their activities can rapidly spiral out of control. Thus vigilante groups set up in response to a specific form of crime may spread their activities to non-criminal behaviour and attack groups they disapprove of (Johnston 1992).

Johnston identifies a number of different circumstances which may give rise to vigilantism. It may be a response to harassment and racially motivated crime by ethnic minority groups who feel a threat to their cultural identity. Thus he gives the example of Jewish youth who formed groups to defend themselves against attack. In other situations, residents, often middle class, have joined together to protect their streets from invasion by prostitutes and pimps, as happened in Birmingham. Vigilante groups may also emerge where the police response to crime is seen as inadequate.

The narrow borderline between such vigilantism and community involvement in policing can be seen in the controversy caused recently by proposals to involve citizens not only in Neighbourhood Watch but in patrolling duties. In 1994 the Home Secretary, Michael Howard, proposed an initiative to extend citizen involvement with police work. He announced, firstly, that members of Neighbourhood Watch schemes would be allowed to patrol areas, acting as the 'eyes and ears' of the police. They would have no powers of arrest, would not wear a uniform or carry equipment and would not receive any self-protection training. Experiments in Washington DC and Sandwich in Kent were cited as a prototype for this development.

The Home Office also indicated an intention to increase the use of volunteers to supplement regular police manpower, and planned to increase the number of special constables from 19,000 in 1994 to 30,000 by 1996. Special constables receive expenses but are not paid. They have uniforms and are trained and sworn police constables with a warrant for the area covered by the police force to which they are attached and to adjoining police forces.

A third means of using volunteer citizens to help with police work is through the extension of the parish constable or parish warden schemes, by resurrecting the parish constable to patrol villages without a police presence. This would involve training unpaid volunteers who would conduct their police work in uniform and would have the power of arrest. The parish warden scheme would require parish councils to establish a list of volunteers who would have no powers of arrest and would merely patrol and record any incident and report it to the police. In 1994 twenty experiments were established to monitor the effectiveness of parish constable and parish wardens.

The Police have objected strongly to proposals that citizens should play a major part in patrolling. A Police Federation statement commented that

> voluntary work can never replace police officers and we are totally opposed to patrolling, uniformed or otherwise, by members of volunteer groups. The dangers of vigilantism are obvious.
>
> (*The Guardian*, 19 April 1994)

Another problem is how effective such groups are likely to be. Johnston (1992), summarising research on the effectiveness of such groups, including the well-known Guardian Angels in the US, comments that it is doubtful whether they have any long-term effect in reducing crime, although they may have some effect on reducing the fear of crime. Like many community crime prevention measures, they are locally based, and may work for a short time, but not in the long term.

In addition, vigilantism arouses many, often conflicting issues. On the one hand, it could lead to the genuine involvement of the community in the tasks of criminal justice, leading to a more genuine community justice. On the other hand, however, it is often seen as a threat to communities as it can all too easily get out of hand. Major fears of vigilantes centre around the issue of who such groups are accountable to and the dangers of untrained and unaccountable citizens attempting to intervene in dangerous or ambiguous situations.

STRATEGIES FOR TACKLING CRIME

Crime prevention

One of the intended objectives of any criminal justice system is to prevent crime by apprehending criminals and by dealing with offenders in a way that deters others and changes the offender's behaviour so that future crimes are prevented. However, this notion of crime prevention is not what is implied by the current usage of the phrase, which focuses upon the prevention of crime before it happens by a number of intervention strategies aimed at reducing the causes of and opportunities for crime. This current emphasis sees very little role for prosecution, trials and sentencing but uses police and community co-operation to curb crime before it has happened. It envisages a limited role for the formal process of criminal justice and a greater role for a broader approach to crime involving schools, transport, neighbourhoods, architects, businesses, with the police seen less as law enforcers and more in an educative or co-ordinating role.

The development of schemes designed to prevent crime has resulted in a growing industry surrounding crime prevention which started in the late 1970s and expanded during the 1980s. Many organisations have responsibility for crime prevention, including multi-agency partnerships involving central government, local authorities, the police, voluntary organisations, business and commerce. A wide variety of measures are involved from simple strategies such as improving locks or installing gates in alleyways to high tech computer and close circuit television (CCTV) screening and changing aspects of environmental design.

There is no one definition of crime prevention. Different strategies imply, or explicitly identify, theories about the causes of crime and offer different types of intervention as a result. Some theories focus on the criminal and offer solutions that seek to change behaviour; others focus on the location of crime and seek to reduce the opportunity through physical changes to the environment – for example, tougher glass, stronger locks and brighter lights – and others seek greater surveillance of public places where crimes are likely to occur, such as car parks.

There are three main models of crime prevention: primary, secondary and tertiary. Primary crime prevention refers to strategies aiming to prevent crime not involving offenders. Secondary crime prevention involves policies which target people considered to be at risk of becoming offenders. Thus a variety of educational and sports schemes aim to divert youth in high crime areas from criminal activity. Tertiary crime prevention aims to prevent those already convicted of crime from continuing with their criminal careers mainly through the sentences of the court.

In the 1990 Blue Ribbon Report in California it was stated that primary prevention aims at a young target population and the importance of social and economic factors and the general welfare of the population in preventing crime are stressed:

> good education, health care, shelter, nutrition, recreation, and employment opportunities represent forms of primary prevention. Unemployment and the lack of formal education are significant contributing factors to the level of criminal conduct in contemporary society. A well-educated and working population are much less likely to be involved in crimes such as robbery, the trafficking of narcotics and other illegal drugs, and certain property crimes such as burglary.
>
> (California State Government 1990: 12)

It goes on to point out that secondary prevention targets individuals who are at risk and have been identified by criminal, welfare or educational agencies as likely to require intervention to prevent a drift towards crime. Tertiary prevention deals with those who have been found guilty of committing an offence, and involves efforts to rehabilitate them.

Recently attention has shifted from tertiary crime prevention through sentencing policy to primary and secondary measures (Pease 1994a). What is often known as community crime prevention mainly deals with the primary and secondary aspects.

Great interest in environmental crime prevention developed during the 1970s. The theme of modern community undergoing decline, undermined by increasing vandalism and lawlessness was taken up in the work of Oscar Newman (1972) *Defensible Space: Crime Prevention Through Urban Design.* He argued that the physical design of estates and public buildings can often hamper the community's surveillance of social space and thus reduces its ability to control crime. Thus high-rise buildings and estates that are built so that windows do not overlook public spaces and buildings with many corridors and exits help to create conditions conducive to crime because they do not provide the opportunity to be able to see or respond to anti-social behaviour.

Reducing the opportunities to commit crime was another approach. In an influential publication the Home Office Research and Planning Unit detailed the potential of a variety of measures for crime prevention (Mayhew *et al* 1976). Some of these involve target hardening, which means making the target of a crime – for example, a car, bank or telephone kiosk – harder to steal, break into or vandalise. Many of these ideas are relatively simple and inexpensive to implement. Other schemes involve altering aspects of the environment – better street lighting, for example, may deter muggers as it increases the likelihood of their being observed and identified. It also reduces

Fig 11.3 Streets, spaces and natural surveillance

A pavement or a street is much more than just a thoroughfare, a way of carrying pedestrians, it is one of the city's vital organs: the most common place of social contact and the key to sustaining a robust and healthy public realm.

By using pavements people become active participants in the dynamics of a city. Successful urban areas are those where people – residents, shop keepers, shoppers, visitors – feel comfortable and able to interact freely with those around them. This sense of safety and comfort is never produced by some external policing agent, it is a function of the multiple interactions which take place in that particular public space throughout the day. Safe streets and pavements are self-policing, through the intricate, almost unconscious network of voluntary controls, checks and balances, sanctions and licences, enforced by the people themselves: the passers by, the people watchers and those whose daily business involves contact with the street, even if this is only through visual contact.

There are a number of important pre-conditions if streets and pavements are to be allowed to police themselves:

(i) There should be a clear demarcation between public and private space. This means that everyone has an equal and unambiguous relationship with the public space they are using and an equal responsibility towards it.

(ii) There must be eyes on the street, a kind of unconscious surveillance. This means, for example, providing places and opportunities for people watching and encouraging visual contact between the indoors and the outdoors. Shops, bars, restaurants, markets play an important role in this respect.

(iii) The pavements must have people on them continuously, across different times of the day. This often means giving people reasons to visit or pass through in those important bridging hours, for example, between leaving work and coming back into town for a recreational purpose.

One of the natural laws of street life – so frequently misunderstood by planners and urban designers – is that the sight of people attracts still other people. They are more likely to be drawn to the buzz of unordered activity than neat, ordered half-empty precincts. Underneath the apparent messiness and disorder of a market or busy pavement there is a subtle order, a set of checks and balances, a mixture of watchers and users, a myriad of social interactions: in short the most effective antidote to crime and fear of crime.

Activity is the key objective: volume of activity, variety of activity and activity across different times of the day.

Source: Urban Cultures Ltd and John Lydall Architects (1993) 'Kings Square: Hammersmith and the Safer Cities Project' December 1993.

the fear of crime among residents. At a more fundamental level redesigning housing schemes may produce more public space – space which people occupy and feel responsibility for. This prevents crime as it means that strangers can be more readily observed and therefore deterred. In any situation in which a crime may occur, levels of surveillance are crucial. Surveillance can be increased informally by altering the design of buildings to ensure greater surveillance by employees or residents, or formally by employing security guards or installing video cameras. Vandalism in schools, for example, could be reduced by using schools in the evening for other activities. An example of this kind of approach is outlined in Figure 11.3, which is an extract from an architect's plan for the renovation of King's Square in Hammersmith.

The potential of these kinds of scheme was quickly recognised and they had a wide appeal. They inspired a more positive approach to crime prevention indicating that something as opposed to nothing worked (Pease 1994a). The slogan 'together we can crack crime' captured this mood. They were consistent with prevailing government policy in that they encouraged the community, industry and commerce to play a part as 'active citizens' in crime prevention, bearing some of the cost and responsibility themselves. The Home Office Crime Prevention Unit, set up in 1983, played a major role in developing many policy initiatives. Other departments such as Transport, Health and Social Security also became involved with crime prevention initiatives and the Department of the Environment plays a crucial role, as much crime prevention involves environmental change in public areas and housing estates (Heal and Laycock 1986).

By the late 1980s many new initiatives were launched. In 1988 Crime Concern, a charity funded partly by the Home Office and partly by private enterprise, was launched. This organisation has been responsible for a large number of crime prevention projects in conjunction with both commercial and public organisations. The Crack Crime campaign and the Safer Cities programme, outlined below, were also launched in 1988. In 1993 a National Board for Crime Prevention was established to bring together representatives of central and local government, business, voluntary agencies, the media, the police and the probation service. The Morgan Report 1991 recommended that local authorities be required by statute to set up community safety departments. While never fully implemented, this report was influential and many local authorities have set up community safety units.

Other schemes aim to prevent crime by targeting particular crimes, criminals or groups of victims. Thus the Home Secretary, Michael Howard, told the 1994 annual conference of the Association of Chief Police Officers, 'Hard facts suggest that targeting crimes, targeting offenders and targeting victims could contribute substantially to the fight against crime' (The Times, 7 July 1994: 5). This is based on a number of studies which showed the importance of concentrating on repeat victimisation (see, for example, Pease 1997). It has been found that victims have a statistically higher chance of becoming a victim in the future than those who have not been a victim. One study found that once a house had been burgled it was four times more likely to be burgled again than a house that had not been burgled (Pease 1991). The 1992 British Crime Survey estimated that 43 per cent of all crime was committed against 4.3 per cent of people who had been the victim of a crime on five or more occasions in a 12-month period.

Another example of successful crime prevention is the Drink Driving Campaign. In 1996, 781,100 motorists in England and Wales were given, or asked to take, a breathalyser test. The percentage of motorists who give a positive test – that is, one which indicates that they have consumed an excess amount of alcohol – or who refuse the test was 13 per cent (100,500 motorists). During the Christmas period there is considerable publicity about the angers of driving and drinking. In December the police carry out more than twice as many tests than in a typical month.

Safer Cities

A major crime prevention initiative followed a series of programmes in the five towns of Bolton, North Tyneside, Croydon, Swansea and Wellingborough, known as the Five Towns Initiative. This was followed by Safer Cities, a larger programme which was linked with the Action for Cities, set up to facilitate the regeneration of inner cities. It incorporated a total of twenty projects funded by the Home Office (Tilley 1993). Safer Cities has three stated goals:

- to reduce crime
- to lessen the fear of crime
- to create safer cities where economic enterprise and community life can flourish.

Safer Cities therefore incorporated not only crime prevention but a concern with other related aspects of community safety. It included the growing concern for victims of crime and the recognition that many live in fear of crime. These issues are interlinked in that a focus on crime prevention inevitably affects the public's estimation of the risks of victimisation. Indeed, some crime prevention schemes can increase the fear of crime by drawing attention to these risks (Tilley 1993). Economic enterprise and community life are also related. If crime rates are high in a particular area and the population have a high fear of crime, they will avoid public places, local shops and community activities. Therefore crime is related to wider socio-economic activity – as indicated in the extract quoted in Figure 11.2.

The structure of Safer Cities, with its local steering committees and organisers, meant that it was involved in a very wide range of programmes. The *Annual Safer Cities Progress Report of 1992/3* states that up to 1993, more than 3,300 crime prevention and community safety measures had been initiated involving £20.4 million Home Office funding. This report also indicates the variety of activities undertaken under the Safer Cities umbrella, which include:

- projects to improve security in homes, businesses and public facilities;
- helping young people as potential offenders, offenders and victims of crime;
- schemes to tackle domestic violence and other women's safety issues;
- action on car crime and racial harassment.

(Home Office 1993: 7)

The use of CCTV has also been a popular method both for preventing and investigating crime. The example in Figure 11.4 gives details of a scheme used on London Underground, as set out in a report on the scheme to the

Fig 11.4 Closed circuit television and crime prevention

The operation of CCTV on London Underground between Royal Oak and Hammersmith Stations

In October 1991, a CCTV system began operating in eight stations on the western end of the District Line, with a monitoring and control room at Ladbroke Grove Station. Before its installation, seven stations on the District line – Royal Oak, Westbourne Park, Ladbroke Grove, Latimer Road, Shepherds Bush, Goldhawk Road and Hammersmith – had the highest rates of crime.

Each station has between ten to eighteen fixed wide-angle lens cameras, covering the platforms and stairways from the booking halls. An operator at the Ladbroke Grove control room has a bank of eight screens showing one picture from each station. The operator can move from camera to camera at each station to show activity at different parts of the stations. Four screens monitor events if a passenger Help/Emergency Line button is pressed at any of the stations. In what is known as a time lapse recording, recordings are made onto a video tape every four seconds. A further monitor, with four-way split screen capability, allows playback from the tapes covering the 150 cameras that are in place. Eight time lapse video recorders, one for each station, cover the pictures sent out every four seconds from each camera. Two time lapse video recorders record pictures sent when the help line button is pressed. The tapes are kept for two weeks. Identical time lapse recordings are made at the British Transport Police office at the Broadway, St James's Park station. As well as recording incidents the operator can alert the British Transport Police or the Metropolitan Police if an incident is seen taking place.

The equipment includes:

- 8 Visual Display Units
- 4 Emergency real time VDU monitors
- 1 Playback, split screen monitor
- 10 time lapse recording VCR machines
- 1 Multiplexer, playback machine
- Radio link with every station

The system cost three and a half million pounds to install. Each time lapse playback video recorder cost £3,500 in 1994, and 24-hour monitoring requires three employees, which is the main operating cost. Other operating costs include top quality video recording tapes and a service contract with Siemens Plessey.

The system provides for a police response to emergency situations and criminal incidents, provided by the British Transport Police. A squad of 20 officers, three sergeants and one inspector covering the seven stations are based near Hammersmith station. At any one time there are typically five officers on duty in mobile police vehicles ready to respond to an emergency. The police have promised a 3–4 minute arrival time for response to the most serious category of incident. Following advice and consultation with the Crown Prosecution Service and the Metropolitan Police as to how tapes could be used in support of criminal investigation and prosecution, a form was designed to permit the tapes to be used in evidence in a court. In a contested case this might involve the control room operator being called to give evidence in court.

Overall, the scheme has proved successful with the manager of the stations involved commenting that 'It has surpassed expectations.' Inspection visits have been made to the CCTV control centre at Ladbroke Grove by representatives of transport systems from Bilbao, Hong Kong, Liverpool, and a Dutch travel authority. What are its main achievements?

Crime investigation

Following a murder on the Sunday of the 1993 Notting Hill carnival, the suspect escaped on the underground. His picture, taken from the time lapse recordings, was printed in the *Evening Standard* the following day leading to his arrest.

Fig 11.4 *(cont'd)*

Crime prevention
On Christmas Day 1993, the operator in the control room at Ladbroke Grove noticed unauthorised personnel at Royal Oak station with spray cans. By using the public address system he was able to announce that the police had been called and were on the way. The potential graffiti was avoided. Now the seven stations have no graffiti on them. The trains are still subject to graffiti but the stations have remained clear since the introduction of the scheme.

Deterrence
Police data on recorded crime shows that in the first full year of its operation, recorded crime was reduced by 83%. From 1991 to 1993 the seven stations have changed from having the highest, to the least, number of recorded crimes for all the London Transport station areas.

Public/employer safety
All staff are issued with a radio and this is thought to have led to an enhanced feeling of safety amongst employees.
Travellers have access to help points on the station that allow for immediate contact with the control room. Visual and radio contact is made with the operator who can call for police backup if necessary.

Public information
The public can use the helpline for passenger information about waiting times for trains. This provides them with useful information and reassures them that someone is available if they need assistance for whatever purposes.

Prosecution
Evidence from the time lapse recordings was used in the successful prosecution of two offenders for serious crimes.
In support of the claims made for this CCTV project it was pointed out by Alan Green, the station manager of the seven stations, that ticket revenue has increased on this section of London Transport's operation and that police recorded crime statistics are down for this sector.

Source: Report presented by the Criminal Justice Centre, TVU, to the Safer Town Centre Committee, Hammersmith, 5 April 1994.

Safer Town Centre Committee, Hammersmith. A survey of losses from shops and retailers in 1994/5 showed a decrease in cheque fraud which was down 53 per cent. This might be explained as customers switch to plastic cards. It is interesting to note that fraud using plastic cards was down 60 per cent and might reflect the methods of surveillance used in stores to monitor customers using credit cards such as CCTVs (Brooks and Cross 1996).

Neighbourhood Watch

Neighbourhood Watch emerged in the early 1980s, based on the principle that the police and the community can work together to prevent crime. Based on local areas, these schemes involve the public looking out for and reporting anything suspicious – being the 'eyes and ears' of the police. By

1987 there were 35,000 Neighbourhood Watch schemes (Heal and Laycoc 1986), and the British Crime Survey estimated that, in 1988, as many as 1 per cent of households were members (Mayhew *et al* 1989). By 1996 the were 150,000 Neighbourhood Watch schemes with 5 million members.

The organisation of individual schemes varies enormously; however, the normally involve groups of residents with a local co-ordinator. Membe produce and distribute newsletters and leaflets giving general crime prever tion advice, often supported by local businesses. Some schemes encourag property marking and security surveys and members are asked to displa their membership by the now familiar stickers on doors.

In conjunction with the Home Office, the Association of Chief Polic Officers, and the National Association for Neighbourhood Watch drew u a 10-point plan to develop a national strategy for Neighbourhood Watcl The aim is to produce a directory of contacts and good practice, provide ir formation on training, and develop a Crime Prevention College to help trai Neighbourhood Watch co-ordinators.

Despite its popularity the success of Neighbourhood Watch has been lim ited. One of its major limitations is that schemes are easier to set up an operate more effectively in the areas in which they are least needed. Thus th British Crime Survey found that schemes were most common in affluer suburban areas, with members being drawn from high status and highe income groups (Mayhew *et al* 1989). The population in multi-racial area and poorest council estates, on the other hand, were least likely to join. Th survey also found that areas where membership was lower also tended to b those where burglary risks were higher. This may have the effect that scheme divert police resources from high-crime to low-crime areas (Heal and Laycoc 1986).

In addition, the British Crime Survey also found that while members c schemes were more likely than non-members to take crime prevention meas ures, many had done so before they joined. Membership of a Neighbourhoo Watch scheme may in reality mean very little and involvement often falls o after initial launch meetings (Bennett 1990). Three-quarters of member interviewed by the British Crime Survey had put stickers or posters in thei windows but 21 per cent had neither attended progress meetings nor knew the name of their co-ordinator. Members reported matters to the police mor often than non-members, and felt a greater sense of security. Many, howeve found it difficult to pinpoint any specific benefits of schemes although ther are some indications that burglary risks were lower after joining Neighbour hood Watch.

Despite the claims made for specific projects and the enthusiasm for crim prevention in general, its effectiveness is difficult to assess. This is partl because we may never know how much crime would have occurred had an initiative not been introduced, and whether any apparent improvement i temporary or long term. Another major problem besetting evaluation is th xtent to which crime may have been displaced to other areas. Evaluation methods can rarely measure this effect (Bennett 1994a; Pease 1994a). For xample, a successful Neighbourhood Watch scheme might prevent crime in ne group of streets, but crime may rise in an adjoining area without such a cheme. One kind of crime may also be replaced by another. Thus would-be urglars deterred by security alarms may turn to car theft, and bank robbers ave turned to the drugs market. It might well be that the benefit of schemes uch as Neighbourhood Watch is to reassure the community that someone is ying to do something about crime.

These problems are related to the assumption underlying much crime revention that crime is essentially opportunist. If, on the other hand, a size-ble proportion of offenders are motivated in some way to commit crime, ney will find a way around prevention measures. Thus a major limitation of ll crime prevention schemes is that they may neglect the underlying roots of rime. If crime is related to diet, family breakdown, alcohol or drug depend-ncy, unemployment and inner city degeneration, crime prevention measures ay offer a slight improvement but can do little to solve these underlying auses.

On a more practical level, the multi-agency partnerships which have been o popular also have problems. In essence these require very different agen-ies with different patterns of organisation, ways of working and cultural ackgrounds to work together. Communications, deciding who is responsible or implementing initiatives and full co-operation have all produced diffi-ulties. There have also been reports that the agencies involved may mistrust ach other. Community groups may mistrust the police who in turn may istrust the social services (Bennett 1994a). In addition, crime prevention ay not be a priority for participating agencies, and, like community polic-ng, it may not be seen as 'real police work' (Heal and Laycock 1986).

Others point out that crime prevention measures are only targeted at some inds of crime. Stanko (1990), for example, comments that they play on omen's fears of 'stranger danger' by focusing on safer streets and public reas, whereas most rapes and domestic violence take place in the home or orkplace. And while there have been some initiatives in the prevention of ommercial fraud, crime prevention measures and Safer Cities programmes ave not so far targeted environmental or corporate crimes which also en-anger the safety of the community (Croall 1998a).

Finally, others have criticised the focus of many crime prevention meas-res on the 'technological fix' of locks, bolts and video cameras. These may ell reduce the fear of crime but can in themselves have an adverse effect on ne environment. Estate residents, for example, may find themselves living mini-fortresses and gates, locks, bolts and bars can themselves inhibit the evelopment of neighbourliness or community spirit (Young 1997). CCTV eans that we are all under far more surveillance than hitherto, leading to ome fears of unduly pervasive policing and loss of civil liberties.

Zero tolerance

A new approach to crime prevention emerged in the 1990s called zero tolerance policing. It was an old idea that had gone out of fashion, the essential
idea being that the police are the community's main weapon against crime
and that if the police were more active and interventionist and did not
tolerate, in the sense of ignoring, so much crime, then crime would fall. The
phrase 'zero tolerance' was coined first within the New York Police Department (NYPD) to indicate that that there would be no tolerance of police
officers involvement in drug taking and corrupt behaviour. If the NYPD
could be cleaned up, then why not New York City?

William Bratton was appointed Police Commissioner of New York in 1994.
Seven thousand extra police had been hired since 1990 under an initiative by
Mayor David Dinkins to cope with the image of New York City as a place
where crime was out of control. Bratton reformed the system of management
so that it was more decentralised. Responsibility and accountability were
pushed downward, empowering local commanders but with instructions to
concentrate on types of crime that were conducive to public anxiety, including those that the police had been ignoring or tolerating in the past. The
police were told to have a more visible profile on the streets and not to ignore
minor infringements. Performance targets were introduced for local precincts.
Considerable success is claimed for this method of policing. William Bratton
writes, 'Over the past three years, the City's crime rate has dropped by 37 per
cent. The homicide rate alone has plummeted over 50 per cent' (Bratton
1997: 29).

The emphasis of zero tolerance policing was not only to reduce crime but
also to restore citizen confidence in New York as a safe place by showing that
the police and not the criminals are in control of the streets. Part of the idea
is to 'Prevent anti-social elements developing the feeling that they are in
charge' (Dennis in Bratton 1997: 3). Norman Dennis wrote:

> Zero-tolerance policing is based on three ideas. One is the simple principle, 'nip
> things in the bud'. Prevent anti-social elements developing the feeling that they are
> in charge. Prevent a broken-down and ugly environment of neglect becoming a
> breeding ground for crime and disorder.
>
> (Dennis 1997: 3)

Tolerating minor crimes, such as disorderly behaviour, encourages the
boundaries of anti-social behaviour. The broken windows thesis (Wilson and
Kelling 1982) states that if minor incivilities, such as drunkenness, vandalism, begging, litter, graffiti and disorderly behaviour, go unchecked then an
atmosphere is encouraged in which more serious crime will flourish. Incivilities
encouraged a more general fear of crime. Graffiti might be seen by some as
the exploration of artistic talent, whereas others might see it as a sign of
urban disorder which drives away the respectable citizens and attracts anti-
social elements.

Subway stations became a shanty town for the homeless and aggressive begging increased, exacerbating a climate of fear, compounded by a significant and notorious decline in the quality of life as a whole.

(Dennis 1997: 33)

The need to include community consultation was central to the project. The police are not able to control crime alone and need the co-operation of the public, and to do this they had to show they were acting in the interest of the public. Community partnership became part of the approach in New York City.

In England the zero tolerance approach has been championed by Ray Mallon, a Detective Chief Inspector in Cleveland. He became the head of the crime strategy unit in Hartlepool and also believes that this approach is responsible for curtailing crime rates in his area. Another higher ranking police officer is not so convinced about the usefulness of this approach. Charles Pollard, Chief Constable of Thames Valley Police, thinks that the zero tolerance approach implies inflexible policing and that over-reacting to minor disorders might provoke greater civil unrest. He also thinks the idea assumes that the police are omnipotent and that they alone can clean up the streets, reduce crime and the fear of crime. Other criminologists claim that the fall in the crime rate in New York, is not attributable solely to this method of policing but to an increase in police manpower, demographic changes in the number of young males in the population and the incapacitative impact of tougher sentencing laws.

CONCLUSION

The debate about the effects of the zero tolerance approach as a method of crime prevention reminds us that responding to crime in a democratic and free society is not the responsibility of any one agency. Professionals, lay groups and the community at large, as well as central government and local authorities, have a responsibility for responding to crime and seeking to prevent it. A truly comprehensive response to crime is unlikely to insist that the answer is found in any one solution, be it CCTV, reducing unemployment or working with criminals and potential criminals. A comprehensive approach would also recognise the crime prevention role played by the law enforcement agencies and the courts in curtailing the activities of the more active criminals and in reassuring the law-abiding public that, if caught and convicted, the criminal will be adequately punished. The public are undoubtedly aware that much crime is not solved and that many criminals evade prosecution. The problem in recent years is that some aspects of the criminal justice system have been seen by some sections as colluding in helping offenders avoid punishment for their crimes. The phrase 'zero tolerance' captures a new and more aggressive public mood in which more is expected from the criminal justice system in its response to crime.

Review questions

1. Below is a list of Home Secretaries over the last 50 years. Use the index t
identify the Home Secretary when the following occurred:

- Introduction of detention centres
- Execution of Derek Bentley
- Abolition of the term 'borstal training'
- Introduction of the term 'Young Offender Institution'
- Publication of the Woolf report
- Sacking of Derek Lewis, the Director General of the Prison Service.

Home Secretaries

1940–1945	Herbert Morrison
1945	Donald Somervell
1945–1951	James Chuter Ede
1951–1954	David Maxwell-Fyfe
1954–1957	Gwilym Lloyd-George
1957–1962	Richard (Rab) Butler
1962–1964	Henry Brooke
1964–1965	Frank Soskice
1965–1967	Roy Jenkins
1967–1970	Jim Callaghan
1970–1972	Reginald Maudling
1972–1974	Robert Carr
1974–1976	Roy Jenkins
1976–1979	Merlyn Rees
1979–1983	William Whitelaw
1983–1985	Leon Brittan
1985–1989	Douglas Hurd
1989–1990	David Waddington
1990–1992	Kenneth Baker
1992–1993	Kenneth Clarke
1993–1997	Michael Howard
1997–	Jack Straw

2. Below are the objectives set by the Home Office and Key Performanc
Indicators (KPIs). Match the KPI with the relevant objective for th
Prison Service e.g. 1 and G.

Objectives

1. Keep prisoners in custody.
2. Maintain order, control, discipline and a safe environment.
3. Provide decent conditions for prisoners and meet their needs, includ
ing health care.
4. Provide positive regimes which help prisoners address their offendin
behaviour and allow them as full and responsible a life as possible.

5. Help prisoners to prepare for their return to the community.
6. Deliver prison services using the resources provided by Parliament with maximum efficiency.

Key performance indicators

A The amount of staff training.
B The number of assaults on staff, prisoners and others which results in a disciplinary adjudication.
C The average cost of a prison place.
D The number of prisoners held in units of accommodation intended for fewer prisoners.
E The rate of positive random drug testing.
F The proportion of prisoners held in prisons where all prisoners on standard or enhanced regimes are unlocked for at least 10 hours on a weekday.
G The number of escapes from prison and escorts.
H The number of prisoners completing programmes accredited as effective in reducing re-offending.
I The number of hours which, on average, a prisoner spends in purposeful activities.

. The Criminal Justice Consultative Committee, established in 1991, has the task of improving awareness and co-operation between the different agencies in the criminal justice system. In what ways could the work of this committee be extended? Answer this by indicating which of the following *key words* and phrases indicate the type of co-ordinating role you would think desirable for the criminal justice system in England and Wales. Think initially in terms of the impact of greater co-operation between agencies working in the same field such as policing. Secondly, how might these key words apply to cross-agency co-operation between different functioning agencies, for instance probation and prisons.

Information exchange
Consultation
Data-sharing
Cross-agency computerisation of data
Joint operations
Exchange of personnel
Establishing common definitions
Agreeing to cross-agency common objectives
Mergers of local units into regional units
Merger of regional units into nationwide units
Merger of national units into European-wide agencies
None of these

Further reading

Bennett T H (1994) 'Recent Developments in Community Policing' i Stephens M and Becker S (eds) *Police Force, Police Service: Care and Contr in Britain*. London: Macmillan

Clarke R V (ed) (1993) *Crime Prevention Studies*, Vol 1. Monsey, New Yor Criminal Justice Press

Dennis N (ed) (1997) *Zero Tolerance: Policing a Free Society*. London: IEA

Gilling D (1997) *Crime Prevention: Theory, Policy and Politics*. London: UC Press

Leishman F, Loveday B and Savage S (eds) (1998) *Core Issues in Policing* 2nd edn. London: Longman

May T (1991) *Probation: Politics, Policy and Practice*. Milton Keynes: Ope University Press

Newburn T (1995) *Crime and Criminal Justice Policy*. London: Longman

Zedner L (1997) 'Victims' in Maguire M, Morgan R and Reiner R (eds) *T Oxford Handbook of Criminology*, 2nd edn. Oxford: Clarendon Press

CHAPTER 12

CONCLUSION

carcely a week goes by without some aspect of criminal justice hitting
he headlines, with topics involving violent crime, young offenders, disputed
entences, miscarriages of justice or lapses in prison security arousing con-
iderable public debate. In reading this book you will have seen that almost
very aspect of the criminal justice system has been and continues to be subject
o a series of reviews, inquiries, commissions and legislation. The effects of
eforms resulting from such discussions remain to be fully determined and it
s likely that there will be many changes in the organisation and functions of
riminal justice agencies as we enter the next millennium. It is hoped that the
nalysis in previous chapters will help the reader to place current events in
he context of past and continuing developments in criminal justice policy. In
his concluding chapter, we will explore some of the major issues and trends
which continue to influence these policies, and consider their effect on key
arts of the system such as the police, the courts, sentencing and the penal
ystem.

The pace of change has in part been a response to perceived crises, in
aw and order, policing, the courts, the prison system, and miscarriages of
ustice. It also reflects changing views on the role and function of criminal
ustice policy. For example, there has been a recognition of the limited im-
act of rehabilitation on individual offenders, and doubts have been cast
bout the ideas that dominated the penal paradigm during the first half of
he twentieth century. Such doubts have led to an awareness that rehabilita-
ion is more difficult to achieve than was previously assumed, concern about
entencing disparities, a noticeable shift in penal rationales from deterrence
nd rehabilitation to punishment and just deserts, and an increased concern
ver the civil rights of prisoners.

In Chapter 3 it was pointed out that only a small proportion of offences
nd offenders are processed through the system, and in Chapter 2 it was seen
hat many of the factors affecting crime lie beyond the reach of the criminal
ustice system. The perspectives outlined in that chapter suggest that crime is
elated not only to the individual circumstances of offenders and their fam-
lies but also to wider social and economic circumstances such as economic
estructuring and the localised effects, particularly on young people, of

unemployment and social exclusion. Thus efforts to reduce crime must in clude policies tackling these issues, and, speaking before the General Elec tion of 1997, the future Home Secretary, Jack Straw, argued that:

> We have to deal with some of the underlying causes of crime such as youth unem ployment, truancy, drug and alcohol abuse, the lack of facilities for young people low income and recession, homelessness and the treatment of the mentally ill.
>
> (Straw 1997:

There has also been a greater concern with the impact of crime on victim and communities, a growing emphasis on crime prevention strategies, and cost/benefit driven reorganisation of criminal justice agencies often describe as managerialism. In this new, more realistic, thinking considerations economic costs, community fears and political realities have shaped develop ments in a way not apparent before. Thus the 1990 white paper preceding the CJA 1991 stated 'a price cannot be put on justice, but it is not without it costs' and then pointed out that the criminal justice system in England an Wales costs £7 billion annually, which represented an increase of '77 per cer in real terms in the last ten years' (Home Office 1990a: para 47.1). In th 1990 white paper the Government also expressed a commitment to get toug on crime, while at the same time wishing to make less use of imprisonmer because of the costs involved. This cost-conscious approach is also reflecte in the Audit Commission reports on the police and youth justice system an has led to the setting of the Key Performance Indicators discussed in earl ier chapters. A combination of cost-effectiveness and political consideration also affected the widespread privatisation of many aspects of criminal justice This was seen as cost-effective by allowing competition and thus a reductio in costs, by cutting down bureaucratic procedures and staffing costs an allowing far greater flexibility. Nonetheless it has been argued that these claims, especially in relation to cost-effectiveness, are exaggerated and tha the exigencies of cost-effectiveness mean less rather than more flexibility.

The increasing focus on cost-effectiveness may also conflict with other influences on penal policy. Governments face a dilemma in pursuing strat egies, often seen as politically desirable, which stress being tough on crim while at the same time taking account of economic considerations. Toughe and more punitive policies may involve higher costs of prosecution and ar increasing use of imprisonment. This has led to a tendency towards bifurcation whereby tougher policies are reserved for more serious offences and offenders while other offenders are diverted from the system at various stages. Some may be diverted before prosecution by the use of cautions and victim offende mediation schemes and diverted from prison by the greater use of commun ity sentences. This can, of course, conflict with notions of just deserts and denunciation and with the interests of victims who see their offenders going unpunished. The Crime and Disorder Act 1998, like many of its predecessors contains a mixture of strategies, providing for a new detention and training order along with more community-based reparation and action plan order.

Many of these strategies have been accompanied by new technologies of control. More offenders can be kept out of prison if they are monitored by what is popularly known as electronic 'tagging' and, as seen in Chapter 11, many town and city centres and other public spaces are subject to surveillance by close circuit television. These are perceived to be more cost-effective and less intrusive than, for example, increasing levels of policing. On the other hand, they have attracted criticism on the grounds that they extend surveillance and control at the expense of civil liberties and will lead to the emergence of the 'punitive city' (Cohen 1985), whereby more people fall into the net of policing and social control and more, rather than less, offenders are subject to interventionist and custodial sentences (see, for example, Cavadino and Dignan 1997).

These trends in policy, which produce new dilemmas, have affected and continue to affect many parts of the system. We will now briefly explore some of the major issues that affect some of the main agencies and functions of criminal justice as we move towards the next century.

Many questions arise when the future role and organisation of policing is considered. Can, for example, the public police continue to be responsible for such a wide range of functions? Can they continue to attempt to prevent, detect and investigate crime along with acting as social servants, traffic controllers, peace keepers, crowd controllers and protectors of the safety of citizens, royalty, governments, businesses, and local neighbourhoods? Reiner (1997) points out, for example, that the British police are unique in having responsibility for crime prevention, detection, peace keeping, order maintenance and the preservation of state security, functions which in other countries are divided between different bodies, and predicts that the policing function will become fragmented.

Reiner also comments, however, that

> The police should be seen primarily as managers of crime and keepers of the peace; they are not realistically a vehicle for reducing crime substantially. Crime is the product of deeper social forces largely beyond the ambit of any policing tactics and the clear up rate is a function of crime levels and other aspects of workload rather than of police efficiency.
>
> (Reiner 1997: 1037)

The application of cost-effective measures to policing is not, however, without problems. The Audit Commission recommended that police efficiency be improved by a more intelligence-led approach focusing on apprehending more serious offenders. One strategy favoured was the use of informers to increase criminal intelligence. Yet one study found that, while using informers could lead to more arrests and the recovery of more property, their contribution to overall cost-effectiveness was less clear cut. They accounted for only a small proportion of arrests and much police time and money was spent recruiting and running informers. Issues are also posed for due process. Informers are sometimes not prosecuted for their involvement in crime and may sometimes act as *agents provocateurs*. Moreover, the necessarily clandestine nature of police relationships with informers makes this largely unaccountable (Dunningham and Norris 1996a, 1996b).

Other dilemmas are outlined by Morgan and Newburn (1997). In the first place they see a conflict between the public's desire for more visible, locally based policing and the auditing perspective that this is not cost-effective. According to Johnston (1994) 'everyday policing' is undergoing a process of restructuring involving the development of many different kinds of policing agencies, including private security organisations hired to patrol particular streets. There has also been an enormous growth of what is often described as 'private' policing. Local authorities increasingly employ security companies and many have their own municipal security – as in, for example, parks – and some have extended this to council property, housing estates and public places. There has also been a growth of Neighbourhood Watch and citizen patrols, along with a growing use of CCTV. Thus in many areas of what is termed 'mass private property', such as large shopping centres, leisure parks, industrial estates, private housing estates and apartment blocks, the role of the public police may be minimal. As Robert Reiner (1992a: 80) comments:

> A police officer is seldom if ever seen in Disneyland or indeed Brent Cross (except as a customer) . . . instead control is maintained by architecture, the technology of surveillance and informal social mechanisms with even the specialist input of private security personnel being vestigial, and primarily concerned with maintaining perimeter security.

These forms of policing are likely to grow, raising questions of how they can be made accountable, and how policing in areas where residents cannot afford private security can be enhanced (Morgan and Newburn 1997). One way of resolving these dilemmas, argue Morgan and Newburn, is to give local authorities a greater role in local policing and to employ auxiliary patrol officers, who would be part of the police service and therefore accountable. The accountability of private and self-help policing, at present open to abuse, could be enhanced by tighter regulation and licensing of the private security industry along with requirements that staff be vetted and trained.

A further dilemma concerns how far the police should be involved in crime prevention. Morgan and Newburn (1997) argue that the primary agency for crime prevention should be the local authority who should, in consultation with enhanced Police/Community Consultative Groups, be responsible for producing a community safety plan. This in turn would form part of the consultation on which local policing plans are based. They further argue that it is possible to retain the advantages of both local and nationally organised policing, envisaging a national police force accountable to Parliament and local police forces accountable to the Home Secretary and to police authorities.

Policy reviews and reforms have, as we have seen, also affected the prosecution process and the courts, which are also affected by considerations of

ost-effectiveness and the process of bifurcation. One way of reducing the
osts of prosecution is to divert less serious offenders, which can be justified
if it is thought that prosecuting many offenders serves little purpose espe-
ally if their crimes have been trivial and only a small sentence would result.
n addition, it may reduce the potential impact of labelling, especially in
espect of juvenile offenders. This raises the fundamental question of how
many offenders should be prosecuted and on what grounds. In addition, to
that extent should prosecution agencies play a role in such diversionary
strategies?

A variety of diversionary strategies have been tried in England and Wales
and elsewhere. In some schemes, such as Caution Plus, cautioned offenders
participate in schemes run by the probation service or voluntary agencies.
Some agencies have implemented schemes like those run in Australia and
New Zealand in which 'conferences' between victims, offenders and their
families discuss and decide upon an appropriate outcome. Reparation may
also be a form of diversion. Other suggestions include a role for prosecutors.
In Scotland, for example, the Procurator Fiscal has powers to impose fines,
the Fiscal fine', and to issue warnings and divert offenders to reparation and
mediation schemes (see, for example, Young 1997). Other proposals include
dealing with more trivial offences by forms of mediation which are more like
civil proceedings. Thus minor disputes between those who know each other
could be dealt with in a neighbourhood mediation centre. In more serious
cases, where this was unacceptable to either side or where the offender denied
guilt, the case could go to court.

Like all strategies, diversionary policies can lead to some public disquiet
on the grounds that offenders may be being let off too lightly and denun-
ciationists might argue that offenders should be publicly tried. In addition,
diversionary policies raise issues of justice and due process in that decisions about these offenders are being made in private and may thus be less
accountable. Offenders, for example, may be encouraged to plead guilty, and
thus clear up the books on the promise of not being prosecuted. This bifurcation may also disadvantage those who choose to contest their guilt and are
seen as taking up officials' time unnecessarily and who may receive a harsher
disposition as a result. It also raises questions of the degree to which some
minor offences may in effect be decriminalised.

The organisation and role of the courts also well exemplifies the tension
between the interests of cost-effectiveness and crime control on the one hand
and due process on the other. Court procedures are lengthy and costly and,
to some, too much emphasis is placed on the rights of the defendant. On the
other hand, from a due process perspective, what are seen as incursions into
the rights of defendants to elect for jury trial, the right to silence and the
provision of legal representation are fiercely resisted. Attempts to streamline
court proceedings by, for example, encouraging early guilty pleas, and defence disclosure of information may give rise to fears of increasing numbers
of what are popularly described as miscarriages of justice, concerns about

which, as we have seen, led to the Royal Commission for Criminal Justice 1993 and the establishment, in 1997, of the Criminal Cases Review Commission. This did not, however, lead to major changes as the commission rejected suggestions that England and Wales should move to a more inquisitorial system, common in other European countries. While establishment the CCRC has generally been welcomed, doubts have been expressed about its reliance on police investigation – given that the basis of the request for review may include an allegation of police misconduct.

We saw in Chapters 8 and 9 that sentencing policy has been affected by the processes discussed above and that, while the CJA 1991 attempted to state clear principles, many of its provisions were vehemently opposed and some were subsequently overturned or diluted. The CJPOA 1994 and subsequent legislation, and the Crime and Disorder Act 1998, all reflect an increasing tendency to be tougher on crime – policies often based on an appeal to public opinion. Yet public opinion may be difficult to define. Thus Ashworth argues that the tendency on the part of the media to sensationalise high profile cases may overplay a 'macho' approach to issues of punishment. In addition, politicians' appeals for tougher sentences, such as the former Home Secretary's claim that 'prison works' or the New Labour promise to be 'tough on crime' may be more concerned with gaining popularity than with a balanced approach to sentencing (Ashworth 1997b). Indeed successive surveys including the most recent BCS, indicate that the public, influenced by coverage of atypical cases and unaware of the 'going rate', underestimates the severity of actual sentences (Hough 1998). When asked about sentencing in general, people tend to think of more serious offenders, yet when presented with the facts of an actual case, they tend to be far less punitive and over half support the use of community penalties to reduce prison overcrowding.

The effect of prison reductionist arguments, the high cost of prisons and the recognition that prisons have only a limited rehabilitative potential raise important questions for the prison system. Should a steady increase in the prison population be accepted, or should steps be taken to reduce numbers in prison? If they are increasingly to be used for more serious, hard core offenders, for largely incapacitative purposes, how should regimes be organised and what should they aim for? If there are few goals other than security and control, popularly expressed as 'keeping them in and keeping them quiet', do they become, as Cohen (1985) argues, effectively 'human ware houses' which may lead to more unrest?

Despite the influence of the prison reductionists' arguments, current official projections suggest that the prison population will continue to rise. By March 1998 the prison population had reached 65,000. It has, for example recently been reported that unless action is taken Britain's prison population could reach 92,000 by the year 2005. Such an increase would mean that more than 20 new prisons would have to be built.

The changes in the training of probation officers, which have downplayed the social work and welfare element, is viewed by many as an unwelcome ift away from the rehabilitative aims of probation and the reparative aims of community service. The orientation of the latter towards notions of punishment in the community have arguably changed the nature of the sentence, conjuring up images of forced chain gangs being visibly punished (Worrall 1997). This has faced resistance within the probation service which also resisted other moves away from rehabilitation, such as the introduction of curfews and electronic monitoring, seen by probation officers as demeaning and as a threat to civil liberties (Mair 1997). There is also a danger that these may also be seen as insufficiently punitive and may therefore make few inroads into the prison population (Cavadino and Dignan 1997).

The emphasis on technological means of surveillance or, as it is sometimes called the 'techno fix', can also be seen in relation to crime prevention, with the enormous growth of video surveillance. This has created new problems of how such technology is to be regulated and controlled. There have been concerns, for example, about the use of such films as 'entertainment', which raises serious issues about the confidentiality of such material. Other problems surround how equipment is used. Who, for example, are the targets of such surveillance? How will this kind of technology develop? In one study of the use of CCTV, it was found that operators, like the police, focus on those they considered to be suspicious or 'out of time and out of place'. Drunks, beggars, the homeless and street traders were among groups so selected. Youth, and in some areas black people, were also disproportionately subject to surveillance. In the future, technological devices may also be developed to identify individuals by pictorial images which could be used to develop data bases for known or suspected offenders (Norris and Armstrong 1997). This raises important issues which need to be addressed.

It is clear, therefore, that in the twenty-first century the criminal justice system faces considerable change and continuing dilemmas. The different models of criminal justice outlined in Chapter 1 continue to influence thinking and remain significant, although the limitations of the system in reducing or preventing crime are more widely recognised. It is clear that criminal justice policy and agencies must be seen in the context of wider social and economic policies. At present, there appears to be a continuing emphasis on being tough on offenders although this works alongside a belief in the values of reparation, mediation and diversion. The system will also use new technologies which are more cost-effective and, in some ways, more humane. On the other hand, the new technology provides opportunity for new ways of committing crime, and for new problems to emerge, both of which may require different kinds of regulation. Issues of public confidence in the criminal justice system provoke individuals to seek redress or the punishment of the guilty outside the criminal courts. The public may use other means to respond to crime which range from vigilantism to using the civil courts to pursue claims that the criminal system has failed to address, a route rarely used, though most famously used in California after the acquittal of O J Simpson in his trial for murder.

In the foregoing chapters, we have addressed issues fundamental to a criminal justice system and descibed how they are dealt with in England ar Wales. Over time, the questions asked on these matters may change and tl answers provided will certainly vary, but the issues themselves will continu to provide opportunity for discussion, study, philosophising and individu and government action in the new millennium.

GLOSSARY OF CRIMINAL
JUSTICE TERMS

Absolute discharge   A sentence of the court in which no further action is taken.

Accused   The person suspected and accused of committing a crime.

Acquittal   Finding of not guilty.

Actual bodily harm (ABH)   An offence of violence where assault results in any physical or mental injury. More serious than common assault but less serious than grievous bodily harm (GBH).

Actus reus   A Latin phrase referring to the acts constituting a criminal offence. It refers to what took place; for example, was a person killed by another?

Adversarial justice   The system of justice based in criminal cases on the assumption that the prosecution must prove the guilt of the person accused of committing a crime by presenting admissible evidence that demonstrates the guilt of an offender beyond reasonable doubt. It is open to the defence to challenge this evidence.

Arrest   An action whereby a suspect is lawfully detained, usually by the police, but in certain circumstances by any individual.

Attorney General   The Government Minister answerable for prosecution policy and the CPS in Parliament.

Automatism   A criminal defence on the basis that the actions of the defendant took place without the defendant being aware of them, as in sleep walking but not drunkenness.

Bail   Release of a suspect or defendant before the conclusion of a case, to return at a specified time to the police station or court, where failure to do so can result in punishment.

Barrister   A professional lawyer who acts as an advocate in the courtroom who can only be instructed by a solicitor.

Borstal   A type of custodial institution which, from 1908 to 1982, sought to rehabilitate young offenders aged from 16 to 21.

Brief   Instructions to a barrister from a solicitor regarding an appearance in court; and also used as a slang term to refer to a defence barrister.

British Crime Survey (BCS)   A Home Office crime victimisation survey covering England and Wales carried out usually every two years since 1982.

Burglary   The criminal offence of illegally entering premises and commit ting or intending to commit acts such as theft, rape, serious assaults an criminal damage. Referred to in Scotland as housebreaking.

Capital punishment   The death penalty as a sentence.

Category A   One of four security classifications that relate to the securit risk of an inmate.

Caution   (1) A formally worded statement made at the time of arrest by th police warning the suspect that whatever he or she says or does not sa may be referred to as evidence in court.

(2) An official caution in lieu of conviction and sentence is a means b which offenders who admit their guilt may be given an official warning b the police and are not sent to court for trial. It is a means of diversion.

Certified mentally ill   A person certified as not criminally liable becaus of the state of his or her mental health.

Clear-up rate   The detection rate expressed as a ratio of crimes cleared u as a percentage of those recorded by the police. A crime is cleared up if person has been charged, cautioned or summonsed, or if an offender ask for crimes to be taken into consideration, or if a prisoner admits to crime, or no further action is taken because the criminal is below the ag of criminal liability.

Closed circuit television (CCTV)   A photographic system used as a mean of security and surveillance.

Co-defendant   A person charged in the same case as another.

Committal   A stage in pre-trial proceedings whereby arrangements are mad to transfer a case from the magistrates' court to the Crown Court for tria or sentence.

Common law   Law developed by court decisions, case law, and not em bodied in statute.

Community sentences   The range of sentences that include a Combination Community Service, Probation Order or in the case of a younger offende an Attendance Sentence Order.

Compensation order   A monetary payment ordered by the court to b paid by the offender to the victim.

Condign   Merited or deserved as in a sentence.

Conditional discharge   A sentence of the court that results in no furthe action for the current offence, but which allows the court to sentence i some other way if another offence is committed within the time specified

Conviction   Formal ascription of guilt in a criminal court.

Coroner's court   A tribunal to investigate sudden or violent deaths preside over by a coroner.

Counsel   Synonymous with barrister.

Court of Appeal   The court to which appeals from the Crown Court agains conviction or sentence generally go.

Crime control model   An objective, or model, of criminal justice whic stresses the aim of reducing crime.

Crimes without victims Crimes that do not have an obvious or direct victim so they are less likely to be reported to the police, for example, prostitution, gambling, drug taking.

Criminal Injuries Compensation Authority (CICA) A board that administers a system of financial compensation in the form of payments for those injured as a result of criminal activities.

Criminal liability Legal responsibility for an offence.

Criminal statistics Officially published statistics of crimes recorded by the police.

Crown Court The higher criminal court that replaced the Assize and Quarter Sessions in 1972 where trials on indictment take place before a judge and jury.

Crown Prosecution Service (CPS) The agency that, since 1986, has been responsible for prosecuting most criminal offences.

Culpability Responsibility of an offender for a crime. Blameworthy.

Curfew Part of a sentence or condition of bail that requires the person to remain in a specified place such as his or her home at specified times.

Custody A sentence of imprisonment, or, for those aged 21 and under, detention in a young offenders' institution.

Defendant The person in the trial who has been accused of committing an offence.

Denunciation An objective of sentencing and punishment where the aim is to reinforce community values by indicating that certain behaviour is regarded as reprehensible and will not be tolerated.

Deterrence An objective of sentencing and punishment the purpose of which is to reduce the likelihood of a crime being committed in the future by the threat or anticipation of a penalty.

Director of Public Prosecutions (DPP) The appointed head of the CPS answerable to the Attorney General.

Dispersal Prison Type of prison designed for high risk, Category A prisoners.

Disposal Another term for a sentence of the court.

Diversion Using strategies such as cautioning to keep offenders out of the criminal justice system.

DNA Deoxyribonucleic acid, a component of all living matter present in blood, hair, bones, fingers, nails and bodily fluids which is used for identification purposes in criminal investigations and at a trial.

Doli incapax The term used to describe children who are deemed in law incapable of committing an offence because they are regarded as being too immature to appreciate the wrongfulness of their actions.

Double jeopardy At risk of being punished twice.

Due process The term used to describe the legally required procedure so as to ensure that a criminal investigation and the trial is conducted in a fair manner and is regarded as protecting the civil liberties of the defendant.

Duress A defence referring to threats which persuade a defendant to commit a crime. It does not apply to murder or treason.

409

Evidential Sufficiency One of the two criteria the CPS must apply in reviewing all case before they may proceed to trial to ensure that sufficient and appropriate evidence has been collected by the police.

Green Paper A preliminary discussion paper issued by a government department inviting comment on proposed changes to the law.

Grievous bodily harm (GBH) Really serious harm such as broken ribs.

Hidden figure of crime Sometimes referred to as the dark figure; the number of crimes that go unrecorded.

Home Affairs Committee (HAC) A select committee of the House of Commons that monitors criminal justice issues.

Home Office The government department responsible for law and order policies and the overall responsibility for the police, probation and prison services.

Homicide Offences involving the unlawful killing of a person, for example murder, manslaughter, infanticide.

Hooliganism Rowdy and disorderly behaviour, usually in a group, that is regarded as threatening by others.

Incapacitation Sentencing or punishment strategy that makes it impossible for the criminal to re-offend by imposing physical restraints such as imprisonment.

Incorrigible An offender who refuses to change his or her criminal behaviour; unmanageable; unreformable.

Indeterminate sentence A sentence that is not fixed in length, such as a life sentence.

Indictable A criminal offence that may be tried in the Crown Court.

Indictment The formal document that contains the charges against a defendant for Crown Court trial.

Inmate A person kept in prison or in a mental hospital.

Joyriding A popular term for the criminal offence of aggravated vehicle taking.

Jurisdiction The geographical and legal extent of the powers of an agency or court.

Jury The twelve adults who are selected to decide, in Crown Court trial, whether from the evidence they have heard the accused is guilty or not. A jury is also used in the Coroner's Court.

Jury vetting Examining the jury list before trial to exclude jurors with extreme political views: only possible in terrorist and national security trials.

Just deserts Sentencing approach in which the sentence should be appropriate for the offence.

Justice model Punishment model based on just deserts.

Labelling The process of stereotyping social categories such as delinquents.

Lay magistracy Justices of the Peace other than stipendiaries.

Litigation Using the courts to pursue a legal remedy.

Lord Chancellor's Department The government department responsible for the courts and the appointment of magistrates and judges.

Magistrates The men and women appointed to decide matters in the magistrates' courts: stipendiaries and lay magistrates.

Magistrates' court The lower of the two criminal courts that try criminal cases.

Mandatory Something that must happen as set down by legislation, for example, mandatory sentences.

Manslaughter A criminal offence of taking life without the intention necessary to be guilty of murder.

Mens rea A Latin term meaning guilty mind, used to cover the various levels of the mental element or intention in an offence, for example, whether the criminal act was the product of an unintended or intended consequence.

Metropolitan Police The police force for London and the surrounding area.

Miscarriage of justice A term commonly used to describe a case where a defendant, after serving a term of imprisonment, is later found to be not guilty. The term is rarely used in respect of mistaken acquittals.

Mitigation Factors that reduce an offender's culpability for a crime without being a defence and thus are used in decisions about sentences.

Mode of trial The way a defendant is tried, i.e. summarily or on indictment, hence the mode of trial decision is concerned with this choice in triable-either-way cases.

Moral panic An alarmed reaction to a social problem. The media is blamed for over-reacting to a type of crime and making it appear more serious or prevalent than it is.

Mugging A commonly used word to refer to a street robbery.

Murder Causing the death of another human being with intent to cause his or her death or intent to cause grievous bodily harm.

Nolo contendere The defendant does not dispute the facts of the case for which he or she is accused.

Notifiable offences These are offences recorded by the police and broadly refers to most indictable and triable either way offences, although a few summary offences are included such as unauthorised taking of a motor vehicle. Not as extensive as the List of Standard Offences.

Organised crime Refers to the serious crimes of organised gangs and criminal syndicates.

PACE Police and Criminal Evidence Act 1984.

Paradigm A way of thinking about a subject of study or professional practice.

Parole Board Body responsible for decisions about parole.

Penitentiary A prison. In earlier use in the USA it was a prison committed to rehabilitative aims.

Plea The answer of the accused to the question of whether he or she is guilty or not to the crime of which he or she has been accused.

Plea bargaining Process of a defendant pleading guilty to certain lesser charges when more serious charges are dropped or an indication of a likely sentence is given.

Plea in mitigation Argument on behalf of an offender after conviction with an aim of reducing the sentence.

Police Complaints Authority (PCA) Name given by the Police and Criminal Evidence Act 1984 to the board that investigates complaints against the police and deaths that occur in the care of the police.

Police Consultative Committee (PCC) A committee comprising representatives of the police and local community to discuss crime and policing in the locality.

Positivism Application of scientific methods to the study of crime.

Pre-sentence report (PSR) A report, prepared by the Probation Service in the case of those over 16 and the social services for those under 16, describing the background and circumstances of the offender with a view to providing information that might be useful in the sentencing decision. It replaced the social inquiry report (SIR) in 1992.

Presumption of innocence The principle that governs the conduct of a trial, and puts the entire burden of proving guilt onto the prosecution. The accused is not required to give any explanation or defence. The outcome of the trial does not lead to the conclusion that the accused is innocent but that he or she has not been proved to be guilty.

Presumptive sentences Sentencing guidelines that are not mandatory but give a strong suggestion as to the sentence appropriate for different types of offences and offender histories.

Prison: Certified Normal Population (CNA) The designed capacity of a prison.

Prison: open A prison with minimum security arrangements, in contrast to a closed prison.

Prison: receptions The annual total of people sent for whatever reasons into the prison system.

Prisoners' Aid Society Founded by Lord Shaftesbury in 1854 to help released prisoners to find work and provide welfare support for their families.

Proactive policing The police initiating inquires without relying on citizen complaints.

Probation: breach Failing to comply with the terms of a probation order.

Probation: order An order of the court that is one of the community sentences that is given for a minimum of 6 months and a maximum term of 3 years.

Professional crime Crimes committed by a career criminal.

Public interest criterion The second criterion that the CPS must apply in determining whether a case should be started or continued.

Queen's Counsel (QC) A senior barrister appointed on the recommendation of the Lord Chancellor.

Rape Knowingly having sexual intercourse with a man or a woman without his or her consent.

Reactive policing The police responding to citizens' reports of crime in contrast to preventative or proactive policing.

Recidivist A persistent repeat offender.

Recorder A part-time judge who presides in the Crown Court; also certain judges with specific administrative responsibilities or traditional duties such as the Recorder of London.

Reformatory A custodial training institution for younger offenders (1854–1933).

Rehabilitation Sentencing objective concerned with the reform of the offender.

Remand centres Place of detention for those remanded in custody before a criminal case is completed.

Remand in custody Detention of a suspect/defendant in custody pending the next stage in his or her case.

Remand on bail Release of defendant pending the next stage in his or her case.

Reparation Making amends for a wrong done; repairing the damage.

Restitution Compensation for the victim of a crime.

Restorative justice An approach that seeks reparation for the victim from the offender.

Retribution A purpose of sentencing and punishment to exact vengeance for wrongdoing. Just deserts.

Right of Audience The right to speak in court.

Robbery An offence that involves the theft of property through the use or threat of violence.

Rule 43 The Prison Rule that allows a prisoner to be held in isolated accommodation for his or her own protection, or because they are disruptive.

Self-report study A survey which asks the respondents about how many offences they have committed.

Silk Synonymous with Queen's Counsel.

Solicitor A lawyer who can be approached directly by the public with rights of audience mainly in the magistrates' court.

Standard list offences A list of offences for which the name of the offender and details of each sentence have been collected by the Home Office. Covers all indictable only, triable either way and some summary offences such as assault on a police constable, and criminal damage under £5,000. Data from this is used for the Offender Index and for reconviction studies. More comprehensive than the List of Notifiable Offences.

Statutory law The law set out in Acts of Parliament.

Statutory sentence A sentence provided for by Act of Parliament.

Stipendiary magistrate A legally qualified and paid magistrate, appointed from solicitors and barristers of at least 7 years' standing.

Strict liability offence A crime not requiring any intention or mental element.

Summary offence A category of criminal offences (one of three). Offences that are tried in the magistrates' court only.

Summary trial Trial in the magistrates' court.

Summons A written notice to appear in court on a specified date to answer a criminal charge.

Taken into consideration (TIC) Offences taken into consideration, i.e. not specifically charged but which the court takes account of when sentencing.

Theft Dishonest appropriation of property belonging to another with the intention of permanently depriving that other of it (stealing).

Total institutions A sociological term for an institution such as a prison in which the entire round of life is conducted within the one place with the same people, isolated from the rest of society.

Triable either way A category of criminal offence (one of three). These offences may be tried either in the magistrates' court or the Crown Court.

Trial Contesting liability in any court.

Vandalism The offence of criminal damage.

Victimology The study of victims of crime.

Victim Support Voluntary organisation concerned with giving advice and support to victims of crime.

Victim survey A survey, such as the BCS, which asks people about their experiences as a victim.

Warrant An order of the court; for example, an arrest warrant which gives power to the police to arrest someone.

White collar crime A term referring to crimes relating to business or professional activities.

White Paper A report published prior to legislation indicating the policy direction of reforms from a government department such as the Home Office.

Younger offender Defined as child (offender aged 10–14); juvenile (offender aged 14–17) and young adult (offender aged 18–21).

Young Offender Institution A custodial institution for those aged between 15 and 21.

Youth Court The name since 1992 of the part of the magistrates' court that deals with younger offenders aged under 18. Previously known as the Juvenile Court.

Zero tolerance A crime prevention strategy of not tolerating or ignoring breaches of the law no matter how trivial.

APPENDIX 1
PRACTICAL EXERCISES

EXERCISE 1: CRIME DATA EXERCISE

You should consider how crime is defined. Look at various sources of information about crime, particularly at the media and official sources. Why are some kinds of crime seen as more serious than others? To understand the creation and interpretation of official data about crime, you will need to examine the processes underlying the reporting of crime – by the public, victims and the police. The reliability of official criminal statistics will depend upon these factors.

Students may wish to consult the following general reading:

Barclay, G (ed) (1993) Digest 2: *Information on the Criminal Justice System in England and Wales*. London: HMSO

Bottomley K and Pease K (1986) *Crime and Punishment – Interpreting the Data*, Chs 1, 2 and 6. Milton Keynes: Open University Press

Colman C and Moynihan J (1996) *Understanding Crime Data*. Buckingham: Open University Press

Croall H (1998) *Crime and Society in Britain*. London: Longman

Home Office (annually) *Criminal Statistics in England and Wales*. An annual report. London: HMSO

Maguire M, Morgan R and Reiner R (eds) (1997) *The Oxford Handbook of Criminology*, 2nd edn. Oxford: Clarendon Press

Mayhew P, Maung N and Mirrlees-Black C (1995) *The 1994 British Crime Survey*. London: HMSO

Mirrlees-Black C, Mayhew P and Percy A (1996) 'The 1996 British Crime Survey: England and Wales', *Home Office Statistical Bulletin*, Issue 19/96. London: HMSO

Interpreting crime statistics

Consult extracts from the criminal statistics and answer the following questions, illustrating your answers with figures taken from statistics. Specify your
source of information. Give the title of the publication you consulted and
indicate which year the data covers:

Title: ....

Year: ....

(a) By how much has the total volume of crime known to the police increased in recent years?

....

....

(b) What percentage of all crimes reported to the police do the following
constitute?

murder   ....
rape   ....
robbery   ....
theft   ....
fraud   ....
car theft   ....

Consider which crimes are likely to be proportionately over represented
and why?

....

....

Which crimes are likely to be under-represented and why?

....

....

(c) Give examples of the variations in the rate at which different kinds of
crimes are 'cleared up' by the police.

....

....

What does it mean to say that a crime is 'cleared up'?

....

....

Why are some offences more likely to be 'cleared up' than others?

....

....

d) Which groups in the population are most 'at risk' from 'personal crime'?

....

....

Should we be more afraid of strangers, acquaintances or family? Why?

....

....

e) What percentage of known offenders are male?

....

....

Taking into account the process of 'creating' statistics – how accurate do you think the ratio of male to female known offenders is?

....

....

EXERCISE 2: VICTIM SURVEY

You should use the following 'Crime Victim Questionnaire' and interviev eight people (four male, four female). Note their age. Try to include a rang of people.

Consider the following:

1. Which offences are respondents most/least likely to be the victims of? Are there any significant age/gender differences?

2. Which offences are more likely to be reported?

3. What reasons do victims give for not reporting crimes?

Crime victim questionnaire

In the last two years, how many times have you been the victim of the following crimes?	If so, was this reported to the police?	If not reported, why not
Theft	....	....	....
of a motor car	....	....	....
from a motor car	....	....	....
of a bicycle	....	....	....
at work	....	....	....
from your person	....	....	....
Burglary	....	....	....
Assault	....	....	....
with injury	....	....	....
no injury	....	....	....
Robbery	....	....	....
in street	....	....	....
in bank/post office	....	....	....
Insulted/bothered by strangers	....	....	....
Any other?	....	....	....
describe briefly	....	....	....

418

EXERCISE 3: MAGISTRATES' COURT OBSERVATION REPORT

We recommend you observe a morning session of a magistrates' court, which will normally start at 10 am and go on until lunchtime. If you are unable to attend during the week it may be possible to find inner urban courts that sit on Saturday and there is at least one evening court in the London area.

1. Name: ....

   Location of magistrates' court: ....

   Date of visit: ....

   Time of arrival: ....

   Time of departure: ....

2. Before you go give some impression of what you expect to see in a magistrates' court.

   ....

   ....

3. How many courtrooms were there? ....

   How many cases were scheduled to be heard in each?

   ....

   ....

4. After 10 minutes, from your time of arrival at the magistrates' court, describe your initial impressions.

   ....

   ....

5. Can you identify the following (*please tick*):

   - Bench ( )
   - Clerk's desk ( )
   - Advocates' seats ( )
   - Dock ( )
   - Witness box ( )
   - Press box ( )
   - Usher's seat ( )
   - Public seating ( )
   - Seating for defendants on bail or summons ( )

6. Personnel in the courtroom

   How many magistrates were there? ....

419

Name the other functionaries.

....

....

Who else was in the court?

....

....

7. Defendants

How many defendants appeared while you were in the court? ....

8. What sort of cases did you observe (*please tick*)?

- a remand ( )
- a decision as to mode of trial ( )
- an adjournment ( )
- a decision to grant bail ( )
- a remand in custody ( )
- a probation order being made ( )
- a disqualification from driving being ordered ( )
- a guilty plea being entered ( )
- a trial ( )
- a fine being imposed ( )

9. How would you describe the types of defendants you saw?

....

....

10. Were there some defendants who seemed unable to understand the proceedings?

....

....

11. Outcomes

How many cases were disposed of, from plea to sentence? ....

How many defendants were remanded in custody? ....

How many defendants were given bail with conditions? ....

How many defendants were given bail without conditions? ....

How many defendants were committed for trial to the Crown Court? ...

How many cases were adjourned to a future date? ....

If they were adjourned, give the reasons why.

....

....

2. What were your impressions of the performance of the Crown Prosecutor?

....

....

3. What was your impression of the magistrates?

....

....

4. What was your impression of the defence lawyer?

....

....

5. Using keywords, describe your general impression of the magistrates' court.

....

....

6. What time did the court commence business? ....

7. Was the conduct of the court efficient in your view? If not explain why not.

....

....

8. Are there any other comments you wish to make about your observations?

....

....

EXERCISE 4: SENTENCING AIMS IN COURT OF APPEAL DECISIONS

In the following three extracts from Court of Appeal decisions on sentencing cases, see if you can identify the aims of sentencing that are referred to by the court. Identify the statement and indicate which theory it represents.

1. R v Decino

....
....
....

2. R v Meggs

....
....
....

3. R v Knight (Colin)

....
....
....

Extract 1

Kiosk theft justifies jail
Regina v Decino

The offence of theft of money from a telephone kiosk was capable of being so serious that only a custodial sentence could be justified, within the terms of section 1(2)(a) of the Criminal Justice Act 1991.

The Court of Appeal (Lord Justice Beldam, Mr Justice Connell and Mrs Justice Ebsworth) so held on April 21 when allowing an appeal by Nicholas Decino against a sentence of 12 months imprisonment imposed on January 8, 1993 by Mr Recorder Williams at Cardiff Crown Court, following his conviction on December 8, 1992 at West Berkshire Magistrates Court of theft of £40.20 from a telephone kiosk.

For that offence he was sentenced to two months, and suspended sentences totalling ten months for burglary and possession of a controlled drug were activated consecutively. The sentences were made concurrent, reducing the total to ten months.

LORD JUSTICE BELDAM says that this was the kind of offence which was capable of depriving members of the public of the use of the public telephone which, to many people, was a lifeline. Of necessity telephone boxes were left unprotected. It was a matter of public policy to deter thefts from such boxes.

There was evidence that the appellant and two other young men provided themselves with the necessary tools and went on a deliberate expedition to rob telephone boxes of their contents.

In their Lordships' view it was, as the recorder has said, an offence capable of being so serious that only a sentence of custody could be justified for it.

Extract 2

Sentencing in cases of incest
Regina v Meggs

Before Lord Lane, Lord Chief Justice, Mr Justice Kennedy and
Mr Justice Hutchinson.
[Judgment February 21]

Cases of incest varied so enormously the one from the other that it was very difficult to derive any assistance from the previous instances which had appeared before the Court of Appeal.

The Lord Chief Justice so stated when giving the judgment of the court on an appeal by Eric William Meggs, aged 50, against prison sentences totalling 10 years passed at the Central Criminal Court by Sir James Miskin, QC, the Recorder of London, on pleas of guilty to specimen counts of incest with two of his daughters, extending in the case of the elder, for more than 22 years. Sentence of three years on one count, which had been made consecutive, was ordered to run concurrent with the other sentences, totalling $7\frac{1}{2}$ years.

Mr William Clegg, assigned by the Registrar of Criminal Appeals for the appellant.

THE LORD CHIEF JUSTICE said that, having made the elder girl pregnant twice the appellant caused her to have abortions. For a time they had lived as a married couple which according to Mr Clegg, was what the neighbours thought they were.

The elder daughter became pregnant by her boy friend but the appellant did not desist from having sexual intercourse with her throughout.

The appellant, throughout interviews with the police, denied that anything improper had occurred.

Such cases varied so enormously from one to the other that it was very difficult to derive any assistance from the previous instances which had appeared before the court.

The court had to mark its disapproval and the disapproval of the community of such behaviour. It had to endeavour to deter other men from behaving in such a way.

It had to punish the appellant for using his two daughters, in particular his elder daughter, simply as a chattel to satisfy his own sexual appetite, regardless of the damage he might do to her welfare

and happiness and, perhaps most important of all, her ability to enjoy a happy married life herself.

Mr Clegg submitted that insufficient regard was given to the plea of guilty and that overall the totality was too great despite the horrifying features of the case.

He pointed out that the appellant was disowned by his family, which was not surprising, but the effect was that he received no visits and was serving his sentence isolated to a great extent from his fellow prisoners.

They were all matters to be taken into account and their Lordships had concluded that Mr Clegg was correct in stating that the totality was too high.

There was nothing wrong with the individual sentences but their Lordships were concerned with the overall total and the proper course was to order that the sentence on a count ordered to run consecutively should, instead, run concurrent, so that the sentence was reduced by three years.

(*The Times*, 22 February 1989, © Times Supplements Limited, 1989)

Extract 3

Punishment for perjury
Regina v Knight (Colin)

Before Mr Justice McCowan and Mr Justice Leggatt.
(Judgment delivered 26 January)

Punishment for perjury had to be condign and commensurate with the gravity of the offence to prevent conviction of another for which the perjury was committed. The Court of Appeal so stated in dismissing an appeal by Colin Charles Knight, aged 32, against a three-year prison sentence passed at the Central Criminal Court by Sir James Miskin, QC, Recorder of London on a plea of guilty to perjury in that, being lawfully sworn as a witness on the trial of a man called Tobin at the Central Criminal Court, the appellant knowingly falsely described a man who jumped down from a crane.

Mr C Y Nutt, assigned by the Registrar of Criminal Appeals, for the appellant.

MR JUSTICE LEGGATT said that the crane was driven by Tobin into the back of a security van to gain access to it by a group of professional armed robbers. The jury disagreed at his first trial.

At the second trial the appellant not called at the first trial, gave perjured evidence in saying that he had been in the area at the time of the robbery and described a man different from Tobin getting down from the crane. In the event Tobin was convicted.

In mitigation of the appellant's offence it was suggested that there had been some inducement and threat by an intermediary.

In passing sentence on the appellant, Sir James Miskin had said that armed robbery, planned with exquisite skill by intelligent, determined men for high profit was one of the most serious crimes known to the courts and there was a great deal too much of it. Those who intentionally gave false testimony on behalf of such men did so intending to mislead the jury into returning a verdict contrary to true justice and the evidence.

Not having seen one whiff of what had happened and for reward the appellant had entered the witness box and told a whole string of purposive lies. Account was taken of the plea of guilty and good character and implicit show of steel on the part of the inter-

mediary. However, perjury was difficult enough to detect and much more difficult to prove. When it occurred it demanded instant prison.

Three years was imposed so that the appellant might be seen to be punished and, even more importantly, so that every single person in this age who contemplated events like giving false evidence in any case, let alone a serious one, or was minded to tamper with a jury, might know it would always be met by immediate, condign punishment.

Their Lordships agreed with every word of the judge in sentencing and, in particular that punishment had to be condign. The purpose of the appellant's perjury was to avoid conviction for a grave offence. The punishment had to be commensurate with the gravity of that offence. The maximum penalty was seven years' imprisonment. The judge having made such allowance as could have been made for the appellant's antecedents and plea of guilty, the sentence was unimpeachable. The appeal was dismissed.

The Times, 4 February 1984, © Times Supplements Limited, 1984)

425

EXERCISE 5: SENTENCING

In respect of the following triable-either-way case consider the sentence you think a court would impose.

Look at the charge(s) in the light of the Magistrates' Guidelines for Mode of Trial. Where should the case be tried? Depending on that decision, what are the court's powers? How would you assess the seriousness of the offence? Consult Figure 8.2 for relevant sentencing guidelines. Is there any mitigation on the part of the offender? Impose your sentence.

Affray

Accused:	DARREN SMITH (22)
	KEVIN JONES (19)
Charge:	On 31 January (this year) used unlawful violence towards others and their conduct was such as would cause a person of reasonable firmness to fear for his personal safety; section 3 Public Order Act 1986.
Maximum Penalty:	On indictment: 3 years, imprisonment and/or fine
	Summarily: 6 months, imprisonment and/or £5,000 fine
Pleas:	Jones pleaded guilty.
	Smith pleaded not guilty and consented to summary trial.
Facts:	The accused with a group of others who have not been traced, were passing a hamburger restaurant when they saw a group of Asian men eating there. The group entered the restaurant and began using terms of racial abuse towards the Asians. The restaurant manager (R McDonald) asked the accused to leave. They refused. An altercation ensued in which Mr McDonald was pushed over, injuring his back. Although the two accused used their fists and a chair as a weapon, no injuries were occasioned to the Asians because of the intervention of other customers. The police were called and arrested the two accused while the rest of the group ran off.

Previous Convictions
SMITH

3 years ago	Magistrates' court: Criminal damage, possession cannabis	Conditional discharge 12 months imprisonment, £80 compensation
2 years ago	Magistrates' court: Threatening behaviour (fight in pub)	Fined £75 and £35 costs
3 months ago	Magistrates' court: Assault actual bodily harm	Probation order 1 year, condition to attend Probation Centre, compensation £250

JONES
No previous convictions

Pre-Sentence Reports (Summary of):
SMITH
Left home when he was 16 because of violence from his step-father. Became involved in alcohol and drug abuse. Drink was involved in last two convictions. He had been drinking before current incident.

Attends Probation Centre under probation order imposed 3 months ago. Also does voluntary work in local psychiatric hospital. Owes compensation from last conviction. Unemployed, on benefit. Lives with girlfriend in rented accommodation. Another probation order is proposed.

JONES
No previous convictions, does not need supervision. Community service available, but suggests financial penalty. Earns £150 per week and has expenses (board, travel to work, etc.) of £70 per week. Lives with parents.

Summary of Mitigation
Both regret stupid behaviour, recognise alcohol partly to blame. Deny they have racist views.

APPENDIX 2

CRIMINAL JUSTICE WEBSITES

Information sources using computers are becoming increasingly important and if you have a link to the internet and a network browser you will be able to access the following websites for which there is no charge. Remember you must be completely accurate when entering the website address and patience is required when sites are busy. The websites listed below will give you access to data and documents such as Acts of Parliament, current news, press releases, annual organisational reports with information about resources, costs, organisational changes and policy developments. Some useful sources are cited below.

1 Statistics on criminal justice

Website address: http://www.homeoffice.gov.uk/rsd/rsdhome.htm

The Research and Statistics Directorate of the Home Office provides data on:

- British Crime Survey
- cautions issued by the police
- crimes cleared up
- cost and staff numbers of criminal justice agencies
- criminal careers
- drugs and crimes
- international comparisons
- offenders
- prison population
- recorded crime
- sentencing

2 Home Office website

Website address: http://www.homeoffice.gov.uk/

A useful site with information about:

● The Home Office: aims, list of all past Home Secretaries, organisational details and a list of associated agencies and public bodies.

● Information about policy developments is provided by copies of press releases and details on developments such as crime and drug prevention, protecting property, Neighbourhood Watch and retail crime. There is practical guidance on creating youth offending teams and crime prevention and details about certain crimes, e.g. drugs and crime.

● Information source on Bills and Acts, policy documents and a list of publications and the full text of reports such as the 1997 White Paper *No More Excuses: Tackling Youth Crime in England and Wales*. The Home Office annual report is available in full on the internet at this site.

3 Information on the judiciary: Lord Chancellor's Department website

Website address: http://www.open.gov.uk/lcd/

Information about legal aid, judges and magistrates including how to apply to become a magistrate or a QC, a list of the names of the senior judiciary, recent judgments and speeches by judges, and legislation and policy changes affecting the judiciary.

There are practice directions for instance on the form of words to be used by judges and magistrates when giving custodial sentence with an explanation of what this means for the sentenced offender. There is information about the Court of Appeal (Criminal Division), plus leaflets and forms that might be of use to a court user.

4 Metropolitan Police

Website address: http://www.met.police.uk/

Very well constructed and useful site with a useful index that will take you to local police stations with local information and their histories; specialist squads such as the Art Squad and the notorious such as Jack the Ripper. There are press releases and current news involving the Metropolitan Police. The history section has information on fingerprinting and the CID. There are policy statements and advice on such matters as crime prevention. The annual report of the Commissioner of the Metropolitan Police is published in full.

5 Current legislation

Website address: *http://www.parliament.the-stationery-office.co.uk/pa/pabills.htm*

Bills before Parliament are available in their latest amended form on the above address. There is a list of all bills currently before the House of Commons and the House of Lords.

6 Crown Prosecution Service

Website address: *http://www.cps.gov.uk*

Information about its history, workload, functions, organisation plus a summary of its annual report. Its liaison role with other agencies is outlined and the Code for Crown Prosecutors is published with details of the evidential sufficiency and public interest tests. The Victim's Charter is included and there is information for witnesses. There is a News Desk with information about recent cases with details about convictions and sentences.

7 Law Commission for England and Wales

Website address: *http://www.open.gov.uk/lawcomm/homepage.htm*

Information about the Law Commission's current projects which in 1998 included: corruption, consent to prosecution, dishonesty and theft, and hearsay evidence.

8 Prison Service

Website address: *http://www.open.gov.uk/prison/prisonhm.htm*

At the time of publication in 1998 this Prison Service website contained information about careers as a Prison Service psychologist and the role of the psychologists in prison.

BIBLIOGRAPHY

dvisory Council on the Penal System (1978) *Sentences of Imprisonment: A Review of Maximum Penalties*. London: HMSO.

lderson J (1978) *Communal Policing*. Exeter: Devon and Cornwall Constabulary.

llen R (1991) 'Out of Jail: The Reduction in the Use of Penal Custody for Male Juveniles', *Howard Journal*, 30 (1): 30–53.

llen R (1998) 'Trends in Imprisonment', *Criminal Justice Matters*, No 30, Winter 1997/8: 8.

lschuler A (1992) *New Law Journal*, 3 July: 937.

mir M (1971) *Patterns of Forcible Rape*. Chicago: University of Chicago Press.

nderson S, Kinsey R, Loader I and Smith C (1994) *Cautionary Tales: Young People, Crime and Policing in Edinburgh*. Aldershot: Avebury.

udit Commission (1996) *Misspent Youth: Young People and Crime*. London: Audit Commission.

shworth A (1989) 'Criminal Justice and Deserved Sentences', *Criminal Law Review*: 340–55.

shworth A (1992a) *The Youth Court*. Winchester: Waterside Press.

shworth A (1992b) *Sentencing and Penal Policy*, 2nd edn. London: Weidenfeld & Nicholson.

shworth A (1993) 'Victim Impact Statements and Sentencing', *Criminal Law Review*: 498–509.

shworth A (1994a) *The Criminal Process*. Oxford: Clarendon Press.

shworth A (1994b) 'Sentencing', in Maguire M, Morgan R and Reiner R (eds) *The Oxford Handbook of Criminology*. Oxford: Clarendon Press.

shworth A (1997a) 'Sentenced by the Media?' *Criminal Justice Matters*, No 29, Autumn 1997: 14–15.

shworth A (1997b) 'Sentencing', in Maguire M, Morgan R and Reiner R (eds) *The Oxford Handbook of Criminology*, 2nd edn. Oxford: Clarendon Press.

agguley P and Mann K (1992) 'Idle Thieving Bastards? Scholarly Representations of the "Underclass" ', *Work, Employment and Society*, 6 (1): 113–26.

aldwin J and Bottomley A (eds) (1978) *Criminal Justice: Selected Readings*. London: Martin Robertson.

431

Baldwin J and McConville M (1979) *Jury Trials*. Oxford: Clarendon Press.

Barclay G (ed) (1995) *Digest 3: Information on the Criminal Justice System i England and Wales*. London: HMSO.

Becker H S (1963) *Outsiders: Studies in the Sociology of Deviance*. New York Free Press.

Bennett T (1984) *Burglars on Burglary: Prevention and the Offender*. Farn borough: Gower.

Bennett T (1990) *Evaluating Neighbourhood Watch*. Aldershot: Gower.

Bennett T (1991) 'The Effectiveness of a Police-Initiated Fear Reducin Strategy', *British Journal of Criminology*, 31 (1): 1–14.

Bennett T (1994a) 'Recent Developments in Community Policing', in Stephen M and Becker S (eds) *Police Force, Police Service: Care and Control i Britain*. London: Macmillan.

Bennett T (1994b) 'Community Policing', *Criminal Justice Matters*, No 17 Autumn 1994: 6–7.

Bennett T and Lupton R (1992) 'A National Activity Survey of Police Work' *Howard Journal of Criminal Justice*, 31 (3): 200–23.

Bentham J (1791) *Panopticon: or the Inspection House*. London: Payer.

Bentham J (1830) *The Rationale of Punishment*. London: Hewood.

Block B, Corbett C and Peay J (1993) 'Ordered and Directed Acquittals i the Crown Court. A Time of Change?', *Criminal Law Review*: 95.

Blom-Cooper L (1988) *The Penalty of Imprisonment*. London: Prison Reforn Trust.

Blumberg A (1967) *Criminal Justice*. Chicago: Quadrangle Books.

Borna S (1986) 'Free Enterprise goes to Prison', *British Journal of Crimino logy*, 26 (4).

Bottomley K and Pease K (1986) *Crime and Punishment: Interpreting th Data*. Milton Keynes: Open University Press.

Bottoms A and McClean (1978) in Baldwin and Bottomley (eds) *Crimina Justice: Selected Readings*. London: Martin Robertson.

Box S (1987) *Recession, Crime and Punishment*. London: Macmillan.

Braithwaite J (1989) *Crime, Shame and Re-integration*. Cambridge: Cambridg University Press.

Braithwaite J and Pettit P (1990) *Not Just Deserts: A Republican Theory o Justice*. Oxford: Clarendon Press.

Bratton W (1997) 'Crime is Down in New York City: Blame the Police' i Dennis N (ed) *Zero Tolerance: Policing a Free Society*. London: IEA.

Brogden M, Jefferson T and Walklate S (1988) *Introducing Police Work*. Lon don: Unwin Hyman.

Brooks C and Cross C (1996) *Retail Crime Costs*.

Brown D (1997) *PACE Ten Years On: A Review of the Research*. Home Offic Research Study No 155. London: Home Office.

Burton A (1994) 'The Demise of Criminal Legal Aid', *New Law Journal*, 28 1491.

Cain M (1973) *Society and the Policeman's Role*. London: Routledge & Kegan Paul.

California State Government (1990) *Report on Inmate Population Management*. Sacramento: The Department of Corrections.

Campbell B (1993) *Goliath: Britain's Dangerous Places*. London: Methuen.

Carlen P (1976) *Magistrates' Justice*. London: Martin Robertson.

Carlen P (1990) *Alternatives to Women's Imprisonment*. Milton Keynes: Open University Press.

Carlen P and Worrall A (eds) (1987) *Gender, Crime and Justice*. Milton Keynes: Open University Press.

Carson W G (1974) 'Symbolic and Instrumental Dimensions of Early Factory Legislation: A Case Study on The Social Origins of Criminal Law', in Hood R (ed) *Crime Criminology and Public Policy*. London: Heinemann.

Casale S (1984) *Minimum Standards for Prison Establishments*. London: National Association for the Care and Resettlement of Offenders.

Cavadino P (1998) 'Juveniles to Stay in Jail', *Criminal Justice Matters*, No 30, Winter 1997/8: 17–18.

Cavadino P and Dignan J (1997) *The Penal System: An Introduction*, 2nd edn. London: Sage.

Chibnall S (1977) *Law and Order News*. London: Tavistock.

Clarke (1980) 'Situational Crime Prevention: Theory and Practice', *British Journal of Criminology*, 20: 136–47.

Clemmer D (1958) *The Prison Community*. New York: Holt, Rinehart & Winston.

Cloward R and Ohlin L (1960) *Delinquency and Opportunity: A Theory of Delinquent Gangs*. New York: Free Press.

Cohen A K (1955) *Delinquent Boys: The Culture of the Gang*. New York: Free Press.

Cohen P (1979) 'Policing the Working Class City', in Fine B (ed) *Capitalism and the Rule of Law*. London: Hutchinson.

Cohen S (1980) *Folk Devils and Moral Panics*. Oxford: Martin Robertson.

Cohen S (1985) *Visions of Social Control*. Cambridge: Polity Press.

Cohen S and Taylor L (1972) *Psychological Survival*. Harmondsworth: Penguin.

Coleman C and Moynihan J (1996) *Understanding Crime Data: Haunted by the Dark Figure*. Buckingham: Open University Press.

Collison M (1996) 'In Search of the High Life: Drugs, Crime, Masculinities and Consumption', *British Journal of Criminology*, 36 (3): 428–44.

Condon P (1994) Address to meeting of British Society of Criminologists, London, January 1994.

Cressey D (1986) 'Why Managers Commit Fraud', *Australian and New Zealand Journal of Criminology*, 19: 195–209.

Crime Concern (1994) *Counting the Cost*. A briefing paper on financial losses arising from crime. Swindon: Crime Concern.

Croall H (1988) 'Mistakes, Accidents and Someone Else's Fault: The Trading Offender in Court', *Journal of Law and Society*, 15 (3): 293–325.

433

Croall H (1989) 'Who is the White Collar Criminal?', *British Journal of Criminology*, 29 (2): 157–74.

Croall H (1991) 'Sentencing the Business Offender', *The Howard Journal*, 30 (4): 280–94.

Croall H (1992) *White Collar Crime*. Milton Keynes: Open University Press

Croall H (1998a) 'Business, Crime and the Community', *International Journal of Risk, Security and Crime Prevention*.

Croall H (1998b) *Crime and Society in Britain*. London: Longman.

Crown Prosecution Service (annually) *Annual Report*. London: HMSO.

Currie E (1996) 'Social crime prevention strategies in a market society', in Muncie J, McLaughlin E and Langan M (eds) *Criminological Perspectives* London: Sage.

Darbyshire P (1991) 'The lamp that shows that freedom lives: is it worth the candle?' *Criminal Law Review*: 740.

Davies K (1969) *Discretionary Justice: A Preliminary Inquiry*. Baton Rouge Louisiana State University Press.

Davies M (1989) 'An Alternative View: Square Deal Punishment in the Community: It is Cheaper But Who Will Buy It?', in Rees H and Hal Williams E (eds) *Punishment, Custody and the Community: Reflections and Comments on the Green Paper*. Suntory Toyota International Centre for Economics and Related Disciplines.

Davies M (1993) *Punishing Criminals: Developing Community-based Intermediate Sanctions*. Connecticut: Greenwood.

Davies M, Takala J-P and Tyrer J (1996) *Penological Esperanto and Sentencing Parochialism*. Aldershot: Dartmouth.

Dennis N (ed) (1997) *Zero Tolerance: Policing a Free Society*. London: IEA.

Dicey A (1959) *Introduction to the Study of the Law of the Constitution*. London: Macmillan.

Dignan J and Wynne A (1997) 'A Microcosm of the Local Community', *British Journal of Criminology*, 37 (2): 184.

Ditton J and Duffy J (1983) 'Bias in the Newspaper Reporting of Crime News', *British Journal of Criminology*, 23: 129.

Dixon D, Bottomley A, Coleman C, Gill M and Wall D (1989) 'Reality and Rules in the Construction and Regulation of Police Suspicion', *International Journal of the Sociology of Law*, 17.

Doig A (1996) 'From Lynskey to Nolan: The Corruption of British Politics and Public Service', *Journal of Law and Society*, 23 (1): 36–56.

Dorn N, Murji K and South N (1992) *Traffickers: Drugs Markets and Law Enforcement*. London: Routledge.

Downes D (1966) *The Delinquent Solution*. London: Routledge & Kegan Paul.

Downes D and Rock P (1995) *Understanding Deviance: A Guide to the Sociology of Crime and Rule Breaking*, 2nd edn. Oxford: Clarendon Press.

Dunningham C and Norris C (1996a) 'A Risky Business: The Recruitment and Running of Informers by English Police Officers', *Police Studies*, 1 (2): 1–25.

Dunningham C and Norris C (1996b) 'The Nark's Game', *New Law Journal*, 22 March: 402–4.

Durkheim E (1970) *Suicide*. London: Routledge & Kegan Paul.

Eaton M (1986) *Justice for Women?* Milton Keynes: Open University Press.

Eaton M (1987) 'The Question of Bail: Magistrates' Responses to Applications for Bail on Behalf of Men and Women Defendants', in Carlen P and Worrall A (eds) *Gender, Crime and Justice*. Milton Keynes: Open University Press.

Eaton M (1993) *Women after Prison*. Milton Keynes: Open University Press.

Eden W (1777) *Principles of Penal Law*. London: B White & T Cadell.

Evans R and Wilkinson C (1990) 'Variations in Police Cautioning Policy and Practice in England and Wales', *Howard Journal of Criminal Justice*, 29 (3): 155–76.

Eysenck H J (1977) *Crime and Personality*. London: Routledge & Kegan Paul.

Farrington D (1992) 'Juvenile Delinquency', in Coleman J (ed) *The School Years*. London: Routledge.

Farrington D (1997) 'Human Development and Criminal Careers', in Maguire M, Morgan R and Reiner R (eds) *The Oxford Handbook of Criminology*, 2nd edn. Oxford: Clarendon Press.

Farrington D and Dowds E (1985) 'Disentangling Criminal Behaviour and Police Reaction', in Farrington D and Gunn J (eds) *Reactions to Crime: The Public, the Police, Courts and Prisons*. Chichester: Wiley.

Farrington D and Gunn J (eds) (1985) *Reactions to Crime: The Public, the Police, Courts and Prisons*. Chichester: Wiley.

Farrington D and Morris A (1983) 'Sex, Sentencing and Re-conviction', *British Journal of Criminology*, 23: 229–48.

Fennell P (1991) 'Diversion of Mentally Disordered Offenders From Custody', *Criminal Law Review*: 333–48.

Field S (1996) 'Crime and Consumption', in Muncie J, McLaughlin E and Langan M (eds) *Criminological Perspectives*. London: Sage.

Fielding N (1988) *Joining Forces: Police Training, Socialisation and Occupational Competence*. London: Routledge.

Fielding N, Kemp C and Norris C (1989) 'Constraints on the Practice of Community Policing', in Morgan R and Smith D (eds) *Coming to Terms with Policing*. London: Routledge.

Fitzgerald M (1977) *Prisoners in Revolt*. Harmondsworth: Penguin.

FitzGerald M and Hale C (1996) *Ethnic Minorities: Victimisation and Racial Harassment: Findings from the 1988 and 1992 British Crime Surveys*. Home Office Research Study No 154. London: Home Office.

Flood-Page C and Mackie A (1998) *Sentencing practice: an examination of decisions in magistrates' courts and the Crown Court in the mid-1990's*. Home Office Research Study No. 180. London: Home Office.

Fogel D (1975) *We are the Living Proof: The Justice Model for Corrections*. Cincinatti: W H Anderson.

Foster J (1989) 'Two Stations: An Ethnographic Study of Policing in the Inner City', in Downes D (ed) *Crime and the City*. London: Macmillan.

Foucault M (1977) *Discipline and Punish*. Harmondsworth: Penguin.

Fox L (1952) *The English Prison and Borstal System*. London: Routledge & Kegan Paul.

Frankel M (1973) *Criminal Sentences: Law Without Order: The American Friend Service Committee 1971 Struggle for Justice*. New York: Hill & Wang.

Garfinkel H (1956) 'Conditions of Successful Degradation Ceremonies' *American Journal of Sociology*, 61 (2): 420–4.

Garland D (1990) *Punishment and Modern Society*. Oxford: Oxford University Press.

Gelsthorpe L and Morris A (1994) 'Juvenile Justice 1945–1992', in Maguire M, Morgan R and Reiner R (eds) *The Oxford Handbook of Criminology*. Oxford: Clarendon Press.

Gill M and Mawby R (1990) *Volunteers in the Criminal Justice System: A Comparative Study of Probation, Police and Victim Support*. Milton Keynes: Open University Press.

Goffman E (1961) *Asylums: Essays on the Social Situation of Mental Patients and Other Inmates*. Golden City, New York: Doubleday.

Goffman E (1968) *Stigma: Notes on the Management of Spoiled Identities*. Harmondsworth: Penguin.

Graef R (1992) *Living Dangerously: Young Offenders in their Own Words*. London: Harper-Collins.

Graham J and Bowling B (1995) *Young People and Crime*. Home Office Research Study No 145. London: Home Office.

Gresswell D and Hollin C (1994) 'Multiple Murder: A Review', *British Journal of Criminology*, 34 (1): 1–15.

Gross H (1979) *A Theory of Criminal Justice*. New York: Oxford University Press.

Grubin D (1991) 'Unfit to Plead in England and Wales 1976–1988: A Survey', *British Journal of Psychiatry*: 540–8.

Hall S, Critcher C, Jefferson T, Clarke J and Roberts B (1978) *Policing the Crisis: Mugging, the State and Law and Order*. London: Macmillan.

Hall S and Jefferson T (eds) (1976) *Resistance Through Ritual*. London: Hutchinson.

Harding C, Hines B, Ireland R and Rawlings P (1985) *Imprisonment in England and Wales*. Beckenham: Croom Helm.

Harman H and Griffith J (1979) *Justice Deserted: The Subversion of the Jury*. London: NCCL.

Hart H L A (1968) *Punishment and Responsibility*. Oxford: Clarendon Press.

Hawkins K (1984) *Environment and Enforcement: Regulation and the Social Definition of Pollution*. Oxford Socio-Legal Studies: Clarendon Press.

Heal K and Laycock G (1986) *Situational Crime Prevention: From Theory to Practice*. London: Home Office.

Hedderman C and Gelsthorpe L (1997) *Understanding the Sentencing of Women*. Home Office Research Study No. 170. London: Home Office.

Iedderman C and Hough M (1994) *Does the Criminal Justice System Treat Men and Women Differently?* Home Office Research and Statistics Department, No 10. London: Home Office.

Iedderman C and Moxon D (1992) *Magistrates' Court or Crown Court? Mode of Trial and Sentencing Decisions.* London: Home Office.

Ieidensohn F (1985) *Women and Crime.* London: Macmillan.

Ieidensohn F (1989) *Crime and Society.* London: Macmillan.

Ieidensohn F (1992) *Women in Control? The Role of Women in Law Enforcement.* Oxford: Oxford University Press.

Ieidensohn F (1997) 'Gender and Crime', in Maguire M, Morgan R, and Reiner R (eds) *The Oxford Handbook of Criminology*, 2nd edn. Oxford: Clarendon Press.

Ientig, H von (1948) *The Criminal and his Victim.* New Haven: Yale University Press.

Iirsch A von (1976) *Doing justice – The Choice of Punishment.* York: Hill & Wang.

Iirsch A von (1986) *Past or Future Crimes.* Manchester University Press.

Iirsch A von and Ashworth A (eds) (1993) *Principled Sentencing.* Edinburgh: Edinburgh University Press.

Iirschi T (1969) *Causes of Delinquency.* Los Angeles: University of California Press.

IM Inspectorate of Probation (annually) *Annual Report.* London: HMSO.

IM Prison Service (annually) *Annual Report and Accounts.* London: HMSO.

Iobbes T (1650) *Leviathan.* Edited by C MacPherson 1968. London: Penguin.

Iobbs D (1991) 'A Piece of Business: the Moral Economy of Detective Work in the East of London', *British Journal of Sociology*, 42 (4).

Iobbs D (1995) *Bad Business: Professional Crime in Modern Britain.* Oxford: University Press.

Iodgson J (1997) 'Justice Undermined', *Criminal Justice Matters*, No 29, Autumn 1997: 4–5.

Ioldaway S (1983) *Inside the British Police.* Oxford: Basil Blackwell.

Ioldaway S (1996) *The Racialisation of British Policing.* London: Macmillan.

Ioldaway S (1997) 'Some Recent Approaches to the Study of Race in Criminological Research', *British Journal of Criminology*, 37 (3): 383–400.

Iollin C (1989) *Psychology and Crime: An Introduction to Criminological Psychology.* London: Routledge.

Iome Office (1895) *Report from the Departmental Committee on Prisons* (chaired by Herbert Gladstone). London: Home Office.

Iome Office (1931) *Evidence to Persistent Offenders Committee*, Vol 3.

Iome Office (1959) *Penal Practice in a Changing Society.* London: Home Office.

Iome Office (1966) *Report of the Inquiry into Prison Escapes and Security* (chaired by Earl Mountbatten). London: HMSO.

Iome Office (1968) *Report on the Regime for Long-term Prisoners in Maximum Security* (chaired by Sir Leon Radzinowicz). London: HMSO.

Iome Office (1977) *Prisons and the Prisoner.* London: HMSO.

Home Office (1979) *The Report of the Committee of Inquiry into the UK Prisc Service* (chaired by Mr Justice May). Cm 7673. London: HMSO.

Home Office (1984) *Criminal Justice: A Working Paper*. London: Home Offic

Home Office (1986) *The Sentence of the Court*. London: HMSO.

Home Office (1988a) *Punishment, Custody and the Community*. Cm 424. Lor don: HMSO.

Home Office (1988b) *The Parole System in England and Wales: Report of tl Review Committee* (Carlisle Committee). Cm 532. London: HMSO.

Home Office (1990a) *Crime, Justice and Protecting the Public*. London: Hom Office.

Home Office (1990b) *Victim's Charter: A Statement of the Rights of the Victim of Crime*. London: HMSO.

Home Office (1991a) *Prison Disturbances, April 1990*. Report of an inquii presented to the Home Office by Lord Justice H Woolf and Judge Stephe Tumin. Cm 1456. London: HMSO.

Home Office (1991b) *A General Guide to the Criminal Justice Act 1991*. Lor don: HMSO.

Home Office (1991c) *Custody, Care and Justice: The Way Ahead for the Prisc Service in England and Wales*. Cm 1647. London: HMSO.

Home Office (1992) *Survey of Prisons in England and Wales*. London: HMSC

Home Office (1993) *Safer Cities Progress Report 1992/3*. Home Office Crim Prevention Unit. London: HMSO.

Home Office (1994) *Home Office Research Findings*, No 14. London: HMSC

Home Office (1995) *National Standards for the Supervision of Offenders in tl Community*. London: HMSO.

Home Office (1997a) *No More Excuses – A New Approach to Tackling Youi Crime in England and Wales*. Cm. 3809. London: Home Office.

Home Office (1997b) *Getting to Grips with Crime – A New Framework f Local Action*. London: HMSO.

Home Office (1997c) *Review of Delay in the Criminal Justice System* (chaire by M Narey). London: HMSO.

Home Office (annually) *Criminal Statistics England and Wales*. London: Hom Office.

Hood R (1965) *Borstal Re-assessed*. London: Heinemann.

Hood R (1972) *Sentencing the Motoring Offender*. London: Heinemann.

Hood R (ed) (1974) *Crime, Criminology and Public Policy*. London: Heineman

Hood R (1992) *Race and Sentencing*. Clarendon: Oxford University Press.

Hough M (1996) 'Drug Misuse and the Criminal Justice System: A Revie of the Literature', *Criminal Justice Matters*, No 24, Summer 1996: 4–5.

Hough M and Mayhew P (1983) *The British Crime Survey: First Report Takin Account of Crime*. London: HMSO.

Hough M and Roberts J (1998) *Attitudes to Punishment: Findings from tl British Crime Survey*. London: HMSO.

Hudson B (1989) 'Discrimination and Disparity: The Influence of Race o Sentencing', *New Community*, 16: 23–34.

438

Judson B (1993) *Penal Policy and Social Justice*. London: Macmillan.

Ignatieff M (1975) *A Just Measure of Pain: The Penitentiary in the Industrial Revolution 1750–1850*. London: Macmillan.

Irving B, Bird C, Hibberd M and Wilmore J (1989) *Neighbourhood Policing: The Natural History of a Policing Experiment*. London: Police Foundation.

Irwin J (1970) *The Felon*. Englewood Cliffs: Prentice Hall.

Irwin J (1980) *Prisons in Turmoil*. Toronto: Little, Brown & Co.

Jarvis G and Parker H (1989) 'Young Heroin Users and Crime', *British Journal of Criminology*, 29 (2): 175–85.

Jefferson T (1990) *The Case Against Paramilitary Policing*. Milton Keynes: Open University Press.

Jefferson T and Walker M (1992) 'Ethnic Minorities in the Criminal Justice System', *Criminal Law Review*: 83–8.

Jefferson T, Walker M and Seneviratne M (1992) 'Ethnic Minorities, Crime and Criminal Justice: A Study in a Provincial City', in Downes D (ed) *Unravelling Criminal Justice*. London: Macmillan.

Johnston L (1992) *The Rebirth of Private Policing*. London: Routledge.

Johnston L (1994) 'Current Developments in Private Policing', *Criminal Justice Matters*, No 17, Autumn 1994.

Jones T, McClean B and Young J (1986) *The Islington Crime Survey*. Aldershot: Gower.

Jones T and Newburn T (1994a) *How Big is the Private Security Industry?* London: Policy Studies Institute.

Jones T and Newburn T (1994b) 'Policing and Democracy', *Criminal Justice Matters*, No 17, Autumn 1994.

Jones T and Newburn T (1997) *Policing After the Act*. Policy Studies Institute.

Joutsen M (1990) *The Criminal Justice System of Finland: A General Introduction*. Helsinki: Ministry of Justice.

Jowell R. Curtis J, Lindsay B, Ahrendt D with Pork A (eds) (1994) *British Social Attitudes, 11th Report*. Aldershot: Dartmouth Puslishing Co.

Kershaw C, Dowdewell P and Goodman J (1997) 'Life Licensees – Reconvictions and Recalls by the end of 1995: England and Wales', *Home Office Statistical Bulletin*, Issue 2/97. London: Home Office.

Kershaw C and Renshaw G (1997) 'Reconvictions of Prisoners Discharged from Prison in 1993, England and Wales', *Home Office Statistical Bulletin*, Issue 5/97. London: Home Office.

King M (1981) *The Framework of Criminal Justice*. London: Croom Helm.

King R and Elliott K (1977) *Albany: The Birth of a Prison, the End of an Era*. London: Routledge & Kegan Paul.

King R and Morgan R (1980) *The Future of the Prison System*. Farnborough: Gower.

Landau S F and Nathan G (1983) 'Selecting Juveniles for Cautioning in the London Metropolitan Area', *British Journal of Criminology*, 23 (2).

Lea J and Young J (1984) *What is to be Done About Law and Order?*, 1st edn. Harmondsworth: Penguin.

Lea J and Young J (1992) *What is to be Done about Law and Order?*, 2nd edn London: Pluto Press.

Learmont J (1995) *Review of Prison Service Security in England and Wales and the Escape from Parkhurst Prison on Tuesday 3rd January 1995*. Cm 3020 London: HMSO.

Leigh L (1997) 'Safeguarding against Miscarriages of Justice', *Criminal Justice Matters*, No 29, Autumn 1997: 16–17.

Leishman F, Loveday B and Savage S (eds) (1998) *Core Issues in Policing* 2nd edn. London: Longman.

Lemert E (1967) *Human Deviance, Social Problems and Social Control*. Englewood Cliffs: Prentice Hall.

Leng R, McConville M and Sanders A (1992) 'Researching the Discretion to Charge and to Prosecute', in Downes D (ed) *Unravelling Criminal Justice* London: Macmillan.

Levi M (1987) *Regulating Fraud: White Collar Crime and the Criminal Process* London: Tavistock.

Levi M (1989) 'Suite Justice: Sentencing for Fraud', *Criminal Law Review* 420–34.

Levi M and Pithouse A (1992) 'The Victims of Fraud', in Downes D (ed *Unravelling Criminal Justice*. London: Macmillan.

Lewis C S (1953) 'On Punishment', *Res Judicatae*, 6, 1952–4.

Light R (1993) *Car Theft: The Offender's Perspective*. Home Office Research and Planning Unit Report No 130. London: HMSO.

Lipton D, Martinson R and Wilks J (1975) *Effectiveness of Correctional Treatment*. Springfield, Mass.: Praeger.

Lloyd C, Mair G and Hough M (1994) *Explaining Reconviction Rates: A Critical Analysis*. Home Office Research Study No 136. London: HMSO

Logan C (1990) *Private Prisons: The Cons and Pros*. Oxford: Oxford University Press.

Lombroso Cesare (1897) *L'Uomo Delinquente*, 5th edn. Torino: Bocca.

Lord Chancellor's Department (1997) *Departmental Report of the Lord Chancellor's and Law Officers' Departments*. Cm 3609. London: HMSO.

Lord Chancellor's Department (annually) *Judicial Statistics*. London: HMSO

Loveday B (1992) 'Right Agendas: Law and Order in England and Wales' *International Journal of the Sociology of Law*, 20: 297–319.

Loveday B (1994) 'Policing the Future', *Criminal Justice Matters*, No 17 Autumn 1994: 4.

Maguire M (1982) *Burglary in a Dwelling*. London: Heinemann.

Maguire M (1997) 'Crime Statistics, Patterns and Trends: Changing Perceptions and their Implications', in Maguire M, Morgan R and Reiner R (eds) *The Oxford Handbook of Criminology*, 2nd edn. Oxford: Clarendon Press.

Maguire M, Morgan R and Reiner R (eds) (1994) *The Oxford Handbook of Criminology*. Oxford: Clarendon Press.

Maguire M, Morgan R and Reiner R (eds) (1997) *The Oxford Handbook of Criminology*, 2nd edn. Oxford: Clarendon Press.

Maguire M and Pointing J (eds) (1988) *Victims of Crime: A New Deal?* Milton Keynes: Open University Press.

Mair G (1997) 'Community Penalties and the Probation Service', in Maguire M, Morgan R and Reiner R (eds) *The Oxford Handbook of Criminology*, 2nd edn. Clarendon Press: Oxford.

Mann K (1985) *Defending White Collar Crime*. New Haven and London: Yale University Press.

Mars G (1982) *Cheats at Work, an Anthropology of Workplace Crime*. London: George Allen & Unwin.

Mathiesen T (1990) *Prison on Trial*. London: Sage.

Mathiesen T (1991) 'The Argument Against Building more Prisons', in Muncie J and Sparks R (eds) *Imprisonment: European Perspectives*. Hemel Hempstead: Harvester Wheatsheaf.

Matza D (1964) *Delinquency and Drift*. New York: Wiley.

May C (1992) *The National Probation Survey 1990*. Home Office Research and Planning Unit Paper 72. London: HMSO.

May T (1991) *Probation, Politics, Policy and Practice*. Buckingham: Open University Press.

May T (1994) 'Probation and Community Sanctions', in Maguire M, Morgan R and Reiner R (eds) *The Oxford Handbook of Criminology*. Oxford: Clarendon Press.

Mayhew P, Clarke R, Sturman A and Hough J (eds) (1976) *Crime as Opportunity*. Home Office Research Study No 34. London: HMSO.

Mayhew P, Elliot D and Dowds L (1989) *The 1988 British Crime Survey*. London: HMSO.

Mayhew P, Maung N and Mirrlees-Black C (1993) *The 1992 British Crime Survey*. London: HMSO.

Mayhew P, Maung N and Mirrlees-Black C (1995) *The 1994 British Crime Survey*. London: HMSO.

McBarnet D (1981) *Conviction: Law, the State and the Construction of Justice*. London: Macmillan.

McCabe S (1988) in Findlay M and Duff P (eds) *The Jury Under Attack*. London: Butterworth.

McIvor G (1991) 'Community Service and Custody in Scotland', *Howard Journal*, 29 (2): 101–13.

Measham F, Newcombe R and Parker H (1994) 'The Normalization of Recreational Drug Use amongst Young People in North-West England', *British Journal of Sociology*, 45 (2): 287–312.

Merton R K (1938) 'Social Structure and Anomie', *American Sociological Review*, 3: 672–82.

Messinger S and Johnson P (1978) 'California's Determinate Sentencing Statute History and Issues', in *Determinate Sentencing: Reform or Regression.*

National Institute of Law Enforcement and Criminal Justice. Washington DC: Government Printing Office.

Metropolitan Police Commissioner (1992) *Annual Report for the Year 1991/9.* London: HMSO.

Miller P and Plant M (1996) 'Drinking, Smoking and Illicit Drug Use Amon 15 and 16 year olds in the United Kingdom', *British Medical Journal*, 31: 394–7.

Mirrlees-Black C, Mayhew P and Percy A (1996) 'The 1996 British Crim Survey: England and Wales', *Home Office Statistical Bulletin*, Issue 19/9(London: HMSO.

Morgan J and Zedner L (1992) *Child Victims: Crime, Impact, and Crimin Justice.* Oxford: Clarendon Press.

Morgan P (1992) *Offending While on Bail – A Survey of Recent Studies.* Lor don: Home Office.

Morgan R (1989) 'Policing by Consent: Legitimating the Doctrine', in Morga and Smith (eds) *Coming to Terms with Policing: Perspectives on Policy.* Lor don: Routledge.

Morgan R (1997) 'Imprisonment', in Maguire M, Morgan R and Reiner (eds) *The Oxford Handbook of Criminology*, 2nd edn. Oxford: Clarendo Press.

Morgan R and Jones T (1992) 'Bail or Jail?', in Stockdale E and Casales (eds) *Criminal Justice Under Stress.* London: Blackstone.

Morgan R and Newburn T (1994) 'Backing up the Police', *Criminal Justi Matters*, No 17, Autumn 1994: 3.

Morgan R and Newburn T (1997) *The Future of Policing.* Oxford: Clarendo Press.

Morris A and Giller H (1987) *Understanding Juvenile Justice.* London: Croo Helm.

Moxon D (1993) 'Use of Compensation Orders in Magistrates' Courts *Home Office Research Bulletin 33/1993.* London: HMSO.

Murphy P (1992) *A Practical Approach to Evidence.* London: Blackston Press.

Murphy P (1997) *A Practical Approach to Evidence*, 6th edn. London: Blackston Press.

Murray C (1996) 'The Underclass', in Muncie J, McLaughlin E and Langa M (eds) *Criminological Perspectives.* London: Sage.

Murray C (1997) *Does Prison Work?* London: IEA and Sunday Times.

Newburn T *Crime and Criminal Justice Policy* 2nd edn. London: Longman.

Newman O (1972) *Defensible Space: Crime Prevention Through Urban Desig* New York: Collier-Macmillan.

Norris C and Armstrong G (1997) *The Unforgiving Eye: CCTV Surveillance Public Space.* Centre for Criminology and Criminal Justice: University c Hull.

Packer H (1968) *The Limits of the Criminal Sanction.* Stanford: Stanfor University Press.

arker H (1996) 'Young Adult Offenders, Alcohol and Criminological cul-de-sacs', *British Journal of Criminology*, 36 (2): 282–98.

arker H, Sumner M and Jarvis, G (1989) *Unmasking the Magistrates*. Milton Keynes: Open University Press.

aterson A (1927) *Report of the Prison Commission*. London: HMSO.

earson G (1983) *Hooligan: A History of Respectable Fears*. London: Macmillan.

earson G (1987) *The New Heroin Users*. London: Blackwell.

earson G (1994) 'Youth, Crime and Society', in Maguire M, Morgan R and Reiner R (eds) *The Oxford Handbook of Criminology*. Oxford: Clarendon Press.

ease K (1991) 'Preventing Burglary on a British Public Housing Estate', in Clarke R (ed) *Situational Crime Prevention: Successful Case Studies*. New York: Harrow & Heston.

ease K (1994a) 'Crime Prevention', in Maguire M, Morgan R and Reiner R (eds) *The Oxford Handbook of Criminology*. Oxford: Clarendon Press.

ease K (1994b) 'Cross-National Imprisonment Rates: Limitations of Method and Possible Conclusions', *British Journal of Criminology*, 34 (Special Issue): 116–30.

ease K (1997) in Maguire M, Morgan R and Reiner R (eds) *The Oxford Handbook of Criminology*, 2nd edn. Oxford: Clarendon Press.

eay J (1994) 'Mentally Disordered Offenders', in Maguire M, Morgan R and Reiner R (eds) *The Oxford Handbook of Criminology*, Oxford: Clarendon Press.

hillips (1978) *Report of the Royal Commission on Criminal Procedure* (The Phillips Commission). Cm 8092. London: HMSO.

ollack O (1950) *The Criminality of Women*. New York: AS Barnes/Perpetua.

ollard C (1998) *The Magistrate*, February.

orter M (1997) *Tackling Cross Border Crime*. Home Office Research Report. London: Home Office.

rison Commissioners (1925) *Annual Report*. London: HMSO.

rison Service (1988) *Briefing*. November. London: HMSO.

rison Service (1993) *Report on the Work of the Prison Service 1991–2*. London: HMSO.

unch M (1996) *Dirty Business: Exploring Corporate Misconduct*. London: Sage.

yle D and Deadman D (1994) 'Crime and the Business Cycle in Post War Britain', *British Journal of Criminology*, 34 (3): 339.

amsay M and Spiller J (1997) *Drug Misuse Declared in 1996: Latest Results from the British Crime Survey*. Home Office Research Study No 172. London: Home Office.

einer R (1992a) *The Politics of the Police*. London: Harvester Wheatsheaf.

einer R (1992b) 'Policing a Postmodern Society', *Modern Law Review*, 55 (6): 761–81.

einer R (1997) 'Policing and the Police', in Maguire M, Morgan R and Reiner R (eds) *The Oxford Handbook of Criminology*, 2nd edn. Oxford: Clarendon Press.

Robertson G, Pearson R and Gibb R (1995) *The Mentally Disordered Offende* *and the Police*. Home Office Research Findings, No 21.

Rock P (1991) 'The Victim in Court Project at the Crown Court at Woo Green', *Howard Journal of Criminal Justice*, 30 (4): 301–10.

Rothman D (1980) *Conscience and Convenience: The Asylum and its Alterna ives in Progressive America*. Boston, Mass.: Little, Brown.

Ruggiero V (1996) *Organized and Corporate Crime in Europe: Offers that Can be Refused*. Aldershot: Dartmouth.

Ruggiero V and South N (1995) *Eurodrugs. Drug Use, Markets and Traffickin in Europe*. London: University College London Press.

Runciman, Lord (1993) *The Report of the Royal Commission on Crimin Justice* (chaired by Lord Runciman). London: HMSO.

Ryan M (1978) *The Acceptable Pressure Group: Inequality in the Penal Lobb* Farnborough: Gower.

Sampson A (1994) *Acts of Abuse: Sex Offenders and the Criminal Justice System* London: Routledge.

Sanders A (1985) 'Class Bias in Prosecutions', *Howard Journal*, 24: 176–99

Sanders A (1997) 'From Suspect to Trial', in Maguire M, Morgan R an Reiner R (eds) *The Oxford Handbook of Criminology*, 2nd edn. Oxford Clarendon Press.

Sanders A and Young R (1994) *Criminal Justice*. London: Butterworth.

Sanderson J (1992) *Criminology Textbook*. London: HLT.

Schlesinger P and Tumber H (1994) *Reporting Crime: The Media Politics c Criminal Justice*. Oxford: Clarendon Press.

Schrag (1944) 'Social Types of a Prison Community. Quoted in Ditchfield (1990)', *Control in Prisons: A Review of the Literature*. London: HMSO.

Schur E (1969) *Our Criminal Society*. Englewood Cliffs: Prentice Hall.

Schur E (1973) *Radical Non-Intervention. Rethinking the Delinquency Problem* Englewood Cliffs: Prentice Hall.

Scull A (1977) *Decarceration: Community Treatment and the Deviant – Radical View*. Englewood Cliffs: Prentice Hall.

Shapland J, Willmore J and Duff P (1985) *Victims and the Criminal Justic System*. Aldershot: Gower.

Shaw S (1998) 'Jack Straw's Prison Record', *Criminal Justice Matters*, No 30 Winter 1997/8: 6–7.

Shawcross (Lord) (1951) House of Commons Debate, Vol 483, 29 Januar 1951.

Skolnick J (1966) *Justice Without Trial*. New York: Wiley.

Smith D J (1997) 'Race, Crime and Criminal Justice', in Maguire M, Morga R and Reiner R (eds) *The Oxford Handbook of Criminology*, 2nd edn Oxford: Clarendon Press.

Smith D J and Gray J (1985) *Police and People in London: the PSI Report* Aldershot: Gower.

Soothill K (1993) 'Sex Crime in the News Revisited', Unpublished pape presented to the British Criminology Conference, Cardiff, July 1993.

oothill K and Walby S (1991) *Sex Crime in the News*. London: Routledge.

outh N (1997) 'Drugs: Use, Crime, and Control', in Maguire M, Morgan R and Reiner R (eds) *The Oxford Handbook of Criminology*, 2nd edn. Oxford: Clarendon Press.

tanko E (1990) 'When Precaution is Normal: A Feminist Critique of Crime Prevention', in Gelsthorpe L and Morris A (eds) *Feminist Perspectives in Criminology*. Milton Keynes: Open University Press.

tephens M and Becker S (eds) (1994) *Police Force, Police Service Care and Control in Britain*. London: Macmillan.

tern V (1987) *Bricks of Shame*. Harmondsworth: Penguin.

traw J (1997) 'The Criminal Justice Crisis', *Criminal Justice Matters*, No 26, Winter 1996/7: 6–7.

utherland E (1949) *White Collar Crime*. New York: Holt, Rinehart & Winston.

veri K (1990) 'Criminal Law and Penal Sanctions', in Snare A (ed) *Criminal Violence in Scandinavia: Selected Topics*. Oslo: Norwegian University Press.

arling R and Weatheritt M (1979) *Sentencing Practice in Magistrates' Courts*. Home Office Research Study No 56. London: HMSO.

aylor I (1997) 'The Political Economy of Crime', in Maguire M, Morgan R and Reiner R (eds) *The Oxford Handbook of Criminology*, 2nd edn. Oxford: Clarendon Press.

aylor, Lord Chief Justice (1993) *17th Leggatt Lecture – What do we want from our Judges?* University of Surrey.

homas D A (1979) *Principles of Sentencing*. London: Heinemann.

illey N (1993) 'Crime Prevention and the Safer Cities Story', *Howard Journal of Criminal Justice*, 32 (1): 40–57.

onry M (1987) *Sentencing Reform Impacts*. Washington DC: US Department of Justice.

glow S (1988) *Policing Liberal Society*. Oxford: University Press.

tting D, Bright J and Henricson C (1993) *Crime and the Family: Improving Child Rearing and Preventing Delinquency*. Occasional Paper 16, Family Policy Studies Centre.

ass A (1990) *Alternatives to Prison: Punishment, Custody and the Community*. London: Sage.

ennard J (1985) 'The Outcome of Contested Trials', in Moxon D (ed) *Managing Criminal Justice*. London: HMSO.

alker M (1987) 'Interpreting Race and Crime Statistics', *Journal of the Royal Statistical Society A*, 150, Part 1: 39–56.

alker N and Padfield N (1996) *Sentencing: Theory, Law and Practice*, 2nd edn. London: Butterworth.

alklate S (1989) *Victimology: The Victim and the Criminal Justice Process*. London: Unwin Hyman.

alklate S (1998) *Understanding Criminology: Current Theoretical Debates*. Buckingham: Open University Press.

almsley R, Howard L and White S (1993) *The National Prison Survey 1991: Main Findings*. Home Office Research Study No 128. London: HMSO.

Warburton F (1993) 'Bail Bandits – A Persistent Minority or the Usua
Suspects?', *Criminal Justice Matters*, No 10, Winter 1992/3: 7.

Wasik M (1993) *The Magistrate*, October.

Wasik M and Taylor R (1994) *Criminal Justice Act, 1991*. London: Blackstone

Watson L (1996) *Victims of Violent Crime Recorded by the Police, England and
Wales, 1990–1994*. Home Office Statistical Findings, Issue 1/96. London
HMSO.

Webb B and Laycock G (1992) *Tackling Car Crime: The Nature and Extent o
the Problem*. Home Office Crime Prevention Paper No 32.

Weigend T (1980) 'Continental Cures for American Ailments: European
Criminal Procedure as a Model for Law Reform', *Crime and Justice*
Vol 2.

Wells C (1988) 'The Decline and Rise of English Murder; Corporate Crime
and Individual Responsibility', *Criminal Law Review*: 789–801.

Wells J (1995) *Crime and Unemployment*. Employment Policy Institute Eco
nomic Report, Vol 9/1, February.

Wessley S (1995) *The Times*, 7 February: 17.

West D (1965) *Murder Followed by Suicide*. London: Heinemann.

West D (1969) *Present Conduct and Future Delinquency*. London: Heinemann

West D J and Farrington D (1973) *Who Becomes Delinquent?* London
Heinemann.

West D J and Farrington D (1977) *The Delinquent Way of Life*. London
Heinemann.

White P and Woodbridge J (1998) 'The Prison Population in 1997', *Home
Office Statistical Bulletin*, Issue 5/98. London: Home Office.

Whitelaw W (1989) *The Whitelaw Memoirs*. London: Arum Press.

Wilkins G and Addicott C (1997) 'Operation of Certain Police Powers
Under PACE: England and Wales 1996', *Home Office Statistical Bulletin*
Issue 17/97. London: Home Office.

Williams K (1991) *Textbook on Criminology*. London: Blackstone Press.

Wilson H (1980) 'Parental Supervision: A Neglected Aspect of Delinquency'
British Journal of Criminology, 20 (20).

Wilson J Q and Kelling G (1982) 'Broken Windows', *Atlantic Monthly*, March
29–38.

Woodcock J (1994) *Report of the Inquiry into the Attempted Escape from H.M
Prison Whitemoor on 9 September 1994*. London: Home Office.

Worrall A (1997) *Punishment in the Community: The Future of Criminal Justice*
London: Longman.

Young P (1997) 'The Peculiarities of the Scots', *Criminal Justice Matters*
No 26, Winter 1996/7: 22–3.

Zedner L (1997) 'Victims', in Maguire M, Morgan R and Reiner R (eds) *The
Oxford Handbook of Criminology*, 2nd edn. Oxford: Clarendon Press.

Zito Trust (1997) *Community Care Homicides*. London: Zito Trust.

446

INDEX

Persistent offenders
  imprisonment, effect of, 320
  rehabilitation, 279
  secure training orders *see* Secure
    training order
  sentencing, 297
Personal injuries
  compensation for, 249
Petty sessions, 178
Phillips Commission, 137
Photographs
  destruction of, defendant's right,
    184
Place of safety order, 165
Plea
  bargaining
    advantages and disadvantages,
      231–2
    charge bargaining, 228
    Court of Appeal decisions, 228–31
    effects of, 231–3
    meaning, 226, 411
    no systematic, 228
    sentence canvass, 228
  decision on, linked to mode of trial
    decision, 193–4, 197
  guilty, of
    cost effectiveness, 24
    decision to give, 226, 403
    discount on length of custodial
      sentence, where, 197, 226–7,
      230, 231
    effect of, 19–20
    lesser charge, to, 226
    procedure, 173, 194, 214
    reasons for, 226–7
    sentencing, 197, 216, 255
  mitigation, in, 44–5, 215, 255–6
  mode of trial decision and, 193–4
  negotiation *see* bargaining *above*
  not guilty, procedure where, 194,
    214–15
Plea and directions hearing, 198
Police
  accountability
    cautioning, 134
    generally, 104–6, 124
    legal, 106
  adversarial system and, 93–4

Association of Chief Police Officers,
  349
Audit Commission Report, 99, 400,
  401
caution and cautioning *see* Caution,
  Cautioning
chief constables, role of, 104–5
community policing *see* Community
  policing
complaints regarding, 104, 106, 107,
  353–4, 371–2
computers, effect of, 97–8, 101
cost of, 8, 91, 366, 401
crime statistics
  comparisons between different
    areas, 85–7
  decisions affecting, 64–5
  influence on, 67, 77–8, 84–8
  recording methods, 85–7
  variations in police practice, 84
  see also Statistics, criminal
Crown Prosecution Service and *see*
  Crown Prosecution Service
culture
  factors of, 122–3, 124
  studies of, 123–4
custody records, 108, 112
deployment of, 117
development of, 94–9
disciplinary codes, 353
discretion
  legal factors, 118
  police station, in, 116, 119–20
  scope of, 116–20, 124
  stop and search, as to, 118–19
  studies of, 117–18
discrimination
  allegations as to, 120
  racial, 120–1
  sexist behaviour, 120
Europe-wide arrangements, 101,
  355
forensic services, use of, 101–4
functions *see* role of *below*
generally, 90–2
images of, 90–2
informers, use of, 401–2
inspectorate, 367, 369–70
Interpol, 101, 356

Woolf Report into 1990 prison
disturbances
background to, 293
introduction of proposals, 322,
331, 340
publication of, 396
recommendations, 17, 338, 364,
370
young offender institutions *see* Young
offender institution
Private Finance Initiative, 367
Private industry, role of, 347
Private prosecutions, 132, 134
Private security firms
role of, 9, 91, 318, 319, 349, 366, 402
Privy Council, role of, 3
Probation order
alternatives to, 289
community sentence, as, 250
mentally disordered offender, 166
offenders sentenced to, 238–9
refusal to consent to, 252
scope of, 250
Probation service
areas, 284
functions of, 9, 283–5
funding, 8
history of, 278, 284
Home Office and, 349, 350
inspectorate, 367, 369, 370
inter-relationship with other agencies,
16
National Association of Probation
Officers, 349
rehabilitative aims and, 283, 289
role of, 5, 9, 23, 256, 273, 275, 277,
284–6
schemes for offenders, 285
Statement of National Objectives for
Probation, 286–7
training, 284, 404–5
Property crime
compensation for, 249
drugs and, 56–7
reparation, 248
statistics, 80
Prosecution
appeal, rights of, 262
caution in lieu of, 348

cost of, 403
Crown Prosecution Service *see* Crown
Prosecution Service
decision as to, criteria for, 127,
139–42
diversion and, 127–8, 144–8
function of, 5
generally, 77, 134
issues of, 127
mentally disordered offenders *see*
Mentally disordered offenders
police, by, 135
policy reviews, 402
private, 132, 134
procedure, 134
regulatory agencies, by, 146–9
Prosecutor
Chief Crown Prosecutor, 138
lay, 138
role of, 8
Prostitution
effect on neighbourhood, 75
reporting, 83, 84
victimless crime, 76
Psychiatrists, role of, 346
Psychopathic disorders, 47, 166, 167, 168
Public
confidence
criminal justice system, in, 405
police, in, 83
impact of crime on, 65–7
relationship with police, 97, 98
reporting of crime
effect of, 88
factors influencing decisions as to,
82–4
statistics as to, 82
safety of, and community care,
169–70
sentencing and, 303, 306–8, 404
tolerance
behaviour, of, changes in, 35
crime, of, 83
Punishment
back-to-back justice approach, 273,
282, 291
capital, 242, 275, 311, 312, 400
community sentences *see* Community
sentence